Freedom Is Not Enough

Freedom Is Not Enough

THE OPENING OF THE AMERICAN WORKPLACE

Nancy MacLean

RUSSELL SAGE FOUNDATION
New York

HARVARD UNIVERSITY PRESS
Cambridge, Massachusetts
London, England   2006

Copyright © 2006 by the Russell Sage Foundation
All rights reserved
Printed in the United States of America

Library of Congress Cataloging-in-Publication Data

MacLean, Nancy.
Freedom is not enough : the opening of the American workplace /
Nancy MacLean.
p. cm.
Includes bibliographical references and index.
ISBN 0-674-01909-1
1. Discrimination in employment—United States.
2. Sex discrimination in employment—United States.
3. Minorities—United States.   4. Segregation—United States.
I. Title.
HD4903.5.U58M33 2005
331.13′3′0973—dc22   2005046445

For Bruce

If you move out of your place everything is changed. If I'm not what that white man thinks I am, then he has to find out what *he* is.

—JAMES BALDWIN, *Conversations with James Baldwin*

Contents

III THE CHALLENGE OF THE NEW ORDER

Illustrations

Freedom Is Not Enough

Prologue: Jobs and Belonging

Freedom is not enough. You do not wipe away the
scars of centuries by saying: Now you are free.
~ *Lyndon B. Johnson*, Commencement Address,
Howard University, June 4, 1965

*L*ESS THAN FORTY YEARS AGO, Wharlest Jackson lost
his life for being promoted to a "whites-only" job. Thirty-seven years
old and the father of five children when he died in 1967, Jackson was a
veteran of the Korean War and treasurer of the Natchez, Mississippi,
branch of the National Association for the Advancement of Colored
People. At the time of his murder, he had just won promotion to mixer
of chemicals after eleven years at the Armstrong Tire and Rubber
Company. Jackson's move into a formerly "white" job meant a great
deal to local blacks, not least to Jackson's family, for the promotion
came with a sizable raise. "My wife and children should have a chance
now," Jackson said to friends. But the entry of an African American into
work long barred to blacks signified something less desirable to others.
As Jackson left the factory after working overtime that rainy Monday
evening, a bomb hidden under the frame of his pickup truck exploded.
The force was so strong that it ripped open the truck's cab and drove
the seat springs into Jackson's chest, killing him instantly.[1]

The coroner ruled the death an accident, although that was prepos-
terous. The Armstrong plant was "infested with Ku Klux Klansmen,"
as the local NAACP put it; so, too, was the police force. The Klan's
campaign of terrorism enjoyed protection among white citizens; some
actively supported it, and others were more concerned that blacks not
upset the established order. For Jackson's promotion was no isolated

1

event. Blacks at Armstrong had been organizing for fair treatment for several years. Jackson's friend and the leader of the Natchez National Association for the Advancement of Colored People (NAACP), George Metcalfe, had lost the sight in one eye and the use of a leg— and nearly lost his life—to an earlier car bomb set while he worked at the plant in August 1965. Having organized to open jobs and desegregate eating facilities, drinking fountains, and washrooms at the Armstrong plant, Metcalfe was also leading a boycott of the town's white merchants. The boycott's wide-ranging demands for fair treatment in all areas of daily life included employment of blacks as salespersons and cashiers in downtown stores and in municipal jobs as police and public workers. Wharlest Jackson's wife, Exerlina, was among those arrested in the boycott for peacefully insisting on equal treatment; she was sent to Parchman Penitentiary. Jackson's murder occurred nearly three years after the Civil Rights Act of 1964 promised an end to employment discrimination.[2]

Yet somehow, Natchez did eventually change, and so did the country as a whole. Indeed, a profound alteration has occurred in American workplaces over the last fifty years. Whereas in 1950 it was rare to see black professionals, or even skilled blue-collar or white-collar workers, employed outside the black community, today such sights are commonplace. The change is wider and deeper than the prominence of a few individual men and women of color, such as Colin Powell and Condoleezza Rice. It appears in most occupational categories—no matter how much remains to be done to achieve the vision of jobs and justice for which Jackson and Metcalfe worked. Clashes between promises of fairness and lived experience persist, not least in the disappearance of many well-paid blue-collar jobs and in the sharp and growing economic inequality that most hurts the long-excluded.[3] But the nation's "common sense" has shifted dramatically—so much so as to constitute a kind of cultural transformation. And the change encompasses, in addition to African Americans, women of all groups, Mexican Americans, and, more recently, Asian Americans and people with disabilities.

What has occurred is a veritable revolution in thinking about race and gender and work. Each time Americans listen to a black male anchor on the evening news, board a bus with a white woman at the wheel, speak with a Latina office manager, or hear a conservative call for "color-blindness," we experience this sea change in the nation's history. The noticeable shift in who does various jobs is but the visible sign of a deeper seismic shift in relations between groups and in the meaning of citizenship. The story of how this came about is the story of America in the second half of the twentieth century, a time of upheaval and repositioning that altered the ground on which we encounter one another, face our history, and meet the challenges of our time.

How DID A SOCIETY that for centuries took for granted the exclusion from full participation and citizenship of the majority of its members (namely, Americans of color and all women) become one that values diversity and sees as an achievement the representation of once excluded groups in prominent positions?[4] Not only workplaces have changed but also the nation's political map. In the mid-1950s, African Americans worked largely in isolation in American politics; among their closest allies were the leaders of Jewish organizations also concerned with fighting discrimination. Women who identified themselves as feminists worked with the National Association of Manufacturers, the Republican Party, and conservative southern Dixiecrats in the hope of winning an Equal Rights Amendment that would wipe out the protective legislation for which pro-labor women and men had fought. Mexican Americans sought to distance themselves from African Americans and gain recognition from Anglos as "white." The conservative movement was new, small, and composed almost entirely of upper-class white Christians. Business organizations fought hard against civil rights measures.

Since the 1960s, nearly all these groups have altered their positions, indeed their very identities, in important ways. Feminist and Latino organizations now follow the lead of progressive black civil rights organizations and ally with them on contested programs. Jewish and black organizations have clashed over key issues, above all affirmative action, and while Jews generally remain far more liberal than white gentiles, the conservative movement now includes many Jewish spokespersons. Although the numbers are still small, some African Americans also play prominent roles in the conservative movement. Meanwhile, some leading business organizations have broken ranks with the right, to join with civil rights and feminist groups in defending affirmative action and extolling "diversity." What brought about this dramatic reconfiguration?

The prime mover was the black freedom movement's fight for jobs and justice.[5] This is not to deny that other forces played a role; they did. But in challenging economic exclusion as a denial of full and fair citizenship, African Americans began a process that shifted the very axis of politics in the United States. When the civil rights movement managed to win a federal ban on employment discrimination, Title VII of the Civil Rights Act of 1964, it created a resource that invited first white women and Mexican American men and later others to rethink their strategies of empowerment. A reform won by a social movement, that is, broadened that movement as it generated others. Legal change invited social action, which itself altered ideas and institutions.

It mattered a great deal that Hispanics and white women followed the lead of African Americans. The black struggle for economic inclusion built on singular resources and had distinctive qualities that can go unnoticed if it is looked at alone. In fact, it is only by bringing other groups into the picture that the remarkable features of modern black politics emerge clearly. Even as victory remained elusive, African Americans had produced by the late 1950s a wide, well-trained leadership group; built lasting organizations with paid staffs and full-time leaders; constructed dense and powerful networks within the labor movement and the Democratic Party; developed ties to potential white allies; achieved relative unity among themselves over goals; accumulated lessons over generations about organizing; and crafted political and moral arguments so compelling as to be finally inescapable. Their leadership in the struggle for economic inclusion had such an impact on the whole political map, in turn, because from their history African Americans developed an unusually radical and universalistic vision of justice and grounded it in mainstream American values. In these years, blacks focused on living-wage jobs for all as critical to advancement, and they worked more than any other population with organized labor. Building broad coalitions, they argued for measures to assist other victims of discrimination and pressed for active effort by the national government to promote economic equality for all Americans to a degree that was not true of other peoples of color, of white women, or of working-class white men.[6] All of this made for matchless organizing and a potentially transformative influence on others, such that African Americans' relations with these groups involved more than simple addition. This was an equation in which changes in quantity begat changes in quality: the meaning of inclusion altered as new actors and arguments entered the field.

One measure of the moral power of the black struggle was the 1965 declaration by an aging white Texan raised under Jim Crow and trained by Dixiecrat mentors, Lyndon Baines Johnson, that "freedom is not enough." The southern-born president, once an enemy of civil rights, urged the heirs of the Declaration of Independence to achieve "not just equality as a right and a theory, but equality as a fact and a result." Justice required the country, he explained, "to give 20 million Negroes the same chance as every other American to learn and grow, to work and share in society, to develop their abilities—physical, mental and spiritual, and to pursue their individual happiness. To this end equal opportunity is essential, but not enough."[7] Johnson's words demonstrated how the black freedom movement had uncorked the bottle. Other groups seeking equality then widened the opening until the genie could no longer be kept inside: the culture had changed too much to return to the old ways. Nearly every movement for equality since then has followed the black struggle in concluding that legal freedom, formal equality, was not enough. Rather, genuine inclusion—full belonging as Americans—required participation in the economic mainstream—namely, access to the good jobs at all levels once reserved for white men alone. And because exclusion had such deep roots in American life, demands to open those good jobs to all altered not just workplaces but the nation's political culture itself, by redefining understandings of race, gender, citizenship, and fairness. Inequality remained, to be sure, but in altered forms and with new dynamics and terms of defense.

This book offers a new interpretation of the civil rights movement and its reverberations through the past half century. For too long, Americans' understanding of the movement has come from journalists, drawn as they are to dramatic showdowns such as the attacks on the Freedom Ride buses, the lunch counter sit-ins, and the brutal beatings of marchers at the Edmund Pettus Bridge. The focus on these climactic confrontations has drawn attention away from quieter struggles on other fronts—above all, from the fight to secure access to good jobs. That effort was less inviting to news cameras, yet still momentous because it sought an essential element of full citizenship and of individual and group self-determination. The quest for jobs and justice, in turn, involved a more robust vision of equality than the legal change evoked by the phrase "civil rights." In the words of Corine Cannon, a North Carolinian who was hired by a textile company as a result of these struggles: "The best thing that has ever happened to black women in the South in my lifetime is a chance to be full-fledged citizens. And that comes from their work. You can't even pretend to be free without money."[8]

Economic exclusion was not simply a matter of financial well-being to those it marginalized. Job segregation restricted their very membership in the mainstream of national life, because the work ethic and the success myth have long constituted the bedrock of American culture. They posited labor as the sure route to the democratic promise of the American dream: the belief that those who worked hard at honest callings, whatever their origins, could better themselves and lift their children's prospects.[9] One political philosopher has identified earning along with voting as the twin pillars that have tacitly constituted true belonging; "earning," she insisted, "is implicit in equal American citizenship."[10] For their part, as individuals, Americans have looked to their jobs for meaning and connection—for companionship, feelings of achievement, and a sense of who they are.[11]

Employment is, after all, a key site in determining personal well-being and communal power. The Charlottesville, Virginia, NAACP clarified why in 1963: "The job a person has is basic to his position in society. To a large extent, it determines the nature and condition of his property, the health and education of his children, the moral environment of his family, and his individual self-respect."[12] So important is labor to self-definition and social relations that Americans routinely ask, "What do you do?" on first meeting someone, a habit that strikes visitors from other countries as strange. Yet since our society's distinguishing promise is that through hard work its citizens can achieve as much as their talents enable them to, that preoccupation makes sense. In recent decades, too, Americans have devoted an ever-increasing share of their waking lives to their jobs. "What we do for daily work shapes—sometimes strengthening, sometimes crippling—our physical bodies, our emotions, our aspirations," observes one of the country's first female electricians, who braved ridicule, hatred, and violence to practice her chosen craft.[13] From slavery forward, not surprisingly given this culture, work has proved a key site for constructing social inequality—

and for challenging such inequality.[14] "We see the economic issues," Martin Luther King, Jr., explained to Congress in 1966, "as probably the basic issue"; addressing them would entail "a restructuring of the architecture of American society."[15]

One core element of that architecture was an entrenched culture of exclusion that long restricted to white men nearly every one of the nation's most desirable jobs at all class levels, whether skilled operative and craft jobs, the professions, or managerial positions. That culture made workplace segregation by race, sex, and sometimes national origin a way of life for most Americans. Members of a single demographic group seemed assigned almost by nature to job categories such as maid, salesman, carpenter, secretary, migrant farm worker, flight attendant, or executive. This segregation gained stability from institutions that grew from it and sustained it. The three most decisive were the sharecropping system that dominated the South's economy from the Civil War to the Second World War, the family wage system that reached its height in the 1950s, and the immigration system that treated Mexican Americans and Asian Americans as outsiders even if they were born and raised in the United States. The nation's "two-track" welfare state deepened the divisions forged in its labor markets, elaborated in its culture, and enshrined in its politics. Just as those excluded from the economic mainstream had lesser citizenship rights, so did they receive second-class treatment in the social welfare policies devised in the Progressive Era and expanded in the New Deal.[16]

What made the exclusion of so many possible for so long was a shared assumption in the mainstream that those who were denied access to better jobs were not important. The white men who monopolized good employment were considered the core of the nation; their needs and interests were taken into account because they belonged. They were the constituency assumed when politicians, business leaders, and intellectuals spoke of "Americans." And they could feel a certain security in advantages taken so much for granted that they seemed hardly deserving of note.

It was different for those who were shut out. Confinement to a restricted range of less desirable jobs—generally menial blue-collar work for men and "pink-collar" service work for women—meant less money, more limited life chances, poorer benefits if any, and less economic security. And it meant stigma—being marked publicly "as a non-person," as some Mexican American activists put it, or at least as less worthy than the white men at the culture's center.[17] The low status of the jobs and the low status of those consigned to them became mutually defining. The result was a kind of ostracism, a public disrespect built into social policy and culture as well as the structure of the labor force. To challenge that imputed unworthiness, to seek to belong to the economic mainstream, was to risk being punished as a trespasser. Although the terrorism that met Wharlest Jackson's and George Metcalfe's ambitions for better lives grew less common, challenging one's assigned range of possibilities attracted enough trouble to deter most people.

And yet mounting numbers of "non-persons" risked retribution, especially in the 1960s and 1970s, and their collective efforts changed the country. They not only gained better prospects and higher incomes for millions of their peers but also altered long-entrenched public ideas and habits. Ultimately, their labors deepened democracy in America and expanded the basic rights of all its citizens. As early as 1963, one writer reported that "the gathering debate over preferential hiring of Negroes is raising questions about the efficacy and justice of the American economic system as nothing else has since the Great Depression."[18] Other than the labor movement's epochal struggle to establish job rights protected by contracts, never was there a deeper challenge to employers' power to hire and promote whomever they wanted on whatever basis they chose.

We forget today what a new and uncharted world opened up when organizers such as George Metcalfe and their Washington allies finally managed, after a quarter century of effort, to get Congress to prohibit discrimination in employment. Title VII of the Civil Rights Act of 1964, which declared discrimination on the grounds of "race, color, religion, sex, or national origin" to be an "unlawful employment practice" and provided redress, was the hardest-won section of that hardwon bill. It passed only after a historic 534-hour filibuster.[19] And it was Title VII's promise of fair employment, more than anything else, that lured white women and Mexican Americans to follow the example of African Americans. This reform created a previously unheard-of resource for social movements for equality: their constituents could now file complaints with the new Equal Employment Opportunities Commission (EEOC) and sue employers for violating their new right to fair treatment. The change in the law encouraged grassroots struggles for jobs and justice, as aggrieved people and their allies in movement organizations and government agencies worked to realize its promise.

Title VII may have promised a new order, but there was no blueprint. Convinced that employment had been unfair and confident that it could be better, the excluded still had much to learn about exactly how they might change the system. What ensued was a vast drama of public innovation. It involved people at every level of society, the institutions they entered, the laws and practices they debated, and the culture they modified. Through their pressure for inclusion, and then for fairness once inside, groups that had been pressed to the margins of American economic and public life challenged their confinement and shook up the established social order.

No one captured the unmooring of the old hierarchy as well as the writer James Baldwin, who once observed: "If you move out of your place everything is changed. If I'm not what that white man thinks I am, then he has to find out what *he* is."[20] Because the United States had confined African Americans for so long to the bottom of the social order and built so much of its culture on rationalizing that violation of its stated ideals, as their struggle gained momentum, it upset every location in the hierarchy. The very identity of whites was built on their notion of blacks: to unsettle that was to bring into question their self-conceptions as well. This was true on a wider scale, too. When African Americans shook the old order, they set off a process of questioning and repositioning among other groups that in time altered the map of American political culture. If blacks were not who whites had so long insisted they were, then not only were most white men not who they thought they were, but also neither were white women, whose standing had long been defined with reference to race, or Hispanics and Jews, whose standing had long been defined as in between that of blacks and whites, or conservatives, who defined themselves by their commitment to the order being shaken. No wonder the struggle to open good jobs to all agitated so many Americans.

This book tells the story of how the culture of exclusion began breaking down after 1955. The commitment of working people such as Wharlest and Exerlina Jackson was part of a larger story of concerted efforts on the part of many thousands of African Americans, Mexican Americans, and white women determined as never before to enter the economic mainstream. The work of inclusion they initiated included grassroots struggle in workplaces and communities, public argument and debate, and private coaching on new ways of thinking and of running organizations. It involved creative social movements, pioneering laws, and cultural innovation. Individuals summoned the courage to do what few had tried before, whether entering the citadels of exclusion or reaching out from within them as allies to newcomers. The work was carried out partly by formal organizations such as the NAACP, the Urban League, the Congress of Racial Equality, the National Organization for Women, the Women's Equity Action League, the American GI Forum, and the League of United Latin American Citizens. It was also conducted informally in workplace caucuses and lunchtime gripe sessions. It was waged through tens of thousands of complaints against discrimination filed with government agencies and innumerable lawsuits. It was pushed through labor unions when they acted as allies, and against them when they acted as obstacles. Inclusion was promoted by arguments over family dinner tables, creative advertising campaigns, and films and television shows that invited insiders to imagine the world through others' eyes.

Only such a vast and varied effort could have altered traditions that had been centuries in the making. As it did so, the quest for inclusion in the workplace contributed to another change: the gradual but striking refashioning of American conservatism, liberalism, and radicalism over the last half century. American political culture is different today from what it was in 1955 or even 1970. The story told here helps explain why.

~ *I*

African Americans
Shake the Old Order

~ 1

The Rightness of Whiteness

$\mathcal{T}$HE CULTURE OF EXCLUSION organized life in the
United States in the early 1950s so thoroughly that it appeared natural
and unremarkable to nearly all white Americans. "You don't have to
look for it to see it," recalled one black paper mill worker. "It was all
right in front of you."[1] Although that culture's operations were most
visible in the South, where segregation was enforced by law, by custom,
and ultimately by violence, it defined all regions of the country. It drew
strength from three institutions that together shaped much of twentieth-century American life: the family wage system, the sharecropping
system, and the system of immigration restriction. The family wage
shored up the place of white men as household breadwinners and the
citizens at the center of public life, as it consigned to secondary status
not only white female earners but also most men and women of color.
Sharecropping undergirded the entire system of segregation and disfranchisement that kept black Americans veritable outsiders in a land in
which they had deeper roots than most white Americans. The system
of racially driven immigration restriction limited Mexican Americans'
and Asian Americans' access to good jobs and, in different ways, undermined their standing as citizens.[2]

Those who upheld exclusion did so in keeping with traditions going
back to the nation's founding. "American law," as the political scientist
Rogers Smith noted, summing up decades of scholarship, has "long

been shot through with forms of second-class citizenship, denying personal liberties and opportunities for political participation to most of the adult population on the basis of race, ethnicity, gender, and even religion." These forms of inferior citizenship existed within the liberal and republican traditions on which Americans have prided themselves. Often, exclusion seemed so powerful as to be an independent third strain, expressed in "passionate beliefs that America was by rights a white nation, a Protestant nation, a nation in which true Americans were native-born men with Anglo-Saxon ancestors." The Constitution itself expressed the fusion: while granting novel self-rule to the white male citizenry, the nation's founding charter decreed that each slave would be counted as three fifths of a human being in determining taxation and representation. Congress "in its first words on the subject of citizenship . . . restricted naturalization to 'white persons,'" as one legal scholar reminds us, a "racial prerequisite to citizenship" not removed until 1952. As a result, for nearly all of its history, a majority of the country's adult inhabitants faced second-class treatment: African Americans, seen first as slaves, then as racial inferiors; Mexican Americans, seen as conquered peoples of the Southwest or illegal immigrants; Asian Americans, seen as "aliens" unfit to assimilate; women, seen as wives and daughters dependent on men; even for a long time Jews and Catholics, seen as outsiders in a culture defined by Protestant Christianity. All found themselves denied full access to rights, opportunities, and recognition in the mainstream economy and polity.[3]

Protected by laws and courts, embedded in the labor force, entrenched through unequal schooling, perpetuated through time-honored everyday practices, and sanctioned by prevailing thinking, the culture of exclusion was a powerful edifice. Its sheer mass deterred most would-be challengers. Yet the appearance of calm that prevailed in the 1950s belied the shifts occurring beneath the surface of a system whose foundations were frailer than ever before.

⌒ THE MAINSTREAM CULTURE of the era sent the message that white men—at least some white men—mattered more than other residents; they belonged in the best jobs and in positions of authority, for they were the real Americans. That culture decreed that what seemed to others to be obstacles to their progress were not in fact obstacles at all but rather evidence of their own unfitness for the positions they desired. Nothing exhibited the underlying assumptions better than the popular imagery of the era. The family was the centerpiece of American mass culture in the mid-1950s and its proudest apostle to the wider world. Always, the lifestyles of abundance that rising real wages—family wages, as they came to be known—afforded such families served as the foundation of their appeal. When Vice President Richard M. Nixon met with Soviet premier Nikita Khrushchev at the American National Exhibition in Moscow, he trumpeted the virtues of the "free world" in front of a life-size model of an American ranch house. Their encounter became known as the "kitchen debate," carried out as it was before that cornucopia of consumer goods.[4]

The families enshrined in public culture did not, in the language of a later era, "look like America." Rather, they were almost uniformly of a single type: white, native-born, nuclear families with male breadwinners, usually living in the suburbs. These were the households featured in some of television's most popular offerings: *Leave It to Beaver, The Adventures of Ozzie and Harriet,* and *Father Knows Best.* In them, only men held jobs, white men held all the desirable ones, and the exceptions proved the rule. The few men of color who appeared in prime time were in character roles, such as Desi Arnaz, the light-skinned Cuban émigré entertainer, whose troubles with English supplied many of *I Love Lucy*'s laughs. The talented Nat King Cole for a time had his own television show, featuring some of the leading figures in contemporary music, until a station executive reprimanded the show's producer, saying, "Nat is a Negro and most of these musicians are white and it looks like the white guys are working for a Negro." Advertisers stayed away for fear of losing white consumers, and the show could not be sustained.[5]

As far as mass culture was concerned, others existed only to serve the white male breadwinner, his homemaker wife, and their dependent children. In these glory years of consumer capitalism, advertising regularly rehearsed these assumptions. Viewers could easily conclude that "all Negroes in America were servants or comic characters," wrote one critic in *Negro Digest.* With Aunt Jemima in her classic mammy attire as the archetypal black woman and Uncle Ben in his white butler jacket as the archetypal black man, "every ad [depicting African Americans] stamps upon the mind the menial, second-class 'place' of the Negro." In the world paraded before Americans, black men and women belonged only insofar as they advanced the comfort of whites. Otherwise, they suffered near absolute invisibility, as one contemporary survey attested: "Not a single advertisement which purported to depict a cross section of the public contained the figure of a Negro. In street scenes . . . in groups of workers, nowhere was a Negro to be found." Advertisers defended their work on the grounds that it portrayed their market: "typical Americans." Blacks were not typical Americans in the view of Hollywood producers, either. "The motion picture industry," as one leader of the NAACP put it, "still treats the Negro as an invisible man, as a menial, as an outworn stereotype."[6] The mass culture of the fifties appears almost cartoonish now, the popular films and television shows as much as the earnest advertisements.

Yet the images captured something important: the family wage system that shaped American social policy. That system built on a long-standing division of labor that assigned women responsibility for child rearing and men responsibility for income earning, exalting the male breadwinner as the provider for his dependent wife and children. First articulated as a goal by reformers in the 1800s, the family wage became a reality for growing numbers of households thanks to improved earnings spurred by unionization after the late 1930s. And yet, even at its mid-century peak, a large share of the population fell outside the system's net—not only widowed and single women, but also less-skilled workers in general and low-wage workers of color in particular.[7]

Believing male labor the norm and female labor an aberration, employers and policymakers constructed a labor market biased toward men, especially white men, and devised social welfare policy that shored up male-dominated households while weakening others. The family wage norm served as a grounding principle for the two-track welfare state built in the Progressive Era and the New Deal years. The superior, entitlement track of this system rewarded male wage earning through policies such as workmen's compensation, unemployment insurance, and Social Security. Its inferior, means- and morals-tested track grudgingly sustained women and children cut off from access to male wages through mothers' pensions, and later Aid to Families with Dependent Children. Well into the 1960s, the pecking order proved self-reinforcing, as the closing of good jobs to women, the lack of reproductive control, and the stigmas attached to divorce and homosexuality bolstered the male breadwinner system, while the exclusion of most families of color from that norm ensured that black women would have to hold jobs throughout their lives.[8]

The partial character of the American welfare state reinforced the prominence of white men and the marginality of others. The New Deal had emerged from compromises that wrote inequality into its component policies, from labor standards and work relief to housing and Social Security. Determined to protect the South's racial hierarchy and low-wage regional economy from challenge, southern Democrats in Congress joined with conservative Republicans to exact their pound of flesh before agreeing to social legislation. As the price of passage, northern reformers had to accept the exclusion of farm and domestic workers from reform legislation and abide the denial of voting rights to blacks in the South. National Democratic leaders felt a need, as the NAACP put it, to "appease the traditional Southerners at the expense of America's Negro citizens."[9] Most white voters in the North, Democrats and Republicans alike, came to think of policies that privileged them and excluded blacks as fair entitlements.[10] With nearly all southern blacks unable to vote until 1965, this system proved all but impossible to fight on its home ground.

There, the long shadow of slavery continued to dim the prospects for Americans of color, denying them benefits that whites took for granted. Cotton, as a sharecropper organizer wrote in the depths of the Great Depression, "to a greater degree than any other product of industry or agriculture rules the South." It also dominated black life. More than two in three African Americans lived in that region in 1950. Trapped in an isolated, low-wage labor market and cut off from New Deal programs, some men still worked behind mules and plows. For their part, more than two out of every five black women in the labor force performed service in a private household, as excluded from the protection of labor law as those who worked the fields. "Negroes of the South have almost all the household jobs and nearly half of the laborer jobs," noted the economist Vivian Henderson in 1963. Only three in a hundred held clerical jobs.[11] In Atlanta, inquiring ministers found that "it is often necessary for Negro girls with one or more years of college training to work as maids. Negro men must take their college diplomas to the Post Office to work sorting mail."[12]

With the exception of tobacco factories and laundries, the same white managers who entrusted their children to black nannies balked at allowing black laborers to work at their machines. Confining African Americans to the occupational ghetto of manual labor, southern whites built fortifications around more desirable jobs so as to "give preferential status to White employees."[13] When non-farm employers hired blacks, it was in a strictly limited capacity: as unskilled or janitorial workers, or occasionally as semiskilled laborers thanks to the efforts of industrial unions in the 1940s and 1950s. There was virtually no "direct interracial competition for jobs" beyond the most "dead-end, isolated work." Even within a single firm, most occupations were known as either "white jobs" or "Negro jobs," with no traffic in between. Blacks who tried to cross the line were rebuffed with the reminder that "this is white man's work." To be accused of "getting out of place" was to risk reprisal, as white vigilantes in the South often targeted those who had managed to achieve some kind of success.[14]

Although the particulars varied by state, sector, and firm, white managers used common methods to keep black workers subordinate. They restricted them to particular job categories with distinctive application forms and segregated lines of seniority, sometimes in collaboration with white workers and their unions. They segregated workplace facilities, too, providing white-only restrooms, lunch rooms, drinking fountains, coffeepots, telephones, even time clocks. As the National Urban League summarized the brutal irony nationwide, "Every labor, management and government device intended to put the right man in the right job or to protect the worker is used to keep out the Negro." One study of North Carolina, the state with the second-largest African American population in the country, found in industry after industry "a rigid pattern of job discrimination based on separate lines of progression, the limiting of all Negroes, however well qualified, to menial job classifications, and the denial of equal seniority rights."[15] Those whose task was to gauge merit were blind to it in blacks. "We do not have a chance of getting a job making a decent salary," Helen Clinton of North Carolina told a committee of inquiry. When responding to an ad for a woman with a high school education (she herself had two years of college), "I was told they wanted white women only." No matter "how much education you might have they won't give you a chance at a job," she said. "It makes you feel awful."[16]

In the North, the division of labor was less stark but still forbidding. Here, blacks had a better chance of securing semiskilled positions as factory operatives, yet the skilled crafts, white-collar jobs in business, and professional positions with white-owned institutions remained largely out of reach. Airlines, for example, the very symbol of modernity, hired blacks for ground jobs only, never for in-flight work. Even in the most liberal locale in the nation, New York City, the racial division of labor in the workplace had long enjoyed the protection of law and custom and was still actively patrolled to keep good jobs a white monopoly.[17] The U.S. Labor Department's official *Dictionary of Occupational Titles* included racial slurs, leading a United Auto Workers union local in 1955 to protest the job title "niggerhead" as "a continuing insult to the millions of Negroes who are citizens of the United States."[18]

A small number of blacks managed to train for and secure better employment through determined effort and luck. In 1950, 2.2 percent of black men and 5.7 percent of black women worked as professionals. This feat was notable, yet the numbers were small, consisting largely of teachers of black children trained by historically black institutions. After graduation, African Americans found that they had to build their own analogues to the white-run professional associations that either refused them membership or kept them subordinate. By mid-century, black professionals had founded the National Bar Association, the National Medical Association, and the National Association of Colored Graduate Nurses, among others. Where African Americans enjoyed success in the business world, it was nearly always in black-owned firms.[19]

Once set in motion, the system of economic exclusion proved self-perpetuating. Parents who led hardscrabble lives and had little social power found it hard to push their children up the economic ladder, while an array of policies cut the ladder off just above its lowest rungs for most black climbers. A segregated educational system that grossly underfunded black schools was one such impediment. Where the slave South had made teaching blacks a criminal offense, the sharecropping South schooled its black labor force as little as possible. To protect planters from challenges and out-migration, southern communities usually spent a third to a half less on education than other regions of the country over the years 1890 to 1940.[20] Needing wages, and seeing no prospect of better jobs through continued schooling, most rural blacks stopped attending school early. In 1940, only 14 percent of black women and 11 percent of black men nationally had completed high school, compared to 40 percent of whites.[21] While professional and clerical jobs were out of bounds, black young people were also denied access to vocational training for skilled blue-collar jobs, allowing employers to claim that black applicants lacked the necessary qualifications for the work.[22] In the North, housing segregation ensured school segregation at the same time that it kept blacks isolated from word-of-mouth information about better positions.[23]

Raised in a world so divided, most whites in the 1950s could not imagine an inclusive workplace, much less operate one. White "children's attitudes toward Negroes," the psychologist Kenneth Clark observed, "are determined chiefly not by contact with Negroes but by contact with the prevailing attitudes toward Negroes." The results were insidious. "The white child in a white milieu," as a group of educators later put it, "builds into his personality a feeling of the rightness of whiteness," a conviction "that whiteness, the way he is, is natural and standard."[24] That conviction infused the culture to the point where most whites could not see obstacles to black mobility that appear, in hindsight, sharp as razor wire.

Other Americans of color also faced obstacles that put the family wage ideal beyond their reach. Mexican Americans were by far the largest minority in the country after African Americans, numbering about 5 million in the southwestern United States in 1960. Mexicans first became part of the U.S. population after the war with Mexico in the 1840s, when American peace treaty negotiators gained for the United States half of its neighbors' country. Thereafter, most Mexican Americans remained in the Southwest, where, like blacks, they were cut off from the huge wave of industrialization that benefited southern and eastern European immigrants in the North in the early twentieth century. Whether native-born or immigrant, Mexican Americans lacked the rights of full citizens, a truth brutally enacted when over 400,000 suffered forced expulsion to Mexico during the Great Depression. Agricultural employers depended on people of Mexican descent as a landless migrant labor force that could be shifted about with little interference. Treated as inferiors by whites and subjected to discrimination, Mexican Americans were nevertheless better off than blacks in having access to many public accommodations closed to blacks by Jim Crow laws, and in being treated as a significant constituency by white public officials.[25]

In the economy defined by these overlapping boundaries, women were almost invariably relegated to the low-status jobs deemed suitable for their sex and race. Black women, those women most likely to be in the labor force, were confined mainly to service and menial blue-collar work at mid-century, with annual earnings half those of white women. Employed Latinas tended to work with their families in the fields, in low-paid factory jobs such as in canneries, or, for lucky second-generation women, in clerical jobs. White women fared better, but not nearly so well as their own brothers or husbands. At mid-century, nearly all women labored in low-level, sex-segregated occupations. When they did gain work as professionals, it was usually in fields that men scorned, such as elementary school teaching, nursing, and librarianship. And although the absolute number of women professionals was growing slowly, women's share of professional jobs had actually dropped since the turn of the century. Married women workers had become scapegoats for job losses in the Great Depression, as fierce attacks on their right to work produced large-scale firings and downgrading that left women who might have aspired to careers demoralized about their prospects.[26] As for graduate education, after a brief opening of doors induced by the shortage of men during World War II, some colleges and universities held down women's enrollment to make way for male veterans. By the 1950s, near-certain discrimination combined with cultural pressure to encourage women to focus instead on their families.[27]

What kept the whole system intact was employers' conviction that they could do as they wished with their own resources, a conviction backed by a legal system that defined the rules of the industrial order. Businessmen had allies beyond their own ranks to defend their understanding of freedom of contract, thanks to the nation's founding commitment to the rights of property—and to the popular success myth that led so many whites to imagine themselves or their relatives someday sitting in the boss's chair. One teacher, for example, argued against fair employment legislation as an injustice because it would violate the "freedom of hiring [that] has been a man's right since the rights of Man were recognized." If an employer "wants a white man, he has the right to have him, regardless of who applies with equal credentials." Similarly, a self-described "friend of the negro" declared, "I cannot subscribe to a doctrine which denies to anyone the right to reject a negro—or a white person either—if negroes—or whites—*are* objectionable to him." Employers, he insisted, "have human rights which should be respected." To deny them full freedom of action, protested others, "savors of slavery"; it would be "socialistic tyranny."[28] This understanding of property rights as the core of liberty trumped claims to fair employment and equal access to jobs. The nation's courts, and most of its white citizens, agreed that American employers had, quite literally, "a right to discriminate."

⟶ YET THE APPEARANCE of stability within the culture of exclusion camouflaged a more complex reality. The supportive social order was weakening in the 1950s in ways that would increasingly invigorate struggles for inclusion in coming years. Political, economic, and social changes under way at the time enabled African American activists to demand inclusion as never before. Even "if he hasn't got the world in a jug," said Congressman Adam Clayton Powell, Jr., "the black man . . . has the stopper in his hand."[29]

In 1940, with World War II looming, A. Philip Randolph, the head of the leading black trade union in the United States, had conceived the first national mass movement against employment discrimination. Announcing to the nation, "We Loyal Colored American Citizens Demand the Right to Work and Fight for Our Country," organizers of the March on Washington movement vowed that ten thousand demonstrators would converge on the nation's capital to protest the use of Jim Crow factories and a Jim Crow military in a war against fascism. The movement won the nation's most active unions to its side when the Congress of Industrial Organizations (CIO) condemned job discrimination as a "direct attack against our nation's policy to build democracy in our fight against Hitlerism." Fearful that the unrest could disrupt military preparations, President Franklin Delano Roosevelt announced Executive Order 8802. The first presidential order to benefit blacks since Reconstruction, it outlawed discrimination by companies and unions engaged in war work on government contracts and created a mechanism to fight it: a federal Fair Employment Practice Committee. As the FEPC helped black workers enter good defense industry jobs, the experience taught a clear lesson: that progress would come from a combination of grassroots organizing and federal action against recalcitrant employers.[30]

The demands of mobilization against a fascist enemy opened all kinds of long-standing prejudices to question and challenge. For the first time, immigrants from eastern and southern Europe came to feel recognized as full Americans. African Americans, too, found new leverage with which to argue for fair treatment. "Prove to us," Walter White of the NAACP challenged white America, "that you are not hypocrites when you say this is a war for freedom." Black activists waged what some dubbed the "Double V" campaign for victory over fascism abroad and racism at home. As the NAACP's monthly journal, *The Crisis*, urged its millions of readers in 1944, "The Dixie octopus strangling the rest of the country must be shaken off."[31]

In the vanguard of the postwar movement stood many black veterans who had sacrificed for "the free world" and now wanted to live in one. Some 500,000 African Americans had served in the military during the war. When they came home, studies found that four in five wanted to escape forever the kind of work they did before the war. They confronted roadblocks at every turn, starting with the Veterans Administration itself. Angry, many became active in the NAACP, the CIO, and other groups fighting for fairness. William A. Ashby, a longtime leader in the Newark, New Jersey, Urban League, described the feelings of thousands of his peers. "They said: 'I'm tired of all this goddam crap. Tired of hearing the white man say, 'I can't serve no niggers in my restaurant,' tired of being told, 'I ain't got no place for colored in my hotel.' Why, hell, I've been to Europe. Hitler leveled his bullets at me. Missed. I went to the Pacific. Mr. Hirohito sent his madmen at me to blow me to hell in their planes. I'm still here. Why don't I tell the white man, 'Take your goddam boots off my neck! Get the hell out of my road so I can pass! I know how to run around you or jump over you.'"[32]

Although white women and Mexican Americans also organized at mid-century, none pressed for economic inclusion as hard as African Americans did. More than others, black activists drew on long-held convictions to deny the legitimacy of the prevailing social hierarchy. In the antebellum era, African Americans who escaped the South and the abolitionists allied with them protested the starkest form of job segregation imaginable, that practiced by "the Slave Power." After emancipation left African Americans an overwhelmingly working-class people, many tried in various ways to gain better terms of employment. In the late nineteenth century, some fought to end a new form of unfree labor based on race, the convict lease system. Others looked to labor unions to improve the jobs they already held. In coal mines and lumber camps, on docks and in laundries, black workers joined together— sometimes in rocky alliance with white workers—to make their jobs pay and to exercise more power.[33]

They were able to mobilize against exclusion as powerfully as they did during the war, owing to a series of profound changes in national life. The most important were those set in motion during the Great Depression, when the country embraced the principle of social citizenship. Along with basic civil and political rights, Americans won social rights, including public provision for common human needs such as old age security, to be guaranteed by the national government, as well as freedom from employer discrimination against union members. Without this prior commitment to the principle of social citizenship, government action to promote the inclusion of black workers would have been unthinkable, for it presupposed a federal right to intervene in businesses and to claim precedence over states in labor-related matters. Just as national New Deal programs helped bring increased parity in wages and working conditions north and south, so government might now be urged to bring convergence between whites and blacks. In an omen of the future, the number of African American federal workers tripled between the Hoover presidency and 1941 to reach 150,000; although most remained in the lowest grades, they still enjoyed more security than private-sector workers.[34]

In their appeals to the federal government, blacks found new allies in the labor movement—or, rather, that part of it forged in the crucible of the depression: the Congress of Industrial Organizations. Its organizers rejected the strategy of exclusionary and segregationist craft unionism that labor had pursued for half a century for a new vision of social unionism. They organized all workers in the nation's mass production industries, unskilled as well as skilled, believing that the security of any worker depended on the involvement of all. On this basis, organizers appealed to black workers as well as white, and by war's end had enrolled four out of every five manufacturing workers. By 1943, some 400,000 black workers had joined, backed by middle-class black leaders as well as white co-workers. CIO unions did not eliminate workplace discrimination, nor did most try. But they provided black workers with powerful tools to tackle it: collective bargaining as a means to compel employers to agree to union demands, seniority to prevent arbitrary firings, grievance systems to appeal violations of workers' rights, and one of the country's most powerful lobbying bodies committed to economic justice and an expanded welfare state. "The CIO has brought more hope for progress to Negroes than any other social institution in the South," wrote the southern-born organizer Lucy Mason Randolph. "Of first significance to Negroes is the acknowledgment of themselves as persons entitled to democratic respect," an acknowledgment that opened the way to national belonging.[35]

The new conditions in turn strengthened black protest organizations as vehicles for economic inclusion as well as civil rights. The NAACP, founded in 1909, had long pursued a gradual strategy of changing the law that placated wealthy white donors while neglecting the pressing needs of its overwhelmingly working-class constituency. But facing criticism and competition from black radicals in the 1930s, the organization increasingly turned attention to the needs of black working people and allied with the CIO. So, too, did the once anti-union National Urban League, whose founding motto was "Not Alms But Opportunity." Calling for "jobs and justice," the League now advised black workers to "get into somebody's union and stay there." It worked with the NAACP, the National Negro Congress, and the National Council of Negro Women to expose discrimination in New Deal programs and push for universal social rights.[36] By the end of the decade, most black leaders came out boldly for an end to Jim Crow. "It is not a question of wanting to sit in the classroom with white students," the legal strategist Charles Houston made clear. "It is a question of vindicating one's citizenship." In 1942 these groups gained a new ally when radical Christian pacifists developed the Congress of Racial Equality (CORE). One founder was James Farmer, who had earned a bachelor of divinity degree at Howard University but abstained from ordination because "I didn't see how I could honestly preach the Gospel of Christ in a church that practiced discrimination." Devoted to direct action for justice, Farmer took from the CIO the idea of "sit-down strikes" and backed the nation's first sit-ins to end segregation in restaurants and workplaces.[37]

The Brotherhood of Sleeping Car Porters (BSCP), a significant force in black and national political life, illustrates the dynamics of social change at mid-century. Black railroad workers faced bitter discrimination in a division of labor so systematic that it later gained notice as

"one of the most highly institutionalized forms of industrial segregation in our land." But in a telling commentary on Jim Crow, the rail-
roads' Pullman car porter jobs were highly desirable because they paid
better than most jobs African American men could get; the tens of
thousands who held them became an esteemed elite in a community
where class divisions remained relatively shallow. After decades of organizing attempts, in the 1930s the porters won a union representation election, led by the brilliant A. Philip Randolph, the Florida-born
grandson of slaves and son of a self-taught minister. Randolph had escaped the South as a teenager by laboring in the kitchen of a passenger
ship bound for New York. There he worked day jobs while attending
night school at City College, and joined the Socialist Party. A staunch
advocate of unions, Randolph was recruited by Pullman porters to
organize their trade. Backed by this well-organized, forward-looking
constituency, Randolph for years led the fight for better jobs and full
citizenship for black workers. Thanks to their unions, railroad men by
mid-century might own their own homes and send their children to
college.[38]

Beginning in the depression, African Americans drew attention to
their desperation for jobs. In New York City, a study commissioned by
the mayor to make sense of the Harlem riot of 1935 found that the
source of the community's problems was that black workers were denied employment that paid a decent living. "The first and most fundamental problem of the Negro citizens of Harlem," the illustrious bi-ra-
cial panel concluded, "is the economic problem."[39] Addressing that
problem, blacks not only in New York but also in other cities such as
Chicago, Detroit, and Baltimore claimed new rights to jobs based on
their standing as consumers. They organized against white employers
in their communities who profited from the purchases of blacks but refused to employ them. Under the slogan "Don't Buy Where You Can't
Work," they picketed offending businesses to demand the hiring of
blacks in proportion to their presence in the area population.[40]

Working in local groups, labor, and government, black activists began to gain a wider hearing among progressive whites and stimulated
them to doubt time-honored ways of thinking. More and more, American scholars were challenging the biological racism spread by nine-
teenth-century intellectuals. The Columbia University anthropologist
Franz Boas led the way in the first decades of the century. Declaring
that "culture makes man, not race," Boas and his colleagues put the

burden of proof on those who claimed that nonwhites lacked ability. Their research modeled a new relativism that demonstrated how environment shaped culture. In the 1930s they at last broke through the old orthodoxy in discipline after discipline, as their research in psychology, sociology, and history amplified the messages of scholar-activists such as W. E. B. DuBois, Louis Adamic, and Carey McWilliams. "Intellectual revolutions can rarely be dated with precision," writes one observer, "yet, clearly the attitudes of social scientists in the United States changed markedly" at this time.[41]

The new ways of thinking reached white readers with the 1944 publication of *An American Dilemma: The Negro Problem and Modern Democracy*. In this massive study funded by the Carnegie Corporation, the Swedish economist Gunnar Myrdal and his team of U.S. researchers concluded that the so-called "Negro problem" was really a problem of whites. "Though our study includes economic, social, and political race relations," they wrote, "at bottom our problem is the moral dilemma of the American" who extolled fairness in the abstract yet systematically denied it to African Americans. The U.S. Supreme Court, hearing lawsuits brought by African Americans, began in a string of decisions after 1938 to chip away at Jim Crow.[42]

⌒ As the New Deal enabled blacks to organize more successfully, it also gave them urgent reason to do so. By paying to reduce production, New Deal farm policy encouraged cotton planters to shed workers as well. And that undermined the sharecropping system that had sustained the exclusion of blacks from power for almost a century. Where once planters had tried to keep laborers tied to the land, restricting their education and their access to the wider world, now they expelled them and, in the World War II era, turned to machines instead. The proportion of black men employed in agriculture, forestry, and fisheries, 42.5 percent in 1939, plummeted to 12.5 percent by 1959 as mechanization plowed under the labor system that black disfranchisement had aimed to protect. Machines picked 5 percent of the nation's cotton in 1950; ten years later the figure was 50 percent, and 98 percent ten years after that. In the space of twenty years a whole social system was all but gone. Nearly 20 million people, black and white, left agrarian life in the 1940s and 1950s in "one of the largest and most rapid mass internal movements of people in history."[43]

Escaping the fields, rural blacks joined wage earners and professionals in cities and towns where organizing was possible with fewer life-threatening reprisals from white supremacist vigilantes. Urban black communities started to amass other resources needed for the battle against exclusion. Between 1930 and 1960, the percentage of black southerners living in urban areas almost doubled to 58 percent. City life offered better jobs and pay as well as more safety, and black incomes in the South, while still very low, improved from 1949 to 1962. As migrants used their greater security and resources to strengthen community institutions, church congregations gained members as well as confidence to speak out on racial injustice. Black colleges grew, too: between 1941 and 1964, the proportion of blacks who had completed college rose from less than 2 percent to over 5 percent. Black voter registration more than quadrupled between 1944 and 1950 to more than half a million, with virtually all the growth in southern cities. In the North and West, black voters acquired the numbers to decide some elections.[44] Together, these changes inspired growing numbers to organize for access to good jobs and the full belonging in the polity they implied.

For a few years after the war, the movement went from strength to strength. As membership in unions and the NAACP alike surged to unheard-of heights, labor and black groups often joined together to fight Jim Crow in workplaces, and sometimes in housing, schooling, and public accommodations. Led by left-wing African Americans in CIO unions, the movement in New York City fought to open good jobs, gain better housing and schools, end police brutality, help free peoples of color worldwide from colonial rule, and more. "It forged the modern urban Black political agenda," notes the historian Martha Biondi, "which included demands from criminal justice reform to affirmative action that would shape Black advocacy for the rest of the century." The vision went beyond civil rights per se to genuine equality in a more robust democracy.[45]

New Yorkers were not alone in this quest. Around the country, increasingly radical organizing for racial equality, backed by African Americans' new power in progressive labor unions, developed in places from Detroit and Los Angeles to Memphis, Tennessee, and Durham, North Carolina. In the South, NAACP membership quadrupled to over 400,000 in 1946, while northern-led black civil rights organizations worked in coalition with Jewish organizations such as the American Jewish Congress, the American Jewish Committee, and the Jewish Labor Committee to work for civil rights legislation that would benefit both groups.[46] By 1948 the movement was strong enough to make racial justice an issue in the U.S. presidential race and split the party of the once Solid South three ways. Running as the candidate of the breakaway Progressive Party, Henry Wallace called "the race problem . . . the South's and the nation's number one problem." As Harry Truman, in turn, struggled to keep black voters loyal to the Democratic Party, he ran on a platform committed to civil rights as never before— so much so that South Carolina's Strom Thurmond led a mutiny of Dixiecrats to form a new States' Rights Party. Short-lived as both third parties proved, the Democratic mainstream would never return to where it had been before; black voters mattered too much in key northern states.[47]

But the momentum soon came to an abrupt stop. As the United States and the Soviet Union clashed after the war, their conflict set off a "red scare" that devastated organizing for economic inclusion. The labor radicalism that had encouraged blacks and Hispanics to fight discrimination turned out to be vulnerable in the cold war because communists, black and white, were among its most passionate activists. As radicals came under attack from white authorities, liberal and social-democratic leaders also shunned them and pushed them out. The situation was complicated; many activists had understandable qualms about Stalinism and Communist Party tactics. But the toll was ruinous. "The leftists were the only ones who could mobilize white supporters to support a black picket and strikes of black workers," one Memphis labor activist later rued. "When they broke up the left coalition, then they began to lose the strikes." The left had also led in advancing black interests on the job. In the recession of 1949, for example, communists pressed hard to preserve the wartime foothold blacks had gained in industry. They argued that seniority should be suspended so as to keep blacks, the last hired, from being first fired. In the two left-led unions that also had a say in hiring, it was the leftists who ensured that one in every four workers placed in jobs was black, argued for work-sharing instead of layoffs, and pushed for what the then rank-and-filer David Montgomery described as "the automatic awarding of two to five years seniority to all Blacks, to compensate for the many decades in which they had been barred from employment in the industries altogether."

After radicals were driven from leadership, no one made such proposals for many years.[48]

By the late 1940s, anticommunism was crippling efforts at jobs and justice. Nationally, leaders of the CIO were terrified that resurgent Republicans in Congress would license an open shop drive like the one that followed World War I. Anxious to stave off a mortal threat as well as to solidify their own control, they clamped down on radicals. Driven by the anti-labor Taft-Hartley Act, passed in 1947, the CIO expelled eleven international unions in 1949 with over 1 million members, among them those that had fought hardest to change employer and union racism. With the CIO debilitated by the purge and drained by ongoing rivalry from the more conservative American Federation of Labor (AFL), and with conservative Republicans and southern Democrats dominating Congress, efforts to win a permanent FEPC came to naught. The NAACP had made this reform its "top legislative priority" in 1949, but the cold war doomed it. The alliance of southern Democrats and conservative Republicans using anticommunism to fight reform was simply too powerful.[49]

In the meantime, to be concerned with black rights was to be suspected of subversion in the eyes of ever more influential anticommunists in and out of government. When fair employment legislation was proposed for New York State in 1945, for example, the popular conservative columnist Westbrook Pegler insisted that "all such proposals . . . are the work of Communists and their kind[,] whose intent is not to open opportunities for Negroes but to cause friction and provoke disorder by creating intolerable personal situations." Within a few years, such thinking had infected the mainstream. "Of course," said the chair of a loyalty review panel in the postal service, "the fact that a person believes in racial equality doesn't *prove* that he's a Communist, but it certainly makes you look twice, doesn't it? You can't get away from the fact that racial equality is part of the Communist line." "Anything that benefited Black people at the time," a woman then doing union organizing explained, "was labeled by our government as red, as communist." Southern segregationists developed a particularly extreme and long-lived anticommunism to paralyze organizing and immunize white supremacy from democratic challenge.[50]

Like the CIO, the NAACP purged its ranks to appease the attackers and ensure national leaders' control. It disbanded branches and dis-

pensed with members who seemed risky—even its founder, the tower-
ing intellectual W. E. B. DuBois. Some branches grew so nervous that
they refused to accept white members for fear they might be leftists.
This menacing climate yielded a weaker and more cautious civil rights
movement in the early 1950s, one fearful of direct action, mass politics,
or economic demands that might draw the ire of red-baiting critics. In
New York City, the epicenter of African American organizing, anticommunism ravaged the cause. Nearly all those involved "suffered
persecution, investigation, repression, or censorship." Most historians
now concur that, as one put it, "anticommunism proved invaluable to
white supremacists during the 1940s and 1950s."[51]

Setting back racial equality in many areas, the red scare especially
hurt the quest for jobs and justice. It enabled northern business interests, represented by conservative Republicans, and southern white supremacists, represented by the Democratic Party, to block expansion of
the New Deal to groups denied its benefits, such as agricultural and domestic service workers, and to prevent the expansion of social citizenship to new areas such as the provision of health care. As the very
idea of economic equality became suspect, resurgent corporate political power brought renewed popular white support for private property
rights over human rights. The years from 1948 to the early 1960s witnessed a revival of corporate sway over public affairs to a degree not
seen since the Gilded Age.[52] With renewed business hegemony, momentum for government-backed equal job rights practically dissolved.

In the name of true Americanism, the National Association of Manufacturers (NAM) and the U.S. Chamber of Commerce fought any interference with managerial autonomy. Eager to reclaim authority and
prerogatives lost in the depression years, those leading business associations were determined to make sure that the federal government
did not gain any new powers, such as the responsibility to enforce
equal opportunity. NAM warned that laws prohibiting employment
discrimination would "overemphasize differences among peoples" and
so "might aggravate—rather than eliminate—antagonism and strife."
By 1952, anticommunism had turned the tide, as the Republican Party
gained control of both houses of Congress and put General Dwight Eisenhower in the White House. "For the first time in twenty years,"
notes one scholar, "friends of business dominated government in
Washington."[53]

Just as the new conservative ethos suppressed challenges to the racial hierarchy, so too did it shore up restrictive gender roles. Mixing older notions that a woman's primary obligation was to her husband and children with a crude Freudian emphasis on biology as destiny, the new ideology assigned women the job of serving their work-weary spouses and attention-seeking children. The focus on family "togetherness" and the emphasis on service to men and children took aim at the autonomy many American women had developed in wartime jobs and experiences. "Women Aren't Men," chided a popular 1950 magazine article, as it summed up the new imperative: "It is for woman as mother, actual or vicarious, to restore security in our insecure world." In private as in public life, the credo of opinion makers was "containment."[54]

So enveloping was the racially specific family norm in postwar culture that it blinded even liberal whites. Social commentators who wrote searching critiques of American society in these years had trouble including African Americans in their thinking. Cut off by segregation from the deepest well of dissatisfaction in their society, white intellectuals found it easy to believe, as Seymour Martin Lipset sunnily declared, that "the fundamental problems of the industrial revolution have been solved." Even sociologists who made their living studying race relations failed to grasp the depth of black discontent, let alone to imagine the mass movement that was about to shatter the manufactured calm of the era. When white liberal intellectuals commented on the black experience or civil rights in the early 1950s, it was to promote what the black journalist Carl Rowan called a "cult of moderation."[55]

What most troubled even radical white critics in these years was not the exclusion of others but the archetypal white man's loss of independence and self-direction—his "conformity." Willy Loman, the tragic hero created by Arthur Miller in his Pulitzer Prize–winning play *Death of a Salesman*, was the quintessential example. Loman held a job to which few blacks had access and lived in a suburban community that would not have allowed them to buy homes, yet he was to stand as the American Everyman. Paul Goodman, author of the irreverent *Growing Up Absurd*, which would become a manifesto for later student activists, skewered the inanity of much adult life in contemporary America. Yet he understood the challenges of work and identity as a problem confronting young white males alone. Faced with a meaningless post as vice president of a company, "an idealistic young fellow would not want to be such a man," Goodman declared. "It's hard to grow up when there isn't enough man's work." The 30 percent of Americans "who are still ill fed and ill housed and more outcast than ever" escaped his notice as actors whose concerns about work, meaningful or otherwise, counted. They appeared, instead, as the "them" for whom "we" could do more. The *One-Dimensional Man* of Herbert Marcuse's influential treatise was likewise assumed to be white and male; the ways in which others might experience the constraints or promises of modern life went unexplored. In C. Wright Mills's brilliant explorations of the new middle class and the "power elite" in postwar America, race was not a category of analysis. Exclusion was taken for granted.[56] Looking north from the South in the 1950s, the view was bleak indeed. "We have such a feeling here," the white progressive Virginia Durr wrote from Alabama, "that we have been abandoned by the rest of the country and by the government and left to the tender mercies of the Ku Klux Klan."[57]

In fact, few white Americans in any walk of life anticipated the challenge that was coming. In 1954 the U.S. Supreme Court shook them from their complacency when it overthrew federal support of black exclusion that went back to the *Plessy v. Ferguson* decision of 1896. Ruling unanimously in *Brown v. Board of Education*, the justices decreed segregation in education a denial of equal constitutional rights. They built their ruling on the legal precedents that NAACP attorneys such as Charles Houston and Thurgood Marshall had amassed in case after case since 1938. Once the high court reconciled itself to the New Deal, it agreed with them that political party primary elections that excluded blacks, segregation on interstate transportation, and inferior Jim Crow graduate and professional education violated the Constitution, and that railroad unions with state-granted exclusive bargaining power owed black members a "duty of fair representation."[58]

A pivotal victory, the *Brown* decision showed how the sword of the cold war might be made to cut two ways. As much as anticommunism had hurt grassroots organizing for inclusion, it also gave the cause unprecedented leverage. As international rivalry shifted from Europe to the nonaligned nations of Asia, Africa, and Latin America in the 1950s, U.S. leaders sought to counter Soviet claims of American racism in order to win support. Harry Truman put the imperative in his own curt way: "The top dog in a world which is 90 percent colored ought to clean his own house." The government's *amicus* brief in *Brown* communicated this recognition to the Court: "It is in the context of the present world struggle between freedom and tyranny that the problem of race discrimination must be viewed." Taking advantage of the opening created by the high court's decision and building on the social changes at mid-century, civil rights seekers rallied. "The magnitude of the decision shocked me," the black scholar Horace Cayton remarked. "A large hole had opened in the dike of segregation, and through it would soon pour a torrent."[59]

~ 2

The Fight Begins

$\mathcal{I}$ N 1955, two insurgent movements broke through the superficial calm. Both claimed to represent the best of the American tradition, but what they valued differed starkly. Each embraced half of the divided heart of a nation pledged to liberty and justice for all, yet founded on slavery and unequal citizenship. African American activists struggling for inclusion stressed the promise of equality, opportunity, and fair reward for earned achievement. White conservatives, aiming to fend off change, stressed the traditions of economic liberty, small government, and privileged access for a minority. Gaining courage from the social developments altering the ground of politics, and confident that the Declaration of Independence represented the true soul of America, the black freedom movement revived from its cold war wounds and, with the Montgomery, Alabama, bus boycott, reestablished civil rights as a mass movement. Over the next decade, the demand for access to better employment would become an ever more vital part of the civil rights movement's grassroots and national efforts. Linking jobs to justice in creative ways immune from the red-baiting that destroyed earlier campaigns, participants built a broad coalition for reform.

Activists proposed a radical departure from the culture of exclusion, yet one anchored in values at the core of American political culture. After Montgomery, an ever-growing minority of African Americans

35

joined with mounting numbers of white allies to pry open the fissures that social change had opened in the foundations of exclusion. Picketing businesses that hired only white workers, they protested the injustice of taking blacks' dollars while denying them the chance to earn more. Training and referring would-be workers, they exposed claims of black unpreparedness as a poor excuse. Testing state fair employment laws, they revealed the impotence of formal equal opportunity in the face of pervasive, long-standing injustice. They worked for something both more tangible and more profound than "color-blind" neutrality in law. They sought to dismantle a whole culture of exclusion and, in its stead, to reconstruct workplaces so as to invite all to achieve their potential. Their efforts fractured business unity, made the labor movement more accountable to its minority members, and ultimately, in 1964, succeeded in getting the federal government to provide black workers a powerful tool with which to open an entry into the economic mainstream: Title VII of the Civil Rights Act.

As African Americans rallied to their cause, white conservatives began organizing to defend theirs. Seeking to shore up exclusion in the face of the many forces eroding it, they venerated not the visionary promises of the nation's founders but their actual practice. The organized right attracted less attention than the black freedom struggle in these formative years, but its intellectual leaders developed a core body of ideas that would in time become influential as they, too, built a powerful movement to change the country. Making common cause with southern segregationists, spokespersons for national conservatism denounced the black movement. Seeking to check its advance at every point, conservatives organized against the *Brown* decision, allied with the white Citizens' Councils founded in Montgomery, and fought passage of the Civil Rights Act.

For the next half century the two causes remained locked in conflict as black activists fought subordinate status. Understanding themselves as hardworking, faith-grounded, education-seeking, law-abiding citizens determined to achieve the American dream, they could not but clash with those whose defense of American history and business impugned them as unqualified and unworthy. As champions of the nation's past, conservative leaders had their own ambitious vision for remaking the nation. Their views on social order, the proper domain of government, the roles of management and labor, the import of the

Constitution, the message of religious faith, and the relation of the United States to the world, let alone race, all led them to oppose African Americans' quest for equality.

~ IN THEIR 381-DAY STRUGGLE, the black residents of Montgomery reclaimed mass direct action as a strategy of popular protest, and so revived American democracy after the contrived calm of the early 1950s. Organizing a city that white residents touted as the Cradle of the Confederacy, movement leaders put traditional ideals to new ends as they made demands for dignified treatment, full citizenship, and racial equality synonymous with love of God and country. The struggle began with the quiet act of an older working woman who exposed southern "chivalry" as a lie when she refused to give up her seat on the bus to a white man who demanded it. Rosa Parks was a committed NAACP leader and veteran of the labor-left Highlander folk school; yet she and other activists emphasized their more orthodox commitments to advance the movement in the daunting climate of 1950s Alabama. Foremost among these commitments were Christian faith, devotion to a better America, and social respectability. Meeting nightly in churches, the Montgomery campaign selected a young clergyman with a doctorate, Martin Luther King, Jr., as its public voice. It gave rise to a new organization led by ministers of the gospel, the Southern Christian Leadership Conference (SCLC), whose participants understood how identifying as "Christian" would not only communicate the faith that sustained them but also act as an amulet against charges of communism. "Everything we did was considered Communist," recalled King's aide Andrew Young. "I think almost to survive we tended to phrase everything in religious terms and to avoid issues that smacked of economic change." When city police jailed King, he declared, "What we are doing is just," and so "God is with us." Whereas, in the late 1940s, anticommunist white supremacists had impugned activists' patriotism, the new movement joined the Christian trinity to the secular one of freedom and justice and equality. "We are not struggling merely for the rights of Negroes," King asserted. "We are determined to make America a better place for all people. . . . It is one of the greatest glories of America that we have the right to protest."[1]

Though it went little noticed in the press at the time or since amidst the drama of their larger struggle for dignity and equal treatment in public accommodations, the tens of thousands of bus boycotters also demanded, in the words of one participant, "a handful of jobs for Negro drivers."[2] The least prominent goal among many in Montgomery, the call for jobs would grow stronger in the years ahead. African Americans had long put their hopes in employment as a route to advancement, understanding economic security as essential to autonomy and justice. Indeed, the massive research project that resulted in Gunnar Myrdal's tome, *An American Dilemma,* had found that of all the forms of discrimination facing blacks, economic discrimination worried them most; issues such as intermarriage that so absorbed whites mattered least to them, barely factoring against their deep yearning for more and better jobs. That desire underlay the alliance built between civil rights groups and industrial unions in the 1930s, and helped make the establishment of a permanent federal fair employment practices committee the leading legislative goal of the NAACP throughout the 1940s. In the South, the life-threatening dangers and daily humiliations of Jim Crow all but forced activists to concentrate on the basic civil rights without which nothing else could be achieved. But in the North and West, where blacks already had formal rights, the quest for better employment opportunities was among the core demands of the movement in the 1950s as before, even if sometimes muted by fears of red-baiting.[3]

As King, representing the southern struggle, developed relationships with Bayard Rustin and A. Philip Randolph, representing the northern struggle, the regional agendas cross-pollinated. King saw, as Rustin counseled, that "economics is part of our struggle." For their part, worried corporate researchers found in the mid-1950s that among "younger Negroes," equal employment opportunity was "rated the No. 1 goal."[4]

A few years earlier, Mary McLeod Bethune of the National Council of Negro Women had anticipated the arguments that would have resonance in the cold war world by tying the quest for good jobs to mainstream white values and concerns. "The right to work," she told an increasingly Republican Congress in 1944, "is a right to live." Ending employment exclusion was the truly patriotic thing to do. The Declaration of Independence, the Constitution, the national faith in free labor, and the evangelical conviction that souls were equal in the eyes of God all pointed in the same direction. "As an American," she said, "I have been imbued with a love of freedom, a belief in the rights of the individual, a respect for and loyalty to our Constitution." How long, she asked, "in the name of American fair play, can we ignore these discriminations, particularly the denial of the right to work at one's highest capacity and capabilities?"[5]

The movement's independent course by the time of the Montgomery struggle was not simply dictated by anticommunism; it was a choice made through collective learning from experience. White liberals had proved valuable allies, but not dependable ones. The national Democratic Party had made peace, albeit a troubled peace, with its southern white supremacist wing as the price of holding power. More wholehearted was the peace white liberals made with racially skewed capitalism as they shed the ambitions for "industrial democracy" that had animated the New Deal in the 1930s. The new liberalism of the postwar years "would not try to redistribute economic power and limit inequality so much as it would create a compensatory welfare system." That retreat on the part of whites from a class-based movement for universal social justice all but ensured that blacks would have to fight for economic justice as a matter of racial discrimination and civil rights. Many liberal organizations, such as Americans for Democratic Action and the American Jewish Committee, had so feared attack from anticommunists that they lost the commitment they once held to thoroughgoing equality. Trying to make headway in the forbidding climate of the fifties, they hesitated to push the class politics that were so vital to black advance and instead depicted racism as a psychological and cultural problem as they pursued gradual change. Some white religious leaders were moved to action by the movement's invocation of a God of compassion yet of ultimate justice for the sinful. But "eleven o'clock on Sunday morning," as King put it, "is the most segregated hour [in] America."[6] The support of such whites was helpful to African Americans, but not enough to justify sacrificing their autonomy.

Seeking to balance their need for allies and for operational freedom, black civil rights groups developed a coalition strategy embodied in the Leadership Conference on Civil Rights (LCCR). An outgrowth of the postwar campaign for a peacetime fair employment practices commission, the LCCR was created by a broad group of civil rights, CIO, and liberal leaders in 1952. Multiplying through cooperation their power to press for change, they signaled that the movement had entered a new era. Especially notable was the NAACP's shift from relying on elite contacts to lobbying with broad-based pressure by allied organizations. Coming together for protection from attack as well as for synergy, the groups stood on their shared American values in place of the particularity that had made organizing vulnerable to opponents in the late 1940s.[7]

Besides the civil right groups, the key participant in the LCCR was the CIO, the main base of liberal power and the repository of radical black hopes in the 1930s. "Organized labor can be one of the most powerful instruments" for fighting racial inequality, as King put it in 1957. Not only had the CIO enlisted the unskilled alongside the skilled, blacks alongside whites, men alongside women. It also understood that full employment, backed by government, was essential to racial justice. At the close of World War II, the black New Dealer Robert C. Weaver had urged that planning for full employment be put at the core of postwar politics. Anything less, he predicted, would take a terrible toll on workers of color, because whites would fear blacks as competitors and resist elementary fairness. In the United States, he warned, "it's work or fight on the color line."[8] After the war, the CIO spoke eloquently on behalf of full employment as it worked hard for civil rights legislation. Corporate researchers found that unions, particularly CIO unions, enjoyed a far better reputation for fairness among black employees than did business.[9]

But civil rights leaders of this era knew that they could not rely too heavily on the labor movement. For one thing, labor represented only a minority of black workers; it left out large sectors such as agriculture and service. For another, unions were divided by race, region, and organizing model. The craft unions in the American Federation of Labor (AFL) building trades earned their reputations as the most hostile to blacks by barring them from skilled construction work. Even in the more egalitarian industrial unions of the CIO, however, national leaders and rank-and-file activists found that they had to tread carefully so as not to lose white members, who, like other whites, were unwilling to give up the advantages they had over blacks in jobs, education, housing, municipal services, and citizenship rights. One Mississippi unionist complained to the AFL-CIO that "if we were to turn out all the people down here who want Segregation we would not have enough of us left to carry our Local's Business much less help others to organize." So many white unionists joined or sympathized with the Citizens' Coun-

cils and the Ku Klux Klan, the Southern Regional Council found, that
southern labor leaders preferred to avoid any discussion of the issue.
Their unions were already in a fight for survival in the region, as the
cold war put labor on the defensive everywhere, especially where it was
weak to begin with.[10]

When the AFL and CIO merged in 1955, commitment to fighting
for the interests of black workers deteriorated. Its dissipation was signaled by the AFL-CIO's choice of a white AFL economist as its director of civil rights; Boris Shiskin spent much of his time defending craft
unions from blacks' complaints and criticizing civil rights leaders. The
federation's top officials hesitated to interfere with affiliates that excluded or subordinated black workers and defended seniority systems
erected on an undeniably Jim Crow basis.[11] Black civil rights leaders
recognized the variety and complexity of the labor movement: while
some unionists acted as irreplaceable allies, others acted as hindrances,
so autonomy was essential to black progress.

Their confidence enhanced by the grassroots determination shown
after Montgomery, union-based civil rights activists challenged labor
leaders to live up to their motto that "an injury to one is an injury to
all." Invited by A. Philip Randolph, seventy-five black trade union officials formed the Negro American Labor Council (NALC) in 1960
to protest discrimination and demand more than "tokenism." When
Randolph reminded the AFL-CIO executive council that "even in liberal New York State it took the intercession of [the] Attorney General
. . . to get one Negro apprentice in the training program of journeyman plumbers in 1961," he was tackling Federation president George
Meany on his home ground. Meany, a plumber by trade and the son of
a plumber, had launched his career from that union. Going on to expose how other forms of racial bias hurt black workers and damaged
the labor movement, Randolph called for an overhaul of the organization's entirely white civil rights department to repair "the crisis of confidence between the Negro community and the labor community."
When Randolph's appeal was answered not with energetic assent but
with outrage and spurious countercharges, King defended him and
begged AFL-CIO leaders to "honestly look to weaknesses in our relationship" in recognition that the causes of "economic justice and the
brotherhood of man" were inseparable.[12] At the NAACP, Roy Wilkins
rejected labor leaders' paternalism, saying that any "unity" between

blacks and labor that could be sundered by demands for elementary fairness must be "a precarious thing." In that case, "its destruction may be regarded as not a calamity, but a blessed clearing of the air." Wilkins pledged that henceforth the NAACP would accept only "honest and adult partnership" with labor.[13]

Thus, after Montgomery, a variety of activists worked pragmatically to open good jobs to African Americans. They often disagreed on strategy and went their own ways: while NALC participants believed that union activism was the best route, the NAACP stressed legal challenges, CORE urged community-based direct action, and the Urban League promoted job training for workers whom it entreated companies to hire. All experimented in the late fifties and early sixties with new campaigns to gain access to better jobs.[14] The labor and industry committees in NAACP branches, aided by the NAACP's labor secretary, Herbert Hill, pressured employers to hire black workers, urged government to use its power of contract to ensure fair employment, and pushed unions to desegregate seniority lines and represent their black members as they did whites. They also joined coalitions, such as the one led by Randolph in 1961 that drew Malcolm X, then a Nation of Islam minister, into a joint rally with trade union and civil rights leaders demanding equal job opportunities and other basic rights.[15] At the same time, CORE revived the "Don't buy where you can't work" activism of the depression, picketing employers from North Carolina to California to New York with demands to hire black workers.[16] The National Urban League, for its part, had always understood employment as the key to racial equality even though it shied away from mass protest. Once Whitney M. Young, Jr., assumed the helm in 1961, the League put growing resources into job training and placement through its National Skills Bank and worked diligently to open up new job opportunities. Martin Luther King, Jr., and the SCLC aided victims of employment discrimination, while some black rank-and-file workers organized caucuses in their unions.[17] From such varied bases, activists widened the cracks in the system of exclusion.

Jobs activists organized education and training efforts to prepare African Americans for new opportunities as they pushed employers toward more aggressive recruitment and hiring. They fused a commitment to "self-help" or "self-improvement" with demands for social reform, matching supply-side preparation to demand-side pressure.

Some organizations took up the work of training job seekers, first on a volunteer basis and later under government manpower training contracts. The flagship program was the Opportunities Industrialization Center, opened by the Reverend Leon Sullivan in 1958. It sought to combat high unemployment among black men by teaching "the skills and training necessary to meet the requirements of industry."[18]

At the same time, the NAACP and the AFL-CIO tried to enlist government backing to open jobs to all. While southern Democrats and northern Republicans joined to defeat a permanent federal fair employment practices commission in the late 1940s, those seeking economic inclusion pushed for state laws barring employment discrimination. By 1964, twenty-eight states had such laws on their books. None was very effective; some lacked any enforcement mechanism.[19] And the laws had no chance of passage in southern states where the most flagrant discrimination occurred. Still, they provided relief to some individuals, and their very existence acknowledged that discrimination was a problem that government could and should address. Helpful as these measures were as steppingstones, activists knew that more was needed. In New York, home of the first such law, frustrations mounted from the time of its passage in 1945 through the early 1960s, as whites discovered that they could avoid opening jobs to blacks by condemning pressure to practice equal opportunity as "discrimination in reverse." The futility of these state laws led NAACP activists in particular to renew appeals to the federal government to prohibit job discrimination.[20]

As the NAACP lobbied for a national law, it also called on presidents to take executive action to deny federal contracts to employers who discriminated, building on the precedent of the wartime FEPC. These contracts involved nearly a third of the businesses in the country, often on highly visible projects. They made good political targets, because arguments about the rights of private property proved less persuasive here. For the government to hand over citizens' tax dollars to employers who shut out black workers was, as a Cincinnati resident later put it, "subsidizing racial discrimination."[21] Responding to activists' pressure, Harry Truman in late 1951 set up the President's Committee on Government Contract Compliance, later called the President's Committee on Equal Employment Opportunity (PCEEO). Corporations, however, simply ignored appeals for fair treatment, and the PCEEO did nothing. When the NAACP in 1958 lodged well-documented complaints of industry-wide discrimination against some of the nation's leading companies, for example, it received no word at all for two years, then was told that the Defense Department was looking into the situation. Another year passed with still no action. That experience was hardly unique. Years after the PCEEO opened for business, federal contractors persisted in unabashed discrimination. A study of nearly three hundred firms with federal contracts in North Carolina found that one fifth refused outright to hire blacks in any capacity; four fifths refused to hire black women. Those that did hire some African Americans placed them in unskilled jobs.[22]

To change employers' behavior, the PCEEO depended on moral suasion. Its Plans for Progress, developed by a white Georgia businessman named Robert Troutman, were voluntary agreements to engage in fair employment. By 1962, some eighty-five companies were enrolled. The federal government held flashy national meetings for participating corporations and published their names in attractive promotional brochures. What the plans did for black workers was less clear. Plans for Progress, the NAACP labor secretary told an inquirer, "was developed as a substitute for enforcement." The program left "it up to the discriminator to decide how much and what kind of compliance there will be with the law," with the result that there was "more publicity than progress."[23] The National Association of Manufacturers even promoted the plans as "protection against pressure from the more militant minority organizations" and a way to ensure "less frequent and bothersome" compliance checks.[24] Activists learned from this experience that unless the government applied sanctions to the recalcitrant, no real change would occur. As they tried to shame contractors into action, the activists kept pushing for a national fair employment law. Yet the prospects looked grim: by the early sixties, Congress had already killed more than two hundred fair employment measures.[25] The need was clear; the path much less so.

⌣ At the very time when the black freedom movement was testing new ways to move forward on the left, a group of intellectuals and journalists set out to rebuild the right. Their cause pitted them against the same developments that had aided the mounting challenge to racial hierarchy. The New Deal state, mass industrial labor unions, anticolonialism, the right to dissent freely and organize nonviolent protest, Social Gospel Christianity and prophetic Judaism, nontraditional scholarship in biology, social science, and history—there was hardly a development on any front that invigorated African American organizing which did not antagonize spokesmen for the conservative cause. The right's architects in these years focused on fighting communism abroad and the welfare state at home. Yet a defense of the racial status quo was part of their cause from the outset, not least because the black quest to promote social justice through mass protest and active government contradicted their vision of the good society and the just state. Conservative intellectuals were a diverse and disputatious group, with some committed to libertarianism, others to cultural traditionalism enforced by government, and still others to a militant anticommunism. But on racial matters, all three strains converged. The consensus was symbolized when the leader widely accredited with achieving "fusion" between the rival factions, Frank Meyer, denounced the *Brown v. Board of Education* decision as a "rape of the Constitution."[26]

Participants and observers alike cite 1955 as the birth date of contemporary American conservatism as an organized national movement fathered by a core group of thinkers, not just a habit of mind or a voting preference. That was the year William F. Buckley, Jr., and his collaborators founded the *National Review*, a magazine that became the organizing center of the cause. At nearly the same time, his compatriots launched two other important journals, *The Freeman* and *Modern Age: A Conservative Review*. Meanwhile, conservative intellectuals were laying the philosophical cornerstones of the new movement in works such as Richard Weaver's *Ideas Have Consequences*, Russell Kirk's *The Conservative Mind*, and Willmoore Kendall's *The Conservative Affirmation*. Before this, recalled one insider, "there did not exist anything in the nature of a broadly principled, coherent conservative movement."[27]

The coincidence of *National Review*'s founding with the Montgomery bus boycott was uncanny though unintentional. From the start, the right's standard-bearers united across the Mason-Dixon line in common defense of the old hierarchical order.[28] In the wake of *Brown v. Board of Education*, the man who spurred the white South to "massive resistance" against school desegregation became a spokesperson for the national conservative movement. James Jackson Kilpatrick, editor of the *Richmond News Leader*, pilloried the Supreme Court and agitated

white southerners to fight implementation of the *Brown* decision. Res-
urrecting John C. Calhoun's proslavery states' rights doctrine of "interposition" for use against federally backed integration, Kilpatrick
exulted in how it was "catching fire across the lower South, and it's
catching fire because it's right." The head of the white Citizens' Councils of Mississippi, one of the most ardent segregationists in America,
praised Kilpatrick as "one of the South's most talented leaders."[29]

The *National Review* made Kilpatrick its voice on the civil rights
movement and the Constitution, as Buckley and Kilpatrick united
North and South in a shared vision for the nation that included upholding white supremacy. The southerners felt a keen urgency about it
that few northerners shared, but no philosophical difference divided
them. Kilpatrick, who described himself as "only a little to the south of
John C. Calhoun," did more than anyone else to make "the militant
South" part of the postwar conservative mainstream.[30] Through him,
Buckley solicited the mailing list of the Citizens' Councils in 1958:
some 65,000 white supremacists who might appreciate the *National Review*. "Our position on states' rights is the same as your own," said
Buckley in thanking William J. Simmons, the main organizer of the
now region-wide group first formed to defeat the Montgomery bus
boycott. Simmons, in turn, praised *National Review's* "contribution to
the cause of political and social sanity."[31]

On both sides of the Mason-Dixon line, conservatives understood
liberty as the nation's slave-owning founders had. They viewed it as
precious and essential to the preservation of republican institutions, yet
something that only certain men, white and with a proper stake in society, were fit to exercise. They therefore aggressively defended private
property rights and the power of employers and sought to shore up the
states against social reforms which they claimed were socialistic pit
stops on the road to communism. Conservatives felt what one described as "a positive hatred of redistributionist schemes" and "anything in the way of mandated equality." Standing against what another
called "the characteristic leveling egalitarianism of the time," they insisted that hierarchy was natural, inevitable, and indeed highly desirable for a good society. So great was the danger that "mediocrity may
trample underfoot every just elevation of mind and character," said the
philosopher and *National Review* columnist Russell Kirk, that "the sa-
gacious statesman of our age must be more acutely concerned with the

preservation of the rights of the talented minority than with the extension of the rights of the crowd." His fellows saw their charge as nothing less than the defense of "the tradition of Western civilization and the American republic," which, as *National Review* senior editor and American Conservative Union leader Frank Meyer later put it, had "been subjected to a revolutionary attack in the years since 1932," when Franklin Roosevelt was first elected.[32] This enterprise demanded religious faith: not the Social Gospel, Sermon on the Mount humane theology that abetted the egalitarians, but sterner stuff, the fighting creed of an Old Testament and martial Christianity. Conservatism, Buckley explained, was "planted in a religious view of man."[33]

The same history that angered African Americans convinced conservatives that their interpretation of the founders' intentions was the correct one. The nation's dual origins in slavery and freedom imbued modern conservatives with a deep sense of cultural authenticity, and northerners and southerners alike held fast against the quest for inclusion. They saw no contradiction between claiming to stand for liberty and opposing the black freedom movement because they revered a tradition that silenced and subordinated blacks. "Integration," said a *Modern Age* writer, "is patently a radical departure from the explicit provisions of the contract between the states which established this federal union." The right vowed support, as Frank Meyer put it, for "the Constitution of the United States as originally conceived"—that is to say, without the later pro-black Fourteenth and Fifteenth Amendments. Conservatives told a tale of declension, of a "nation [that] has strayed from the values which once made it strong," in the words of American Conservative Union president and *National Review* stalwart M. Stanton Evans.[34]

Conservative spokesmen gained confidence in the justness of their cause from a number of presuppositions. First, they were unable to imagine African Americans as full members of the polity. When Buckley urged his readers to empathize with "the Southern community," he most assuredly did not understand blacks as part of it. They were, rather, troublemakers with "their eyes on the jugular vein of Southern life," a way of life whose protection required control, "at least for the time being, by the white majority."[35] The "White community," Buckley wrote approvingly in 1957 in defense of the denial of voting rights to blacks, "will take whatever measures are necessary to make certain that it has its way." Willmoore Kendall, a teacher of Buckley's before becoming his colleague on the *National Review*, proclaimed that one of the things that made liberals so odious was their "*egalitarian* principle," their deplorable belief in "one-man one-equal-vote." Seeing it as "manifestly dangerous" for "the inferior group" to be "granted political equality," *National Review* staffer James Burnham thought it eminently reasonable to "continue to want my group to have more than its arithmetic share in running things."[36]

Like most white Americans of the 1950s, the conservative leaders had learned in school that the Reconstruction experiment in black citizenship rights was a terrible mistake, but they went further. Even the northerners promoted an interpretation of those historic events that supported the South's case for states' rights. Some rejected the Union and the antislavery cause in the South's own terminology, speaking of "the War between the States."[37] All actively promoted the slave owners' perspective on America's bloodiest conflict to make their case for rolling back social reform. Explaining his support for whites who deprived blacks of the vote, Buckley announced approvingly, "The Fourteenth and Fifteenth Amendments to the Constitution are regarded by much of the South as inorganic accretions to the original document, grafted upon it by victors-at-war by force."[38] Kendall declared that the contemporary "war" between liberals and conservatives "began as a war of aggression, launched . . . by the Liberals," who had attacked "the victims' territory in the 1860's and 1870's" in the form of "emancipation of the slaves in the name of equality, [and] the post-Civil War 'equality' amendments to the Constitution."[39]

Indeed, conservatives portrayed the South of their day as a kind of Shangri-la, a utopia of order and civilized values. Defending the South's devotion to the "principle of exclusion" and an "aristocratic" social order, Richard Weaver equated the "heavy assault" on "the regime of the South" by "Liberalism" with what he saw as the self-destruction of the larger society by the same forces. Writing for the *National Review* in 1958, Anthony Harrigan praised this region of "essential conservatism" for its "built-in power brake." To Michigan-based Russell Kirk, the South was "the citadel of tradition," the frontline of defense for "civilization," which "need feel no shame for its defense of beliefs that were not concocted yesterday."[40]

Across regional lines, conservatives took for granted that the segregation of blacks and whites was natural. It was simply the "realistic" way for a society to handle two fundamentally different populations living side by side. Kirk urged readers to consider "the immense problem which must exist whenever two races occupy the same territory." Buckley spoke of segregation and discrimination as "traditional American patterns for racial assimilation and conciliation." According to Donald Davidson, realism dictated that "the alien element" needed to "be strictly controlled" in order to ensure "democracy for white people." For Davidson, "the race problem" was one not of equity but of coexistence. The South's system of "parallel societies" was "a practical solution to [this] most difficult of all problems."[41] A rare female conservative writer championed segregation as "Christian, moral, and no violation of human dignity." It was merely a law of nature seen also in the relations of "wife to husband, servant to master, employee to employer, [and] child to parent," for "in every contract there are principal and subordinate positions."[42]

Segregation appeared natural to conservatives because of another axiom on the right that needed little discussion: blacks were inferior. Not the victims of discrimination, they were if anything the beneficiaries of white generosity. Some conservatives set out to "strike a fair balance" on slavery by recognizing the "benefits" blacks gained from it and the "substantial advantages" they enjoyed as a result. Buckley thus urged recognition of "the conditions from which American Negroes were rescued years ago" when taken captive and sold away to America. Opinions on the right varied as to whether it was biology or culture that caused the purported inferiority, but the practical import was the same: government need not ensure African Americans the same chances others enjoyed because they lacked either the ability or the will to succeed. "The Negro," wrote Weaver, discussing the postbellum South with reference to Haiti and Jamaica, "had shown that his tendency, when he was released from all constraining forces, was downward rather than upward." No wonder southern whites treated blacks as they did: they knew better than to accept the North's "dogma that the Negro had the white man's nature and capacities." What made "the White community" in the South "entitled" to use any means necessary to keep blacks from voting, Buckley explained, was that "it is the advanced race," so its "claims of civilization supersede those of universal suffrage."[43]

Actively promoting prejudices that might have dissipated without their goading, conservative opinion makers in the 1950s honed these antipathies into tools to advance their traditionalist, anticommunist, and anti–big government cause. Leveraging the power of race to summon loyalty, the right worked from 1955 forward to realize far-reaching goals. Its leaders championed the conservative coalition in Congress that blocked expansion of the New Deal, a coalition which united southern Dixiecrats with northern Republicans to protect the culture of exclusion at home and wage the cold war abroad. Friendly toward business organizations such as the National Association of Manufacturers and the Chamber of Commerce, conservatives helped to shape the emerging corporate conversation about race in the workplace. Some conservative opinion makers, Kilpatrick among them, wrote for business publications such as *Nation's Business*, the official journal of the Chamber of Commerce, where they pressed the case that, as the popular conservative economics writer Henry Hazlitt proclaimed in 1964, the "market is color-blind."[44]

As Jim Crow remained the law of the land, conservative writers provided whites who resisted inclusion with arguments that translated their prejudices into ennobling political premises. The right's main focus in these years was always anticommunism, but as the white supremacists who retained control in the South well appreciated, anticommunism offered the best defense for segregation, so the two causes were mutually reinforcing.[45] At a moment when white Americans were being urged by the growing civil rights coalition to consider making up for centuries of active injustice, the founders of the conservative movement worked to ensure that they would not. *National Review* had a circulation of 25,000 in 1958, but those readers tended to be avid and actively engaged in the larger conservative project. Through words and action, the right's spokesmen cultivated political identities on their side much as activists for inclusion were doing on theirs. One conservative, skeptical of the right at its founding, looked back on what its organizers had wrought: "*National Review*, it turns out, was part of a larger movement that created institutions which shaped and trained several thousand young conservatives, not so much to go forth and proclaim the gospel, as to go into the Republican party and gain control of it."[46]

Starting with massive resistance to *Brown*, conservative spokesmen worked to convince wavering whites that blacks had not earned the hearing they were beginning to receive in the court of public opinion. The moment of truth came in Birmingham, Alabama, in 1963. As African Americans demanded equal treatment on a scale never before seen and won the sympathy of millions of whites, the right proceeded to do what William F. Buckley had announced as its purpose in the charter issue of the *National Review:* "stand athwart history, yelling Stop."

⤳ ONE HUNDRED YEARS after the Emancipation Proclamation, Birmingham blacks organized for "freedom now." Local white officials in this Deep South industrial hub boasted of running the most segregated city in the nation. The governor, George Wallace, had welcomed the new year with a pledge of "segregation now, segregation tomorrow, segregation forever!" A few months later, the city became the site of a pivotal battle for the gathering black freedom movement as the thirty-four-year-old Martin Luther King came to town to shore up local activists such as the Reverend Fred Shuttlesworth. They had begun a campaign for fair treatment soon after the *Brown* decision and the Montgomery movement, which now appeared in danger of defeat. Their calls to be treated with dignity on city buses and to attend better schools were answered by white mobs with beatings and with eighteen bombings in six years. Birmingham's devotion to unapologetic white supremacy made it an inviting target for a movement gaining skill at using the media to bring the southern struggle to a national audience, so King accepted Shuttlesworth's invitation to come help. "We believed that while a campaign in Birmingham would surely be the toughest fight of our civil rights careers," King explained, "it could, if successful, break the back of segregation all over the nation."[47]

It did. The viciousness of white Birmingham's response to the nonviolent appeal from blacks to be granted the basic human respect enjoyed by whites attracted national media coverage as never before. Arrested and jailed with hundreds of local activists, King wrote the "Letter from a Birmingham Jail," his stirring answer to "the white moderate, who is more devoted to 'order' than to justice." When the campaign sputtered in the face of bitter resistance, children enlisted. Unlike their parents, young people could not be fired for their activism or have their credit cut off by banks and businesses. They took up the baton in May. As thousands marched for justice, Commissioner of Public Safety Eugene "Bull" Connor directed his police to attack the protesters with dogs and fire hoses so powerful they stripped the bark from trees. The nightly footage of police brutality, described by participant Andrew Young as free "educational t.v.," woke the world to the heroism of black activists and the cruelty of their opponents. As pressure mounted, one State Department official warned that "the picture of a dog attacking a Negro, of a police officer pinning a Negro woman to the ground— these pictures have a dramatic impact on those abroad who listen to our words about democracy and weigh our actions against those words."[48]

The savage response to the protesters made nonviolence hard to sustain. Working-class black spectators at the demonstrations, themselves having suffered chronic police abuse and now facing worsening unemployment, began to fight back. Fearing chaos, white businessmen negotiated a truce with the SCLC. They agreed to end Jim Crow at "lunch counters, rest rooms, fitting rooms and drinking fountains," and to accept the "upgrading and hiring of Negroes on a nondiscriminatory basis throughout the industrial community of Birmingham," notably in downtown clerk jobs that had been a white monopoly. The Ku Klux Klan, furious at compromise, bombed the motel where King was staying. When the police beat the blacks who gathered in outrage, a riot broke out, the first of a series of increasingly devastating upheavals nationwide, fueled by long-contained rage among those who had the least and endured the worst. As slum residents destroyed storefronts and set fires, movement leaders were powerless to stop them; chaos had descended, provoked by white resistance to elementary fairness, and this radicalized the situation. Convinced that stalling was now more dangerous than action, President John F. Kennedy declared on national television on June 11, 1963, that civil rights was a "moral issue" which could no longer be dodged.[49]

Civil rights was indeed a moral issue of the first order, but the Birmingham events made clear to close observers that addressing the challenge would require more than a pledge to stop sinning. It would require a wide-ranging agenda of social change that included, centrally, access to good jobs. King listed in his letter from jail the many reasons, as the title of his best-selling book title put it, *Why We Can't Wait*, and one of them was watching "the vast majority of [our] twenty million Negro brothers smothering in an airtight cage of poverty in the midst of an affluent society." Already, the year before, King had told SCLC's hometown supporters that "we must get better jobs in order to help our children to better education and housing, and in order to enjoy some of the entertainment and eating facilities that are now open to us." That was the consensus that various wings of the movement had reached in the years since Montgomery. Now, the Birmingham struggle dramatized the quest for national audiences as it brought poor urban African Americans into the struggle, testing its limits as never before. As King explained, "the Negro today is not struggling for some abstract, vague rights, but for concrete and prompt improvement in his way of life."[50]

For many contemporaries, the desire of blacks to escape unemployment and menial jobs was one of the clearest messages sent by the Birmingham events. The courage of Birmingham's people had invigorated activists all over, including the weary NAACP labor and industry committee in Harlem, which exulted that, thanks to its Alabama brethren, "our struggle has taken on a greater militancy and force."[51] The director of the NAACP Legal Defense and Education Fund declared that "full and nondiscriminatory employment are crucial to meaningful exercise of the ballot" as well as to educational achievement.[52] In the string of sympathetic protests across the nation, demands for jobs were often an element, and sometimes the key element, of participants' calls for change in their own communities. Justice Department figures counted 1,412 different demonstrations across the nation that summer in what some scholars call "a brushfire of 'little Birminghams.'" Thereafter, even organizations not involved in the Alabama events, such as CORE, began pressing harder for good jobs.[53] CORE leader James Farmer echoed King in arguing that "it will be a hollow victory, indeed, if we win the important rights to spend our money in places of public accommodation, on buses, or what have you, without also winning the even more vital right to earn money."[54]

The national business press realized that Birmingham called for action on employment. What so many had risked so much for was not just formal equality but real change, and that included better lives for themselves and a more promising future for their children. *Fortune* magazine called the Birmingham events "a major watershed in the history of U.S. race relations." According to one of its editors, "the entrance of the poor into the Negro protest movement has profoundly altered its direction and temper." Perceiving the mood at the grass roots, he went on to predict that "the problem of race relations may become a major—at times *the* major preoccupation of top management for a number of years to come." Other observers agreed. "The summer of 1963 may well go down as a landmark in the history of American industry," noted *Business Week*. "With a forcefulness few businessmen ever expected," its editors reported, "Negroes nationwide are pressing, individually and in well-organized groups, for more jobs and better jobs. In its drama and impact, the campaign is comparable to the American worker's drive to unionize at the turn of the century."[55]

From the beginning, most activists recognized that opening up the economic mainstream would take more than a declaration of equal opportunity. In effect, they relearned the lessons their predecessors had mastered in the movement that fell victim to cold war repression: that equality demanded the kinds of targeted compensatory measures that would later be named "affirmative action."[56] Countering the established ideology that what employers did with their property was their own business and that what happened to black workers was their own doing, movement spokespersons saw the need to counterbalance generations of advantages for whites. They had found that the most potent barrier to black access was less malicious, intentional discrimination than a habitual employer preference for whites: the unthinking assumptions bred by long acceptance of exclusion.[57] One study found that half of southern whites and 45 percent of northern whites believed at the time of the 1963 Birmingham struggle that blacks already had "as good a chance" as whites "to get any kind of job for which they are qualified." Even back in 1956, more than half of whites questioned in one corporate survey believed that "companies give Negroes a good break [in hiring]." Whites maintained this even as seven in ten also responded that "their own employers do not open up certain types of jobs" to blacks. More to the point, fewer than one in four whites believed that companies should follow the same rules in hiring blacks and whites. And although whites regularly maintained that blacks lacked adequate qualifications, almost half opposed any "special steps to train" them.[58]

Even those white employers who believed that they were doing nothing wrong simply assumed white entitlement and black incapacity. A 1962 study of Atlanta employers found that evidence of unthinking bias was rife. "This is just a sales and service office," said one corporate official to explain the absence of blacks. "We don't have any manufacturing in Atlanta." Even managers proud of their hiring records "repeatedly" referred to "the 'fact' that Negroes were not suited for any but production jobs." Some told investigators that "their work was extremely technical, implying that it was too technical for a Negro." One manager found the notion of a black salesman "ridiculous" for a firm with white customers. Graciously, investigators for the Southern Regional Council noted "some apparent confusion over the meaning of the phrase 'equal employment opportunity.'"[59]

A veteran African American judge, Francis Rivers, explained how preferential hiring of ethnic whites served to block opportunity for blacks even in the nation's most liberal city. Looking at how certain white ethnic groups came to dominate particular occupations in New York, such as the "almost wholly Irish Catholic" job of court attendant, Rivers observed that "this restrictive employment situation . . . did not result from discrimination *against* Negroes, or Italians, or Jews, or Puerto Ricans—it resulted from discrimination *in favor* of the Irish Catholics—from preferential treatment of the Irish Catholics." The implication was that "it would be difficult for one Negro, and still more difficult for a number of Negroes . . . to prove that the failure to hire had been *because* of his *race* or *color*." And that meant that "traditional imperatives like 'equality of opportunity' are useless for securing new employment opportunities, but can only serve to extenuate and rationalize" a "Negro-excluding job system." The task for policy was to figure out how blacks could get jobs without having to prove "that employment was denied them solely because of race or color."[60]

To counteract favoritism for whites, a variety of movement leaders came to advocate what some called preferential hiring for blacks, at least for a time, until more fairness prevailed. This would be one of the variety of measures that came to be summarized collectively as affirmative action, among them also targeted recruitment and training efforts. King made the case succinctly in his Birmingham manifesto as he urged "some compensatory consideration for the handicaps" blacks had "inherited from the past." The burden of history on the present put blacks at a continuing disadvantage. "It is impossible to create a formula for the future which does not take into account that our society has been doing something special *against* the Negro for hundreds of years. How then can he be absorbed into the mainstream of American life if we do not do something special *for* him now, in order to balance the equation and equip him to compete on a just and equal basis?"[61] Some black labor leaders, fearing anything that might jeopardize seniority, drew back from the idea of preferential employment. But they, too, wanted more than color-blindness. Randolph argued that "Negro labor needs and is entitled to special and preferential treatment, in the form of preparation in training and education to enable it effectively to move forward."[62]

Success should be measured, activists from across the spectrum agreed, not by declarations of equal opportunity but by outcomes in the form of better lives for black Americans. Reasoning that long operation of "the deliberate 'color-consciousness' of a prejudiced and unconcerned white majority has placed the Negro at a competitive disadvantage," the New York City Commission on Human Rights in 1963 similarly urged "preferential treatment" of "qualified" blacks "for a limited period" to close the gap. "Society must work affirmatively for integration rather than negatively for desegregation," the commissioners insisted. "Color consciousness . . . is necessary and appropriate." A CORE activist succinctly summed up the spreading conviction that "after three hundred years of discrimination . . . there is obviously no immediate solution that does not involve some kind of 'preferential hiring' system."[63]

What made aggressive effort especially urgent now was that those bearing the injuries inflicted by generations of state-backed subordination had to board a moving train: an economy undergoing the early stages of a process now known as de-industrialization. The NAACP had turned away from efforts to improve agricultural work for blacks in the 1940s and placed its hopes on industrial work.[64] Yet the decline of manufacturing employment by the early sixties boded ill for all lessskilled workers, in industry as elsewhere. Throughout the nation, a process that came to be known as "automation," sometimes "cybernation," was transforming industry as it created today's labor market, in which workers without advanced education or vocational training faced ever-dimming prospects. By every measure African American workers lost ground relative to whites between 1945 and 1960—whether income, rates of employment, or jobs held. By the mid-fifties, two blacks were out of work for every white American. The timing of sharecropping's decline had proved tragic. A half century earlier, it might have freed blacks to benefit, as European immigrants did, from the North's labor-hungry industries. But blacks were heading toward central cities at the very moment when waves of whites were spilling out to the suburbs, with businesses hurrying after them. "There is an irony in this for the Negro," noted a Chicago Urban League forum in 1964: "He may be winning the right to get a job at just the time when the job itself is disappearing." As some spoke of a "Negro depression," it was clear that the economic situation of blacks, while better relative to their own past, was not advancing nearly as fast as that of whites.[65]

Fearing disaster ahead, movement spokespersons called for access to better jobs so as to save unskilled blacks from poverty and welfare with no hope of escape. In early 1963 the SCLC's Operation Breadbasket started trying to open good jobs to blacks in the belief that automation was creating "a desperate situation" for the unskilled worker. "The impact of automation upon Negroes in the United States has been allowed to reach crisis proportions," brooded John Feild, a Kennedy administration strategist for equal employment.[66] Even African Americans who held jobs in established industries such as auto manufacturing and meatpacking began losing them to technological change in large numbers by the early sixties.[67] In 1961 this "job crisis" brought together black leaders as diverse as A. Philip Randolph, Percy Sutton, Louis Micheaux, and Malcolm X to publicize the issue. Three years later, some of them alerted the country that just as Reconstruction had been undone in the industrial revolution, so was the civil rights movement in danger of being undone in the automation revolution.[68] The country's inaction, Herbert Hill admonished, would create "a permanent black underclass," a group of "permanent unemployables." Americans had "choices to make," Whitney Young summed up. "Either we make these people constructive citizens, productive and healthy, or they are going to be destructive dependents," and "we [shall] pay the cost of our shortsightedness."[69]

Activists wanted the wider public to recognize the harm that white power had inflicted on blacks for so long and commit to counteract it. The discrimination came not only from individual employers, after all. It came from an entire social system that had systematically, over many generations, worked to put blacks in a weaker competitive position, creating disadvantages as cumulative for them as the advantages were for whites. Brought up in segregated housing that produced high rates of illness, deprived of good medical care, confined to the worst schools,

denied access to advanced training, cut off from the cultural mainstream, exposed to relentless deprecating messages from the larger society, and met with violence if they lost patience and rebelled, African
Americans seemed all but doomed to the lowest rungs of the labor
market.[70]

All wings of the movement knew this; the injustice fueled their fight
for change. In the midst of the clashes in Birmingham, they gathered
together for the historic March on Washington in August 1963. Its
purpose was to call for "Jobs and Freedom," a demand that united the
southern wing of the movement, with its focus on freedom, and the
northern and western wings, with their focus on jobs. The black trade
unionists who conceived the event and the marchers who answered the
call believed that access to good employment on both sides of the Mason-Dixon line was vital to full inclusion in a fair America. Randolph
posed as the key task for follow-up "a nationwide drive for massive
public works," providing "fair employment and full employment," to
be built with "billions of dollars of federal funds." One economist approved, saying that the "real success" of the civil rights movement was
"the fact that it has, almost single-handed[ly], wrested America out of
the apathy in which it was mired and forced it to face the problems of
unemployment and inadequate education, the problems of poverty, and
the long-run dangers of cybernation."[71]

As the grassroots struggle helped white Americans recognize the
need for deep change, the movement's confidence grew. "We have progressed as a nation," the National Urban League had earlier declared,
"to the point where only bigots would publicly espouse the position
that a man is not entitled to get and hold a job commensurate with his
talent, education and performance." Now, emboldened by Birmingham and "the Negro revolution," as King called it, the League called
for more: a Domestic Marshall Plan, evoking the ambitious, expensive,
and stunningly successful reconstruction of Europe after World War
II, which particularly lifted America's former enemy, Germany. "Special effort," the League urged, "is required to overcome the damaging
effects of generations of deprivation and denial" and afford blacks a fair
chance in this "increasingly complex and fast-moving economy." The
plan called for large infusions of money to build better housing and
provide health care as well as strenuous efforts to change the occupational profile of African Americans by training the jobless to rebuild
blighted areas and supply needed services.[72]

The need to undertake such active efforts to assist black citizens was difficult for many white voters to accept. With empathy, Whitney Young identified the sources of the uneasiness the movement caused those who still wanted to believe that American society was fair. "The concept of special effort for Negro citizens may be difficult for the majority of white citizens to accept for three reasons," he said. It meant, for one, acknowledging that the nation had treated African Americans unjustly, an acknowledgment unlikely to occur unless one accepted them as fellow citizens with the same needs and rights. It also meant recognizing that "whites themselves have been the beneficiaries of a preferential system—and nobody really wants to admit this." Lastly, Young noted, "it is extremely difficult for a society that has only recently begun to adjust itself to affording equal opportunity for all its citizens to find itself suddenly called upon to offer special treatment as well."[73]

Movement activists and their sympathizers tried to ease that recognition by rooting the cause in widely shared values. One day, King predicted from Birmingham, the country would see that the jailed black protesters "were in reality standing up for what is best in the American dream and for the most sacred values in our Judaeo-Christian heritage, thereby bringing our nation back to those great wells of democracy . . . the Constitution and the Declaration of Independence." Activists applied the founders' principle of no taxation without representation, asking, "Does the State to which I pay taxes offer me full opportunity for employment?"[74] Arguing that their purchases entitled blacks to the same dignity as their white counterparts, movement leaders helped shape the "consumer's republic" of the post–World War II years. They argued that a social order based on mass consumption should bring equal entitlements and obligations.[75] Spokespersons for the jobs and justice effort appealed also to popular dislike of welfare and to whites' economic self-interest. Over and over again they pointed to employment with the prospect of upward mobility as a way for people to help themselves, the best alternative to "welfare dependency."[76]

That argument gained strength from the conviction, nearly universal in the 1950s and early 1960s, that families should be headed by men. For a family to be headed by a woman, like those receiving welfare through Aid for Dependent Children (ADC), struck many black men and women as well as most whites as aberrant, even destructive of social order. Indeed, what sealed the case for economic inclusion among many whites in the era of the hit television series *Father Knows Best* was the gender component of the struggle. High rates of participation in the labor force among black women notwithstanding, male civil rights leaders commonly portrayed their campaign as being for "the Negro worker (and his wife)," as Roy Wilkins put it. If this usage jars today, it was one that contemporary whites understood. Among white movement allies, a man deprived of his status as household head and compelled to share power with a female breadwinner was a scorching indictment of employment exclusion. One white supporter of the quest for jobs claimed that "the reversal of roles almost invariably poisons the marital relationship." He, like others, proposed combating "matriarchy" by opening good jobs to black men as "the greatest need Negroes have." Jobs are the "fulcrum," this sympathizer explained, "on which a strengthening of the family, and through the family, of the Negro's role in American society, ultimately rests."[77] Such arguments for male dominance had grown more shrill in the postwar years among blacks as well as whites, while women's independence was construed as threatening much-needed racial solidarity.[78]

So appealing was the undertone of gender conservatism in the case for economic inclusion that it moved Hollywood directors to spread the message. Films that addressed racism in employment nearly always did so by depicting men whose inability to get a job with decent pay and dignity undermined their manhood. In 1950, for example, Sidney Poitier debuted in *No Way Out* as the first black doctor in a city hospital, forced to deal with the taunts of a psychopathic white criminal patient while proving his professional competence. In the 1961 film version of Lorraine Hansberry's play *A Raisin in the Sun*, the racism of the job market ate like acid at a husband and father's sense of self, turning him to drink, cynicism, and spousal abuse and driving him to chase fantasies of economic autonomy that harmed the whole household. A few years later, similar themes animated the plot of *Nothing but a Man*. Ivan Dixon starred in this allegory of the damage done by economic exclusion to a man who could only maintain his dignity in the Jim Crow South as a footloose railroad worker in the company of other single black men. When he fell in love with a preacher's daughter, married, and tried to settle down, the humiliations of menial work under the white man's thumb deformed his once winning personality. Debased at work, he degenerated at home; no longer warm and playful, he became bitter and cruel, nearly repeating his father's pathetic demise.[79]

The demand for economic inclusion fit the prevailing ethos in another way that is harder to document. It bespoke a public optimism difficult to recapture in our more skeptical, pessimistic era. Its hopefulness about the prospects for African American mobility and the future of interracial relations grew from widespread confidence in the capacity of government to promote the common good. Before the war in Vietnam and the exposures of Watergate undermined public trust, whites as well as blacks believed in social progress directed by democratic government. Four in five Americans polled in 1964 expected the government to "do what is right all or most of the time." On a global scale, never was there greater faith in the ability of public officials to initiate positive change, from the state-run societies of the Eastern bloc, to the nationalist reform governments in the developing world, to the welfare states of postwar Europe and the United States.[80] Appealing to the prevailing spirit of possibility, the civil rights movement became almost irresistible in a culture that enshrined progress.

YET THAT VERY ETHOS, the faith that government could advance social justice, helped make the evolving movement and its ambitious calls for change anathema to the nation's conservative leaders. "It is possible to pinpoint the time and place when the Negro movement became a revolution," wrote the economist Murray Rothbard. The time was "May, 1963, the place, Birmingham, Alabama." Among the features of the revolution were the rapid spread of the movement "throughout the country," the demands for what he called "forced hiring of Negroes in various jobs," and the growing involvement of "the poorest strata of the Negro workers." His hope was that it "might be crippled and defeated." The jurist Robert Bork sided with white "citizens" against the black "mob coercing and disturbing other private individuals in the exercise of their freedom." As police fire hoses blasted children down Birmingham streets, Bork declared that for anyone to tell these white citizens "that even as individuals they may not act on their racial preferences" was "unsurpassed ugliness."[81]

At the *National Review's* Manhattan office, Frank Meyer fulminated against the Birmingham movement. Deploring the "sentimentality" of the nation's response, Meyer drew attention to "what, without exaggeration, can be called a revolutionary situation." To subdue it, he intimated, police power on a so far unseen scale was overdue. (Privately, he elaborated that the *National Review* staff "should have discussions with the few Negroes we know" in hopes of initiating "a counter-movement.") Blaming the crisis on the movement, the Supreme Court, and the president rather than white supremacists, Meyer sided with "local law-enforcement agencies, which have quite successfully and humanely suppressed mob action." He allowed that "the Negro people have suffered profound wrongs," but insisted that the movement against segregation was "destroying the foundations of a free constitutional society." Like the hostile Supreme Court in *Plessy v. Ferguson*, he genuflected to "equal treatment before the law," yet maintained that "social, cultural and economic relations of the races" were "another matter." Here, government must stay out. Fair employment laws would be "an equal monstrosity" to statutory segregation.[82]

Conservatives opposed the black freedom movement's tactics as well as its goals, especially Martin Luther King, Jr.'s, signature action: civil disobedience in the name of a higher law. While urging the white South to respect the Bill of Rights and allow "peaceable" assembly, William F. Buckley, Jr., insisted that right "does not rank above the need for public order." "Repression is an unpleasant instrument," he said, "but it is absolutely necessary for civilizations that believe in order and human rights. I wish to God Hitler and Lenin had been repressed. And word should be got through to the non-violent avenger Dr. King, that in the unlikely event that he succeeds in mobilizing his legions, they will be most efficiently, indeed most zestfully, repressed."[83] Others agreed. "We need not be ashamed," declared one, "for invoking the armed power of the state to preserve public order."[84] While some conservatives packaged their opposition in race-neutral language warning of chaos or encroaching socialism, others forthrightly appealed to racism to turn white America against racial reform.

Some argued black incapacity explicitly, injecting the idea into the discussion whenever the chance arose. Since they took as an unquestioned premise that the market was fair and free and traditional institutions just, how else to explain disadvantage? If blacks didn't do well, the problem must be in them. "Most poor people in America today are poor because they want to be," summed up a *National Review* writer. "They make themselves the way they are by being lazy, uneducated, sick, undependable"—because "they cannot or *will not* compete." Richard Weaver, described by a colleague as "the pioneer and protagonist of the American conservative consensus," dismissed "the dogma that the Negro had the white man's nature and capacities." Praising Weaver, Meyer called the "unjust" society one "which allots to one sort of nature rights and duties that properly belong to other sorts of human beings."[85] Blacks simply had a lesser capacity, such men believed, for "civilizational achievement."[86]

Answering Birmingham, James Kilpatrick, the rising star in the conservative firmament, made his movement's premises more explicit. "This precious right to discriminate," he argued, "underlies our entire political and economic system." As for the Negro claiming the right to inclusion, why, he had sat out the whole industrial revolution. "He is still carrying the hod . . . still digging the ditch," because that's all he had bestirred himself to do. "The hell he is equal," Kilpatrick exclaimed. "He has no right . . . to favored treatment in employment, promotion, or anything else." White Americans should rise in "resentment," he urged, against "those who demand in the name of race what they have not earned in the way of worth."[87] Pioneering "in-your-face" politics, Kilpatrick used the podium at a conference on the centennial of the Emancipation Proclamation to force into public discussion "inquiry into the possibility of some innate inferiority in the Negro race." He complained that blacks were being "petted and pampered, cuddled and coddled" by "reverse racism," an interesting line of attack, since simple equal opportunity, much less affirmative action, had not yet been accepted as public policy. Far from rendering Kilpatrick marginal, such outbursts won him a lucrative platform as a national spokesman for the cause. In 1964 the Newsday syndicate hired him to write a weekly column, "A Conservative View," soon carried by fifty newspapers. By 1970 it was appearing three times a week in 170 newspapers across the country; its author would be invited to dine at the Nixon White House, was featured as a writer for *Nation's Business*, and was given a weekly television spot on *60 Minutes*.[88]

And so the lines were drawn, as the civil rights movement and its conservative opposition both sought to win over the wavering white voters in between them. As African Americans pressed harder to be treated as full citizens and granted access to good jobs, conservative spokesmen countered with arguments that they were incapable. Frank Meyer circulated newspaper accounts of research purporting to show that heredity produced lesser intelligence among African Americans, underlining key passages for his colleagues at the *National Review*. Ernest Van den Haag, a *National Review* contributing editor and Fordham professor whom Buckley praised as a "tuning fork of reason," relished theories of genetic inferiority drawn from fringe pseudo-science. Effective learning demanded the separation of students "according to ability," he said, "and this means very largely according to race." Well into the 1970s, he argued that the lower average scoring of blacks on intelligence tests was "largely genetic," and used this "empirical actuality" to argue against government attempts at equity. Like Kilpatrick, Van den Haag was rewarded, appointed a Distinguished Scholar at the Heritage Foundation and then Olin Professor at Fordham University.[89] Buckley, for his part, blamed culture rather than biology for why blacks got the short end of the stick. But they all reached the same conclusion: using public policy to help blacks advance was wrong.[90]

Not only opponents but even some sympathizers criticized conservative leaders' racism. "Your editorials" on the South, one woman wrote to the *National Review*, "strike me as not so much conservative as aristocratic." A few others complained that on matters racial, the magazine was not just mistaken but "appalling." It "degrades the conservative cause," said one man of Van den Haag's writing on race and intelligence. "I am ashamed to subscribe to the magazine any longer." Another reader found the piece "about as scientific" as Nazi racial theory.[91] A self-described white Presbyterian "registered Republican" wrote to "protest" Buckley's claims that the Constitution was on the side of Jim Crow's upholders. "You are prone to defend the causes of the white southerners who have rejected the Constitution whenever it did not suit their cause," he chastised the editor. Although "you accuse the Supreme Court of fanaticism," he charged, "you are the fanatic." Irving Kristol thanked Buckley for sending Van den Haag's article, but warned that to oppose school desegregation "in terms of racial differences" was "political folly."[92] Even a *National Review* colleague who claimed to "strongly suspect that the negro is inferior intellectually" still thought it wrong that Kilpatrick "attacks the [entire] negro race" in print. "It surely won't destroy the whole fabric of society for the white to realize that some negroes have a lot on the ball."[93] Nevertheless, despite scattered words of protest, most conservatives hewed to the party line.

⟶ THE ANTAGONISM conservative leaders expressed toward black activists stands out all the more because millions of other whites responded so differently to Birmingham and the national protests that followed. As the images of Bull Connor's brutal police conveyed the evil of white supremacy to worldwide audiences, messages of shock and outrage deluged the White House and persuaded John F. Kennedy to make a civil rights act a priority. "We face a moral crisis," he told the nation in June 1963; "it is time to act in Congress." The bill the president proposed addressed many of the areas in which activists had pressed for change. Yet Kennedy, fearing the combined opposition of Republicans and southern Democrats, concentrated on the southern evils that were most in the public eye, such as Jim Crow restaurants, theaters, and stores. His bill ignored employment discrimination and voting rights, and failed to ban segregation in all public accommodations or to act decisively on school segregation. Still, it was the most substantial civil rights legislation yet proposed.[94]

With meaningful federal reform now on the nation's agenda, movement activists and their opponents mobilized on a scale that dwarfed previous efforts, with thousands upon thousands going into action. The broad labor and liberal civil rights coalition that United Auto Workers president Walter Reuther called the "coalition of conscience" summoned all its resources to lobby for the bill and make it stronger by adding a fair employment provision and an Equal Employment Opportunities Commission to oversee implementation. "We need the power of the federal government to do what we are not fully able to do [by ourselves]," AFL-CIO president George Meany told Congress. NAACP and AFL-CIO lobbyists were joined by a wide array of liberal social reform organizations. Among them were predominantly white mainstream women's groups, such as the League of Women Voters, that saw the need to alleviate black poverty and open access to jobs. By 1960, more than seventy organizations belonged to the Leadership Conference on Civil Rights, which oversaw the lobbying campaign.[95]

The core coalition gained allies from the religious community, as nearly all the nation's mainline denominations joined in the effort. The Jewish community supplied the most dependable allies of longest standing, its leaders having cooperated with black civil rights groups since the end of World War II from a common interest in winning anti-discrimination policies and a philosophical commitment to equal opportunity. Experiencing unfair treatment themselves, particularly in higher education, corporate management, and the professions, many Jews felt moved to action by revelations of the horrors of Nazism. Jewish organizations such as the American Jewish Congress regularly joined with black civil rights groups in the postwar years to organize for fair treatment for all.[96]

By the mid-1960s, significant numbers of mainline white Christians also came to the aid of the black freedom struggle. Breaking a half-century habit of abstention from politics, leaders of the major liberal Protestant denominations worked through the National Council of Churches to change racist attitudes, stop discrimination, and organize for reform. Lobbying hard for the Civil Rights Act, they applied pressure that shifted otherwise hard-to-move Midwestern Republicans, such as Senator Everett Dirksen of Illinois.[97] In the wake of Birmingham and Vatican II, liberal Catholics also organized for economic inclusion. The National Catholic Conference on Interracial Justice created Project Equality, an interfaith body, to promote equal employment. Working on the premise that "religious institutions have an obligation to spend their money in a moral manner," namely, "in a manner consistent with the Torah and the Gospel," Project Equality pointed out that the combined purchasing power of religious congregations was second only to the federal government's, and urged them to press suppliers to cast off discrimination. With the cooperation of Catholics, Jews, and Protestants in localities across the country, by 1966 Project Equality had enlisted ten thousand firms in twelve cities. Its agreements suffered from the same problems as the Plans for Progress, but its overwhelmingly white participants spread the word that job discrimination was "the major root of all the racial injustices" and that opening good jobs to all was the duty of "a moral society."[98]

Even in the business world, the sector of society most allied with conservatives, a few came around. Most who did were afraid that prolonged domestic unrest would hurt the economy, but a few urged their fellows to acknowledge injustice and commit themselves to change. Charles E. Silberman is the best example. An editor of *Fortune* magazine, the nation's premier business periodical, he became a veritable radical in 1963, answering Birmingham with a manifesto titled *Crisis in Black and White*. Silberman understood how the growing involvement of the poor was adding urgency to the civil rights movement's calls for color-conscious hiring. "It is inevitable," he wrote, "that Negro organizations should use their power to increase job opportunities for Negroes *qua Negroes*. Indeed, Negroes are not content with equal opportunity any more; they are demanding preference, or 'positive discrimination' in their favor." What is more, this opinion maker endorsed the demands as necessary "to overcome the tendencies to exclude the Negro which are built into the very marrow of American society."[99] Corporate leaders in general proved less ideological and more pragmatic than the *National Review* set. "Few will insist that the situation is morally justifiable or consistent with democratic and Christian ethics," one report observed, even though "the white employer who will take voluntary action" to change things was "so rare as to be practically nonexistent."[100]

Still, Silberman's reaction was quite atypical in the business world, where vehement opposition to the Civil Rights Act was the norm. The U.S. Chamber of Commerce presented Title VII as the road to dictatorship. NAM cribbed from Kilpatrick and other segregationist writers in describing the act as "perhaps the greatest encroachment ever undertaken by the Federal government into the personal and private affairs of individual citizens." The "Socialist Omnibus Bill" was what it was, an opponent complained, "the antithesis of freedom." Any law that required fairness to blacks, NAM insisted, would lead employers to "discriminate in reverse against all other employees."[101] Discounting the seriousness of the problems blacks faced, NAM also sought to make a case for "free market solutions." African Americans' "rapid" progress from "savagery," it claimed, "demonstrates the quickness of growth in a relatively free society." The key was for blacks to improve their "motivation" to raise themselves to "the stage of development" whites had reached. The organization found a black businessman, S. B. Fuller, who was willing to tour with its multi-city "Minority Program" and make its case. A once-poor southerner with a sixth-grade education who had become an entrepreneur, Fuller served as "the vehicle into the Negro community" for the "free enterprise story." He offered arguments rare in black communities but pleasing to his white business audiences. The real cause of blacks' problems, he proclaimed, was "lack of initiative, courage, integrity, loyalty and wisdom," to say nothing of "hat[red of] work." What was needed, NAM underscored, was "motivation of the individual" through "the free enterprise system."[102]

The insincerity of such arguments became manifest when business spokesmen showed no interest in helping blacks help themselves improve their qualifications. To silence the public outcry over automation, for example, NAM acknowledged "the need for a greatly expanded program of education and training" to equip Americans with "the most fundamental skill of all: the skill to learn new skills quickly." Yet the organization never pressed to ensure blacks an equal education, much less compensatory education. For its part, *Nation's Business* questioned "whether industry should be forced to train people if the job market can produce the applicants needed." Conforming to a common pattern, one corporate representative complained that the combination of civil rights pressure and automation "increases the problem of hiring and even advancing persons without adequate background, education, experience and ability."[103] While powerful white opponents claimed that blacks lacked qualifications, almost none tried to assist them in becoming qualified. "We cannot hire people who are not qualified, nor can we lower standards," the Bank of America told CORE protesters demanding jobs in the San Francisco Bay area.[104] The truth was that most managers did not want to be bothered, and were at best indifferent to injustice. As NAM put it, "companies feel that training is the responsibility of the individual negro." Resenting pressure for change, the business-friendly weekly *U.S. News and World Report* complained of "legislation that compels employers to hire Negroes, and treat them the same as whites," as nothing but "forced hiring of Negroes."[105]

Business opponents of the Civil Rights Act gained confidence—and sometimes the language for their resistance—from the conservative intellectuals who worked together with southern segregationists against civil rights. Nowhere was the discord between blacks and the liberal left on the one side and the conservative movement builders on the other more evident or more lastingly important. One simple fact speaks volumes: whereas the business world had at least a few liberals such as Charles Silberman, not one prominent conservative opinion maker supported the most important victory for racial equality since Reconstruction. On the contrary, the right's premier publication, the *National Review*, embraced the case against the Civil Rights Act developed by leading southern defenders of Jim Crow. As Buckley later reminded the magazine's publisher, "I feel a considerable debt of gratitude to the [Virginia] Commission [on Constitutional Government] for permitting us to publish free of charge and without assigning them the credit, the[ir] extensive analysis of the civil rights bill." The act, commission member Kilpatrick wrote, "would undermine the most precious rights of property." If "the citizen's right to discriminate" should "be destroyed," he said, "the whole basis of individual liberty is destroyed."[106]

According to conservatives, the Civil Rights Act was an affront to America that would abrogate its liberties and undo its finest traditions. "The right to own, and possess, and manage property is vital," Kilpatrick insisted in a campus debate with Roy Wilkins of the NAACP, portraying any restriction on owners' rights as a death threat to the principle itself. He even ventured that "this bill is going to create a race consciousness where none has existed before." The Civil Rights Act, he said on another occasion, would surely force Americans "into a form of society less free, and more regimented, than any we have known in the past," even a "totalitarian" state.[107] Robert Bork argued that distinguishing between property rights and human rights was spurious; property rights were human rights of the highest order, and "individual liberty" depended on their sanctity. The issue, he said, "is not whether racial prejudice is a good thing but whether individual men ought to be free to deal and associate with whom they please for whatever reasons appeal to them."[108] Conservatives in Congress did everything they could to derail the proposed civil rights bill. Filibustering against it, Richard Russell, the powerful Georgia senator, railed that "no member of the Reconstruction Congress, no matter how radical, would have dared to present a proposal that would have given such vast governmental control over free enterprise in this country so as to commence the process of socialism."[109]

Polarized between advocates and opponents of the Civil Rights Act, Congress dithered. It held back even after white supremacists bombed the Sixteenth Street Baptist Church that served as headquarters for the Birmingham movement one Sunday morning in September and killed four girls attending Sunday school. Only with the assassination of John F. Kennedy in November did the calculus change. As Lyndon Johnson assumed the presidency, he pledged to fulfill his predecessor's mission by passing a strong civil rights bill. As vice president, Johnson had chaired the President's Committee on Equal Employment Opportunity and knew firsthand the defects of its reliance on voluntary compliance by employers. Demoting property rights from their privileged place, the newly added Title VII became the most contentious section of the act. Johnson engaged in a no-holds-barred, two-shifts-a-day lobbying effort to pass the stronger bill. "Politics," the new president believed, "is the art of making possible what seems impossible." In July 1964, after three months of debate, his legislative artistry helped the Civil Rights Act become law by a vote in the Senate of 73 to 27.[110]

But the artistry included concessions with long-term import for economic inclusion. One would widen its base in unanticipated ways. Seeing that property rights were losing their power to defeat human rights, desperate Dixiecrats sought other ploys to stop the legislation. The most cunning was the attempt of eighty-year-old Virginia representative Howard W. Smith to sink the bill by making it ridiculous in his colleagues' eyes through the addition of one word to the list of proscribed grounds for discrimination: "sex." Taunting the bill's sponsor in committee meetings, Smith called the legislation "as full of booby traps as a dog is full of fleas." He had indeed put proponents in a difficult spot, not least because his amendment threatened protective legislation for women that progressives in labor and social reform circles had long supported in a hostile job market. What Smith failed to anticipate is that some women, finding the provision a boon, would persuade the bill's sponsors to leave it in, in the process laying the groundwork for a feminist movement for inclusion. Even with Smith's amendment, Title VII won passage. Johnson personally called to thank the act's advocates for achieving "the most comprehensive civil rights bill in history."[111]

It was that, but it was also less powerful than what activists had fought to win: the final version was hedged with restrictions that would assist later efforts to nullify its promise. Diehard southern segregationists alone were not powerful enough to kill the act; its passage hinged on the votes of moderate Republicans, long the defenders of business prerogatives, so Johnson and the bill's sponsors had to enlist their support. Senate minority leader Everett Dirksen proposed a slew of amendments to limit Title VII's power to achieve what it promised. He succeeded in denying the new Equal Employment Opportunity Commission (EEOC) the ability to file suit in its own right (a power not gained until 1972) and to issue cease-and-desist orders to put an immediate stop to lawbreaking. In addition, his amendments built in waiting periods and other restrictions, exempted schools, and held down the new agency's budget. Finally, language built into section 703[j] barred efforts to deduce discrimination from numerical "imbalance" and forbade "preferential treatment" to correct imbalance, stipulations originally prompted by challenges from southern segregationists in Congress who opposed any form of desegregation. Johnson's Senate allies had no choice but to accept the amendments in order to have any chance of passing the bill.[112]

Essential to passage, Dirksen's support was also a Trojan horse. The result was that the reform's ability to deliver justice was enfeebled. Not only would those suffering employment discrimination not gain immediate relief, but also one of the approaches that grassroots activists saw as essential for racial equality would be embattled from the start—commitments to award set numbers of jobs to eligible African American applicants, as in the Birmingham settlement. Hamstrung before they set to work, government equal employment officials would have only imperfect tools to assist those who so desperately needed help. While seekers of inclusion focused on the spirit of the bill for which they had worked so hard for so many years, the restraints built into Title VII emboldened its critics for years to come.

At the time, though, what stood out was not the containment but rather the scale of the achievement. African Americans were elated; "finally," declared Roy Wilkins of the NAACP, Congress was acknowledging "that the Negro is a constitutional citizen."[113] Defenders of exclusion no longer set the terms of the debate. A deep struggle over the moral imagination of the nation had taken place as the Birmingham movement helped many northern white liberals and fence sitters see truths to which they had been blind, among them that white supremacy was wrong and the civil rights cause was just. Fusing old themes and new dreams in a way that made the package's appeal nearly inescapable, activists found great strength. The civil rights cause was now so irrefutably associated with the core values of the wider culture that the right could no longer isolate it. Millions of whites saw in inclusion a way to more social amity and economic development, less public assistance and crime, and the fulfillment of America's founding promise. As empathy for African Americans spread, polls found substantial majorities in favor of civil rights legislation for voting rights, jobs, housing, schools, and public accommodations. By the time Title VII passed, only 15 percent of Americans opposed equal employment opportunity.[114] Cramped as the powers of the new agency the law created were, seen from the perspective of cold war conservatives, the passage of Title VII was indeed an epic shift.[115]

⟋ BECAUSE IT CHALLENGED assumptions and privileges that whites had taken for granted since the nation's founding, the Civil Rights Act was bound to spark some resistance. In a zero-sum perception of the stakes of change, a significant minority of whites interpreted simple equal opportunity as an illicit taking from them. Even before the act passed, some whites in the North had fought the mere proposal of a government-backed end to exclusion, whether in postwar housing developments or in school systems that sought to implement *Brown v. Board of Education.*[116] Simple fairness seemed to such people a loss for themselves and an undue privilege for blacks.[117]

What was not inevitable, however, was the encouragement that wholly predictable backlash gained from conservative elites who deepened and protracted the conflict. For several years a grassroots right had been growing among middle- and upper-class whites, especially in the new suburbs of the Sunbelt, and its participants avidly consumed the books and articles of the intellectual conservatives. Right-wing activists believed that the moderate Republican president Dwight Eisenhower and his liberal successor John Kennedy had aggravated the communist threat through appeasement. At first, when grassroots conservatives undertook activism, they focused on local issues such as school curricula, but the Civil Rights Act controversy drew their attention to questions of national power. With a presidential election looming in the fall of 1964, conservatives at all levels turned to electoral organizing. Defeating their moderate rivals for control of the Republican Party, they made Senator Barry Goldwater of Arizona, a leading opponent of the Civil Rights Act and an outspoken anticommunist, the GOP presidential candidate in 1964.[118]

For all that Goldwater as a western libertarian differed from the southern segregationist Kilpatrick, Martin Luther King believed him "the most dangerous man in America." Goldwater "talked soft and nice, but he gave comfort to the most vicious racists and most extreme rightists in America."[119] Goldwater attacked the Civil Rights Act as "special appeals for special welfare" and insisted that it would lead to "the creation of a Federal police force of mammoth proportions." He asserted, "Our right of property is probably our most sacred right."[120] Lyndon Johnson thrashed Goldwater at the polls, winning the most stunning presidential victory to date, with 61 percent of the popular vote and more than nine times as many electoral college votes as his opponent.[121]

Yet the right's attacks on the Civil Rights Act mattered a great deal. They agitated whites already hostile to change, limited Congress's commitment to inclusion, and established the groundwork for later, more successful resistance as conditions changed. The case made by conservatives convinced whites who saw any advance for blacks as an unfair infringement that they were right, and that obstruction was an honorable pursuit. "I like what you write very much," one New Jersey man wrote to William F. Buckley. "The white population is not ready, not inside less than a year, to recieve the negro in every way of life, to dictate the unions, to push the white man around, take there jobs, by law of the land."[122] When Buckley invoked "the now all but inflamed resistance of the white population at large" just prior to Goldwater's thundering defeat, he was conjuring a future, not reporting accurately on an existing constituency. Some on the left also saw that future coming. Just after Johnson steered the Civil Rights Act through passage, he remarked ruefully to an aide, "I think we just delivered the South to the Republican Party for my lifetime and yours." From the clash over civil rights came future white GOP leaders committed to rolling back reform. For southern conservatives the Goldwater-Johnson contest, a later Senate majority leader, Trent Lott of Mississippi, would say, was "the first time that we really started thinking, 'Gee, maybe we are Republicans.'" In 1964, in his once solidly Democratic state, 87 percent of voters, still overwhelmingly white, had a similar epiphany.[123]

Undeterred, the president outlined the work ahead in one of the most significant speeches in American history. Addressing graduates of Howard University in the spring of 1965, Lyndon Johnson condemned the complaints about qualifications being used to raise drawbridges at the castles of privilege. Borrowing a metaphor from King, the president declared: "You do not take a person who, for years, has been hobbled by chains and liberate him, bring him up to the starting line of a race and then say, 'you are free to compete with all the others,' and still justly believe that you have been completely fair. Thus it is not enough just to open the gates of opportunity. All our citizens must have the ability to walk through those gates." Even with the new legislation, the struggle was just beginning, because "freedom is not enough." Simply and eloquently, Johnson explained why more than color-blind neutrality was needed for the Civil Rights Act to realize its promise.[124] For the first time since Reconstruction, the blinders of racial exclusion had been lifted; an American president had seen African Americans as equal citizens and human beings worthy of the kind of targeted benefits that other groups of Americans took for granted.[125]

The right had lost an epochal battle, but the struggle was far from over as all sides reconfigured themselves in the decade between Montgomery and the Civil Rights Act. Faced with an entrenched system of exclusion, fortified by McCarthyism and an automating economy, black activists took stock and devised new strategies. As they prepared to build on advances like *Brown*, the right's leaders propounded an ideology that made white advantage appear natural, while they helped agitate into being a newly self-conscious constituency to defend it. Failing to prevent passage of the Civil Rights Act, conservatives had managed to ensure that the effort to open better jobs to blacks would always be a struggle, and would require strong methods.

These formative encounters set up an abiding relationship of conflict. The conservative answer to blacks' efforts to achieve inclusion was to say that the opportunity already existed but blacks lacked the qualifications, or even the capacity, for such achievement, while at the very same time they worked to close off opportunity and stunt the growth of such capacity, for example, through massive resistance to school desegregation. The right's relentless claims of black incapacity, in turn, deeply affected those seeking access to the mainstream. It made compromise impossible and even dialogue difficult. Civil rights activists, meanwhile, were understandably wary of admitting that some African Americans might lack the preparation for the jobs they desired because that would seem to be giving ground to those who stigmatized all blacks as undeserving and inferior. After years of hearing talk of their lack of preparation used as an excuse for inaction rather than an argument to actually improve education, activists learned to recognize it as at best stalling, at worst as an ugly insult designed to sustain exclusion. In a common dynamic of social change, the intransigence of the privileged radicalized the newcomers, pushing them to develop measures strong enough to make headway in the face of such resistance.

In the escalating contest over opening good jobs to all, neither side's stance makes sense without the other's. Defenders of the old order were right: more was being done for blacks than ever before. And yet, activists for jobs and justice were right also: far too little was being done relative to the scale and severity of the problem. Each side's perception of the situation incited continued struggle. But when southern white conservatives insisted that the Civil Rights Act was "destructive of the very essence of life as it has been lived in this country since the adoption of the Constitution," they were in a sense correct.[126] Something fundamental had changed. The culture of exclusion was no longer secure.

～ 3

Civil Rights at Work

*E*QUAL EMPLOYMENT became the law at a time when white employers viewed their habits and hierarchies as the natural order of things. Now, suddenly, they were to change. But as Herbert Hill alerted NAACP branch presidents, *"Title VII is not self-enforcing."*[1] No one really knew the full magnitude of the task ahead or the practical steps needed to end racial exclusion. People had the text of the law but few guideposts for implementing it. Though less epochal than the challenge of defining freedom after the Civil War ended slavery, defining equal employment echoed the participatory democracy of that process. Immediately after President Johnson signed the new law, aggrieved African Americans began filing complaints of employment discrimination. Whereas public officials had expected a few hundred cases, they numbered in the thousands. From 9,000 in its first year of operation, the EEOC was tackling 77,000 cases by 1975—and still leaving many unaddressed.[2]

The insistence of so many ordinary workers on fair treatment helped create an innovative and effective national policy: affirmative action. In place of lip service to equal opportunity, it called for active effort and measurable results. African American workers and their advocates could not have achieved what they did if Congress had not changed the law and if the courts had not backed them in demanding accountability. Yet it was their willingness to put the law to work that changed the country. In filing the complaints that forced public officials to act, these workers were themselves setting national policy. They established an agenda for affected employers and for government watchdogs by explaining what they believed discrimination was, and spelling out what constituted fairness. Like the runaway slaves who presented themselves to courts as claimants on the nation's promise of liberty, the women and children who demanded protection against family violence, and the depression-era labor organizers who exhorted their fellows that "the president wants you to join a union," black working men and women claimed democratic ideals as their own and strove to enact them in everyday life.

Their efforts required allies. Civil rights attorneys and agency staff at the EEOC and the Office of Federal Contract Compliance (OFCC), established in the Labor Department by President Johnson in late 1965, aided workers in applying the new law. These staffers served as brokers of inclusion, intermediaries who maneuvered between those seeking change and those resisting it. With unique resources and skills, they helped workers navigate government bureaucracies and taught employers to see things differently. Powered by the law, the brokers raised questions and fashioned procedures that opened once unimaginable conversations and altered powerful institutions. As anger at continuing racial inequality exploded in deadly and costly urban riots across the country in the second half of the decade, such brokers grew in number and determination; they gained the cooperation of liberal leaders who realized that delivering results through orderly processes of law and government action might stave off worse division and disorder. Most EEOC staff members had a sense that the moment would not last, so they had to work hard, quickly, and well. "In those days," noted Ronnie Blumenthal of the EEOC, "every decision was precedent-setting."[3]

Two industries—southern textile manufacturing and northern construction—illustrate how workers and community activists, aided by movement lawyers, agency employees, and sympathetic judges, brought the law to life. Both industries offered good blue-collar jobs for their regions, jobs long denied to black Americans. Each became the premier site of the jobs campaign the civil rights movement waged in its region. Owing to generations of Jim Crow, people with limited education made up the majority of the black population, and placing them in better jobs was the activists' primary concern. The surprising contrast in the outcomes in the North and South reveals the complex forces that determined who would benefit from the new law.

⌒ TWO MONTHS AFTER the EEOC began work, the labor secretary of the NAACP called on the commission to investigate "the entire southern textile manufacturing industry." The new agency received 869 complaints from North Carolina, the industry's center, more than from any other state. The appeals prompted the EEOC to conduct its first public hearings on the textile industry. Held in Charlotte in January 1967, the effort included on-site visits to mills. Plant managers acted out their hostility to government intervention on behalf of blacks by arriving as much as three or four hours late for appointments. "Meanwhile, the employees who were there in the office," a staffer remembered, "would talk to the manager on the phone at intervals and tell him, 'This nigger is still sitting up here waiting for you . . . Yes, she's here.' They would call you 'nigger' and think nothing of it." On occasion, a carload of men trailed the investigators' car with "the barrel of a shotgun in an open window." Just the sight of teams of blacks and whites "wearing coats and ties when it wasn't even Sunday" signaled "trouble" to many southern whites. Some harassed the EEOC visitors, showing special venom for "nigger lovers." On a few occasions, locals arrested investigators. They drove one out of town at gunpoint. Wilma Hudgens of the EEOC recalls the period as "the insulting years": "Nobody," she said of whites, "really respected EEOC."[4]

No knowledgeable person at the outset of the 1960s would have predicted success for black workers and their allies in the textiles campaign. Centered in the Piedmont region at the foot of the Appalachian Mountains stretching from the Carolinas through north Georgia and western Tennessee into Alabama, the mills had hired almost all whites since the industry's take-off in the 1880s. Mill owners prided themselves on offering poorer whites of the up-country South, descendants of the old yeomanry, a respectable alternative to debt-strapped farming. Hiring whole families, women and children along with men, industrialists built company towns that supplied Jim Crow housing and churches as well as factories. South Carolina barred blacks from production jobs by statute; from 1915 to 1960, its legislature prohibited the manufacture of textiles by "operatives . . . of different races . . . together within the same room." The industry locked out black women completely (except for cleaning bathrooms for white women), and confined black men to dirty or dangerous janitorial and warehouse jobs. "We were doing the work that the white man didn't want to do," recalled Johnnie Franklin Archie of Rock Hill, South Carolina. "That's the only reason we were there."[5]

White workers had long colluded with management in these practices. Their employers designed them a segregated workplace, and they labored to keep it that way. Sharing the views of most whites in the South, they felt themselves superior to blacks and stood firm against racial egalitarianism in the labor movement.[6] The last time the mills had hired blacks, as temporary workers to keep up with military demand during World War II, some white workers had actively, even violently, protested. Keeping the textile industry white helped define who the workers were and where they stood in their communities. Blacks sometimes recognized this in the way they spoke about white workers. Said one North Carolina NAACP official about those in her community, "especially the poor ones," who resisted black civil rights, "White is all they had, and they were fighting for that white."[7] White mill workers were little prepared to accept blacks on their once exclusive terrain.

Textile mills were by far the largest manufacturing employer in the South and the largest non-farm employer of workers with limited education, supplying more than half of all industrial jobs in the Carolinas and Georgia. That commanding position made the mills a target for the advancing civil rights movement. Most textile jobs could be learned quickly by people with little education, as several generations of rural whites had found. The work was hard, low-paying, and stressful, and it could lead to deadly brown lung disease. Yet it was far better than what most blacks had: in 1967, the average wage paid by a North Carolina textile mill was more than twice the annual income of half of the state's nonwhite *families*. Most black women could find work only as domestics, laboring "10 hours a day, 6 days per week," as one woman recalled. "Before the mills opened up for black women, all they had was washing and ironing and cooking for white people." That was true even for some who had attended college.[8]

In March 1961 President John F. Kennedy issued Executive Order 10925; announcing fair employment as a national goal, it set up the

President's Committee on Equal Employment Opportunity. The previous year, as student-led lunch counter sit-ins had begun in North Carolina and swept across the South, Kennedy's statement of support for them and for Martin Luther King, Jr., had attracted a record proportion of black votes. Knowing the importance of good jobs to this constituency, the new president called for "affirmative action" to achieve "equal opportunity" in firms operating with federal contracts. What either phrase meant was not exactly clear yet, but mill managers felt a push to stop turning away black applicants.[9] Pressure from the federal government caused the industry's leaders to worry about the cost of stonewalling. As early as 1963, one North Carolina activist with the Merit Employment Program of the Quaker-based American Friends Service Committee (AFSC) who had worked for ten years with local employers "stated categorically" to an interviewer that the opening up of new positions to blacks "was due directly to the 'Compliance' provision of Federal government contracts." Indeed, 1963, the year Birmingham roused Washington, was the year many black workers themselves cited as the beginning of their entry into the textile industry.[10]

Mill managers, for their part, faced a mounting labor shortage in the early 1960s as higher-paying industries new to the Sunbelt began luring away white workers, especially men, just as the demand for textiles surged. Prompted by the government, and tempted by their own need for new sources of labor, some mills began hiring a few blacks for entry-level positions.[11] So novel was the idea that some applicants feared to speak of it in public, knowing it was dangerous to express ambition within earshot of whites. Corine Lytle Cannon, then working in a chicken processing plant, recalled the collective excitement produced when word spread that Cannon Mills would start hiring black operatives: "I had heard that black people were going to be allowed to go to sign up for work in the mill. . . . So I went back to work that Monday and told everybody. So when we got off work we all went over to the mill, and we all walked in. . . . We all signed up. All women. . . . We whispered it, you know, there was some things that you just didn't talk about. It was just a new area that was opening up for blacks and you just didn't talk about it."[12] As workers sought what they had never dared try for before, branches of national organizations such as the NAACP and the AFSC and local groups such as the Durham Committee on Negro

Affairs urged employers to accept them. In South Carolina, one black minister, the Reverend B. J. Gordon, used a church bus to drive women out to Oneita Mills to apply for work, reassuring them in the face of threats from the white families who employed them as domestics.[13]

Such efforts increased after the passage of the Civil Rights Act. With labor shortages and federal pressure to back them, black workers used Title VII to pry open the doors to the mills. It enabled individuals such as Sallie Pearl Lewis to believe that their initiative in seeking good work might at last yield results. Lewis had first applied to the textile manufacturer J. P. Stevens in 1966, when she was thirty-two years old. For the next five years she kept riding the bus out to the mill and applying over and over again, but to no avail. Unable to get even entry-level industrial work, Lewis had to rely on stopgap jobs such as "setting out pine trees" in the late winter and picking peaches in the summer—a job that left her only six hours out of every twenty-four when she wasn't either working or taking buses back and forth. Lewis, like many who had come through rural South Carolina's Jim Crow schools, had only a seventh-grade education. But she understood why she wasn't being hired while legions of similarly educated white women were. When she learned of Title VII, she sought help from the EEOC. She told her story and brought others forward to tell theirs. "The colored folks had to live," she later said, "and I had to get some work to do." Seven years after her quest began, Lewis became the lead plaintiff in class-action lawsuits against two major textile companies. She and other like-minded, low-income black women joined together to remake the industry through their legal cases. Most of Lewis's co-plaintiffs had similar profiles: little schooled but able to read and write, often thirty-something, with children, and desirous of jobs that would do more to improve their day-to-day lives and their families' futures than the ones they had as domestics, farm laborers, or hospital maids. What moved them was not only the need for work and the difference in pay, but also the pain of racial exclusion. "You see, every time we go [to apply for a job]," explained Lewis, "the black folk had to leave with a hanged head down, aching heart and we had to wonder [where] we was going to get another meal at."[14]

The new visibility of the federal government in their region encouraged many black citizens to lift their heads. The EEOC hearings provided a nationally publicized forum in which black workers could be heard describing how white mill managers had treated them and explaining why it was wrong. These hearings were a kind of public theater in which customary relations of power were momentarily reversed: low-wage workers found respect and sympathy while the region's self-styled "best men" were shamed in what one trade journal complained was "a government-financed 'Turkey-Shoot.'" Invited to testify, black workers became, as one witness put it, more "conscious and vocal about the inequalities they observe."[15] Identifying as urgent public problems practices that had been tolerated for years, their testimony broke through the racial etiquette which had long silenced challenges. In late 1967, moreover, the EEOC began a publicity campaign to urge African Americans, especially women, to apply for textile jobs and offered its support if they met resistance. In the same year, the OFCC chose ten large textile companies for a pilot program to enforce equal employment among government contractors.[16]

Enemies of the change agreed on its source. "It's the Government contracts, pure and simple," said one white small business owner in a textile town in 1969, angry that other whites were, in his perception, "bending over backwards for the Negro."[17] Two features of the textile industry made its leaders unusually susceptible to oversight: their reliance on big Vietnam-era Defense Department contracts for fabric to clothe and shelter soldiers, and their desire for federally imposed import quotas to shield their firms from foreign competition.[18] Johnnie Archie, a South Carolina plaintiff, conveyed the impact this way: "One thing about the southern white man, if the stick was big enough he obeyed it, but if the stick was small he'd try to take it and bend it." Those white men "feared the federal government, no doubt about it," he said. "If it had not been for the federal government we would probably still have had slavery in this country."[19]

That stick also tamed white laborers. After years of hostility to the idea of working alongside blacks, numerous whites described their understanding that now, finally, resistance was futile. Was the entry of blacks "a problem," a worker at Burlington Industries was asked. "No," she said. "We knew we had to accept them." Even the most hostile white workers grumbled but in the end gave in. When her foreman made his rounds one day and said he'd be bringing black workers in soon, Mildred Edmonds recalled, some of her co-workers swore they would quit. "They wasn't working with no nigger." But in the end, not one left. "They didn't like it too much but they didn't say too much" either.[20]

Even some white textile workers committed to Jim Crow outside of work came to see it as only fair that blacks have the chance to earn a decent living. "I think you can just fall in and accept it, and just think, 'Well, they want to live, too,'" mused one woman. Said another, "I feel they're entitled to work as much as I am. . . . They have families to raise as much as I do." Women's predominance in the mill labor force probably contributed to the accommodation, because by tradition and training women were less given to public assertion, much less violent displays of racism, than men. "They bunch up and talk to their selves," observed one disapproving white co-worker about those who objected to the presence of blacks. "You can hear them very often making remarks after they get out." They would stare belligerently, whisper menacingly, and resort to name-calling: hateful conduct, to be sure, but not as intimidating as actual violence.[21]

Another, ironic contributor to the relative smoothness of the transition was the lack of union power in the industry in the 1960s. Poorly organized as they were, hostile white workers lacked a vehicle to obstruct change. Right through the 1950s, the main union in the industry—the Textile Workers Union of America (TWUA)—had upheld white supremacy, particularly at the local level. Had such a caste-ridden union wielded more power, desegregation would likely have been less extensive, slower, and uglier. As it happened, the few times white workers walked out in the 1960s to protest the hiring of black workers, instigators were fired instantly, dissuading imitators.[22]

Yet if conditions were propitious for change, it was anything but automatic. Believing that their firms did not discriminate—that blacks were just unqualified and prone to raise objections—mill executives, let alone floor supervisors, resented pressures for civil rights compliance. Many branded the plantwide seniority and numerical racial hiring goals imposed by the courts to ensure equity "reverse discrimination" unfair to white workers. J. P. Stevens, which had long refused to hire or promote blacks, claimed that its accusers wanted to impose "a total regime of pro-black and anti-white discrimination." In fact, these policies ensured that blacks would get fair consideration from whites incapable of recognizing their competence. A case in point: systematic data collected by Dan River Mills, one of the industry's leaders, found that its black workers were actually better educated than whites and had higher productivity and lower quitting and absentee rates. Yet the year before, the personnel manager had described black employees as people who "are shiftless, lazy, don't want to work and leave as fast as they are hired."[23]

In the face of such hostility, workers needed support to realize the potential of the new law. The NAACP Legal Defense and Education Fund (LDEF) started a project in late 1967 to which other groups contributed, called TEAM. The acronym stood for "Textiles: Employment and Advancement for Minorities." Headquartered in Greenville, South Carolina, it acted as the community organizing arm of the textile jobs campaign. It paid field workers, most of them men and women from the areas they served, to visit textile mills, urge managers to open jobs, and organize local people to apply for them. The organizing was needed because, much as people wanted better work, it took great courage to apply. In communities such as Abbeville County and Aiken County, South Carolina, the Ku Klux Klan was still menacing blacks. And employers and creditors might blacklist those who tried for "white man's work." Fighting fear by working with local black clergy and NAACP activists, TEAM sought to promote "affirmative action" at all levels in the industry, director Mordecai Johnson told the press. The son of a Florence, South Carolina, minister, Johnson had worked his way through the state's black schools, taught in them, married and fathered four children, earned law degrees from Howard and George Washington universities, and assisted the general counsel of the U.S. Commission on Civil Rights before taking on this project. That varied training helped in this complex challenge. Prodding employers to change voluntarily and encouraging workers to claim their rights, TEAM acted as the carrot; in the role of the stick were class-action lawsuits.[24]

Whereas the challenge for black women was to get in, for black men it was to move up from the hard, dirty, low-paying work to which the mills had long consigned them. In Stanley, North Carolina—a small town where blacks and whites "stay[ed] to themselves" and African American public officials were still unheard of—A. C. Sherrill was in early 1968 the first black man promoted to a production job in the J. P. Stevens plant. With the highest output on his shift, he was told by his supervisor that he was a "great doffer." But when he started asking two years later about a promotion to supervisor, things changed. The head supervisor told Sherrill "he didn't think it was time for blacks to be moving into a position like that." The plant superintendent warned Sherrill that whites wouldn't like it. Harassment soon started: trash in his car, threats of violence, then a white co-worker took a knife to him. Some whites told him that the town would not abide his seeking advancement, and "the NAACP can't help you a bit." Finally, after a December 1971 meeting with a roomful of white supervisors, some in "a rage" against him for pressing for promotion, Sherrill left the company. But the abuse followed him to another mill in a nearby county, as whites spread the story of his attempt to rise. In 1973, he acted as the lead plaintiff in a class-action suit against J. P. Stevens on behalf of all blacks whose promotion had been blocked.[25]

At the time Sherrill sued, few blacks had reached skilled positions, and even fewer had been hired as clerical workers, salespeople, managers, or professionals. Willing to integrate unskilled jobs because it served their own interests, mill managers continued to block entry to the higher grades, which they still viewed as "white man's work." The Dan River Mills management recognized the problem in an internal memorandum in 1970 as the company faced a loss of federal contracts for its practices. "White supervisors," it reported, "discriminate without realizing that they are discriminating because they dislike blacks." A black Fieldcrest worker vented his anger over his employer's practices to the EEOC: "Just because I am black I am not suppose to better myself. I think that I am capable of doing this job but he won't give me a chance to even try." Persuading management to adopt even simple changes—such as the posting of skilled job openings where all employees could see them—could require a formal complaint to a government agency and the threat of legal action. Many managers considered promoting only blacks who were well liked by whites (not "pushy"), overqualified, and light-skinned.[26] Whitney Young mocked such charades: "I'm asking you not just to hire the Phi Beta Kappas and Lena Hornes," he told other businessmen. "[You need] to let apply, and to hire, dumb Negroes as you do dumb white people, and mediocre Negroes as you do mediocre white people. We need these jobs at all levels."[27]

In the face of employer recalcitrance, Title VII's award of the right to sue for fair treatment was a precious resource. "It was difficult to do anything before the Civil Rights Bill was passed," remembered Joe Moody, one of the local organizers of the class-action suit against J. P. Stevens in Roanoke Rapids, North Carolina. There "wasn't anything *to* do, you were scared to talk." With the new law as support, aggrieved workers obtained services from committed attorneys. Serving as brokers between the grass roots and the state, the attorneys began building up a body of case law in support of economic inclusion. The two most important contributors to legal counsel were the NAACP, which had more branches in North Carolina than in any other state in the late 1960s, and the NAACP Legal Defense and Education Fund, an independent organization. The Fund, its director counsel at the time, Jack Greenberg, later noted, "brought virtually all the cases that gave the [Title VII] law its bite."[28]

Between 1965 and 1971, over 1,200 such class-action lawsuits reached the courts. The Fund, with a staff grown to seventeen and a wide network of cooperating attorneys, led in pushing the courts to enforce the Civil Rights Act. Its lawsuits covered issues including separate seniority lists that locked blacks out of good jobs, discriminatory hiring and promotion procedures, biased recruiting, segregated locals in union workplaces, and the use of testing and job requirements unrelated to job performance that excluded blacks from competition. Those changes, Greenberg believed, were in legal terms "almost on a par with the campaign that won *Brown*." He later recalled, "Many black workers came to meetings clutching wrinkled, decades-old smudged bits of paper—one railroad worker had saved documents for twenty-six years— records of how they had been passed over in favor of whites, denied that most fundamental ideal of democratic capitalism, the opportunity to sell their services in an open and fair marketplace." The participation of people like this man imparted some of the spirit that made this legal struggle a collective, communal endeavor.[29]

As brokers of inclusion working with the Fund, Julius Chambers and James E. Ferguson II, partners in a Charlotte law firm, carried out the lion's share of the local work. Chambers knew Jim Crow from the inside. He had grown up in Mount Gilead, North Carolina, where he was born in 1936. When a white trucker refused to pay Chambers's father for repair work he had done, the elder Chambers could find no attorney willing to bring suit for a black man against a white to recover the money. After attending a black college in the state, Chambers earned an M.A. in history at the University of Michigan, where white preference again cut him off: Michigan's law school accepted only one black student a year, and that one had already been chosen. Returning home, Chambers earned his law degree from the University of North Carolina Law School in 1962, and then became the first intern at the Legal Defense Fund's New York headquarters. Two years later he returned to the South, to Charlotte, where he became chair of the NAACP's regional legal committee in the Southeast and established the first integrated law firm in the state by bringing in a Jewish partner. Within a year, Chambers initiated almost sixty lawsuits in North Carolina for racial discrimination in jobs, schools, hospitals, and public accommodations. Defying whites who bombed his home and set fire to his law offices and his father's shop, he became by the early 1970s the foremost civil rights attorney in the region.[30]

The firm's mission was to end "labor apartheid," said the Asheville-born James Ferguson, who joined in 1967. He explained how "these cases would grow out of a total community effort." It took exacting research and follow-through: in the *Sledge v. J. P. Stevens* case, for example, attorney T. T. Clayton interviewed each of the three thousand plaintiffs in his makeshift office at Horne's Motor Inn in Roanoke Rapids. From the passage of the Civil Rights Act to the late 1970s, black workers and their attorneys filed dozens of such suits; some lasted well over a decade, absorbing thousands of hours of labor from attorneys who went unpaid until they won, if ever. Because of them, companies such as J. P. Stevens, Cannon Mills, Cone Mills, Dan River Mills, Fieldcrest, and Burlington had to answer to judges and juries for how they treated blacks. One local worker later said, "We should put up a bronze figure of Julius Chambers in this town."[31]

The textile industry effort radically altered the lives of tens of thousands of black citizens. The head of the North Carolina NAACP had announced at the beginning of the campaign that it would mean the most to "mothers who are breadwinners of families, who go to work at 7:00 o'clock in the morning and come home late at night," women like Sallie Pearl Lewis. Before the mills opened to them, such women were treated as though they existed only to clean up after others, to do the work white people disdained to do for themselves. Mill jobs were far from ideal, but they helped countless black women escape personal service. Going from "a white woman's kitchen" at fifteen dollars a week in

1968 to a Georgia job that paid "minimum wage," Bobbie Harrison recalled, "was a great difference," adding, "That year I bought my home."[32] Years later, many spoke about what the jobs had meant for their children. "One of the things that the mill did," Johnny Mae Fields reflected, "was give me an opportunity . . . to give my kids a college education. They couldn't have gone to school if I'd still be working in that cafeteria." Even a woman who loathed mill work, comparing it to "living in slavery without having a master," reported high hopes for her daughter, whose "advantages" and "alternatives" came in part from her mother's having used the mills to escape the cotton fields. Corine Cannon, who was over forty years old when she took up mill work, found deeper meaning. "The best thing that has ever happened to black women in the South in my lifetime is a chance to be full-fledged citizens," she said. "And that comes from their work. You can't even pretend to be free without money."[33]

Even though the change fell short of both needs and hopes, the industry—so long a bastion of white supremacy—was transformed. Described by one economist as "a virtual revolution" and by black workers who lived through it as "the change," the turn in hiring was sharp. By 1970 blacks made up approximately 15 percent of the textile labor force in the Carolinas, and almost half of those hired were women.[34] Manufacturing employment such as this, moreover, contributed much to the improved overall economic status of blacks in the South after 1960. Whole communities felt the results in better education for children, hitherto unheard-of home, furniture, and car purchases, and in the new willingness of adult children to stay near their parents. "A whole lot of black people were pulled up, made their living a whole lot better," William Suggs, a retired worker, told an interviewer. "I bought this old house here," he noted, and "I sent three of my children to college." Thomas Pharr described how textile work "uplifted the whole community" and marked "a step into the mainstream of America."[35]

As it improved lives, Title VII also worked its magic on institutions, above all the labor movement. Because it made unions, as well as employers, liable to charges of discrimination and to lawsuits for redress, it made textile unions at last understand that "an injury to one is an injury to all." So altered was the industry by the act that the TWUA (later ACTWU, now UNITE HERE) found it had to remake itself in order to win union elections and strikes in a context in which it enrolled fewer than one in ten southern textile mill workers. Operating in a fiercely anti-union industry in a pro-business region, the union had always faced devilish choices. But before, those choices had made even antiracist unionists fear alienating whites. After Title VII, union leaders came to see greater danger in running afoul of black workers backed by the federal government.[36] When finally admitted to the mills, African Americans proved so pro-union that their propensity for organizing was the one thing on which both unions and management could agree. "The consensus opinion" of mill officials, reported an industry journal, is that "as the percentage of Negro employees increase[s], so does a mill's chances of union organization."[37]

Pushed at first against their inclinations, a significant minority of white workers in time came to respect and appreciate their black co-workers. They cooperated toward common goals, sometimes ate lunch together in a region where that kind of socializing had been taboo, and even became friends in ways that would have been unthinkable twenty years before. "You'd be surprised," the retired Corine Cannon said. "I can call up those white women I worked with or they call me up and we just talk. See your work, and this goes for white people and black, is what you are. . . . The mill is a way of life. When we black women came in there, this was just a new area of life that was opened up to those white women as well as for us.[38]

The transformation in textiles was a dramatic instance of a process changing lives around the country, especially in the South between 1965 and 1975. No one saw this better than the longtime civil rights strategist Bayard Rustin. In 1975 Rustin slammed the stereotype that blacks were either "poor" or "bourgeois." What was regularly forgotten in such thinking, he said, was the "black working class," yet "perhaps the most dramatic, and largely unnoticed change brought about by the civil rights revolution was a massive transformation in the composition of the black work force." Whereas before the movement blacks were almost totally confined to low-paying jobs without prospects of advancement, by the end of the 1960s "a combination of anti-discrimination laws, federal manpower programs, and a rapidly growing economy acted to pull most black workers out of the ranks of the working poor and into the solid working class." It was, he said, "a shift in occupational status unprecedented in its dimensions and rapidity."[39] Indeed, systematic studies found "significant change" in the occupational patterns and earnings of employed African Americans and gave affirmative action policies aimed at realizing the promise of Title VII significant credit for the improvement. Although progress varied, it proved "much greater than in previous decades."[40]

⌐∿⌐ BUT THE ADVANCE was nonexistent in some areas, as Vincent Whylie learned when he came north in 1962, as tens of thousands of African Americans had before him, determined to make a better life than he could in the Jim Crow South. An experienced wire lather by trade and a member of an AFL-CIO local in Daytona Beach, Florida, he moved to Brooklyn with his wife, five daughters, and high hopes. "The life of a lather is a hard one," Whylie admitted of his work installing support frameworks for buildings. He didn't expect things to be easy; the job was "hazardous," often done outdoors during "months of rain, sleet, cold and snow," though at least with a union there was decent pay, "security," and a "future." But not for all workers: Local 46 of the Wood, Wire, and Metal Lathers, which controlled all the construction jobs in Whylie's trade in New York, had no interest in admitting black members. With six thousand men on its rolls, the union counted no active black members, and simply refused Whylie's transfer card. Turning to the NAACP for help, he landed a job on a post office building project. But he soon lost it on the pretext of a layoff—only to see a white man hired as he left. Outraged, Whylie took his case to the New York Human Rights Commission. It found "gross discrimination" and ordered the local to admit him immediately, but it stonewalled. He had "reached such a point of desperation" by 1970 that he wrote to President Nixon, "most respectfully Sir," as he put it, "for your help." Whylie told him, "I have fought with the Union in every way," and "even gone on bended knees, but without success." While this dispute dragged on, his children sometimes "went without food," he had nearly lost his home, and because of all this turmoil he "became very ill and had to have a major operation." What Whylie wanted was "a chance to earn a decent living so that I will not have to rear my children on Welfare." He begged the president "to give me an opportunity of better working conditions by doing whatever may be possible to help me to get in Local 46." Whylie's experience reveals why, as one observer noted, "today, there are fewer Negro plumbers or electricians than Negro Ph.D.s."[41] "Exclusion in the craft unions is so complete," the director of the Chicago Urban League declared, "that segregation would be a step forward."[42]

As their southern counterparts focused on the textile industry, northern civil rights activists set their sights on construction in the early 1960s. The trades seemed a logical place to look for the jobs needed to achieve full citizenship for low-income African Americans, because construction was, as Herbert Hill of the NAACP said, "a huge industry with vast growth potential." It also paid the nation's highest wages for blue-collar work. Hiring essentially began anew with each building project, so low turnover and seniority did not pose the barriers they did elsewhere. Moreover, the big projects tended to be accessible to central city black populations in a way that much newly suburbanized manufacturing was not. Even more than the South's textile industry, construction seemed to offer hope of upward mobility to working-class African Americans. A thriving sector with revenues of over $100 billion in these years, it accounted for 14 percent of GNP, and depended on public goodwill because government projects constituted so much of the work. Publicly funded all-white construction projects infuriated community residents, for they maintained labor apartheid in the most insulting way. A West Coast NAACP leader gave voice to that anger when he complained that the new Oakland post office was "being built with federal dollars in an American Negro neighborhood without a Negro electrical worker, Negro plumber, Negro sheet metal worker, or other crafts too numerous to mention."[43]

There was another force behind the focus on the building trades that did not arise from rational strategic calculations: perceptions of injured manhood among black men, who were seen as emasculated by racism and in need of a boost. Hill shared his concern for black masculinity with a congressional subcommittee. "Jobs in the building trades are for men," he said. In the "highly important symbolic sense" these were "male jobs," and such "'manly' jobs" with "high status implications" were "especially important for Negro men." Building on widely shared ideas about gender, the argument found scholarly support in *Tally's Corner.* That popular 1967 study poignantly showed how some poor black men's inability to secure any but menial, intermittent jobs as laborers undermined their marriages, soured their relations with their children, depleted their faith in themselves, and left them reliant on a "street-corner society" of other defeated men who provided "sanctuary" for one another.[44]

The powerful lure of construction jobs—plentiful, skilled, lucrative, public, and coded as manly—drew civil rights organizers across the North in the 1960s. In city after city, they petitioned, lobbied, demonstrated, picketed, and sat in on job sites in order to open up the trades to men of color. Encouraged by the Birmingham struggle, NAACP branches in Philadelphia, Cleveland, Newark, New York, and Pittsburgh all organized in 1963 against Jim Crow construction sites and for the inclusion of blacks and Puerto Ricans in the building trades. In ensuing years, dozens upon dozens of communities saw such organizing, often lasting years.[45] Sometimes protesters practiced civil disobedience with "lay-ins" on job sites. One such action in Philadelphia "received nationwide publicity and TV coverage," noted the nervous director of the AFL-CIO civil rights committee, as he sided with the construction unions, imagining progress where there was none.[46] Such grassroots organizing was essential to success and yet was no guarantee of it.

Again and again, aspiring entrants and activists came up against unyielding counter-pressure from contractors and from white workers and unions. A few protracted conflicts illustrate the impasse. In Brooklyn in the summer of 1963, thousands of people joined in a month-long campaign for jobs for blacks on a big public building project, the Downstate Medical Center, near the impoverished Bedford-Stuyvesant neighborhood. At times it looked like the southern freedom movement, with hundreds of demonstrators sitting in and singing freedom songs as they blocked deliveries to the site. Led by a broad-based group called the Ministers' Committee for Job Opportunities, it was, above all, an attempt to unlock the trades to blacks, who made up 22 percent of the local population but only 2 percent of apprentices. Yet thousands of hours of labor, myriad miles of picket lines, and seven hundred arrests produced virtually no results.[47] An impregnable fortress, the industry absorbed all the artillery outsiders could fire and left them spent, still outside, and counting their losses while life went on as before within the walls.

Sometimes, white tradesmen engaged in their own forms of massive resistance to change. St. Louis construction workers conducted a veritable hate strike in 1966 over who would work on the Gateway Arch that was to become the symbol of the city. Long puzzled over how to deal with the well-documented racial exclusion in the building trades and embarrassed by the protests of local activists, OFCC officials had decided that the arch project was a place to start. The agency awarded a contract to a firm that promised to practice equal employment opportunity, and turned to non-union plumbers because the AFL-CIO had no black members to send. At that, five building trades locals, long unwilling to train black apprentices or accept black members, walked off the job in a wildcat strike, refusing to work with the black craftsmen. (They claimed race was irrelevant to their fight against "union-busting.") Work on the arch stopped for months. Faced with this militancy, and pressured by the NAACP and others, the Justice Department filed its first "pattern and practice" suit under Title VII against the city's building trades. It took this major lawsuit and a federal court injunction to make the white tradesmen consider admitting a few blacks to their unions. Once again in construction, as a New York CORE leader put it, "maximum action" yielded minimal gains.[48]

Whereas textile work was largely unskilled, dull, low-paying, and family-based, the building trades were skilled, high-paying, satisfying, and all male. Owning most of the tools they used, and looking for employment not to contractors but to union hiring halls, tradesmen had far more autonomy than most other workers, blue or white collar. Not surprisingly, given the wages the trades paid and the satisfactions they offered, they were so prized that they became a kind of property that could serve as an inheritance, as one contemporary put it, "handed down like heirlooms from father to son to grandson." Even where the father-son pattern gave way as sons went to college, an unusual work culture still thrived. Male co-workers bonded with one another in daily displays of technical competence, physical prowess, and virility. These performances insinuated whiteness and maleness into definitions of skill, insider status, and labor militancy.[49]

Yet these jobs had significant drawbacks that were equally defining of the shop-floor culture. The work was dangerous: rates of accidental injury and death ran higher in construction than in any other American industry. Workers needed to trust one another to feel secure where risk was so routine; ensuring high-quality work was a safety precaution as much as a matter of pride. The work was also episodic and seasonal, such that annual earnings could be much lower than hourly wages implied, and worry about where the next job would come from was constant. Each new project usually meant new employers, which made the union hiring hall vital to finding steady work over the course of one's life. The advantages and the insecurities of construction work thus combined to make workers fiercely loyal to profoundly exclusive institutions.[50]

After more than a decade of fighting with the AFL-CIO building trades unions, Herbert Hill of the NAACP described them as "narrow, restrictive protective associations" that had "more in common with medieval guilds than with labor unions [in] . . . a twentieth century industrial society." At the core of the old American Federation of Labor, the craft unions managed to pull the AFL-CIO rightward after the two bodies merged in 1955. Presiding over the new federation was George Meany, the portly, cigar-smoking plumber who once boasted that he had never walked a picket line, so tight was his union's control of access to its trade. The unions' strict rules of entry facilitated white nepotism, much as grandfather clauses kept blacks from voting in the South. One asbestos workers' local that found itself in the courts in the sixties, for example, required applicants to have written recommendations from three current members and a majority vote from the membership in a secret ballot, as well as four years' experience as a "helper," a job restricted to "sons or close relatives living in the households of members."[51]

While admission practices varied across the fiercely independent trades, their common purpose was to limit labor supply while steering scarce jobs to the family members, friends, and associates of those already inside. For some craftsmen, race may not have been an issue, or at least not the primary one, yet for most it clearly was. Although white strangers might find their way into the trades through on-the-job experience as laborers or helpers (the route more than half of white tradesmen took), black strangers almost never gained access this way. Their path, like Whylie's, was blocked at every turn. As the battles over exclusion escalated, white workers reacted as if blacks were looking for handouts when they sought work. Faced with men chanting "Jobs . . . Now!" at their worksites, some white workers exploded. "Everybody else waited half their lives for a job and they want jobs now," said one worker. A crane operator voiced the common white interpretation of blacks' protest: "They want our jobs."[52] Against such a phalanx, direct action was not enough.

Recognizing the power of the building trades unions and their determination to control apprenticeship, some civil rights activists tried to bore from within. Ernest Green, one of the nine students who had integrated Central High School in Little Rock in 1957, now fresh from college at Michigan State, was one. He became assistant director of the Joint Apprenticeship Program operated by the Workers' Defense League (WDL) and the A. Philip Randolph Institute, founded in New York in 1964 to bring blacks into the building trades through the front door. Backed by coalition-minded social democrats such as Randolph, Rustin, Norman Thomas, and Michael Harrington, the WDL worked with the AFL-CIO Civil Rights Department to open the federation's member unions. Beginning with his brother Scott, the first black apprentice in a New York sheet metal workers' local, Green and his coworkers prepared hundreds of blacks for apprenticeships and in time claimed to have placed two thousand in the trades. "We had played by the union's rules and defeated them," he later said.[53]

But most contemporary activists found such union-supported outreach efforts grotesquely short of what was needed, if not cynically cosmetic on the part of the unions. A fierce debate raged between the AFL-CIO officials who posed the problem as merely an atavistic one of "pockets of discrimination" and outsiders who agreed with Herbert Hill that exclusion was systematic in the craft unions. In the end, the results were so disappointing that blacks turned increasingly to government for help. They fought through the courts, as the textile campaign had done, waging a series of lawsuits against construction contractors and unions that widened the scope of Title VII. Green's brother, for example, gained entry to the union for sheet metal workers because a court had insisted it open its apprenticeship program.[54]

⌒ As DIRECT ACTION and legal cases drew attention to the industry, would-be workers got help from an unlikely source. In September 1969, the Nixon administration issued the revised Philadelphia Plan. The plan promised to bypass all-white hiring halls and put non-union minority craftsmen on city jobs where unions refused to provide them, as well as to decertify union-run apprenticeship programs that excluded blacks. The effort had originated with the Johnson administration, which ultimately shelved the idea for fear of clashes with unions, construction contractors, and conservative critics alike. Nixon had less to fear than Johnson from organized labor and was in a better position to handle conservative opponents.[55]

There was another problem for the emerging policy of aggressive federal affirmative action marked by the Philadelphia Plan. Thanks to those conservatives in Congress, especially the business-protective Republican Everett Dirksen, Title VII contained an explicit prohibition of quotas to achieve employment equity and of proportional representation as a gauge of fair hiring. Yet these were precisely the solutions that the movement for inclusion increasingly believed essential to economic advance for African Americans, while continuing riots underscored the danger of inaction. The revised Philadelphia Plan sought to solve this quandary by avoiding inflexible quotas in favor of target ranges for employment. It identified numerical "goals" with timetables for achieving them, coupled with a proviso that failed "good faith" attempts to meet the goals would not be punished. By specifying numerical target ranges for blacks in each of the crafts, the plan offered a way to break through the barrier of the closed-shop hiring hall. Now contractors would have to enlist numbers of black workers within the ranges specified, or at least show that they had tried to do so in "good faith." The goals were modest: the percentage of minority employees on Philadelphia Plan projects was to rise to 4 to 9 percent in 1970 (from 1.6 percent), and 19 to 26 percent by the end of 1973. All were to be hired to fill new vacancies; no white workers were to be displaced. In effect, the plan followed the path that courts were charting in response to black workers' suits. In the case of the asbestos workers, the court prohibited the discrimination and nepotism that produced segregation, as it ordered the union to develop objective, job-related criteria for membership and to alternate white and black referrals for jobs in the interim. In effect, the court introduced meritocracy and numerical goals at the same time. Veteran civil rights leaders such as Whitney Young and Herbert Hill, along with much of the black press, commended the president and rallied around the plan.[56]

The man Nixon charged with overseeing the construction effort, Arthur Allen Fletcher, brought a deep commitment to employment inclusion. As assistant secretary of labor for wage and hour standards,

Fletcher was the top black official in the Nixon administration. He knew discrimination firsthand, having been raised in a series of West Coast ghettos by foster families because his parents could not care for him. His father was a career cavalryman with a Jim Crow unit of the army; his mother, who had college degrees in nursing and teaching but could not find a professional job, became a live-in maid, and had to give up her son. Becoming a star football player in high school, he went on to play professionally, but he was traded by the Los Angeles Rams in 1950 because the team had exceeded its ceiling quota of five black players. Unable to find a coaching job after he left the league, Fletcher had to rely on menial and factory work as he earned a postgraduate degree. Meanwhile, he became director of a manpower development project for the "hard-core unemployed" that became a model for the Republican Party's "black capitalism" initiative in 1968. In the spring of 1969, Fletcher joined the Labor Department, where he helped design and implement the Philadelphia Plan. A wounded combat veteran of World War II, a football hero, and a daily Bible reader, at six feet four inches tall and 240 pounds, Fletcher was an imposing figure. To make the case for vigorous affirmative action, he took the 1969 moon landing as a model of what Americans could do when they tried. He pointed to the Apollo mission as an unparalleled "*social* achievement" that engaged thousands of people, who persevered even after eight of the first ten launches failed and three astronauts lost their lives. Alluding to the numerical remedies in the Philadelphia Plan, Fletcher attributed the moon landing's success to having "a *clear, concrete, measurable* goal," "a timetable for achieving it," and the resources needed to do the job well.[57]

Opponents howled. What the Philadelphia Plan really meant, said the construction unions and contractors and their congressional allies, was "quotas" and "reverse discrimination." Senator Sam Ervin of North Carolina was among the first to complain, and his forceful efforts to derail the plan's guidelines as unlawful "quotas" won him warm praise from NAM. The organization's general counsel blasted "the growing tendency of the government to seek to accomplish by executive decree objectives which the Legislative Branch of the government has either failed or refused to authorize by statutory authority." Showing new solicitude for workers' rights, NAM fretted that the plan "would inevitably result in discrimination against some qualified non–

minority group workers." The ironies were stark. Ervin and his allies had done everything in their power to defeat the Civil Rights Act and its commitment to bettering the job prospects of black workers. Failing in that quest, they doggedly pushed to enforce only one small fraction of that law—the section opponents had inserted to weaken its effectiveness.[58]

At this stage, however, such critics of affirmative action appeared less as guardians of meritocracy than as defenders of white privilege. Among their ranks was George Wallace, the segregationist former governor of Alabama and now a presidential aspirant, who warned of the danger to apprentice and seniority systems and supported the construction unions' fight against integration. It was "clear as the noonday sun in a cloudless sky," wrote the journalist Tom Wicker, mocking remarks by Ervin, that the construction unions and their southern segregationist and northern business allies "were standing fast for one of the most important remaining strongholds of racial discrimination." That was a truth "no amount of rhetorical camouflage" could hide.[59] Congress itself rejected their arguments in December 1969; by a vote of 208 to 156, the House upheld the numerical goals of the Philadelphia Plan. Yet the unusual alignments in the vote marked fault lines that would deepen in years ahead, as many labor-based Democrats opposed a civil rights measure and usually anti–civil rights Republicans supported the authority of the president.[60]

The odd lineup reflected some of the Machiavellian motives that led Nixon to side with the NAACP and black workers here but nowhere else. Since the Johnson years, the White House had shared business leaders' alarm over high construction wages as a source of inflation. "There was general agreement," reported top advisers to Johnson, "that we have to find some tools to get at the labor unions in the construction area" to keep overall wages in check. One idea was to promote more job training in the trades. In late 1968, *Fortune* magazine pressed the theme with an article on the "murderous bargaining strength" of the "most powerful oligopoly in the American economy today." Blaming the "unchecked power" of the construction unions for the era's "wage-price [inflation] spiral," *Fortune* identified union control over training and hiring as the cause. It called for several reforms, among them the abolition of the union hiring hall and a shift away from union-run apprenticeships to on-the-job training. The last in the seven-item list was *"new legislation against discrimination,"* a law to decertify unions that excluded minorities. A NAM publication titled *Chaos in the Construction Industry* concurred on the "urgent" problem ("unavailability of enough skilled craftsmen") and on the culprit ("excessive union bargaining power"). The situation seemed so serious that NAM urged opening jobs to blacks as a way to break down craft union restrictions on labor supply.[61]

Business was overcoming its aversion to government intervention because it could not solve the industry's problems on its own. So fragmented was construction—with nearly 900,000 contractors, 10,000 local unions, and 30,000 separate labor agreements—that voluntary solutions were doomed. In a rare admission, the president of the powerful Bechtel Corporation—Labor Secretary George Shultz's future employer—announced, "The private sector alone cannot do the job."[62] In early March 1969, Nixon asked some of his assistants to confer about construction. "Working quietly" alongside White House staff was Roger Blough, the influential business leader who headed the corporate Construction Users Anti-Inflation Task Force, which would evolve into the Business Roundtable. One idea that attracted wide internal support was to have the government run a vast training effort to turn out skilled workers in a fraction of the time required by apprenticeships. Such an initiative, noted one official, might "fit in well with the program for non-white employment and also for the returning Vietnam veteran."[63]

Nixon's people added to their economic calculations some political ones. The president and his staff were delighted to find themselves upholding a civil rights initiative that made much of labor and many liberals queasy. They tweaked the sanctimonious *New York Times* for its refusal to endorse the Philadelphia Plan. After the Senate fight over the plan, one White House aide exulted to another, "The key issue is that we have laid bare the split between the Blacks and the trade union movement," adding, "A wedge has been driven into the liberal Democratic ranks which should be exploited for the confusion it puts them in." He suggested that the Justice Department work with the Labor Department "to keep the pot stirred." (Actually, the labor movement split on the issue. Some industrial unions, including the United Auto Workers, "felt that the craft workers were getting away with murder," and lobbied for the plan as a way to "undercut the Meany position.")

Nixon insiders rejoiced that the alliances "between civil rights and labor people"—alliances that Martin Luther King, Jr., had done his best
to foster between the country's two main progressive constituencies—
"are going to come apart."[64]

Some warned that a policy subject to such intrigue might go out of
favor as fast as it came in, and they were right. Two leaders of a state labor council with a good record on training minority apprentices challenged the president in late 1969 to stop bashing labor for political advantage and instead do something real for black workers. "Isn't it just a
bit hypocritical," they queried, to push for the Plan and then immediately curtail federal construction spending so that it was harder for everyone to find work?[65] For its part, the AFL-CIO accused the Nixon
administration of applying the law selectively, and pointedly urged
tough affirmative action for police forces that not only excluded African Americans but also acted as "instruments for the repression of their
legitimate aspirations." In any event, important as the construction industry was, it accounted for only 2 percent of the labor force; surely
other sectors needed attention. Yet the Nixon administration fought
adequate funding and enforcement powers for the EEOC and the
OFCC.[66] Perhaps most revealing of White House cynicism was the announcement, nearly simultaneous with the promulgation of the Philadelphia Plan, of a 75 percent cutback in federal construction, alluded to
in the unionists' letter. Blacks were being promised employment in an
industry that was about to hemorrhage jobs.[67]

In the end, the construction effort ran aground for other political
reasons. The president realized that his foes on the Philadelphia Plan
might be his best allies on Vietnam. After George Meany blasted the
plan on national television in January 1970 as an attempt to win
"Brownie Points" with civil rights groups, the president observed to an
aide, "This hurts us."[68] A few days later, when Daniel Patrick Moynihan, the Harvard sociologist (and future U.S. senator) turned personal
adviser to the president, observed to his boss that little advantage had
come of his initiatives for blacks and urged a policy of "benign neglect"
instead, the president observed that other advisers had been "directing
our appeal to the wrong group (both in case of Negroes and whites)."
They should aim, rather, at the conservative, pro-business elements
in each group.[69] Soon Nixon was reaching out to the building trades
unions and trying to make amends. Professing agreement with them on

the need for "voluntary" approaches, the administration backpedaled from the Philadelphia Plan and promised no "undue zeal" in putting it into practice.[70]

Building trades union officials supplied the muscle for "hard-hat" support of the president's policy in Southeast Asia, and became the focus of his bid to cultivate an uneasy white lower middle class. In 1970, encouraged by their union officials and by contractors who paid them for the time off work, two hundred helmeted New York City construction workers attacked a peaceful Wall Street demonstration to condemn the invasion of Cambodia and the killings of college students at Kent State and Jackson State. Injuring seventy people, the "hard hats" trumpeted their support for America, its war, and its president. It was, Vice President Spiro Agnew enthused, an "impressive display in patriotism." When the head of the New York Building Trades Council then presented Nixon with a hard hat labeled "Commander in Chief" at a White House meeting, the president praised it "as a symbol" of "freedom and patriotism."[71]

Soon the president assigned Charles Colson to "move hard, fast and extensively" on solidifying relations with conservative union leaders. "Picking them off one by one," he tried the Teamsters, the firefighters' and carpenters' unions, and the Maritime Union. Even George Meany's daughters were invited for tea at the White House to secure their father's favor. Relishing his task, Colson targeted right-leaning rank-and-file workers, including those "keenly aware of the race question," such as "the Wallace hard core in the UAW." He also tried to rescue corrupt pro-Republican union officials from prosecution by the Justice Department, urging instead "a major attack on left wing/commie infiltration of the labor movement." But Colson looked to the building trades as "clearly our most fertile ground." The strategy paid off when many more conservative union members walked away from the Democrats in the 1972 elections; more than one in two union households voted for Nixon's reelection.[72]

Always less a firm commitment than a means to other ends, the Philadelphia Plan could not survive these intrigues. Within less than a year of its proclamation, word spread that it was to die a quiet death. The Urban League reported that "little progress has been made in translating the promise of the Philadelphia Plan into actual jobs." In place of serious results-oriented efforts, the administration turned to "hometown plans" for American cities, voluntary programs for self-monitoring by unions and contractors whose lip service to equal opportunity convinced no one, certainly not the black workers whose continued exclusion was now certain. The turnaround in policy was complete when the president chose Peter Brennan, the New York building trades leader who organized the "hard-hat" demonstrations, as secretary of labor. Now there would be an unyielding champion of exclusion inside the cabinet. Soon thereafter, the director of the OFCC resigned over its "illusionary and cosmetic policies."[73]

After the demise of the Philadelphia Plan, activists continued organizing to get black and Latino men—and later women—into construction work. Coalitions and independent organizations kept up the pressure in many northern cities. In New York, for example, the Harlem-based group Fight Back, which started work in 1964, pushed for years for access to construction jobs. In New Haven, a broad-based Black Coalition—which included organizations from the Elks to welfare rights activists, black schoolteachers, and the Nation of Islam—pressed hard to win job "entry and upgrading" on behalf of "oppressed minorities." The Urban League worked nationally on the issue through its Labor Education Advancement Program (LEAP), begun in 1966 in collaboration with unions, the Workers' Defense League Joint Apprenticeship Program, and Labor Department government contractors.[74] Because of efforts such as these, the number of black men in the skilled trades crept up incrementally in the 1970s.

In the meantime, though, the resistance from contractors and co-workers also continued, and government did little to stop it. "As far as can be determined," reported a *New York Times Magazine* investigation in 1972, "no public construction project anywhere in the country has ever been canceled because of civil-rights violations, as required under Federal law, although dozens of courts have documented violations." Even if those responsible for enforcing the law had wanted to do so, it was hard to see how they could have. The entire New York regional OFCC office consisted of three people: a director, his assistant, and a secretary. Between them, they were to ensure compliance from the thousands of government contractors and dozens of unions in the whole of New York State—as well as New Jersey, Puerto Rico, and the Virgin Islands. What that meant, said James Haughton, the founder of Fight Back and the son of a construction worker himself, was that "the only contract compliance in New York is when the brothers throw up a picket line." Years of earnest effort had brought little to celebrate. Nationwide, while the percentage of black carpenters grew from 3.5 percent to 6.6 percent between 1960 and 1980 (from 29,000 to 53,000), the percentage of African Americans in other crafts rose only from 6.5 percent to 7.8 percent (from 112,000 to 149,000).[75]

Thus, in the end, the southern, conservative, small-town industry became more inclusive than the northern, urban, unionized one. For all its historic dedication to white supremacy, the textile industry proved more permeable than construction. Staffed largely by unskilled workers who could be fully trained within a month, the mills were hungry for labor. They were also relatively concentrated: the handful of large corporations that dominated the industry offered big sitting targets for class-action lawsuits and agency monitoring. As seekers of protective legislation against textile imports, these firms were also vulnerable to bad publicity and government pressure. Equally important, their existing workforce had little to lose besides its sense of racial superiority from opening access to entry-level jobs; workers' desire to keep the jobs white got no added fillip from the desirability of the work.

It was different in construction. There, thousands of contractors jostled for position, virtually free of accountability, and they needed amity with powerful craft unions to complete their projects. Decentralization and project transience made for murky lines of authority and accountability. Skilled tradesmen liked their jobs, far more so than other working-class Americans: they prized the work itself, the good wages, the camaraderie, and the sense of belonging to an exclusive fraternity of autonomous white men. No matter what outsiders said about fairness, they aimed to keep the benefits of this preserve for themselves, their relatives, and their friends. More to the point, they had the power to restrict access to jobs through their control of certification and hiring. The only thing that might have broken this monopoly was strong federal pressure with penalties, such as the Philadelphia Plan provided, but that did not happen.

⌒ Across the country, Title VII emboldened workers to challenge exclusion in multiple ways. Thousands filed charges against employers, sometimes with NAACP backing; hundreds, if not thousands, complained to or of their unions.[76] Others built workplace caucuses and rank-and-file groups to press for fair treatment, holding mass meetings, issuing newsletters, and developing links with counterparts elsewhere. Using tactics honed in the Birmingham crusade, activists in a number of Deep South communities—including Natchez, Mississippi, where Wharlest Jackson had lost his life for gaining a better job—organized black citizens to refrain from shopping in downtown stores until they hired African American cashiers and workers.[77] Under the leadership of Martin Luther King, the SCLC set up Operation Breadbasket in Chicago, run by the young Jesse Jackson; its mission was to win jobs for blacks and enable some to establish their own businesses. Sometimes the mere threat of a boycott was enough, as in a major victory with the A&P grocery chain in Chicago, which promised seven hundred new jobs and agreed to turn to black-owned companies for some services. Success there inspired efforts in more than a dozen other communities from Brooklyn to Los Angeles. In 1972 Jackson created his own organization, Operation PUSH (People United to Save Humanity), which negotiated hiring and purchasing agreements with companies.[78] The NAACP, for its part, sponsored a "field-labor director" to organize for jobs and justice. The Birmingham-born labor and civil rights activist Grover Smith, Jr., traveled all over the South, helping workers register complaints, meeting with employers and contractors to encourage hiring, and speaking about equal employment on the radio and in public meetings in places from Boomer, West Virginia, to Florence, Alabama.[79]

As some activists worked to open up particular workplaces, others sought to reshape the nation's political economy. Labor-affiliated civil rights workers led by A. Philip Randolph began a campaign for the Freedom Budget, a visionary attempt to cure the deep structural inequalities in American life. "Freedom from want," proponents declared, "is the basic freedom from which all others flow." They called the budget "a practical, step-by-step plan for wiping out poverty in America during the next ten years" by creating federally funded jobs to improve housing, schooling, and community life at a cost of $180 billion. Backing it was a broad coalition of well-known civil rights spokespersons, including Randolph, Rustin, Whitney Young, James Farmer, Dorothy Height, John Lewis, Roy Wilkins, and Martin Luther King, as well as leaders of the country's more progressive trade unions, religious bodies of all denominations, scholars, and "forward-looking business leaders." With full employment to end poverty as its goal, the Freedom Budget outlined the kinds of broad-ranging reforms that had been proposed earlier by the National Urban League's Domestic Marshall Plan and King's Bill of Rights for the Disadvantaged. The vision was of a far different kind of capitalism from that America had known, more democratically controlled, socially beneficial, and egalitarian in its outcomes. Only this, they believed, would address the racial inequities that were rooted in and perpetuated by class inequality.[80]

Proponents also understood that a wider social justice agenda addressing class inequality was vital to win over working-class whites who might otherwise be persuaded by the right that advancement for African Americans would come at their expense. As King had pointed out in 1963, the nation's majority needed what only a bold new approach could provide: "a massive program by the government of special, compensatory measures." King asserted that "the deprivation and the humiliation of poverty" was in some ways "more evil" for "the white poor" because "it has confused so many by prejudice that they have supported their own oppressors."[81] Promising betterment for all those struggling, not only for those long excluded by race, the Freedom Budget could light the way to new cooperation for mutual benefit. "In this, the richest and most productive society ever known to man," said Randolph, "the tragedy is that the workings of our economy so often pit the white poor and the black poor against each other at the bottom of society." He noted, "Not only the poor . . . but all Americans, are the victims of our failure as a nation to distribute democratically the fruits of our abundance. . . . We shall solve our problems together," he warned, "or together we shall enter a new era of social disorder and disintegration."[82]

The riots that ripped across the country in the second half of the 1960s, which some called "rebellions" to emphasize that participants were expressing long-standing grievances, drove home the urgent need for action. The deadly eruption in the Los Angeles community of Watts in the summer of 1965, just as the EEOC opened for business, electrified the country; many more followed. When the Department of Justice calculated "riots and civil disorders" for 1968, it tallied 366 in the first nine months of the year alone. As the department's community relations field staff investigated, again and again jobs issues—whether the lack of work or the low-paying, menial quality of the employment open to blacks—emerged as key causes of distress.[83]

Movement leaders interpreted these events for white Americans, whose fear and hostility the riots inflamed. To avoid "further social chaos," A. Philip Randolph advised the president, "the major responsibility for all of us is . . . to make work available for those in the ghettos." Martin Luther King agreed. "Every single outbreak without exception," he telegraphed Johnson in 1967, "has substantially been ascribed to gross unemployment, particularly among young people." King urged the president to set up "a national agency that shall provide a job to every person who needs work, young and old, white and Negro." The historic report of the blue-ribbon National Advisory Commission on Civil Disorders—known as the Kerner Commission—came to the same conclusion in 1968: job segregation and institutional racism fueled the riots. In internal White House discussion, Johnson aide Harry McPherson was by then referring to employment discrimination as "our currently most serious domestic problem."[84]

Some movement leaders took the case right to businessmen, skillfully demolishing common excuses for not hiring African Americans. The Urban League's Whitney Young traveled the corporate circuit telling audiences that "I frequently meet white people these days who tell me that they were once immensely sympathetic to the Negro cause but that they no longer feel as sympathetic now because of the riots, cries of 'black power,' etc." His response was to ask the person, "And what were you doing in the days when you were sympathetic? How many Negroes did you hire or train?" After an awkward silence, "it usually turns out that he didn't do anything, that he has simply found a new, and respectable, excuse for indifference. If all the people who claim a previous sympathy had been performing accordingly during that period, it's fair to assume we would not have had any riots."[85] On occasion, appeals to conscience did move employers. Stanley Marcus, head of Neiman Marcus department stores, in early 1968 shocked the corporate world by alerting the chain's nine thousand manufacturers and suppliers that the chain would henceforth "favor" those who hired minorities in awarding contracts.[86] But more commonly, as in textiles and construction, employers fought change.

And that resistance radicalized the contest, prompting advocates of inclusion to devise more aggressive measures.[87] In the view of many, perhaps most, corporate officials, the changes taking place were radical, wasteful of time and resources, and without compelling justification. Echoing conservatives in Congress, NAM and many businessmen claimed that federal anti-discrimination efforts had "far outdistanced clearly stated Congressional policy" in Title VII. Promoting superficial adjustments while resisting deeper change, NAM and the Chamber of Commerce sought to limit the reach of the new law.[88]

Facing such obstruction on one side and a flood of worker complaints on the other, equal employment officials switched from a "retail" to a "wholesale" strategy. Instead of reacting to complaints one by one, which required vast resources for tiny and evanescent gains, they turned to system-wide measures to open up recruitment, training, and promotion, as had the campaign in textiles and the Philadelphia Plan. The near impossibility of proving intentional discrimination helped drive the change. As activists saw in the early 1960s, it was a Herculean feat to prove that employers had acted with malice toward blacks. Few recorded their motives, and finding such evidence was beyond the resources of those who suffered. "Negroes are losing faith in the complaint system," noted a West Coast NAACP official in 1967, because "it is virtually impossible to satisfactorily prove and win a case before the investigative officers, hearing officers and appeal bodies."[89]

Taking the offensive, activists and their allies developed a wide array of techniques that could be calibrated to specific situations; together they became known as affirmative action. Their common purpose, as participants in a formative White House conference in 1965 put it, was "to provide not only equal opportunity but the opportunity to be equal." Among the possible components were active recruitment of potential employees through institutions and media in black neighborhoods (as opposed to reliance on word of mouth or walk-ins), training to give otherwise qualified workers the specific skills they would need on the job, eliminating requirements and hiring tests that had no bearing on job performance, job posting and personnel counseling to encourage existing employees to prepare for and seek better jobs, restructuring of job ladders to make mobility from lower grades possible, and sometimes, as in the Philadelphia Plan, hiring preferences for hitherto excluded workers.[90] Above all, the approach signified aggressive efforts to find, welcome, and prepare black applicants. To aid employers in effecting change, the EEOC offered a Technical Assistance Division, and the OFCC advised on new procedures.[91]

Understanding grew with experience. One outgrowth was that the concept of institutional racism quickly made its way into popular understanding. Given its name by Stokely Carmichael and Charles Hamilton in 1967, it codified ideas that were developing among antiracists. Unlike "individual racism," institutional racism was "less overt, far more subtle, [and] less identifiable in terms of *specific* individuals committing the acts." But for all that, it was "no less destructive of human life." It, too, relied on pervasive assumptions of blacks' inferiority and whites' entitlement to prevail, but it did its work through ostensibly neutral procedures which had the effect of either excluding blacks altogether or keeping them in menial, subservient positions. Because it built the advantages of whiteness into organizational practices, Carmichael and Hamilton found policies based on "color-blindness" to be "totally unrealistic." "Emphasizing race in a positive way," they said, aimed "not to subordinate or rule over others but to overcome the effects of centuries in which race has been used to the detriment of the black man." Others elaborated. "Racism will not be ended," wrote the social scientists Louis Knowles and Kenneth Prewitt, "by the normal working of institutions whose very normality is itself the foundation of the racial problem." Those habits needed to be disrupted and their white practitioners brought to awareness if meaningful change was to occur.[92]

As the pressure for inclusion confronted the inertia of long-established habits, new approaches to hiring developed. Agencies prodded employers to think about what training and skills were truly necessary for particular jobs. Very often firms had set the bar arbitrarily, and the result was to shut out people who were disadvantaged to begin with. For example, one campaign convinced the courts that the height requirement for New York City sanitation workers not only was inessential for the work but also kept out Puerto Ricans, who tended to be shorter than Anglos. NAM explained to its member companies that they needed to consider whether job applicants were "*capable of doing the job being recruited for*"—to shift their focus "from developed ability to apparent potential."[93]

As it had in the textile and construction cases, litigation enabled workers and their allies to outlaw practices that produced exclusion, most dramatically in the Supreme Court's milestone decision *Griggs v. Duke Power Co.* The case arose when Willie Griggs and thirteen other black janitors were rebuffed when they applied for better jobs at the

Dan River, North Carolina, power plant where they worked. The men contacted the NAACP, which aided them in filing complaints with the EEOC in 1966 and achieving victory in 1971. The Court, ruling unanimously, outlawed "barriers" to inclusion such as tests for applicants that were unrelated to the job and "favor[ed] an identifiable group of white employees." In the words of an EEOC official involved in the case, the "decision restricts employers from translating the social and economic subjugation of minorities into a denial of employment opportunities." The Court thus moved away from a notion of discrimination as constituted by isolated acts on the part of hostile individuals and toward an understanding of how ostensibly neutral industrial-relations systems might hurt historically excluded groups. In Title VII, the Court said, Congress had aimed at "the *consequences* of employment practices, not simply the motive." Specifically, the Court declared that where testing, educational, and other requirements disproportionately excluded minority workers—where they "operate as 'built-in headwinds'" with what came to be known as "adverse effect" on minority applicants—*and* where they could not be shown to be needed for the work as performed, they were discriminatory. The employer had to demonstrate a "business necessity" for such a practice or change to keep within the law. Now the burden of proof was on Goliath.[94]

Griggs gave the blessing of the nation's highest court to an increasingly common feature of settlements in discrimination cases: numerical hiring and promotion goals and timetables akin to those imposed on the textile industry and in the Philadelphia Plan. The EEOC, the OFCC, and the courts turned to stronger medicine when, by the late sixties, it had become clear that, given the lack of enforcement, simple prohibitions on discrimination failed to end exclusion. After Congress and the courts upheld the Philadelphia Plan, the Labor Department issued an order that spread the plan's methods to all federal contractors. The numbers set were almost never rigid demands but, rather, flexible targets requiring that those hired be "qualified" (if not the "best qualified"). "The 'best qualified' never had any legal right to employment," one architect of the new system reminded critics, because American law had long granted the employer the "discretion to hire and promote at his will." So "where [employer] discretion has been used to exclude," he urged, "it would be a tragic misuse of the principle of equality if it could not now be used to *include*." What was being asked of employers was simply "good faith" effort, a concept taken from collective bargaining that stressed "a process, not a result." These facts, along with the pejorative imputation of incompetence that accompanied the "quota" allegation, led supporters regularly to distinguish goals from quotas. "The 'goal' that we refer to," explained the U.S. Commission on Civil Rights in 1972, "is nothing more than a description of what the labor force would look like absent the effects of illegal racial or sexual discrimination, and the 'timetable' is the informed estimate of time needed to achieve the discrimination-free labor force without disrupting the industry or denying anyone the opportunity for employment."[95] Congress reaffirmed the legitimacy of such goals in 1972.[96]

Where earlier voluntary efforts and EEOC conciliation agreements had failed to convince many employers, mounting court-imposed back pay settlements began to. "The new message the awards sent," Jack Greenberg recalled, was that "the longer you discriminate the more it will cost you." Corporations began to worry. Most *had* excluded blacks, or confined them to the worst jobs, and their senior management knew it. Now they faced the prospect of embarrassing publicity and steep settlement costs. In a 1974 article titled "Running Scared," the *Wall Street Journal* reported that American corporations "are spending huge sums to ferret out and eliminate questionable—or downright discriminatory—hiring and promotion practices." Some were "making fundamental changes in the way they do business," such as driving home the need for change to middle managers by linking their raises to affirmative action success.[97]

Systematic scholarly studies by economists working with large data sets found that numbers-oriented affirmative action plans were aiding the advancement of black workers. Research on personnel records from numerous companies to assess the impact of government antibias policy found "overwhelming" evidence that it was central to the significant progress blacks made in the labor market after 1964. Another economist found a modest but telling impact on federal contractors that grew in the second half of the 1970s, most dramatically among firms that underwent federal compliance reviews. "Direct pressure," he concluded, "does make a difference."[98]

As economists looked at the effects on overall employment, some sociologists revealed how federal pressure changed the way firms operated. In response, personnel managers constructed new internal labor markets. Whereas the old ones presupposed occupational segregation and dead-end positions for minority men and women, the new systems treated all employees as interested in mobility. Reducing managerial discretion so as to insulate firms from charges of discrimination, they formalized the mechanisms that governed promotion in a way that made more mobility possible. The new formal position descriptions, performance reviews, and salary classifications systems were, in effect, "organizational formulas for inoculation against EEO litigation." At a deeper level, the new policies furthered a sea change in American culture by presuming and encouraging striving for achievement among all employees, no longer only a favored few.[99]

Aggrieved workers came to rely heavily on litigation because, owing to their limited scope and budgets, the government agencies that were to help them lacked the power to get the job done. The compromises that went into the Civil Rights Act's passage had left the EEOC, as one study put it, "a poor enfeebled thing."[100] Because the agency lacked the ability to enforce the conciliation settlements it secured, companies felt free to violate the terms of agreements they had signed. Through "low visibility" funding decisions, hostile forces in Congress could further obstruct justice, as when Congress cut Lyndon Johnson's first proposed EEOC budget by half. Although the law specified a lag time of no more than two months between complaint filing and investigation, by the end of 1968 an overtaxed EEOC was taking eighteen months just to open cases, long after trails were cold, and at the cost of "irreparable damage to the individuals concerned." Never thereafter did the EEOC enjoy sufficient funding or authority to succeed in the work designated for it by Title VII. Quite the contrary: it developed a backlog of cases that snowballed to over 53,000 by 1972. As NAACP head Roy Wilkins observed in lobbying for increased funding, "It is one of the oldest truisms that a law can be nullified as effectively by lack of resources for enforcement as it would be if it were repealed."[101] Similarly, the Department of Justice lacked appropriations sufficient to carry out its responsibilities under the law. Almost half the regions under its jurisdiction devoted no resources at all to employment discrimination in 1968—not for lack of demand but for want of money.[102]

Part of the problem, the A. Philip Randolph Institute pointed out in 1969 after a year-long study, was that "civil rights are unique in that they appear to be the one group of constitutional rights most readily temporized, evaded and delayed." Government reluctance to apply sanctions was chronic in civil rights. "Proponents of the laws tend to rest on their victories," the report explained, while "the opponents of the laws, Southern members [of Congress] mostly, work tirelessly to undermine them." Their unusual seniority built on black disenfranchisement, these southern opponents wielded vast power through their control of key congressional committees, including those that could undermine civil rights by beggaring the agencies charged with enforcement. Thanks to such funding decisions, the ratio of contract compliance personnel to contracting firms was approximately one to one thousand; in the area of defense, twenty officials were charged with monitoring some ten thousand facilities. If in theory the government contract compliance effort touched one in every three jobs in the economy, in practice the number was far, far fewer. The system "simply does not work," summarized the head of the EEOC in 1970, "any more than traffic regulations would without traffic cops."[103] Across the country, others were learning this just as aspiring construction workers had.

The vast, committed, and creative effort of so many people across the country had produced, at best, circumstantial justice. What determined the outcome in any particular workplace or industry was not a fair reckoning of the harm inflicted and the remedies needed but circumstances beyond the control of the injured: the power of the movements pushing for change, employers' labor needs and public relations concerns, the stance of the workers already employed, the interests of the unions involved, and above all, the rigor of government intervention, itself a function neither of law nor of fairness but of the resources of the contestants.[104] As dramatic and important as the changes were, indubitably the brakes were being applied in some areas even as the gains mounted in others. Their many well-reasoned and eloquent calls notwithstanding, movement activists never persuaded white leaders to adopt an ambitious program of full employment or broader social reconstruction, or even to apply the law and federal contracting power as rigorously as need demanded.[105] These were the limitations of accomplishments that depended so heavily on backing from the courts and government. Partial and imperfect though they might be, the results so outstripped anything gained previously that on balance, the strategy appeared a winning one, even as its ability to deliver depended more than many contemporaries could see on the mass mobilization of the era.

In fact, from the time Title VII became law, black workers and their supporters had pressed to make its promise come true. They shaped it inside workplaces and in community campaigns; in union halls, personnel offices, and courtrooms; in textiles, construction, and dozens of other industries; in mass meetings and individual confrontations. They invented new ways of assessing qualifications and making decisions that helped break down a centuries-old culture of racial exclusion. Their efforts changed the way businesses and government operated and altered the thinking of countless whites. They opened the American labor market and broadened the labor movement. They altered the course of tens of thousands of individual black workers' lives, opened new vistas to the children of such workers, and bettered whole communities. Yet they still had much farther to go to achieve equality.

Into this tense situation—of limited resources to meet almost unlimited need—would come new challenges: other populations with their own long histories of exclusion and legitimate claims for public redress. For black civil rights activists quickly gained company in the quest for access and equity, and the fragile foundation beneath them was called upon to carry much more weight. When other groups to whom Title VII had offered the promise of inclusion began to use it, women of all groups and Mexican American men foremost among them, affirmative action would change not just in scope but in meaning and prospects as well.

~ *II*

Others Reposition Themselves

~ 4

Women Challenge "Jane Crow"

$\mathcal{T}$HE PROMISE of an end to sex discrimination on the job transformed American feminism as it healed a long-standing and bitter split. After winning the right to vote in 1920, politically active women had divided over how to seek the full citizenship they still lacked. While some concentrated on winning an Equal Rights Amendment (ERA) to the Constitution, others sought practical measures that would relieve the strain of combining employment with child rearing and homemaking. The question whether to seek abstract equality in law or substantive equality through reform split women by class: well-educated women who could compete with men for professional and managerial jobs and meet domestic obligations by hiring others found the formal equality of the ERA attractive, while working-class women found its titular fairness not simply hollow but actually threatening to hard-won legislation protecting women through measures such as limits on working hours. As long as employment discrimination was legal, the conflict over sameness versus difference seemed inescapable: while some women lost opportunity by stressing women's difference from men, others lost security by stressing their similarity.[1]

The dispute was furious, abiding, and nearly inevitable given the real differences of interest in the mid-century legal context. As the main self-designated "feminist" organization, the National Women's Party (NWP) had made the Equal Rights Amendment its sole goal for half a century. It allied with employers, and their National Association of Manufacturers, who hoped for the elimination of protective legislation as a victory for laissez-faire economics. In Congress, the main backers of the ERA were northern pro-business Republicans and conservative southern Democrats who embraced the call for "no special privileges" in hopes of undermining targeted social welfare. Allying with them left the country's most visible feminists cut off from trade unionists and civil rights reformers for almost half a century, and made the very name "feminist" anathema to those women and men who were working for broader social justice. NWP members demonstrated their narrow loyalties when, as the Civil Rights Act was being debated in Congress before the ban on discrimination by sex was added, they unanimously criticized the draft bill for failure to extend protection to "a *White Woman, A Woman of the Christian Religion,* or a *Woman of United States Origin.*" There was clearly no natural, inevitable affinity between civil rights and feminism among white women; the sense of common purpose that had united antebellum abolitionists and feminists was sadly rare.[2]

But Title VII cut the Gordian knot. By promising substantive fairness, it did not solve the sameness versus difference dilemma but did alter its terms so as to allow diminution of the old conflicts. Doing away with gender-based protective laws while at the same time promising working women equality with working men, it allowed women to define themselves as full earner-citizens and to build new alliances. Much has been said about the class and race biases of second-wave feminism, yet when the focus of inquiry turns from the youthful women's liberation activists, often students, to the usually older working women who mobilized around issues of employment and focused on changing public policy, the movement looks more diverse and more attentive to bread-and-butter needs.[3]

In fact, the women who most appreciated the potential of Title VII were those who had benefited least from the family wage bargain. Many black women of all classes and wage-earning women of all backgrounds experienced firsthand both the underside of an order that promised family wages to men only and claimed to protect women while treating them as lesser beings, and the limitations of color-blind and gender-neutral formal equality. Because neither of the strategies white feminists had been pursuing met their needs, black women activists had for decades sought instead social policies that recognized mothers' need for well-paid work and for support in their familial obligations.⁴ Participation in civil rights struggles also made some acutely sensitive to the dangers of the separate-but-equal tack pursued by labor-affiliated white feminists and more willing to demand an end to exclusion. "I just want equal treatment," said the labor and civil rights activist Dollie Robinson. "Whatever the men get, I want."⁵ Moreover, now that the civil rights movement had won broad support for the idea of opening up all jobs, employment organizing benefited from a built-in momentum that other feminist projects such as reproductive rights lacked.

That momentum, in turn, enabled workplace activists to pose powerful challenges to widely accepted norms and practices that held all women down, among them the division of labor by gender and the sexual objectification of women. As they worked on the job and through activist groups, government agencies, court challenges, and other means to win equal citizenship at work, their organizing changed the way millions thought about women's and men's capacities. They altered American culture's common sense about gender, just as black activists had its notions about race. As they inspired women to redefine their identities, allegiances changed too, and the novel idea spread that the women's movement and the civil rights movement were natural allies. The reforms they won—not only access to new jobs but also pregnancy leave, the outlawing of sexual harassment, and greater support for parenting—led to increased inclusion of women in all areas of public life. Throughout, outsiders and insiders worked together, as grassroots protesters and sympathizers passed the initiative back and forth "like running a relay."⁶ Once again, Title VII did not itself bring change, but it did provide a resource that enabled activists to chip away at the foundations of exclusion in so many areas that they caused the whole structure to stagger.

AMONG THE FIRST to appreciate Title VII's potential to improve women's lives, especially black women's lives, was the attorney Pauli Murray. Identifying herself as a member of "the class of unattached, self-supporting women for whom employment opportunities were necessary to survival," Murray became one of the most influential voices for including women of all groups in Title VII's ban on discrimination. Having crossed many boundaries in her own life, she saw ties that others overlooked. Descended from slaves, slaveholders, and Native Americans, Murray was orphaned at an early age. Raised in the South, she made the North her home in adult life. Influenced deeply as a young adult by the radical left, and a participant in the first sit-ins in the 1940s, she forged at that time a friendship with Eleanor Roosevelt which gained her access to power. A deeply spiritual person—later she became an ordained Episcopal priest—and a poet, she felt herself to be also "a warrior." Married only briefly and disastrously, she built her world around strong, independent women in the age of the feminine mystique. But what most affected Murray's identity was the combined force of race and gender. A brilliant and accomplished student, she found herself denied admission by the University of North Carolina in 1938 because of her race, and by Harvard Law School in 1944 because of her sex. When she entered Howard Law School, where some of the country's most brilliant legal minds honed the challenges that would lead to *Brown v. Board of Education*, she learned that her male civil rights colleagues thought sex discrimination humorous, even when turned against a co-worker in the cause. It was then, in the 1940s, that Murray coined the phrase "Jane Crow" to capture the injustices to which women were subject. "The rationalizations upon which this sex prejudice rests," she declared, "are often different from those supporting racial discrimination in label only." As she would say later, "the two meet in me," and from that standpoint she widened public understanding of what real freedom meant.[7]

Murray was "overjoyed" when the word "sex" was added to the Civil Rights Act "because, as a Negro woman, I knew that it was difficult to determine whether I was being discriminated against because of race or sex." She belonged to a network of progressive women who in the 1950s and 1960s began to explore different strategies for achieving fairness for their sex in the absence of a mass movement. In 1963 some succeeded in persuading Congress to pass the Equal Pay Act, the first federal anti-discrimination legislation. Yet their victory showed that formal equality was not enough: since job segregation had kept women in low-paying occupations different from those held by men, the key problem was not unequal pay for the same work but different work for women that was accorded lower market value. When a southern congressman, Howard Smith, proposed an amendment to the Civil

Rights Act of 1964 to bar sex discrimination in Title VII, these women pounced on the opportunity. "Smith insisted he was serious," writes one observer, "but his comments appear to have been aimed at satirizing the logic behind the civil rights bill, which, in the view of Smith and many conservatives, was attempting to defy human nature." Representative Martha Griffiths of Michigan used the ribaldry that greeted Smith's proposal to shame her male peers: "I presume that if there had been any necessity to have pointed out that women were a second-class sex, the laughter would have proved it." Other female House members, few as they were, rose to support Griffiths with arguments about the prevalence of sex discrimination in employment. Meanwhile, self-defined feminists who had weathered the years since women's suffrage in the National Women's Party lobbied in support of women's inclusion in the bill. The amendment stayed in, by a vote of 168 to 133. And thus it was that the historic Civil Rights Act outlawed discrimination against women, but only in employment.[8]

Behind the scenes, what persuaded the law's sponsors to keep the sex discrimination provision, notwithstanding Smith's hostility to the bill's purpose and their own fear of "diluting" black civil rights, was neither the NWP nor Griffiths but Pauli Murray. She drafted a memorandum that the women's network distributed to every member of Congress, the attorney general, and other key players, among them the president's wife, Lady Bird Johnson. "If sex is not included," she argued, "the civil rights bill would be including only one half of the Negroes." Her logic convinced in part because she brought people to see how the case being made for opening jobs to African Americans concentrated on men while slighting women's needs. Advocates were so concerned to shore up black men's masculinity and familial authority through breadwinning jobs that they utterly neglected the plight of the tens of thousands of black women struggling on their own under the most challenging conditions. Murray used the same data others used on family breakup to make a very different, feminist case. "Negro women *especially* need protection against discrimination," she pointed out, because they are "heads of families in more than one fifth of all nonwhite families." For them, there was no such thing as a protective male family wage. Besides, since women of all groups now made up a third of the nation's labor force, it was time to understand that "women's rights are a part of human rights."[9]

Murray keenly appreciated how full-time employment could change women's sense of themselves and their options. She and a circle of other black women wrote critiques of gender relations in the 1940s that anticipated the sexual politics most observers associate with the 1960s, just as black women's need for good full-time jobs anticipated the future for nearly all American women. "What's wrong with Negro men?" asked the novelist Ann Petry. Ignore the impassioned avowals of progressive politics from "the average Negro male," she urged, and "observe his actions at home." Although his wife "works forty hours a week," he expected a "cook, chambermaid, waitress, cleaning woman, valet and butler," owing to his belief in "the God-given superiority of the male." The black woman "is obviously in a state of revolt," announced Pauli Murray in 1947, explaining "why Negro girls remain single." Noting that black women of necessity worked outside the home, she observed that "college-trained and professional women" in particular found rare the "Negro male [who could] accept the Negro female as his equal and treat her accordingly." Most black men suffered from the prevailing "mis-education of the sexes" that trained men "to act as if they are the lords of creation." As the poet Gwendolyn Brooks elaborated in "Why Negro Women Leave Home," a woman with her own income was unlikely to endure being treated as "a chattel or a slightly idiotic child." If a male partner could not "treat her as a fellow laborer, deserving of his respect and tact," then she might well "prefer to live alone."[10]

The male leaders of civil rights organizations and trade unions similarly tended to assume that men's needs were more important than women's. Although black women carried much of the burden of the civil rights struggle at the grass roots, they repeatedly found themselves unheeded, even disrespected, by the men at the helm. Ella Baker, one of the most visionary grassroots leaders, left the NAACP in part because of such obtuseness, only to find that the male clergymen of SCLC seemed incapable of regarding women as equals in the struggle. Women were similarly discounted in the call for speakers at the March on Washington for Jobs and Freedom, the eloquent protests of some notwithstanding. While serving as executive director of the NAACP, Roy Wilkins indulged a kind of argument about gender inequality that he fought furiously where race was concerned. "Biologically," he said of women, "they ought to have children and stay home. I can't help it if

God made them that way."[11] Even the United Packinghouse Workers, a progressive labor union with the best record of fighting racial discrimination, favored men; black women had to argue and organize for gender equity in wages, job assignments, seniority, and protection from layoffs.[12] In short, few progressive men recognized that, like black men, black women also needed good jobs and deserved the dignity of full citizenship. "The Negro woman," Murray concluded in 1964, "can no longer postpone or subordinate the fight against discrimination because of sex to the civil rights struggle but must carry on both fights simultaneously."[13]

Murray transmitted her commitment to the dignity of "self-supporting" women to a new wave of activists in the mid-sixties. Title VII provided them a wedge with which to open up the whole gender system to question. It served as the mechanism with which once-private grievances could be turned into classically political issues, the subjects of public debate and policy. Now able to work on problems they never before had tools to fix, feminist activists challenged the very foundation on which gender was constructed.[14]

Yet articulating a vision and including women in legislation were only the beginning; the hardest struggle would be to make the law actually work for women. That would never have happened but for working-class women such as Lorena Weeks, a middle-aged white mother from small-town Georgia. Weeks, who had given nineteen years of "exemplary" service to Southern Bell as a telephone operator, took courage from Title VII and applied for the much better paid position of "switchman" in March 1966 in hopes of a shorter commute, allowing for more time with her children. Because she was a woman, the company denied her request outright and gave the job to a man with less seniority; Weeks then suffered unrelenting harassment. When efforts at conciliation by the Equal Employment Opportunity Commission failed to persuade the company, Weeks sued. She was not alone. When the EEOC opened in the summer of 1965, observers were stunned at the number of complaints it received from women: they made up more than one fourth of the total. Some 2,432 women in that initial year alone, overwhelmingly wage-earning and often union members, challenged refusals to hire, unequal wages, sex-segregated seniority lists, unequal health and pension coverage, biased recruitment and promotion policies, and more. Like the African American would-be textile and construction workers whose appeals helped shape the EEOC's mission, these women showed why their treatment, so long accepted as "just the way things were," was an injustice that demanded righting. In Weeks's case, Southern Bell claimed allegiance to a state protective law that prevented working "women and minors" from being required to lift more than thirty pounds; Weeks pointed out that her typewriter, which supervisors made her move, weighed more than that. The Court of Appeals ruled in her favor against laws based on "stereotyped characterization" that excluded women from good jobs. Title VII, the judges observed, "rejects just this type of romantic paternalism as unduly Victorian and instead vests individual women with the power to decide whether or not to take on unromantic tasks"—an autonomy "men have always had."[15]

Weeks's case and others like it exposed a pattern of workplace "sex segregation," a term that did not exist prior to the Civil Rights Act. Emerging as it did from the struggle against Jim Crow, Title VII put the spotlight clearly on job ghettos. Although women unionists had questioned their lower wages and lesser benefits before the mid-1960s, the sexual division of labor had remained sacrosanct: that men and women should hold different jobs required no explanation. Breaking out of what some feminists came to call "the pink-collar ghetto" was unthinkable because hardly anyone recognized the walls that enclosed them. "We never questioned it when they posted female and male jobs," recalled one woman who was active in the labor movement before the 1960s. "We didn't realize it was discrimination."[16]

Thanks to Title VII, activists could better identify how this division of labor restricted human possibility for both women and men, much as the racial division of labor did for blacks and whites. The issue came up in the very first Title VII case, which concerned airline stewardesses, as they were then called. In arguing against the airlines' case that only women could properly provide service and comfort to passengers, NOW activist Mary Eastwood noted wryly that the airlines were unlikely to hire "the star of the girls' basketball team, even [if] she were a compassionate, sensitive woman and would be great at throwing coats up on the shelf and balancing martinis." Eastwood then proposed a way to settle the issue that would become the essence of the "self-analysis" required of government contractors by affirmative action programs. In each job where such stereotypes operated, she urged, "it should be re-

quired that a very objective analysis be made of the specific requirements of the work and the actual ability of the particular individual
who seeks the job. If one must be compassionate to be a flight attendant, then an individual female or male who seeks this job should be
tested for compassion. For the airlines to assume that any female automatically has this characteristic and all males do not is the very essence
of sex prejudice."[17] By asking why only men were thought able to do
certain jobs and only women others, Title VII activists opened foundational questions about gender.

Such questions, let alone their answers, were anything but obvious at
the time Lorena Weeks and the flight attendants filed their complaints.
Herman Edelsberg, the EEOC's executive director, called women's inclusion in Title VII a "fluke" and mocked it as "conceived out of wed-
lock."[18] His was at first the majority opinion at the new commission,
blessed by Vice Chairman Luther Holcomb, a white Baptist evangelist
from Dallas, before his appointment to the new agency. These men saw
no problem with airlines that hired women for the same jobs as men
but gave them a different job title and smaller paychecks, and then fired
them when they married or turned thirty-two, because, said Holcomb,
"the practice represents the unanimous judgment of an entire industry." The public liked "to be ministered to by women rather than men,"
airline surveys found, and after all, "Congress did not seek to abolish
the differences between the male and female sex." If a business acknowledged those differences by restricting a particular job to one sex,
Holcomb could see no "discriminatory purpose" in that. "Common
sense" dictated that women could better please passengers and make
them "*feel* well cared for."[19]

Like Holcomb, most businessmen at the time thought women fundamentally different beings, much more unlike than like men. An electric company executive thus warned of "accelerated physical, if not
emotional, failure and increased claims for compensation" if women
were hired. He invoked mysterious "instabilities of women," as well as
their "interruptions for child bearing" and "the ever present possibility
that a woman will quit to let her husband be the breadwinner," as unfair burdens on prospective employers. A Georgia manufacturer agreed
on the dangers of "forced equalization of employment opportunities between the sexes" as "destructive of free enterprise." He wanted
government to remember that "women are different biologically, phys-

ically, and emotionally" and so could not do men's jobs; to pretend otherwise was to squander money, defy nature, and debase the Constitution. Women's incapacity for "men's work" seemed such a foregone conclusion that NAM insisted it was a waste of time and money for Congress to require corporate recruiters to visit women's colleges.[20]

One could further gauge the seismic shift under way from the reaction of conservatives, who alternated between nervous ridicule and rage. At the *National Review*, Ernest Van den Haag thought it appalling that a man "may not even be allowed to advertise for a secretary of determinate sex." It marked gross interference with "freedom of association." Van den Haag admitted that "women often get lower paying jobs than men of equal competence." But this was "because their career life is interrupted by motherhood." And since "women seem to like to become mothers," there really was no problem at all. "Those who are, and act as mothers must expect an interrupted career and, usually, lower earnings." Other leading conservatives were as contemptuous of what Russell Kirk called the "anti-feminine feminists," suggesting that women who sought equality mocked nature. One writer made the shared logic explicit. "Roles don't limit men and women; roles protect them," he warned. "It's a bitter truth that Christians know."[21]

The debate over whether the gender division of labor was a decree of God or nature or an artifact of exclusion drove a prolonged fight over whether job advertisements in newspapers could be lawfully segregated by sex. Where white supremacists had long claimed that racial differences made blacks suited only to menial jobs, so defenders of male privilege claimed that sex segregation was merely a kind of species specialization. The majority of EEOC commissioners at first thought it quite reasonable that newspapers should divide want ads by sex—as in "Help Wanted, Male" and "Help Wanted, Female" listings. That was merely a "convenience" to all concerned: women and men had no interest in each other's lines of work, Commissioner Holcomb reasoned in 1968, so "neuter columns" would only produce "havoc" for personnel offices. The deeper issue was the unquestioned belief among most women as well as men that gender determined capacity, that being a man or a woman fit a person for one kind of work but not another. It was not simply a theoretical problem. Because most jobs were closed to them, women suffered what one legal activist called "a sort of reverse monopoly." Their crowding into a small number of "female" occupations such as secretarial work created an oversupply that reduced wages for all.[22]

Yet sex segregation affected culture and identity as well as pocket-books. The confining of women to a narrow range of jobs in which they nearly always took direction from men and often literally served them could not help but shape both parties' sense of themselves, each other, and their respective places in society. Television news stations demonstrated this point when they refused to hire women reporters through the early 1970s because "no one would take the events of the day seriously if reported by a woman." Such beliefs illustrate how gender, as one labor historian puts it, "is created and recreated at work."[23] Using the new law to demand, as Pauli Murray did, the right "to achieve as *persons*," working women and their allies in the feminist movement interrupted the ceaseless rehearsal of limiting portrayals of gender. In exposing how the cycle worked and how it might change, they transformed the options open to both sexes and so revised the gender system.[24]

〜 THE FORCE that helped shift the EEOC from the employers' side to the feminists' side of this contest was one of the commission's own female employees, Sonia Pressman. Having immigrated with her parents to the United States as a child in 1933 to escape the perse-cution of Jews in Berlin as Hitler came to power, Pressman felt rac-ism acutely, whoever was involved. Yet she was no feminist when she moved from the National Labor Relations Board to a job as assistant counsel at the EEOC in October 1965. She merely read the law she was charged with enforcing and tried to enforce its directives, includ-ing the prohibition on sex discrimination. For this, her new boss, EEOC general counsel Charlie Duncan, called her a "sex maniac"; other staff members ridiculed and obstructed her. "Basically," said Pressman, "I was battling the whole commission, except for the few people [Aileen Hernandez and Richard Graham] who felt as I did." But having braved her parents' opposition when she chose a career in law instead of marriage, Pressman knew how to stand her ground.[25]

The second time the journalist Betty Friedan, newly famous author of *The Feminine Mystique,* came to the EEOC to inquire about what it was doing for women for an article she was writing, Pressman pulled Friedan into her office and told her the truth. That was the beginning of a collaboration that produced the founding the following year of the National Organization for Women (NOW), which set as its first task making the government honor its new obligation to stop sex discrimination at work. The idea for an action group for women's rights had been circulating among a network that included Pauli Murray, who wanted "something a little more attuned to the Space Age than the NWP."[26] Newspaper reports of a speech by Murray announcing that Title VII would be a dead letter unless women organized as blacks had done gave Friedan the idea to seek her out. After the meeting, Murray introduced Friedan to her own network of activists, the women who would soon found NOW.[27] Inspired by the black freedom movement and lured by Title VII, NOW described itself as a "civil rights organization" for women, "the N.A.A.C.P. of women's rights."[28]

Once the new feminist organization was up and running, Pressman became a kind of double agent. By day, she pushed women's cases at the EEOC; at night, she secretly met NOW leaders at homes in Washington to divulge to them exactly "what the commission had *not* done that day" so that NOW could write a formal letter of complaint. In addition, Pressman passed information to the attorney Marguerite Rawalt for use by lawyers who were aiding female plaintiffs in "precedent-setting" sex discrimination lawsuits. "Let me tell you," she informed an interviewer, "it took letters, it took picketing, it took lawsuits to get the commission to move in the area of women's rights." The White House recognized the radicalism of "these women" in its own way: one Johnson aide complained, "Nothing you can say will satisfy them."[29]

Employers also paid backhanded tribute to their audacity. At first, they treated the issue as a joke; many simply couldn't believe that women were serious about undoing sex segregation in employment. "Hire male [Playboy] bunnies?" guffawed *Nation's Business*, the publication of the U.S. Chamber of Commerce. But soon it was the other side that was laughing, as business discovered the extent of the coming challenge. A nationwide survey of employers by the National Association of Manufacturers in 1965 reported that "where problems [of applying Title VII] have arisen, they are largely centered in the area of sex, rather than race." Whereas women were now "almost universally excluded" from executive training programs, the *New York Times* alerted business readers, they would in future "have to" have access. It might even no longer be legal to set compulsory retirement for women at age sixty-two and men at age sixty-five. Only half kidding, a vice president of NAM warned leaders of the nation's corporations, "When those women's magazines get hold of this law and start telling their readers about the 'new rights' of women, why the Emancipation Proclamation will be a pygmy by comparison." Still insisting that the many policies that were "highly discriminatory toward women" arose "mainly because of their chemistry," he predicted that the prohibition on sex discrimination "could be a headache to employers long after the last of the race complications have been solved."[30]

As working women and their activist allies unsettled beliefs about who could do what, they also defied prevailing understandings of employers' prerogatives by using Title VII to fight sexual objectification. Today, nearly all histories of second-wave feminism mention the women's liberation protest at the Atlantic City Miss America pageant of 1969. What they miss is that two years before, other women had *already* challenged such imagery. Working with the flight attendants two months after its founding, NOW demanded that the nation's airlines cease treating the female worker "as a sex object" to be fired when she was no longer judged pleasing to males—when she was no longer nubile, got married, or gained weight. NOW backed up flight attendants' protests at the way the airlines used them to lure male customers in the same way strip clubs might. National Airlines, for example, ran an ad campaign featuring beautiful young women saying, "I'm Debbie, Fly Me," or "I'm Cheryl, Fly Me," and required female crew members to wear buttons inviting passengers to "fly me."[31] Aided by NOW, some of the workers went on to form Stewardesses for Equal Rights and others the Stewardesses' Anti-Defamation League. (One bumper sticker taunted "National, Your Fly Is Open.")[32] This was just the first of many campaigns against advertising that treated women as mindless sexual instruments. Through its Images of Women Task Force, NOW identified and fought numerous battles against such ads.[33]

Like the slow abrasion of waves on stone, the arguments of female petitioners, the initiative of brokers of inclusion, and the experience of seeing women do as well as or better than men in jobs once off-limits proved "a revelation" to male EEOC staff, including Tom Robles, director of the Albuquerque regional office. "It was like somebody turned on a light in the dark," he admitted. Even Edelsberg saw that light within a few years, and later acknowledged Murray and Pressman for "having turned him around." The about-face at the agency was striking, as its staff members both manifested and advanced the national sea change in attitudes about gender justice in these years. Be-

tween 1968 and 1971 it issued a series of decisions and new guidelines
to promote gender equality and began collaborating with NOW on
joint efforts. Pressman boasted of having written the EEOC's first *Annual Digest of Legal Interpretations*, which advised the nation's employers
that the only jobs for which sex legitimately created a monopoly were
"sperm donor and wet nurse."[34]

Learning of the agitation rousing the EEOC to action, other women
began to fight practices that had long bothered them but until then had
seemed untouchable. "Their very presence in the streets," one AT&T
employee turned activist later said in acknowledging feminists, "enabled us inside."[35] Responding to news of the Civil Rights Act, a factory
worker named Alice Peurala recognized, "Here's my chance." Peurala
had worked at U.S. Steel's South Works plant in Chicago doing quality
testing since 1953, an occupation a few women managed to stay in after the company let most women go at the end of World War II to
open jobs to male veterans. Born to Armenian immigrants in St. Louis,
Peurala was a radical. Her father, a devoted unionist, had admired
the Soviet Union for its aid to Armenians against Turkish aggression;
stamped by his example and her own employment experiences since
she took her first job at age eight, Peurala became a labor organizer.
Though not a feminist, she was an active antiracist; she joined CORE
in the 1940s and took part in early sit-ins to open St. Louis lunch counters to black patrons. In the 1950s Peurala found sanctuary for her values and resources for organizing in the ranks of the left. As embattled
as it then was, it trained and sustained Peurala and others in an outsider
counterpart to the reform network that nurtured Murray and other
NOW founders. What kept Peurala at U.S. Steel, however, was not
leftist politics but a failed marriage. When her husband became an abu-
sive alcoholic, she left him. In order to raise her infant daughter, she
needed higher wages, and the night shift at U.S. Steel paid much better
than did female-dominated occupations, even with a third of her pay
going for babysitting. From the time her little girl reached school age,
Peurala kept trying for a day job at the mill, but to no avail. The jobs
were never posted; they just "all of a sudden" went to men. At the end
of 1967, when a man she had trained, who had ten years' less experience, landed a day job in the main lab, she protested. Her boss admitted, "We don't want any women on these jobs," and the union sided
with the company. That was when, laying claim to Title VII, Peurala
filed suit.[36]

Her experience illustrates both the drawbacks and the potential of legal challenges. On the one hand, her case dragged on for years; it wasn't until 1974 that Peurala actually got the job she sought. On the other hand, it paved the way for a larger lawsuit a few years later, when thirty female steelworkers in Gary, Indiana, joined with Chicago NOW to form Steel Workers NOW and pressed for broader changes in the industry. At the same time, Pennsylvania NOW members and Baltimore NOW steelworkers filed suit against steel companies after fourteen years of fruitless complaints about the persistent preference shown to males with less seniority. They benefited from a landmark consent decree in 1974 that settled 408 cases pending with the EEOC, following decisive legal victories by the NAACP on behalf of black steelworkers. The decree opened nine leading steel firms to black men and all women as never before, particularly in the skilled crafts from which they had been most particularly excluded.[37]

While women like Peurala worked to open "men's jobs" and others supported them by changing the culture, allies in government used the resources they had at their disposal to try to clear away obstacles. At the EEOC Phyllis Wallace and others began to see a pattern as they considered tens of thousands of appeals: the worst discrimination went on where the segregation was so sweeping that victims rarely recognized it. An example of such "institutional" discrimination was "the secretarial ghetto," the clerical work that was the prime job category for women. To concentrate on a complaint-by-complaint approach, said one EEOC chairperson, was "like trying to drain a swamp with a teaspoon." As NOW summarized the developing consensus in 1971, "everyone involved in the civil rights movement agrees that individual complaints are not the way to solve the problem of job discrimination."[38] Activists and the EEOC alike turned instead to industry-wide problems such as those at "Ma Bell," the nationwide telephone monopoly for both local and long-distance calls. The Bell System, which included AT&T, was then the biggest single employer of women, accounting for one out of every fifty-six in the labor market, among them Lorena Weeks. Having drawn its internal race and gender lines sharply, Bell became the target of an ambitious research project for a landmark lawsuit to uproot occupational segregation; the effort was led by Wallace, who, as chief of technical studies, was the EEOC's top researcher.

Phyllis Wallace understood racial steering in employment well, for she had resisted it in her own life. She had become an economist mainly to escape the Jim Crow system of higher education in her home state. To forestall desegregating the all-white University of Maryland, the state government began paying out-of-state tuition for black students who could not study their chosen fields at its black college. So as a high school student in Baltimore, the eldest of seven children in the depression years, Wallace sat down with a stack of college catalogues and compared the majors. Hoping to get far away from Maryland, and finding economics only at the white schools, she chose that major, and went off to New York University, where she graduated magna cum laude and Phi Beta Kappa in 1943. She then earned a Ph.D. at Yale in 1948. Along the way she learned four foreign languages, including Russian, which landed her a job as a CIA analyst studying the Soviet economy. The secrecy requirement hurt her personal life, however, so it was a relief for more than one reason when she decided to move to the EEOC in 1965. "I have decided," she would say of her new focus on discrimination, "to say what I see." At the EEOC Wallace arranged the historic textile industry hearings and set up interdisciplinary teams of scholars who uncovered how employee testing was used to exclude qualified workers from better-paying jobs. The findings of her research staff contributed to the landmark *Griggs* decision that required employers to do away with the systematic advantages white applicants enjoyed by tailoring evaluation systems to jobs. Fresh from that success, they took on AT&T.[39]

That single company accounted for 7 percent of the EEOC's complaints by 1970, over 1,500 in all. Under Wallace's direction, the agency scoured over 100,000 pages of internal AT&T records to uncover company practices. Her team produced a report in late 1971 that provided a meticulous demonstration of systematic discrimination by sex, race, and national origin in over 25,000 pages of proof and 5,000 of testimony that showed how favoritism for white men permeated all phases of employment: advertising, hiring, training, promotions, pay, benefits, career ladders, and vacation leave. Every single wage-earning job was classified as male or female. In comparison to similarly qualified men, women employees of the company lost over $500 million a year from these practices. "The Bell monolith," the government study found, "is, without doubt, the largest oppressor of women workers in the United States." So sharp was the rebuke that change was swift. "In the fall of 1971, AT&T scoffed at the idea of male operators," let alone female linemen, one member of the EEOC team observed. "By 1972, they admitted the possibility and by January 1973, there were goals and timetables" for hiring in both areas. By then, the company had reached a consent decree with the agency that transformed its personnel policies and provided restitution to thirteen thousand female and two thousand minority male victims of its practices in the nation's largest back-pay settlement to date. Other businesses took notice. Said an attorney with the U.S. Chamber of Commerce, "Fear is not too strong a word to use about the way the companies feel about the EEOC now."[40]

Complaints, activism, and agency policies alone, this experience demonstrated, would not bring change; getting the courts to interpret the law and punish violators was essential. Indeed, litigation became as important a resource for the women's movement as it was for the civil rights movement. For such lawsuits to work, plaintiffs needed committed and well-trained attorneys to translate their grievances and the movement's demands into language that could sway judges and juries. Hundreds around the country would contribute, some through the NOW Legal Defense and Education Fund, modeled on the NAACP Legal Defense and Education Fund, others as freelancers. In the lead as the 1970s began was Ruth Bader Ginsburg at the American Civil Liberties Union (ACLU). Her way was prepared by others, as from the first, activists with legal training had helped advance the new movement. Pauli Murray had joined the board of directors of the ACLU in 1965 and pressed for it to address gender inequality. Eleanor Holmes Norton, a younger African American attorney who had known Murray at Yale, joined her at the ACLU later that year as assistant counsel. They helped persuade the ACLU to make gender equity its first priority in 1971 and to establish a Women's Rights Project to spearhead the fight against the whole tradition of second-class citizenship that kept women out of good jobs.[41]

Like Pressman and Murray, Ginsburg enjoyed class advantages that working-class women like Lorena Weeks and Alice Peurala did not. Yet gender had kept Ginsburg an outsider to the access enjoyed by the male students with whom she attended school, and it continued to make her an "outsider within" male-dominated institutions. An excellent, hardworking student, Ruth Bader won admission to Harvard Law School—only to have a dean there make the nine women in her class of five hundred describe to skeptical faculty what they would do with their legal training that would vindicate their taking up places that would otherwise go to men. Ginsburg tied for top student honors in her graduating class and served on the *Harvard Law Review* and, later, the *Columbia Law Review*. Yet when she applied for work, not one firm tendered an offer. Seeking clerkships, she learned that the nation's premier judges, men she had long admired, such as Felix Frankfurter and Learned Hand, refused to hire women. When she did at last land a position, her male colleagues thought nothing of meeting in men-only clubs to discuss cases; some belittled her for questioning the practice. After she read Simone de Beauvoir's *The Second Sex* in 1969 and female students asked her to teach a course about women and the law, a colleague recalled, she "caught fire." Researching more and more avidly, she was shocked to find that the common law, court decisions, state and federal laws, and administrative rulings had all consigned women to second-class status.[42]

Ginsburg worked to demolish the legal edifice sustaining the idea that women were lesser, weaker beings unable to stand on their own. As co-director of the Women's Rights Project, she oversaw a vast methodical effort to topple a centuries-old legal tradition, choosing cases for maximum impact and cumulative effect. She and her staff created a pool of do-it-yourself filing guidelines and other resources to assist victims of employment discrimination and their attorney allies. She took as her first ACLU case a woman challenging a state law that stipulated the discharge of any public school teacher who became pregnant. That was the first of many; by the mid-1970s, Ginsburg had argued six cases before the U.S. Supreme Court and won five of them, yielding the Court's first declarations that sex discrimination could make a state law unconstitutional. Ginsburg and her co-workers took aim at the family wage system's grounding "stereotype": "the idea that husbands are always and necessarily breadwinners for their families and that their wives are always dependent upon them for survival." Those in power, she said in one case, must be brought to see "how the notion that men are this way (frogs, snails, puppy dog tails) and women are that way (sugar, spice, everything nice) ends up hurting both sexes." To demonstrate this argument, two thirds of the cases she litigated featured as plaintiffs men who were hurt by the family wage norm, such as a widower denied the Social Security benefits earned by his wife. Such practices, Ginsburg persuaded the Court, kept women "second-class earners."[43]

Yet it was not simply protective laws that made women "second-class" but also employers' long-standing practice of penalizing women for motherhood. What rights, if any, did workers expecting children have? Until 1965, none. "This was all uncharted territory," remembered Sonia Pressman. Prior to the movement's emergence, it was common for women to lose their jobs for having a baby or to be required to take lengthy, undesired, unpaid leaves with no guarantee of reemployment. Ginsburg found herself demoted in a civil service job because of her first pregnancy; as one of the first twenty female law professors in the country in 1963, she took care to hide her second pregnancy with baggy attire.[44] "For women to be forced to take leaves of absence five months or more before their anticipated date of delivery of a child," argued another woman, "and to remain out of employment for six months or more after such a delivery, when their physician attests to their physical and psychological capacity to continue to work, is as blatant a case of discrimination as to deny a man a job because he is black, or Catholic, or of Mexican-American heritage."[45] While individual women found their livelihoods threatened by such forced interruptions, companies found in them a rationale to deny opportunities to all women. Why bother training women or placing them in challenging positions, employers argued, if they were only going to leave to have babies? Many company officials were shocked to find that, under Title VII, pregnancy might not be grounds for firing a woman. "There may come a day," attendees at an early NAM seminar on Title VII were told, "when we will have to give pregnancy leaves to executives." In 1964 a pregnant executive was such an oxymoron that even the idea of one could bring gaiety to a grim discussion.[46]

The laughter turned to anxiety as activists pushed the issue from many directions: grassroots organizing, legal challenges, media exposure, and union contracts and grievances. Some union women had pioneered the defense of pregnant workers as early as the 1940s, using contract negotiations to secure maternity leave without loss of seniority. But Title VII gave the effort a huge boost by giving other working women legal grounds for demands that labor women had made part of NOW's agenda from the outset. Dorothy Haener of the UAW, for example, urged NOW to fight for "paid maternity leave as a form of social security for all working mothers, and the right [of a new mother] to return to her job." Under pressure from NOW, the EEOC in early 1972 issued guidelines for employers to treat pregnancy like other temporary disabilities, which meant that pregnant workers could receive leaves of absence and be entitled to reappointment without giving up seniority or benefits on their return. Beginning in 1972, Ginsburg and other feminist attorneys took up the cases of women who fought employers' practice of "punishing pregnancy" and built a body of case law that enumerated new rights to fair treatment on the job. By 1978, a coalition of labor women, feminists, civil rights organizations, and liberal groups persuaded Congress to pass the Pregnancy Discrimination Act, which amended the Civil Rights Act to protect pregnant women from unfair treatment.[47]

From understanding that pregnant workers deserved rights, it was a short step to the question of child care. Here again, black activists and trade union women had paved the way. For decades, married black women had been more likely than their white counterparts to be in the workforce; accepting that mothers needed to hold paying jobs, black women's organizations had pioneered in setting up day nurseries for children. In the postwar labor movement, female activists and leaders pushed for the establishment of both employer-provided and publicly supported day care facilities. Seeing how the unpaid work women did in their homes undergirded gender inequality in the workplace, they sought to minimize the strain on women by providing quality care for their children. Similarly, civil rights leaders pushed for "child care centers for working mothers" to aid poor women who wanted to enter the labor force but feared for their children's well-being.[48] Following these leads, NOW had called for universal child care from its founding. In its first Statement of Purpose, the group demanded "a nationwide network of child-care centers and other social innovations to enable more women to work while raising a family, as well as national retraining programs for women who join the work force after their children have grown." Its Bill of Rights called for such facilities to "be established by law on the same basis as parks, libraries, and public schools . . . as a community resource to be used by all citizens from all income levels." Within a few years, organizers began pointing to men as co-parents responsible with women and society as a whole for rearing children.[49]

Led by labor feminists and the civil rights veteran Marian Wright Edelman, now of the Children's Defense Fund, a broad coalition managed to get slim majorities in Congress to pass the Comprehensive Child Development Act in 1971 to provide quality child care to a broad range of working parents on a sliding scale basis. Their victory fell victim to realpolitik calculations as President Nixon, whose own appointed task force on women had recommended such action, vetoed the measure in a speech written by Patrick Buchanan, which aimed at pleasing social conservatives in the right wing of the Republican Party. Denouncing the act as a "radical piece of social legislation," he charged that it ignored a "keystone of our civilization," that child rearing should be done by mothers, not through "communal approaches." Never again would the government show such support for broad child care legislation. Thereafter, while wealthier women in the labor force found solutions in private care for their children, wage-earning women continued to struggle with the double day and worries about the quality and reliability of their child care arrangements. Hobbled by conservative opposition, public and employer policy failed to keep pace with rapidly changing popular ideas about gender justice.[50]

The ongoing gender upheaval that so rattled the right gave women trade unionists and their male allies unprecedented leverage to achieve change on the shop floor. For years since World War II, women in more progressive unions such as the United Auto Workers, the United Packinghouse Workers, and the United Electrical Workers had tried to achieve fairness. "Women's lib—this wasn't something new," noted Mildred Jeffrey, the first director of the UAW women's bureau in the 1940s. Building on the precedent of black civil rights work in the unions, and often enlisting its veterans, they made headway on equal pay, especially in the postwar years. "If there had not been a few people like us doing the kinds of things that we have done," one of these women insisted, "much of what we have seen happen in the women's movement might well not have happened." Yet without law on their side, they could do only so much: employers, male co-workers, and union leaders alike were free to ignore women's arguments if they so chose with scant fear of consequences. "It was an impossible situation," recalled one activist, but "now [after Title VII] it's no longer a moral issue. Now it's the law."[51] The difference was huge. Like other institutions, labor organizations persisted in favoring men, as Lorena Weeks and Alice Peurala learned.

But in a few unions, the embrace of change was dramatic and accounted for much of feminism's momentum on job equity. Unions had collective bargaining agreements and grievance procedures to enforce fair treatment in workplaces that neither the EEOC, with its cramped authority, nor the feminist movement, operating on the outside, had. Making use of such power, the International Union of Electrical Workers (IUE) became a leader in seeking gender equality after the passage of Title VII. Rank-and-file women initiated the push for change in their grievance filing and formal complaints to the EEOC and received support from female staff members in the union's international headquarters, such as Gloria Tapscott Johnson, an African American economist from Howard University who became the point person on women's issues after her hiring in 1954.[52]

Yet women's most effective ally in the IUE proved to be a white man: Winn Newman, its legal counsel after 1972. A longtime antiracist and a former EEOC staff member, he now brokered women's complaints with the IUE using the specter of costly lawsuits to convince skeptical male leaders that supporting equity was in their best interests. Failing to act decisively, he advised, "could result in the financial ruin of the Union." And he told the union president in no uncertain terms that women members were encountering "substantial harassment" for filing complaints. Some union officers, for instance, "called them lesbians" for not behaving as the men thought women should. Newman reported numerous "incidents involving women who tried to get men's jobs": "slashing of tires of women, guns shot in their homes, placement of rats on machines, a strike when women went on jobs for the first time," and more. Rather than simply reacting to trouble as it arose, Newman developed an aggressive policy to uproot discrimination. The three-part program required local unions to collect data to identify problems, push for redress though grievances and contract negotiations, and, if these failed, file formal charges with the EEOC or the National Labor Relations Board or else initiate lawsuits. "He really was a revolutionary," the head of NOW's Legal Defense Fund later said of Newman. "He was a master at using litigation for social change."[53] Yet as significant as the contribution of some unionists to gender equity was, most women had no union representation.

Change in non-union workplaces often came through ad hoc organizing by the women's movement. At the hub of it was Lynne Darcy, chair of NOW's national compliance task force in the early 1970s. Even after the national organization decided to concentrate on the ERA, a significant minority of its members continued to organize grassroots action for justice on the job for women. Exhibiting a self-assurance unthinkable a decade before, one activist declared, "We will win," adding, "If the government will not help us, then we will picket, sue, confront, lobby, and demonstrate until it does its job." Darcy, a young white woman with a B.A. in chemistry and a fulltime job at RCA Laboratories, who also chaired the Princeton, New Jersey, Commission on Civil Rights, kept local activists engaged as she corresponded with fifty to sixty people each week.[54]

These activists were scattered everywhere, it seemed, not only in big coastal cities but also in places such as Tulsa, Oklahoma; Kalamazoo, Michigan; Columbia, South Carolina; and Pensacola, Florida. They picketed local newspapers over sex-segregated want ads, filed complaints against companies, distributed information, called and wrote legislators, testified at hearings, exposed discrimination at employment agencies, ran how-to workshops, pressured the EEOC on cases, worked with churches in stockholder campaigns against companies, organized demonstrations, and ran advice hot lines for women facing job discrimination. (The New York City NOW chapter had fifteen women answering phones, but they couldn't keep up with the number of calls for assistance.) "The more work I do, the more shit I uncover," wrote one tired but jubilant Toledo, Ohio, activist to Darcy of a local Ford dealership that had advertised for "salesmen who are 'married, with families, and have non-working wives.'" "I suspect it is company policy," she said, urging nationwide action if so. NOW carried out numerous such campaigns, including multi-city organizing to back up the EEOC's case against AT&T. (The picket signs used by the New Orleans branch read "Dial 'O' for Oppression.")[55]

Another nationwide effort was aimed at Sears Roebuck & Company to get across "the needs and problems of women who are the working poor." Then the country's largest retail firm, Sears was the biggest employer of low-wage female sales workers, and the second-largest employer of women after AT&T. Chicago NOW members Ann Ladky and Mary Jean Collins-Robson coordinated the effort, which at its peak involved over one hundred chapters and drew in Sears workers. They exposed the low wages that anti-union Sears paid to female clerical and sales workers, its sex-segregation of jobs that gave men a monopoly on big-ticket commission items, the lack of opportunities for women to advance to better-paying work (only 4 of 840 managers were women, for example), and the efforts Sears was making to weaken the EEOC and the OFCC. Winning changes at Sears, the campaign also yielded one of the nation's leading organizations for clerical workers when Ladky helped found Women Employed. By the late 1970s, a dozen such groups were operating with a membership of eight thousand women.[56]

Meanwhile, sympathizers in the media used their skills to publicize such struggles, broadcasting the Title VII fight to the wider public. By the early 1970s, television, magazines, and newspapers were carrying stories about sex discrimination in employment and women's struggles against it. Some journalists actively aimed to help the movement. Carol Kleiman wrote a column at the *Chicago Tribune*, for example, that stimulated discussions among those active in the women's rights committee at the local Bell Labs. Sometimes inspired by the articles, committee members met almost daily to talk about issues affecting women—from job concerns to advertising, religion, and literature. At lunchtime they fanned out to tables in the company cafeteria to seed "consciousness-raising" discussions among other employees.[57]

Emboldened by the movement, women organized within major media outlets to change them. When *Newsweek* magazine's editors assigned a cover story on women's liberation to the non-staff wife of a senior editor, annoyed female employees began discussing their grievances over lunch. The gripe sessions brought out complaints about how management confined virtually all women to what they called "the 'research' ghetto" and had hired only one woman among fifty-one writers. Armed with Title VII, the women organized, enlisted the ACLU and the EEOC, and impelled change at the magazine.[58]

At the *New York Times*, a women's caucus formed in 1972 challenged the newspaper to practice the fairness it preached to its readers after nine female employees in the news departments got together to compare experiences over lunch. The *Times* had once boasted in an advertisement that one of the women, then a copyeditor, had a "passion for facts." Now the facts so carefully collected by eighty women and verified by Betsy Wade, a caucus leader, documented sex-based salary inequities, the confinement of women to lower-paying jobs, the failure to promote female employees even after years of exemplary service, and women's total exclusion from non–classified-advertising sales, management, and policymaking positions. When "nothing happened" in response to their petition, the women found a lawyer, filed charges with the EEOC, and eventually undertook a class-action suit for sex discrimination on behalf of more than 550 women in all job categories at the newspaper. As the suit wound its way through the courts, the caucus held meetings, put out newsletters, and continued to agitate. In 1978 the women won. Settling out of court, the *Times* compensated the plaintiffs for past discrimination and legal costs and adopted a strong affirmative action plan with numerical goals for representation of women in jobs previously closed to them, from entry-level to top positions. "Considering where we were in 1972," said one activist, it was "the sun and the moon and the stars."[59]

Others exerted pressure from the outside to end the mass media's stereotypical portrayals of gender. NOW cooperated with the National Council of Churches, for example, in circulating lists of corporations that demeaned women in ads and employment and urging churches to withdraw their vast investments.[60] Looking not just to the insulting commercials but to the publicly licensed television networks that aired them, NOW locals around the country, supported by the ACLU, lobbied the Federal Communications Commission to deny license renewal to stations that failed to practice equal employment for women and that routinely denigrated them in programming. That meant most stations in the early 1970s. At ABC News in New York, for example, the twenty-one producers, seven associate producers, five production assistants, four directors, and eighteen film editors were all men; the thirty-three secretaries were all women.[61] Using the leverage of Title VII, NOW lined up support from other women's organizations for its argument that television "promotes a low image of women, thereby perpetuating employment discrimination."[62] The most arresting critique came from the NOW Legal Defense and Education Fund (LDEF) in 1973. With pro bono help from advertising professionals, it mounted a novel public service ad campaign that used humor to undercut sex discrimination's appearance of naturalness. Conveying the absurdity of the criteria often used for female job candidates, one cartoon showed a middle-aged man in a suit lifting up the his trousers with the caption "Hire him—he's got great legs."[63]

As an alternative to the mainstream media, Gloria Steinem and others founded *Ms.* magazine in 1971. Each month it ran a column called "No Comment" that reprinted egregiously sexist advertisements collected and sent in by readers eager to alter the culture that encouraged the ads. At *Ms.*, journalists were free to take women's side. Susan Davis covered the rise of women's caucuses in a 1972 piece, "Organizing from Within: Justice on the Job and How to Get It." Describing the caucuses "known to exist in more than a hundred companies," she instructed readers on how to augment that list.[64]

As feminist arguments entered the daily news, the questions posed by the movement spread far beyond its ranks. At the time of the Apollo moon landing, for example, one stumped ninth-grade science class inquired of the president, "Why aren't there women astronauts?" Two sixth-graders wanted to know, "How come girls can't sign up for certain jobs?" For that matter, "why can't there be a woman president?" Feminist challenges had brought into children's view the forces steering the sexes to differently valued and rewarded jobs. Through them Americans learned how, as one Title VII scholar puts it, "women's work preferences are formed, and created, and recreated in response to changing work conditions." Schooling was one of those forces, so NOW activists pushed to open wood, metal, and auto shop classes to girls and sewing and cooking classes to boys.[65]

With the case law established, the agencies converted, organizers showing the urgency of action, and media coverage spreading the struggle, program builders like Carmen A. Estrada were able to attract government funding to help low-income women in local communities. Estrada, an attorney, directed the Chicana Rights Project founded by the Mexican American Legal Defense and Education Fund in 1974. The next year, the organization collaborated with NOW in San Antonio after a local NOW study found pervasive discrimination against Chicanas in San Antonio's municipal hiring and training programs, and the two groups worked together to monitor a new affirmative action plan for the city. Such efforts were sorely needed, because of the way in which War on Poverty job training programs targeted men as opposed to women. The flagship Opportunities Industrialization Center, for example, prepared men for an array of skilled trades while placing "girls" only as waitresses. In New Orleans in 1967, one investigator reported that in government-funded training programs "approximately 80 to 85 percent of the applicants are female and [yet] job development has been pointed toward male workers." Estrada's program filed complaints and lawsuits to help Mexican American women enter apprenticeships in nontraditional craft jobs, clerical work, bank jobs, and more.[66]

As these efforts convinced some corporate officials of the need for change, unexpected allies appeared. When a female division manager of the Celanese Corporation filed suit, the company's female associate general counsel read through the charges "and promptly filed a sex-discrimination complaint on her own behalf."[67] When the companies looked for specialists to staff the new compliance programs they had to create, they not infrequently turned to activists in organizations such as the Urban League and NOW. Radicals saw such hiring as an effort to co-opt their own, which it was. Some companies, like Sears, tried to lure activist leaders right off the picket lines with job offers.[68] Yet these hirings brought into the managerial ranks people who often remained deeply committed to inclusion. One NOW member whose role at the Polaroid corporation had "progressed from that of feminist pressure group organizer to a senior administrator helping to enforce compliance within the corporation" volunteered to help Lynne Darcy with compliance work.[69] Others who went on to do this work included NOW's first president, Aileen Hernandez; Sonia Pressman of the EEOC; and Lois Herr, a founder of the Bell Labs women's rights committee.[70] Even where the power of personnel employees was limited, as it usually was, they became resources for workers with complaints and for EEOC staffers seeking information, as well as voices of conscience in their companies. Such specialists used personnel journals and conferences to set the terms of debate within the corporate world, reframing affirmative action as in management's interest when the policy came under attack from white male critics. "What was radical," noted one participant, "became routine."[71]

By the time Eleanor Holmes Norton assumed leadership of the EEOC in 1977, the old lines between radical outsiders and officialdom had blurred. A self-described "political, radical activist," the new government agency head was not only a Yale-trained attorney and a protégée of Pauli Murray, but also among the last cohort of black students to attend Washington, D.C., schools segregated by law. Norton entered politics by founding a CORE chapter in New Haven while a student, helped mobilize the 1963 March on Washington for Jobs and

Freedom, organized with SNCC in Mississippi, served as assistant counsel at the ACLU, represented the women who took *Newsweek* to court in the first class-action lawsuit for sex discrimination, cofounded the National Black Feminist Organization in 1973, and brought together civil rights organizations, feminists, unions, and community groups to combat discrimination as head of the New York City Commission on Human Rights from 1970 to 1977. She was a vocal feminist from early on. "What more telling evidence" could there be of discrimination against women, this committed antiracist demanded in 1970, "than that white women are paid less than black men?"[72] Norton argued that black women could not simply seek "the empty treasures white women are today trying to turn in"; rather, African Americans should lead the way to the future by "remak[ing] the family unit," starting with "our conception of the black woman." Without provisions for child care, Norton later explained, using a practical illustration close at hand for someone who had raised a young son and a daughter with Down syndrome while leading this important government agency, "the right to work is more mythical than real."[73] Under her guidance, the EEOC stretched Title VII to fight what was coming to be known as sexual harassment.

Insisting that women be taken seriously as workers proved to be the best ground for fighting an age-old problem: men's use of power to coerce sex. Because such behavior was legal, women had risked being blamed and losing their jobs if they complained. But Title VII helped some feminists to name the problem and imagine solutions. In Ithaca, New York, they organized a public "speakout" that launched organizing as women in a wide range of jobs testified to the treatment they endured and why it was wrong and had to stop. Encouraged, working women themselves filed complaints against perpetrators, whose acts ranged from whistling and invasive touching to stalking and rape. Black women again led the way. Vulnerability to a virulent racialized form of sexual harassment had plagued black women in slavery and domestic service (Norton's own enslaved great-grandmothers had been raped by their owners); defamation of them as Jezebels who invited sexual advances was a core element in the ideology of white supremacy. This history led some to an acute awareness of such harassment as a social problem rooted in power relations, while civil rights activism and unions offered many ideas about how to fight it. Half of the plaintiffs in the first six cases to reach the courts were African American women, and their litigation built on the precedents set by racial harassment cases, although at first judges discounted the sexual variant as "natural" and "personal" and sometimes mocked the plaintiffs as overly sensitive to what was merely flattery.[74] Blue-collar women pioneers in jobs long considered "men's work" similarly pressed some of the victorious lower court cases.[75] By 1980, with Norton at the helm, the EEOC spelled out for the nation's employers why sexual harassment was a form of illegal job discrimination and coached them in how to prevent it. The EEOC guidelines in turn influenced the Supreme Court to conclude in 1985 that such practices violated the civil rights of women. Within a decade, activists had created potent remedies for what had so long seemed a blight of nature.[76]

In an agency whose founders originally insisted on white male directors, Norton proved the best leader the EEOC had ever had in the eyes of most who worked with it. In only a few years, she had thoroughly reorganized the embattled agency and virtually solved its huge problem of case backlog. (When she took the job in the underfunded agency, 130,000 charges awaited, stacked so high on the shelves that her staff found moldy files wedged under loose ceiling panels). She improved relations with both employers and unions even while pushing both sides to adopt aggressive, proactive affirmative action policies; she supported pay equity policies for women who remained in sex-segregated occupations; and she imbued the work of the nation's leading voice for fair employment with her own profoundly inclusive vision. In New York, she had tried to bring into the economic mainstream blacks, Latinos, and women alike, and secure fair treatment for ethnic Euro-Americans and lesbians and gay men faced with discrimination.[77] By the time Norton left the EEOC, American workplaces looked and felt very different than they had in 1964 when Title VII was passed.

The new law and efforts to implement it did more than reform workplaces; they opened once unimaginable prospects of personal and sexual autonomy to women. Inviting experimentation in daily life, the law helped refashion identities. One of the first female guards at a U.S. Steel plant sounded like many other women who braved the gender boundary line. "When I first took this job," she said, "I had to prove to them [the men] that women could handle it." But it was not only the spectators whose minds changed. "Before this, I had been brought up to think women were inferior and I believed it. It wasn't actually until I started doing what they considered a man's job and found out that I could do it just as well that I actually began to believe."[78]

Like young radical women students, older women workers attempted things they had once thought impossible and talked to one another in ways that changed their sense of themselves and how they deserved to be treated by others. New York NOW, for example, ran "rap sessions" for women to discuss employment problems. The founding conference of Stewardesses for Women's Rights included a panel on "consciousness-raising," run by Kathie Sarachild, the women's liberationist best known for explaining the technique.[79] Without using that rubric, other working-class women engaged in similarly empowering discussions. Whether in formal settings such as the founding conference of the Coalition of Labor Union Women, women's caucuses, or casual small-group lunchtime conversations, women re-scripted the stories of their own lives.[80]

Expecting better treatment at work, many also changed their relationships at home. One focus was the gender division of household labor, which created a double burden for most working women. Even before Title VII and the women's movement, said the auto worker Florence Peterson, "I resented" doing all of the housework and child care and "felt it was unfair. But I always thought that's the way life was." Fighting for change at work ended that sense of inevitability. "Most of us worked in three spheres, at least," recalled one AT&T activist, "trying to change our personal lives, our workplaces, and our world." Some working women activists learned that their growing confidence was "a threat" to the men they had married. Speaking for many, one found herself saying, "I don't need this"—and leaving. "Everybody likes to be loved," she observed, but there were limits to how "tolerant" she felt now. Others found partners who welcomed their growth. A key reason why Ruth Bader Ginsburg was first attracted to the man she later married was that "Martin was the only boy I knew who cared that I had a brain." He also learned to cook well. "A supportive husband who is willing to share duties and responsibilities," she said, "is a must."[81] For some, intimate sustenance came from other women. A few NOW activists therefore organized for "lesbian rights" and campaigned for city ordinances that included "sexual preference" among other categories for protection from discrimination. One Chicago activist argued that gay women would benefit from organizing for "basic economic issues such as adequate jobs and job related benefits, affirmative action, child care." "For no women are jobs, housing, child custody, and child support more crucial," she observed, "than for lesbians who daily face the threat of losing any or all of these" as punishment for their sexual orientation.[82] Justice proved indivisible: settling one problem yielded the resources to name and face others.

∼ As activists put it to use, the law also made new political identities possible. One could see its impact in women's adoption of affirmative action as a prime strategy for inclusion. When activists insisted, as NOW did, that "women neither wish nor require separate consideration apart from other victims of discrimination," they were articulating a new understanding of women's place in the polity.[83] Pushing for women to be added to Executive Order 11246, the main affirmative action order covering federal contractors, NOW leaders echoed Murray: "The excuses used by employers practicing sex-based discrimination are not substantially different from excuses regarding racial bias" and "can best be met by the same laws, agencies, investigators and government officials." Activists mounted steady pressure, including letters, meetings, hearings, and demonstrations, until, eventually, the federal government issued "sex guidelines" like those dealing with race: employers would be required to develop "goals and timetables" for hiring and promoting women, too.[84] Today's organizers take for granted the pressure for identical reforms and for inter-group collaboration against discrimination, but that outcome was anything but inevitable given the prior history.

The idea that large numbers would believe such unity desirable itself presupposed an upheaval in social conditions, law, and activists' thinking. In outlawing sex discrimination in a statute aimed primarily at racial discrimination, Title VII had led feminists to connect issues of gender and racial discrimination as it invited white women to ally with African Americans in seeking solutions. In the mid-sixties, the latter had better organization, larger numbers of experienced activists, and more radical movement intellectuals, as well as more legitimacy as aggrieved parties in the public eye. They were also the most progressive population in the country—the group with the most robust conception of social justice—and now white feminists were apprenticed to them in the affirmative action struggle. The new law thus shifted the axis of progressive politics by making novel alliances possible. White women as individuals usually had more social power than black men or women, but now feminists as a group needed to affiliate and cooperate with black civil rights forces to make political headway. The result was a historic 180-degree change in the relationship between the women's movement and the civil rights movement since the days of the National Women's Party.

The Title VII struggle had undercut the policy basis for the division between white middle-class feminists on one side and people of color and unionists on the other. As applied by activists, the new law transformed women's relation to the rest of the polity, defying head-on the legal and cultural model that the United States had inherited from British common law. From the colonial era forward, that model made men legally the real earner-citizens and subsumed women under their husbands' headship as supportive dependents, a fiction that corresponded less and less to lived experience. The historian Linda Kerber has argued that this tradition of "substitut[ing] married women's obligations to their husbands for obligations to the state" proved "the central element in the way that Americans have thought about the relation of all women, including unmarried women, to state power." Such thinking resulted in a pattern of American social policy that, as one political scientist puts it, "supported individualism, independence, and self-reliance for some people (primarily men) and dependence and reliance on paternalism for others (primarily women)." For generations, most white reformers thus treated women as different from men: as mothers, or potential mothers, in need of special "protection" through policies that granted unique exemptions from such burdens as overtime, heavy lifting, and night work, but at the price of excluding women from better jobs and marking them as a dependent class incapable of full citizenship.[85]

NOW took aim at both the culture and the legal traditions sustaining this system in its founding Statement of Purpose. It rejected "the current assumptions that a man must carry the sole burden of supporting himself, his wife and family, and that a woman is automatically entitled to lifelong support by a man upon her marriage." Instead, it proposed that "a true partnership between the sexes demands an equitable sharing of the responsibilities of home and children and of the economic burdens of their support."[86] By spurning the family wage system that had never included most women of color and now failed to provide for growing numbers of white women, and by claiming instead access to all jobs and the right to be rewarded as equals, activists overthrew the tradition of "coverture" and enabled women to be recognized as self-reliant earners and citizens, as persons with constitutional rights.

The alteration in women's standing effected by Title VII revised the algebra of American alliance politics, as women's newly recognized autonomy made for a new relationship to the most powerful institutional base of progressive politics: the labor movement. In making moot protective legislation aimed at women alone and encouraging gender-neutral fair labor standards while giving women new power to protect themselves, Title VII erected a bridge over the half-century split between feminists and the leading voice for low-income Americans. With women no longer treated as wards unable to organize in their own right, they came to figure more prominently in the labor movement's calculations, just as blacks had in the textile industry after the passage of Title VII. William Pollard, the director of the AFL-CIO's civil rights department, offered backhanded acknowledgment of the new situation when he posed to a convention of unionists the question "What do women want?" and answered, "The same as men in the workforce." In case anyone missed the point, he warned delegates to "take [women's] complaints seriously for they are more likely to sue than minorities." Marking the national turnaround since Howard Smith had created hilarity by adding the word "sex" to Title VII, Pollard warned that sex discrimination "is no laughing matter." The dramatic rise in women's involvement in the labor movement since then—such that they now account for about 40 percent of all union members—is testimony to the change that Title VII organizing wrought.[87]

To stress the change is not to deny that potent divisions remained; those involving race proved especially sharp. As much as they were radically changing the world, white feminists were also products of a deeply segregated society that routinely discounted the experiences and perspectives of people of color. Most assumed their own problems and goals to be the universal norm in ways that infuriated black women. The domesticity that appeared a kind of confinement to a white suburban woman like Betty Friedan looked like enviable luxury to black women compelled by necessity to leave their children for menial jobs, while the intimate sexual politics that so engaged young feminists seemed to some, as the writer Toni Morrison derisively put it, nothing but "a family quarrel." African American women, she observed, "look at white women and see the enemy. . . . [T]hey know that racism is not confined to white men." Many blacks of both sexes resented white women's appropriation of the vocabulary of civil rights, particularly because their advance was occurring at a time when the black struggle faced severe repression. Distrust was the prevailing sentiment, a fear that, as one critic expressed it, white feminists would exploit "the black movement as a stepping-stone to opportunities in a highly competitive economy."[88] And in fact, many white activists continued pursuing their own unmodified agendas even in the face of the rebuke that a feminism which does not try to "free all women" is "not feminism, but merely female self-aggrandizement."[89]

A classic example arose when Betty Friedan worked with a small group at NOW's 1967 convention to force through a plank in support of the ERA despite pleas by labor and black feminists that this would pose "intolerable political choices" for them and might even hurt worse-off women; because the fate of protective legislation was still unclear, their organizations opposed the ERA. Describing herself as "almost inconsolably" saddened, Pauli Murray quit NOW's leadership in "revulsion" at the lack of consideration for women facing other kinds of oppression. "As a human being," she said, "I cannot allow myself to be fragmented into Negro at one time, woman at another, or worker at another." Murray wanted a movement that would be "unifying" of these identities, not divisive of her very person. The union activist Dorothy Haener similarly recoiled at "the narrow parochial professional direction" of the single-minded ERA push and urged a campaign for wider "social justice."[90] That particular conflict waned as Title VII led to the adoption of more uniform labor standards for both sexes, and as unions and liberal groups became strong supporters of the ERA in the 1970s. But the kind of self-absorption shown by the Friedan group would reappear among white feminists in ensuing years, to the consternation of black women, Latinas, and white working-class women whose efforts to promote the movement's goals in their communities were set back by these displays.[91]

Even as conflicts persisted, however, a convergence began to arise among some activists on both sides. Most accounts of black women and feminism have concentrated on Friedan and on antagonism between young women's liberationists and Black Power activists, and have missed what others were doing. The somewhat older activists whose story is told here were less interested in ideological competition than in changing values and winning practical reforms, and one result was that their work appealed across racial lines. Indeed, even when they disliked particular white feminists, black women were significantly more likely than whites to support the policy goals of the women's movement.[92] They did so not only from the strategic orientation to universal equality that characterized black civil rights organizations, but also from their distinctive needs as black women. As a group, they were more likely than white women to be in dual-earner relationships or heading households on their own, and because of racism, they faced extreme versions of the problems that concerned feminists, from low wages, poor benefits, and exclusion from better jobs to lack of good child care and protection from sexual harassment. Attuned to potential solutions by participation in civil rights, labor unions, and liberal organizations, activist black women came to offer notable leadership in pioneering policies that benefited all women and their families. "You don't go into coalition because you just *like* it," explained Bernice Johnson Reagon, but "because that's the only way you can figure you can stay alive."[93]

Work on employment issues was itself no guarantee of improved relations between feminists and other progressive groups. As Audre Lorde astutely observed, in a hierarchical, competitive society in which being viewed as different put those so viewed at a power disadvantage, "we have no patterns for relating across our human differences as equals." It would take committed individuals, hard discussions, and experimentation to learn how. Still, the challenge of "using human difference as a springboard for creative change" proved beyond the imaginations of many.[94] Not a few white feminists perceived their own advance in a kind of rivalry with African Americans, with civil rights remedies a scarce resource to be divided. Those from business backgrounds seemed especially inclined to think of social change in competitive terms, as when Joan Hull, who led NOW's "corporate feminism" task force, urged members to fight "any increase in appropriations" to equal employment agencies until they appointed more women.[95] Such feminists failed to grasp that at least some of the resistance to addressing discrimination against them came from the legitimate fears that already underfunded agencies were seeing their client population multiply without additional resources to meet the new demands. One result was that white women privileged by race and class gained an advantage over African Americans in the quest for good jobs. "Instead of baking a bigger pie and giving everyone decent portions," Vernon Jordan complained, even as he vowed solidarity with women and other "new minorities," the establishment was "slicing the same old pie of economic opportunities thinner."[96]

Sexism on the part of some men of color fueled such rivalry. Some accused white women of taking jobs that, said one, "rightfully and justly belong to other minorities." In one government agency where minority men became hostile to white women activists, exasperated feminists pleaded for a truce: "While we're hassling each other at the bottom of the ladder, the white men are laughing at us from the top." Many black nationalists especially ridiculed gender injustice as trivial and suppressed black women as they pressed their case that invigorating black manhood would lift the race.[97] Still, powerful cross-currents notwithstanding, a historic shift was under way.

To hold both white women and black men accountable to more inclusive visions of equality, moreover, there was now a critical mass of black women empowered by these same developments. As "a black, female, low-income working person," said the laundry worker turned labor and civil rights leader Dollie Robinson, "I always felt like I represented every minority on the face of the earth." That understanding of the intertwining of identities and the necessity to challenge the mutually reinforcing social hierarchies of American capitalism for all to be truly free became a hallmark of black feminist theory and activism. "By asserting a leadership role in the feminist movement," Murray predicted, "the black woman can help keep it allied to the objectives of black liberation while simultaneously advancing the interests of all women."[98] Pushed by women of color, major women's organizations began examining how they got to be so white and practicing internal affirmative action to become more inclusive.[99] At the same time, black women organized their own wing of the movement through such groups as the National Black Feminist Organization, established in 1973, as did Latinas and Asian American women.[100]

As a result of all this activity, cross-pollinating coalitions became built in to the architecture of American reform. From the early 1970s forward, in fact, activists on all sides routinely examined the effect of their work on other potential coalition partners, and then reached out to involve them. In the AT&T campaign, for example, NOW, the NAACP, MALDEF (the Mexican American Legal Defense and Education Fund), and the EEOC worked together to call attention to the injustices all of their constituencies faced in that corporate empire. Black and Latino groups denounced the discrimination affecting women, many of them white, as NOW denounced the discrimination affecting "Blacks and Spanish Americans."[101] Explained the leader of NOW's federal compliance efforts, Ann Scott, "We consider the attitude that holds race and sex discrimination as mutually exclusive to be both short-sighted and self-defeating."[102]

Newly recognized as allies, civil rights organizations reciprocated. When, in 1971, NOW called on the FCC to include women in the affirmative action guidelines it required of licensees, the NAACP and MALDEF came to its aid. Sharing resources made for synergy, as a coalition of thirteen black, Chicano, and women's rights groups learned in producing a study of "corporate apartheid" in California that same year. For its part, NOW urged its jobs and justice activists to be "deeply concerned about institutional racism" as they fought "institutional sexism" and to press for "specific objectives for each minority group" in the affirmative action programs they won.[103] Examples of reciprocity multiplied over time.

Feminists' entry altered the stakes of the struggle for economic inclusion, as they expanded the challenge first posed by African Americans. Women's numbers and their distribution through all groups helped their challenge penetrate the culture's very core, including, ultimately, the white upper-class elite. Now it was not a minority but a majority demanding access. Now it was not about allowing black men to head conventional families but about allowing all adults to support themselves and raise children on their own if it came to that. No longer figured as dependents of men, women found that their relationship to the wider polity changed as well. The results were not always good for individual women, or for the most vulnerable women with the least promising prospects. As lifetime employment became the norm for most women, and as feminists won them the right to be considered as individual earners apart from family commitments, popular support for public assistance for mothers remaining outside the paid labor force waned, and the welfare program Aid to Families with Dependent Children became more politically vulnerable than ever.[104] But however uneven the outcome, it was clear that a male-dominated economy had lost the legitimacy it once enjoyed.

All of this revised understandings of gender long embedded in American culture. It also won results that mattered to millions, even those oblivious to the source of the changes. The 1970s saw the first notable decline in sex segregation in the United States in a century.[105] By the time women's push for economic inclusion was in full rig, the more mainstream, family wage argument for affirmative action raised by male civil rights activists was in tatters. In its place was a new vision of universal access to transformed workplaces. When white women— so long the beneficiaries of the family wage and "protection"—demanded to stand on their own two feet and chose African Americans as allies, the culture of exclusion started to give way as never before.

~ 5

Are Mexican Americans "Whites" or "People of Color"?

*I*N THE SPRING OF 1960, a convention of Mexican American political activists in California divided over a proposal to form "coalitions with other nonwhite minorities." Most delegates, Bert Corona recalled, "were not prepared to come out front and state that we considered ourselves nonwhite. This question of whether Mexicans are whites or people of color has been a thorny issue for years."[1] As the largest minority group in the United States after African Americans then and the largest now, Mexican Americans were from the outset the main Hispanic constituency, making up over half of the otherwise varied group. About five million Mexican Americans lived in the southwestern United States in 1960, the vast majority in Texas; in some areas, such as in California, they outnumbered other peoples of color. After blacks, they were also the best-organized minority, with an array of organizations that by then included the League of United Latin American Citizens (LULAC), the Community Service Organization (CSO), the Mexican American Political Association (MAPA), and the American GI Forum, a veterans' group that led the movement for access to good jobs.[2] As the leading Hispanic constituency in both numbers and relative power, they also accounted for nearly all the "national origins" complaints filed with the EEOC, in a historic struggle that has been overshadowed by the dramatic farm workers' campaign led by César Chávez and Dolores Huerta. Because Mexican Americans

155

fought employment discrimination far more actively over the past half
century than did Puerto Ricans, Cubans, Dominicans, or other Latinos, this story is their story.[3]

Mexican Americans' difficulty in deciding how to identify themselves said much about the national climate. For whether they were an
oppressed race or ethnic whites facing language difficulties and cultural
prejudices was less an empirical debate than a political one, and less an
issue of identity than one of strategy.[4] State policy played a preeminent
role in race-making in Mexican American history before and after Title
VII. Although Anglo elites treated Mexican Americans as an inferior
race from their first encounters forward, by a quirk of international
diplomacy they had been classified officially as white since the 1848
Treaty of Guadalupe Hidalgo. The government of Mexico had insisted
that they be eligible for U.S. citizenship, and since the Naturalization
Act of 1790 stipulated that only whites were eligible, they became
nominally white. Given the devastating system of Jim Crow erected on
a black-white binary, for most of the twentieth century Mexican American civil rights activists concluded that, in order to hold on to some of
the benefits white classification conferred and to fight discrimination,
they needed to resist efforts to mark them as nonwhite. There was a
steep price to be paid for being identified with African Americans,
for that would invite worse domination than they were already experiencing—if not the sweeping denial of citizenship per se that Asian
Americans experienced, then certainly the full disfranchisement and
the greater segregation and violence that afflicted African Americans.[5]
Whereas Mexican Americans' intermediate social position between
blacks and whites virtually dictated a go-it-alone strategy before 1965,
especially in Texas, where most lived, by contrast, blacks' situation at
the bottom of the hierarchy led African Americans to seek allies by
pressing for fair treatment of others even before these groups organized in earnest. A social order that created incentives for Mexican
Americans to separate themselves from other minorities of color inclined even mainstream African American organizations toward strategic inclusiveness.[6]

Government policy thus steered Mexican Americans to define themselves publicly as white and to seek advancement through assimilation
and respectability; the strategy seemed commonsensical to the largely
middle-class and lighter-skinned American citizens who led the ma-

jor Mexican American civil rights groups. Sometimes the appeal to be recognized as "Caucasians" was plaintive, as when Houston Mexican Americans protested being classified by the Social Security Board as nonwhite in 1935 as a form of "discrimination [that] is humiliating to their pride and unjust to their proper status" as people who "belong to the white race."[7] For three decades thereafter, civil rights activists fought as "error" any attempts to categorize them as "colored" or "nonwhite." Even small infractions aroused angry protests, as when one leader denounced doctors who used "the same rooms for the Mexican American people and the Negroes." "This is wrong," he fumed, just as a later draft board classification as "nonwhite" was "illegal."[8] For a brief time in the 1930s and 1940s, a radical labor movement offered another route in a militant class-based challenge to all racial discrimination using a strategy of solidarity among outsiders, but that was crushed by McCarthyism, leaving Mexican Americans no other promising avenue for seeking change but to claim white standing until the law changed.

When it did, Mexican American activists recalibrated their strategy in the light of new possibilities. The Civil Rights Act and the movement that produced it expanded their options in ways that proved radicalizing. No longer did Mexican Americans have to choose sides in an either-or situation in which the penalties for aligning with blacks were huge. Title VII, in particular, provided a practical incentive to identify as people of color as a strategy for advancement. Mexican Americans no longer had to follow the white European immigrant model of seeking assimilation in the hope of ultimate recognition as equals. Now they could position themselves as the "brown" counterpart to blacks in a vigorous assertion of their right to good jobs. As the law changed the rules of politics, affinities changed with them. No longer driven toward an isolated, assimilation-seeking strategy, Mexican Americans could more freely embrace a pride in Mexicanness—a cultural identity as "La Raza," a brown people or race—that they had long felt but could not express politically because the penalties were too great. The new situation did not necessarily produce alliances among people of color and women of all groups; on the contrary, tension and competition remained. But it did make solidarity a potentially rewarding option to consider in a way that it simply had not been before. Shifting sharply leftward as had white feminists, Mexican Americans also followed the lead of a group more expansive in its vision of citizenship, more bold in its tactics, and more aware of how wealthy whites pitted disadvantaged groups against one another in order to stay on top. In this way, employment organizing marked a historic turning point: a choice to follow the lead of blacks instead of whites.[9]

⌒ For decades, the strategy of insisting on recognition as whites went largely unquestioned because it seemed so sensible, given the conditions of Mexican American life. Whereas the African American experience took shape from a collective history of two and a half centuries of slavery, a brief taste of political power during Reconstruction, and then generations of Jim Crow, the Mexican American experience derived from two divergent streams: foreign conquest and immigration. As Johnson administration officials acknowledged, "the Mexican American was an American long before this land became the United States." Mexican Americans first came under the sway of the U.S. government when it seized over half of Mexico's land area in the mid-nineteenth century. But by far the largest influx of Mexican Americans came in the next century as immigrants from Mexico to what had become the United States. Precise numbers are elusive, yet one demographer called this "the greatest historical mass migration to the United States from a single country." In 1960, about one in three people of Mexican descent in the United States was foreign-born. The Mexican-born proportion would surge after 1965, as many continued to commute between the two countries.[10]

This history of conquest and of often unofficial immigration made for a unique relation to citizenship in which Mexican Americans were, as one observer put it, "neither fully accepted nor fully rejected by the dominant Anglo community." Their intermediate standing in the nation's racial hierarchy found expression in law and practice for generations. The law viewed Mexican Americans as "white," but sometimes only in order to deprive them of grounds for an equal protection claim under the Fourteenth Amendment, as for jury representation. As Mexicans came to constitute a majority of those charged with illegal immigration, the word "illegal" began to cling even to Mexican Americans born in the United States. "Casting Mexicans as foreign *distanced* them both from Anglo-Americans culturally and from the Southwest as a region," immigration historian Mae Ngai points out. "It stripped Mexicans of the claim of belonging." And this, in turn, helped render them somehow "illegitimate" and therefore "a disposable labor force."[11] Mexican Americans and Anglos both spoke of established residents and newcomers alike as "Mexicans," an expression that was a declaration of cultural affinity for the former and a racial designation for the latter. "There was general agreement" among Anglos of different groups, concurs the historian David Montejano, "that Mexicans were not a legitimate citizenry of the United States." They might be used as workers but not included as partners.[12]

The U.S. government for decades treated Mexicans as lesser workers unfit for citizenship. During the Great Depression, the government cooperated with groups such as the American Legion to coerce some 400,000 workers of Mexican descent into leaving the country—about one in three Los Angeles Mexican Americans among them, citizens as well as noncitizens. During World War II, the government set up its *bracero* program to provide for labor-hungry growers a supply of cheap workers with only limited rights by law. The program brought an average of 350,000 Mexicans to the United States each year, and a total of 5 million by the time it ended in 1964. When workers left their designated employers or stayed on in the country after their contracts expired, the government punished them by way of another unique policy, "Operation Wetback," begun in 1953 and named after a racial slur. During the program's lifetime, some 3.8 million Mexicans and their American-born citizen children were deported, nearly all without a hearing.[13]

Those who stayed in the United States were steered into inferior schools, segregated by custom if not by law, that failed to prepare them for good jobs and thereby condemned nearly all to the lowest rungs of the labor market. As one Texas grower explained, "educating the Mexican is educating them away from the job." In urban areas, Mexican Americans often found themselves turned away from employment offices on the basis of their accents. Other times, those with limited English had to undergo written tests for jobs that involved no writing. Many employers denied opportunities to Mexican Americans by demanding higher levels of education than their positions required, such as a high school education for manual labor; even the well-educated could rarely secure white-collar jobs outside their own community.[14] Among the help wanted advertisements printed in San Antonio newspapers in the 1960s were these: "Maintenance: 30–45 Anglo, local, married, $250," and "Waitresses, Colored or Latin." On the job, "insulting remarks"—"this job is nothing a Mexican can not do" or "go back to Mexico"—were common to silence protest. Thus, poverty, poor education, and discrimination together conspired to consign three quarters of Hispanic men in the Southwest in 1960 to manual labor. They worked in semiskilled, private household or other service, laborer, or craft positions held by fewer than half of the Anglo population. Nevertheless, what was distinctive about the pattern was that, in contrast to blacks, Mexican Americans managed to secure some more skilled jobs for men and some clerical jobs for women. Moreover, although they averaged significantly less education than blacks, their earnings were higher. Summing up their position, one scholar concluded that Mexican Americans were "better off than the Negro and worse off than the Anglo."[15]

Mexican Americans' experiences varied sharply from place to place. In New Mexico they wielded enough political power that the state constitution recognized Spanish along with English as official languages. California was more open and fluid than the Deep South. And when Mexican Americans moved to Midwestern cities after the 1920s, they encountered discrimination, though in forms less absolute than those facing African Americans.[16] But the vast majority of Mexican Americans, three in five in 1960, lived in the Southwest, above all in Texas. There, pervasive racism and legally mandated Jim Crow prevailed, ensuring that to be associated with blacks was to suffer. A conservative region, it was run by Dixiecrats and low-wage growers whose power depended on widespread political disfranchisement and on preventing workers from building unions. Unlike in the urban, industrial North, mass organizing here was seldom a real option. To achieve anything, Mexican Americans had to seek allies among the powerful Anglos in positions of control.[17]

Mexican history prepared them for the complexities of such intermediate standing. Unlike the rigid American racial system, in which "one drop" of "black blood" designated a person for discrimination, Mexico had a far more finely calibrated racial hierarchy linking indigenous Indian peoples to Spanish settlers. Intermarriage *(mestizaje)* could improve one's position, producing whitening by association *(blanqueamiento)*. Within the United States, Mexican American leaders had for decades sought to advance by separating themselves, as American citizens, from Mexican immigrants hired by employers to lower wages and undercut rights, in a racially charged variation of the old-timer versus newcomer tensions common in migrant communities. In the same way, middle-class people sought to differentiate themselves from poorer Mexican Americans, knowing that, as the saying went, "money whitens." LULAC, the most mainstream and middle class of Mexican American organizations, had from its founding in 1929 claimed the name "Latin Americans" as a way of dissociating from more marginalized Mexicans. Both Mexican tradition and U.S. government policy prior to the Civil Rights Act thus encouraged people of Mexican descent to adhere to the strategy of seeking recognition as whites.[18]

Mexican Americans also lacked the resources for mass protest that blacks had developed. The long African American struggle for justice in the United States, beginning with abolition, made for a strong infrastructure of activism. Although black activists could count on few white allies in the difficult years between the end of Reconstruction and the rise of the modern civil rights movement, in comparison to Mexican Americans they had many more inroads to power. By the 1940s, left liberals and industrial unionists had begun to recognize that racial fairness and economic democracy were dependent on each other: unless blacks regained the vote and turned the Dixiecrats out of office, social progress beyond the New Deal would stall. Blacks' ability to acquire such allies both reflected and enhanced the strength of their own institutions, among them black-run primary and secondary schools, and independent churches that encouraged widespread basic literacy as they trained leaders and fostered community action. Mexican Americans had not a single higher education institution of their own to compare with the network of historically black colleges and universities, many aided by white philanthropists, which groomed the "talented tenth" whom W. E. B. DuBois viewed as vital to group advance.[19] Where whites recognized the plight of Mexican America at all, they tended to treat it as a regional rather than a national concern, and one of little importance to others. Mexican Americans had no civil rights analogue to the NAACP, supported by white liberals, or the Urban League, funded by corporate contributions. The occasional nods to Mexican Americans in the Anglo press appeared under titles like "Texas' Forgotten People" and "A Minority Nobody Knows." As one popular *barrio* say-

ing went in the sixties: "There are only two kinds of Anglos who are interested in us—the sociologists and the police." "For the Mexican-
American," summed up one educator, "there are no liberals."[20]

Illustrating this, blacks and Chicanos looked to different institutions
for support at mid-century. With their migration away from southern
sharecropping, blacks had become an important constituency in urban
politics, in national elections, and in major industrial unions as black
civil rights groups constituted a key component of the national liberal
coalition. They could count on the labor movement and several largely
white groups to lobby for racial fairness as part of a broader vision
of progress. Mexican Americans, in contrast, tended to rely on the
Roman Catholic Church, which the scholar-activist Ernesto Galarza
once called *nuestra madre*, "our mother." Yet members of other ethnic
groups dominated that church and allowed little leadership space for
Mexican Americans. The church did in time back several organizing
initiatives—such as the Community Service Organization—so long as
they forswore radicalism. But the Catholic Church was a profoundly
different institution from the laity-shaped black churches, labor
unions, and community institutions that anchored the civil rights
movement.[21]

Whereas African Americans had looked to Washington, D.C., for
aid against injustice in the states from the American Revolution onward, Mexican Americans remained understandably wary that such
overtures would bring trouble rather than help. The U.S. government
had conquered northern Mexico and gone on to subjugate Mexican
Americans as lesser workers through the *bracero* program and Operation Wetback. Such practices reinforced some immigrants' Mexican
nationalism and their unwillingness to give up their home country citizenship, for the Mexican government was a more helpful ally than any
Anglo institution. It could and sometimes did intervene to protect its
nationals' rights and property. Immigrants, who constituted a large
share of the population, proved especially hesitant about engaging in
political activity which might threaten their status. In neither Mexico
nor the United States had their experience of politics been rewarding,
and one result was an enduring pattern of low voter turnout. Concentrated in a conservative region and a Jim Crow state, fearful of losing their citizenship, and lacking independent bases of power, Mexican Americans took for granted that claiming rights as assimilating

and respectable white Americans was the best way to improve their standing.[22]

⟶ FOR A BRIEF TIME in the late 1930s and 1940s, an alternative strategy developed. The wartime labor shortage enticed several hundred thousand Mexican Americans away from rural areas to jobs in cities or suburbs. Over 375,000 joined the armed forces, through which they traveled far from home and encountered a wider world with different notions of race and citizenship; they took great pride in helping to defeat fascism. Owing partly to the war, Mexican American communities began developing new strengths as blacks had, including a growing if still small number of college graduates and alliances with labor and progressive Anglo civic activists. The GI Bill helped members of the community obtain housing and education loans. These resources aided in building more democratic organizations responsive to local needs.[23] Above all, with greater engagement came new thinking. "Mexican Americans no longer saw themselves as visitors being mistreated but as natives who were denied full equality," writes one observer. "Returning to Mexico was no longer an option."[24]

The CIO and left-wing activists encouraged Mexican Americans to challenge the Anglo habit of viewing them as "alien" laborers with lesser rights by waging an open struggle for equality. Building on earlier efforts, militant CIO unions in the Southwest in the 1930s and 1940s attracted large numbers of Mexican American workers who participated in historic strikes in agriculture, canneries, furniture making, mines, and mills. Joining the labor movement to the wider community, they built new pan-Hispanic civil rights organizations such as El Congreso de Pueblos que Hablan Español (the Congress of Spanish-Speaking Peoples), founded in 1938. It united well over a hundred community groups and union locals with Anglo allies on the left. Devoted to solidarity between established residents and newcomers as between Mexican Americans and the wider labor movement, delegates joined antiracism to political rights and economic improvement for all. "Instead of demanding that Mexicans prove their loyalty to American values, ideals, and institutions," explains one historian, "congress members argued that [white] Americans themselves should begin to live up to the high democratic standards and principles they claimed to venerate." The congress dissipated during the war, yet in 1949 a new organization took up its cause, the Associacíon Nacional México Americana (ANMA), and organized in like ways for a radical democratic vision.[25]

As important as its challenge to race and class hierarchy was the left's opening of new space for Mexican American women as independent actors. Some helped found and lead the radical CIO cannery workers' union and the Spanish-Speaking People's Congress and through them advanced an employment-linked feminism.[26] As a result, for the first time, Mexican American organizing benefited from one of the factors that made the African American civil rights movement as strong as it was: a high level of female involvement that drew whole family networks into politics, promoted rank-and-file leadership, and helped sustain activism at the grass roots by attending to the personal relationships of trust on which communal daring is built. Mexican American organizing had tended to be profoundly male-dominated in ways that contributed to its relative weakness. Now Mexican American women were mobilized as activists and leaders.[27]

The onset of the cold war and domestic anticommunism, however, devastated the left among Mexican Americans, as elsewhere, and stifled the feminist thrust. Key leaders of the new movement suffered deportation or fled the United States to avoid persecution, including Luisa Moreno, the female founder of the Congress of Spanish-Speaking Peoples, while ANMA and the left-led unions faced destruction as "subversive organizations."[28] The force of the red scare pushed Mexican Americans back to seeking recognition as whites, which implied rivalry with blacks in the South at least, as they felt defending their American-ness and respectability to be urgent. Protecting the cause from the American Legion's suggestions of ties to communism, one leader told redbaiters to "rest assured" that "this is a nonexistent problem among this minority group."[29]

The minefields notwithstanding, many Mexican Americans desperately wanted to better their situation, and some found an innovative way to do so. The sleepy port town of Corpus Christi along the Gulf Coast of south Texas might seem an unlikely site for a social movement that would bring Mexican American needs to national attention. Yet there was a poetic justice to it, because conflicts over the surrounding land had triggered the Mexican-American war a century earlier. The local resident whom a later biographer would call "the most successful organizer that the Mexican American community ever produced, with

the exception of César Chávez," was himself an immigrant, Hector
Perez García, the child of schoolteachers who fled the upheavals of the
revolution in his native country. García graduated from the University
of Texas, a rarity for Mexican Americans, especially in the depression,
and then began medical school, urged by his father to seek a dignified
livelihood that would be secure from Anglos. He enlisted in the army
in 1942 and, after initial disbelief among Anglo officers that a man
named García could be a trained physician, earned a Bronze Star for
outstanding service as a medical officer in Europe and North Africa.
Upon his return to the United States, he opened a medical practice in
Corpus Christi, where he provided care to veterans and low-cost or
free services to those in the *barrio* who could not afford to pay. Dr.
Hector, as his neighbors called him, felt immense pride in his World
War II service to his country.[30]

García and other veterans stood on that record of sacrifice to assert
Mexican Americans' fundamental rights as American citizens in the
new American GI Forum. A kind of Latino NAACP, it became the
leading Mexican American civil rights organization. Unlike earlier
communal organizations, which had served the better-off, the GI Forum drew a more working-class membership. Self-consciously breaking with the elitism that characterized LULAC, the GI Forum was
soon attracting several hundred people to meetings to discuss their
concerns. At first, the group focused on veterans' issues such as challenging discrimination in benefits, getting medical care, and securing
federal civil service jobs. But during its second year, a funeral home's
refusal to allow use of its chapel for a Mexican American soldier's memorial provoked fellow veterans, led by García, to appeal to their U.S.
senator, Lyndon Johnson. Sympathetic to Mexican Americans from his
years as a schoolteacher in rural Texas and outraged over the insult to
servicemen, Johnson within a day organized a funeral with full honors
at Arlington National Cemetery. Energized by that vindication, the GI
Forum tackled broader civil rights issues such as substandard education
and lack of political power.[31]

These male veterans of the U.S. armed forces defined the vanguard
of the postwar movement. They waged their campaigns for equal treatment from deep within the dominant culture, appropriating classic
conservative themes of family, religious devotion, and patriotism in
their quest for justice. Such positioning immunized the group to the

charges of communism leveled at other civil rights efforts in the cold war years. Whereas red-baiting had devastated the labor-oriented black and Latino radicalism of the 1930s and 1940s, this new approach proved untouchable. Presenting themselves as "this most valiant, faithful and loyal group," GI Forum members organized as a traditional, patriotic fraternal order, replete with a Ladies' Auxiliary and a Junior Forum. It was an organization akin to the American Legion or the Veterans of Foreign Wars—only eager to fight for Mexican American rights. Indeed, the GI Forum backed President Kennedy's Latin America policy even after the Bay of Pigs debacle and the war in Vietnam, showing little interest in either Third World or domestic radicalism.[32] Always, the movement would bear the stamp of its regional origins. Members proudly wore their military uniforms, opened their meetings with a prayer and the Pledge of Allegiance, and sponsored their own military band for public events. This was civil rights Tejano-style.[33]

Its activists pressed for changes on many fronts, including Mexican Americans' need for jobs and justice. From its Corpus Christi base, the GI Forum in 1961 helped forty postal employees and customers challenge the postmaster's "daily belittlement of Latins." Targeting the government that had counted on them for the nation's defense, the organization demanded that people "of Mexican descent" be "treated as equals." The Forum also pressed for fair hiring and access to training in local industrial plants that had won government contracts. The Mexican American Political Association (MAPA), which became active at about the same time in California, worked on community issues to build a base for electoral politics. As one member recalled, "we took on the military establishment regarding jobs for Mexican-Americans" as well as car dealers and repair outlets that hired Mexican Americans for only low-wage jobs.[34] In early 1963, the organization advocated for the hiring of Mexican American teachers in the California state college system, where they made up just 1 percent of the faculty and administration; MAPA charged that they were being excluded for "arbitrary" reasons. Most tellingly, native speakers could not find work as Spanish-language instructors. MAPA "categorically" rejected the claim of state education officials that "there are no *qualified* Mexican American" potential candidates, a claim that had so often been used to try to silence African Americans' calls for inclusion as well. The GI Forum warned that Latin Americans would be shocked to learn of Hispanics' treatment in the United States.[35]

Yet even as Mexican Americans pushed harder for full citizenship, that drive at first produced little affinity with African Americans among any but leftists. Tellingly, LULAC's 1963 convention voted down a proposal by its Minnesota state body to declare support for the Birmingham civil rights campaign, with most delegates insisting on limiting attention to "our own problems." In a position paper that scorned "the present craze" of "groups banded together to create chaos and confusion," LULAC's then president, Paul Andow, denied that the black movement was "acting for the general welfare." Although "we believe that every American citizen has a right to demand full and equal protection under the laws," he elaborated, "we also emphatically believe that these rights must be met with certain unavoidable responsibilities." Sounding much like white conservative critics of the black movement, he intoned, "We believe that an individual must earn and merit" his rewards, not gain them through "mass hysteria." The GI Forum also condemned civil disobedience.[36]

Some sought differentiation from blacks not simply as a strategy but out of prejudice, believing themselves better than African Americans. A survey in San Antonio in the mid-sixties found that more than a third of *barrio* residents disdained the idea of eating with blacks, two thirds looked down on dancing with them, and almost nine in ten scorned the idea of marriage between Mexican Americans and blacks. Faced with a local black civil rights movement, some San Antonio Mexican Americans took part, but most residents and their organizations stayed aloof, unable to see how their interests would be served by blacks' advance. Even in the absence of racism, blacks and Chicanos tended to be cut off from each other, especially in the Texas heart of the movement, where the "historical divide" between the two groups and their organizations remained wide.[37]

Yet on the eve of the Civil Rights Act, this strategy of separation had yielded few results relative to the pressing needs of so many. Mexican Americans' visibility in agriculture notwithstanding, 80 percent resided in urban areas as early as 1950, where they lived for the most part in *barrios* on the fringes of city life. In 1960 Mexican Americans in the Southwest averaged 7.1 years of education (4.4 in Texas), compared to 12.1 for Anglos. Mexican American unemployment rates ran double those of whites, and fewer than one in five Mexican American men held a white-collar job. One third of their families lived in overcrowded housing.[38] Hearing testimony about the Southwest, Mrs. Frankie Freeman, a black member of the U.S. Civil Rights Commission, thought that "you could close your eyes" and believe it concerned blacks. Or, as another observer put it, Mexican Americans had "arrived at the same dead end by a different route."[39]

This impasse created an opening for those who argued for a new approach—one based on emulating black activists instead of powerful whites. The people pushing for it tended to come from outside Texas and from the left, such as Bert Corona, who worked with the CIO and the Congress of Spanish-Speaking Peoples in the 1940s. In 1960 he pressed the case for alliance at the California MAPA convention. LULAC, however, seemed uninterested in organizing collective action against discrimination until blacks made some headway. Rather, as the black freedom movement surged forward in the early 1960s, LULAC chapters concentrated on education, English instruction, charity, beauty contests, and Mexican food fairs, treating civil rights as the domain of its attorneys, not ordinary members. Meanwhile, GI Forum leaders, packaging Mexican Americans as the country's most dutiful minority, not infrequently drew contrasts with another minority rarely named but signaled as a foil. Rudolfo Loa Ramos thus pressed in 1963 for investigation of the hiring practices of federal contractors, complaining of the President's Committee on Equal Employment Opportunity's "98% plus direct work for one minority group." Seeking to expand not the size of the pie but rather his group's slice, Ramos asked for no increased outlays. He wanted government efforts allotted in proportion to the size of affected minority groups, "not geared at one deserving group at the expense of others equally as deserving." Ramos jostled for favor: "Please notice that we do not publicize every event to which we have legitimate complaints as opposed to the group mentioned in paragraph one." By contrast, "[we] do as much as we can to solve our own problems."[40] What sealed the case of those pushing for a different strategy, in the end, was a massive alteration in the political environment.

⌒ LIKE LIGHTNING, Title VII lit up the path to new territory. In its glare, Mexican American activists saw two things: that suddenly blacks, long beneath them in the nation's racial hierarchy, now had a way to rise, and that whites in power were not thinking of including other minorities in this ascension. Government was focused on blacks' capacity to disrupt business as usual and create embarrassment for public officials proclaiming freedom and democracy in a land of Jim Crow. "The only thing they [Anglo officials] understand is marching and demonstrating," said Albert Peña, a Mexican American politician, about the Washington officials charged with ensuring equal employment.[41] It was not simply the moral example of the civil rights movement that led Mexican American leaders to change strategy, but rather the practical new tool for change which blacks had won that tipped the balance. With that tool, Mexican Americans could envision better results. As with white feminists, it was not black struggle alone but black success that persuaded Mexican Americans to shift their strategy.

The leap came in the spring of 1966, as Mexican Americans learned of the new Equal Employment Opportunity Commission. At a San Francisco regional EEOC conference, the agency's executive director, Herman Edelsberg, had infuriated the western Mexican Americans in attendance. Asked why the EEOC was doing "nothing" about the problems of their people, Edelsberg had answered that Mexican Americans were "distrustful of agencies," so little could be done. He even told his listeners that their people had "no such proverb as 'the wheel that squeaks the loudest gets the grease.'" At that, one listener leapt up and shouted, *"El que no grita, Dios no lo oye"* (The one who doesn't cry, God doesn't hear). Stuck in a binary black-white understanding of discrimination, Edelsberg stumbled as badly with the Mexican American men in attendance as he had with the women who founded NOW. EEOC chairman Franklin Delano Roosevelt, Jr., failed to grasp the danger ahead. When the agency convened a similar conference in Albuquerque a few weeks later, to which fifty Mexican American leaders traveled at their own expense from across the Southwest, the young Roosevelt did not appear. Instead, he sent the offending Edelsberg, along with a commissioner who knew little of the problems of Mexican Americans. The southwestern delegates caucused until nearly 3 AM. The next day, after hearing out the agency's representative, they condemned the EEOC's "total lack of interest and understanding" and walked out as a body. Pointing out that none of the agency's five commissioners was Mexican American and its daily work ignored them, the delegates urged President Johnson to reorient the EEOC and institute "affirmative action" for Mexican Americans. After years of patient efforts at persuasion, confrontation felt liberating. "For once in this person's lifetime," one delegate exulted back home, "we Mexican-Americans united and demonstrated that we can work on a national level." To have taken part was a "privilege."[42]

The unity of the Albuquerque walkout was exhilarating. Until then, Mexican Americans' experience varied so much between states and locales and by class and citizenship status (whether native-born or immigrant, legal or illegal, temporary or permanent) that coordination proved hopeless.[43] "In a way, I thought the [Equal Employment Opportunity] commission people had done us a favor by turning their backs on us," reflected a veteran of the Albuquerque walkout, "since many Mexican-American professional people and educators who had never before displayed their anger and disgust with the government were now coming out to protest. I had never seen some of these people from LULAC and the American GI Forum speak so militantly."[44]

As the Albuquerque revolt signaled, the Civil Rights Act and its Title VII invigorated Mexican American activists. Indeed, the jobs issue galvanized their civil rights movement as they, like African Americans and feminists of all backgrounds, came to see access to good employment as the measure of full citizenship and discovered new leverage with which to seek it. Nowhere was the "castelike position of the urban Mexican" clearer than in the barriers that kept him from good jobs.[45] Having watched the black struggle, Mexican Americans began to organize for fairness and equal treatment by embracing "minority" status.

After Albuquerque, their organizations came together as never before to press for economic inclusion. The newly convened Mexican-American Ad Hoc Committee on Equal Employment Opportunity joined the American GI Forum, LULAC, MAPA, and PASO (the Political Association of Spanish-Speaking Organizations) to insist that the government act, and charged the EEOC with employment discrimination against Mexican Americans.[46] No longer politely requesting justice, they now demanded it. In early 1967 MAPA joined with other groups for a noontime picket line at the Los Angeles postal service to protest discrimination against Mexican Americans, American Indians, and Filipinos. Soon the pickets spread to a dozen post offices, and stayed for more than thirty days. This fight led to the creation of a unique affirmative action program in which the agency helped 800 people to prepare for the postal hiring test; 640 passed and got jobs. A few thousand other Mexican Americans that year won inclusion in training programs for better jobs at higher wages. The GI Forum, for its part, began to pry open jobs in many areas: utility companies, telephone exchanges, insurance agencies, city halls, courthouses, and private businesses of all kinds. Hector García, much like Herbert Hill at the NAACP, aimed a steady stream of complaints at the federal government, insisting that it compel employers and unions to treat Mexican Americans fairly.[47]

Such organizing, in turn, elicited more attention from government. By mid-1967 it had convinced President Johnson's cabinet that "there is no more fundamental problem facing the Mexican American community today than the need for good jobs and job training." Johnson appointed as one of the five commissioners of the EEOC a past president of the American GI Forum, Vicente T. Ximenes, whose forebears had become U.S. residents when a defeated Mexico ceded their land. Also in answer to broadening protest, the president set up a cabinet-level Inter-Agency Committee on Mexican-American Affairs (IACMAA), headed by Ximenes, to coordinate federal efforts. In October it held public hearings in El Paso that, like the EEOC's textile hearings in North Carolina, provided a platform for a long-suppressed population to speak in its own name and enjoy public respect. For the first time in U.S. history, national leaders came to listen to Mexican Americans explain their problems and help devise solutions, among them affirmative action, manpower programs, farm labor projects, bilingual education, and more.[48]

The new strategy of civil rights confrontation proved its value by bringing much better results much faster than older methods. The government began funding a job-training program for less-skilled workers as a form of affirmative action, similar to some Urban League manpower initiatives. Run jointly by the GI Forum and LULAC, it was called SER/Jobs for Progress (after the Spanish verb for "to be," and short for Service, Employment, and Redevelopment). SER worked with private employers to prepare thousands of workers for better blue-collar and white-collar positions in cities throughout the South and West.[49] Such initiatives sometimes changed lives. One Mexican American woman studying to become a nurse's aid, for example, wrote to thank President Johnson "for the education I have received under your equal employment opportunity program." She told him, "I have had to work since I was 9 years old," and "sent my three daughters to school by working in the fields," so "this is the first time I have had a chance to learn to read and write English." Completing the training program "was the only graduation many of us ever had," said a south Texas sheet metal worker trained by SER and employed in an aerospace job. "Today, I look at my children and I know they will finish high school and maybe go to college. . . . I see my family and I know the chains are broken."[50]

As had African Americans, some Mexican Americans turned to sympathetic unions to open good jobs, rediscovering the strategy of labor solidarity against discrimination that was crushed in the cold war years. A southwestern EEOC Trade Union Conference held in Albuquerque in 1968 attracted 110 union delegates. Addressing the group, Commissioner Ximenes sounded like Martin Luther King, Jr., when he called unions "perhaps the most powerful advocate the Mexican American race can have in [its] fight to break down race prejudice." As participants described the "subjugation of Mexican Americans" in their industries, AFL-CIO civil rights director Donald Slaiman promised to push affiliates to act.[51] Some unions were already taking action. Near San Antonio, the International Association of Machinists struck U.S. Gypsum. "At the heart of the dispute," said one observer, was the anger of the mostly Mexican American strikers that "Anglos are given preferential treatment by management in hiring, promotion, pay increases and other benefits." The company also maintained separate housing settlements, which management justified by saying that "Mexican-Americans [were] not sufficiently civilized to live in the Anglo housing area."[52] In Lubbock, Texas, Mexican Americans and blacks worked through the United Packinghouse Workers of America to fight a federal contractor that obstinately defended discrimination at the bargaining table. The company routinely paid Chicanos and blacks less than Anglos for the same work, refused to promote deserving laborers as foremen and supervisors, rejected qualified applicants as clerical workers, and excluded nonwhite employees from its coffee shop and bowling league.[53]

Some Mexican American leaders began to push for deepening civil rights with demands for far-reaching economic reform. Echoing the Domestic Marshall Plan and the Freedom Budget, they called for "immediate and massive federal investments" to move Mexican Americans "out of poverty and into the mainstream." They pressed for "aggressive and affirmative" efforts to employ them, for a higher minimum wage for farm workers, for job training and "compensatory" education, for low-cost housing, and more. Hundreds of Chicanos led by the Denver activist Rudolfo "Corky" Gonzales participated in the Poor People's Campaign led by Martin Luther King in Washington, D.C., in 1968, demanding job training and placement programs for Chicanos and insisting that "racist placement tests be dropped" in place of criteria that "relate only to the qualifications necessary for that job." Impatient with empty talk, by the summer of 1970 the major Mexican American organizations were urging the White House to establish "specific *federal* employment quotas" to hire 55,000 additional Hispanics within the year.[54]

As older Mexican Americans embraced minority standing and confronted Anglo elites as never before, young people also grew more radical and carried the cultural challenge into a new strain of identity politics. Inspired by the turn to Black Power among their peers, younger activists conceived Brown Power and renamed themselves Chicanos, adopting a term used by poorer workers. A California "Brown Power Conference" in early 1967 drew six hundred delegates claiming to represent hundreds of thousands of Mexican Americans. No longer willing to be excluded from public jobs on the basis of English language ability, the delegates urged that civil service exams be given in Spanish as well as English. (Answering such appeals in 1970, the EEOC issued guidelines—later upheld by the Supreme Court—barring the use of English-language tests in cases where they were not "job related.") The tone of the Brown Power conference was set by the esteemed, graying Dr. Ernesto Galarza, who, like King, tied domestic progress to changing foreign policy. To rousing applause, Galarza proclaimed that "far too much American wealth is spent making war and, in the case of Latin America, suppressing revolution."[55]

The Chicano youth movement, itself aided by the changes that followed the Civil Rights Act, embraced mass direct action as well as claims of Mexican-ness. Student strikes hit four southwestern cities in 1967 to protest practices that young people connected with their high dropout rates, among them the schools' failure to hire Mexican American teachers. A unique characteristic of the Hispanic population was its large youth component—almost one in every two was under eighteen years of age in 1971—such that a huge generation of young people was entering college at the high-water mark of campus radicalism. Deeply influenced by the Black Power movement's call for solidarity among Third World peoples, a significant minority of Chicano students grew critical of an Anglo culture that disdained them, yet in which they felt more at ease than earlier generations. Calling the Southwest "occupied America," they built new bodies to work for self-determination: the Mexican-American Youth Organization (MAYO), El Movimiento Estudiantíl Chicano de Aztlan (MECHA), La Raza Unida Party, and others. No longer apologetic for their language and Mexican-ness, they identified themselves as a "conquered people" who had fought oppression against long odds. Collective identity and culture became critical terrains of struggle, as a radical nationalist "Chicanismo" came to define "el movimiento" after 1968. Eclectic and romantic, sometimes crude and contradictory, Chicanismo exuded pride and defiance. As one observer noted, established groups such as the GI Forum "welcomed MAYO as an ally for an understandable reason": it "says what they cannot afford to say"—much as Malcolm X had said what Whitney Young and Roy Wilkins could not.[56]

Chicanismo brought new spirit and imagination to the movement as it made community empowerment a cardinal virtue. By valorizing Spanish language and indigenous identities, it encouraged bilingual education and cultural reclamation and innovation. It helped transform university curricula and create Chicano Studies, analogous to Black Studies. It excited young people and energized campuses to the point where even high school students became politically active—most dramatically in East Los Angeles in 1968, when ten thousand waged one of the biggest student strikes in American history. "Kids out in the streets with their heads held high. With dignity," remembered Sal Castro. "It was beautiful to be a Chicano that day."[57]

Yet in some ways Chicanismo sapped the jobs struggle. As young people venerated ancient Mexico and the qualities that made Chicanos different, efforts at equal employment appeared to them hopelessly integrationist and dull. Hector García found himself scorned as a "Tio Taco," a Mexican American Uncle Tom; young activists saw him as a "finger pointer" giving unwanted advice and derided his "big Cadillac" and his unrequited love for the United States. Police brutality and Anglo domination in education riled young protesters more than economic exclusion.[58] Some older activists looked with sadness on their notions of efficacy and radicalism. Bert Corona, whose labor-focused activism connected the 1930s to the 1970s, mused that they "used much more radical rhetoric to challenge the system," but "in the end, their rebellion was a personal rebellion" because "they didn't understand where the power was."[59] When taking up workers' issues, the student activists were more likely to support the United Farm Workers movement, infused with vibrant rural-based Mexican nationalism, than the struggles of urban Mexican Americans seeking inclusion in the U.S. mainstream.[60] The youthful nationalists also venerated the ancient Aztec warrior culture of Aztlan, a modern military revolution in Mexico, and a machismo they saw as their cultural patrimony. "*Machismo* means manhood," proclaimed Corky Gonzales, among the most popular Chicano leaders, and "to the Mexican American man *machismo* means," among other things, "to run his house, to control his woman, and to direct his children." Such devotion to male domination pushed Chicanas toward feminism, as similar posturing among black nationalist men had alarmed Pauli Murray and other black women.[61]

Still, tensions notwithstanding, there was much cross-pollination across generations. As youth staged school walkouts, adults established new organizations such as the National Council of La Raza. Its founding conference in San Antonio in 1968 was a community event "bubbling with excitement," one resident said. He witnessed "a willingness on the part of the organizations to help each other [such] as I have never seen before," which augured "a new era for Mexican-Americans in the Southwest." Among the broad range of goals identified by the 1,200 participants were calls for action by the EEOC against federal contractors who discriminated and for the media to stop representing the Mexican American "as a servant or a field hand."[62] The GI Forum launched a lawsuit and boycott against the Frito-Lay Company's "Frito Bandito" advertising icon, claiming that it "makes the typical Mexican American look like a short, squatty, dirty, ill-kept, thief and clown." Comparing the gunslinging corn chip thief to the Sambo character blacks opposed, activists reported that the ads had led Anglo schoolchildren to call their Mexican American peers "banditos."[63]

～ EVEN AS THE MEXICAN AMERICAN struggle grew more militant, however, contrasts with African American organizing for jobs persisted. Mexican Americans filed vastly fewer complaints with the

EEOC than blacks: 72 as compared to 3,067 in the agency's first year, a disproportion that narrowed but endured.[64] They also selected a more limited range of targets, with most campaigns aimed at public employment through appeals to government bodies. Above all, they built on their record for patriotism and disproportionate service in the armed forces to challenge discrimination in employment at military facilities such as Kelly Air Force Base in San Antonio, Texas, and government agencies such as the postal service.[65] They undertook few multi-city campaigns against private corporations like those that black civil rights groups waged against U.S. Steel, General Motors, and General Mills. Mexican Americans were also much less likely than African Americans to organize rank-and-file caucuses within the labor movement, although some 200,000 belonged to unions in the 1960s. And there appear to have been no well-coordinated citywide boycotts for access to jobs in stores and municipal government like those waged by blacks in Birmingham and numerous other communities, North and South. In part, this difference was the result of the weaker infrastructure of protest. "Even the sturdiest and longest-lived of the [Mexican American] organizations," one observer noted, "have very little in the way of paid staffs. If you want to see the head of some group, you phone his place of business or his house, because it is quite likely that there isn't any headquarters." Lacking the money for staff let alone Washington offices, LULAC and MAPA relied on Mexican American federal employees "to moonlight as lobbyists."[66]

But politics also played a role, as the old habits of leveraging liminality in competitive jockeying for position rather than practicing solidarity continued to make the Mexican American struggle more conservative than the African American in its ideas and methods. Many, especially among the older and more assimilation-minded leaders, felt a core ambivalence as to whether to ally with blacks against white Anglos or climb over them by proving their mainstream credentials. They often seemed to gauge their progress relative to blacks, not whites. One attorney illustrated the frame of reference when he complained that the government had apparently "concluded that Mexicans are entitled to something less from the Constitution than are the black people." Throughout the era it often seemed less Anglo hostility than African American progress that was prompting Mexican American initiatives. Receiving a press release announcing that President Johnson had appointed the first black woman to a federal judgeship, Rudy Ramos forwarded the notice to García, scrawling across the top, "Hector: where are our people?"[67] Complaining of favoritism to blacks, Los Angeles GI Forum members wanted "a separate agency to conduct War on Poverty programs in the Mexican-American community." When Mexican Americans eventually turned to direct action, they chose not Anglo-run corporations or even Congress but the EEOC as the target for their first "walkout," and the 1966 White House Conference on Civil Rights and the U.S. Civil Rights Commission as sites for picketing.[68] The Mexican American Ad Hoc Committee on Equal Employment Opportunity protested as "shameful discrimination" not the seats on the EEOC reserved for whites but those allotted to blacks.[69]

It was not only leaders who engaged in such competitive jostling but sometimes the rank and file as well. The black Chicago steelworker activist Frank Lumpkin recalled that when affirmative action began in his mill, "the Latinos said, look, if you're gonna get a black, you gotta get a Latino. So they *centered* not on the white, but on the weakest link in the chain: 'If the blacks gonna get up, We wanna get up.' I says, 'Look, they got twenty white foremen and only one black foreman, and you arguing about the one black that come up.' It's not that they're fighting the black, they're fighting for the *just end*, but it seems that we're fighting against each other."[70]

Yet in light of the long history of division, the real surprise is less the competition and clashes than the leap toward cooperation for mutual benefit in the new era opened by Title VII. The best example of the new potential was the high point of Mexican American movement organizing for access to good jobs: the decade-long struggle against Coors Beer. After the Colorado activist Corky Gonzales alerted GI Forum leaders that the Adolph Coors Company, the fourth-largest beer maker in the nation, was "a racist company," what they found persuaded them to declare a nationwide boycott. Although the company refused to release exact figures, inquiries found that of the 1,330 workers at the Golden, Colorado, plant, only 27 were Mexican Americans, at a time when they numbered well over 100,000 in the greater Denver area. Coors hired few Mexican Americans and confined those to low-level jobs. To determine whom to hire, managers subjected applicants to a polygraph-tied personality and values test to detect possible troublemakers. Perceiving hostility, minority workers hesitated to apply.

They suspected that the questions aimed "to 'weed out' minorities." For two years, the GI Forum protested the hiring policies of Coors, only to be ignored. Community resolve hardened when Coors began using its delivery trucks to aid western growers boycotted by the farm workers and then donated a surveillance helicopter to the Denver police that was used to teargas a Chicano protest. The boycott galvanized urban activists to hold press conferences, issue news releases, distribute bumper stickers and buttons, and rally the support of all the main communal organizations: the Crusade for Justice, LULAC, MAPA, MALDEF, and MECHA. They also enlisted white support, making Mexican American issues nationally visible in new ways.[71]

As the boycott stretched into the 1970s, it helped to break down the historic isolation of the Mexican American cause. One leaflet boasted that "working people, Chicanos, Blacks, Anglos, Orientals, and Native-Americans are only some of the groups of people who refuse to buy or drink Coors." Because the company also held down black and female workers, the civil rights and women's movements became allies, and the NAACP and NOW resolved support. Having broken a big strike in 1968 and locked out seventeen unions, Coors had made comrades of labor activists united against a common enemy. Given that the firm's patriarch, Joseph Coors, was a leading benefactor of the right-wing Heritage Foundation and the Committee for the Survival of a Free Congress, Anglo liberals took more interest than they might have otherwise. The emerging gay liberation movement had its own grievances against Coors, and one of the most successful sites of the boycott proved to be San Francisco's Castro district. A beer boycott offered an apt focus for campus activism, too. Led by Chicano student groups in Colorado, individual colleges took up the issue, and the National Student Association pledged its support in 1969. In short, the boycott brought varied groups—some never before in conversation—to recognize common interests.[72]

Through the Coors struggle, Mexican American organizers learned valuable lessons. Unapologetic now about being nonwhite, they gained confidence to emphasize the distinctive problems Mexican American workers faced, especially language barriers. By the mid-1970s they were pressing Coors to set up "a bilingual-bicultural section" within its personnel offices. The movement also learned how to get action from government, in particular the once aloof anti-discrimination agencies.

Their appeal moved the Colorado Civil Rights Commission to rule in August 1970 that Coors had indeed discriminated, and activists drew in the EEOC as well. Its complaint prompted the U.S. Supreme Court to rule against the company in 1973, making possible a full-scale EEOC investigation and a civil lawsuit in 1975 charging that Coors denied opportunities to Mexican Americans, African Americans, and "females" because of their "race, sex and national origin." It required affirmative action to open employment opportunities to all. Coors settled, and the GI Forum ended the boycott at its 1979 convention. "By any standard," said one participant, it "had been an overwhelming success."[73]

Yet the Coors campaign also revealed the vulnerability of the movement. One aspect was the difficulty of reaching a varied and far-flung population with unpaid volunteers. Even a decade into the boycott, Coors still proved the best-selling beer among Mexican Americans in some communities. More disturbing than disarray was vocal opposition from some in the community, particularly those leery of the new, more militant strategy. The GI Forum felt a need to remonstrate with those "who objected" to direct action and felt "ashamed" about speaking Spanish or listening to mariachi music. It urged such people to "do one of two things": either "move farther out into suburbia" or "make yourself a CIVIL RIGHTS [ACTIVIST] NOW!"[74]

At stake were rival understandings of the collective future, some of which hurt the struggle. Coors, for example, tried to get the GI Forum to lift the boycott by offering "certain Mexican Americans Coors Beer distributorships." The GI Forum called it "an insult to Chicanos" to imagine that their movement could "be bought off with money-making opportunities to a few." But while many took offense, some took the bait. Manuel Fiero, president of the National Congress of Hispanic American Citizens, declared in a joint press release with Coors that the company's "contribution toward our community" was without peer incorporate America. The erstwhile president of LULAC, Joseph Benites, outdid Fiero. He first talked his organization into quitting the boycott and then accepted a $25,000 grant for LULAC, and for himself "a top staff position" in the company's public relations department. "We feel fortunate getting a man with the leadership qualities of Benites," gloated Coors. GI Forum activists and some LULAC members outside the national office were "appalled."[75] Coors had carried out a divide-and-conquer ploy that took advantage of the main weakness of Mexican American politics. The long habit of jockeying for advantage instead of solidarity and of patron-client relations instead of group struggle meant that there would always be the temptation for some in the community to cut private deals with Anglo business and political leaders—especially the better-off, light-skinned, and more assimilated Mexican Americans, who could reap the greatest gains.[76]

Some in the Republican Party saw Mexican Americans as a promising constituency for just this reason. In the wake of the 1966 Albuquerque walkout, Senator John Tower of Texas promised to push for a Mexican American appointment to the EEOC and assured them that "political independence" would be rewarded. "These people are watching us," Barry Goldwater told Richard Nixon, "to see if we will treat them the way the Democrats have." After all, if 80 percent of Mexican Americans had voted for Kennedy and Johnson, 20 percent had not. Those numbers could grow. At the same time, some Mexican Americans were warning Democrats not to assume their loyalty, most dramatically through La Raza Unida.[77] Later, when faced with foot-dragging on federal employment, one leader warned President Johnson, "If our Democratic friends do not show concern for our problems with affirmative action, we shall work just as hard toward their defeat as we did for their victories."[78] The ability to make such a threat gave Hispanic activists leverage in electoral politics that blacks lacked, because they for so long had connected their struggle to broader reforms that their voting Republican in significant numbers was unimaginable.

Nixon's abysmal showing among Mexican American voters in the 1968 elections, which one southwesterner called "the worst defeat of a 'gringo' since the battle of the Alamo," persuaded the new president to embark on what one journalist called "the Chicano Strategy." He courted votes with federal jobs and more high-level Mexican American appointments than in any previous administration. Republican tacticians also saw aspects of Mexican American life that might work in the GOP's favor. "A close family, their church and their pride in their ancestry and their identification with it," said one operative, "seem to make them a bit more conservative in certain basic things." By 1969, Nixon had designated "Mexicans" (alongside "Italians" and "Poles") as the three "key ethnic groups" for courtship by his administration, telling the Republican National Committee to stop fawning over "middle

Europeans."⁷⁹ Through his staff the president also learned that the
Mexican American population "is strategically located in politically
doubtful states." Soon the administration announced a "Sixteen-Point
Program to Assist [the] Spanish-Surnamed."⁸⁰

Four years later, when one quarter of Mexican American voters
backed Nixon's reelection bid, his aides saw LULAC and the GI Forum as "most cooperative" and sufficiently "supportive of this Administration" that they could be counted on against "maverick" troublemakers. Hoping also to divide Mexican Americans from African Americans,
Nixon operatives in Chicago schemed about how to foment the "*black/
brown* issue" by encouraging the belief that "blacks get preference."
The best strategy for reaching "Spanish Speaking" voters, they concluded, was a "negative campaign."⁸¹ Some Mexican American leaders
also tried to use this relative conservatism to their advantage, as when
Vicente Ximenes appealed to Nixon by noting, at a time when more
black leaders opposed the war in Vietnam, that "we don't burn draft
cards because we have none to burn—we volunteer."⁸²

Yet the benefits of moderation came at a price. Such positioning
helped ensure that the current of economic democracy and universal
rights in the Mexican American community's politics remained anemic
compared to its black counterpart. Advocates, important as their voices
were, fought for a hearing for progressive ideas in arenas more conducive to a mix of Mexican nationalism, American patriotism, and
economic individualism. While still mainly pro-Democratic, Mexican
American organizations by the 1980s had found favor with the Reagan
administration, while blacks remained out in the cold. Even Hector
García, a lifelong faithful Democrat, received a Presidential Medal
of Freedom from Ronald Reagan. Through these years, the GOP
achieved only limited success with Mexican Americans, not least because they offered benefits to a few leaders but not to the ranks. Yet history and ongoing liminality meant that aligning with more conservative whites remained an option in the future. And lures would be
plentiful. In 1974 García condemned the "increased indebtedness due
to 'gala' and 'impressive conventions'" of the order he had founded.
Worried that "we have changed our thinking," he beseeched his colleagues "not [to] lose sight of the fact that the strength of the American
G.I. Forum, for these 26 years, has been the poor Mexican-American
family."⁸³

⌒ IN COMING YEARS, the ambivalence in Mexican American movement activism would find expression in electoral politics. In effect, the Democratic Party appealed to Mexican Americans as brown people facing discrimination and poverty, seeking advance through solidarity with blacks in a common quest for economic inclusion won through social-democratic means such as labor activism, civil rights, and demands for government programs to promote equality. The Republican Party, by contrast, appealed to the more conservative, assimilationist tradition among Mexican Americans, speaking to the change-wary side of their religious faith, their pride in military service and patriotism, and the anti-feminism associated with the Catholic Church and the armed forces, as it invited them to advance in comparison to blacks through economic individualism and cultural conservatism.[84] As the surge of Mexican American activism broadened the struggle for economic inclusion, it thus also introduced new complications.

The umbrella rubric under which the government recognized Mexican Americans signaled those complexities. Variously referred to in the early years as Spanish-speaking Americans, Spanish-surnamed Americans, Hispanics, and Latin Americans, they were considered part of a broad category that included others of Spanish descent. "There is no common basis for discrimination against Hispanics," observe several legal scholars; as the courts have acknowledged, it "may result from physical appearance, national origin, language use, surname, cultural identification, or a combination of these elements." The largest Latino populations in the United States after ethnic Mexicans were Cubans and Puerto Ricans. In all but their use of Spanish, the two groups diverged sharply, in ways analogous to the two poles of Mexican American politics.[85]

Cuban Americans, the third-largest Latino group, occupied the right-hand pole of Hispanic politics in these years. As descendants of white Spaniards and better-off conservatives who had fled their homeland after the Cuban Revolution, few suffered the kind of discrimination that Mexican Americans experienced, and almost none organized civil rights challenges. Most abstained from identification with other Hispanics and were seen by them as "elitist." Whereas prominent Mexican Americans had organized Viva Kennedy and Viva Johnson committees, the Cuban American television personality Desi Arnaz chaired the Viva Nixon Committee. Their white European ancestry

combined with their anticommunism to make Cubans politically conservative. Leaders in the Republican National Committee, understanding this and seeing them as "one of the strongest sources of Republican
support in the Hispano movement," urged that the president "'reward'
them" with "policy-making positions."[86]

Occupying the left-hand pole of Hispanic politics were Puerto Ricans. Descended largely from African slaves, so they more readily identified with African Americans, they also looked on the United States as
a colonial power dominating their island homeland since the war of
1898. There was no chance that Puerto Ricans would vote Republican
in notable numbers; conservative assimiliationism was a viable option
for very few. In 1950 there were 300,000 Puerto Ricans living on the
U.S. mainland; by 1970, after what some called "the great migration,"
their presence reached two million. They came, as one put it, "because
the U.S. is in Puerto Rico." Unique among immigrants in holding U.S.
citizenship from birth, Puerto Ricans were nonetheless the most disadvantaged minority, apart from Native Americans. Almost one in three
households had an income below the poverty level; some of their
neighborhoods, one observer noted, "resemble the ruins of postwar
Europe, but without the hopes of a domestic Marshall Plan." Puerto
Ricans also had weaker schooling than blacks and Chicanos. In 1960,
87 percent of those over thirty-five had not completed high school;
fewer than 1 percent had finished college.[87] Thus, they remained overwhelmingly working-class and, like growing numbers of African Americans, trapped in unskilled jobs in declining sectors of the manufacturing economy.[88] To the extent that they organized for better jobs, Puerto
Ricans seemed less comfortable in alliance with Mexican Americans
than with African Americans, because the black movement in New
York, where most Puerto Ricans lived, had long included demands for
Puerto Ricans, too. In late 1966 the White House had to hold two separate conferences on Hispanic issues because, according to one aide,
"the Mexicans are very reluctant to accept the Puerto Ricans, and the
latter expect (rightfully) some attention of their own."[89]

As if the political landscape were not complex enough with altered
identities, shifting allegiances, and rival pulls, some white longtime
Democrats and liberals began rethinking their historic affinities as they
realized the magnitude of the challenge posed by African Americans'
push for economic inclusion. Now the fight involved not only access to

the nation's laboring mainstream for a widening array of groups, but also new forms of competition in the professions and the educational gateways to them. As white feminists were turning left and Mexican Americans were embracing minority status, an influential group of Jewish men broke with their previous allies in civil rights over the extent of the changes that affirmative action should bring.

Wharlest Jackson was murdered for being promoted to a "white" job three years after the Civil Rights Act of 1964 promised an end to employment discrimination. His eleven-year-old daughter heard the bomb explode in her father's truck as she waited to play their nightly game of jacks. Now grown and still awaiting justice in the case, Denise Ford visits his grave. (Courtesy Newsday Photo/Ari Mintz)

Join Your Local Branch of the NAACP Today and Help Finish the Fight!

During World War II, African Americans waged a "Double V" campaign, for victory over fascism abroad and victory over racism at home. After the war, a permanent federal Fair Employment Practice Committee was a top priority for the NAACP, which invited support for the campaign in this 1950 brochure. (Courtesy Library of Congress)

Conservatives appealed to cold war–era anticommunism in an attempt to stir up hostility against civil rights. In 1962, the Louisiana State Sovereignty Commission published the comic book from which this panel is taken, in an effort to turn white children against federal efforts to open schools and workplaces to African Americans. (Courtesy Special Collections and Archives, Marquette University, Milwaukee)

The Birmingham, Alabama, struggle that prompted Martin Luther King, Jr., to call for affirmative action–like measures in 1963 spurred more than a thousand demonstrations in other cities around the country. Many demanded the opening of good jobs to African Americans, as did participants in this nonviolent civil disobedience campaign led by the Ministers' Committee for Job Opportunities for Brooklyn at a major construction site in New York. Scores of people were arrested for participating in civil disobedience to stop work on the Downstate Medical Center. (Courtesy Corbis)

At the historic August 1963 March on Washington for Jobs and Freedom, where Martin Luther King, Jr., delivered his "I Have a Dream" speech, southern activists' call for basic civil rights merged with the decades-old push by northern and western black activists for good jobs and full employment. (Courtesy Leonard Freed/Magnum Photos)

When segregation was legal, many black men and women with college degrees could be found sorting mail at facilities such as this one, the Main Post Office in Washington, D.C. Compared with the alternatives open to them, it was such good work that the image was used in a story on the "middle-class Negro." (Courtesy U.S. News and World Report Photo Collection, Prints and Photographs Reading Room, Library of Congress)

The Civil Rights Act of 1964 granted full citizenship rights for the first time in U.S. history to African Americans. After defeating two hundred earlier efforts, Congress at last outlawed employment discrimination and created resources to help ordinary workers fight it. For the black freedom movement, the new law was a landmark victory, celebrated by President Lyndon Johnson and Martin Luther King, Jr., at the July 1964 signing. (Courtesy Corbis)

Few downtown stores in the South employed blacks prior to the civil rights movement—or even after passage of the Civil Rights Act. In Bogalusa, Louisiana, where black activists organized more than a hundred marches in 1965 and 1966 for equal treatment in jobs and politics, the Ku Klux Klan, very active in the area, picketed to protest their hard-won successes. (Courtesy Danny Lyon/Magnum Photos)

Working with the Equal Employment Opportunity Commission, the civil rights movement waged a major campaign to open up jobs at textile mills to black men and women. Here EEOC staff members review complaints, after receiving more in their first year of work from North Carolina, the center of the textile industry, than from any other state. (Courtesy U.S. News and World Report Photo Collection, Prints and Photographs Reading Room, Library of Congress)

Social activism and government intervention with employers produced dramatic improvement in the economic standing of black workers in the South from 1965 to 1975. The new conditions also made possible a kind of fellowship across racial lines that had been impossible in the years before the Civil Rights Act, as evoked in this photograph of co-workers at a union furniture plant in Andrews, North Carolina, in 1981. (Courtesy Earl Dotter, photojournalist, *www.earldotter.com*)

In the North, the skilled trades offered the nation's best pay and benefits for blue-collar work. The civil rights movement targeted the construction industry in a campaign to open good jobs to black men in order to fight the poverty that plagued black families. Here, in a 1965 march at New York's City Hall Park, Herbert Hill, labor director of the NAACP, advocates equal employment. (Courtesy New York Times Photo Archives)

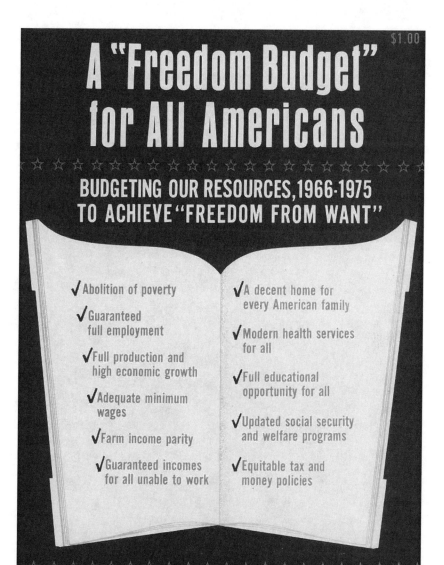

As jobs moved to the forefront of the civil rights agenda, leaders like Bayard Rustin and Martin Luther King, Jr., demanded full employment to better the lives of all Americans, white and black. They proposed a "Freedom Budget" that would create jobs so as to improve housing, schooling, and community health. Although unsuccessful, the campaign helped many Americans understand that "freedom from want is the basic freedom from which all others flow." (Courtesy George Meany Memorial Archives)

Many white male workers, over the long period when segregation was legal, came to think of particular types of work as belonging to them by right. Nowhere did they fight harder to preserve their monopoly than in construction, where a sense of entitlement merged with racism among workers such as these Pittsburgh picketers in 1969 who opposed the entry of African Americans into the trades. (Courtesy Corbis)

As civil rights activists opened up better jobs, they also ran training programs to help people take advantage of the new opportunities. Here a recruiter for the Opportunities Industrialization Center works the streets of North Philadelphia in the spring of 1968. (Courtesy U.S. News and World Report Photo Collection, Prints and Photographs Reading Room, Library of Congress)

Sex segregation of U.S. workplaces was a way of life until feminists used the Civil Rights Act to challenge what the black activist and attorney Pauli Murray termed "Jane Crow." Here, another activist attorney, Florynce Kennedy, and other women demand that the *New York Times* stop steering women to low-wage jobs through sex-segregated help-wanted ads. One protester's costume mocks the newspaper's "old-fashioned" thinking. (Photo by Renoux)

The phone company wants more operators like Rick Wehmhoefer.

Rick Wehmhoefer of Denver, Colorado, is one of several hundred male telephone operators in the Bell System.

Currently, Rick is a directory assistance operator. "So far, my job has been pleasant and worthwhile," he says. "I enjoy assisting people."

We have men like Rick in a lot of different telephone jobs. Both men and women work as Bell System mechanics, truck drivers, installers and engineers.

We want the men and women of the telephone company to do what they want to do, and do best.

Today, when openings exist, local Bell Companies are offering applicants and present employees some jobs they may never have thought about before. We want to help all advance to the best of their abilities.

AT&T and your local Bell Company are equal opportunity employers.

The struggle to break down the ghettoization of jobs opened new options for everyone, including white men. Advertising campaigns that unsettled conventional wisdom about gender, race, and work were part of the affirmative action programs instituted by large employers such as AT&T in response to challenges from their workers and the EEOC. (Property of AT&T Archives. Reprinted with permission of AT&T)

The campaign to open good jobs to all was the driving force behind much of the broader transformation of American culture in those years. No longer discouraged from building strong bodies or being competitive, women surged to the forefront in sports, and girls gained a wider range of role models from which to choose. Here, one girl reads *Wonder Woman* in the Boston women's bookstore New Words. (Copyright © Ellen Shub, 2005)

Mexican Americans encountered severe racism and discrimination in the Southwest, if not the full-fledged, government-mandated segregation that helped thwart black mobility. Here a South Texas restaurant in the 1940s excludes Latinos through methods reminiscent of the "white" and "colored" signs that steered African Americans to Jim Crow facilities. (Courtesy Russell Lee Photograph Collection, Center for American History, University of Texas at Austin)

The American GI Forum, founded after World War II, here shown taking part in a 1968 Independence Day parade, led the Mexican American struggle for access to better jobs. Its veteran members employed the classic conservative themes of patriotism, family, and faith to conduct a distinctly southwestern civil rights campaign. (Courtesy Special Collections and Archives, Bell Library, Texas A&M University–Corpus Christi)

The Mexican American movement lacked the infrastructure of the black civil rights movement yet accomplished a great deal with scant resources. Pictured here in the 1980s is GI Forum founder Dr. Hector Perez García, who carried on his medical practice in Corpus Christi, Texas, providing low-cost or free services to *barrio* residents while he led civil rights work for more than four decades. (Courtesy Special Collections and Archives, Bell Library, Texas A&M University–Corpus Christi)

BOYCOTT COORS!

REPRINTED FROM SEDITION /MARCH/ 1975 SAN JOSE

Life is not so golden in Golden, Colorado, where the Coors brewery, largest in the world, with sales last year of $440 million, is located. Especially if you're a Chicano! Chicano unemployment there is over twice that of whites. There are about 120,000 Chicanos living around Denver, but at Coors in 1966 out of a total work force of 1330, only 27, about 2% were Chicano. When Coors hired 490 more workers only 47 1% were Chicanos, and they all serve in the most menial jobs.

The Colorado GI Forum (a chicano veterans' group) called for a boycott of Coors products in 1966, and were joined by many Chicano groups. In 1969, the Equal Employment Opportunity Commission filed a complaint charging that Coors was engaging in unlawful employment practices againts Chicanos and Blacks. In 1970, the Colorado Civil Rights Commission found the Coors Co. guilty of racial discrimination

COORS WORKERS SUFFER TOO

Hovever, life isn't a whole lot better for Coors workers! In 1959, there was an 118 day strike by the Brewery Workers. Later each worker had to personally apologize to the head of the company, saying s/he went on strike, and promissing s/he would never strike again! Coors does its own building and contruction, and pays 20-25% less than prevailing wages in the Denver area. In 1968, 13 construction crews struck the brewery, with Coors refusing to recognize the union. The strike still continues today. William Coors claims that unions are one of the "special interests" putting "our political system out of balance." The brewery looks like a big Attica prison. BREWED WITH THE BLOOD OF CHICANOS

In Fact, things aren't a whole lot different in the 11 Western states where Coors is sold. To join the company, distributors must sign a contract binding them to use scabs in the event of strikes. So the most anti-union people are attracted to Coors distributorships.

About a year and a half ago, Coors refused to sign a new contract with Local 888 of the beer drivers' local of the Teamsters Union. One of the local's demands was an "affirmative action" program where all job openings for the next 6 months would be filled by Blacks, Browns, Native Americans and women.

Coors refused even to discuss it, and the beer drivers struck. Coors then brought in scab workers and got the National Labor Relations Board to schedule a representation election, allowing the scabs to vote. Naturally enough, the scabs voted for no union, and Local 888 was decertified in Oakland, Alameda, Hayward and Sacramento. MORE GRIPES

A former Coors attorney, Irwin Lerten, is given credit for getting the load limit per driver eliminated from contracts, making driving a lot more hazardous to truckers.

Coors, unlike all other major brands of beer, is not pasteurized, causing it to go stale if not refrigerated or within a month em e in an icebox. Non-pasteurized beer has been banned in Oregon since 1968, as a health hazard.

During the United Farmworkers strike in the late '60's Coors trucks were used to haul scab grapes. This last summer they were hauling scab grapes again.

These actions are lightweight compared to the Coors family's role in beefing up the police department to harass the Chicano movement in Denver. Adolph Coors personally donated a police helicopter which the Denver P.D. has put to good use in persecuting the peoples' organization, Crusade for Justice. In April 1973, police armed with shotguns, automatic rifles, and impact grenades--without provocation devastated an apartment house where activists, teachers in the Crusade's free school, and innocent families lived. One man died (Luis Jr. Martinez) and 19 were hurt in the seige. Last year, 5 militants were killed when a bomb exploded in their car. These right wing attacks are directly linked to the Coors' family's leadership in bringing about racial inequality and hostility

Coors is still the best selling beer in the West, and, here in San Jose, is the 1 beer in the chicano community. Apparently a lot of people are still unaware of the racist and anti-union policies of the Coors Family. Put his article up where you shop or work, tell your friends, and BYPASS COORS!

La vida no es si dorada en Golden, Colorado, donde la cerveceria Coors, la mas grande del mundo, con ventas de $440 Milliones en ano pasado, esta localizada. Especialmente si eres Chicanas/o! El porcentaje de chicanas/os desempeados es mas del doble de blancos desempleados. Hay aproximadamente 120,000 Chicanas/os en Denver pero en la cerveceria Coors en 1966 de 1330 empleados solamente 27 (2%) eran Chicanos y los 27 tenian los empleos menas prestigiosos. Cuando Coors empleo a 490 trabajadores mas solo 47 (1%) eran Chicanos y otra vez estos tenian los empleyos peores.

En 1966 el Foro "GI", de Colorado, un grupo de veteranos Chicanos, hicieron una llamada para boicotear los productos de Coors y fuero resaldados por la Crusada para Justicia, UMAS, MECHAS, Coalicion del Lado Oeste, MAYA, MAPA, El Foro GI Nacional. En 1969, La Comision de Oportunidad Inqual de Empleos hizo cargos contra Coors, quejando que esta cerveceria estaba discriminando contra Chicanas/os y negras/os contra la ley en cuanto a empleos. En 1970, la Comision de Derechos Civiles de Colorado encontro que Coors era culpable de discriminaccion a base de raza. LOS OBREROS DE COORS

Sin embargo, la vida no anda mucho mejor para los obreros de Coors. En 1959, hubo una huelga de 118 dias por los trabajores de la cerveceria. Al terminar la huelga cada empleado tuvo que disculparse ante la caberzra de la campaniadiciendo que sentia mucho que habia participado en la huelga y que prometia nunca mas holgar. Coors hace sus propias construcciones y consistentemente pa a 20-25% menos que los salarios que prevalen en la area de Denver.

En 1968, 13 gangas de construccion salieron en huelga contra la cerveceria y Coors se nego a reconocer la union. La huelga continua todavia.

A punto, las cosas no son muy diferentes en los once estados del oeste donde se vende Coors. Para que la cerveceria tenga control de los distribuidores, ellos tienen que firmar un contrato nuevo con Local 888, un local de manejeros de cerveza de la union fue un programa para accion afirmativa, por la cual solo negras/os, Chicanas/os, Americanas/os y Nativas/os y mujeres aggarraran empleos durante los 6 meses siguentes. Coors nego aun a discutirlo, y los manejeros Salieron en huelga. Coors empleo a esquiroles y logro a hacer las Comision Nacional de Relaciones de Labor arreglar una eleccion representativa, en la cual los equroles votaron.

Naturalmente, los esquiroles votaron contra una union y Local 888 fue decertificado en Oakland, Alameda, Hayward, y Sacramento. MAS GRIPAS

Durante la huelga de los obreros chavistas a fines de los pesentas, se usaron camiones de Coors para mover unas cosechadas por esquiroles. El verano pasado, se usaron estas camiones para los mismos uvas cosechadas por esquiroles otra vez.

Estas acciones son pequenitas si se mira al papel de la familia Coors en ayudar al departamento de policia de Denver en sus es fuerzos molestar el movimiento Chicano de Denver. Adolph Coors personalmente dio un helicoptero a la policia, lo cual el departamento ha usado efectivamente en su persecucion de la Crusadia para Justicia, la organizacion del pueblo. En Abril de 1973, 60 policias, bien armados incluyendo grenadas, sin provocacion, destruyeron una casa de apartamentos donde vivian activistas, mastros en la escuela libre de la Crusadia, y familias inocentes. Un hombre murio (Luis Jr. Martinez) y 19 fueron heridos en este ataque. El ano pasado 5 Militantes fueron matados cuando una bomba destruyo su carro. Estes ataques del derecho estan juntados directamente al papel de la familia Coors en la aumentacion de la inegalidad y la hostilidad a base de raza.

Coors todavia se vende lo mejor en el Oeste, y aqui, en San Jose, es la Cerveza numero uno en la comunidad Chicana, Evidentemente muchas personas no se dan cuento de la posicion y de la practica racista y anti-sindicalista de la familia Coors. Ponga Vd este articulo en la amigos y la proxima vez que quire una cerveza fria: CHALE CON COORS!

A nationwide boycott of Coors beer in the 1970s, prompted by leaflets like this one, assisted Mexican American civil rights advocates in building new alliances. Activists created a broad coalition to end the firm's discrimination against Chicanos, African Americans, and white women and stop its unfair treatment of trade unions. Co-owner Joseph Coors funded several conservative causes in the 1970s and helped rally business backing for Ronald Reagan's successful presidential bid. (Courtesy Bolerium Books, San Francisco)

BLACK vs. JEW
A Tragic Confrontation

TIME

After World War II, black and Jewish civil rights organizations worked together to secure antidiscrimination laws and policies that benefited both groups. Yet in the urban crisis of the 1960s, growing class tensions and political differences produced clashes between some Jews and some blacks that sapped the struggle for inclusion of its momentum, as captured in this story from the January 31, 1969, issue of *Time*. (TIME Magazine © 1969 Time Inc. Reprinted by permission.)

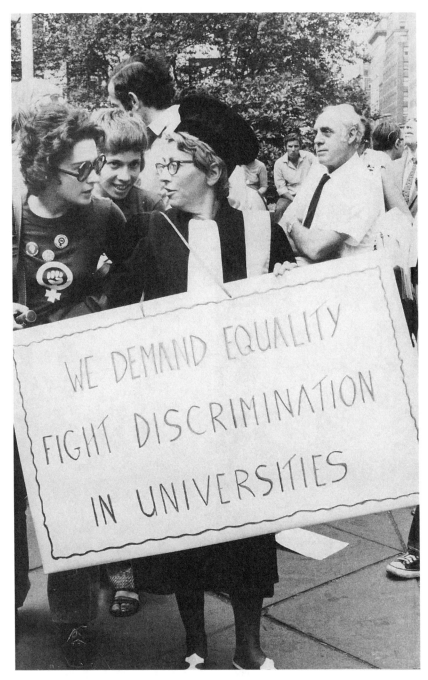

Women eagerly pursued higher education in the 1960s and 1970s but then encountered blatant discrimination when they applied for faculty positions. A nationwide campaign to secure fair treatment, promoted by this marcher in a 1971 New York City rally for women's equality, persuaded the government to apply affirmative action to colleges and universities. (Courtesy Bettye Lane)

The Civil Rights Act encouraged new coalitions between feminists and black and Latino civil rights activists. But they fought an uphill battle in the late 1970s and 1980s, when conservatives used the charge of "reverse discrimination" with growing success to attack the reforms of the civil rights era. (Photo by Wayne Glover for Pathfinder Press, Courtesy Pathfinder Press Collection, Hoover Institution Archives)

By 1983, women held more than 100,000 construction jobs, thanks to feminist organizing to help low-income women escape poverty by training them for well-compensated "nontraditional" occupations requiring only a high school education. Most tradeswomen loved the work itself, and many persisted, as did these Chicago workers, in the face of hostility from employers and co-workers. As one female electrician put it, "we believed that the path we were opening would eventually become an ordinary road." (Photo by Henriquez Studio, Courtesy Chicago Women in Trades)

MR. PRESIDENT! THE SUPREME COURT UPHELD OUR POSITION ON AFFIRMATIVE ACTION!

THIS MEANS THAT WOMEN AND MINORITIES CAN'T PUSH QUOTAS...

CAN'T FILE CLASS ACTION SUITS AND CAN'T SAY WE'RE IGNORING THE LAW

CAN THEY STILL VOTE?

Progress stalled when Ronald Reagan, the standard-bearer of the conservative movement that had been fighting inclusion since the 1950s, was elected president in 1980. As the White House tried to rescind the reforms that had proved most effective in achieving equality, cartoonists skewered his administration's hostility toward the cultural transformation of the preceding decades. (Courtesy Dan Wasserman, Copyright 1986, Tribune Media Services. Reprinted with permission.)

Even as the skilled trades in general resisted desegregation, a minority of white male workers acted as allies on whom women and men of color could rely for support. This photograph of three union emergency-response workers after the 9/11 attacks on of the World Trade Center suggests an alternative America—the one that might have been if the federal government had continued to back equal employment. Black men and all women are rare today on construction sites because of the failure to enforce fair hiring. (Courtesy Earl Dotter, photojournalist, *www.earldotter.com*)

The combination of conservative hostility toward civil rights enforcement and the economic restructuring that decimated better-paying manufacturing jobs in recent decades wiped out many of the earlier gains that working-class men of color and white women had made through affirmative action. Smokestacks are all that remain of U.S. Steel's Homestead Works, which supplied Pennsylvanians with jobs as steelworkers for more than a hundred years. (Courtesy Earl Dotter, photojournalist, *www.earldotter.com*)

The widening inequality of rewards in the new service economy has led many activists to see economic justice as *the* civil rights challenge of the new century, since blacks, white women, and Latino and Asian immigrants suffer most in the expanding low-wage service sector. Anna Amaya, an office cleaner in Washington, D.C., worked with the "Justice for Janitors" campaign of the Service Employees International Union in 1991 to win, among other changes, a wage increase to $6.50 an hour, health insurance, and respect for the dignity of workers. (Courtesy Earl Dotter, photojournalist, *www.earldotter.com*)

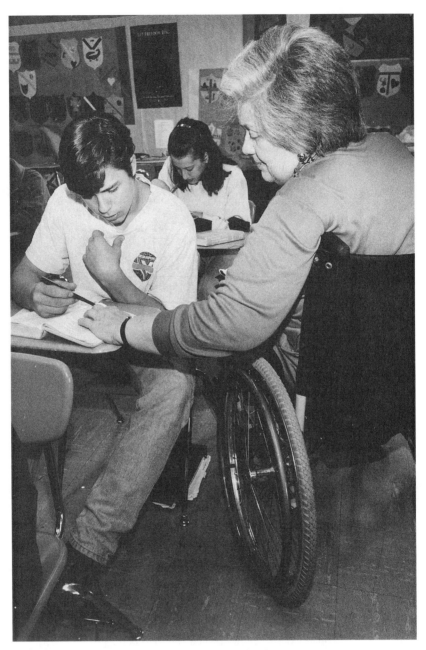

Thanks to the 1990 Americans with Disabilities Act, people with disabilities have made notable progress in gaining fairer treatment over the past decade. The protections from discrimination that they and older Americans have won would have been impossible to achieve without the long struggle for economic inclusion begun by the black civil rights movement. Here, a teacher in Montgomery County, Maryland, assists one of her high school students in 1998. (Courtesy Earl Dotter, photojournalist, *www.earldotter.com*)

~ 6

Jewish Americans Divide over Justice

"FREEDOM IS NOT ENOUGH," Lyndon Johnson had warned in 1965. After centuries of injustice, he said, the United States must work to achieve "not just equality as a right and a theory, but equality as a fact and as a result."[1] In the tumultuous years that followed passage of the Civil Rights Act, tens of thousands of Americans of all backgrounds worked for that equality of result. They used affirmative action measures in particular to open the workplaces and the schools that served as gateways to jobs with the most promise in the new economy. Even as conservative critics, business organizations, and craft unions tried to discredit them, their efforts attracted significant establishment support, notably among faculty and administrators in higher education, who worked hard to recruit faculty and students of color.[2]

In 1972, however, those efforts met opposition from surprising quarters: the nation's major liberal Jewish organizations, key members of the civil rights coalition. With one voice, the American Jewish Committee (AJC), the American Jewish Congress, the Anti-Defamation League of B'nai B'rith (ADL), and other, smaller organizations, saying that the push for equality of result was going too far, mobilized against what they called "quotas." Together, their opposition proved formidable. More than earlier critics, they made the invidious quotas label stick and popularized the related notion of "reverse discrimination." By mid-1972, a leader of the National Jewish Community Relations Advisory Council reported that "no domestic issue has been higher on our collective agenda during the past year." "Black-Jewish relations have reached [their] nadir in the United States," said Alexander Miller of the ADL at year's end. "Preferential treatment" was "in danger of becoming a Black-Jewish issue."[3]

As feminists and Mexican Americans were turning left, the Jewish agencies had turned right, and in doing so set off a conflict not only with those struggling for inclusion but also among Jewish Americans over what constituted equity in post–Civil Rights Act America. Exposing the fragility of inter-group bonds and trust, the episode revealed the tendency of Americans of all backgrounds—not just women or people of color—to fall back on identity politics when feeling embattled. Identifying "the Jew as a victim," in the speech AJC leader Morris B. Abram used to rally contributors, the campaign joined a particular understanding of group self-interest with a particular interpretation of the American liberal tradition.[4] The pursuit of justice and respect for intellectual rigor both being central to Jewish tradition, Jewish Americans turned a spotlight on the gray areas of affirmative action and debated them with passion.

The climax came in August 1972, when the AJC issued a widely publicized open letter to both candidates in the upcoming presidential election, Richard Nixon and George McGovern, calling on them to "reject categorically the use of quotas and proportional representation" in civil rights efforts. That public appeal, dubbed the Hoffman letter after its author, AJC president Philip Hoffman, stood as the centerpiece of a mobilization that targeted hiring and admissions in higher education but affected all government affirmative action efforts. Both candidates, but Nixon with most alacrity, denounced quotas and vowed not to tolerate them. Some AJC staff considered the exchange "one of the most significant events in the long and illustrious history" of the organization, and predicted it would be remembered as "one of our most important contributions to American society as well as to Jewish interest."[5] Six national Jewish groups followed up these efforts several months later with a joint protest to the Department of Health, Education, and Welfare (HEW) over "reverse discrimination" against white males in higher education.[6] Within six months, the *Chronicle of Higher Education* was reporting a "substantial backlash."[7]

The agencies were reacting to the application of affirmative action to hiring and admissions in higher education after Congress's passage of Title IX of the Education Amendments Act of 1972, which outlawed discrimination in educational institutions receiving federal support. In March 1972 another amendment to the employment title of the Civil Rights Act brought under Title VII's umbrella the four million previously excluded personnel in academic institutions.[8] Under pressure from feminists in particular, HEW had challenged leading universities on their records of hiring minority and female faculty. Most dramatically, its officials threatened to block contracts that accounted for as much as one third of the budgets of Harvard University, Columbia University, and the City University of New York (CUNY) if they refused to demonstrate good faith in trying to achieve inclusion. Schools accustomed in the postwar years to a feast of federal funding now faced the prospect of famine. The pressure produced no mass hiring of African Americans, Mexican Americans, or white women, and some of the reforms required were as basic as open advertising of jobs to replace the old-boy system. But the pressure did prove sufficient to rouse many inside—and above all outside—academe to defend established ways of operating. In June, the American Jewish Congress and the ADL sharply criticized the affirmative action hiring requirements HEW had imposed and called on it to repudiate "preferential treatment." The Hoffman letter followed.[9]

What was new—and grabbed headlines—was the criticism of efforts to achieve equality coming from groups whose members had long suffered discrimination and advocated civil rights for all. The coalition of business leaders, conservative Republicans, and southern Democrats that for decades had opposed any form of fair employment legislation had always insisted that it meant preferential treatment and quotas that violated the individual rights of white men.[10] But never before had charges of "reverse discrimination" against whites been made by people with such credibility as proponents of fairness. As Aryeh Neier, a Holocaust survivor and the director of the American Civil Liberties Union, put it, precisely because Jews had done so much for racial equality and were looked to for leadership, "when Jews are antagonistic it makes everybody feel less responsible for doing their part." The reversal was "no worse than anybody else's retreat," he made clear. "It's just that the perception of the role of the Jews [as leaders in this area] gives it a larger significance." The black Democratic Party activist Patricia Roberts Harris agreed. Noting that Jewish intellectuals had long led in "progressive change" in the United States, she explained that "when this group appears to have deserted the cause of remediation for the black community . . . it is very serious," because "it sends a signal to the political side of the progressive community that this is not an issue that the political side has to deal with."[11]

The civil rights movement to which Jewish thinkers and activists contributed so much had succeeded in turning the vast majority of Americans against discrimination, such that by 1972, to advance a plausible claim of discrimination was to play a trump card. But now, in effect, the Jewish critics of affirmative action were using their standing as a historically oppressed group to limit the measures that other excluded groups were counting on to achieve equality. This staggered black civil rights groups and feminists—and many Jews, who remained liberal and antiracist in far larger proportions than gentile whites throughout these years. Divisions ensued between the organizations and the constituency in whose name they spoke and between and within the organizations themselves, so charged were the new politics. The spectrum ranged from the hard-line ADL, which rejected any attempts at race-conscious redress, including special appeals in recruitment, to the more social justice–minded AJC, which pledged support for affirmative action outreach and training but opposed any racial preference in hiring or admissions. Ironies abounded in the Hoffman letter episode, but surely the greatest was that HEW had been prompted to action in the first place by a Jewish woman seeking to end the blatant discrimination against women, disproportionate numbers of them Jewish, that was rife in higher education.[12] Another, deeper irony was that these liberal Jewish agencies furthered the shift to the right among the overwhelmingly gentile white voters who elected Richard Nixon in 1968 and 1972.

⁓ THE ACTION of the six agencies proved a watershed in part because their open break with longtime black allies was such a shock. For decades, the American Jewish Committee and the American Jewish Congress, in particular, had contributed to the nation's broad civil rights coalition. Together with organizations such as the NAACP, they had put their shoulders to the wheel for a wide range of reforms, including a permanent Fair Employment Practices Committee and the

Civil Rights Act. American Jews were and remained far more committed on average to social justice than gentiles. Their liberal voting traditions and disproportionate activism issued from long-held principles of
fairness as well as self-interest, as victims of anti-Semitism, in ensuring
that people would be judged not on their heritage but on ability and
achievement. Their commitment won appreciation from black leaders.
"It would be impossible to record the contribution that the Jewish people have made toward the Negro's struggle for freedom," Martin Luther King, Jr., once commented, "it has been so great."[13]

Jewish Americans had also proved some of the most effective white
advocates of affirmative action. At the time of the Birmingham movement in 1963, *Fortune* editor Charles Silberman had pushed the nation
to recognize blacks' desperate need for better jobs. He explained that
"preference, or 'positive discrimination' in their favor" to give them a
leg up was a matter of simple justice "to overcome the tendencies to
exclude the Negro which are built into the very marrow of American
society."[14] Herbert Hill at the NAACP and Jack Greenberg at the
NAACP Legal Defense and Education Fund were at the forefront of
the fight for good jobs and better education to realize the promise of
the Civil Rights Act. The two were but the figures most often featured
in the news among the thousands of Jewish American activists working
alongside African Americans to break down barriers in various arenas.
On campuses, Jewish faculty members often organized the effort to admit more black students and hire more black professors; in business,
Jewish corporate leaders were more likely than their gentile counterparts to mentor African Americans. At the grass roots, polls regularly
found Jews to be far more liberal than gentile whites, especially those
of like economic standing. As one pundit wisecracked, "Jews live like
Episcopalians but vote like Puerto Ricans."[15]

The action of the six agencies was perplexing, too, because it was not
black civil rights groups that were pushing the government to act but
feminists, with a Jewish woman in the lead. Having just earned a Ph.D.
from the University of Maryland in 1969, Bernice Sandler, a forty-one-
year-old married woman, was told that her department had refused to
consider her for open faculty positions. When she asked a friendly professor why, "he was truthful, and simply said, 'Let's face it, you come on
too strong for a woman.'" Sandler remembered discouraging remarks
her adviser had made about women in the professions, and recalled that

she had been turned down for a supposedly merit-based fellowship because she was married, which then went to a man who "needed" it
more because he was married. She noted, too, that no woman had ever
received tenure in her department, and that the male graduate students
"went on to good full-time jobs while the women students had no offers, or were only offered temporary and/or part-time jobs." Provoked,
she joined the Women's Equity Action League (WEAL) and proceeded
to research sex discrimination at the University of Maryland and elsewhere. Sandler's conclusion was stark: "Whether by design or accident,
the effect is the same: women are second class-citizens in academia."[16]

Colleges and universities had indeed been treating women abys-
mally. Although 49 percent of college-age women were enrolled, compared to 55 percent of college-age men in 1970, their numbers steadily
decreased as one moved up the status hierarchy. Many leading graduate
and professional schools simply refused to admit women or maintained
low ceilings for them well into the 1960s. Daniel Patrick Moynihan
joked to President Nixon in 1969 that probably "there are proportion-
ately more women in the Marine Corps than on most University faculties." The numbers were stark. At Harvard, an early HEW target, of
the 411 tenured professors in 1970, only one was female, and she held a
chair earmarked for a woman. At another targeted university, Columbia, the future U.S. Supreme Court justice Ruth Bader Ginsburg in
1972 became the first woman in the law school to hold a full-time post
above lecturer.[17] Studies based on systematic data found that even when
researchers concentrated on women with degree paths and publications parallel to men's, the "women generally hold lower ranks and
make lower salaries, however comparable their backgrounds, work activities, achievements, and institutional work settings." Several documented how the identical résumé or presentation would be rated more
critically when ascribed to a woman. So open was the scorn that many
Yale faculty members gathered at a men-only restaurant, Mory's, to recruit new colleagues, network over lunch, and even hold department
and committee meetings.[18]

The campaign widened when Sandler discovered a trigger for federal action that had eluded others. The presidential executive order
that required affirmative action goals and timetables on the part of federal contractors did not cover just blue-collar work such as textiles and
construction, as most people assumed. It could also apply to higher ed-

ucation, and in 1971 it had been revised to include women. WEAL filed a class-action suit against the entire U.S. higher education system, charging an "industry-wide" pattern of discrimination against women. Representative Edith Green of Oregon held hearings in Congress in the summer of 1970 that documented the case in nearly two thousand pages of testimony and publicized it to all women's groups and each member of Congress. NOW sued Harvard University in the same year, moved against the whole state university system of New York, and produced a do-it-yourself "Academic Discrimination Kit" for would-be plaintiffs. Pauli Murray, then a faculty member at Brandeis University, began organizing women there to fight for equal treatment.[19]

Naming the problem in public "was enough to open the dikes," Sandler observed, and the ensuing torrent of complaints forced HEW to act.[20] Yet when it asked for information to determine whether the allegations were true, university officials stonewalled. Only when faced with the loss of federal contracts did the administrations of Harvard, Columbia, the University of Michigan, and Cornell begin to cooperate with investigators and establish affirmative action hiring programs. Officials at CUNY stonewalled for some twenty months, once declaring that they would give up government money before they would allow HEW to examine employment records.[21] The men's recalcitrance radicalized women activists and set off a sweeping challenge to sexism in all aspects of education. The CUNY Women's Coalition brought together almost seven hundred women from sixteen campuses to monitor HEW's intervention, while other feminists built women's caucuses in dozens of disciplinary professional organizations and created countless faculty and staff women's groups on their home campuses.[22] While WEAL worked with the government and NOW agitated in communities, the caucuses monitored hiring and treatment and pushed for wider changes in the culture of academe.

Yet the damning findings of gender inequity that Sandler and others adduced were all but lost on the Jewish organizations' leaders. The exposés of sexism in higher education crossed their desks but failed to register as significant. The agency leaders never addressed the rigged searches and nonprofessional criteria for appointment revealed by the women nor criticized some male faculty members' resistance to reforms that would create a true merit system, such as rules that jobs be advertised to invite the largest pool of candidates. They ignored the research documenting hostile attitudes on the part of male peers that kept female scholars from doing their best work. And they played ostrich about the structural inequities feminist activists had uncovered in funding, salary determination, parental leave, health insurance, pensions, curricula, and more. Several months before the Hoffman letter, a nascent feminist network within the AJC had urged that "we not refer only to Jewish men when we ask 'What will be the impact [of HEW affirmative action policies] on Jews.'"[23] But this appeal, too, fell on deaf ears.

One obvious reason why the agency leaders failed to "get" the gender issues was that nearly all of them were men, and they imbibed the sexist assumptions common in postwar America. A Detroit woman who protested the Hoffman letter pointed out that in recognizing female talent, "the Jewish [agency] record is dismal." She noted, "Even enlightened groups like the American Jewish Committee are extremely male-oriented."[24] As feminism swept the nation, some women staffers complained that "most of AJC's women still play hostess and pour tea," granted even this menial ceremonial role thanks to "their husbands or fathers or financial position." Women on the payroll suffered "real inequities" in all aspects of personnel policy and found their complaints answered with "condescending joke[s]."[25]

But as important a reason why the agency leaders ignored the gender issues and set off a national alarm about race instead was that HEW's action stirred anxieties about racial matters which had been growing for several years. Privately, AJC director Bertram Gold distinguished "affirmative action for [white] women from affirmative action for minorities" in the belief that "a qualified female labor force exists to take advantage of the removal of discrimination" in a way that was not true, he said, of minority populations.[26] Indeed, because being white meant access to schooling and resources that few children of color could match, white women filed more complaints about faculty hiring than members of all minority groups put together.[27]

Class differences exacerbated by segregation had also generated tensions between some blacks and some Jews. In the North, both groups overwhelmingly lived in cities, sites of both day-to-racial conflicts and, after 1964, devastating riots. Leaders of the two communities discussed the clashes and the anti-black racism and black anti-Semitism they sometimes engendered. In New York especially, home to the largest concentrations of both groups in the country, blacks daily encountered Jews as employers, merchants, landlords, teachers, school administrators, and social workers—"generally not happy" relationships in these years, one dialogue noted. Moreover, because Jews had a history of suffering prejudice, "more was expected of" them than other whites, in ways that compounded resentment. Bad feeling grew, in addition, because, in the words of an observer, "Negroes today had come to distrust 'liberals'" in the civil rights movement as "not completely committed to the concept of equality," and Jews, "perhaps more than any other group, were identified as liberals in the white community." One American Jewish Congress member concluded after a meeting with Harlem leaders that "unless . . . we are able to demonstrate by deeds that we are ready to help in some of their difficulties we are not likely to retain their trust for very long." At the grass roots, a major study found in 1960, "the Negro community is completely dissatisfied with the present rate of progress toward equality," and that, faced with black neighbors, "Jews act, in the main, like other whites." Trouble loomed because, "despite the deep commitment of Jewish community relations agencies and their genuine efforts to preach and teach equality, there is a wide and alarming gap between the leadership and the rank and file in the Jewish community; and in the Negro community, too." It was inevitable, concluded one leader, that "we are in for a period of mutual irritation and misunderstanding."[28]

At first, as the agencies worked to alleviate the tensions, they remained confident about the future because Jewish Americans had never been more secure politically or better off economically than in the decades after the Second World War. In the first half of the century, they had faced substantial discrimination. Some white gentiles had trumpeted their anti-Semitism with job advertisements announcing "No Jews Apply" or "White Protestants Only." For decades, elite colleges, professional schools, and the corporate world adopted subtler ways of discriminating, above all ceiling quotas to keep Jews from the access they would otherwise have earned. The impact was devastating. The proportion of Jews in Columbia University's medical school, for example, dropped from 47 percent in 1920 to 8 percent in 1940. By 1945, three in four gentiles who applied to medical school were admitted, as against only one in thirteen Jews. In wartime New York, anti-Semitic discrimination was so rife that the Fair Employment Practice Committee won by black civil rights activists received nearly half its complaints from Jews.[29]

Yet as postwar revelations of the Nazi death camps confronted gentiles with the heinous crimes that anti-Semitism produced, it lost legitimacy. Polls recorded hostility to Jews diminishing to record-low levels in a continuing trend after 1947, and political anti-Semites found themselves pushed ever closer to the margins. "Pockets of exclusion still remained in large industrial corporations, utilities, and banking," observed one survey, yet overall, as barriers fell, "Jews showed an extraordinary mobility as they concentrated increasingly in the professions, in managerial, executive, and proprietary positions." Moreover, having enlisted in the military in large numbers to defeat Hitler, Jewish men benefited from the GI Bill, which aided veterans in obtaining college educations and mortgages. Housing discrimination also began to relax for Jews after NAACP attorneys persuaded the Supreme Court to outlaw restrictive covenants in 1948. Although the decision did little for blacks, one in three Jews left the cities over the next two decades as part of the headlong rush of white Americans to the booming suburbs. Moving upward as well as outward, Jews attended college in proportions twice as high as non-Jews to obtain the advanced education that assisted their extraordinary mobility.[30] The postwar era produced such good news overall that it became known as the "golden age" of American Jewish history.[31]

Yet some saw signs in the 1960s that the halcyon times might be ending. The radicalization of the black movement and the wider New Left included currents that scared many whites, but proved particularly unsettling to some Jewish Americans. "The general failure to bring racial and economic justice to the American Negro," noted the American Jewish Congress's executive director in 1968, "opened a wound in American society more serious than any our country has known since the Civil War." That failure, which was partly due to the draining away of resources by the divisive war in Vietnam, was enervating the center of American politics as it energized the far left and the right. Two years later, violent clashes on the home front over Nixon's invasion of Cambodia and the rise of his no longer silent majority sharpened the polarization. Observing the spreading rage was "an American Jewish community troubled as Americans and troubled as Jews—the most highly educated, professionally successful, affluent and secure Jewish commu-

nity in history, yet pervaded with a profound malaise." Such social polarization and civic violence had historically spelled danger for Jews, associated as these developments were with lurches into anti-Semitic
scapegoating and pogroms.[32]

Moreover, at the very moment when most Jewish Americans rallied
to Israel after the 1967 war, movement activists, blacks prominently
among them, were turning left and linking racial injustice in the
United States to neocolonialism in the Third World. When growing
numbers of activists denounced Zionism as a form of racism and Israel
as an oppressive settler state, sometimes in anti-Semitic terms, many
liberal and some left-wing Jews recoiled in horror at the hostility to a
land they had come to believe guaranteed Jewish security in the wider
world.[33]

Within a year after the 1967 war, Jews and blacks came into conflict
in New York City as never before in a dispute over the public school
system that exacerbated the tensions. Nathan Glazer noted the city's
uncomfortable demographics in 1963: "Only one of some 800 school
principals in the New York system was a Negro, and only four of the
1,200 top-level administrative positions in the system were filled by
Negroes! But as significant as these ridiculously tiny percentages is the
fact that most of the *other* principalships and administrative positions
are filled by Jews who poured into the educational system in the 30s
and are now well advanced within it, while thousands of Negroes, comparative latecomers, have inferior jobs."[34] At the same time, black parents and community leaders, angry at the schools' failure to educate
their children, were pressing for community control. When the Ocean
Hill–Brownsville community in Brooklyn gained control of local
schools in 1968, the new school authorities had numerous white teachers transferred out to other districts. Seeing the transfers as a violation
of due process and contractual agreements, and fearing that community control would devastate union power, the United Federation of
Teachers, the vast majority of whose members were Jewish, struck.
Tempers flared on both sides. Black activists accused the strikers of being racists indifferent to the well-being of their children, and the strikers, led by Albert Shanker, accused their opponents of being radicals,
militants, and anti-Semites. There were a few instances of ugly anti-
Semitism in the black community, and of ugly anti-black racism among
the striking teachers. Yet numerous local black and Jewish leaders

viewed the charges and countercharges as evasions of the real core of the conflict: black aspirations to economic inclusion in labor markets locally filled by Jews. Similar competition was arising in the social work profession in New York, where an overwhelmingly Jewish administrative and supervisory staff presided over an increasingly black workforce and clientele. "What was essentially a competition for available professional positions," according to those working to heal the breach, "became translated into and obscured by a fight over anti-Semitism and anti-black feeling."[35]

〜 AMONG THOSE MOST SURE that recent developments boded ill for America in general and Jews in particular was a group then becoming known as neoconservatives. The luminaries of the new political tendency were scholars such as the philosopher Sidney Hook and the sociologist Nathan Glazer, but its most avid proponents were the pundits Norman Podhoretz, editor of *Commentary*, a magazine of broad appeal sponsored by the AJC, and Irving Kristol, senior editor at Basic Books. Already vehemently anticommunist before the 1960s, and now alarmed about the future of both Israel and America, the neoconservatives began to believe that the greatest dangers no longer came from the right but from the left. Passionately committed to liberal ideals as the highest expression of Western civilization and the best security for Jews in a gentile-dominated world, they believed the United States to be a haven of opportunity and the rule of law, and they bristled as radical criticism mounted. By 1968 Kristol was writing a column in *Fortune* magazine, and by 1970 he had joined a monthly lunch group with William F. Buckley, Jr., and leading media figures which they called "the Boys Club." With *Commentary* and a new publication, *The Public Interest*, to spread their ideas, the neoconservatives articulated a distinctive politics grounded in strong backing for the United States in the cold war and for Israel in the Middle East, and in anger at the New Left and black activists at home. Convinced that the coalition between Jewish organizations and black civil rights groups was no longer desirable, neoconservatives reached out to white gentile defenders of established practices.[36]

Most of the neoconservatives were Jewish Americans, with some important exceptions, such as Daniel Patrick Moynihan and Paul Seabury, and they assessed the interests of the Jewish community in ways that validated their move to the right. Evoking the history of European anti-Semitism culminating in the Nazi genocide, Nathan Glazer, for example, worried over the prominence of Jews as intellectual critics of American society, left-wing student activists, and agents of the spreading "moral revolution." He warned of "the rise of a stab-in-the-back myth" in the American "hinterland" akin to that seen in Weimar Germany. In a context in which government was losing authority, anti-intellectualism was growing, tolerance was waning, and social violence was more and more "accepted," trouble was likely for "a small minority whose very security is based on the rules of civilized intercourse." Unless Jews began to dissociate from the left, he warned in 1971, "the potential backlash" might be devastating.[37]

Yet Glazer and the neoconservatives faced a conundrum. The isolationism, anti-intellectualism, and sometimes open anti-Semitism of the old-style interwar American right was repugnant to them, but neither were they enthusiastic about the new-style conservatism Buckley was fashioning at the *National Review*. At the outset of the 1960s, it was the "neo" in "neoconservative" that marked their core difference with the *National Review:* their own continuing commitment to the New Deal welfare state inaugurated by Franklin Roosevelt, however queasy they might have been about Lyndon Johnson's Great Society. In addition, several neoconservatives had made their mark in print with critiques of McCarthyism as a bigoted, backward-looking populism run amok, dangerous to intellectual life, Jews, and civil liberties alike. Buckley, by contrast, condemned academic freedom in his first book and in his second praised Joseph McCarthy. Catholic anticommunism such as his frightened Jews, who suspected kinship with the demagogic Father Coughlin.[38] To make matters worse, Buckley's movement chose the bellicose segregationist James J. Kilpatrick as its spokesperson on civil rights, and featured others, like Richard Weaver, whose devotion to ascriptive social hierarchy led them to romanticize medieval Europe, hardly a Jewish paradise. The literary critic Lionel Trilling mocked such conservatism as little more than "irritable mental gestures which seek to resemble ideas."[39] Repelled by biological racism and bullish on modernity, Kristol, Podhoretz, and their fellows began developing a new conservatism, devoted to classic liberal ideals and "free of nostalgia."[40]

It was neoconservatives who first interpreted affirmative action as a violation of liberal values that threatened Jewish Americans. As moderator of a *Commentary* forum on "liberalism and the Negro" in March 1964, Norman Podhoretz announced that "American liberals are by now divided into two schools of thought." One believed in simply removing barriers to individual mobility, he claimed, and the other was a "radical" innovation of the past few years. Its alleged novelty was trying to raise blacks as a group through measures such as the Domestic Marshall Plan and "preferential treatment" in employment. Podhoretz and the other neoconservatives depicted individual opportunity as the essence of liberalism.[41] They spoke in general political terms initially, but a few months later Nathan Glazer made the case that the division involved race and ethnicity. "Preferential hiring," he argued, was one sign of the peril posed to Jews by "a radically new" strategy of integration. He equated their interests with both "the democracy of merit" and the right to maintain "Jewish exclusiveness" in institutional life, perhaps having in mind pressure on publicly funded Jewish social work agencies to accept black children on an equal, nonsectarian basis and on historically Jewish-led garment unions to include the now black and Latino rank and file in positions of leadership. Over the ensuing years, others elaborated on his arguments, producing the discussions that led the Jewish agencies to attack HEW.[42]

Ironically, it was the Irish Catholic Daniel Patrick Moynihan who sounded the alarm most powerfully for a new conservative Jewish identity politics that marched under the banner of color-blindness. "If ethnic quotas are to be imposed on American universities," Moynihan warned in a widely noted 1968 speech, "the Jews will be almost driven out."[43] Other neoconservatives spread this interpretation of affirmative action. Alleging "the reinstitution of discriminatory measures against the Jews," Podhoretz in 1971 called it a symptom of a fearsome new anti-Semitism by which Jews must inevitably be harmed.[44] The zero-sum, groupthink perspective which the neoconservatives urged on affirmative action was nowhere more bluntly stated than in Podhoretz's 1972 goad: "Is It Good for the Jews?"[45] When the AJC constructed a timeline of "activities and statements" surrounding the Hoffman letter, it began with neoconservative critiques of affirmative action by Milton Himmelfarb, Earl Raab, and Paul Seabury in *Commentary*.[46]

The neoconservatives argued in no uncertain terms that affirmative action in higher education imperiled Jewish Americans' recent success.

The professions and academe had proved a kind of haven for Jewish men in the gentile-dominated economy, a place where, unlike in the corporate world, their achievements were judged on their merits and they could expect to succeed through learning and hard work. For two generations now, large numbers had headed for the professions not only for their intrinsic appeal but also as a strategy for enabling children to match or better the standing of their parents. According to ADL figures from these years, 85 percent of college-age Jews were enrolled in college, and among Jewish graduates from four-year colleges, 47 percent went on to graduate or professional school. While making up about 3 percent of the country's population, Jews accounted for 9 percent of its college and university faculties and 17 percent of those in the top universities. In some New York institutions, two of which were HEW targets, the proportions ran even higher. Given how academe had become a secure arena for achievement in the larger, less-welcoming economy, some edginess about the idea of proportional representation as a gauge of racial equality was hardly surprising, especially among men of Hook's generation, who had grown up in the quota era.[47] Jewish American organizations, for their part, had always opposed the quotas that biased gentile-run institutions had used to keep Jewish participation down.

As affirmative action hiring goals for blacks spread in blue-collar and lower-level white-collar employment in the sixties, the agencies were watchful yet remained supportive. When the prospect of affirmative action goals in admissions to selective schools was first raised in the American Jewish Congress in 1969, the balance of opinion was in favor. "We should direct ourselves to achieving equality of results even if this means some sacrifice in the quality of education," said the liberal scholar and leader Leonard Fein.[48] The agencies resisted the fearmongering of the neoconservatives until about 1970.[49] But as selective law schools, medical schools, and graduate programs—pushed by black campus activists demanding faculty role models and more relevant curricula—began aggressively recruiting young men and women of color for limited places in student admissions, they grew nervous.[50]

Complaints that Jewish youth were being hurt in admissions competition by "preferential treatment for the blacks" kept the issue simmering. Just as hopes for their children had moved African American and Mexican American parents to push for inclusion, so, now, concern for their children led some Jewish American parents to seek to enhance their options by marking limits.[51] Within the AJC, convention work-shops a few months before the Hoffman letter were animated by "the conviction that the concept of group rights which seems to be find-ing increasing acceptance today poses a threat to Jews." Participants "unanimously rejected" the idea of "proportional representation" of long-excluded minorities in higher education, both in principle and from fear of "some Jewish displacement."[52]

As membership organizations dependent on grassroots backing, the agencies feared the cost of ignoring attacks from what some staff called "angry Jews" in their constituency. Urban Jews who had "become vic-tims" of the spiraling urban crisis, said one leader, were especially likely to "charge that our agencies would rather help the blacks than fellow Jews" and to demand that they "protect specifically *Jewish* interests." Among those pushing for a new, more narrow and identity-driven course were public school teachers who believed that they were "being by-passed for promotion" because of government policies "giving pref-erential treatment to individuals less qualified than themselves. These Jews feel that the Jewish community has forsaken them in failing to in-sist that promotions be made on the basis of merit." In higher educa-tion, the agencies encountered "severe criticism" for failing "to protect the interests of Jews" as their missions mandated.[53]

Religious leaders seemed especially concerned. At a National Com-munity Relations Advisory Council discussion, "the rabbinic groups," reported one attendee, "chided the lay agencies for having neglected and alienated the Jewish community."[54] In New York, two Orthodox professors led a Jewish Rights Council that condemned not only af-firmative action but also school busing for integration, scattered-site public housing, and antipoverty programs targeted at blacks.[55] The most recent arrivals in the academy, Orthodox Jews tended to be more socially conservative and to define communal interests narrowly. Ber-nard Fryshman, of the Association of Orthodox Jewish University Fac-ulty, was one of the first to fight affirmative action. For "several years" prior to 1972, he complained, "Orthodox Jews were alone in reacting to the burgeoning problem." He excoriated the wider Jewish commu-nity for its "silence" after "each new erosion of the rights of Whites" and attributed that silence to the way, until 1972, the professions were still "untouched" by pressure to hire minorities. Fryshman derided lib-eral Jews who failed to recognize the problem as one of "Jewish rights."

He portrayed the Orthodox as uniquely "suffering" from affirmative action as the poorest and "the last of the Jewish groups to enter the professions," and, because of their religious commitments, "never 'one of the boys.'" Emanuel Rackman, past president of the Rabbinical Council of America and a prominent voice of so-called modern Orthodoxy, agreed. He called affirmative action possibly "the greatest threat to the Jewish community especially in New York State."[56] ADL leader Benjamin Epstein later reflected that what stirred the "strong anti-black backlash" among some Jews was a "primitive" reflex of self-preservation: "Jews have said, 'Sure, let's make sure that blacks get equal treatment, but not at our expense.'"[57]

Perceiving danger in current events, those who felt that reflex also read the past in ways that demanded aggressive action. These were years of newly public Holocaust remembrance in the United States, as events in Israel and in America produced a consensus on the need to commemorate the Nazi persecution and genocide. Such commemoration often included criticism of "'our timidity,' 'our cowardice,' and 'our failure'" to combat anti-Semitism. While attention to history kept many Jews on edge, the behavior of Israel after 1967 provided a new model of tough self-regard that some found inspiring.[58] In an indication of how world events affected domestic views, when the 1972 AJC convention leading to the Hoffman letter devoted a day to "the pursuit of equality," one facilitator summarized the discussion in her group thus: "If we are concerned with the well-being and security of Jews in Israel and Russia, should we not be equally concerned about the displacement of Jews [by blacks] in New York City or anywhere Jews are in trouble not of their own doing?"[59]

Seeing vigilance as a necessity, some critics of affirmative action took their arguments to startling extremes as they tied a moderate New World reform for blacks to Old World persecution of Jews. The recently founded Jewish Defense League (JDL), led by Meir Kahane, was the most extreme. With "Never Again!" as its battle cry, the JDL called Jews to arms with advertisements stating that they "should not be forced out of their jobs by hoodlums" or allow themselves to be "victims of quota systems and reverse discrimination in schools." "We Are Speaking of Survival!" screeched JDL appeals to combat black demands. "Nice people build their road to Auschwitz." The JDL remained a fringe movement abhorred by major Jewish organizations.[60]

Yet even figures in the mainstream echoed the theme of imminent peril to Jews from affirmative action. Sidney Hook linked it to European anti-Semitism. "Its logic points to the introduction of a quota system, of the notorious *numerus clausus* of repressive regimes of the past. If blacks are to be hired [by universities] merely on the basis of their color and women merely on the basis of their sex," he reasoned with exaggeration common among critics, "before long the demand will be made that Jews or men should be fired or dismissed or not hired as Jews or men, no matter how well qualified, because they are *over*represented in our faculties." A sociology professor at Wayne State University likewise equated the city of Detroit's 1972 affirmative action plan with "the quota system of the old Austro-Hungarian Empire." She urged her peers to shed their "ultra-liberal and assimilationist" illusions and recognize that "submissiveness invites aggression." That spirit of belligerent identity politics infused the conflict.[61]

Still, reactions from the mainstream agencies were measured—until HEW demanded that institutions of higher education open their books to show what they were doing in the way of hiring women and minority men as faculty members. That set off the wave of *Commentary* articles, internal debates, and government lobbying that resulted in the Hoffman letter. In May 1972, AJC staff joined with the five other Jewish organizations in a meeting with HEW secretary Elliot Richardson to convey their concerns. They conceived the Hoffman letter, conducted "preliminary soundings with Nixon and McGovern representatives," and then announced the action. The decision to use an open letter to pin down the candidates was made in awareness that Republicans were "targeting Jewish voters as an important constituency" which came out to the polls in numbers "almost as strong as blacks" and was "active politically . . . [and] trained to give." Delivery of the letter was set up in advance with "good connections in both camps" for maximum impact.[62]

Once the candidates denounced "quotas," the AJC disseminated the news far and wide. "We cooked up a real storm," observed the AJC's representative in Washington, Hyman Bookbinder, to a group of twenty participants invited to discuss "where we go from here."[63] The outcome of the letter was "spectacular," he boasted to his boss and colleagues a few weeks later. "Way beyond our wildest expectations, the issue of de facto 'quotaism' is being not only discussed but being tackled. Literally scores of top government officials are involved in evaluating, modifying, [and] monitoring the various programs." Pointing to the extensive press coverage, he said with satisfaction, "We have started a full-fledged national discussion of the subject" and "helped to create a new climate."[64]

Indeed, the AJC had publicized the issue by feeding information to various media outlets, distributing hundreds of copies of the letters between Hoffman and the candidates, and urging discussion in the "internal newsletters" of white-led organizations with which the AJC worked, among them Jewish groups, labor organizations, inter-group organizations at the state and local level, and youth centers.[65] "The subject was a 'natural' for political and social analysts," exulted a staff member soon after, "and many of the nation's major columnists latched on to it." In fact, "the exchange of letters was carried in practically every major paper and on every network throughout the country. . . . Syndicated columnists had a field day with it." Numerous newspapers had "credited AJC with upholding the merit system."[66] The organization began an outreach effort to enlist "Jewish academicians," a group long uninterested, but viewed as open to involvement now that their "ox is gored."[67]

Led by the neoconservatives, the mobilization affected not only HEW and higher education but also the wider culture, in particular the way white Americans came to remember the civil rights movement. The critics made their case to restrict affirmative action on the grounds that color-blind equal opportunity was the movement's historic tradition and the only just and fair course for liberals. They insisted that race-conscious methods to achieve the goal of equality of results, in contrast, were a recent deviation that could only bring trouble. In the lead were the *Commentary* writers who had already "declare[d] full-scale war" on the wider "Movement" of the sixties. They now made affirmative action a key theater of battle against "false ideas of social justice."[68]

Representing themselves as premier authorities on the authentic liberal tradition, the budding neoconservatives Norman Podhoretz, Sidney Hook, and Nathan Glazer tried to corset equality's in-built and historic expansiveness by reducing the civil rights tradition to the pursuit of color-blind law and policy. Equating race-conscious efforts at equality with "quotas," and branding quotas a hijacking of that tradition, they constructed a narrative that became ever more central on the national stage. Like any bid for hegemony, it offered a creation myth to explain how the society had reached the point it had. According to the neoconservatives, seeking strict nondiscrimination and "equality of opportunity" for individuals was the movement's true essence, while affirmative action was an illegitimate late-sixties attempt at totalitarian-inspired "equality of results."[69] The sociologist Daniel Bell framed the policy as part of a destructive "leveling" reaction against the necessary "meritocracy" of post-industrial society. "What is at stake today," he declared, "is the redefinition of equality." Furthermore, "the claim for equality of result," he maintained, "is a socialist ethic," not a liberal or American one.[70] Similarly, a Columbia faculty member who backed the neoconservatives' call for "a color- and gender-blind policy" criticized HEW's policies as "redistributionist" rather than "anti-discrimination." They constituted "a policy of confiscation."[71] Having depicted equality of result as historically groundless, the critics had to explain how the government's enforcement apparatus came to be. Writing on HEW and the universities for *Commentary*, Paul Seabury cast the agency as a deus ex machina wheeled into action by "middle-range bureaucrats" bent on expanding their power "like Alice in Wonderland's Red Queen." As was typical of a whole genre of attacks on affirmative action, never once in more than a dozen pages did he acknowledge that real, living women with carefully documented and legitimate grievances had invited the government's intervention.[72]

The neoconservative interpretation of equality would resonate with the most cherished ideals of America, advocates insisted. "We are on a collision course with militant blacks on this issue," as Philip Perlmutter, an AJC leader from Boston, later put it, but "most of [white] America will be with us."[73] As much prescribing as describing, Glazer wrote, "Jews found that their shift against the positions of the major Afro-American civil rights organizations not only did not do violence to their principles—it defended their principles." What he meant was that Jewish Americans in the North had long supported equal opportunity in pursuit of color-blind merit as the fairest strategy for allocating scarce goods. Where they parted company with African Americans was over the latter's belief that some kind of proactive, compensatory effort was needed to break through race-based institutional discrimination, an effort that might award some blacks positions that would otherwise go to whites.[74]

Using the frame of the rule of law and respect for individual as opposed to group rights, neoconservatives and leaders of the Jewish agencies thus crafted a new language of opposition to affirmative action. Spurning the bigotry of segregationists like Kilpatrick and the nepotism of the "hard hats" then fighting the Philadelphia Plan, they argued with high-minded talk of justice, due process, and equal opportunity for all.

⟳ YET THE NEOCONSERVATIVES and the Jewish agencies that followed their lead were advancing a version of liberal activism that artificially narrowed a broad, capacious, complex, and evolving stream in American politics to one current. Drawn from a selective reading of history, it was less a dispassionate account than a vehicle for their political project of trying to pull Jewish Americans to the right. That idiosyncrasy was evident in the opposed reading of the nation's premier voice of liberalism, the American Civil Liberties Union, which also counted many Jews in its ranks and which supported HEW's efforts and vigorous affirmative action more generally. Its Equality Committee, presumably versed in that concept, rejected the notion of reverse discrimination, and explained that those whites and men adversely affected by affirmative action "are deprived not of their rights, but of their expectations, expectations grounded in discriminatory practice."[75] Throughout the decade, as the Jewish agencies parted company with former allies to join with neoconservatives, the ACLU stayed true to them.

In fact, what the neoconservatives and the Jewish agencies were describing as *the* civil rights tradition had been *a* civil rights tradition—their own. They had, over the preceding decades, developed a civil rights strategy for American Jews that rejected social-structural approaches to ending exclusion. "As cold war liberals they fought a rearguard action aimed at conserving the achievements of the New Deal without seeking to extend the social safety net," one student of these organizations writes. As anticommunists in the McCarthy era, they had come to frame bigotry as a psychological problem and to de-emphasize its ties to economics and class in part as a way to distance their civil rights work from that of the Communist Party.[76] For Jewish Americans, as whites of European descent who arrived in the United States with urban experience and a level of education that was unusual in the

era of mass industrialization, the enforcement of anti-bias laws to ensure individual equal opportunity was enough.[77]

Because of their very different history, black activists saw early on
that a color-blind civil rights strategy alone would not work for them,
necessary as it was to fighting racial segregation. Centuries of slavery in
which black literacy was a crime, followed by a century of sharecropping, disfranchisement, and state-backed inferior employment, housing, and education, had put blacks in a far weaker competitive position
than European immigrants. They also knew the evil that could be
shrouded by the veil of race neutrality. The white South had denied
blacks the vote for more than a half century through the ostensibly
color-blind machinery of the grandfather clause, the poll tax, and literacy tests. For that matter, some of the worst attacks on blacks' rights after the Civil War, first from President Andrew Johnson and later in the
Supreme Court's devastating Gilded Age rulings, came in the name of
upholding race neutrality. The unique fusion of class, race, and state-
sponsored discrimination in the plight of African Americans had driven
a quest for affirmative action–like measures for decades. Their clashes
with American Jews over how to achieve justice were not new in the
1970s, but went back to the "Don't buy where you can't work" campaigns of earlier decades and to rival interpretations of the first fair employment law in the country.[78] What was at stake was as much opposed
strategies derived from contrasting histories as a clash of ideals.

African Americans' distinctive experience led them to a different
kind of struggle for inclusion. For them, the supreme goal was not formal fairness through the simple elimination of barriers to competition,
but rather a real alteration of power in the United States through substantive change. Most black activists saw color-blind laws as vital in the
struggle against segregation—and saw race-conscious remedial measures such as affirmative action as equally vital against the inequality
created by generations of preferential treatment for whites. For them,
the goal of racial equality took primacy over the particular tactics used
to achieve it, whether color-blind or color-conscious. And that is why
most felt wholly justified in pushing for extra help in the labor market and school admissions—sometimes referred to as "preferential
treatment"—as remedial action to counter long exclusion.[79] Their approach, ironically, was in keeping with that of the individual who first
introduced the phrase "color-blindness" to the U.S. Supreme Court,

Albion Tourgée, the radical Republican Reconstruction activist. Serving as Homer Plessy's attorney in the formative *Plessy v. Ferguson* case, he had urged the court, in vain, to judge a law by its "concrete" impact, not by its "abstract" claims.[80]

However instrumental the version of the civil rights tradition advanced by the neoconservatives and the agencies that followed their lead, it did highlight ethical gray areas of affirmative action that hitherto had attracted little national discussion. The critics' reckoning of costs stressed three themes. One involved principle: the liberal values of equal opportunity and due process to protect the rights of individuals. While they agreed that it was fair to help African Americans rise, critics insisted that it was unfair for other individuals to lose opportunities they might have enjoyed but for affirmative action. And they therefore allied with white men who alleged "reverse discrimination" in the belief that they should have been awarded positions that went to African Americans in universities seeking more black faculty. The AJC took pride in backing the first such case to result in a monetary "penalty." In this case, Martin Goldman, a young Jewish scholar of African American history, protested the failure of Temple University's Institute of Afro-American History to interview him for a post in 1971 because he was not black, although he was told that "his qualifications were the best of all applicants." Although his AJC supporters worried about the breach with blacks that might result, they still publicized the case "as a warning to academic institutions around the country that reverse discrimination is also subject to monetary penalties."[81] For their part, affirmative action advocates acknowledged that it might cause "some hardship" for some whites, as a liberal Catholic leader put it, but insisted that "it is self-deluding to advocate the promotion of civil rights for Americans who have been economically exploited by our society, without expecting some consequences to that society."[82]

A second cardinal theme of the new liberal case against affirmative action was a call to uphold "standards of excellence." Jewish organizations were devoted to the merit systems first introduced in the late nineteenth century to put an end to political patronage appointments; they believed that such systems, with rare exceptions, produced fair competition that lifted the whole society to new levels of achievement. "The merit concept," said Benjamin Epstein of the ADL, "was the dream that made America so meaningful to the underprivileged Jew when he came to this country."[83] The dream was, as Paul Seabury put it in *Commentary*, that persons would advance "according to ability and accomplishment, rather than according to status, preferment, or chance."[84] In the conflict over affirmative action, the agencies and their backers insisted that only the best-qualified person should take the prize of a job or an admission; to choose anyone less qualified was to lower standards. "Merit alone must govern," insisted one writer. "To allow one qualified Jewish student to be denied admission to the university of his choice" so as to enroll "someone who is less qualified is to negate the many years of effort expended to eliminate quotas."[85]

Some also claimed that affirmative action was elevating incompetent African Americans to the detriment of all concerned. One academic couple who wrote to Podhoretz to praise his "sensible, courageous" position asserted that they had been denied teaching jobs for which they were told they were "eminently qualified and would be hired immediately if only we were members of an underprivileged minority." Both partners claimed to have personally witnessed how, because of HEW, "incompetent, ill-prepared minority instructors have overshadowed the good work of other minority faculty." As a result, "students have suffered from incompetent instruction," and "double standards have been established for salary, promotion, hiring."[86] As institutions rushed to right decades-old, even centuries-old, exclusion of a population long denied the same quality of education as whites and ostracized from the mainstream, no doubt they made some weak appointments to which critics could point in good conscience. Moreover, competition for the relatively small number of black scholars also lifted the salaries of the most productive above those of their white counterparts. In a market so long rigged against African Americans, the laws of supply and demand were now working for a few, and the differential rewards caused resentment among some white peers.[87] Such developments were predictable, and seemed to advocates a small price to pay for the larger good achieved.

But the critics disagreed, and in their fear and anger over the changes they increasingly insisted that race must never be a criterion and that only formal qualifications should ever matter. Some now turned against affirmative action in blue-collar settings such as construction which had never before been associated with the merit principle. Even the strongest defender of affirmative action at the AJC came to fret that the Philadelphia Plan might achieve results "at the cost of bypassing non-minority employees with greater seniority and/or greater quali-fications"—a rather astonishing concern in light of the brazen and now illegal racial exclusion practiced in the building trades.[88]

A third theme of the mobilization against HEW, and the most prom-inent in internal discussions, was identity politics, namely, concern that affirmative action would adversely affect Jews in particular. AJC direc-tor Bertram Gold thus called current policies "a grave threat to the future welfare and status of the Jewish American community," espe-cially "because past discrimination against Jews has caused them to be concentrated in certain vulnerable employment areas" such as college teaching, law, and medicine.[89] "Infusing all of the discussions" at the spring AJC convention before the Hoffman letter was a belief that the quest for equality of results for blacks "poses a threat to Jews," in the words of a convention report that also noted "a new candor in protect-ing our own interests."[90] Perhaps the best summary formulation of the reasoning behind the agencies' action was "defense of Jewish interests within the broader context of defending the democratic process."[91]

Those against whom the neoconservatives and agencies mobilized patiently repeated over and over again that quotas were already illegal by the terms of the Civil Rights Act, and that the affirmative action guidelines applied by HEW simply called for reasonable, flexible goals and timetables for meeting them—what the business world calls man-agement by objective. If an institution failed to meet its goals but could show that it had made a good faith effort, no punishment would ensue. HEW officials insisted that they were not "seeking racial, ethnic, or sexual balance in faculties," nor were they interested in "lowering stan-dards," let alone doing away with "excellence." The hiring plans typi-cally assumed that significant change would take two to three decades. The real difference was to be found, rather, in how those promoting the plans rejected the insiders' assumption "that traditional modes of faculty selection have resulted in . . . as good a world as we might aspire to, and thus any change in these modes must be for the worse."[92] Sup-porters of change pointed to what one philosopher called the "radi-cal difference of moral intent" between the quotas of the past and affirmative action: whereas quotas sought to keep out qualified peo-ple, goals aimed to bring in those whose qualifications might go over-looked.[93]

Such distinctions struck opponents of the plans as the cant of petti-foggers trying to obfuscate the truth. When the man at the center of the storm, Stanley Pottinger of HEW's Office of Civil Rights, insisted that "goals are not quotas, and the difference is not a matter of seman-tics," the critics laughed. "If you can count up to 100," retorted one, "it is obvious that a quota *for* one group is a quota *against* another." The ADL agreed. "Asking for numbers," one spokesperson insisted, "is a clear request for a quota." Indeed, some concluded that even talk of "underutilization" or "deficiencies" should be barred because the words might imply proportionality as a goal.[94] In their complaint to HEW, the six agencies cited thirty-three cases of schools accepting black applicants with lower test scores and grades than most whites who were admitted, of setting aside a certain number of places for mi-nority applicants, of explicitly pledging to hire minority or female fac-ulty, or of seeking to match the proportion of their minority hires to the minority population in question. HEW insisted that the exam-ples resulted from "excesses of zeal" on the part of people unversed in the law.[95]

HEW and its backers charged the critics with exaggerating in ways that poisoned discussion, as in Sidney Hook's declaration that universi-ties were being forced "to hire unqualified Negroes and women" or the claim of others that HEW was aiming to "end any role for individual merit in higher education."[96] There was, observed Bernice Sandler of the hand-wringing over imperiled excellence, "a not-so-covert assump-tion [among the critics] that women and minorities are, almost by definition, not 'qualified.'"[97] Indeed, while the lion's share of new jobs still went to white men, and race and gender discrimination remained common, the leader of a faculty group fighting affirmative action de-clared that it was now "good to be black, valuable to be a woman, and bad luck to be both white and male," as he proclaimed that affirma-tive action was "destroy[ing] academic standards." Said a disgusted ob-server, "One might have expected more rationality and respect for evi-dence in the academy of all places."[98]

In fact, the public clash of inflated criticisms and defensive parries obscured the substantive heart of the dispute: the cases in which black candidates met threshold standards but did not have records quite as strong as those of the whites with whom they were in competition. The debate was not really over the "qualified" versus the "unqualified"; it was over the "best qualified" versus the "also qualified." As they tried to fend off distorting attacks, HEW and its supporters tended to focus on the easier case to make, for "soft" affirmative action policies of expanded recruitment and newly rational personnel procedures that were creating a real universal merit system for the first time. The critics, by contrast, focused on "hard" affirmative action, on cases in which less formally qualified applicants gained positions that in its absence would have gone to highly credentialed white men, especially Jewish men, whose parents or grandparents might have encountered the old ceiling quotas on Jews. Yet even in the most extreme case of "preferential treatment" identified by the AJC, a University of Pennsylvania School of Social Work program that sought to admit 50 percent black students to meet desperate appeals for black social workers from riot-torn cities, "the officials indicated that all persons accepted into the school had to be qualified regardless of racial considerations."[99]

Supporters of HEW policies, including many Jewish Americans, argued that if only the best qualified were selected, those long excluded would never get in because there was no way they could beat competitors groomed with far more privilege in a highly unequal society in which advantage and disadvantage snowballed over time. As one American Jewish Congress leader pleaded in an internal discussion, given the self-reinforcing "cycle" of a racist social structure, "so long as the sole criterion for selection was the highest level of qualification, 'you have doomed the blacks forever.'" A Columbus, Ohio, woman protesting the Hoffman letter pointed out that "in the United States there are enough Caucasians to fill the jobs—and well-qualified ones, also." Given this oversupply and employers' resistance to hiring minorities, "the quota system was the only hope of any Negro employment at all (even of highly qualified persons), and now that is gone."[100] Within the agencies, some acknowledged the truth of these predictions. "The main argument made by our critics is true enough for us to be concerned," noted Bookbinder: "that until the government talked about numbers, there was little if any progress in many places." He acknowledged that the "new climate" the Hoffman letter created "also contains the danger of hurting entirely legitimate efforts to expand equality of opportunity."[101]

⌒ THE CONSEQUENCES of the Hoffman letter were indeed harmful. The feminists who had been pushing hardest to change faculty hiring practices were stunned. At the very moment when they had forced the government to recognize sex discrimination as a problem in higher education and promote affirmative action to rectify it, the critics had changed the discussion to race and undercut reform. The National Organization of Women joined with the NAACP to condemn the resulting "retreat in equal employment," and a delegation of NOW leaders met with AJC officials to protest.[102] Answering the agency's fear that goods would be allotted based on groups' proportions in the wider population, former EEOC commissioner and NOW founder Aileen Hernandez explained that when feminists demanded "51%" women, "that's a bargaining tactic"; in reality, "we take what we can get." One woman AJC staffer at the meeting urged the legal director that "we should recognize at least among ourselves the difference between rhetoric and a fully developed philosophical position in support of proportionality." Arguing against over-literal interpretation of political bluster, she pointed out that the AJC itself "implicitly used proportions as a measuring rod" in gauging whether corporate employers were treating Jews fairly.[103]

While gentile feminists seemed dumbfounded by the opposition from the Jewish agencies, some Jewish feminists, more aware of how neoconservatives were vying against liberals and radicals for the hearts and minds of their community, fought back directly. Congresswoman Bella Abzug, elected in 1970 as the first Jewish female U.S. representative, was furious. Abzug was a veteran of the labor–left–civil rights alliance that neoconservatives wanted Jews to jettison, and she understood how these critics were using a new kind of identity politics to lure Jews to the right. "I would like to remind my brothers that in attacking affirmative action programs in higher education as producing reverse discrimination against Jews," she argued, "they are talking about and speaking for Jewish *men*, not for Jewish women." The latter's long exclusion had roused no such "indignation and concern." Abzug complained from experience, having been, like Pauli Murray, denied admission to the all-male Harvard Law School in the 1940s.[104]

Abzug was not the only one to question the men's credentials as arbiters of fairness. By 1973, Bernice Sandler, who had first invited HEW to look into higher education hiring practices, urged Jewish women to "write letters to counter the campaign undertaken by some Jewish men's groups against affirmative action," observing, "Nobody seems to have been asking Jewish women who have been held back in academe because of their sex what *they* think about affirmative action."[105] What further infuriated her was that at the very moment when HEW was scaling back its enforcement of equal employment in the wake of the Hoffman letter, and had agreed to create an ombudsman position to treat as "top priority" Jewish agency complaints of "reverse discrimination," "more than *100* cases of individual women who filed charges one and two years ago are still lingering in the files and have *not* been investigated." She branded "such differential treatment for males and females" a blatant violation of equal protection. She made the case with such "embarrassing and troublesome" cogency that AJC staff feared a "polarization in which Jews would appear to be championing the rights of white males against the interests of women."[106]

While feminists felt blindsided, black civil rights advocates felt bereft, abandoned, and devastated at an already difficult time. An impromptu coalition of the best-known leaders of the major civil rights organizations protested to HEW. They bemoaned the retreat from enforcement caused by "the spurious attack on quotas" and complained that they had been frozen out of discussions convened under "demagogic auspices." It was "regrettable," they declared collectively in a letter drafted by the attorney Marian Wright Edelman, "that the recency of gains by some minorities long barred from equal access to university faculties, and their continuing insecurity result in their criticizing goals necessary to open up access to other minorities." John Morsell of the NAACP sent a copy to the AJC, reiterating yet again that "we do not embrace a rigid quota of jobs or its corollary—rigid proportional representation on jobs," and "we are emphatically opposed to any procedure which would fill jobs with unqualified people who have nothing but their race or sex to advance as qualifications." But, he underscored, "the fact is that we simply have no confidence whatsoever in so-called 'good faith' approaches to job discrimination, whether in the building industry or on the university campus." The historical record on the kind of soft affirmative action programs the Jewish agencies were advocating was "quite clear: nothing happens unless you beat people over the head," and goals and timetables were a way to accomplish that.[107] U.S. Representative Louis Stokes, chair of the Congressional Black Caucus, rued the fact that "the very allies" who had together won civil rights legislation were now "pitted against one another in a class and economic struggle."[108]

"As one would expect," noted an AJC staffer, "the Black press and Black broadcasters resented" the Hoffman letter.[109] For some, that was putting it mildly. Ethel Payne of CBS News called the AJC's insistence that its efforts would not harm legitimate affirmative action "pure, unadulterated hogwash," and demanded, "With friends like it, who needs enemies?" Payne tossed down the gauntlet: "Take your choice. Shall it be welfare? Or shall it be jobs?"[110] The black columnist William Raspberry described himself as "flabbergasted." Because quotas had never been government policy to begin with, he noted, attacks on affirmative action as "quotas" could only be interpreted as a call to do less of what little was being done. "Let the Civil Service Commission say no more quotas," he wrote, "and the most realistic interpretation is: The pressure to hire black folks is off."[111]

Few blacks saw the existing system as the meritocracy the neoconservatives and their Jewish agency allies insisted it was. They saw the alleged meritocracy instead as an ideology which had worked well for some white people but never for even the most meritorious blacks—and which was now being used to defend an unfairly constructed social hierarchy that locked others out and defamed them as incompetent. "Structural inequality along racial fault lines exists from the moment of birth," notes the civil rights attorney Theodore Shaw, "so that supposedly objective measures of merit and ability ultimately reflect something other than who is truly deserving of opportunity. Usually they reflect the benefits of privilege, in a self-reifying process of unnatural selection that becomes enshrined as 'merit.'" Accordingly, some civil rights advocates tried to broaden the conversation about what constituted merit away from a focus on how individuals performed on tests to consideration of their lives and society's needs. They asked whether the law school applicant with the highest LSAT score was "necessarily the one with the most merit." Wasn't there merit in a public university designing its admissions so "that all ethnic groups have lawyers, doctors, and engineers"? Might not a policy "designed to see that no already disadvantaged people remain forever hewers of wood and drawers of water" be meritorious?[112]

Black leaders were especially aghast at the behavior of their erstwhile allies. Without any advance notice, they had publicly attacked a reform seen as crucial to black well-being. Cheered on by Vernon Jordan of the National Urban League, the attorney Patricia Roberts Harris blew up at Hyman Bookbinder of the AJC, whose conduct, she said, made her sympathetic to the "people [who] avoid 'coalition politics.'" She lamented, "I have spent all my life with people who are not black telling me and other blacks what is best for us," but no more. No longer did the AJC seem "the champion of all the oppressed"; now it seemed "the representative of very selfish, very short-run interests." Julius Hobson, a federal contract compliance expert, echoed her sentiments. "The people at my side have always been Jewish," he said, "but I can't sit back any longer and listen to this nonsense about quotas." According to one observer of the NAACP convention that met the day after the Hoffman letter became public, "many blacks thought that the Jews had declared political war on them." For "just as America seem[ed] to be on the verge of recognizing" that "since we were deliberately handicapped, perhaps we must be consciously assisted," suddenly "we hear Jewish cries of abhorrence of discrimination in reverse, quotas, and preferential treatment."[113]

Such African American leaders felt that Jewish opponents of affirmative action were willfully refusing to listen to its advocates. In vain did mainstream figures such as Jordan "speak with the bluntness of a true friend" in telling Jewish audiences that "the issue that has most visibly separated the Jewish community from the black community is the issue of affirmative action." When Jordan denied that a merit system was already in place, he knew whereof he spoke. Having chauffeured wealthy whites and worked his way through college partly as a bus driver, he well appreciated that "the way people survive in this society is through work." He saw affirmative action as vital for blacks to secure "a decent job with a decent wage." Jordan begged that "the word 'quota' . . . be forever expunged from this discussion," and with it the imputation that supporters of inclusion aimed to hire "unqualified persons" and elevate "incompetence." But his patient exposition of black "fears of Jewish abandonment" went unheeded. Instead, those he aimed to reach rubbed salt in the wound by continuing to use "quotas" as a synonym for affirmative action.[114] From the Deep South, an NAACP field director accused the AJC of being "not in touch with the reality of the Black experience" in the labor market. Of its claims of "discrimination in reverse," he said, "I hear this same argument by white racists, who claim they would employ Blacks if they could find them in Mississippi. Yet, they use the very system you endorse (merit) to keep Blacks from certain positions."[115]

What made the sting worse was that those working to institute affirmative action were rarely the Third World–identified radicals who criticized Israel and romanticized armed struggle, but rather the so-called responsible leaders who always sought constructive solutions. The NAACP, for example, was a committed advocate of alliances with whites, a supporter of Israel, and a vocal critic of anti-Semitism. The National Urban League was similarly moderate, as were other organizations shocked by the Hoffman letter, such as the National Catholic Conference for Interracial Justice, which criticized the AJC for "provoking a public uproar in the midst of a presidential election." Advocates such as the NAACP leaders believed that the Jewish agencies were exaggerating the extent of anti-Semitism in the black community and misconstruing how best to deal with it, but they were loyal allies who felt the horror of the Holocaust and did not shrink from denouncing prejudice against Jews. Indeed, they denounced it far more often than white gentile leaders, and certainly more than figures such as Nixon, whom the agencies were treating as a friend.[116]

Because of that loyalty, some black leaders were deeply scarred by the whole episode, as Patricia Harris explained in a 1974 interview that she had sealed until her death. Her anger at the label "quotas" was palpable. The purpose of affirmative action was not to exclude anyone, she said, but rather to establish a set of "remedial programs to bring blacks to where they would have been in the absence of 300 years of discrimination." That meant sometimes hiring someone a bit less qualified, perhaps in the "eighty-ninth" rather than the "ninety-ninth percentile," but not someone who was incompetent, as the campaign's rhetoric implied in ways that invigorated racists. As upsetting to Harris was the "unilateral" way the AJC had acted, not even alerting allies of "sixty or seventy years in this cause," who considered the policy "essential to changing blacks' position" in society. That behavior she found "contemptuous." What cut as much was to find herself maligned as anti-Semitic for criticizing the agencies' conduct. "This is a very dangerous area to deal with," she noted. "I am very concerned about the inability of people who are black to debate this issue without being accused of being an anti-Semite." Harris believed that all these "deadly" consequences flowed from the failure of the agencies to seek "consensus" before breaking ranks. It was "very hurtful to me," she confided, because "if I didn't have any Jewish friends, I might not have any white friends at all," for "there is a way in which people like me tend to have greater comfort, greater sense of identity of interest, partly because of the holocaust, with people who are Jewish and intellectuals." After the Hoffman letter, many such relationships suffered.[117]

Joining black activists and white feminists in protest over the agencies' actions were a number of Jews. Even within the agencies' membership, some protested. The ADL's Wisconsin vice chair told the press that the attack on HEW was "immoral" and would "drive a flesh-tearing wedge" between minorities and the Jewish community.[118] At a forum of the National Conference of Christians and Jews, the social work educator John Slawson worried that the controversy would promote "backlash" against blacks' urgent quest for employment.[119] The longtime civil rights attorney Joseph Rauh chastised those who "now oppose the only effective method by which blacks can be assured jobs from which they have been so long excluded." He called the "quotas" label "at best confusing and at worst deliberately misleading and said he was "sick and tired" of people who promised support but practiced obstruction.[120]

Such advocates weighed the relative risks of affirmative action very differently from the neoconservatives and the agencies. At a discussion convened after the Hoffman letter, Bill Taylor, the former staff director of the Civil Rights Commission, spoke for many when he said that "he felt the danger of continuous denial of rights to be worse than [the danger of] codifying quotas." There was nothing wrong with "preferential treatment" for a "qualified" applicant, said Rauh. "In light of the real mistreatment" of blacks, "the misuse of goals was slight."[121] The most incisive formulation came from the president of the mid-Manhattan branch of the NAACP. "To be sure," he said, "there are negative aspects in the use of quotas. Does the fire burn? Can sharp knives maim?" Sometimes they did. But "the proper use of these items has been a boon to civilization," just as "the proper use of quotas can help right some ancient wrongs and promote the kind of equitable society the A.J.C. and the NAACP are striving for."[122]

The outcome of the episode was that a gulf opened between the two sides, and agreement over even the meaning of common words proved beyond reach. Once the label "quota" was attached to the policy, it proved an irrepressible impediment to reasoned exchange, let alone give-and-take negotiations. Most efforts at "dialogue" only worsened matters, for each side saw its understanding as just, obvious, and nonnegotiable. Asked to speak for the National Industrial Conference Board on "the problem of quotas" in employment, the highly regarded social scientist Kenneth B. Clark opened by dismissing it as "an essentially spurious issue," another example of the "racial code words and phrases" that "were never intended to illuminate any serious social problem" but rather to rally whites to defend their privilege.[123] For many Jews, however, once the term "quotas" was affixed to the policy, it became an anathema to be avoided at any cost. The impasse endured because the conflict of interests and ideas existed in a world of vastly unequal power. The trouble was less the words than the world in which they did their work.

～ THE CATASTROPHIC SCENARIOS conjured by the neoconservatives and the agencies never came to pass. In fact, between 1968 and 1973, blacks' share of total university faculty jobs grew from 2.2 to 2.9 percent; with historically black colleges and universities removed from the calculations, blacks made up only 0.9 percent of the professoriate. Over the next twenty years, black representation among full-time faculty members grew only .05 percent.[124] Even the numbers of women hired in the peak years of HEW pressure were negligible. Between 1968 and 1974, their share of faculty positions grew by approximately one tenth of a percent.[125] The federal government had barked but never bitten in academe as in construction: by 1980, not a single college or university in the country had lost federal monies for failure to comply with anti-discrimination law.[126] A few leaders later acknowledged that affirmative action had caused no discernible loss of jobs for Jews, and that, quite to the contrary, Jewish women had benefited.[127] Surveying the "impact of affirmative action on Jews" in 1976, an AJC leader concluded that it "has not had a catastrophic impact," though particular individuals might have "suffered mightily." How many, though, "nobody seems to know," as no one had bothered to collect any data beyond the anecdotal. Nor had anyone adduced figures proving that Jewish students had lost out across the board in admission to law or medical school.[128]

If affirmative action proved not to be a calamity for Jewish Americans, the Hoffman letter did have the effect that antiracist activists worried it would: it proved a setback from which the quest for inclusion never recovered its earlier momentum. The anti-quota directive

President Nixon issued in response to the letter became, said Hyman Bookbinder, "the basic bible" for all government agencies. "I have significantly affected the policies of the Civil Service Commission, the Civil Rights Commission, the 'four-agency' policy statement, and other Federal operations," he chided an American Jewish Congress critic who accused him of dovishness.[129] Try as he might to convince civil rights critics that such changes strengthened affirmative action by ending what HEW officials had called "excesses of zeal," the factual record said otherwise. The Hoffman letter produced retrenchment. It helped to sink the Philadelphia Plan, already floundering in Nixon's courtship of the building trades unions. The candidates' widely publicized condemnation of quotas emboldened companies accused of discrimination, as it demoralized the government brokers of inclusion. The EEOC reported that many companies charged with discrimination "were refusing to engage in settlement attempts on the ground that the Administration's policy had changed." Calling the furor over quotas "the Sleeper Issue of '72," *Newsweek* noted that it had inaugurated "the 1st respectable backlash since the Civil Rights Movement began."[130]

After their success with the Nixon administration, the agencies joined *DeFunis v. Odegaard,* one of the first nationally prominent legal challenges to affirmative action in professional school admissions. Reaching the Supreme Court in 1974, the case drew more amicus briefs than any other case in the history of the Supreme Court. Marco DeFunis, a Jewish student, claimed that but for the affirmative action policy at the University of Washington Law School, he would have gained admission, and the ADL, the AJC, and the American Jewish Congress all rallied to his side. Two ADL leaders insisted that "the closing of a door in the face of a Marco DeFunis . . . is no more justifiable, no less wrong, than the closing of a door in the face of a James Meredith" by the all-white University of Mississippi in 1962.[131] In denying that affirmative action goals were a legitimate tool of social justice, DeFunis's attorneys employed racist arguments to make their case. "Any observant person knows that certain races have certain bents or inclinations," their brief stated. "The predominance of Whites in the University law school may well be explained by a lack of inclination or aptitude on the part of Blacks for such studies." The Jewish agencies continued to support his challenge, while "privately . . . explain[ing] our concern about this kind of language."[132] They had moved a long way in a few years.

In aligning with a lawsuit designed to gut affirmative action, the agencies found themselves in other new company. Their allies against the law school program included the National Association of Manufacturers, the U.S. Chamber of Commerce, and the anti–Philadelphia Plan AFL-CIO national leadership, dominated by the building trades. At the same time, they pitted themselves against the progressive alliance that Title VII had made possible: African American and Latino civil rights organizations working alongside feminists and traditional liberal groups together with the most progressive labor unions in the country. Briefs supporting the University of Washington's affirmative action plan came from a coalition that included the SCLC, the American GI Forum, the National Urban League, the NAACP Legal Defense and Education Fund, the NOW Legal Defense and Education Fund, MALDEF, the Puerto Rican Bar Association, the Japanese American Citizens League, the ACLU, the UAW, AFSCME, the United Mine Workers, and the United Farm Workers.[133]

As in the fight against HEW, the agencies' choices divided them not only from feminists and other civil rights organizations, but also from the progressive Jews who took the other side and rushed to fend off the challenge to affirmative action in higher education. "The fundamental issue," said Jack Greenberg, head of the NAACP's Legal Defense and Education Fund, "was whether the country could afford to have a profession in which virtually no blacks were graduates of elite universities." And "would it be good for Jews," Greenberg asked, "if that condition resulted from Jewish activism?" Among the dissenters were also Reform rabbis of the Union of American Hebrew Congregations (UAHC) and, most vocally, the National Council of Jewish women (NCJW). Writing in amicus against DeFunis, they insisted that "the risks of discretionary preferences—though real—are not so large as the risks of endangering all necessary affirmative action programs to bring disadvantaged and minority groups into the mainstream of educational life."[134]

The NCJW's decision to challenge Marco DeFunis's lawsuit exposed how deeply the fracture in the Jewish community now ran. Irate at their officers, some in the NCJW's ranks—and sometimes even their husbands—sounded off. One father sarcastically demanded copies of the organization's brief to give to his son and daughter when they applied to colleges and were turned away. A sense of proportion was not always in evidence. The executive board of the Brooklyn branch complained that "in the last few years many of our own sons, daughters, and close relatives have been systematically excluded from admission to professional schools." Still, the National Affairs Committee stuck by their support of affirmative action, concluding after strenuous debate that it "was the only moral and ethical position" they could take in this case.[135]

In the biggest Supreme Court case of the decade a few years later, similar splits ensued as the male-led Jewish agencies again pitted themselves against the country's civil rights and feminist organizations. This challenge featured a white male, Allan Bakke, who claimed that affirmative action in medical school admissions at the University of California–Davis had discriminated against him. Now the agencies, allied in amicus with right-wing white ethnic organizations of central European heritage long hostile to black civil rights, and sometimes to Jews as well, made the case that institutions should not consider race at all. Instead, they argued, only "true disadvantage" should count. "It was no coincidence," Nathan Glazer wrote soon after, "that the two great conflicts on which the [civil rights] alliance broke up were the cases of Marco DeFunis—applying to law school—and Allan Bakke—applying to medical school. Law and medicine are the two Nirvanas toward which Jews strive. . . . A new principle of selection, one that took minority status into account and reduced, even moderately, Jewish chances to get into these highly selective institutions, was sure to arouse Jewish defense organizations—and Jews generally. And it did."[136] Glazer portrayed a unanimity among Jews that did not exist. Like *DeFunis*, *Bakke* divided them. Albert Vorspan of the UAHC, warning in vain that "no one will gain from emotionalism, vituperation, and polarization on this issue," allied in amicus with the ACLU, the UAW, the UMW, AFSCME, and others against Bakke's complaint.[137]

Yet Glazer had captured the extent to which, terrified of racial proportionalism, the Jewish agencies had turned against racial justice. To make the case that color-blind hiring and admissions were the only fair approach, they denied that being black in America carried any cost or disadvantage in its own right, apart from poverty. As ever, the ADL was the most "hawkish," as its more coalition-minded counterparts put it. But even the more liberal AJC, which supported affirmative action goals while denouncing quotas, felt the pull. Its leaders came to believe that public policies granting any recognition whatsoever to race constituted a menace to Jews in particular and to liberal ideals in general. So much did they want to outlaw race as grounds for positive attention that some even suggested that a "means test for charity," as a critic put it, be applied to gauge "an *individual* applicant's past deprivations due to discrimination." They also developed rhetorical tropes to discount the impact of racial oppression on the life chances and daily experiences of African Americans. The children of black doctors, they said, ought not to gain places that might otherwise go to poor "Appalachian whites," the recurring example, or to "the son of non–English speaking impoverished Russian immigrants." Disgusted, the editor of *Jewish Currents* protested that the American Jewish Congress seemed "willing to take everything into account except race" in its campaign to deny that "discrimination against Blacks . . . [is] a group problem that needs to be faced as such."[138] Although the AJC had in 1972 upheld affirmative action goals as different from quotas, within a few years attitudes hardened, and Bookbinder found himself having to defend not only hiring and admissions goals but also the "positive recruiting" earlier considered eminently reasonable but now subjected to "nit-picking."[139]

Facing challenges now from longtime liberal allies as well as from conservatives, disoriented affirmative action supporters grew defensive. As the 1970s wore on and the "reverse discrimination" challenges spread, they became less willing to acknowledge any weakness that might encourage their opponents. Bombarded with cruel exaggerations about "quotas" for the "unqualified," they became self-protective, and in their caution less open and honest about why hard affirmative action was needed, for fear of giving ground to those who implied that all blacks were underprepared. The Supreme Court furthered the shift. Even as it delivered a body blow to the quest for racial equality in *Bakke*, it profiled new, nonremedial grounds for defense of affirmative action. "Racial and ethnic distinctions of any sort are inherently suspect and call for the most exacting judicial scrutiny," Justice Lewis Powell wrote in explanation of his tie-breaking vote. But where the state had a "purpose or interest" that was "constitutionally permissible and substantial," then some consideration might be given "race or ethnic origin." Powell found "the attainment of a *diverse* student body" to be such a compelling interest, because "the atmosphere of 'speculation, experiment and creation'—so essential to the quality of higher education—is widely believed to be promoted by a diverse student body." A history of exclusion was therefore no longer sufficient grounds for affirmative action goals and timetables, except where there was a clear finding of discrimination by the institution in question, along with identifiable individual victims to be made whole, but race or ethnicity could be considered as a factor in admissions in the service of institutional enhancement. Indeed, in the interest of "diversity," Powell argued, "an Italian-American" might do more for "educational pluralism" than "a particular black applicant."[140] Pushing questions of redistributive justice aside, the Court turned attention away from the disadvantages suffered by minorities and toward the benefits to institutions thus altered. At one level, then, *Bakke* was devastating to proponents of affirmative action. Yet at another, this approach did imply a future for the policy, and even relief from the hostile scrutiny being turned on its beneficiaries. Supporters grasped at the new language as at a life raft on a perilous sea.

In the end, though, the most momentous outcome of the 1972 panic over quotas was the lesson it taught the conservative movement builders who had been organizing since the mid-1950s. What one AJC staffer hoped to avert—that "the bad guys will take advantage of our actions"—came to pass. As he noted, "our many years of genuine, effective work on behalf of equal opportunity never got the kind of space [in the news] that our anti-quota stand is now getting."[141] That was because their anti-quota stand altered the arithmetic of the struggle for inclusion, which at the outset of the 1970s had appeared to involve only addition as feminists and Latino activists joined blacks in pushing for change. The very measures that these groups' leaders now concurred were vital to opening the economic mainstream to all had helped shatter the coalition needed for political success. As the critics advanced an anti–affirmative action argument articulated in terms of fairness, egalitarianism, and opposition to "discrimination" in any form, they provided conservatives with more persuasive grounds from which to oppose inclusion.

Over the next several years that formulation would rescue the conservative movement from what had until then seemed a conundrum:

how to oppose civil rights initiatives without appearing to be selfish, backward-looking, and bigoted enemies of reasonable egalitarian reform. Precisely because of Jews' history of persecution, their organizations spoke with a moral authority on civil rights matters that the established right lacked. Jews, as Eleanor Holmes Norton put it, "were far and away the best whites."[142] When Jewish organizations argued cogently against affirmative action in the name of civil rights tradition, gentile conservatives took note and began to recast their arguments. After 1972, men like Kilpatrick and Buckley turned the label "quotas" into a kind of talisman whose deployment could stop discussion of injustice. Stigmatizing the means used to achieve equality, it aborted efforts at redistribution of opportunities and resources. The quota scare so narrowed the range of permissible discussion about how to address inequality that the creation story first developed by neoconservatives became widely believed as a true account of civil rights history. Spread far and wide as it was, that interpretation blanketed the more complex reality. In time, sheer repetition convinced many whites that the movement had been "hijacked" away from its founding purpose.

The Jewish organizations that fought affirmative action in the name of racial justice at least proposed other routes to inclusion, such as greater investment in primary and secondary education and expanded job-training programs. As the American Jewish Congress put it in criticizing "preferential admissions" policies for minority students, "we have an obligation to offer alternatives."[143] They put little effort into working for such alternatives compared to what they expended in seeking to limit affirmative action, but they did at least acknowledge injustice that needed righting. The non-Jewish conservatives whose sails filled with wind from the flap in academe would do nothing of the sort. They found in the new anti–affirmative action discourse a tool to block genuine equality and a magnet to attract a popular white following in their own quest for power. The battle over higher education thus tutored the right in what had eluded its standard-bearers throughout the glory years of the civil rights movement: a morally and politically legitimate language for continued racial and gender exclusion.

~ 7

Conservatives Shift from "Massive Resistance" to "Color-Blindness"

*W*HEN INVITED TO WRITE on conservative prospects in early 1972, James Kilpatrick seemed almost morose. "How fares American conservatism today?" the syndicated columnist was asked. "Poorly," he answered. "The cause is not lost," he insisted. "But mostly we fight and fall back, resist and give way." Even with Republican electoral success, liberalism just kept advancing. In the eyes of movement conservatives, nothing seemed to stop "encroaching statism." Richard Nixon's first term was a grave disappointment to them, the congressional conservative bloc was in "disarray," and Supreme Court decisions were making it difficult to govern the country. "The virus of egalitarianism by government decree" was contaminating more and more areas of American life. For his part, William F. Buckley, Jr., portrayed himself at the opening of the new decade as "a conservative grown up in the knowledge that victories are not for us." Yet somehow the outlook changed; at mid-decade, one conservative marveled that his fellows had become, "of all things, optimistic."[1] By 1980, Buckley, Kilpatrick, and their fellows had achieved what once seemed impossible: the Goldwater wing of the GOP was about to gain the White House, with the right's standard-bearer, former California governor Ronald Reagan, elected president.[2] How did this reversal of fortune occur?

Faced with sweeping realignments among the long excluded, some

225

conservative intellectuals engineered a new defensive alliance against the model of society and government that black civil rights activism had popularized. Just as supporters of inclusion had learned that the road to eliminating inequality went through race-conscious and gender-conscious policy, so defenders of exclusivity now learned that its best protection could be found in the embrace of formal equality.[3] Reaching out to pull in neoconservatives and business leaders along with many white working-class people, conservative movement strategists began pushing back (but never out) the openly racist southern conservatives who had proved so important to their movement in the 1950s and who had joined the GOP en masse after passage of the Civil Rights Act. Their eclipse, in turn, enabled the right to appropriate the language of civil rights and racial justice, turning its power against its original bearers in a kind of political jujitsu. Less and less frequently did conservatives argue that affirmative action violated property rights or elevated racial inferiors, as they had before. Rather, they insisted that it abused the civil rights of others and was itself discriminatory, with Jews and later Asian Americans put forward as victims. Once having made this shift, the right could do what it never had before: attract highly educated people of color. Their numbers in the movement were not large, but their presence persuaded many wavering whites that the conservative cause was no longer tainted with racism.

Appearances could mislead, though, for at the very moment when conservative leadership was becoming more demographically representative, both the movement and the GOP lined up more sharply against policies to promote inclusion of minorities and women. The party that had presided over the Philadelphia Plan and for decades backed the Equal Rights Amendment for women now turned against both. Minorities were welcome only if they opposed affirmative action, and women only if they defended the gender ideology against which feminists had rebelled. Meanwhile, the conservative cause attracted new interest from business leaders and many white workers, if for very different reasons, owing in part to the economic crisis of the early 1970s. Acquiring resources from corporate leaders, conservatives copied techniques from the movement for inclusion in order to reach the rank and file. In particular, they found sympathetic plaintiffs for lawsuits to overturn anti-discrimination policies. In *Weber v. United Steelworkers of America*, the star player would be a white working-class man who accused his union and his employer of discrimination for their joint effort to bring women and black men into the economic main- stream. Even as affirmative action policies continued to spread in the 1970s, their critics mobilized more effectively than ever before.

～ NONE OF THIS was foreseeable at the outset of the decade when Kilpatrick and Buckley brooded about the movement's prospects. On the contrary, the impasse they had reached notwithstanding, con- servatives persisted in habits developed in the 1950s. Writing in 1972 for the conservative quarterly *Modern Age*, the historian Clyde Wilson railed against the "coerced mingling of the races." He upheld "a favor- able view" of American slavery to counter the "negative stereotype" of the plantation South he found spreading in scholarly histories. The real problem for blacks, he said, was their "deterioration after slavery." Other neo-Confederate conservatives assailed inclusion in the same pages. The English professor M. E. Bradford took pride in being an "impenitent conservative Southerner" still angry about the outcome of "the War between the States." Any intentional effort by government to assist blacks was doomed to disaster—whether emancipation, Recon- struction, or the current civil rights effort. "Millennial schemes for the mechanical elevation of racial minorities," he insisted, "are the most dangerous of all reformist undertakings."[4]

Conservatives affirmed interest in and respect for the body of thought which asserted the biological incapacity of African Americans for more demanding employment. Richard Herrnstein condemned what he viewed as an all-pervasive "extreme, unrestrained environmen- talism" sustaining "the egalitarian orthodoxy." He tried to blast away the foundations of then-current civil rights policies by drawing atten- tion to "the role of genes in human society." That role was a simple, even inescapable "biological reality," he explained: "the inheritance of intellectual capacity." Herrnstein pronounced his research on intelli- gence "lethal" to hopes for a more egalitarian society. While several conservatives defended "the hardheaded analysis" of Herrnstein and like writers, no leading conservative criticized their work.[5] Rather, a few looked to racist states abroad for better models of dealing with what they claimed was inevitable inequality. The "Bantustans" of South Africa seemed to James Burnham a much "more promising" way to ac- commodate black demands than "forced integration."[6]

Neo-Confederates and some northern conservatives saw much ground for hope in the electoral unrest with which the new decade opened. Looking to the South, they took heart from the conversion of white voters to Republicanism spurred by the Civil Rights Act. The GOP was now attracting not only conservative businessmen but also white textile workers angry at the desegregation of their plants and their children's schools. George Wallace gave voice to that anger in his 1968 and 1972 presidential campaigns. Wallace polled well not just in the South, where he was known as the Alabama governor who had stood in the schoolhouse door vowing, "Segregation now, segregation tomorrow, and segregation forever!" but in parts of the North as well, where his blend of rough populism, racial resentment, and aggressive patriotism touched many white voters across class lines. For a time in the early fall, some were predicting that he might win as many as one hundred votes in the electoral college. In the end, he lost ground to a retooled Nixon-Agnew campaign, but he had made his point. At least 10 percent of the electorate outside the South and more within it was willing to defy the major parties for a right-wing alternative. Though not enough to win an election, that was plenty to alter the national political debate.[7]

In 1969, a young political analyst named Kevin Phillips, who advocated a "populist conservatism," offered Republicans a region-by-region guide for exploiting white dissatisfaction with the Democrats over "the Negro socioeconomic revolution." The election of 1968 had registered "an epochal shifting of national gears," Phillips said. "The Negro problem" had split the New Deal bloc and opened the South to Republicans. "The new popular majority is white and conservative," he advised. With this "New Right," as he christened it, the party of Lincoln no longer had to worry about black votes; it could win with whites alone. Heeding Phillips, *National Review* publisher William Rusher embraced George Wallace as "the leading spokesman of social conservatism." Rusher hoped to win the former governor's following for a new conservative "majority party" that would unite "economic and social conservatives" in hostility to the "non-productive" classes, among them welfare "parasite[s]" and the professoriat. His social imaginary pitted "establishment WASPs plus their minority group allies [on one side] against middle Americans and hyphenated [white] ethnics," on the other.[8] Richard Viguerie volunteered to organize Wallace's direct mail campaigns, raising some $7 million between 1973 and 1976. Wallace's appeal, he said, showed how populist-sounding talk could build the right. "We are no longer working to preserve the status quo," declared Viguerie. "We are radicals working to overthrow the power structure of this country."[9]

Yet not everyone on the right was pleased. William F. Buckley scorned Kevin Phillips. The two accused each other of what each one prided himself on: "elitism" for the former, "populism" for the latter. Indeed, Phillips aimed to distinguish his "New Right" from the "Old Right" of "Squire Willy" and his "Ivy League five-syllable word polishers."[10] Buckley himself was horrified by the crude populism of the rough-cut Alabamian George Wallace, whose very "uncouthness" and air of racial violence seemed the source of "his general popularity." Style aside, in economics Wallace was a New Deal Democrat, and Buckley attacked him for his "enormous enthusiasm for federal handouts."[11]

Wallace repelled other elite Americans as well. A *Human Events* poll in 1968 reported that the vast majority of leading conservatives spurned his bid for the presidency. Some no doubt remembered how Barry Goldwater's candidacy had sent big business rushing to the Democrats, who understood that multinational corporations required a powerful federal government. After moving toward the Democratic Party in the mid-1960s from fear of Goldwaterism and shock over the depth of black anger, large corporate interests began to rethink their interests in the 1970s.[12] Also, in adapting to a post–Civil Rights and Voting Right Acts polity, in which black voters might determine the fate of allies such as Senator Strom Thurmond of South Carolina, some conservatives likely grew edgy about having their cause represented by a man widely derided as an open hatemonger. The doubters sensed that they were heading toward a dead end, lacking even suitable language for debating politics in a nation in which most people had come to think basic equality a fair proposition.

The strategic-minded could see other social changes that might advance or retard the conservative movement, depending on how its leaders played their hands. More and more Americans were quitting the "Rust Belt" areas of Democratic strength in the Northeast and Midwest for the Sunbelt, itself long a home to various strands of conservatism. Ever weaker in American workplaces since its peak in the mid-1950s, organized labor was less and less a powerful voice in politics, creating a vacuum the right could fill. As important for long-term calculations, the spiraling population in the suburbs across the United States was changing the electoral base of both parties.[13] Whereas demagoguery offended white suburban voters, mild-mannered moderates appealed to them. So, too, did a "color-blind" approach to the defense of privilege that stressed the legitimacy of "earned" class advantages such as acreage-zoned communities and locally funded, socially homogenous suburban public schools.[14]

No one better sensed the flaws of the old conservative approach than the movement's founder, a skilled sailor used to tacking in fresh winds. William F. Buckley, Jr., began framing conservatism in a new way in 1969—as a defense of old-fashioned liberalism. The "new conservatism," he argued, must go beyond fighting communism and championing capitalist enterprise to uphold traditional American commitments on which liberals, he claimed, had lately defaulted. These included "the democratic process," "due process," and "upward mobility," all of which came into play in civil rights efforts in post–Jim Crow America. He observed the work of the neoconservatives with mounting admiration and excitement as Irving Kristol, for example, argued that conservatives were defending liberal institutions from liberals' own mounting complaints. By 1974, Kilpatrick could speak of "contemporary Conservatives" as "old-fashioned 18th Century Liberals" who believed that "'equality' ought not to be achieved by state coercion."[15]

The liaison between old and new conservatives began tentatively, the awkwardness owing to long-standing Jewish fears of anti-Semitism on the right.[16] Yet having for years personally sought to rid his cause of anti-Semitism, Buckley could court Jews in good conscience. He was helped by the upheavals on college campuses. They narrowed the distance that once prevailed between conservatively inclined Jewish intellectuals and the movement he was building, which was populated almost entirely by Christians. "There is nobody in America doing better than you what so much needs to be done," Buckley praised the philosopher Sidney Hook, then leading the fight against affirmative action in academe.[17] Other new friends of the right included Irving Kristol, co-editor of *The Public Interest*, and Norman Podhoretz, editor of *Commentary*. Buckley also won their gratitude by defending the scholarship of Daniel Patrick Moynihan and Nathan Glazer from allegations of racism. Looking back, Moynihan said, "Glazer and I began to notice that we were getting treated in *National Review* with a much higher level of intellectual honesty" than in liberal and left publications. Jacob Neusner of Brown University told Buckley that "on the educational matters which mean so much to me, *NR* stands for the truly liberal position and for reason." In fact, he found "the range of agreement . . . far wider" than the remaining differences.[18]

When James Buckley, William's younger brother, won the U.S. Senate race in New York as the candidate of the Conservative Party in 1970, he took aim at what he called the "affirmative action shock troops" and pronounced their efforts "wrong, wrong, wrong." The policy, he said, went against "everything that the civil rights movement has sought to achieve." If the younger Buckley echoed the critics of inclusion in higher education, it was partly because he had studied their texts. Indeed, he had the *Commentary* articles and speeches of Sidney Hook, Earl Rabb, Paul Seabury, and others entered into the *Congressional Record*. Condemning "quotas" as "reverse discrimination," the senator declared that they "reward the untalented or lazy."[19] Affirmative action proved critical to this developing alliance because it was one issue on which all neoconservatives agreed and, furthermore, saw eye to eye with old-style conservatives.

The issue also offered political opportunities that others simply did not. In fighting "reverse discrimination," conservatives could achieve ideological victories of wider value. To see how, one needs to appreciate the strategic savvy of some on the right. Years before, in a confidential memo to fellow core staff at *National Review*, Frank Meyer had explored how the movement might use particular issues as "transmission belts" to spread a general worldview from their small group to "people at all levels of society." The biggest challenge was "bringing into action and effectiveness wide forces who, while they do not think of themselves as conservative, can be led in effective struggle on specific issues where the bankruptcy of the Liberal leadership of the nation makes their policy obviously disastrous." In short, the trick was to find issues that would allow "the magnification of the influence of [the conservative] movement through 'united front' tactics." Or, to put it more bluntly, the aim of the united front approach was "to reach those who would otherwise not listen to us."[20]

A dozen years later, conservatives looked to affirmative action for

just such an effect on "those who would otherwise not listen to us"—
and got it. As a practical matter, affirmative action was a far lower priority for them in day-to-day organizing and argument than waging the
cold war abroad and attacking the welfare state at home. In point of
fact, the toll of the policy was not large, either, because so-called reverse discrimination occurred on an inconsequential scale. Of those
cases that reached the courts, presumably the strongest, one later Labor Department study found that "several were brought by whites or
males who were less qualified than the females or minorities who obtained the position."[21] Moreover, not all conservative-minded Americans frowned on such policies. Some bulwarks of social order such as
the U.S. Army seemed to have made their peace with the need for
greater inclusion and with affirmative action as a tool to achieve it.
That such a hierarchical, traditional organization run by men known
for conservative temperaments remade itself into the nation's most integrated major institution in these years and, as two military sociologists note, "the only place in American life where whites are routinely
bossed around by blacks" underscores the singularity of the political
right's crusade.[22]

Attacks on affirmative action, in fact, had strategic utility for the
conservative cause. Here was a handle that could turn other gears, that
could "reach those who would otherwise not listen to us," for conservatives stood for goals that alienated many potential followers. They opposed widely enjoyed entitlements from New Deal and Great Society
programs, sought to reverse reforms such as civil rights that had majority support, and aimed to undo federal regulation not just of discrimination but also of old-age insurance, labor relations, pollution, consumer fraud, occupational health and safety, and more. The builders of
the right used their attacks on affirmative action to accomplish ends
whose value to them went well beyond the matter at hand.[23]

For conservatives, then, pushing back civil rights gains was both a
goal in itself and a step necessary to other ends. Citing affirmative action "quotas" as a heinous case in point, M. E. Bradford observed that
"the 'civil rights revolution'" was uniquely dire because it more than
anything else had got Americans over their national aversion to using
federal power to achieve social betterment. Conservatives wanted to
restore that aversion, and this issue proved an ideal wedge to widen
suspicion of all state efforts to promote equality. Senator Orrin Hatch

of Utah framed it this way: "Affirmative action is a symbol and a symptom of the regulatory socialism which, sprouting with the New Deal, has grown like a kud[z]u vine until our institutions and their classical liberal inspiration are on the point of vanishing." Whereas the old screeds against the New Deal state had tangled conservatives in trying to argue the majority of whites out of government help to which they felt entitled, the affirmative action attacks employed more favorable math. A large number of white males (and, thanks to shared racial attitudes, almost as many white women) could be persuaded that efforts at remedying exclusion had harmed them, their children, or their friends, however weak the empirical evidence. Conservative movement intellectuals encouraged such resentments. When one Atlanta man complained that the problem since *Brown v. Board of Education* "was not race, but the have-nots taking what the haves had produced and achieved," to the point where many "of us middle class people" have been "liquidated," Kilpatrick sympathized. "I know what it is to have one of my sons refused a job for which he was qualified, merely to give the job to a less qualified black."[24]

The conservative effort made the most mainstream, achievement-oriented, work-seeking solution of the social movements for inclusion look like a venal bid for "handouts" from innocent whites. The policy of affirmative action, lectured education professor Allan Ornstein, "rewards the dumb, lazy, and unambitious at the expense of the smart, talented, and ambitious."[25] With such arguments against affirmative action, conservatives reassociated minorities (and, to a lesser degree, women) with the "undeserving" label that the movements for equality had fought free of in the sixties and early seventies. For all the talk of color-blindness, their arguments made clear to minority and female newcomers that their race and gender would never be overlooked but, rather, would regularly be thrown in their faces as alleged evidence that they had entered illegitimately. By repeatedly insisting that these newcomers could not be respected, white critics sought to ensure that they *would not* be respected. If beneficiaries of affirmative action could be framed as undeserving claimants of special "privilege" trying to get something for nothing, government's attempt to achieve greater equality lost its justification, and the state itself became suspect. Senator Jesse Helms of North Carolina situated efforts at inclusion on a continuum that included the New Deal and ran all the way to socialism. "For forty years an unending barrage of 'deals'—the New Deal, the Fair Deal, the New Frontier, and the Great Society, not to mention court decisions tending in the same direction," he charged in 1976, had "installed a gigantic scheme for redistributing the wealth that rewards the indolent and penalizes the hard-working."[26]

As conservatives claimed that affirmative action was wrong, they rejected all talk of disadvantage, of deep-rooted social inequality built on race or gender, and what many anti–affirmative action Jewish Americans had recognized as "the debt society owes to those previously discriminated against."[27] Kilpatrick and his fellows told those aspiring to better jobs and lives to rely instead on the blind beneficence of the market in human labor. And they suggested that anyone who remained excluded simply lacked the capacity or the determination to advance. Whereas some liberals had criticized affirmative action while backing other reforms, conservatives criticized it in order to end reform altogether.

Attacking affirmative action on grounds borrowed from neoconservatives offered an additional advantage for a movement known to have been on the wrong side of the now widely honored civil rights struggle and hostile to its most beloved leader, Martin Luther King, Jr. Conservatives could finally acknowledge that injustice to minority men and all women had once existed (as Ernest Van den Haag put it, "in the distant past"), while aggressively denying that it still existed and insisting that "current generations can bear no responsibility" for what their predecessors did "other than to discontinue it." Conservatives thus used affirmative action to achieve modernization without reform, deserting their former battlements to accommodate shifts in public sentiment, while still refusing to let in those who were outside, beyond the castle wall.[28]

The affirmative action struggle also offered a way to escape the unpopularity caused by long-standing conservative contempt for equality, a value the right had universally abhorred as a threat to social order, limited government, and the standing of men like themselves. As late as 1969, Kilpatrick insisted that "the international obsession with egalitarianism" was one of the curses of the day. The very idea of "egalitarianism" was a "perversion" of Western and Christian traditions of individualism, Frank Meyer preached. It was an abomination that "leads inexorably to barbarism and darkness."[29] In a nation whose founding text proclaimed that "all men are created equal," let alone in a world overthrowing colonialism, such elitism was a recipe for marginality. The neoconservatives who mobilized against affirmative action in the early 1970s lighted a way out of this trap. Their careful parsing of the meaning of equality made equality of opportunity alone legitimate, while stigmatizing equality of result as a socialist-inspired anathema. So dangerous was "the New Equality," said Robert Nisbet, that it was producing a "new despotism" in America, "the greatest single threat to liberty and social initiative."[30]

The constriction of equality, in turn, allowed for an interpretation of racial fairness with which defenders of the existing social order could live: "color-blindness." By mid-decade, even Patrick Buchanan, one of the more incendiary voices on the right, was extolling color-blindness while railing against blacks: "As for an end to racial conflict in America, the first step along that road is to make the government of the United States color-blind." The vision of procedural equality in a system in which race was irrelevant had roots in the campaign of Jewish agencies to make only achievement, not background, relevant to access. But color-blindness also had a less savory prehistory on the right, in strategies of "nonracial" opposition to the inclusion of African Americans that were very much concerned with shoring up white privilege. In masterminding "massive resistance" to school desegregation, for example, Kilpatrick had exulted in his constitutional theory of "interposition"—which posited that state governments had the right to deny the authority of federal policies such as the desegregation mandated by *Brown v. Board of Education*—as an approach that "transcends the race issue."[31] When invited in 1986 by the law professor Randall Kennedy to comment on whether he had "reconsidered" his views, Kilpatrick answered, "In recent years I have concentrated my efforts on urging a color-blind view of the law," pointing to his opposition to affirmative action and busing as examples. To another writer Kilpatrick affirmed that he had "long ago repudiated the 'racism' [his quotation marks] with which I was identified at one time"—a repudiation that was less than ringing.[32]

The vision of "color-blind" formal equality thus helped conservatives refashion their appeal for a new era. Many now moved in campaigns against affirmative action and school busing for integration from proud anti-egalitarianism and celebration of hierarchy to a populist-sounding stress on equal rights that was striking for its sudden avidity. Conservatives had worked to kill or curb key reforms "the people" had fought for in the past: New Deal social programs, labor's right to organize and strike, federal support for the schools, consumer and environmental protections, civil rights, and more. Now, oddly, men who had taken part in this offensive were all at once clamoring for the ear of the common people. Irving Kristol explained the newfound charm of the masses this way: "Populist dissent today," he said in the late seventies, "is directed against liberal politics" that were "too committed to equality."[33] Without the race factor, the turnabout makes no sense.

Above all, leading conservative spokesmen began moving away from open racial animus. Realizing the ground to be gained by giving up the defense of prejudice and discrimination, they found a better way to oppose egalitarian social policies than simply red-baiting advocates as enemies of property, a practice that seemed ever more atavistic. "Color-blindness," in contrast, created a pleasing sound of fairness that could persuade anti-elitist whites while obscuring the history that had produced demands for race-conscious solutions. Its simple catechism could be easily learned; "I am getting to be like the Catholic convert," Kirkpatrick marveled, "who became more Catholic than the Pope." He admonished a supporter of affirmative action, "If it is wrong to discriminate by reason of race or sex, well, then, it is wrong to discriminate by reason of race or sex." Color-blindness could even be used to paint the "egalitarians" as "worse racists—much worse racists—than the old Southern bigots." Kilpatrick claimed in 1979 that "the bureaucrats of HEW have done more to destroy good race relations in the past ten years than the Ku Klux Klan did in a century."[34]

The conservative bid for power in the 1970s elaborated on the creation myth about affirmative action first advanced by neoconservatives. This story had to explain how the inclusive measures promoted by HEW, the EEOC, and the OFCC came to exist. Its burden was to show that the impetus for affirmative action came not from victims of injustice and social movements of ordinary people seeking fairness, but rather from a sinister alliance of scheming government operatives and ivory-tower academics. "This growing national problem," Senator James Buckley told Congress, "is entirely the creation of over-zealous bureaucrats." The best storyteller was Ernest Van den Haag.

While allowing that affirmative action policies were "aided and abetted" by guilt-ridden whites and supported by "groups which, rightly or wrongly, felt discriminated against in the past," he avowed that "in the main these are creatures of the federal bureaucracy and judiciary." The "bureaucracy," he said, "actually gave birth to the illegitimate child; the judiciary adopted and legalized" the "monstrosity."[35] In one swoop, this story excised from historical memory the popular struggles that had produced the policy, undercut with its allusions to sex and bastardy the moral standing of those who had developed tools to combat the problem, turned sympathetic brokers of inclusion into power-mad authoritarians, and, not least, set the sights of those who had qualms about the policy on the much bigger conservative prize of shrinking the federal welfare state. The creation story could not accommodate those such as Wharlest Jackson and George Metcalfe who had risked their lives for good jobs, or Sallie Pearl Lewis, who had to sue in federal court to get dangerous, low-wage textile work, let alone the Mexican American workers passed over for good factory jobs, the flight attendants who were fired for marrying, or the female scholars barred from professions for which they had spent years training. They no longer existed in the tale that conservatives related to Americans.

Painting those who sought fair treatment and a chance at upward mobility through work as arrogant elitists, even thieves, was a perverse but effective strategy. Pinning a collective name on the troublemakers in order to focus aggression, Kristol argued that all the fuss about equality was coming from "the new class": bureaucrats and intellectuals with suspect motives. "It is not really equality that interests" members of the new class, he asserted. Rather, they "pursue power in the name of equality" in a scheme to usurp authority from the "business community."[36] Like a wave washing over writing in the sand, this revisionist account erased the grievances of women and minority men as it implied that all the trouble came from outside agitators, meddling government bureaucrats, and ivory-tower academics. Since African Americans themselves (let alone Mexican Americans or white women) had never sought economic inclusion with affirmative action, the logic went, repeal would therefore hurt no one but the elite "new class." In making efforts at inclusion appear the actions of a power-hungry state invading private life, conservative leaders played to traditional American fears of autocratic government.

As a rhetorical strategy, such arguments proved infinitely more effective than the case against civil rights as an infringement on property rights and white superiority which conservatives had advanced in the 1950s and 1960s. Indeed, as declaring oneself in favor of color-blindness became a more common ploy, those who continued to argue on the grounds of violated property rights, such as Robert Bork and the Young Americans for Freedom, came to seem increasingly archaic and exotic.[37] Moved in part by hatred of affirmative action, many neoconservatives, over time, grew less "neo" and more like old-style conservatives in their antipathy to government as an agent of social justice and their enthusiasm for unrestrained markets and corporate power.[38]

Just as the right was developing more unified, popular, and persuasive grounds for attacking liberal government, many in the corporate world, roused by the economic crisis that began in late 1973 and extended into early 1975, were feeling a need for new political allies. Many scholars describe the ensuing seventeen tough months of recession as a turning point, "a watershed event in American political economy." Not only was it the worst downturn since the Great Depression; it was also the closing parenthesis on the long boom the United States had been enjoying since the end of World War II. As such, it aggravated existing fears about deeper structural problems: declining productivity, runaway inflation, and falling profitability in newly competitive world markets. It opened a frightening era of "stagflation," a new word coined to capture a mystifying combination of inflation and stagnation, the Scylla and Charybdis between which macroeconomic policy had long sought to steer. Sharply rising oil prices imposed by the Organization of Petroleum Exporting Countries (OPEC) compounded the sense of anxiety and weakening American power.[39] By 1975, writes one business historian, "a genuine sense of crisis existed among the nation's leading CEOs." Reacting to a felt emergency, they rallied to a degree never seen before, and looked to conservatives for intellectual guidance. In hopes of restoring profitability and increasing the competitive edge of U.S. firms in world markets, they set out after 1973, in effect, to reverse those aspects of American politics and policy most identified with the New Deal. Business interests and conservative ambitions thus coalesced in what one writer has called "a realignment of elites."[40]

Uneasy in a sagging economy, many businesspeople bristled at government regulation and came to see that just as the social movements had to organize to get redress, they too would have to organize. The new laws to open good employment to minority men and women of all groups in the sixties, after all, had stimulated a much larger turn to more active government, which resulted in workplace safety laws, environmental and consumer protections, energy use guidelines, and other efforts to enact evolving popular visions of the good society. Within a few years of the EEOC's creation came other such federal agencies: the Environmental Protection Agency (EPA), the Occupational Safety and Health Administration (OSHA), and the Consumer Product Safety Commission. All had busy staff and a modicum of power. Now, big business leaders set about creating their own unified mobilization.[41] One of those who goaded the Chamber of Commerce to engage in politics was a staff member, the future Supreme Court justice Lewis Powell. In a strategic memo he warned that "business and the [free] enterprise system are in deep trouble." Powell urged the Chamber to use the courts more aggressively to advance business goals and to cultivate academics who could bring back legitimacy to corporate interests. The larger purpose was "the preservation of the system itself." Powell wrote, perhaps reflecting on the centrality of litigation to the cultural transformation sparked by the widening struggle for inclusion, "The judiciary may be the most important instrument for social, economic, and political change." Following his advice, the "sleeping giant" of American business roused itself. Over the decade, the Chamber of Commerce quadrupled in membership, tripled in budget, and became immensely more influential in Washington.[42] It was, one observer said, "a revolt of the haves."[43]

With prodding from movement conservatives, business leaders began to subsidize a whole infrastructure of institutions to reshape the national debate. Joseph Coors is a case in point. Won to conservatism in the 1950s when he read Russell Kirk's *The Conservative Mind*, he fought off fair employment boycotts by Mexican American groups and labor in the 1960s and early 1970s. Angry at the direction the nation was taking, Coors urged his corporate peers to recognize that "our system of free enterprise is being threatened" and "our own government is causing most of our headaches." To fight the "outrageous anti-business legislation" of OSHA, the EPA, and the EEOC, he donated thousands of dollars to the Committee for the Survival of a Free Congress as an "investment" in the future, and he contributed to Ronald Reagan's first presidential bid. He also gave Paul Weyrich over half a million dollars to launch the Heritage Foundation in 1973.[44] Most of today's conservative think tanks got their start in the early 1970s: after Heritage came the Manhattan Institute for Policy Research and the Cato Institute, both in 1977.[45] Others, already established, attracted more generous funding, including the Hoover Institution, begun in 1919, and the American Enterprise Institute (AEI), founded in 1943. By 1979, the AEI had a staff of 160 and a budget of nearly $10 million, and was "matched brain-for-brain" with the mainstream Brookings Institution. As "federal regulation" became "a major preoccupation" of the AEI, the ratio of corporate to private foundation funding that kept it going rose from 25 percent to 38 percent over the 1970s. That funding enabled the institute to communicate the conservative perspective through a broadly aired television roundtable program, a weekly radio show run by six hundred stations, op-ed articles in one hundred newspapers every few weeks, a number of periodicals, and fifteen resident scholars. The first was "senior fellow" Irving Kristol, soon joined by other neoconservatives whose social science credentials were especially valued.[46] The foundations funded and aggressively promoted conservative books that changed public policy discourse, including those by Charles Murray, Jude Wanniski, George Gilder, Dinesh D'Souza, Robert Bork, and David Horowitz. All in all, by the mid-1970s the right was gaining what the left was losing: activists, money, institutional support, political momentum, and confidence. Collectively, conservatives had mounted what one commentator describes as "a sustained attack on the use of government money and regulation to solve social problems."[47]

Between the new egalitarian-sounding conservative arguments and the lushly funded think tanks, the right had resources to lure a new constituency: conservatives of color. The first and most formidable was the UCLA economist Thomas Sowell, whose life embodied the complexities of class mobility in postwar black America. Born to working-class parents in North Carolina, he moved to Harlem, where he left high school to take factory and delivery work to help his family. He then entered the Marine Corps during the Korean War. Thanks to the GI Bill, he later went to college at Howard University, then Harvard, and went on to earn a Ph.D. at the University of Chicago in 1968, where his mentor was the free-market economist Milton Friedman. Sowell entered the national affirmative action debate in 1972, when he took offense at a mimeographed letter from Swarthmore College announcing a search for "a black economist." He wrote back in protest that "many a self-respecting black scholar would never accept an offer like this." "You and I both know that it takes many years to create a qualified faculty member of any color," he wrote, "and no increased demand is going to increase the supply immediately unless you lower quality." He asked, "Now what good is going to come from lower standards that will make 'black' equivalent to 'substandard' in the eyes of black and white students alike?" As a man who had struggled hard against the odds to achieve success, he was a powerful messenger for the right's argument. The American Enterprise Institute commissioned Sowell to do more research on the subject, and he soon became a prolific polemicist. He brought his supply-side explanation for the problems of black America to wide audiences in books and newspaper columns in which he blamed welfare, affirmative action, rent control, and the minimum wage for blacks' difficulty in getting ahead. The only route to freedom, he insisted, was self-reliance and a slow accretion of education, skill, business knowledge, and capital. By the end of the decade, he had won appointment as a senior research fellow at the Hoover Institution, which enabled him to devote himself to writing full-time.[48]

Sowell's example inspired others, among them Clarence Thomas, who considered Sowell "not only my intellectual mentor but my salvation." Before reading Sowell, he said, "I thought I was totally insane." Others followed, among them Glenn Loury and Linda Chavez, a Latina mentored by the neoconservatives Albert Shanker and William Bennett.[49] Whereas Nixon-era Republicans of color, such as Art Fletcher, had helped to develop affirmative action, the new cohort gained fame by seeking its abolition.

∾ TO WIN OVER election-swaying numbers of working-class white Americans was more of a challenge for conservatives than amassing a tiny retinue of spokespersons of color. Fortunately for the right, the tighter economy after 1973 set many lower-income white Americans on edge. As layoffs reached levels not seen since the 1930s, especially in manufacturing industries, job anxiety mounted. By early 1975, more than half of the Chrysler Corporation's employees had been laid off and were out of work. "Does anybody in his right mind believe we can solve the civil rights revolution in the framework of mass unemployment?" the labor leader and civil rights backer Walter Reuther had asked a dozen years before. "We will tear asunder the fabric of American democracy if the contest is going to be whether a white worker is going to walk the streets unemployed or a black worker is going to walk the streets unemployed."[50]

The layoffs and the long-term economic restructuring that was under way hit the struggle for inclusion in its weakest spot: the failure of the broader social reform program from which affirmative action had come. Advocates had pushed for what Martin Luther King called "radical restructuring" not simply because they believed it the only way to deliver justice to blacks for centuries of deprivation, but also because they understood it as vital to avert white backlash. White men had enjoyed privileges denied others for so long and with so much cultural support that some reaction to ending those advantages was predictable among white working-class men, who also suffered from inequality and feared for their families' security. That was why when King in the Birmingham struggle insisted that "something special" must be done for blacks, he did so in the context of calling for "a broad-based and gigantic Bill of Rights for the Disadvantaged." Taking the idea from the GI Bill of Rights, which gave such generous government help to veterans after World War II, King insisted that his program include the "millions of white poor" who were so "confused . . . by prejudice that they have supported their own oppressors," warning that "nothing would hold back the forces of progress in American life more effectively than a schism between the Negro and organized labor."[51]

This understanding of the inseparability of racial justice and class justice animated efforts from the National Urban League's Domestic Marshall Plan and the A. Philip Randolph Institute's Freedom Budget to King's participation in the Poor People's March and the ongoing coalition pushing for full employment legislation in the 1970s.[52] Awareness of the need to alleviate all inequality reached beyond the ranks of activists, as when the writer James Baldwin described white working people of the South as "the real victims" of what he called "one of the most cunning bargains ever struck in history."[53] Yet white America at large proved more sympathetic to appeals to tear down unfair barriers to competition than calls to construct greater equality of rewards. Activists were unable to amass powerful enough backing to overcome fierce business and conservative hostility to the kind of radical transformation needed to achieve equity for the excluded without backlash from less well-off whites.

Thus it was not difficult for conservatives to paint affirmative action policies as taking from white men, for the lack of wider redistribution made zero-sum interpretations plausible. With them a right that had seemed so marginal only a few years before made unprecedented headway. By decade's end, its spokespersons had persuaded a majority of voters to support a candidate whose policies would produce across-the-board shifts in resources and power that benefited corporations at the expense of working-class people. Arguing against affirmative action and related policies and promising a strong America in an uneasy world, conservatives built a following for a once unpalatable program.[54]

The contribution of men such as Kristol and Podhoretz proved critical in winning sizable numbers of white working people to the right, for, having grown up in working-class and lower-middle-class neighborhoods, they understood the residents far better than elite old-timers like Buckley. For one thing, they appreciated the pull of communal affiliation. They could defend commitment to preserving neighborhood homogeneity and local schools against fair housing and school busing initiatives in more respectable terms than white supremacists such as George Wallace. Still appealing to tribal emotion, they did so in a register of pride rather than hatred. "Jews find their interests and those of formally less liberal neighbors becoming similar," Nathan Glazer wrote in 1964. "They both have an interest in maintaining an area restricted to their own kind; an interest in managing the friendship and educational experiences of their children; an interest in passing on advantages in money and skills to them." Neoconservatives appealed to less affluent Americans not in class terms, as the left did, but in ethno-religious terms, cultivating a new kind of right-wing populist identity politics to counter the identity politics on the left. The American Jewish Committee applied this approach to affirmative action when its legal director sought support for the *DeFunis* reverse discrimination lawsuit from leaders of "white ethnic organizations" of Poles, Italians, Lithuanians, Ukrainians, and others.[55]

Such ethnic organizations had become increasingly vocal in their own right, voicing resentment about blacks' gains and anger that their own concerns went unaddressed. In the wake of the 1965 Howard University speech in which Lyndon Johnson told fellow white Americans that "freedom is not enough," Paul Deac of the National Confederation of American Ethnic Groups (representing some forty different nationalities) contacted the White House. "Perhaps because U.S. ethnic groups have never been 'pushy' or made noises like other groups, preferring to earn their way, they are a woefully 'forgotten man,'" he said—unlike "Jews, Negroes and now even women." The push for racial equality was producing "anti-European attitudes" that troubled the "loyal, law-abiding, hard-working citizens" he represented. Like Deac, other whites began expressing their ethnicity as a claim to inclusion in a pattern one anthropologist calls "competition through emulation."[56] "While you have made some spectacular Negro appointments," White House staffer Jack Valenti thus prodded the president, "let us not forget that the largest ethnic group in this country (larger than the Negro) is the Italian." The organizing was effective enough that headcounts of Italian Americans, Polish Americans, Yugoslav Americans, Slavic Americans, and others in the executive branch ensued.[57]

The growing clamor to address discontent in the "white working class" or "lower-middle class" became linked in Republican minds to such ethnic politics, which ranged from "me-tooism" to outright backlash. As early as 1964, the Republican National Committee pursued city-dwelling whites of central and eastern European and Italian descent. Members of various ethnic groups habitually appealed for ethnicity to be a criterion in selecting federal judges. Pat Buchanan chided his boss, President Nixon, in 1969 for going "too far" in abjuring regional, religious, and ethnic balance in Supreme Court appointments. No group should have a seat reserved for it, Buchanan argued against Jewish claims, *"but the broadest representation on the High Court is essential to the broadest acceptance of controversial decisions."* On that basis, Buchanan urged Nixon to think about appointing "a Catholic Italian American" to take the vacated "Jewish seat on the Court."[58] Antonin Scalia seems to have come to the attention of a later White House through similar ethnic advocacy. Scalia, the arch-foe of affirmative action, apparently felt comfortable having Italian Americans promote him as an ethnic "first" on the court with the backing of "probably the largest ethnic minority in the country."[59]

By the 1970s, the thrust would shift from claims that ethnics also faced bias to the assertion that blacks held a "privileged" position. "As the American ethnic remembers his past," a writer for a Catholic weekly intoned, "there was no welfare state for him," only "long hours and back-breaking work." In fact, white ethnic Americans' greatest progress had come as a result of the New Deal, with its two-track social policies that disadvantaged most blacks and Latinos and its mortgage backing for segregated housing in red-lined communities, which enabled even wage-earning whites to amass capital to which people of color were denied access, as well as the later GI Bill, whose education benefits favored whites disproportionately because so many Jim Crow colleges lacked accreditation.[60] Yet, however belied by the historical record, the spirit of grievance rallied people and organizations claiming to represent white ethnics—some fifty million, if the fourth generation was included, and mostly Catholic Europeans (for neither Jews nor Protestants were at first thought of under this rubric)—to speak out loudly in the 1972 elections. "America is not a melting pot," declared Barbara Mikulski, then a Baltimore city councilwoman. "It is a sizzling cauldron for the ethnic American who is overtaxed and underserved at every level of government." Among the reasons offered were the "black-oriented social programs" for which the ethnic American "pays the bill" and "fears that blacks will displace ethnics in jobs." In corner bars, reported the journalist Pete Hamill, the talk was even tougher. "None of them politicians gives a good goddamn" about the problems of guys like him, complained one ironworker Hamill offered as typical. "Everything is for the niggers . . . and they get it all without workin'."[61]

Building a bridge between the tavern and the podium, leading conservatives encouraged such hostility. Why, demanded Pat Buchanan in a rage against his own burlesque version of affirmative action, "should Americans, whose great-grandparents came to this country to escape famine, pogroms, poverty and persecution, now submit to discrimination in favor of Americans whose great-grandparents were slaves?" Buchanan denounced "the rape of the merit system" even as he urged Republican Party leaders to "discriminate in favor of the Democratic minorities we can win," such as in Irish Catholic South Boston, at the time a site of anti-busing militancy. No one kindled the fury of self-styled "innocent victims" of black advance better, however, than Antonin Scalia, law professor and American Enterprise Institute scholar in residence. He exonerated "white ethnic groups" as "themselves the object of discrimination by the dominant Anglo-Saxon majority." Evoking his hardworking father as an archetypal immigrant scorned by that Anglo-Saxon majority, he complained that "it is precisely *these* groups" who were called upon to bear the greatest burdens for "restorative justice" to blacks. His rallying cry was, "I owe no man anything, nor he me, because of the blood that flows in our veins."[62]

⌒ As men on the right reached out to white "ethnics" with populist appeals that turned anti-elitism against blacks especially, they found unexpected allies among the minority of women still reliant on the family wage bargain codified in 1930s social policy. Here, too, the inability of the movement for inclusion to match cultural transformation with improved economic security for all left its gains politically vulnerable. Congressional passage of the ERA and the Supreme Court's legalization of abortion coincided with the recession-driven right turn to alarm homemaking wives already apprehensive that in a world of liberal sexual mores, widespread contraception, improved female employment, and easy divorce, they were an endangered species. One journalist aptly called theirs "the fear that feminism will free men first."[63]

No one gauged the potential fervor better than Phyllis Schlafly, a talented leader in the conservative wing of the GOP who had produced a best-selling case for Barry Goldwater in 1964. She modeled for male leaders an issue-driven strategy to tap grassroots energy. Using her newsletter to mobilize in 1972, she started a new national organization called STOP ERA to cultivate housewives' political identities as victims of inclusive policies. Recruiting white Christian women in a gender counterpart to the ethnic mobilization of white men, the campaign warned that feminism would undermine "the rights women already have," above all, "the right to be a housewife." As the right now nurtured conservatives of color to argue against pro-equality policies, so did it begin to feature women. Feminism, Schlafly warned, threatened to end the cultural authority of the already faltering male breadwinner system, diminishing the claims of women who depended on it. Schlafly's shrewdness, along with feminists' own left turn after Title VII, persuaded male conservative leaders to take up these issues. Whereas in the years between 1920 and 1965 self-described feminists had aligned with business, anti–social welfare Republicans, and conservative southern Democrats to promote the ERA, by the early 1970s that had changed. Backed by labor unions, civil rights groups, and voices for wider social justice as well as feminists, and advanced in a much-altered world for women and families, the ERA had taken on a different meaning. No longer would its passage appear to help business or the right. In 1980 the GOP reversed its longtime support of the amendment.[64]

Appealing to those made uneasy by the demise of the family wage system and the associated changes in gender and sexual norms, the right argued that women benefited uniquely from the status quo and should not surrender the advantages sex conferred. Why, Schlafly demanded, "should we lower ourselves to 'equal rights' when we already have the status of special privilege?" Her answer to the devastating recession of the mid-seventies was simple: not government-backed social reform but "job preference" for breadwinners, a program that shrewdly spoke to the fears of women reliant on men's wages as it led them to see men of color and independent women as the source of their vulnerability. Buckley echoed Schlafly as he warned that the ERA "would result in the loss of as many special privileges . . . as the ladies would gain." George Gilder argued that men's support of their families was the basis of social order, and so opening careers to all amounted to "wastage and abuse of women," for "whatever discrimination against women" takes place, he reasoned, "the offenses do not constitute a significant social problem."[65] By portraying feminists as the antagonists of ordinary married white women, conservative leaders thus managed to construct the women's movement as an elite cause in much the same way that they positioned affirmative action as the creation of a "new class" of mandarins.

Indeed, in these family politics conservative movement organizers also found a lever to move a vast resource base into the right's court: the growing numbers of Americans turning to religious orthodoxy. Schlafly demonstrated the potential as she recruited churchgoing evangelical women against the ERA. The anti-abortion movement that galvanized so many conservative Catholics alongside evangelicals drove the lesson home: there was gold for the right in popular fears about the future of household arrangements in a society that was rife with inequality and undergoing profound cultural change involving gender roles and sexual mores. Evangelical Protestants and conservative Catholics moved in the greatest numbers to the right's camp, but Jews experienced an analogous polarization. The more tradition-minded among them also found the spread of feminism frightening. Conservative and Orthodox Jews were especially anxious about Jewish continuity in this era of rapid assimilation, and least willing to accept that Jewish men and Jewish women might have different interests. Their strategy for group cohesion required conventional gender roles, in particular, that women bear several children and raise them in the Jewish tradition. Among some, feminism became "perceived as a threat to Jewish survival."[66]

Tapping into faith-based concerns, the neoconservatives propounded anti-feminism in these years as part of their larger agenda. "The real trouble" America faced had nothing to do with inequality, Irving Kristol announced; "it is not sociological or economic at all" but rather "a religious vacuum" produced by the fallacy of "the death of God," which allowed the "new class" to fill the vacuum with its dangerous notions of equality.[67] Milton Himmelfarb, a contributing editor of *Commentary*, had earlier insisted that Jewish "survival" required "2.5 or 3" children per household, a cause he continued to champion through the 1970s, as he fretted about how the trends toward later marriage as a result of professional training and contraceptive use was diminishing Jewish women's fertility. Kristol branded feminists "women who do not wish to be women," freaks of nature notable for their "identification of sterility with vitality." For Midge Decter, a leading female neoconservative, feminism was all "self-hatred," a yearning for the "freedom demanded by children . . . the freedom from all difficulty."[68]

By decade's end a fundamentally new alignment in U.S. politics became visible. A right-leaning ecumenicalism, it marked a sharp departure for a nation whose conservatives were traditionally Protestants, often given to anti-Catholicism and sometimes anti-Semitism as well. Yet now, as large numbers of practicing Catholics and smaller numbers of religious Jews left their traditional home in the Democratic Party for the GOP, the emerging fissure was no longer between the major faith traditions but rather within them. It ranged the more orthodox within all faiths on one side against religious liberals and secular citizens on the other.[69]

With these amassed forces—new allies, more favorable socioeconomic conditions, wealthy business backers, new counter-institutions, growing ranks, religious conviction, and a more varied white follow-ing—conservatives argued against affirmative action and an array of re-forms old and new with growing gusto. Having snatched the vocabu-lary of civil rights, they now mimicked its tactics with jujitsu moves in the legal realm as well. Now that conservatives had mastered the talk, why not copy the walk of such bodies as the NAACP Legal Defense and Education Fund, Mexican American Legal Defense and Education Fund, and the National Organization for Women's Legal Defense and Education Fund? Some on the right did, setting up their own advo-cacy-driven law firms, such as the Pacific Legal Foundation, estab-lished in 1973 to litigate "nationally on behalf of a free enterprise, pri-vate property rights viewpoint." Joseph Coors, for his part, launched the Mountain States Legal Foundation in 1977. Their strategy, as an architect put it, was to "try wherever possible to find a plaintiff whose plight outrages people."[70]

THESE VARIED CURRENTS joined in a legal challenge that reached the Supreme Court in late 1978, *Kaiser Aluminum & Chemical Corporation and United Steelworkers of America, AFL-CIO v. Brian F. Weber*. The case's very title became a symbol for the new politics, sum-moning as it did the image of a large corporation and a big labor orga-nization together bearing down on a lone white working man. Called by some pundits the "blue-collar *Bakke*," in reference to the better-known challenge to affirmative action in higher education, *Weber* was the most important Supreme Court case involving economic inclusion since the 1971 test, *Griggs v. Duke Power*. Now, however, those seeking inclusion were playing defense. For this was one of a small but growing number of cases mounted by white men charging "reverse discrimina-tion" that violated their rights in the effort to remedy injustice against others.[71] Offering an opportunity to broadcast the new-style conserva-tive argument to a much larger audience, the case drew the right's in-terest.

Like the grassroots white "ethnics" drawn to conservatism, Brian Weber felt aggrieved. A laboratory analyst in his thirties at the Kaiser Aluminum plant in Gramercy, Louisiana, Weber applied to a new training program in 1974, the year of the *DeFunis* case. Whereas the company had traditionally hired craftsmen from outside its ranks—in-

deed, until 1974 it had required five years' experience of anyone seeking such a position—now, in cooperation with the plant's union, the
United Steelworkers of America (USWA), Kaiser offered opportunities
for advancement to its unskilled production workers, black and white.
The new program came about after decades of struggle for inclusion by
black steelworkers, and after a recent government contract compliance
review of the plant had revealed stark job segregation. Blacks made up
46 percent of the local population in this rural area between New Orleans and Baton Rouge and 39 percent of the plant's employees. Yet
they held only 1.83 percent of the high-paying skilled positions: 5 black
to 268 white craftsmen. Moreover, the company's hiring practices all
but guaranteed that blacks would remain stuck in low-level jobs. The
skilled trades had so long excluded them that there was almost no place
in Louisiana where they could acquire the prerequisite experience or
vocational training. Brought to recognize this by the OFCC, and hoping to avoid lawsuits from black employees, the company and the union
had agreed on the training program. It would admit workers according
to seniority, with the reservation that until blacks' representation in
the crafts came closer to their representation in the local labor force,
they would get 50 percent of the trainee positions. This arrangement
seemed fair to both sides at the bargaining table.[72]

   But Brian Weber viewed the situation differently. He saw not a history of shutting out blacks but a practice that denied him something to
which he felt entitled. He had more seniority than some blacks admitted to the program, and this seemed wrong to him as a white man with
six years at Kaiser. There was no reason why he "should be made to
pay for . . . what someone did 150 years ago." An active member of
the USWA local and the chairman of its grievance committee, Weber
knew how to read contracts. Studying the text of the Civil Rights Act of
1964, he discovered a clear prohibition on discrimination—Title VII
made it illegal "to discriminate . . . because of . . . race"—and in this
prohibition was his opportunity. Wasn't *any* race-conscious affirmative
action plan "reverse discrimination" and "a quota system," as his suit
would label it?[73] Describing his own racial views as "basically conservative," he complained that blacks had moved beyond desegregation:
"They've crossed over into taking our jobs." His lawyer, Michael R.
Fontham, filed a class-action lawsuit on behalf of Weber and other
white male production workers. The case appealed to the new conser-

vative legal foundations, and when Weber went before the high court in Washington, three such enterprises filed amicus briefs: the Pacific Legal Foundation, the Southeastern Legal Foundation, and the United States Justice Foundation.[74]

Conservatives looked to the case as a way to steer both business and industrial labor unions away from making peace with affirmative action, which they seemed to be doing as the decade opened. From the perspectives of many pragmatists in each camp, it seemed wiser to accept than fight the thrust for inclusion. While those like Joseph Coors repulsed change fiercely, other corporate leaders saw reason to welcome affirmative action. Systematic searches of the broadest possible labor pool could ensure access to the best candidates, while having an affirmative action program in place was an excellent defense against costly court-imposed penalties for race and sex discrimination.[75] The *Wall Street Journal* found unremarkable that which conservatives called outrageous. "It is no mystery why this system has developed its tough, punitive, numbers-oriented character," it observed of the *Weber* case. "Before the civil rights legislation of the 1960s, normal processes of group accommodation were manifestly not working for black Americans. That is why the civil rights movement was forced to rely so heavily on the courts, the law, national opinion and federal action."[76] In staking their claim for Weber, conservatives urged the federal government (via the courts) to tell private parties, businesses included, that they could not undertake voluntary action for shared purposes or choose whom to train for what positions.[77]

As *Weber* went to Washington, the stakes were huge. "The great bulk of affirmative action occurs in employment," explained EEOC chair Eleanor Holmes Norton to the NAACP convention in 1978, "and it is in employment where most is at stake." At issue were the plans of some thirty thousand private firms for the economic inclusion of African Americans, Hispanics, and women of all groups. Some thirty-five million workers would be affected by the case's outcome.[78] In his own notes on the case, President Carter wrote that *Weber* was "probably more important" than *Bakke*. Indeed, labor organizations representing twenty million workers had taken a stand in defense of workplace affirmative action in the case, alongside the NAACP, NOW, the American GI Forum, and many more. If Brian Weber won, unions might not be able to negotiate contracts with affirmative action clauses to break down long-standing patterns of job segregation. Realizing the stakes, some civil rights, labor, and feminist activists came together in coalitions in New Orleans and nationally to defend the workplace policies they had fought so hard to win.[79] In the end, the Supreme Court sided with the union and Kaiser against Weber's challenge, though it ruled narrowly, finding that Title VII's ban on discrimination "does not condemn all private, voluntary, race-conscious affirmative action plans."[80]

When individual conservatives argued about the case in public, they seemed to be reading from a common script, so ritualized had their habits of thought and argument become. A look at the shared features of their discourse can illuminate their point of view. For one thing, conservative commentators ignored women at the plant entirely as they assured the public that blacks had never suffered discrimination at Kaiser, when actually the facts of the case proved no such thing: the district court had never been asked to rule on prior discrimination. In discussing the case, Terry Eastland and William J. Bennett, for example, declared that "since its opening in 1958, Kaiser's Gramercy plant had hired its employees without regard to race." No one on the right saw anything suspicious in the assertion that a company operating in rural Louisiana six years prior to the Civil Rights Act had never discriminated. But, then, their movement had denied discrimination back then, too, when Jim Crow was law. As believers in the magic of the market, conservatives found unfair treatment a faulty argument and pointed to African Americans as the authors of their own troubles. "Discrimination is costly," as Orrin Hatch told a Heritage Foundation audience, so it was axiomatic that business would avoid it. In a free market world, "you will ultimately be paid approximately what your work is worth." Therefore, if some group failed to do well, its members should look to themselves for reasons. After all, "different cultures have different attitudes to work and leisure," and "traditions do not dissolve overnight."[81]

The truth was that it was in the interest of both Kaiser and the union to remain silent on past discrimination, for acknowledging it would make them liable for back-pay claims. But as Justice Harry Blackmun pointed out, the company "concedes that its past hiring practices may be subject to question." Kaiser's requirement of five years' experience for access to craft jobs, for example, which had never been shown necessary to perform these jobs, could easily have been found arbitrary and discriminatory by virtue of its disparate impact on black applicants. In any event, as unions supporting the plan pointed out, in 1970 blacks made up one in five of the available pool of "craftsmen and kindred workers" in the cities of New Orleans and Baton Rouge, so a determined effort might have recruited some. Their brief also pointed out that Kaiser had in the past hired whites who lacked the "required" experience, and that one of its nearby plants in Chalmette, Louisiana, was found guilty of prima facie discrimination by an appeals court in a 1978 Title VII case. For women the case was open and shut: they had been denied all but secretarial positions at Kaiser until 1973, yet if Weber won, the training program would end before they had access to the 5 percent of positions it provided them. Blacks' alleged lack of "skill" was the outcome of a history of very intentional discrimination, such as the "segregated and inferior trade schools for blacks in Louisiana" and their willful exclusion by all-white building trades unions there, as elsewhere in the country. The problem with the trial record that came to the Supreme Court, Blackmun noted, was that none of the participants in this case "had any incentive to prove that Kaiser had violated the Act"—not the company, not the union, and certainly not Weber himself. Now, in effect, Weber and his allies on the right were using the result of historic exclusion, the small number of black craftsmen, to absolve the company and the union of any responsibility for changing it.[82]

Ironically, the training opportunity to which Brian Weber felt entitled would not have existed for anyone, white men included, but for these efforts to break down job segregation. Before 1974, the company had simply hired craftsmen from outside; the success of Weber's challenge in the lower court ensured that no one would benefit from the internal outreach program after its first year in operation. As one black activist in New Orleans put it after Weber's victory in the lower court, "Weber's actions have shut down the very affirmative action program he was trying to gain entrance to." None of this prevented his supporters from bemoaning "the injury done Brian Weber" and denouncing court support for affirmative action as "justice debased."[83] Readers of conservative pieces on the case would conclude that race was a real advantage to blacks: in their tracts, all that distinguished blacks at Kaiser from white co-workers was privileged access.

The shared label "blue-collar" hid much about the divergent life histories of Weber and the aspiring black workers against whom he and the right pitted themselves. One such co-worker was Jim Nailor, who had as much seniority at Kaiser as Weber when he gained admission to the training program in 1974. Nailor grew up on a nearby plantation, where his mother harvested sugar and many black workers still called their bosses "master." "We didn't have any running water," he recalled, "and we had to hustle up wood for our own fire." As a child, he walked to his Jim Crow school, as did other black children, some from as far away as seven miles, while white kids rode by on their school buses and mocked them from the windows. At his school, "we got handed-down books," sometimes "with the pages ripped out"; his town, Vacherie, had no high school for blacks. Wanting better for their son, his parents worked extra jobs to send Nailor to a high school run by the Tuskegee Institute, after which he moved to California and put himself through a junior college. As his parents aged and could no longer work as hard, he came back to help out. Yet he quickly learned that little had changed in Vacherie. "The trade unions wouldn't let you in," he found, and no utilities or other companies would hire him, so he finally had to accept a "pick-and-shovel" job. "I was depressed all the time," he said. "Here I am, I thought, digging a ditch, and I've completed junior college." Finally, facing affirmative action pressure, Kaiser hired him as a laborer. Hoping for more, he attended night school in New Orleans to enhance his skills. When he was admitted to the new training program in 1974, his pay suffered during the apprenticeship, but it was worth it, he felt, to become a licensed electrician making $25,000 with overtime—the only African American electrician out of thirty-seven at Kaiser. "I've got more money now," he told an interviewer. "I added on to my house, I got furniture, I drive a pretty decent car, [and] I have more money to send my kids to school." For all this, some whites hated him. "Quite a few in some of the departments don't even speak to me," he reported. Although Nailor's story appeared in the *New York Times*, no conservative supporter of Weber ever mentioned him or showed the least curiosity about Kaiser's black workers.[84]

Studiously oblivious to injuries to blacks and women, conservatives, in their effort to win broader support, continued to portray white working men as victims of all the evils their movement pledged to fight. Illustrating how the affirmative action issue could be used to undercut loyalty to unions and the New Deal, one veteran of the fight in higher education portrayed the case this way: "Big Labor has indeed paired with Big Business, Big Government and the Big Left to deprive Brian Weber and others like him of equal opportunity." If nothing else, invoking a "Big Left" in 1979 portended mischief. Senator Hatch similarly tried to use affirmative action to divide "union members" like Brian Weber from "union bureaucrats." Their "outright betrayal," he insisted, marked "the most radical assault upon the principles of equal protection and of liberty since our Republic was founded"—a rather strong claim given the competition—and this from a man who led the assault against legislation to end illegal union-busting and blocked full employment and fair housing laws. But in Hatch's view, affirmative action, along with other "federal regulations," was the cause of the American economy's plight after 1973: those covered by it were parasites trying "to get society at large to pay them a subvention."[85]

Other conservative critics of the *Weber* decision agreed that what was happening to white men like Weber was as bad as or worse than anything done to blacks. Editorializing, William F. Buckley, Jr., claimed that the purpose of Title VII had "quickly" become "discriminating against different people." Antonin Scalia equated the reasoning of those who supported Kaiser's program with that of the antiheroes of George Orwell's *Animal Farm:* "All animals are created equal but some are more equal than others." "Reverse discrimination is not an invention or a hypothesis yet to be confirmed," exhorted another writer; "it is a sociological and legal fact." Some suggested that the practice they alleged of substituting incompetent blacks for deserving whites had gone so far as to endanger public safety. In its amicus brief, an organization of conservative professors thus urged anyone concerned about "the way buildings are 'put up' nowadays" to consider that the faults might be due to government pressure on the construction trades to hire black men, while Hatch implied that it was minority hiring that had caused the Chrysler Corporation to require a bail-out from Congress in 1979.[86]

Another feature of the right's discussion of the *Weber* case was its bid to rewrite the history of the Civil Rights Act, legislation the conservative movement had opposed, so that it allowed only formal equality to individuals. They sought to contain the meanings of all the key words in the debate over economic inclusion so as to render them as thin and de-limiting of action as possible. Weber's lawsuit pivoted on what the Supreme Court's majority spoke of as "a literal construction" of Title

VII that reduced it to a single part of Section 703, the anti-quota language inserted in compromise with congressional opponents. That interpretation refused either to acknowledge the law's aim of undoing the systematic exclusion of black Americans or to engage the legislative history which showed that Congress understood race-conscious measures as one way to achieve inclusion. "It would be ironic indeed," wrote the Court's majority in *Weber*, "if a law triggered by a Nation's concern over centuries of racial injustice and intended to improve the lot of those who had 'been excluded from the American dream for so long' [quoting from the debate in Congress] constituted the first legislative prohibition on all voluntary, private, race-conscious efforts to abolish traditional patterns of racial segregation and hierarchy." To William F. Buckley, in contrast, the language of "the great Civil Rights Act" (whose passage he had fought) was "about as ambiguous as 'John hit the baseball.'"[87]

Conservatives' interest in fairness focused exclusively on white men, and even, one could say, on violations of white men's expectations of entitlement, as when Weber complained that blacks were getting "our jobs." Buckley, long a stern critic of unions, developed a sudden affinity for the labor movement's principle of seniority in this case, where the union in question supported affirmative action over strict seniority for white members.[88] In fact, seniority was the only thing that distinguished Weber from the blacks who made it into the training program; they were "as fully qualified" as whites but had less time in the plant. Had entry been awarded according to length of employment at Kaiser, no blacks would have been admitted, then or in the near future. Yet this did not stop critics like Scalia from posing the issue as that of "discrimination against better qualified employees."[89] Once again, while framing the other side as elitists acting on behalf of incompetents, conservatives styled themselves populist friends of white working men like Brian Weber.

No doubt some conservatives genuinely embraced color-blindness, in a change of heart as thoroughgoing as the "born-again" spirit that moved so many of the religious faithful in the 1970s. Yet the embrace of color-blindness was cost-free. One did not need to surrender antipathy to blacks to argue in the new way; one merely had to exercise restraint in expressing it. Brian Weber himself told reporters early on that, avid supporter of one clause though he was, he opposed other parts of the landmark Civil Rights Act. "I never agreed with making restaurants serve blacks," he told the press. "If you choose not to serve them, that's your business." Other signs suggested that conservatives were embracing the language of color-blind fairness not so much from ethical conversion as from calculation about what would serve best to advance their overall agenda. Spokespersons for the right were more forthcoming in discussing foreign affairs, for example. In southern Africa, where blacks formed majorities sufficient to make policy, if only they had the right to vote, conservatives rejected color-blindness and unabashedly defended white power and apartheid measures until the end. Discussing Zimbabwe the same year Weber's case reached the Supreme Court, James Burnham deemed it quite reasonable that "white votes will count more than black votes."[90] Consumers of conservative tracts at the grass roots spoke still more bluntly, as when one branded "remedies to correct non-existent wrongs" as nothing but "the rape of the whites' pocketbook."[91]

It required steady herding by movement leaders to keep such rank-and-file followers "above" racism when it was racial antipathy that had attracted so many to the right in the first place, a tutoring best revealed to posterity in personal correspondence. When criticized by an annoyed segregationist for apologizing for "your former views regarding racial integration," Kilpatrick hastened to set the "record straight": "I did not say I was sorry for my former views on racial integration. I said, very carefully, that I was sorry I ever defended the practice of State-sanctioned segregation. There is a world of difference. Neither did I 'belatedly come to the conclusion that I was wrong about my former stand on equality of the races.' As I tried to make clear, I belatedly came to the conclusion that I was wrong about my former stand on the rightness of State-sanctioned discrimination."[92]

Even as the conservative movement nudged vocal segregationists out of the national limelight after the mid-1970s, moreover, it never tried to eject them from the cause. Nor did it denounce their racism, which it regularly insisted that African American leaders must do in cases of anti-Semitism among blacks. Men such as M. E. Bradford remained valuable contributors to the overall effort, even as he, for example, called emancipation of America's slaves a historic blow against "liberty" and warned that civil rights "could not be digested." This did not prevent sixteen Republican senators, among them Jesse Helms, Orrin

Hatch, Strom Thurmond, and Trent Lott, from recommending Bradford in 1981 as an "impeccable" scholar to serve as head of the National Endowment for the Humanities, or keep Russell Kirk, William F. Buckley, and M. Stanton Evans from backing his appointment. The politicians who supported Bradford were not exactly consistent in their enthusiasm for color-blindness. Trent Lott, for example, was a proud member of the Sons of Confederate Veterans and soon-to-be participant in the Council of Conservative Citizens (descendant of the white Citizens' Councils that fought the southern civil rights movement). Still disappointed by the Union victory in "the War between the States, the War of Aggression," Lott was pleased that the party of Lincoln now stood for "things that Jefferson Davis and his people believed in," proud to have voted against making Martin Luther King, Jr.'s, birthday a national holiday, and sorry that other "members of Congress caved in on that one." Such "paleo-conservatives," as they came to be known, faced challenge mainly from "East Coast neoconservatives," as when Irving Kristol opposed Bradford, successfully promoting fellow neo-conservative William F. Bennett instead.[93]

Seen in this broader context, conservatives' new solicitude for Asian Americans appeared less altruistic than instrumental. One Asian American conservative at the time of the *DeFunis* case observed that, like Jews, his peers were "over-represented in the sciences and the professions. 'Affirmative action,' then (at least as practiced on the West Coast)," he argued, "ends in 'reverse discrimination' against Orientals."[94] In fact, however, many Asian American activists, like Latinos, saw their future as in alliance with blacks and feminists. Their oldest and strongest organization in the 1970s, the Japanese American Citizens' League (JACL), alone among the ethnic organizations invited by the AJC to support Marco DeFunis, refused. Its leaders argued that "Asian Americans are subject to the same racism, repression, and social injustices that are so much more obvious with most other minorities." The JACL supported the Kaiser-USWA affirmative action plan against Weber's challenge, as did the Asian American Legal Defense and Education Fund.[95]

Yet because of the recency of large-scale immigration from Asia and the historic vulnerability of Asian Americans' citizenship, they were as likely to be spoken about by whites as to speak for themselves in the public debate on affirmative action in the 1970s. Asian Americans had strategic appeal to white conservatives, who now understood that WASP prerogatives could no longer trump minority claims for justice. Some thus propounded the stereotype of Asian Americans as a "model minority" to use against the demands of blacks. A 1966 *U.S. News & World Report* feature on Chinese Americans anticipated the genre. Praising them for "hard work," energetic learning, strong families, and abstention from crime and public assistance, the piece contrasted their virtues with the alleged vices of blacks. "At a time when it is being proposed that hundreds of billions be spent to uplift Negroes," the newsweekly intoned, "the nation's 300,000 Chinese-Americans are moving ahead on their own—with no help from anyone else." Over the coming years, the right exaggerated Asian American success to diminish that of blacks and deny their worthiness to receive redress. Shifting the discussion from political economy to purported cultural values, proponents of the stereotype used it to argue that just as Asian Americans lifted themselves up, so others held themselves down.[96]

Employing a language first developed to depict Jews as victims of affirmative action, neoconservatives tried to convince Asian Americans that aid to African Americans came at their expense. When Asian American activists organized against apparent quotas that kept their college admissions down in favor of less qualified white students, the right changed the subject to the ways in which not whites but blacks benefited. Owing both to a history of discrimination against them and to the model minority image of hard work and family devotion, reports one study of these efforts, "compared with whites, Asians constituted more sympathetic victims of affirmative action in the public eye." Conservatives used stories of struggling immigrant families to put liberals on the defensive. After reviewing the litigation record, one legal scholar concluded that claims that Asian Americans suffered as a result of affirmative action amounted to "an intentional maneuver by conservative politicians to provide a response to charges of racism."[97]

Conservative movement architects had come a long way since beginning their work in the mid-1950s. After fumbling their opposition to the early civil rights movement—enhancing that movement's appeal and influence with their attempts to defend exclusion on the grounds of property rights, states' rights, anticommunism, and belligerent racism—they finally looked outward for direction. It came from those who opposed affirmative action in the name of liberal individualism and other minorities long discriminated against. Observing such efforts in the early 1970s, leading conservatives updated their own arguments. More and more they spoke of color-blindness, of even-handed treatment, and of justice rather than embattled privilege. It was an astute choice. It allowed the right to appeal to a much broader popular audience than ever before, and provided a rare occasion to portray its cause as one of fairness and justice. The new approach helped persuade record proportions of traditionally Democratic voters—notably white trade union members, Catholics, and Jews—to join with a majority of other whites in voting for Ronald Reagan, their movement's standard-bearer, in the presidential contest of 1980.[98]

The change in discourse, dramatic as it was, did not require a change of heart from the movement's founders. As Kilpatrick indicated, one did not even have to apologize for the harm one had inflicted or commit to working for across-the-board fairness. All one had to do was stand with a polite smile at the gateway to jobs, schools, and other contested resources and preach the virtues of formal equality. Conservatives had come to understand that they no longer needed de jure segregation to keep their cherished hierarchies in place; with affirmative action and like measures gone, de facto segregation would suffice. Shifting their tactics, they managed to change the very terms of debate on affirmative action. Whereas in the mid-1970s the public usually encountered the issue as one of "remedial action" to right a history of discrimination, within a few years that would give way to "reverse discrimination" as the most common frame. And where once the media had tended to interview openly racist opponents of the policy, they now presented critics who condemned it in the appealing cadences of anti-racism.[99] The new package sounded so reasonable to most white voters that they came to think of conservatives as fair-minded defenders of ordinary Americans from Washington-sponsored injustice—thus luring more of "those who would otherwise not listen to us."

In this way, affirmative action gave movement conservatives traction in their climb to political power from a mid-sixties nadir. More generally, conservatives and business together—in unsteady but potent collaboration—found the means to shift public discourse and policy from the direction they had followed since the Great Depression. Notwithstanding powerful odds, as Thomas Edsall points out, "the political stature of business rose steadily from the early 1970s, one of its lowest points in the nation's history, until, by the end of the decade, the business community had achieved virtual dominance of the legislative process in Congress." In fact, corporate lobbies that lost power in the decades after 1965, a business historian points out, "fought most opponents to a standstill in 1975–1978" and scored important victories thereafter in the Carter, Reagan, and Bush years as well.[100] In the climate thus created, small groups of women embarked on one of the most courageous challenges to economic exclusion since Wharlest Jackson and George Metcalfe had fought for industrial jobs in the Deep South: an effort to enter the skilled construction trades long marked as "manly." These women became canaries in the mineshaft of the emerging national political order, gauging exactly how serious America was about inclusion.

~ III
The Challenge
of the New Order

~ 8

The Lonesomeness of Pioneering

$\mathcal{A}$S CONSERVATIVES ASSERTED that affirmative action was preventing the United States from being a color-blind and gender-neutral society, Melinda Hernandez, a twenty-two-year-old Puerto Rican from the Bronx, tested that proposition. She began by sleeping out on a New York City sidewalk for five nights in the summer of 1978 in order to secure an application for apprenticeship with the electricians' union. The applications were to be given out Monday morning; to get them, thirty other women and hundreds of men began lining up on Wednesday. Those nights presaged much about the future. As "the sons of electricians" lined up in this neighborhood so much theirs that it was spoken of as "Electchester," the men couldn't imagine what women were doing there. Some grew ornery. "They pissed on some of the women's sleeping bags," said Hernandez. A few even drove a car up on the sidewalk where the women were sleeping—anything "to get us off the line," Hernandez recalled. "I've never been exposed to such direct hatred like that."[1] Like the border guards of a wealthy country, the aspiring tradesmen tried to drive the would-be entrants back.

Their indignation signaled the radicalism of the challenge, for the effort to open the skilled trades to women proved to be a landmark that extended to a new frontier the struggle under way since the 1950s. It was an audacious initiative: an attempt to place women in the most desirable blue-collar jobs—and the most carefully guarded by well-orga-

265

nized men known for their machismo. And it managed to achieve its
goal in significant numbers. By 1983, women held about 105,000 construction jobs in the United States. Only 2 percent of the industry's labor force, the number was nonetheless greater than the memberships
of many social movement organizations.[2] Foregrounding the needs of
low-income black women and Latinas, the initiative built on the campaign of black men for building trades jobs as a model for advancing
the autonomy of women. Defying the association of construction skills
with whiteness and manliness, it sought to re-make gender by breaking
down the sexual and racial division of labor in the best blue-collar work
to be had. The campaign's means were as cutting-edge as its goals:
it depended on the new, post–Title VII coalitions between feminists
and black and Hispanic civil rights groups to pressure employers and
win government backing. In the face of growing conservative power,
jobs-minded activists persevered to make headway for working-class
women, tens of thousands of whom jumped at the chance for a better
life.

Puerto Ricans like Hernandez were among the most disadvantaged
Americans. Many observers agreed that the dire straits of Puerto Rican
women impoverished the larger community, because two out of every
five Puerto Rican families were now headed by women, and most were
poor. In 1978, only 4.1 percent of Puertorriqueñas had graduated from
college; fewer than half completed high school. Although they had at
one time been more likely to be employed than white or black women,
by the late 1970s their rate of participation in the labor force was declining, owing to the closing of urban factories. Those concerned concurred that, as one community leader put it, "job skills training in fields
that allow upward mobility [is] a very major priority." No wonder,
then, that when Hernandez and three other women graduated from
their apprenticeships to become the first female electricians in New
York City, they were proud. They organized a dinner dance at the Gramercy Park Hotel, with a "magnificent turnout" of two hundred family
members, friends, tradeswomen, and other supporters. Now journeymen, in the language of the trades, they would enjoy the high wages
and benefits that had long been a male monopoly in working-class
communities.[3]

The women's achievement was more than an individual triumph: it
resulted from the most active national campaign for economic inclu-

sion of the late 1970s and 1980s. These tradeswomen, like many others in New York City, found training and support in an organization called All-Craft. This and similar groups learned from and allied with anti-racist groups such as Harlem's Fight Back, which was working to get black men into the industry. One of many such new groups for women, All-Craft served as a kind of midwife for tradeswomen, offering pre-apprenticeship classes, helping women to navigate the complex and hostile job market in construction, and teaching them to use such government and union resources as existed for them. NOW had prepared the way by pushing for women to be included in the federal executive order covering government contracting in construction and insisting that goals and timetables be set for women of all groups. Even as the national organization and many chapters began to focus on the ERA in the 1970s, members in some areas, New York City among them, continued the fight to open up nontraditional work as a feminist anti-poverty campaign. In 1980 construction was the largest sector of the American economy, accounting for more than one tenth of the gross national product, and offering the highest-paying, most interesting jobs someone with no more than a high school education could find. In addition, government supplied much of the work for the larger contractors, making possible public oversight to ensure democratic access. Just as some feminists staffed the clerical worker organizations that spread in the early 1970s, others now founded groups to assist women, especially low-income women of color, in getting and keeping nontraditional blue-collar jobs. The year Melinda Hernandez slept out to become an electrician, minority women made up three out of every four women served by her All-Craft program. Four in five of its trainees headed households, nearly half of which were on welfare.[4]

Their struggle was not only for the future of women; it was also, in effect, a struggle for the souls of white men. For ultimately, as hard as Hernandez and other tradeswomen worked, the fate of their effort was in the hands of the men who ran the construction industry, those who filled the building trades, and those in government who oversaw the industry. Would they be willing to make this prime earning territory equal access? While many tradesmen fought the entry of women into their occupation, some acted as allies who enabled the hardy to persevere. In the end, what determined who would predominate were the actions of government, management, and union offices. Where shop-floor resistance was greatest, women such as Hernandez discovered, as black men like Vincent Whylie had before them, that government backing was the key variable on which progress depended. Because of the changes in the national political landscape since the early 1970s, that backing was becoming less reliable just as the guests at the Gramercy Park Hotel were gathering to celebrate the first class of female electricians. The story of tradeswomen's shift from exuberant trailblazers to "endangered species" opens a window onto the new challenges facing the struggle for inclusion and the progressive forces that had earlier sustained it in the aftermath of conservative success.[5]

～ THE EFFORT TO OPEN what came to be known as nontraditional work to women had its roots in the first years of the feminist revival. From the outset, NOW had envisioned what a UAW member and early employment task force chair called "a campaign to open new avenues of upgrading and on-the-job training for women now segregated in dead-end clerical, secretarial, and menial jobs." The effort sought both to achieve justice by opening good jobs to all women and to fight the poverty that was increasingly concentrated among low-income women and their children, particularly women of color. Since skilled "men's jobs" usually paid at least twice as much as the men's sisters might earn in the jobs that were open to them and included much better benefits, the stark difference in rewards created a powerful incentive for working-class women to break down sex segregation. If large numbers of women left the pink-collar job ghetto, it would relieve the downward pressure on their wages caused by oversupply of labor. Also, as NOW pointed out early on, owing to better technology, brawn was no longer needed for most occupations, so exclusion of women could not be justified on those grounds.[6]

A pioneer organization, Advocates for Women, was founded in San Francisco in 1971. Convinced that "economic power is the foundation for all other power, and organization is the key" to achieving it, the group attracted more than a hundred volunteers and built a diverse staff. It modeled itself on similar services for minority men, worked with some of their experts, and took advantage of newly available federal training funds. Directed by Dorothea Hernandez, a Latina activist, the apprenticeship program aimed to reach "women of all races and cultures with emphasis on low-income women who must support themselves and their families." Its leaders believed that the best way to relieve women's poverty was to raise their earnings, not urge them to rely on men's support or miserly welfare assistance. But the traditionally female occupations wouldn't pay enough to escape poverty, particularly for those with limited education. Advocates for Women reasoned that since the skilled trades had long offered a good income for men with only a high school education, they could do the same for women—if they had government backing, advocacy, training, and support.[7]

Challenged by urban upheaval, feminism, and the welfare rights movement of the early 1970s, some established, largely white women's organizations joined the effort, most notably Wider Opportunities for Women (WOW) in Washington, D.C. It began in 1966 as a resource for college-educated housewives seeking volunteer opportunities, society matrons who to a woman went by their husbands' names (as in Mrs. Harold Fleming). Yet by 1972, the group had shifted its focus to poor women, particularly "poor minority women," aiming to supply the training and backing they needed to secure craft jobs. WOW particularly wanted to help women avoid typical "marginal jobs which cannot sustain even minimum family needs." With more and more single mothers raising children without help from men, the organizers sought to steer those entering the labor force "away from traditional, poorly paid, often-glutted fields and into new and promising areas of work."[8]

Backed by WOW and a coalition of feminist groups, Advocates for Women acted as the lead plaintiff in a lawsuit that brought employment goals for women to construction. Just as black men had found that they needed to sue to get access to the building trades, so did women. The exclusion of women from the trades was absolute until *Advocates for Women v. Ussery*. The 1976 case aimed to compel the Department of Labor to enforce Executive Orders 11246 and 11375: to take action against federally funded construction contractors practicing sex discrimination, which until then it had refused to do, claiming that women had no interest in these jobs. Many women had gone into nontraditional blue-collar work of various kinds in recent years, and some had made their way into the skilled trades in manufacturing, such as the automobile industry, but construction work was off-limits until this lawsuit. It was settled out of court when President Jimmy Carter in April 1978 issued affirmative action regulations setting specific goals for hiring women. All construction contractors would be expected to try to meet them or else explain why they had failed. The goals were modest: 3.1 percent at the outset, to be increased to 6.9 percent over three years. The women's groups had demanded 40 percent, to match women's share in the overall labor force, but to gain any specific commitment was a real achievement. Any woman who later found employment on a large building project owed her position to the class-action lawsuit that moved Carter to issue the order. As the federal government for the first time stood behind women seeking to enter the construction industry, their numbers took a quantum leap upward.[9]

Government support proved critical, because Advocates for Women and WOW represented a new kind of organization, distinct from earlier direct action protest groups. Like the Urban League's LEAP program and Mexican Americans' SER/Jobs for Progress, which aimed to help minority men get into skilled labor, these did the same for women. Because the newcomers required extensive training and ongoing oversight to ensure fair treatment, these groups needed reliable staff and resources. To get money for these services, the organizations turned to foundations and to government contracts from the Labor Department under the Comprehensive Employment and Training Act, or CETA, passed in 1973.[10] Even where the groups had membership dues, these could rarely meet the overhead. CETA, in contrast, was sending $400 million a year into New York City alone in the late 1970s, money earmarked for training. As it became the leading source of funding for training programs, the federal government underwrote the movement. In New York, for example, CETA funded both All-Craft and Nontraditional Employment for Women. The VISTA program, the domestic counterpart of the Peace Corps, supplied staff for some women's work organizations.[11] Some foundations also helped, among them the Ms. Foundation, the Ford Foundation, and, having its own interest in nontraditional women, the Playboy Foundation.[12]

With such backing, over the next decade scores of programs to train women for the skilled trades and sustain them there came into operation across the country. They included Women in Apprenticeship (San Francisco), Mechanica (Seattle), the All-Craft Center and Nontraditional Employment for Women (New York), Women in Trades (Chicago), Hard-Hatted Women (Pittsburgh), YWCA New Jobs for Women (Philadelphia), Better Jobs for Women (Denver), Women in

Skilled Trades (Detroit), Skilled Jobs for Women (Madison), Southeast Women's Employment Coalition (Lexington), Women in Construction Projects (Boston and Washington, D.C.), Women and Employment (Charleston, West Virginia), and Work Options for Women (Wichita, Kansas, and Raleigh, North Carolina). With foundation support, over ninety organizations concerned with women's work from twenty-seven states joined a WOW-led initiative to launch the Women's Work Force Network in 1979. It ran a Construction Compliance Task Force of twenty-two groups to aid the entry of women into the building trades, especially economically disadvantaged women.[13]

The early response to the opening of construction was exuberant, and word traveled fast. One woman was advised by a friend who worked for the Missouri Unemployment Office to think about the trades. "They've got apprenticeship programs. Go down and check it out," he told her in late 1977. "They're starting up affirmative action and this thing is going to open wide up." Some received alerts from civil rights organizations such as the Urban League that contractors were now under pressure to hire women of all groups as well as minority men. Many had a sense of being part of a historic endeavor. "When people in the women's movement were talking about women doing men's jobs and why shouldn't they be able to do it, it made sense to me," said Cynthia Long, a Chinese American who enrolled in a pilot program in New York. A few gave credit to President Carter. A concerted effort was made to attract recruits, with ads about the opening of the trades appearing in the newspapers and on television. One woman, "fed up" with her clerk job, saw a poster in a train that exhorted, "Women Build Your Own Future." Curious, she enrolled. Women's employment programs did extensive outreach. Tapping into other networks, they distributed information to public libraries and visited classes and community groups.[14]

Skeptics doubted that women would choose to go into the trades. Blinded by stereotypes, they ignored the fact that skilled journeymen earned far more than those in traditional "women's jobs" and enjoyed good low-cost health insurance and retirement plans. When Advocates for Women first advertised, 1,100 women applied so quickly for the 125 positions available that the group had to cancel further notices in order to manage the inquiries. For one welder with four children and an unemployed husband, the initial attraction was that "the wages were just absolutely unbelievable." Consuela Reyes, one of the first female carpenters hired in Manhattan, put it even more bluntly: "These jobs pay damn well. Try supporting yourself and a few children on the salary from a clerical job." In addition, the typical workday, 7 AM to 3:30 PM, was well suited to parents of school-age children.[15] By 1980, the traditional women's magazines had signed on. *Women's Day* opened the decade with a feature on tradeswomen and their wages. "The best jobs for women in the 1980s are, quite simply, men's jobs," the magazine declared. "Nontraditional jobs are where the money and the opportunities for advancement are."[16]

Although some tradeswomen crossed gender boundaries only for the pay or other benefits, those drawn to the satisfaction of the work far outnumbered them. "I hated my work," said one carpenter of her days as a secretary; as soon as she heard that the trades were opening to women, "my imagination went with it." Carpentry was "creative" and "applicable to your daily life," and it promised "independence." A former receptionist who "had been sitting at a desk for 12 years with my ear pressed to the phone" decided, "I wanted a career I could grow in— something where I could continue to learn" and also "move around and work with my hands." A woman who had hated having to rely on tips while waiting tables ("it's a little like being a prostitute") was now driving a concrete truck. Construction was "a whole new world," a Seattle woman marveled. People in the trades "help each other and cooperate." Without having to say, "'Let's lift this thing,' they automatically do it."[17] Whether "working as a cook or working with people, it's real hard to see what you did that day," noted another woman working construction. But "carpentry is concrete" because "you have this thing you can touch and see and experience" and that lasts.[18] Still others savored their children's pride in their work, and the pleasure of having, as one put it, a daughter "who thinks all mothers fix things in the house when they break."[19]

Tradeswomen were gaining not only income and dignity but physical strength, too, as they changed their bodies to cross the gender divide. Typically, construction workers had to be able to pick up and move up to seventy pounds. As training groups would point out, "any woman who's ever carried children or groceries can carry 70 pounds." For those unable to at the outset, women's training programs offered physical conditioning courses. "We were running five miles every other day. We were lifting weights," remembers one Massachusetts woman. "We were ready to take the world on!" Some women liked the trades precisely for this reason. The attraction of plumbing, said one, "was being able to use my body and be physical, which I love to do, plus being able to use my mind" in a practical, applied way. "My body feels in shape," a former minimum-wage short-order cook told an interviewer. "I feel very healthy." Tradeswomen's groups fielded softball teams and organized basketball, volleyball, or bowling; a few members became champion weight lifters.[20]

The timing was perfect: physical aptitude mattered to feminists in the 1970s. As the anti-rape movement got under way, its activists turned to self-defense with the motto "Fight Back!" In 1975 some launched a magazine called *Fighting Women News*. Dozens of others put out books, manuals, and training films with titles like *Fear into Anger* and *Nobody's Victim*. Hundreds set up classes to train women in self-defense and martial arts which attracted thousands of recruits.[21] The idea of self-defense focused interest on the body. By achieving physical prowess that was once a male monopoly, women could avert assault without sacrificing their freedom.

Not just feminists but others touched by the movement began to imagine how women might use their bodies in new ways. Sports were transformed. In 1972, when women won the right to equal access to athletics in Title IX, there had been little popular pressure for it. But support soon grew. "Without Title IX, I'd be nowhere," said Cheryl Miller, one of the leading players on the gold medal–winning women's basketball team at the 1984 Olympics. The numbers of women involved in intercollegiate athletics grew fourfold from 1971 to 1995. Among high school students, the age group most likely to go directly into the building trades, the numbers leaped from 300,000 to 2.4 million between 1971 and 1995.[22] Growing physical confidence spurred women to consider work that required some brawn as well as brains.

⌒ THE TRADES HAD BECOME potent cultural symbols. After President Nixon's retreat from the Philadelphia Plan and some tradesmen's well-publicized rallies in support of the war in Indochina and against busing in Boston, male "hard hats" became emblems of the populist conservatism energizing the New Right. But the women joining the trades sent a different signal. Doing their jobs alongside men on sites open to public view, they became icons of the remaking of gender that was under way. Clad in jeans or coveralls and sporting tool belts and hard hats, they flouted stereotypical femininity by projecting physical power and competence where women were said to have none. Just going about her job, the tradeswoman seemed to be avenging the injuries of others. "I remember, particularly in those first years, the enormous encouragement I felt from women on the outside, as though I represented them as well," recalled electrician Susan Eisenberg. "Women driving past my jobsite who would notice me and honk and give me a raised fist."[23]

The influx of tradeswomen seemed to right an old wrong that still rankled. As scholars in the new field of women's history reminded Americans, in World War II "Rosie the Riveter" had excelled at nontraditional work, but employers, co-workers, and government stole her success away when the men returned from war. In the 1980s the documentary *The Life and Times of Rosie the Riveter,* with its dual message that women could master any work if given the chance and that their exclusion was a shameful injustice, became one of the most popular feminist films ever produced. Tradeswomen's groups showed it to teach members their history and open discussions of ongoing problems. Leaflets promoting affirmative action referred to the story; activists sold Rosie the Riveter paraphernalia to raise money and remind women that they now had another chance to show what they could do.[24] Performing the pliability of gender by taking up tools coded male in spaces once closed to their sex, Rosie's heirs signaled a change in the whole structure of power perpetuated by assigned roles for men and women.

The women most interested in the new options were often those least likely to benefit from the male-oriented family wage system, especially low-income women raising children on their own. "All I'd ever been was married," recalled a white North Carolina woman who trained to become a plumber. "I had separated from my husband, had a small child to support, no skills. I was a high school dropout. . . . The night I graduated from that program I was on cloud nine. It was the first time in my life that I had completed something that was important to me. . . . When I think back to how I used to be, it's real scary, and I wouldn't ever want to be back there again." According to a Boston woman, "It was very exciting to have a skill, to feel as though I didn't have to depend upon the state, welfare, to support myself and my kids." Bordering on religious conversion testimonies, such expressions from newcomers pervade the sources on nontraditional work. "I'm glad I went to jail," said a participant in a program to train female ex-convicts for the trades. "If I hadn't, I wouldn't have found WOW and my new life." Other women described how their new jobs and income altered relationships with husbands, friends, and children, even acquaintances, and helped them achieve a novel sense of competence. "One of the biggest rewards of a high-paying construction job has been to feel less trapped by traditional gender roles at home," said one. "My husband and I have been able to switch back and forth between being the primary income-earner and being the primary home- and child-care person."[25]

Among the women for whom the family wage was a mirage were lesbians. Although heterosexual women accounted for the majority, large numbers of gay women entered the trades. Perhaps having braved scorn for their unorthodox sexuality in youth helped some lesbians acquire the inner strength needed to persist. Or perhaps those women who had developed a "butch" transgender identity, or who, like Melinda Hernandez, had been "tomboys" as youths, found construction work especially attractive. For lesbians coping with a male-dominated gay rights movement and with heterosexual feminists fearful of what Betty Friedan called "the lavender menace," the trades may have promised new authority. Whatever it was that drew lesbians in, when six hundred tradeswomen gathered in San Francisco in May 1983 for the first National Conference of Women in the Trades, there was enough interest that a workshop was offered on "being 'out' as a lesbian on the job."[26]

~ YET WOMEN WHO WENT into construction found their initial euphoria difficult to sustain. The timing of President Carter's executive order could not have been less propitious. The movement to gain access had begun in the midst of the long economic boom of the 1960s, but the prospects were much less promising by 1978, when the government finally announced goals and timetables for women in the trades. Also, even if women were enthusiastic, most of the men they encountered on the job were not. The seventeen-month recession of the mid-1970s that had galvanized business leaders and conservatives produced layoffs that decimated the ranks of construction workers. The United Brotherhood of Carpenters alone lost 68,000 members between 1974 and 1978.[27] The dread of job loss became the lens through which many white men in the trades eyed newcomers. A woman taking the plumbers' exam in California with three hundred men reported that one came up to her fuming, "Not only do I have to compete against all these guys, I have to compete against you, too." Women were entering the industry in the wake of much hardship; no one knew whether the recovery would last.[28]

The nature of tradesmen's occupations and their organizations led them to be wary of newcomers. Construction unions were not industrial unions open to all but craft associations. By restricting access to training, they controlled the size of the labor force and thereby sustained wages and conditions for members. Skill was to them a kind of property, like the tools craft workers owned and brought to their jobs; it protected their autonomy and nourished a camaraderie found in few other occupations. Tradesmen called their organizations brotherhoods (as in International Brotherhood of Electrical Workers) in honor of the premodern fraternal guilds on which their founders modeled them. Because employment in construction was so volatile, the brotherhoods tightly controlled access to the trades. This was especially true in the 1970s: unions took on only as many apprentices as they believed could find steady work, numbers that dropped as unemployment rose.[29] Construction work was also seasonal and job-specific; the end of a job meant the start of a new set of negotiations with unfamiliar foremen and co-workers. Staying regularly employed thus required initiative. Safety was a consideration, too. Construction was highly dangerous work. There were times when partners had to hold ladders or rope lifts for one another, for example, so it was hardly irrational to want a strong partner. Fear that newcomers, especially women, might lack the capacity to do the job well was a reasonable concern.[30]

Skepticism that women could do "men's work" was a product of everyday experience over the years. Helping fathers around the house, playing on sports teams, working on cars: this was the lore of growing up male in the postwar years. Few women had such informal training. While steering boys to wood, metal, and auto shop classes, schools assigned girls to sewing, cooking, and typing. In 1977 NOW was just starting to campaign to open shop classes to girls. "Some of these guys [on the job] had been with their dads for years and years," said carpenter Lorraine Bertosa, "but I'd never done any hammering." "I came into the trades with absolutely no knowledge of how to work with tools," said another, who nevertheless managed to become "a good carpenter." Tradesmen could sense that unfamiliarity. Although the trades required more mental skill than physical power, and although machines and prefabricated products had reduced taxing labor, each trade still had its share of heavy materials that needed to be lugged around worksites: pipes, steel, lumber, glass, and concrete. A large man paired with a small woman could reasonably fear that they might be less productive as a team, or that he might have to pick up the slack. One woman recalled how the journeyman she was assigned to "hated it. I was too skinny, I wasn't strong enough." Practical considerations aside, few men in construction had ever worked with a woman, so women's entry stunned them: it was antithetical to a lifetime's experience.[31]

But if surprise and some wariness were predictable, the fury that greeted pioneering tradeswomen was a shock. They were never allowed to forget that, as one put it, "you are entering an area [the men] have designated as their own." Many men simply refused to work with women. Others refused to talk to them, let alone train them. If they acknowledged the female newcomers at all, it was to stare at them in silence or belittle them to other men. "She can work," one told his foreman, "but we will not be partners." Such a freeze could last weeks, and might occur without another woman anywhere on the worksite to offer support.[32]

Foremen and co-workers expressed their hostility in ways that ranged from petty to life-threatening. "If a foreman comes up to a group, he'll look at everyone but you," one woman gave as an example; "he'll delegate jobs to everyone but you, and then you have to go up and ask him." Virtually all tradeswomen interviewed had been on at least one job where the men routinely ignored them and refused to eat lunch with them. "We were finally forced to actually bring our lawyer with us when we took these fully trained, competent women down to the hiring halls," a program staffer who worked with laborers in the mid-1970s recalled, "so that [they] could legally document the numerous incidents of outright discrimination." And this was in a union that cooperated in getting women into the trades. Supervisors at another company "just rolled on the floor with tears in their eyes—they thought it was the funniest thing in the world" that women wanted jobs. Several women reported violent opposition: one team who went to apply for jobs had a brick thrown at them; others were shoved down steep hills or into holes, falls that might have hospitalized them, or were sent into poison oak, exposed to potent electric currents, or sabotaged in other ways. One man walked up to a car full of tradeswomen eating lunch and urinated on it. When a Boston woman completed her training, she was told outright by a union hiring agent, "We had the colored forced down our throats in the '60s and we'll be damned if we'll have the chicks forced down our throats in the '70s."[33]

The hostility flowed from a visceral reaction: the men simply refused to believe that women were there just like them, to do the job. When Susan Eisenberg arrived at a downtown Boston bank to assist a journeyman electrician, the security guard denied her access. "He'd figured I was a terrorist planning to bomb the bank. In 1978, that seemed more likely than that I might actually be an apprentice electrician." One pipe fitter reported, "I wasn't allowed to do certain types of jobs." If she tried, some of the men would take the tools out of her hands. Not able to get proper training, some women suffered injuries; then, the accidents would serve as "an amulet to frighten women into leaving" or as evidence of their inability to do the job.[34] As women stretched to claim for themselves the physical prowess, competence, and camaraderie the skilled trades signified, men blocked their way. Though they complained that women didn't know how to do the job, they repeatedly refused to train female apprentices along with their male counterparts. More than half of all tradeswomen in one survey reported this kind of treatment. On her first day on the job as a trainee, Paulette Jourdan waited and waited for her co-workers to give her something to do, finally asking, "Aren't you guys supposed to train me?" They stared at her, she recalled, "and two of them said at the same time, 'We ain't got to show you shit.'"[35]

Women of color like Jourdan faced the worst hostility. White tradesmen who had fought so hard to keep out black men were not about to accept their sisters. "I am the only black woman on my site," reported a journeyman carpenter on a Manhattan project. There is "a great deal of racial name calling directed at blacks. It's very up front!" A white ironworker confirmed, "I see a lot of prejudice towards blacks." What black men faced was hard enough, but "a black female—God help her."[36] One Mexican American woman said, "Race played a big role [in men's hostility]." "If you were not white, you were not good enough. Just because you had a different shade meant you were dumb or an idiot or ignorant." Some of her white co-workers did inferior work, "but just because they were white it was all right for them to make mistakes." Mercedes Tompkins, an African American woman, "felt really unsupported" even by "the white women" at her first job, who seemed willing to accept harassment as something "that happens" when "you're an apprentice." Yet "as a black woman," for whom servitude had added meaning, she found that the treatment "was really affecting my self-esteem." She finally left the trades. The abuse was so bad, confessed another black woman, that "I have this hatred for the white male. Every night, every morning, I ask the Lord to take this hatred from me. This job has changed me so much."[37]

That gender anxiety and not just fear of job loss drove the men's reactions was obvious in their efforts to humiliate female newcomers. Sexual harassment was just acquiring that label in the years when women first entered construction, as feminists organized against it and created a legal analysis of how it violated women's rights to fair employment under Title VII. Men's sexual attention to women in the workplace, such activists contended, aimed to drive women from desirable jobs, affirming these workplaces as men's exclusive terrain.[38] No other industry bore out that analysis as starkly as construction. One woman recalled of her apprenticeship training that "the instructor used to let the guys bring in porno movies" and watch them at lunchtime. That level of complicity was unusual. What was more typical was men posting pornographic images on jobsites. Such images had long been part of shop-floor culture, but once women arrived, the display was aimed deliberately at them. "As soon as I came on the job," said Mercedes Tompkins of her first job, working on the Prudential Center in Boston, "the pin-ups went up, the naked ladies and the jokes—the works." Sometimes when women complained and had the pictures taken down, even more would go up in response.[39] The men sought through such acts to subdue the threat female co-workers posed to their own gender identity. They issued a tacit warning: if women ceased to be "ladies" and refused individual men's "protection" by claiming a place as equals, then any man could treat them as sexual prey.

If only a minority of men put up such images, they did so on the majority of worksites, and few of their peers ever tried to stop it. Melinda Hernandez felt especially bitter that when one co-worker harassed her with pornographic photographs, the other men "were laughing." No one protested, not even the "born-again Christian, [sitting there] reading a Bible." Sometimes unions came to the women's aid, but often they sided with the men. "One time I ripped some porno off the wall, a poster-size crotch shot of a woman," recalled a Seattle plumber, "and the apprenticeship coordinator said . . . that I had to understand I was in a man's trade, and that the men shouldn't have to live by my rules." When more smut "disappeared," he warned her that she might be "sued by the union for taking personal property." No one expressed the men's attitude better than the shop steward who told a woman protesting the hiring of a stripper for a birthday party in the jobsite shack, "Just because we have to take you in, doesn't mean anything has to change because you're here."[40]

Some men used more than sexual imagery against women. In the one systematic survey extant, 83 percent of tradeswomen reported unwelcome sexual comments and 57 percent reported men asking for sex or touching them inappropriately. In a federal study, more than five in every ten women in nontraditional jobs reported having experienced sexual harassment. It ultimately led many to leave the trades; those who endured unwanted touching were likeliest to go. In addition, supervisors told some women seeking work that, as a Kansas City apprentice carpenter put it, "if I would fool around with him, he'd give me a job." Some men tried to intimidate women and drive them out by talking with other men about sex in their presence. "There were a couple of guys who, whenever I was within earshot, would get into this loud and disgusting rap about all the horrible things they had done to women," remembered a plumber of her first job, and then "glance over to . . . check out the reaction." They also baited their female workmates by calling them "dykes." "They take refuge in the belief that we are all lesbians," noted one Albuquerque electrician.[41] For all the men's bravado, there was more than a little panic in their efforts to convert the women from threatening co-workers to sexual quarry.

The struggle was not only over what women could do but also over what manhood meant. "Somehow if a woman can do [the job]," observed one tradeswoman of most men's reactions, "it ain't that mascu-

line, not that tough." There was a dominant model of masculinity in
the trades, but it was not authoritative enough to inhibit competitors.
In fact, there was a variety and evolution of male responses in construction as in other jobs: the nice guys rarely outnumbered the hostile ones,
but they did deprive them of total victory. "There was this one guy," recalled a North Carolina plumber, "who actually believed that a woman
could make it, who gave me the benefit of the doubt. He kept telling
me that if I'd just quit listening to the bullshit and do my job I'd make
it." Particularly after the novelty passed and women had been on the
job for several months, rare was the workplace in which they confronted a phalanx of uniformly hostile men. Studies of women in nontraditional blue-collar work more generally in the early 1980s argued
that "men who strenuously oppose working with women are probably
in the minority." At least a fifth of men in some nonconstruction blue-
collar work "strongly approved" of having women in craft jobs, according to the estimates of female co-workers. Stories surface regularly of
male mentors or allies on the job as a source of respite that kept the
women going. Some fathers, moreover, encouraged their daughters'
interest and helped them get training and jobs, much as fathers had
long sponsored sons in construction.[42] Like co-workers, husbands varied in their attitudes. Some women described their spouses as "very
supportive" at every stage. Others enjoyed the income but showed little
interest in their wives' work. Still others were so threatened by the high
wages and male co-workers that they tried to make their wives quit in
contests that led to divorce. A woman Hernandez began with quit after
"her husband beat her up because he refused to let his woman work in
construction."[43]

Because the spectrum of male responses was wide, day-to-day politics mattered, for which side would prevail was an open question. No
one knew in the early years who would win over the unpredictable middle. "We believed that the path we were opening," recalled an early
electrician, "would eventually become an ordinary road."[44] Could a
tradeswoman or her male ally persuade others and even win over a majority on a given jobsite so as to improve day-to-day quality of work life
for women? No one could be sure in advance. Women in the trades had
to give much thought to such everyday politics, and some of their strategies were inspired. Cynthia Long was apprenticed to a journeyman
who, determined *not* to teach her how to be an electrician, kept her

running pointless errands and turned his back to her when doing complex work she needed to observe. "So what I did is, I tried to figure out, what was he interested in? He was into model trains. So I'd ask him questions about model trains. He'd be happy and talking about his model trains, then I'd throw in a question. 'People keep talking about galvanized pipe—what is it?' He would answer it because he was already in a good mood. I would get information out of him that way." Then, "once it sank into him that I was going to try, his attitude gradually changed," Long said. "He decided that I was going to be his proof to the union that he was a good electrician, 'cause he was going to make me 'The Best Electrician.'"[45] When camaraderie came, it could be intoxicating. "I just started walking taller around these ironworkers," said Lorraine Bertosa in explaining why skyscraper work was "heaven." "I got respect from them. They weren't afraid to hand it out if you deserved it."[46]

As women gained experience, they learned to predict which men were most likely to become allies. Black men, who also struggled for access, tended to be most supportive of the women's right to work, although some engaged in sexual harassment.[47] More surprising, older men proved more accepting than younger men. "It's been my experience," said one carpenter of men under thirty, "that they are threatened by a woman doing a man's job." Perhaps older men's seniority made them feel less threatened, or perhaps their age reduced sexual tension or anxiety about manhood. That hypothesis gains support from the immunity many married women enjoyed from co-workers' advances. One woman noticed an instant change once she married; men who had crudely tormented her became "friends."[48]

Most of all, though, age seemed to yield a more empathic imagination, inducing the older men (most of them fathers) to picture female co-workers as daughters. That metaphor came up again and again. "I think it's easy, for a white man especially," mused a plumber in accounting for a "wonderful" foreman she'd had, "to put a white woman . . . in the role of their kid. Even if they don't think it's good for you to be doing the work, they have a family feeling for you."[49] Showing such feeling, the man who helped one woman withstand her apprenticeship continued to send her anniversary cards every year, well into his retirement, to mark the day she became a journeyman. Paulette Jourdan fondly remembered the union apprentice coordinator who, after she suffered much misery during her apprenticeship, took the time to explain, with drawings, the things no journeyman plumber on her first jobs had taught her. "It was like *The Miracle Worker* when the deaf girl finally understands what all those finger movements were about. . . . After that I was fine." There are many such stories of "exceptional" men. "That's how I got through it," said one woman: "guys like that."[50]

‿ ACTIVIST WOMEN who entered the trades often proved especially able to relate to supportive men in part because of their shared commitment to unions. They, more than others, were driven by the hope that, as one put it, someday "we'll grasp arms and sing *Solidarity Forever* without a list of exceptions." Experiences varied from place to place and from trade to trade, but over the next generation the Seattle local of the IBEW became a model of what could be achieved. By 1993, its new class of one hundred apprentice electricians included twenty-seven women. Over time, a group that had started as an unwelcome handful had converted the local to recruiting large numbers of women, providing child care at union meetings, holding a national women's conference, and using contract negotiations to require foremen to take sexual harassment and racial discrimination training. "I think that the real Neanderthals are getting to be the minority," said one of the women responsible.[51] That the Neanderthals and not the newcomers became the endangered species in her local proved the value of the micro-politics practiced by activist tradeswomen.

In the meantime, the activists helped keep up the spirits of others by creating new forms of mutual support. United Tradeswomen, for example, sustained Melinda Hernandez and other New York pioneers. In such groups, female hard hats could overcome, at least temporarily, the despair caused by isolation on the job and share strategies for coping with opposition. Through them, tradeswomen forged a collective identity as well as new individual ways of expressing who they were and what they stood for on the job. They used humor and satire to sustain morale, as when United Tradeswomen sponsored a "Blue Collar Fashion Fantasy Show and Dance." Hundreds bought tickets to see tradeswomen decked out in gender-and-labor fantasy wear—like the disco electricians wired with flashing lights, the S&M electrician sprouting wire whips, and the tradeswoman with the hard hat that looked like a giant breast (to demonstrate the way she felt at work). "It was such

a great spirit," recalls an organizer, "taking on the culture and transforming it into something that we could really deal with and have fun
with."[52]

Similar in many ways to the consciousness-raising groups that spread
the word of women's liberation and the caucuses that infused anti-
racism and feminism into workplaces, these mutual support groups
partook of another model increasingly familiar in American life. The
self-help group was its prototype: a quasi-confessional forum in which
peers came together and emerged stronger from sharing their weakness and anger in emotional exchanges that solidified their commitment to shared goals. The reason she participated in Women in the
Trades, explained one carpenter, was that she needed "that sympathy,
that understanding, and to share the feelings of accomplishment." Such
support could be enough to deter a woman from quitting the trades in
surrender.[53] The groups worked their magic in simple ways: monthly
potluck dinners, local newsletters, national conventions, and *Tradeswomen Magazine*, which allowed women to process and share their experiences in poetry and prose.[54] Because of them, pioneers could feel
like part of something historic and worthy of sacrifice.[55] Helping
women stay in the trades, support groups equipped them to shape
change in day-to-day interactions with male co-workers on the job.

Nevertheless, there were sharp limits to what could be achieved at
the micro-level by support groups, let alone by individual women and
their individual male allies. Even more than other lines of work, construction was not about to be refashioned by one-on-one encounters.
In an industry fragmented among hundreds of thousands of contractors and thousands of local unions, with unparalleled turnover as hiring
began anew with each project, voluntary efforts were doomed. Construction employers had recognized as much when they appealed for
government backing to help weaken the building trades unions in the
Nixon era. Tradeswomen and their allies understood that, ultimately, it
was not micro-politics but macro-politics that would prove decisive.[56]

Most construction employers were initially as hostile to affirmative
action as were working men afraid for their jobs. Contractors had projects to complete on deadline, with innumerable elements to juggle.
Sexism aside, the last thing they wanted was new obligations or paperwork. This was all the more true in the 1970s, when their industry was
taking much of the blame for runaway inflation. One contractor who

held $15 million in government contracts in 1981 and employed no women told researchers that setting affirmative action goals and time-tables was "the only way" to open the industry. "Contractors are not going to do it voluntarily." Some smaller contractors simply refused to have women on the job. Large contractors were rarely on site to prac-tice the in-your-face resistance of workers, but they were far more powerful. Their trade group, the Associated General Contractors, fought hard to prevent federal agencies from enforcing inclusion. While lobbying the White House to end affirmative action, in the meantime they also urged the OFCC not to enforce goals and timeta-bles for women's and minority men's participation in the trades.[57]

Over time, women's employment groups found that employers' level of commitment to inclusion was the single most important factor in de-termining how women would be received by co-workers. "The mes-sage has to be unequivocal," explained one veteran, "that driving these particular women out is not going to keep women out. If these particu-lar women go away, we're going to hire more." From firm to firm, there were radical variations. On one side was Stein & Company, a Chicago developer with a woman president and a strong commitment to affirmative action. By the early 1990s, it was known for having sev-eral dozen women on large jobsites, for training supervisors to estab-lish an inclusive workplace, for disallowing pornography and sexual graffiti, and for providing clean and locked separate toilets and chang-ing facilities for men and women.[58] Given how decisive management attitudes were, the women's groups worked to shape them with hand-somely produced materials detailing the measures needed for genuine inclusion.[59] By the early 1980s, WOW had established an Industry Ad-visory Committee for its nontraditional jobs program and was invit-ing funding support and advertising assistance from corporations. "Choosing cooperation over confrontation," announced the appeal, "WOW has served over 30,000 women and hundreds of employers."[60]

Contractors, for their part, took their cues from government. "Nu-merical goals," one union official admitted to an investigator, are "the only way to get people to hire women. If we would do the right thing to begin with, government wouldn't have to make us." The signals from Washington, however, changed with the larger political climate.[61] After Nixon and subsequent Republican leaders recognized the potential for blue-collar conservatism, they curried support in particular from hard hat union leaders, encouraging white tradesmen's notions of their own entitlement as well as their devaluation of newcomers. Conservatives then presented blue-collar white men like Brian Weber to the public as victims, insisting that they had suffered personally because of affirmative action "handouts" to unqualified men of color and women. Indeed, no sooner had women's training groups opened their doors than some began to lose federal job training funds for alleged "reverse discrimination" against men.[62]

The men of the construction industry were also encountering the prospect of female co-workers at a time when a powerful anti-feminist movement led by Phyllis Schlafly and backed by the wider right was preying on popular anxiety about the breakdown of the family wage. Real women did not want more challenging jobs, they maintained; those who did were unhappy oddballs with axes to grind. Many in the New Right were determined to reverse the wider gender revolution in which tradeswomen braved the minefields that deterred others. "What really worried homemakers about the ERA," concluded one political scientist, "was the way it seemed to promote a public image of women having the same needs and capacities as men." That was precisely the message the tradeswomen's movement embodied; the right framed that core feminist proposition relentlessly as a danger to male breadwinners, female homemakers, and society at large.[63] Even some men who worked well on the job with women hesitated to mention their presence to their wives for fear it might cause friction, presumably fear of adultery and desertion. After six months of friendly partnership with an older journeyman, one tradeswoman found that he hadn't told his wife he was working with a woman. "I told her," he said, "that I work with a guy named Frank."[64]

One could gauge the impact of the shifts in national politics in how far short of its initial expectations the tradeswomen's movement fell, despite the initial exuberance and widespread interest among women. Even the limited nationwide goals announced by President Carter in 1978 were never met. The proportion of women among the nation's skilled tradespeople reached just under 2 percent by the early 1980s but then stalled, climbing only to 2.5 percent by 1996. The lack of strong, consistent backing from government had taken its toll and strengthened resistance. Still, the variations in outcome showed that the bleak overall picture after twenty years was in no way inevitable: greater inclusion was possible.[65]

⁓ THOSE WHO HAVE the audacity to believe the world can be made better by collective effort never know in advance whether they will be proved right. They take what is necessarily a leap of faith and then work to realize their vision. The notion that "the time was ripe" for success emerges only with the comfort of hindsight as we gaze back on success that was entirely unpredictable when the activists set to work. In many ways, conditions looked ideal for the tradeswomen's struggle in the late 1970s. Feminism had become the most vibrant social movement of the era, and seemed to be going from victory to victory. More than ever before, Americans expressed commitment to universal equal employment opportunity. Government was acting on that commitment by including women in federal affirmative action programs. Formerly excluded groups were allying in new ways and making headway in the progressive wing of the labor movement. There was a constituency of women who needed the income the skilled trades could provide, who wanted the challenge and satisfaction of the jobs themselves, and who were winning over a significant minority of white male co-workers. And advocate allies were developing an infrastructure of groups with expertise in opening such employment to women. Yet things did not work out as envisioned; in the end, other unforeseeable elements of the evolving context favored their opponents. In this, the tradeswomen's story illuminates the fate of broader progressive reform efforts after the mid-1970s, which sputtered and stalled for reasons that still mystify those who lived through these events.

As the corrosive recession of mid-decade energized the right, it disoriented and divided the left. But before it hit, some labor unions had made striking headway in advancing the inclusion of men of color and women. Among them were the American Federation of State, County, and Municipal Workers (AFSCME), the hospital and health care union Local 1199, and the United Farm Workers (UFW). They undertook aggressive new organizing drives, lobbied for a more generous welfare state, aided in the passage of civil rights legislation, and secured anti-discrimination commitments in their contracts with employers. Some defended affirmative action in the courts from lawsuits alleging reverse discrimination. Their women members acquired and wielded power through them, winning protection from pregnancy discrimination and from pay disparities for men and women doing the same work, securing grievance procedures for job-related injustices such as sexual harassment, striking over pay equity, and more. The unions that delivered the most for their female and minority male members had common characteristics. They often operated in the public sector, had strong national centers able to take action against locals that failed to serve all members, involved less-skilled workers, and enrolled large numbers of workers of color and women, who made up pluralities or even majorities of their membership. To be progressive and inclusive made sense for them, even in the short term. Attracted by such efforts, women joined in growing numbers, until they accounted for 37 percent of all union members by the outset of the 1990s. Yet the layoffs of the mid-1970s and the era's fiscal crisis in the public sector hit all of labor hard. Coming at a pivotal moment, the impact disrupted the momentum toward inclusion. Survival, not innovation, became the pressing issue for American unions.[66]

As the economy worsened, bruising clashes over how to deal with layoffs spread; they alienated both parties in the labor–civil rights alliance that had been the heart of postwar progressive reform. Every union ranked the defense of seniority above affirmative action in the recession of 1970s. As the only thing that protected workers from the arbitrary whims of an employer, seniority was sacrosanct. In vain did Eleanor Holmes Norton at the EEOC plead with unions either to grant "super-seniority" to minority men and all women to compensate for past exclusion or to adopt work-sharing strategies to save the newcomers' jobs. The AFL-CIO's leaders refused to consider such alternatives. Respecting seniority, the Ford Motor Company laid off six hundred women and General Motors laid off four hundred in 1975. This, rued one NOW leader, amounted to "nearly all the women who had been hired in recent years through affirmative action." An AFL-CIO Civil Rights Conference held in April 1975 lined up the membership against innovative job-sharing proposals to share the burden of the crisis. As one attendee summarized what it taught, "Layoffs are the worst possible occurrence, but four-day weeks, forgoing raises, etc. are also abhorrent to union workers."[67] The lack of commitment of labor's top leaders, let alone most white Americans, to aggressive job creation and creative job defense policies in turn pushed civil rights organizations to rely more and more on race and rights-based strategies for winning jobs, strategies then criticized by labor and liberals for not being "universal."[68]

The officials pointed fingers in part because they had few positive

ideas for addressing their own ever more obvious weaknesses. Organized labor itself was undergoing a pronounced long-term decline in
these years that muted it as a voice for working people and for progressive politics more generally. Less and less did the AFL-CIO succeed in
moving social justice legislation such as the Civil Rights Act, or even in
organizing the unorganized. Even as some affiliate unions and rank-
and-file activists practiced creative social unionism, the ostrich-like response at the federation's headquarters overshadowed their efforts in
the public eye. From representing almost one third of the workforce in
the mid-1950s, unions declined rapidly after 1975 to the point where
they now include little more than one in ten workers. A rapidly restructuring economy and changing labor market and the rising power of the
anti-union Sunbelt states were among the forces that weakened labor.
At the same time, labor lost moral authority as the AFL-CIO's top officials gave their blessing to the war in Vietnam, presided over undem-
ocratic, even tyrannical bureaucracies, dragged their feet on pushing
recalcitrant affiliates to obey civil rights legislation, and failed to take
seriously their own movement's crisis. By the mid-1980s, all signs
pointed, as one observer sadly put it, to "a labor movement that has lost
its bearings and has no strategic outlook."[69]

As the climate changed and labor floundered, the once helpful link-
ages between organizers and their sympathizers in government grew
strained. If Nixon had let conservatives down, Carter now did the same
to progressives. This was true in many areas, but the most significant
for the long term was economic policy: nothing else so set back the
struggle for inclusion at work, dependent as it was for success on full
employment. With labor enfeebled and social movements demoralized, the Carter administration carried the Democratic Party to the
right in an effort to appease business interests and white suburban voters. In the end, Carter ignored the call of labor and all the main movement organizations for an aggressive jobs policy that would expand
employment. Instead, faced with devastating stagflation, he decided,
as Secretary of Labor Ray Marshall put it, "to use unemployment to
check inflation." As job losses mounted, zero-sum thinking gained in
popularity.[70] Not that there wasn't popular demand for full employment: it was the "number one priority" for 79 percent of Urban League
affiliates according to a 1977 survey and the goal of a vigorous campaign that involved a wide array of liberal groups along with labor.[71] In

addition, Carter failed to deliver on labor law reform, which unions desperately needed because companies were finding it cheaper to pay fines for violating the law against breaking unions than to engage in honest collective bargaining. One aide reminded the president, in vain, that labor law reform was especially sought by "the 'progressive' unions" which "represent our real base of support in labor," not the "stale" building trades–based leaders of the AFL-CIO.[72]

But the challenge went much deeper than recession and the question of which party was in office: the whole political economy was altering in profound ways that flummoxed organizers. The recession of the mid-1970s spurred a fundamental restructuring of capital, labor relations, and the welfare state. Some stark numbers hint at the larger story. "Between 1958 and 1968," reports one labor historian, "there were four million new manufacturing jobs; in the period 1978–83 the manufacturing sector of the economy lost three million jobs." The sources and nature of the changes are much debated and remain beyond the scope of this work, but that tectonic plates were shifting seems beyond dispute. One economic geographer sums up the research by noting, "The only general point of agreement is that something significant has changed in the way capitalism has been working since about 1970." In effect, the very conditions that the earlier successes of the struggles for inclusion had presupposed were being altered in ways that enervated the effort. The civil rights movement and all those who followed its example had depended on the New Deal regulatory state, the vision of social citizenship it embodied, the faith in the power of government to serve justice that produced it, and the membership organizations that tried after the heyday of the New Deal to deepen and broaden the quest for equality. Now changes in the nation's economy and politics were weakening them all. The impact could be seen in a general decline of progressive grassroots activism that debilitated organized labor and movement organizations alike after the mid-1970s. As workers grew less likely to strike, so supporters of equality were less likely to attend demonstrations, let alone carry on the daily, unheralded face-to-face organizing that kept the cause going.[73]

Even the large national membership–based organizations that initiated these struggles, such as the NAACP and NOW, changed. They soldiered on with thousands of members, hundreds of branches, task forces, and annual conventions, yet they felt the loss of grassroots energy. As meaningful ties to their constituents waned and with them such accountability as had existed before, leaders trying to keep their groups afloat looked to business to fill the vacuum. The NAACP, one of the only surviving national civil rights groups, struggled as membership fell from an era high of half a million to 100,000 in 1974. Its executive director, Benjamin L. Hooks, declared: "The age of the volunteer is coming to an end. The problems are getting beyond the scope of volunteers to deal with." One reporter found a new focus at the NAACP's 1978 convention on such issues as "industrial productivity" and "the effects on minorities of changes in the prime interest rate and the need for a more dynamically growing economy." Perhaps concern with economic growth marked an advance. But it came as well from the organization's overtures to corporations in the new context. NAACP board chair Margaret Bush Wilson, for example, served on several corporate boards as she pushed for less reliance on government and more on the private sector.[74] The roster of the Puerto Rican LDEF's annual banquet in 1980 suggested in the extreme how such relationships could change those who built them. Chaired by the president of New York Telephone, it honored the president of Chase Manhattan Bank, the former chairman of the board of J. P. Morgan, and the former CEO of the New York Bank for Savings—but not one person active in the Puerto Rican struggle.[75] LULAC degenerated into a veritable extortion agency. Demanding contributions from companies and threatening boycotts if they failed to deliver, its national leaders grew more adept at the enterprise under the tutelage of Jesse Jackson and Operation PUSH.[76] NOW looked less to corporate donors, yet it too changed as direct mail solicitation to support professional lobbying efforts replaced grassroots involvement in a pattern that was becoming common among all kinds of groups.[77]

What was happening in these groups was part of a national shift toward accelerated professionalization in organizational life. "For the first two-thirds of the twentieth century, a powerful tide bore Americans into ever deeper engagement in the life of their communities," wrote the political scientist Robert Putnam in 2000, "but a few decades ago . . . that tide reversed and we were overtaken by a treacherous rip current. Without at first noticing, we have been pulled apart from one another and from our communities."[78] Across the country and the spectrum of issues, membership-based organizations gave way to those run by professionals, funded largely by foundations and government contracts or direct mail entreaties, overseen by boards made up of business representatives and characterized by weak member involvement, if any. Much of their contact with "members" was no longer person to person or in meetings but through the mail, making them, in effect, "organizations without members." A study of Dayton Working Women, one of the few histories of a local feminist organization in the 1970s, found that while its "leaders did build ties with other clerical organizers, government officials, and private philanthropists . . . ties with their own members, who became accustomed to having programs delivered to them ready-made, were the crucial and neglected ones."[79] The shift from protest to advocacy was partly an adaptation to the information age, as politics came to be dominated by information processors engaged in research programs, public relations, competition for funding, lobbying, and leverage-jockeying. As volunteer activism waned by the late 1970s, this new form surged, not least because it proved hardier than other models under the new conditions.[80]

Those most committed to continuing the struggle made do as best they could in this changing environment, and the women's employment groups illustrate both the successes they achieved and the strains they bore as obstacles mounted and members and volunteers stopped participating in the numbers they once had. On the one hand, professional advocates multiplied, because once the movements won changes in law, the tasks facing reformers changed. There was no way that the old direct action–driven groups could meet the complex challenges of, for example, securing women's access to construction work. Informal groups of volunteers lacked the ability to monitor business and oversee government enforcement efforts in an ongoing way. Nor could they supply reliable expertise such as trained personnel to walk would-be tradeswomen through the rigors of apprenticeship and the hazards of securing work. A similar logic drove the rise of the progressive advocacy groups elsewhere. They grew not only because they could secure funding and resources but also because they met real needs.[81]

On the other hand, the gains came at a cost. Foundations provided the money they desperately needed to operate. Their program officers' advice often enhanced day-to-day efficiency and saved grantees from having to reinvent the wheel. Sometimes, foundations even radicalized the organizations. The National Council of La Raza (NCLR), for example, "reluctantly admitted women and learned to accept and work with them as peers" as a result of Ford Foundation prodding. Yet foundation involvement could limit as well as license: it could discourage fresh thinking, risky alliances, and disruptive behavior. At a minimum, it favored action through established legal channels and employer contacts.[82]

Foundations, and with them Labor Department contracts for job training, tamed the messy struggles that came out of the sixties. Making organizations more similar to one another, they muffled the once bold talk about inequality, power, class, and justice and lured activists away from the disruptive tactics they had used at first. The groups' felt need to win favor likely increased when the weak economy of the late 1970s shrank the foundations' stock portfolios and thus their grant-giving capacity. For as organizations came to depend more on funding from the government and private foundations, they could find themselves expiring if their money streams did. Survivors learned not to scare the grant-givers with too much radicalism.[83]

Reliance on external funding was a symptom of a deeper change: a loss of democratic participation. Following a staff-led, service-based model, these were no longer social movements in the strict sense. Supporters might help as donors or be called upon for shows of strength for the media, but neither volunteers nor client populations were likely to take part in day-to-day operations and decision making. However imperfect democratic control had been in mass membership groups such as NOW and the NAACP, the mechanisms for it existed. But the new groups ran more like businesses whose managers were accountable to investors (in this case foundations, government contractors, and boards of directors) than like assemblies accountable to their constituencies. These distinctions between staff and constituency remained muted in many women's organizations, in which feminist ideals stressed participation and bridge building. Elsewhere they were starker. When PRLDEF, for example, found itself faced with a union drive among disaffected employees in 1983, the board fired nearly the entire staff. Forming a Coalition to Save the Fund, the workers complained that the board did not represent the community and that clients lacked a voice in it. "A constant complaint is that the board is overpopulated by wealthy Latinos," reported one journalist. "The president's job was becoming a place for Latino executives to 'park' while looking for high-level jobs."[84]

The pressures of the new situation were contradictory. On the one

hand, as achieving change increasingly depended on staff success in
winning over government, corporations, foundations, and courts—at
the very moment when the growing conservative movement was pull-
ing these institutions rightward—the arguments for change altered in
ways that widened the split between staff and client populations. The
All-Craft Center thus told prospective funders that a graduate of their
program "becomes an example for her children and the youth of her
community." With a well-paying job, "she is no longer on welfare, taking funds out of the system, but has become a taxpayer and makes a
contribution." If its programs were funded, "there will be fewer numbers on the welfare rolls in future generations." The grant writers even
hinted that tradeswomen would take better care of subsidized housing.[85] Petitioners of the incoming Reagan Labor Department understood that to hold up "program models which have successfully helped
disadvantaged women move into economically self-sufficient jobs" was
to lead with a strong suit.[86] Other projects held out the promise of reducing rates of crime and prison recidivism. Making themselves brokers of other women's fortunes in this way, the organizers were perhaps
also subtly modifying their own conception of whose interests they
were serving and toward what end. Feminist ethics often mitigated the
logic of the situation, as many who had built these groups worked to
get tradeswomen on staff. At Wider Opportunities for Women, trainees who went through the program created an alumnae association to
advise staff, serve as "sisters" offering peer counseling to new entrants,
and promote the program in the wider community. Yet working tradeswomen rarely had a voice in policy making.[87]

Meanwhile, centrifugal pressures within the organizations also grew,
such that even keeping staff members together proved a challenge. The
movement's very successes in making it easier and less costly to be a
woman in the wider society freed other kinds of concerns to come to
the fore. Such unity as existed in the euphoric early days of the movement dissipated as women discovered their differences in practice and
saw how much they mattered. The slogan "Sisterhood is powerful" galvanized white heterosexual middle-class women who had the luxury of
focusing on gender alone. But it made others, less privileged by race,
class, or sexuality, suspicious that their interests would be compro-
mised. Black women and Latinas called for more attention to racism,
wage-earning women and welfare recipients called for more atten-

tion to class inequality, and lesbians called for more attention to homophobia. The pressure was a sign of progress: as long-silenced groups gained some voice and power, friction was inevitable. It also stimulated vital debates on how to broaden appeal and deepen analysis and strategy. Yet activists were coming to terms with their differences and conflicts in a climate in which they were less able than before to mobilize others and achieve new gains. As they sought to explain why, they not infrequently blamed one another. The particular way that issues of race, class, and sexual orientation found expression in this era, in other words, said something about the general loss of direction vis-à-vis the world beyond the organizations. The process was sometimes so personal that it drew attention away from the larger context shaping individual behavior, and so quick to point fingers that it destroyed the trust and the will to cooperate on which mass politics depended. Feeling nearly paralyzed by the scale of the public challenges they faced, many activists turned on one another in place of the more distant and unyielding targets at which they had originally aimed. Conflicts that might have sharpened ideas, redirected goals, and broadened allegiances were instead often handled in such a way as to decimate the ranks in a process that came to be known as "trashing" for the wreckage it wrought.[88]

As organizations that bridged race, class, and sexual orientation, tradeswomen's groups were especially vulnerable. Women on building sites had to cope every day with the cruelest of sexism, racism, and homophobia from some male co-workers. Since understanding and solidarity from other women was so vital to enduring these hardships, failures cut deep and left scars. Tradeswomen's organizations tried hard to raise consciousness and build solidarity. In May 1983, for example, when members gathered from across the United States for their first national conference, there were workshops on "unlearning racism," "affirmation of women of color," and "being 'out' as a lesbian on the job." United Tradeswomen held its first "Gay Women's Rap" in 1981 to open a series about lesbian concerns. Participants identified "a gap of understanding between gay and straight women" and looked to find ways of "building a working relationship" between the two. The group also planned "a newsletter written by and for women of color" to discuss the specific issues that affected them in training, at work, and in their unions.[89]

Yet conflict persisted, and activists found it hard to stick to and advance their social change agenda. When the Southeast Women's Employment Coalition (SWEC) held a workshop on homophobia at a 1986 retreat, the discussion seemed remote from the goal of achieving employment inclusion which had brought participants together. No one even mentioned how homophobia operated on the job, let alone in the wider economy. Instead, the discussion was soul-searching, individualistic, and intensely personal in ways that mirrored the therapeutic culture spreading throughout the country in the 1970s. As one participant described her earnest efforts in the encounter group–style meetings, it was like "shedding your skin from the inside out." Others grew defensive. "Am I homophobic [because] I resent that Lesbian Issues are injected into an already developed agenda?" asked one woman. Another wondered how to keep homophobia from "detracting" from other serious issues. The full impact of the diversity they were seeking seemed to have settled in and raised a host of new issues that disturbed participants and drew attention away from their earlier agenda. Managing internal transformation while staying committed to external projects became almost impossible. "In the pursuit of a greater understanding" of internal "barriers," a staff member observed, "we have in some ways lost the original context," namely, the aim of "achiev[ing] economic equity for women in the Southeast."[90] In its disorientation SWEC was a microcosm of the wider progressive movement in the new era.

In that wider movement, too, as a more daunting context loomed, ideas and goals shifted in ways that weakened the struggle for economic inclusion. As movement organizations, labor unions, and government proved less able to deliver results, the pulls of other kinds of politics grew stronger, and with them skepticism grew about whether workplace organizing of any kind mattered. Excluding the staff-led advocacy organizations, most activists for equality at the grass roots turned away from labor. Many had concerns that reached far beyond the workplace: the questions of identity and sexuality that engaged radical feminists and lesbian and gay rights activists, for example, and of intra-community life and culture that engaged Black Power and Brown Power advocates. And some issues transcended conventional class politics even as they took working-class victims. Police brutality blighted whole communities and attracted much organizing energy; among Chicano groups it was the main focus in the late 1970s, eclipsing schooling and jobs. For their part, many feminists desiring a radical, multiracial women's movement more attentive to reproductive politics and domestic labor began to distance themselves sharply in the mid-1970s from liberal feminists. In seeking to account for the depth and persistence of male domination and racism, theorists turned their sights toward new questions about language and subjectivity. Given how deeply employment matters affected their constituencies' well-being, however, the spreading lack of interest in political economy among many antiracists and feminists remains striking, however much it was encouraged by union leaders' default on their issues. In turning their backs on labor, they were turning away from work as a key source of identity and potential collective power. This disengagement had consequences yet to be fully understood, because the labor movement, however troubled, was and remained not only the largest membership-based force for social change but also "the country's *most* integrated major social institution." Scorning it meant forsaking the political promise present in that diverse membership.[91]

The new context of the late 1970s and early 1980s, so different from that at the time the Civil Rights Act passed, exaggerated the weaknesses of the struggle for inclusion, which before had been counterbalanced by its strengths. In the early years, the grassroots activists and the brokers of inclusion in advocacy organizations, law offices, and government agencies worked together in ways that maximized the effectiveness of all sides and created a synergy that seemed unstoppable. The popular pressure meant that the constituency most affected by and most invested in change was itself actively driving the process. In the context of the dramatic confrontations and devastating riots of the late 1960s that put the nation on edge, the grassroots mobilization focused the attention of elites in government and the judiciary on employment problems and the need for real solutions. For a time, the machinery of law and regulation delivered in ways that transformed lives and communities, as in the southern textile industry. Litigation in sympathetic courts made it possible for workers to beat hostile employers and change recalcitrant unions. But as grassroots involvement receded and brokers could no longer evoke the specter of disruption to convince skeptics of the need for change, at just the point when conservatives were effectively mobilizing new sources of power on their side, the whole calculus changed. The ties between the brokers and the base frayed, and the advocacy groups found themselves relying more and more on law and lobbying and less and less on grassroots mobilization as the courts and government turned away from righting historic injustice. In short, activists grew more dependent on a strategy that was less able to deliver. Perversely, the new situation turned those who had begun as radicals into preservationists. Trying to protect hard-won gains, they no longer felt free to speak the truth as plainly as they once had. The reforms they had won changed the terrain on which they operated.[92]

⟝ The tradeswomen's story offers a dramatic example of the dynamics of desegregating an occupation. In its very extremity, it casts light on the challenge of inclusion in more commonplace situations. To fight exclusion required a lure: interesting work with good wages and benefits that would make braving the unknown inviting. It also required a vision, and in the heady days of the 1970s, as feminism became common sense to more and more people, the prospect of good work no longer restricted by gender inspired experiment. The conviction that women could do anything, that they could escape stereotypes, enter new worlds, and develop long unimaginable skills invigorated workers, advocates, funders, and bystanders alike. Had they been men, the women who entered the trades might be celebrated today as quintessential Americans, explorers whose hunger for challenge led them to brave dangerous frontiers in the hopes of better, fuller lives. Instead, they found themselves treated as freaks and threats by hostile men who blocked their path in defiance of the law.

Yet large numbers did stay. Tens of thousands proved they could do the jobs and do them well. Most poignantly, and most interestingly for students of social change, some managed a moral feat akin to that of the early civil rights activists: through the witness of their dignity and their hard work, they changed the minds of some opponents. In their dedication to their craft and resourcefulness in defusing hostility, they showed how dramatic change can happen in one-on-one encounters in ways that enrich both parties. These micro-histories of women's successes with once hostile co-workers and local unions offer glimpses of an alternative history that might have had a happier ending, not only for the women but also for a nation that claimed to value equal employment and justice for all.

While the record is replete with small-scale triumphs, for the most part the campaign to open the skilled building trades to women is a story of collective defeat. Those committed to exclusion largely won; those who wanted fair access never had the backing to open the door very wide. In other ways, too, these years left a troubling legacy for the future. The ties that once linked fights against discrimination to a broader social justice agenda of full employment and improved wages and conditions for all had been severed. High unemployment was accepted by a Democratic administration as the price of holding down inflation. And social action groups of all descriptions had so changed by the early 1980s that whatever struggles arose now would take place on very different footing. Women's employment groups and tradeswomen felt not so much vanquished as wearied, beset by "battle fatigue" and perplexed about how to secure the fairness that was still so manifestly lacking. The simple human truth of their constituents' story is breathtakingly sad: a group of workers who were determined enough to suffer hatred, bullying, and even violence to pursue a craft they loved, who pushed mightily to decode its mysteries and master its skills, and who labored daily to produce work with undeniable social value may not survive in their chosen vocation. Tradeswomen may go extinct as a social group, much as the wartime Rosie the Riveters did before them, for one simple reason: no one (neither government, nor employers, nor unions, nor co-workers) was willing to enforce their right to do their work. "It was the lonesomeness of pioneering that broke her resistance," wrote an electrician poet, "like the slow eating away of acid on metal: the damage only visible over time."[93]

One lesson the experience made inescapable was that the federal government's backing was essential if women were to find even limited inclusion in the construction industry. It was not the only ingredient for success: women's interest in entering the trades, the organizations that supported them, and the responses they met from tradesmen and unions also affected the outcome. But nothing else other than the economy so shaped the field on which these varied players met as government. What it did, how it did it, and with what seriousness of purpose mattered. Government action or inaction would be the deciding variable. When the conservative movement that had long fought inclusion elected one of its own to the presidency in 1980, this heralded, as two feminists put it, a "long decade in the wilderness."[94]

~ 9

The Struggle for Inclusion
since the Reagan Era

$\mathcal{S}$OON AFTER HIS INAUGURATION as president, Ronald Reagan addressed a gala gathering of the nation's conservatives. In the audience were leaders of such movement institutions as the *National Review*, the American Conservative Union, the Fund for a Conservative Majority, *Human Events, Conservative Digest*, and Young Americans for Freedom. Reagan regaled them with a reminder of "just how far we have come" since Barry Goldwater showed the way in 1964, since men such as Russell Kirk and Frank Meyer first fashioned "modern conservatism," and since the *National Review* was "ridiculed by the intellectual establishment" in 1955. What "a victory of ideas" his election marked, said Reagan. Reagan's new GOP majority differed from that which had prevailed until the 1960s: party leaders no longer felt a need to join forces with the liberal Republicans of the East Coast, whose acceptance of the New Deal state and civil rights remedies had been anathema to the wing of the party that produced Reagan's candidacy. The right exulted, and William F. Buckley, Jr.'s, brother James declared the election a sign that "God continues to love the United States after all."[1]

While Reagan concentrated on foreign affairs and the economy in his first term, some in his administration read his reelection in 1984 as authorization to roll back progressive changes in domestic life which they had long opposed. Just as activists for inclusion had relied on government brokers to advance their project, those on the other side now did the same to reverse a quarter century of policies to promote inclusion. In August 1985 Reagan's close friend and attorney general, Edwin Meese III, along with William Bradford Reynolds, the head of the Civil Rights Division of the Justice Department, set out to effectively rescind Executive Order 11246, and even to prohibit the collection of statistical data to assess whether discrimination existed. The order required affirmative action of all federal contractors: the 15,000 businesses that together employed twenty-three million workers at 73,000 worksites in the United States. One of the greatest victories of the black freedom movement, the contracting program had also opened up new jobs for Mexican American and Puerto Rican men and backed the hiring of women in workplaces from universities to construction sites. Issued by Lyndon Johnson in 1965 and reaffirmed by every successive president, the order built on a principle dating from World War II of using contracts paid with taxpayer dollars to end discrimination.[2]

Seeing the program as an example of big government in action, administration spokespersons denounced its goals as quotas. Making the label stick was essential to the enterprise, because as pollsters found, three quarters of Americans supported affirmative action for women and minorities, "provided there are no rigid quotas." When framed as quotas that hurt others, however, such policies provoked fierce hostility. Using the "reverse discrimination" charge that had proved its superiority to earlier arguments in the 1970s, conservatives insisted that the contracting program discriminated against white men, burdened employers with paperwork and regulations, and failed to help poor blacks. To their mind, it was a case of Uncle Sam coddling those who neither needed nor deserved help at the expense of white men of all classes.[3] The Reagan initiatives, one White House staffer promised, would "wipe out the effect of nearly twenty years of quota programs." The beauty of it, she said, was that "the only community that can be expected to oppose such a change is the entrenched civil rights leadership." This was not a constituency on which the president counted, having won less of the black vote than any previous Republican presidential candidate since the party's founding.[4]

By early 1986, however, the Reagan administration was realizing just how complex the borders between the mainstream and the margins had become in American life. Although they held the White House and controlled core mechanisms of public power, the Reaganites overestimated their strength. For their effort to undo this hard-won reform aroused what one veteran called "the largest coalition ever on a civil rights issue."[5] From the movement-based membership organizations and advocacy institutions of blacks, women, and Latinos, to unions, representatives of the nation's higher education system, and even leading business associations, a storm of protest met the attempt to rescind the order. Expecting an easy time, White House operatives had trouble keeping up with the hostile mail.

Yet as effective at blocking a rollback as they turned out to be, participants in the affirmative action coalition faced challenges of their own that reflected how much ground they had lost. For all the broad support their values enjoyed, cultural authority proved difficult to translate into practical public power. They had won over much of the corporate world to the idea of "diversity," but in the process they had lost the initiative. The grassroots activism that might have fulfilled the whole of the agenda they had originally envisioned, in which freedom and good jobs for all would make for a more equal and better America, no longer existed as it once had. Their ranks had been demobilized and their programs changed by the remodeling which had enabled them to survive and keep working in the face of strong opposition.

Even if the Reagan administration could not eliminate affirmative action, it could, as one student of the presidency notes, "recast civil rights to a degree not seen since Lyndon Johnson."[6] Lacking enough popular support to revoke the reforms outright, opponents found other ways to nullify them. They starved enforcement agencies of resources and subverted them from within by appointing leaders hostile to their missions. The result was the stalemate that has characterized American public life ever since: while inclusive employment retained cultural legitimacy, active enforcement waned. Respect for the law became, in effect, voluntary. Unless the aggrieved were willing to sue in court—an expensive, time-consuming, personally draining, and risky course of action, especially as the courts grew less sympathetic—it became less and less likely that offenders would face any significant penalty for favoring whites and men. "If the tax laws of the United States were enforced as slackly as the antidiscrimination laws currently are," one economist said in 1986, "very few people would pay taxes."[7]

⁓ As outsider activists on the left had depended on allies in government, so did their opponents on the right. No one would do more for them than William Bradford Reynolds, the president's choice to run one of the key agencies of civil rights enforcement, the Justice Department's Civil Rights Division, whose mission was to advocate for those facing discrimination. Just under forty at the time of his nomination, Reynolds had no experience with civil rights policy or law before assuming the position. His own work was in commercial litigation and antitrust law, but even before his swearing in, he took aim at Executive Order 11246. Breaking ranks with every federal appellate court that had ever addressed the question, Reynolds declared to Congress that the Justice Department would no longer push for goals and timetables or any form of "preferential" hiring as redress for job discrimination—regardless of the particulars of the case. With the 1980 Republican platform as his guide, he viewed all such remedies as discriminatory practices that prevented the United States from being a "color-blind" society. Brandishing a copy of the Constitution in his suit pocket ready for citing, Reynolds—in the apt words of the NAACP's director Benjamin Hooks—understood "the law as a very formal set of syllogisms."[8] The Constitution is color-blind, Reynolds reasoned, and the Civil Rights Act forbids discrimination. Affirmative action acknowledges race, gender, and national origin. Therefore, affirmative action violates the Constitution and must go.

Reynolds set about his task infused with confidence from ideas that conservatives had been developing since the 1950s and updating over the previous decade. They believed that claims of discrimination against men of color and women had always been exaggerated; to the extent that it once existed, it was now for all intents and purposes gone. America's employers were eminently fair. The explanation for continuing inequality was simple: exclusion was a supply-side matter. Women were not interested in good jobs because they were by nature focused on motherhood, while men were more aggressive and so did better at work. Blacks—let alone Mexican Americans—were unqualified for the positions they coveted; if they were qualified, no one would bar their way. Employers, government, and white men as a group had done no wrong and had no reason to change because they were already, in Reynolds's terms, "color-blind and sex-neutral." All suggestions to the contrary came from self-interested bureaucrats and freelance agitators whose careers depended on what George Gilder, one of the president's favorite theorists, called "the myths of racial and sexual discrimination." As Gilder summarized the conservative consensus in the *National*

Review, "Discrimination has already been effectively abolished in this country." If anything, there was "discrimination in favor of blacks," a "racial spoils system" that was "odious" to "principle."[9] Reynolds agreed. Such policies were "a free handout" that favored the "barely mediocre" over the "damn good."[10]

Signs of these beliefs abounded in Republican Washington. One Department of Justice official defended his attempts to rewrite civil rights law on the grounds that "racial and other stereotyping is declining and most people now accept the legal and moral imperative to treat people equally." In the Senate, Orrin Hatch convened hearings in June 1981 to discredit affirmative action as more harmful than "inject[ing] heroin in the bloodstream of the Nation." After Vilma Martinez of MALDEF testified to continuing exclusion in American life, a startled Hatch responded, "The one comment that you make is the one that bothers me. That is that there is discrimination in America." Unfazed, this proud son of a construction tradesman continually pressed the administration to overthrow Executive Order 11246.[11]

With Reynolds in the lead, the Reagan Justice Department used its vast power to seek a virtual reversal in American civil rights policy, an end to the government-backed efforts at inclusion developed by both Democratic and Republican administrations since the early 1960s. Perhaps spurred by criticism of the administration in *Commentary* magazine for having "dithered and equivocated" on affirmative action, Reynolds moved to turn post-election proposals from the Heritage Foundation for strict "color-blindness" into law. In this view, only evidence of "willful action" proved discrimination, not evidence of institutional racism or sexism; and only identifiable individual victims, not groups, could legitimately complain of it. Employers should even be "forbidden" to take note of employee demographics. Within twenty months of Reagan's first inauguration, a liberal lawyers' group charged in a major report that the civil rights division had "completely reversed its previous position concerning the appropriate relief in Title VII cases." Angry at the continuing spread of affirmative action despite the right's expanding power, Reynolds had pledged to find a case that would invite the Supreme Court to overthrow the *Weber* decision upholding voluntary policies on the part of employers. This, the attorneys noted, "is tantamount to an announcement that the Civil Rights Division will not enforce the law of the land." In perfect symbolism,

Reynolds joined a lawsuit by some white policemen in Birmingham, Alabama, against what they alleged to be a "quota" for black hiring under a consent decree.[12] After President Reagan won reelection, the time seemed propitious to rescind the federal contracting program.

The effort delighted some longtime affirmative action critics. Representing small businesses that found almost all regulation odious, the U.S. Chamber of Commerce called the repeal proposal "a positive step." Employers must have "the right to employ or promote the best qualified worker," the Chamber insisted, "and race or gender considerations should not be part of that decision making." Working with the Heritage Foundation, the Anti-Defamation League, the Eagle Forum, the Committee on Academic Nondiscrimination, the Associated Builders and Contractors, and the American Subcontractors Association, among others, the Chamber built the Ad Hoc Coalition against Quotas and pressed for a meeting with the president.[13] The effort united Patrick Buchanan, scourge of the left-liberal intelligentsia, with the university professors' association that had fought hardest against inclusive hiring on campus. "Fantastic! The best news to come from Washington in 1985" exclaimed the chair of the Conservative Action Forum, who urged Buchanan to "keep the fight going." The *National Review*, for its part, cheered Reynolds as "one of the heroes of the Reagan revolution"; his "victories" over "oppressive nonsense" involving civil rights "were among the most important domestic achievements" of Reagan's first term.[14]

Even more enthusiastic were the white construction contractors who wrote the president in support of Reynolds and Meese. From Mississippi and Alabama, Vermont and Kansas, Wisconsin and Oregon, from far and wide, builders thrilled to the prospect of not having to hire minority men or any women. "The issue," declared the Associated General Contractors of America, "is one of prime importance to the construction industry."[15] Some police officers and firefighters, occupations nearly as resistant to inclusion as the building trades, wrote to praise Meese and Buchanan for what one called "your concern for the white male" and opposition to the "handout." For their part, the two thousand self-described "conservative business leaders" in the U.S. Business and Industrial Council applauded the proposed revision of Executive Order 11246 as the route to "a genuinely color-blind society."[16]

On the other side, the groups which had fought for inclusion since the 1950s now mobilized en masse to defend affirmative action in federal contracting, which had done so much to advance that goal. Among the members of what one called "an umbrella parliament" were the leading organizations that remained of the black freedom struggle: the NAACP, the SCLC, the Urban League, and the National Council of Negro Women, as well as the Leadership Conference on Civil Rights and the National Black Leadership Roundtable. Executive Order 11246, the Indiana State Conference of Branches of the NAACP told President Reagan, "has been the single most important means of minorities and females overcoming discriminatory hiring and promotion practices in private industry in this country for the last 20 years."[17] The order's work was not yet done, the National Black Leadership Council explained to the president, not when black unemployment was running at two and a half times the national average and black median family income was about half that of white families. The Congressional Black Caucus and black state legislators spoke out too. At the A. Philip Randolph Institute, Norman Hill begged the president not to "unravel 20 years of progress." From the NAACP Legal Defense and Education Fund, one attorney declared that "if President Reagan signs the proposed executive order [overturning 11246], it would be the most anti–civil rights step taken by a President since Woodrow Wilson issued orders requiring the segregation of offices and other facilities in Federal Government buildings."[18]

Latinos also protested, insisting that the policy was vital to realizing the promise of America. The president of the League of United Latin American Citizens, Oscar Moran, warned Reagan that "voluntary compliance" was "doomed to failure." Quoting the text of the existing order, Moran demonstrated that the order's critics "are simply wrong." Closing with a reminder to Reagan that Hispanics were "the one ethnic group in which your administration made the greatest [electoral] gains," Moran asked for better from "the party of Lincoln." The entire Congressional Hispanic Caucus wrote the president to urge him to consider how every presidency since 1965, Republican and Democratic, had sought to "strengthen these much needed provisions."[19]

Having battled the Reagan administration over women's employment, women's organizations now rallied, too, to defend the order. For over ten years, support for affirmative action had been building far beyond the ranks of NOW, which had been the first to push for it, to include groups from the Girl Scouts to radical feminists and all points on the spectrum in between. "This proposal would declare war on equal employment opportunity," Nancy Kreiter of Women Employed proclaimed on behalf of the consensus. "It is a brazen attempt to negate 20 years of slow, progressive improvement in employment opportunities for women and minorities."[20] The League of Women Voters, the voice of civic-minded moderates, reviewed the great good the executive order had accomplished, and reminded Reagan that "the dismantling of a pervasive system of discrimination takes work—and commitment." The National Commission on Working Women elaborated further. Said its director, "Affirmative action has been the single most effective tool for desegregating the American workplace and opening up higher-paying jobs to qualified minority and women workers—jobs that were formerly held exclusively by white males." The National Federation of Business and Professional Women's Clubs, with more than 140,000 members and a tradition of relative conservatism, agreed. Why, the federation asked, *shouldn't* the nation's government "refrain from commerce with contractors who cannot demonstrate a commitment to equal opportunity"?[21]

More unsettling to the Reagan appointees was how the attempted recision had begun to unravel their own coalition. The GOP had little popular African American support to begin with, and this effort was now alienating those few whom the party had attracted. "I am Black and I have been a registered Republican for twenty-five years," wrote one California man, but the threat to the executive order left him with "deep concern and serious anxiety." He pledged to fight it "by every and any means at my disposal." The Council of 100, an organization of black Republicans, registered dismay. The proposed change in the executive order, they predicted, "will be harmful and destruct[ive] to the interest of Council of 100 members, American Blacks, and the future of our country." The board of the National Black Republican Council voted unanimously to condemn the attorney general's plan. Two black advisers patiently explained to Reagan that "Executive Order 11246 is important to your Presidency" because it helped secure what Reagan said he wanted for black Americans: "lasting, meaningful jobs in the private sector" to make them "more economically independent."[22]

Many members of Congress called it the same way. Numerous U.S. senators and representatives signed strong letters against the proposed plan: 194 representatives by late November 1985, and by early 1986, sixty-nine senators. Some assured the president that "minorities and women have finally begun to be included in the American main-stream," but "only because of bipartisan cooperation" for the common good. Twenty-six others, from the Connecticut moderate Lowell Weicker to Dan Quayle, wrote as concerned Republicans. They feared charges of GOP unfairness, and worried, too, that the change would set off "a proliferation of litigation and legislation" causing "instability in the business community and a serious disruption of the legislative process." Charged with leading the president's troops in Congress, the Senate majority leader and the House minority leader expressed near disbelief. "Leave it as it as," implored Senator Bob Dole. Robert H. Michel, his House counterpart, agreed: "When it works, you don't fix it."[23]

The administration had miscalculated the support of white male citizens as well. No doubt remembering the higher education clashes of the 1970s, at least one White House operative, Linda Chavez, protégée of the neoconservative spokesman Albert Shanker, assumed that Jewish organizations would support the attack on affirmative action. But that calculus failed to factor in one of the most intriguing developments of the decade: the success of feminism in penetrating all the major institutions of American life. The American Jewish Committee, for one, had undergone a feminist revolt that had "quite vociferously and effectively" been challenging the organization's male leaders since their campaign to limit affirmative action in higher education. So changed was the AJC that it hired its old nemesis, Bernice Sandler, to lead its work on "women's issues." She, at the same time, rediscovered and re-valued her Jewishness; finding in it the root of her lifelong commitment to "justice" and "learning" alike, she studied Torah on Saturdays while testifying in defense of affirmative action in Congress during the week.[24] Prompted in part by dawning recognition that, as even one hard-line male leader put it, "there has probably been more discrimination against Jewish women because they were women than there has been against Jewish men either because they were Jewish or because they were white" and that "white males are still favored," numerous Jewish community leaders concluded that it had been wrong to present affirmative action as such a threat to Jews.[25] When Reynolds and Meese made their bid to undermine it, all the major Jewish agencies except the

ADL opposed them, saying that they had come to believe that the policy's value outweighed the problems. The AJC now came to the defense of "numerical goals and timetables." In cases where "goals" became treated as "quotas," its leader said, "the answer must be rigorous supervision and correction, not the eradication of the programs themselves." The American Jewish Congress issued a like appeal: numbers, it said, were needed to learn whether contractors were really "hiring and promoting qualified minorities." If the administration feared quotas, it simply needed to do a better job of "polic[ing]" the programs.[26] Some Catholics, a key Reagan constituency also influenced by feminism, spoke out too. Saying the recision would be "a major regression," leaders of Project Equality pointed out that "white males" had enjoyed "preferential treatment for decades."[27]

Leaders in higher education, the site of the earlier challenge by Jewish agencies to affirmative action, rallied now in the policy's defense. The president of the American Council on Education credited Executive Order 11246 for the "substantial progress" colleges and universities had made. Saying that it had "broadened the pool of recruits, expanded internal training programs, and transformed our faculty and support staff with the infusion of individuals with new ideas and backgrounds," he urged the president to leave a good system alone. Individual college presidents and faculty representatives such as the American Association of University Professors and the American Association of University Women agreed that ending or diluting the program would have "disastrous effects on the progress this country has made."[28]

Some in labor's ranks also balked. Progressive unions were vocal in opposition. The public workers' union, AFSCME, called on the president not to undermine fairness "in taxpayer-financed jobs." The Newspaper Guild, too, which had supported the women's and minority caucuses at the *New York Times*, now urged continuation of a program that "has worked well." The International Union of Electrical Workers, where Winn Newman pioneered programs against sex discrimination, pointed to the "dramatic improvements for women and minorities" in the workplace that twenty years of the executive order had made possible. Recision, the union's president said, "would be a giant step backward." Having worked to promote affirmative action for more than a decade, the Coalition of Black Trade Unionists, organized in 1972, and the Coalition of Labor Union Women, organized in 1974, also protested. For its part, the AFL-CIO denounced the plan as "a giant step backward in the fight against employment discrimination." Arguing that "those who opposed civil and women's rights are also opposing labor's rights," the federation's civil rights committee pressed affiliates to defend affirmative action.[29]

Even some craft unionists who might have been expected to welcome the government's retreat from affirmative action did not, perhaps having been won over by the determined and hardworking women and minority men in their ranks. The president of the United Brotherhood of Carpenters and Joiners of America, Patrick Campbell, wrote Reagan "to protest." Calling the executive order "a key weapon" in "the battle against discrimination," Campbell insisted that it "must not be abandoned." Hard hat unionists like Campbell mattered very much as the president's people pursued what one staffer called an "urban/ethnic/Catholic strategy" to court the "blue-collar vote," so such opposition no doubt registered.[30]

But the greatest shock to the Reagan people came from corporate leaders, their core constituency. Business had helped make such a conservative administration possible: it was the mobilization of large corporations in the 1970s that helped transform the country's electoral landscape and reorient its policy debates. White House strategists had expected business to be "relieved" by the gutting of affirmative action in federal contracting.[31] They were wrong: some top business voices claimed that the administration was going too far. The Business Roundtable, which had spearheaded corporate organizing to break construction unions, undo the regulatory state, and restore profitability, now told the White House that "this Executive Order has served American society, workers, and government contractors well for the past 20 years." Setting goals and using numerical measures "are a basic fact of how business operates." The organization had some concerns about the way the program operated, but giving up the effort seemed far worse. The National Association of Manufacturers showed how far it had come since fiercely opposing the Civil Rights Act of 1964. "Companies affiliated with NAM," its president wrote—and these accounted for 85 percent of American manufacturers—"have consistently expressed the belief that the Executive Order has served as a major impetus in achieving a diverse workforce." NAM did call for "fine-tuning of the implementing regulations," but the order itself and the goals and statistics it employed were applauded as "sound policy" that received "enthusiastic support from our members." Even some textile manufacturers, once the fiercest opponents of inclusion, defended the program. As a headline in *Fortune* magazine put it, "Businessmen Like to Hire by the Numbers."[32]

As the business press noted, there were sound reasons for the about-face. Above all, corporations dreaded the prospect of the federal government ceding questions of discrimination to fifty different and potentially conflicting state programs. They also feared a deluge of lawsuits from both sides: disgruntled white men, women, and men of color all might sue for discrimination if federal policy moved in the direction championed by the Reagan administration. Over five thousand lawsuits charging discrimination under Title VII, more than a third of them large class actions, had already been decided by the federal courts by 1981. Faced with the possibility of more such expensive, embarrassing litigation, business leaders wanted, in the parlance of their legal departments, "a defensible performance appraisal system" calibrated to the content of jobs and able to shield them from costly lawsuits. From such considerations, many leaders of large corporations, traditionally more able to absorb regulation, now bucked a friendly administration. A *Fortune* magazine poll in 1989 captured the split: "43% of CEOs polled say they remain fully committed to affirmative action, 59% say they don't plan to change their established programs, and 68% characterize the effect of the programs on U.S. business as good, very good, or outstanding." Some companies were also starting to see such programs as tickets to growing minority consumer markets, and to realize that a majority of their future hires might be white women and people of color. No wonder, then, that *Fortune* described "the mortar binding CEOs to affirmative action" as "a compound of social conscience, fear, and self-interest."[33]

Clearly, Meese, Reynolds, and Buchanan were taking aim at a practice that had become deeply entrenched in American institutional life. They did so with little knowledge of or interest in the employment history or current experience of long-excluded groups. Rather, the effort to rescind the executive order issued from ideology and responded to pressure from conservative supporters to move against civil rights remedies. "The government's offensive," wrote one stunned scholar, "is occurring despite the successes of affirmative action, without the support of public employers and the business community, and in the face of overwhelming acceptance of affirmative action by the federal courts."[34] "Meese and Reynolds are relentless," agreed *Business Week*, declaring that the "arch-conservatives" were "taking a jackhammer" to "an accepted part of U.S. corporate practice." When civil rights supporters called Reynolds, Meese, and Buchanan "extremists," the charge was thus more descriptive than rhetorical.[35]

Seeing how they were dividing the White House from the mainstream, Reagan's advisers came to realize the wisdom of retreat. "The best solution," the White House chief of staff conceded in the spring of 1986, "may be to do nothing." The previous fall, reports had emerged of a deadlock in the administration. On one side were those—led by Meese, Reynolds, and Buchanan—who wanted to end the program in the name of killing "quotas." On the other side were those who believed that the program should be retained—led by Labor Secretary William Brock, and ultimately including cabinet secretaries Samuel Pierce, Jr. (Housing and Urban Development), Margaret Heckler (Health and Human Services), Elizabeth Dole (Transportation), George Shultz (State), James Baker (Treasury), and Malcolm Bainbridge (Commerce). "Impassioned" and unable to reach agreement, the contestants finally sent Reagan three separate and conflicting recommendations.[36] A president who had announced in January 1986 to a jamboree of right-wing luminaries, "Fellow conservatives, it took us more than 20 years," but now "we're rockin' and we're rollin'," had learned that whatever his showings at the polls meant, it was not that the nation wanted to roll back the modest progress it had made toward economic inclusion.[37] Quite the contrary, the maneuver had divided the administration from opinion makers in most walks of life.

That impasse led to dependence on another strategy. In federal contracting as in other civil rights areas, the Reagan administration found quieter ways to subvert agencies it disdained. One was to appoint heads opposed to their missions, all the better if they were African American. To chair the U.S. Commission on Civil Rights, Reagan appointed Clarence M. Pendleton, Jr., a protégé of Edwin Meese in San Diego. The first black head of the commission, Pendleton gained headlines by opposing school busing for desegregation, denouncing affirmative action as a "bankrupt policy," and calling comparable worth policies for women, based on the idea that work of equal value should receive equal pay, "the looniest idea since Loony Tunes."[38] For the all-important Equal Employment Opportunity Commission, Reagan chose the thirty-three-year-old Clarence Thomas, who, during his tenure from 1982 to 1990, presided over a steep drop in job discrimination lawsuits approved. He also returned the agency to strategies whose proven ineffectiveness had by the early 1960s encouraged the turn to affirmative action, namely, a focus on intentional discrimination and individual complaints instead of institutionalized exclusion.[39] Thomas understood that for African Americans to succeed with white conservatives, "you must be against affirmative action and against welfare."[40]

Another way to undermine agencies from within was to deprive them of the resources needed to fulfill their missions. Job losses resulting from budget cuts shrank the staff of the Office of Federal Contract Compliance Programs by half between 1979 and 1985, for example.[41] "They conceive a limited role for government in civil rights," explained the attorney William L. Taylor, "and they are carrying it out by not enforcing the law." A former assistant attorney general documented what he called "the Reagan Administration's failure to uphold settled law" in the area of civil rights. "No matter how purposeful, longstanding, or widespread the discrimination, and no matter how recalcitrant the employer," Taylor noted, "the Reagan Justice Department will limit itself to remedies that history illustrates are unlikely to provide effective relief to minorities and women." The harm "easily done in four years," he warned, "may take a generation to repair."[42]

Scholarly studies supported these predictions. Economists, who produced the only large empirical studies of the impact of Executive Order 11246, highly rigorous examinations involving data from tens of thousands of firms, largely concur in seeing a pattern. The affirmative action requirement gave a significant boost to inclusion, especially in the 1970s. "Despite vigorous contention and weak enforcement," concludes one major study, "affirmative action appears to have played a major role in improving the economic position of minorities and females." This was true in unskilled jobs as well as skilled and white-collar employment. Yet once the Reagan administration took over, progress dwindled. "Affirmative action under the contract compliance program," writes a leading scholar, "virtually ceased to exist in all but name after 1980." The result was not simply "stagnation, but . . . an actual reversal of black advances."[43] Other studies reached similar conclusions about the affirmative action remedies used by the EEOC: they contributed in a limited yet significant way to the gains made by minority men and women of all groups in the 1970s, but that effectiveness ebbed in the 1980s. Such thorough studies of the impact on women have been fewer in number. But it is well established that job segregation by sex declined more dramatically in the 1970s than ever before or since (10 percent in ten years), presumably at least in part because of affirmative action. The gap between women's and men's wages shrank as well.[44] Now that momentum slowed.

The clash over the executive order illustrated not only how opinions and alignments had shifted since the 1950s, but also how the dynamics of social change had altered. The mass grassroots participation that had animated the movements of the 1960s and persuaded establishment leaders to recognize the legitimate grievances of the long excluded had ebbed. Now it was staff professionals, almost alone, who acted as bodyguards of the movement's victories. The 11246 rollback effort had attracted little popular attention. However important the stakes, it aroused at the grass roots and among the young people most inclined to activism in the 1980s nothing like the response that, for example, attacks on abortion rights did among feminists or that police brutality and campus racism did among antiracist activists. The "alternative" press covered the attacks on the federal contracting program, to be sure, and criticized them sharply, but galvanized no collective mass protest.[45] With their constituencies focused on other matters or perhaps even complacent with their gains, the advocacy groups worked in their now customary fashion: staff members issued press releases, made calls, sent off letters, secured media attention, testified at government hearings, and lobbied wherever they might have influence. Whatever the effort may have lacked in popular participation, it worked: the Reynolds-Meese-Buchanan team had to retreat. And that was a hugely important achievement, because it left the reform on the books to await a friendly administration that might again enforce it. But the impasse revealed much about the changed politics of inclusion.

THE MOVEMENT to open good jobs to all had converted many in the ranks of corporate America: having fought affirmative action when it came into being, numerous employers now enlisted in its defense. Pushed by earlier activists, coaxed by advocacy organizations, threatened by lawsuits, enticed by new markets, and persuaded by their own personnel departments, some had indeed come a long way. As they took on the issue, however, they also changed it, above all through "diversity management." Today the rhetoric of diversity has become so prevalent that few remember it first came not from the movement but from a rightward-listing Supreme Court in the *Bakke* case of 1977. In that "reverse discrimination" lawsuit, Justice Lewis Powell, who delivered the tie-breaking vote that saved affirmative action, had called use of race as a criterion in admission policy "inherently suspect"—save where there was another government "purpose or interest" that was "constitutionally permissible and substantial," such as "the attainment of a *diverse* student body" to enhance education.[46] Shoving history and remedial justice to the side, the Court urged attention to the possible benefits of inclusion for institutions thus altered.

That was a fundamental change in the rationale on behalf of affirmative action, away from its original purpose of remedying the continuing exclusion that resulted from historic discrimination. It came in part from the push by neoconservatives and Jewish agencies through the 1970s to deny that being black was itself a source of disadvantage and therefore a justification for race-conscious assistance. And it answered the charges of reverse discrimination by pointing to the common good. Yet in shifting the ground from history to diversity as justification, Powell opened a Pandora's box of new claims that the critics of the earlier approach, ironically, would also reject, notably from new immigrants to the United States. If inclusive policies were not about righting wrongs but about promoting variety, then why should immigrants *not* be included? Indeed, as institutions changed to accommodate the new political and legal reality, they began to expand their policies to target newcomers from Latin America, Africa, and Asia, some quite well off, and even the children of international adoption by white parents, as they did African Americans and Mexican Americans, whose unfair treatment in the United States went back centuries. "The eligibility of 80 percent of immigrants to America for affirmative action programs," as one critic put it, "made a mockery of the historic rationale that minority preferences compensated for past discrimination." The new Americans benefited from resources originally intended for those historic victims of unequal U.S. citizenship.[47]

If the Supreme Court first made diversity a trump card, however, it was corporations that played it to greatest effect for their own ends. They were helped to see its value by a corps of inclusivity entrepreneurs, race and gender personnel specialists who set up consulting firms. One was R. Roosevelt Thomas, who minted the phrase "managing diversity." He established at Morehouse College in 1983 the American Institute for Managing Diversity. Consultants such as Thomas marketed their expertise to corporations anxious to avoid charges of discrimination.[48] A landmark in the shift in perspective was the publication of *Workforce 2000*. A joint effort of the Reagan Labor Department (then defending affirmative action from the Justice Department) and the conservative Hudson Institute, this publication warned business leaders that their fortunes in the global era would depend on how successfully they accommodated an ever more varied labor force, clientele, and network of suppliers. In 1991 the National Industrial Conference Board chose as the topic for one of its five Diamond Jubilee Symposia "In Diversity Is Strength: Capitalizing on the New Work Force." An organization that "understands and values diversity," explained a Conference Board researcher of the new thinking, "has a competitive edge in developing and managing business relationships, not only with employees and customers but also with vendors, suppliers and governments worldwide." A survey of 406 leading U.S. companies in 1991 revealed that three of every five were practicing "diversity training" and more planned to. Indeed, by century's end, *Fortune's* business rankings came to include "diversity leaders," while Merrill Lynch was offering investors a corporate diversity-based stock portfolio ("the Principled Values Portfolio"). Some inclusion had become chic.[49]

The growing popularity of diversity management hinted at changes in the corporate culture since the 1950s. Then, ascribed differences of race, sex, and national origin among workers were viewed as visible signs of where each fit into tightly rigged company hierarchies, most commonly a management track reserved for white men, secretarial pools filled by white women, menial service functions assigned to men and women of color, and production facilities that separated working-class people by race and gender. No one imagined "difference" from white men as having innate worth then. Its only value was in making the matching of workers to jobs easier for managers, for where the "different" went could be read in good part from their faces. By the 1990s, however, management had bowed to the reality of a labor force in which those long held down now had tools with which to resist confinement. Lured by images of boundless global markets, prodded by judges and fears of litigation, coaxed by their personnel specialists, and perhaps even tugged by conscience, growing numbers of executives began to question what one called "the military model which dominated corporate life for so long," which had yielded a "white male order [that] was hierarchical and authoritarian." "Without differences of opinion and perspective," explained this proponent of diversity, "you risk having an environment where everybody thinks alike, acts alike, and comes to the same conclusions. That's what got us into trouble in the first place."[50] The new value that management put on diversity thus fit with the appeal of teamwork and chaos theory: letting sparks fly could move stale work groups toward innovation in an ever more competitive environment.

The change was a genuine advance. It implied that to be black or female or both was no longer to be a perpetual outsider to the mainstream. The new thinking acknowledged that a mother might be a success at work, that black employees might know some things that whites did not, and that a native Spanish speaker might be an asset. Claiming that everyone's experiences and ideas mattered, it marked a radical departure from traditional corporate styles. It even implied that dissent at work could be healthy, an idea almost unthinkable in the gray flannel culture of the pre–civil rights era. When companies instructed that "the most important lessons for trainees" in these programs were "a greater awareness of self and others and how differences can enhance or inhibit relationships and the way work gets done," or that they would make all concerned "better listeners" and teach them "empathy," who could object?[51]

This new thinking contributed to opening once-locked gates. The decades since the 1960s have seen great advances for some, especially the better educated and those seeking inclusion in sectors vulnerable to consumer pressure. The expansion of the ranks of the better-off black working class and middle class and the tiny but growing black elite since the peak of the civil rights movement is one of the great success stories of recent history. Viewed in the aggregate, the changes are arresting. A former government official with wide experience in the EEOC, the Department of Justice, and the federal contract compliance program estimated in 1995 that "more than five million people of color and six million women are in higher occupational categories today than they would be if we still distributed people through the labor force the way we did in the sixties." The result has been not only a growing, ever more accomplished black professional class and elite, but also significant advances for many working-class black people, who are now able to buy homes and send their children to college. "The story of the past two decades," summed up one civil rights attorney in 1986 of the rapid advances since the Civil Rights Act, "is one of individual and collective progress exceeding that made by blacks in any other period in American history." The greatest convergence, moreover, was occurring where the racial disparity in rewards to training and experience had long been the most pronounced: between college-educated blacks and whites.[52] Such advances strengthened families, uplifted communities, and enhanced individual life satisfaction.

An analogous story could be told for women of all groups, but white women especially. By the opening of the new century, women made up nearly half of all law school students—up from one in ten in 1970—and 46 percent of students entering medical school. Along with minority men, women continued to expand their share of managerial jobs over the 1980s, to about 12 percent for white and Asian women, nearly equal to the share of the overall labor force in management positions, although black and Hispanic women still lagged at about 7 percent. With full-time working women by the late 1990s supplying nearly half their families' income and nearly one in five providing the household's sole support, even conservatives began deserting the battlements over whether women with children should work. One economist summarized in 1998, "Women have made substantial progress towards gender equality over the past 25 years" in areas ranging from labor force participation rates, to differences between the sexes in education and occupations, to the gender wage gap, to wage inequalities within marriage, and even—to a lesser degree—in fairer distribution of household labor between men and women among married couples.[53] The changes that occurred have bettered the lives of millions.

Yet success in making movement goals so mainstream also came at a cost. For in the process, access to good jobs was cut loose from the rest of the agenda that was required to make affirmative action on the job fulfill its original aim. That was to advance equality of result: to help those who had been hurt by the cumulative toll of long exclusion while at the same time making life chances fairer across the board through complementary policies to desegregate housing, improve schooling, and expand public services. None of the activists who first pushed for affirmative action had imagined that it could do its work alone, without these other measures and without full employment to prevent zero-sum rivalry with whites. Operating without these supports in a society of unchecked and growing overall economic inequality, affirmative action necessarily became distorted as the tool eclipsed the goal.

Now corporate spokespersons were redefining the issue of equal employment for the advocacy organizations rather than the other way around. The truth was that for corporations, talk of "diversity" became a way to focus on the future by submerging the long past history of economic racism and sexism. "The supposed newness of diversity," as one critic puts it, "allows the corporation to ignore the fact that it was instrumental in keeping American business more homogenous than American society." Managers were interested not in the antiracist egalitarian project that had guided the movements for inclusion but rather in "us[ing] diversity to create a long-lasting cross-racial class alliance" in the corporate world. Some diversity spokespersons took pains to differentiate the two. "Affirmative action is a workforce issue; managing diversity is a competitive issue," explained the CEO of Allstate Insurance. Diversity, said another CEO, "isn't affirmative action with its talk of helping people who are disadvantaged." Instead, it turned "people from diverse backgrounds" into "the helpers." As a result, "companies aren't helping them; they're helping companies to succeed."[54] This argument for inclusion was based on corporate interest and not the social justice vision that had inspired the movement in the first place. By uncritically absorbing the corporate language and way of thinking, advocacy groups lost the power to advance that vision through activism, let alone to win over whites who feared that they might be hurt by the policies.

With talk of exclusion, subordination, and power—and especially of good jobs for all as a route to full freedom and genuine equality—out of the way, discussions of "difference" threatened to become trivial, even pernicious.[55] The implication that the value of "the helpers" came from their difference from the white men, who still served as the implicit norm, was retrograde. "Everyone's *not* the same," *Industry Week* tutored its readers. "To get maximum productivity," managers had to recognize this and adjust their techniques accordingly. At one level so obvious as to be banal, the point also had the potential to generate a new kind of essentialism, a new way to reduce workers to their demographics. One might feel pressure to bring an "authentic woman's voice" to the table, for example, or fear losing position for having failed to enhance diversity, now the justification for one's presence. In that sense, diversity policies might lead to exaggerating differences among groups. When one state-of-the-art publication predicted "a greater emphasis on diversity-specific skills" in coming years, those wary of the dangers of racial and gender essentialism had reason for concern. They might well have been especially nervous when a firm such as the Bechtel Corporation, the huge construction-engineering company that undermined union power in the building trades, urged frontline managers in its "Diversity Awareness" class to "practice looking for distinctions between people"; to "pay attention to people who are different from you"; to "note what these differences seem to be"; to study "posture," "eye contact," "marital and parental status," and "language and accents."⁵⁶ One thing was clear: what was being valued was not the righting of injustice against those long shut out; it was discovering how institutions might prosper by opening their gates.

This was far from the vision of people like Wharlest Jackson, Sallie Pearl Lewis, James Haughton, Pauli Murray, Hector García, Alice Peurala, Bernice Sandler, Paulette Jourdan, and many others. In fact, the mounting popularity of the "diversity" frame was a sign of a broader shift, subtle and yet momentous. As the affirmative action effort professionalized, subdivided the work, lost active members, and came to depend on foundations and government contracts to survive in more conservative times, it became decoupled from the broader social justice mobilization that first produced it. No longer was the policy visibly linked to an overall push for a more equal America, as signified by Martin Luther King, Jr.'s, Bill of Rights for the Disadvantaged, the National Urban League's Domestic Marshall Plan, or the campaign for a Freedom Budget, all of which linked breaking down job segregation to improving the life chances and communities of all Americans with wide-ranging reform of housing, health, and education.

In the hard times of the late 1970s and 1980s, that engine never left the station. It stalled before the work was done. The United States remains far from achieving full and fair inclusion. For all the invocation of color-blindness and the need to get beyond "vague and ancient wrongs," exposures of unabashed racism in American workplaces continue. Texaco, Shoney's, Denny's, Abercrombie & Fitch: each of these major corporations has acknowledged in recent years, under suit, pervasive hostility to African Americans and sometimes Latinos as well. Texaco's practices came to light only because a senior executive and later whistleblower was secretly taping meetings for his own purposes; at the time he joked that "all the black jelly beans seem to be glued to the bottom of the bag." The only rare aspect of the Texaco situation, one columnist concluded sadly, was "that it was reported."[57]

Such cases result in part from the still large numbers of Americans openly committed to racism by the strictest definition of that term. When in the 1990s the National Opinion Research Center polled white Americans on whether they would like to see laws prohibiting interracial marriage, 26 percent of southerners and 17 percent of Midwesterners answered yes (in the more liberal Northeast, 12 percent answered yes). In other words, about one in five whites opposes allowing other people to choose their own spouses. "If only 20 percent of whites are blatant racists," as one social scientist puts it, "that's still 30 million people—as many as there are black people." Some of those thirty million whites are making decisions about whom to hire or promote; others are shaping the climate in their workplaces. One *Newsweek* poll in 1995 found that three out of four American adults thought it wrong to choose "qualified blacks" over "*equally* qualified whites" for jobs or college admissions; twice as many considered white losses from affirmative action a "bigger problem" than black losses from racial discrimination.[58]

Such attitudes help to protect the discrimination that persists in American workplaces. In one of the few published studies based on the investigations of a large pool of "testers"—blacks and whites of equally matched ability and qualifications who applied for the same advertised jobs in several cities—the Urban Institute found that where discrimination occurred, it was three times more likely to benefit whites. In one out of eight cases, the white team partner was offered a job while the black partner was not (in only one of twenty cases did the reverse happen). The researchers concluded that "unequal treatment of black job seekers is entrenched and widespread." ABC's *Prime Time Live* found a similar pattern when its reporters followed black and white testers with hidden cameras in St. Louis in 1991. In every setting—applying for an advertised job, trying to rent an apartment, shopping in a store, and buying a car—the black man faced discrimination. "The positions are taken," he was told about jobs moments after the white man was invited to apply.[59] Two social scientists studying inner-city joblessness in the Chicago metropolitan region commented, "We were overwhelmed by the degree to which Chicago employers felt comfortable talking with us—in a situation where the temptation would be to conceal rather than reveal—in a negative manner about blacks." Another study employing black and white testers found racial bias worst in low-wage, entry-level jobs, such that a white ex-convict proved more likely to receive an interview than a law-abiding black man.[60]

No such studies exist on men and women applying for the same jobs, no doubt partly because the national discussion of affirmative action has been so effectively racialized by opponents. Yet there is much evidence that women continue to face barriers and demeaning treatment that men do not. Even as the numbers of women in law school steadily rose, for example, the numbers of women making partner in large law firms or winning judgeships failed to rise as fast, for a complex of reasons involving ongoing prejudice, disproportionate child care commitments, and hypercompetitive organizational cultures established by men that turn off some women. Similar patterns appeared in the business world, giving rise to the phrase "glass ceiling," as women gained access in ever larger numbers but also reported facing bias that limited their advance. And in some stereotypically male fields such as engineering that women had entered in the 1970s and 1980s, an "exit" began in the 1990s. Although talk has spread about how sexism and sex discrimination, like racism, have grown covert and insidious, many women learned that open hostility persisted, too, and blocked their progress. In 2002, for example, a Morgan Stanley Dean Witter employee, among the leading women on Wall Street, reported to the EEOC not only a glass ceiling but also "a working environment in which men swapped off-color jokes and tales of sexual exploits and treated their female colleagues as inferior—and with impunity."[61]

A far more common and debilitating problem for most employed women, as for men of color, was being trapped in low-wage jobs. Even as some working-class and professional women gained access to traditionally male fields and improved their situation, a leading economist found that women with less education and skill faced essentially the same opportunities their mothers had in the early 1970s: low-wage service and clerical jobs.[62] In Chicago, researchers for Women Employed found in 1990 that fewer than 4 percent of women working full-time held jobs in the seven leading traditionally male occupations. By and large, most women remained stuck in the low-paying jobs that were losing more ground over these years, while overall wage and salary inequality grew. As the new century opened, economists determined that sex discrimination and other gender-related factors explained less of the ongoing income gap between the sexes than did the highly unequal overall wage structure in the United States. American women, explains one researcher, "were essentially swimming upstream in a labor force increasingly unfavorable to low-wage workers." As some better-off women advanced relative to their brothers, the gap in earnings and opportunities widened among women themselves and put into sharper relief class differences long contained by gender discrimination.[63] For low-wage women, the weakness of the American labor movement is of particular concern, because far-reaching collective bargaining agreements in other countries have raised the relative wages of women by lifting the floor for all low-income workers. Surveys offer glimpses of how these growing differentials produce sharp divergence in quality of life. One found in the mid-90s that "among [employed] women who were college graduates, 95 percent said that things were going at least fairly well, compared with only 3 percent of the women who had not completed high school."[64]

Now, moreover, advocacy groups have less power to sound the alarm effectively. In the absence of large numbers of active members, and in the face of vastly diminished government support, they have to rely more and more on private funding, and few corporations or foundations were likely to welcome plain talk about class inequality. In 1982 Vilma Martinez of MALDEF signaled the changed orientation when she urged fellow members that "all of us" need "to be much more creative" in arguing for affirmative action than in the past. "Valid though it is," she said, "the argument of past discrimination is of no interest to [white] Americans these days." Instead, "we must let private industry know that affirmative action programs make good, solid, profit-making sense."[65] The impasse became self-reinforcing as the chatter about "diversity" drowned out serious discussion of unfairness and power that might have attracted more popular involvement. In accepting corporate language as their own, advocacy groups signaled that although they had not been defeated, they had suffered from waging such a protracted struggle to hold ground. Playing good defense for so long by petitioning the state on its own narrowing terms made it hard to get back on the offense. "Our side," Eleanor Holmes Norton noted sadly, "lost the art of the fight to take the initiative."[66] At the opening of the new century, the vocabulary of the opposing sides proved eerily similar and sadly narrow, as critics of affirmative action charged violation of "equal opportunity" through "reverse discrimination" and defenders responded with paeans to "level playing fields" and the competitive advantages of "diversity." Under such banners, the rivals dug in for what military strategists might call a war of position: a conflict neither side was likely to win soon.

Holding back the tides of conservative pressure that threatened to submerge the achievements of years, activists found it hard to advance vital issues that were harder to get a hearing for, notably those that involved the changing economy and labor market. For one thing, affirmative action worked only where there were jobs to allot. Where jobs disappeared—as many of the best-paying working-class jobs did in growing numbers after the 1960s—such policies had no answer. Worse, many if not most of the gains that working-class men and women had made through affirmative action programs in the 1970s fell like hay before the tractor of economic restructuring in the 1980s and 1990s in the auto, steel, meatpacking, telecommunications, and textile industries, to take only obvious cases. The threat that "automation" posed to low-income African Americans once had been a key rationale for affirmative action. Yet in the end, changing technology and labor force demand proved more powerful than those policies, and resulted in what one sociologist called, with little exaggeration for some inner-city communities, "the disappearance of work."[67] In 1974, just under half of all African American men between twenty and twenty-four years of age in the labor force held what one sociologist calls "well-paid, blue-collar, semiskilled crafts positions." A dozen years later, that proportion had been halved.[68]

In some communities the devastation was palpable. In New York City, as half a million manufacturing jobs disappeared, the rate of labor force participation among young black men dropped by more than 50 percent between 1950 and 1980, and barely grew thereafter. In the twenty years after 1967, Chicago lost 226,000 jobs in manufacturing; neighborhoods such as North Lawndale had poverty rates as high as 50 percent by 1990. Job loss also affected the premier site in the making of a black middle class since the 1960s: government employment at all levels. In contrast, the areas that have produced the greatest growth in jobs since the early seventies, among them the high-tech industries, small firms, and the suburban employers that accounted for so many net new jobs, remained little touched by the civil rights movement.[69]

As some young people of color acquired better education and skills that helped them move forward, their achievement put in starker relief the plight of those who remained behind. When the caste-like restrictions ended, allowing new mobility for some, class differences among African Americans—and among other populations of color and all women—loomed larger. By 1980, according to a number of social scientists, "background differences" stemming from generations of racial inequality had become a stronger hindrance to progress for young African Americans than racial discrimination per se. While those with better training and from "more advantaged family backgrounds"— measured by parental schooling and occupational attainment, reading patterns, type of residence, and whether households included a male parent—continued to advance, those from less advantaged households fell behind. At the same time, the black poor became isolated and concentrated in central cities to a historically unprecedented degree, which magnified problems always associated with poverty: crime, family breakup, weak schools, cultural and linguistic distance from the mainstream, and all the rest.[70] America's unwillingness to invest in the life chances of the poor proved especially critical to blacks because, as one researcher points out, "compared with gender inequality, racial inequality is much more clearly tied to class advantage and disadvantage." Inferior schooling and the decline in real wages for nonsupervisory workers from the 1970s through the opening of the new century both boded ill for the majority of African Americans, who remained working class.[71]

∿ THE NEW SHAPE of inequality sparked controversy about strategy at the end of the twentieth century. The liveliest debate took place among African Americans and antiracists, who had acted as guides in the drive for jobs and justice from its outset. Their quest had inaugurated the remapping of American politics, inspiring white feminists and Mexican Americans to identify with them, spurring some Jews to align with anti–affirmative action white gentiles, and inducing conservatives to talk of "color-blindness" to counter their initiatives. Now some blacks opened searching exchanges about gains and losses. Although many points of view were aired at the turn of the new century, most clustered around two poles. One school of thought would try to silence specifically black claims in a search for common ground in progressive coalitions with whites to achieve social-democratic reforms that would bring more equity all around. The second urged more active pressing of race-conscious politics, notably a campaign for reparations to blacks for hundreds of years of slavery and segregation.

Among those who best made the case for seeking allies in the AFL-CIO and among low-income and progressive whites was the social scientist William Julius Wilson. In a pathbreaking 1978 book Wilson turned discussion about racial inequality to what he called "fundamental problems that derive from the intersection of class with race." Wilson argued, "The problem for blacks today . . . is that the government is not organized to deal with the new barriers imposed by structural changes in the economy." Threats to low-wage workers such as labor-saving technology, plant shutdowns, the migration of businesses to the suburbs, the waning of manufacturing, and the waxing of service employment were beyond the reach of civil rights measures aimed at racial bias alone. Wilson saw as vital to the future of racial equality such measures as government-backed full employment, massive public investment for equity in education, and training programs that would teach job skills matched to new opportunities—"programs based on the principle of equality of life chances." Arguing that such change would come about only if the white majority could be persuaded to support improvement for everyone, he urged less emphasis on racially charged politics and more on seeking common ground for progressive reform coalitions. Along the way, he discounted affirmative action (based less on any empirical research than on the political positions of those from whom he took his bearings, such as the AFL-CIO–linked Bayard Rustin and Tom Kahn). Over the years, Wilson has tried to draw public attention to the plight of the unemployed and low-wage African Americans for whom no current policies are working well.[72]

For all his wisdom, Wilson had a knack for depositing land mines on the road to reconciliation. Titling his first book *The Declining Significance of Race* and his second *The Truly Disadvantaged*, he angered many antiracists who heard in these provocative phrases a justification for ending race-conscious reform just when it seemed most under attack. If this fear led many to overlook Wilson's important arguments about employment and social structure, it was not unjustified. Wilson drew acclaim from white conservatives who never seemed to read his work but found in those titles and his stature as a renowned black scholar support for their quest to rescind affirmative action and other race-conscious reform policies.[73] Encouraged by Wilson's seeming dismissal, which was often cited by conservatives to show that their case was reasonable, the idea spread that affirmative action had benefited only the better-off. Many came to believe that it had come into being not as an achievement of grassroots struggles but as a Trojan horse conjured by the sinister Richard Nixon.[74] Ironically, a section of the left now echoed the creation story that conservatives had spun in the 1970s to discredit affirmative action—and with it all government-backed progressive reform.

For their part, those urging continued support for race-conscious measures read both history and the present differently. They saw a tradition of preferences for whites and racism so deep that most white Americans refused to support universalism even when it seemed obviously in their own interests to do so, and thus a history in which race and gender helped define the very meaning of class. As early as 1967, Stokely Carmichael articulated the problem that many saw in the liberal emphasis on coalition building: "There is in fact no group at present with whom to form a coalition in which blacks will not be absorbed or betrayed." Years later, Adolph Reed, Jr., came to a similar conclusion in evaluating the "new orthodoxy" among scholars and centrist Democrats who blamed blacks and affirmative action for the demise of the New Deal coalition. "When does a call for pragmatic coalition building," Reed asked, "become a call for accommodating the maintenance and reproduction of white racial privilege?"[75]

It was not at all self-evident, to this group, why race-targeted programs could not accompany universal ones. The black scholar-activist Kenneth Tollett, a veteran of the higher education fight, accused people like Wilson of harboring "a modified Gerald Ford syndrome," as-

sociating them with the former president's supposed inability to do two
basic things at once. "The issue," Tollett said, "is whether it is better
to avoid confronting this problem [of racism] by trying to finesse it
with race-neutral policies or whether it should be confronted with targeted programs." He concluded that both should "be pursued simultaneously."[76] By the 1990s, with conservatives regularly and disingenuously invoking Martin Luther King, Jr.'s, name to sacralize their attacks
on affirmative action, his widow, Coretta Scott King, felt moved to remind the white public that "my husband unequivocally supported such
programs." The radical left, small but energetically activist, seemed
much more able than liberals and social democrats to embrace *both* universal policies to address the needs of all working people *and* targeted
policies to aid those with a history of discrimination. For all the fierce
disagreements among its varied groups, collectively they stood out for
their belief in the complementarity of the two streams of reform. What
all these approaches shared, in fact, was agreement that either/or formulations (if class becomes more salient, race must be less so) obscured
the true challenge of the new situation: that race and class were inter-
acting in new ways not reducible to either, and which required real
commitment to both universal programs and targeted efforts.[77]

By the opening of the new century, others rejected the long-running
debate over universal-versus-targeted measures as a futile distraction
and instead built a mass campaign demanding reparations for slavery
and government-backed segregation. Some black leftists and liberals
joined nationalists in pressing the case. They called not for payments to
individuals, which would have broken open a hornet's nest of legal,
practical, and ethical problems, but rather for what the scholar-activist
Manning Marable described as "a reparations trust fund" for "closing
the gap between whites and blacks." Interest was prompted partly by
the success of other reparations initiatives in achieving recognition of
grievous wrongs done and securing some form of restitution: for Jewish victims of the Holocaust and of Nazi-era slave labor practices, Japanese Americans interned in the United States during World War II,
Korean women forced into sexual slavery by the Japanese army in the
1940s, and other well-publicized instances of public policies that attempted to redress historic group injuries.[78] By the turn of the new century, a book on reparations had made the bestseller list, a bill proposed
by Democratic representative John Conyers of Michigan for a com-

mission to reckon the toll of slavery and segregation appeared to gain ground in Congress, and debate on the issue spilled into such mainstream venues as the *New York Times*.[79]

But the impasse over affirmative action and economic racism also contributed to interest in reparations. Anger at whites' resistance to what seemed simple fairness and resentment at the momentum lost to arguments about "reverse discrimination" animated nearly all calls for reparations. One treatise on reparations opened with the declaration, "Affirmative action for Black Americans as a form of remediation for perpetuation of past injustice is almost dead." It went on to argue for reparations as "a new mass-based antisubordination agenda" that avoided the pitfalls of the older civil rights agenda. Some thus began looking to reparations in part as a way to restore what had been lost since the 1970s. They were seeking not only an effective tool for addressing persistent black poverty that remained beyond the reach of affirmative action, but also some recognition of African Americans' unique history, injuries, and needs stemming from 350 years of slavery and government-supported discrimination. Advocates sought to move public discussion beyond history-blind platitudes about diversity and level playing fields to a serious engagement with the present import of the nation's past. If Americans could recognize how the past shaped the present, they might then imagine just solutions to the accumulation of advantages on one side and of harm on the other.[80]

Reviving bold talk of injury and justice, reparations activists aimed to dislodge the idiom of personnel administrators and poll-wary politicians. Instead, they spoke of "economic human rights." Most abhorred the terms the affirmative action debate had adopted since the 1970s, with opponents deriding the policies as "undeserved racial preference" and supporters responding ever more cautiously, even disingenuously, in seeking to protect it. Reparations, in contrast, promised public discussion on different terrain: that of history and present social reality, rather than abstract ethics or interpersonal questions that obscured both. Even if the campaign failed, many felt, the substantive debate over "the principle that the victims of unjust enrichment should be compensated" would be a step forward.[81] The campaign for reparations thus emphasized how generations of special privilege for whites and compulsory exclusion and subordination for blacks had exacted human and social costs that needed reckoning. Regardless of whether it pre-

vailed in the end, the effort was important for the way it was rein-
vigorating seekers of racial justice after two decades on the defensive.

Political activists feel a need to choose between such opposed poles
of debate, but historians have the luxury of a longer view that highlights what the coalition seekers and reparations advocates shared.
Their common ground has much to tell us about America at the outset
of the new millennium. Each believed that American ideas about government had changed fundamentally since the sixties, such that ethical
appeals for racial equity seemed to hold little chance of success at the
very moment when judicial pressure for color-blindness was blocking
efforts to address the deepest roots of inequality. One law professor put
it this way: "As surely as the law has outlawed racial discrimination, it
has affirmed that Black Americans can be without jobs, have their children in all-black, poorly funded schools, have no opportunities for decent housing, and have very little political power, without any violation
of anti-discrimination law."[82] Addressing such disparities would require
massive resources and much work from many parties, at a time when,
after decades of Vietnam, Watergate, and Reaganism, faith in the efficacy of government as a tool for good has ebbed lower than ever. It
was the popular Republican Reagan who, after all, taught Americans
from his inauguration onward that "government is not the solution
to our problems; government *is* the problem," while Democrat Bill
Clinton announced that "the era of big government is now over."[83]
Both sides in the debate over reparations sensed also that a strategic
political tool for people of color in the postwar era was now gone, as
the end of the cold war brought the end of the competition between
the United States and the Soviet Union.[84] In this altered world, hewing
to old approaches seemed a sure way to lose over the long haul.

Most important, both the social democrats and the reparation advocates recognized, in their different ways, the changes that had occurred
in race and class (and, one might add, gender). For all their deep and
fiercely maintained differences, both sides felt frustration with the
mainstream debate over racial inequality. They agreed that affirmative
action had value, but argued that the defensive focus on it was leading
to stasis in the face of a world becoming ever harder for low-income
people, blacks especially. Supporting fairness for all once excluded
groups, they nonetheless worried that white American citizens and
public officials were losing sight of the unique history and situation of

African Americans. Other groups' claims to justice and fair treatment, legitimate as they were, seemed to have sapped the utility of affirmative action for the descendants of slaves. "The concept of affirmative action essentially is a euphemism for reparations," as the columnist Salim Muwakkil put it, "and this point is lost when its advocates urge its expansion across race lines."[85]

Perhaps the most striking commonality between the social democrats and the reparations advocates was their shared concern for the problems that had been left to fester unattended. Both government and what remained of the movements for equality had neglected issues pivotal to the future of equality in the United States: the massive loss of well-paid working-class jobs, ongoing segregation, declining real wages, and the resulting poverty and community crisis in poor areas. Some of the challenges stemmed from the economic restructuring of the previous half century, mounting with the globalization of the nation's economy and its shift to services. Both sides, in other words, wanted to do something about class injustices that affected blacks most, as they reproduced and in some areas deepened racial inequality.

Black feminists, meanwhile, offered a synthesis between the two poles of debate that stressed both difference and coalition. Identifying the tension as an existential reality of modern life, they rejected the polarity of "class politics" versus "identity politics" as a false dichotomy. They recognized what the men leading both rival camps failed to see: that the complexity of all political identities, white men's included, derive from experiences not only of race and class but also of gender, sexuality, and more. Beginning in the dog days of the 1980s, as activists wrestled with the differences that divided them in the harsh conditions of the Reagan era, activist intellectuals such as Barbara Smith, Audre Lorde, and June Jordan warned of the futility of "ranking oppressions" because so many people, black women especially, experienced them in "simultaneity" as "interlocking" systems that relied on one another for reinforcement. Expanding on ideas that Pauli Murray had first advanced years before, they drew out the practical import of this social reality: the need to move beyond hostility-producing either/or formulations that demanded of people what was impossible—to be only female, or only black, or only working class, or only gay or lesbian. Instead, black feminists urged creative experimentation with alliances that could address shared goals while leveraging differences as sources of enriched understanding for all parties in the quest for equality. They argued for such coalition building not from romantic notions of inevitable unity but rather from "our actual need for each other" if anyone was to succeed. "It is not our differences that separate," explained Audre Lorde, "but our reluctance to recognize those differences and deal effectively with the distortions that have resulted from the ignoring and misnaming of those differences." In a climate so little conducive to successful activism of any kind, it was hard to test such ideas on a large scale. Yet black feminism's wise critiques and capacious humanism won it a wide hearing among progressives. The challenging vision of inclusive social justice its advocates held out inspired many to try to make a difference.[86]

After conservatives appropriated the idiom of civil rights, and public talk about race and gender shifted from equality to diversity, African Americans interested in social justice looked elsewhere for a language of struggle that would be morally compelling and practically urgent. One group found it in a discourse of coalition and common ground, another in a discourse of injury and debt, and still another in discourse based on recognition of difference as an unavoidable reality and of alliance as an inescapable necessity. All were saying, in effect, that freedom is not enough. It is good that publicly, at least, the principle of equal opportunity is now almost universally accepted, and that enthusiasm for diversity is greater than ever before: those are important changes. But they were never all that the movements for inclusion sought. The purpose of equal opportunity is, as one philosopher reminds us, "to regulate the competition for advantage."[87] As competition has grown fiercer and the gap between those who gain advantages and those who lose has opened wide, it is no wonder that some activists and intellectuals are raising basic, foundational questions about what the conditions of the new order imply for the next phase of the struggle for inclusion. This kind of rethinking and remodeling after a huge leap forward met a big shove backward was just what enabled their predecessors to come out of the devastating 1950s stronger than ever before.

Epilogue

> I pondered . . . how men fight and lose the battle, and the thing that
> they fought for comes about in spite of their defeat, and when it
> comes it turns out not to be what they meant, and other men
> have to fight for what they meant under another name.
> ~ *William Morris, 1892*

𝒥N GREEK MYTHOLOGY, the character Sisyphus spoke truth about power. For that act of hubris he was condemned for eternity to push a boulder up a steep hill—only to see it roll back down as soon as he reached the top. The seeming futility of his fate made Sisyphus a hero in the eyes of the philosopher Albert Camus. Intention, effort, and integrity seemed to avail so little: what a perfect metaphor for the human condition in a century in which each leap forward was matched by a fall back, in which the most modern technology enabled the barbaric regimes of Hitler and Stalin. But Camus saw that there was more to the story of Sisyphus than tragedy—more, too, than ceaseless, barren labor. The very spirit of rebellion that had led him to speak the truth in the face of danger made Sisyphus "stronger than his rock."[1] The same is true of the spirit of inclusion whose uneven advances have been traced in these pages.

It is not difficult to understand why many people today feel defeated about the prospects for genuine economic inclusion. Particularly among lower-income Americans of color and white women, high hopes have taken a beating. The nation that spawned a movement which inspired struggles for justice around the world in the 1960s and 1970s, from South Africa to Northern Ireland, now tolerates unprecedented levels of inequality, unmatched anywhere else in the industrialized world. The nation's wage earners, a group that includes most men

of color and the majority of women, today take home less in real wages
than they did at the peak of the struggles recounted here, and many
have less secure employment, benefits, and old age provisions. More
women are in good jobs across the class spectrum than ever before, it is
true, but the vast majority still hold "pink-collar" jobs with little future.
Their options dwindling, many Americans have lost hope of entering
the nation's economic mainstream. Almost a million African Americans
are further cut off from it than before, trapped in a prison system
whose growth is so lucrative that it draws Wall Street investors. "The
thousands now in prison for drug dealing," one scholar-activist rightly
points out, "are exiles from a job market that largely excluded them and
a school system that failed them."[2] When more young black men are in
jail than in college, despair is an understandable response to the history
of recent decades. Surely this is not the world that activists imagined
their labors were ushering in.

Yet just as there is a deeper truth to the story of Sisyphus, so, too, is
the reality of recent years different from what the discouraged imagine.
Far from accomplishing nothing, the struggle for inclusion achieved so
much that it reconfigured the nation's political culture and so changed
the terrain on which future activists would operate. Work-related
struggles for equality have driven much of the revolution in American
thinking about race and gender since the 1950s. They did so under the
radar in the very years we are told marked the demise of the civil rights
movement. Yet in fact, the years from 1965 to 1980 were the time when
the work of inclusion began in earnest, in a new and distinctive wave of
activism, as ordinary people at the grass roots began to use the reforms
that activists had won. As the stories of people like Vincent Whylie,
Lorena Weeks, Sallie Pearl Lewis, Alice Peurala, Hector García, Bernice Sandler, and Melinda Hernandez show, affirmative action was not
a bureaucratic abstraction cooked up high in the courts and down remote corridors of government agencies, but a realistic remedy for exclusion devised by common citizens facing unfair obstacles and ugly
treatment, who creatively enlisted the democratic process to achieve
some justice.

Beginning with limited numbers and little power in the mid-1950s,
activists made remarkable use of the resources they had. Building
wisely on social changes that were working in their favor, they appealed
to some of the nation's deepest values to tear down a culture of exclu-

sion hundreds of years in the making. In just a few decades, they improved the life chances of millions as they changed popular thinking, reconstructed law, altered established practices, and invented policies to promote equity and inclusion. African Americans began the struggle virtually alone, yet found inspired ways to attract white allies and achieve potent reforms whose promise recruited other long-excluded groups to their side. As large numbers of white feminists turned left and allied with blacks, Mexican American activists ceased seeking to prove that they were white and instead embraced brownness. For peoples so long cut off from power, they effected a stunning amount and variety of change.

They roused a nation lulled by McCarthyism to remember that there was greater purpose to public life. They convinced a majority of Americans that access to good jobs was a basic need and right of all, and that in this area, at least, human rights mattered more than property rights. More than ever before, large numbers came to appreciate that freedom is not enough: liberty and justice for all required more than abstract equality before the law. They required what for at least a hundred years the nation's leaders had either not considered or had explicitly denied: that access to good jobs was necessary for full citizenship, and that full citizenship was the birthright of all Americans, not just some. Economic security, these struggles taught, is vital in order to exercise the personal autonomy Americans value so dearly and to build the strong families and communities they also desire.[3] Activists brought new elements of representation, due process, and public oversight to a realm of American life where autocracy was long the norm: the corporation. Building on the legacy of the labor movement's long fight for fairness at work and on the institutional apparatus the New Deal offered to attain it, they extended hard-won rights and communal norms to new arenas of life and to groups long denied those benefits.

They revitalized the labor movement, such that nearly all its progress since 1955 has been in some way stimulated by the developments described here. The unions that have grown most as others stumbled and shrank under the new conditions are those that have attracted large numbers of workers of color and white women. Trying to organize blacks, Latinos, Asian Americans, and women of all groups, they have infused their understanding of class fairness with a commitment to racial and gender justice and worked hard to involve populations long overlooked. Among the most successful are the public workers' union AFSCME, the service workers' union SEIU, and the garment industry and hospitality workers' union UNITE HERE, all deeply affected by the changes Title VII wrought in American workplaces. Today the labor movement offers the best hope to the people of color and low-wage white women still desperately in need of change, and that is in part because some in its ranks have learned from the wider social movements since the 1960s and applied that learning to their organizing. Indeed, the egalitarian vision of the early movements for inclusion survives most intact today among progressive labor activists, many of whom see the widening economic gap as *the* civil rights challenge of the new century. As the right now seeks cultural hegemony through embrace of nominal equal opportunity, no wing of the earlier movements has better adapted to the new environment and held aloft the vision of substantive equality than the unions actively organizing low-wage workers.[4]

The struggle for economic inclusion also altered the culture in ways that continue to inspire others to claim fairness and inclusion. Many groups have since articulated new rights to fair treatment on the job: older Americans, people with disabilities, lesbians and gay men, and Asian Americans have all become more vocal and cohesive. If today most Americans think it is wrong to fire an employee simply because he or she is no longer young and cheap, or to refuse a job to someone who moves in a wheelchair, or to hound a co-worker for his or her sexual orientation, that is because affirmative action activism redefined our collective sense of right and wrong where jobs are concerned. None of these more recent claimants to fair treatment could have made their cases plausibly without the scaffolding of law afforded by Title VII and the alteration of culture achieved by the civil rights and feminist movements.[5]

Even when they are simply going about their daily work, millions of Americans—whites, men, Anglos, and the able-bodied among them—enjoy the fruits of these struggles in fairer, more rational personnel procedures and in grievance systems for non-union as well as union employees.[6] Americans today also enjoy protection from pregnancy discrimination and sexual harassment that would not exist but for the struggles described here. That our political culture no longer remembers how such policies came into being demonstrates "the remarkable rhetorical power of the market in the United States," a power that has "blinded many to the role of the state in improving opportunities for disadvantaged groups."[7] So much did the movements alter both the state and the culture that these changes survived the concerted efforts of the Reagan administration to undo them in the 1980s. But they prevailed at a cost. As they became absorbed as "diversity" policies to benefit businesses and institutions, their grassroots origins were muted and the original vision of which they were just one part was obscured.

If low-income people of color and white women are still struggling, it is not because movement activists did not know or care about their situation. On the contrary, that injustice drove many to work for change and kept them going even in the face of exhaustion and daunting odds. But they were aiming at a moving target. As the Chicago Urban League phrased the sad irony early on, they seemed to be "winning the right to get a job at just the time when the job itself is disappearing."[8] At the very moment when activists had convinced Americans that freedom was not enough and that everyone deserved access to good jobs, jobs changed in ways that made the vision for which these movements fought harder to realize.

The "automation" that worried early civil rights leaders proceeded apace, despite their best efforts, in ways that distorted their victories. Changing rapidly since the 1950s, the nation's labor force now bestows once unheard-of rewards on some who have advanced education and training while it harshly victimizes those with less. And that is why today it appears—wrongly—that the movements helped only middle-class people: because the industries where they made the greatest headway in opening good blue-collar jobs to all were devastated by the economic recession of the 1970s and subsequent restructuring. To remember the characters in this story is to evoke industrial graveyards, whether the railroad work from which A. Philip Randolph launched the first mass movement to break down job desegregation, the meat-packers who supported Martin Luther King, Jr., the textile workers like Sally Pearl Lewis and A. C. Sherrill, the communications workers like Lorena Weeks, the steel workers like Alice Peurala, the auto workers like Dorothy Haener, and a host of others. Soon after they broke down the barriers to good jobs, industrial restructuring wiped out most of those gains.[9] Perhaps if job loss had been the only cause of the impasse, they might have sustained the momentum for change by meeting the challenge, as many tried to, with public policy measures such as government-backed full employment through public works, an increased minimum wage, health care coverage, and expanded support to education for all.[10]

The more ultimately decisive obstacles, however, were political. They came from a conservative movement which surged forward in that same decade of economic crisis.[11] Recruiting formidable business support, conservatives also mastered a kind of political jujitsu by appropriating the language of the movement for inclusion to win over wage-earning and middle-class white voters and block further progress. Repackaging themselves as opponents of discrimination, they accused affirmative action supporters of backing unfair "quotas." They were not wholly successful, as the defeat of the Reagan-era effort to end federal affirmative action showed. But they did manage to block rigorous enforcement of the rights of minority men and all women and to change the terms of debate about such policies. In the 1980s, systematic underfunding of government anti-discrimination agencies and conservative control of them created a situation in which respect for the law became, in effect, optional. Companies that see a self-interest in inclusion are likely to practice affirmative action, among them the consumer or world market–oriented firms such as McDonald's and General Motors that top the new "diversity rankings."[12] Others, less driven to reach diverse markets, learned that they could do pretty much as they liked, particularly as newly appointed and increasingly powerful conservative judges made the nation's courts more hostile to affirmative action and other egalitarian initiatives by the late 1980s. As important for the long run, the right defeated the kinds of reforms that would have improved life chances for all young Americans—measures such as open housing, a living wage, and equalizing school funding to raise the quality of education in poorer districts to match that enjoyed in better-off districts.

Along with their practical political victories, conservatives made important cultural conquests. Resisting the unflattering reflection of themselves and the social order they exalted that came from the movements for inclusion, they invented their own version of the past. It actively sought to erase the reality of deep-rooted and continuing discrimination with a new creation myth that attributed affirmative action to a power-hungry liberal elite, in a manner reminiscent of the way an earlier generation of conservatives had ignored African American drive and initiative and blamed Reconstruction on "carpetbaggers." Through well-funded sponsors and active promotion, conservative spokespersons managed to make their story about public policy measures for inclusion the most widely believed interpretation of this history, such that it is now nearly universal among white Americans. Through sheer repetition of it, they convinced many whites that the early civil rights movement had achieved all it set out to, and that later, scheming government bureaucrats tried to hijack that victory with measures like affirmative action. Numerous mainstream scholars, too, have accepted this creation myth and spread it. Ignoring the social movement origins of such policies, and looking only at government officials, they perpetuate the misconception that there was no popular push for affirmative action. Remarkably, the notion that it was imposed from above rather than produced in a dialectic between grassroots outsiders and sympathetic insiders working together against powerful conservative resistance is now the conventional wisdom among social scientists and historians.[13]

Reducing this mainstream movement victory to a misguided thrust by extremists and arrogant elites, conservative leaders have managed to turn an earnest quest for decent jobs into a radical, even surly demand for a giveaway. In this context it is worth remembering how in the 1960s the effort to open good jobs seemed a relatively conservative strategy for redressing racial injustice. The call for affirmative action looked quite tame next to the withering scorn of Malcolm X for American institutions, the armed militancy of the Black Panther Party, the demand of the National Welfare Rights Organization for federally funded "jobs or income now," the self-styled "revolutionary union movement" that grew up in Detroit's auto factories, or Martin Luther King's campaign in his last years to wipe out poverty in America though the Poor People's Movement. It proved far more acceptable to the white mainstream at the time than these other ideas—cheaper, safer, and more in keeping with dominant values. Yet over the ensuing decades, conservative leaders managed to employ against this bid to share in the American dream of success through hard work the same racial stereotype that served them so well in the fight against welfare: the idea that blacks, in particular, were trying to get something for nothing. In a work-obsessed nation hostile to "free handouts," that alchemy has enabled the right to discredit the most mainstream, achievement-oriented, assimilation-minded, and hopeful branches of the movements for equality—those who, as Whitney Young put it, wanted to "'revolt' into partnership" with the dominant society.[14]

The myth about affirmative action's origins spun by men such as Norman Podhoretz, Irving Kristol, and Ernest Van den Haag, and promulgated far and wide by others since, has reinterpreted these historic events for most white Americans. Many now genuinely believe the ventriloquist's tale that an early color-blind movement, interested only in formal legal equality, was later rerouted by bureaucrats and intellectuals bent on gaining power for themselves. The right even commandeers Martin Luther King, Jr., whom conservatives disparaged when he was alive, into a posthumous cameo appearance in this fantasy. King's hope that his children would "not be judged by the color of their skin but by the content of their character" is endlessly repeated, while the occasion on which he spoke these words, a mass March for Jobs and Freedom, is ignored, as is the powerful call he made for affirmative action in the same year and his commitment to use the power of government to end poverty for all Americans, white as well as black. Yet none of those active in working for justice, Martin Luther King, Jr., included, saw the strict color-blindness preached by today's late converts to equal opportunity as an answer. As King said in 1967, "the Movement must address itself to the question of restructuring the whole of American society."[15] Seeing how equity required more than legal equality, every group seeking inclusion and nearly every specific campaign to bring fairness to the workplace came to demand affirmative action–like remedies to redress the long-standing and self-perpetuating culture of preference for some white men and the exclusion of all others.

In that affirmative action has served as the wedge in the right's attack on all government efforts to redress social injustice and promote equality, the success of the creation myth is little short of breathtaking. If a policy so hard-won by so many, so historically, practically, and ethically justified, and so in keeping with the core cultural value of work as the route to a better future cannot survive, what beyond mere lip service to fairness can? It is no coincidence that today the opponents of equal citizenship for lesbian and gay Americans rely on the weapons honed against affirmative action to accuse those seeking fair treatment of demanding "special rights."[16] Even conservatives' critics must acknowledge that they have been stunningly successful in changing the terms of debate by erasing public memory of the history recounted here. The right's leaders understand that whether and how we remember the past shapes our analysis of the present and our visions of the future. "If there isn't a problem," notes one scholar of public opinion on race and policy, "you don't need a solution."[17]

Having airbrushed from popular memory the long struggle for economic inclusion, the right has scored another cultural success that needs reckoning. Neoconservatives first pioneered a therapeutic language packaging affirmative action as a hazard to the self-esteem of and public respect for its intended beneficiaries, without ever consulting those in whose name they spoke. As Sidney Hook proclaimed in a classic illustration, "intelligent, self-respecting Negroes and women would scorn such preferential treatment."[18] In effect, such critics portrayed those hired through affirmative action as not simply unqualified, lazy, and illegitimately rewarded but also as self-loathing, even pathological. The right's relentless accusations against the policy's beneficiaries gave new respectability to old stereotypes used to demean men of color and all women. The notion that African Americans lacked ability and drive was not new, after all, but a staple theme of racism. In the late nineteenth century, the abolitionist and reformer Frederick Douglass lamented that whenever an African American sought a career in a profession, "the presumption of incompetence confronts him, and he must either run, fight, or fall before it."[19] By so relentlessly attaching those presumptions of incompetence to the most effective policy for achieving inclusion, the right has succeeded in tarnishing it in the eyes of many of those who have gained from it. Not knowing affirmative action's grassroots origins, and experiencing such cruelty and hostility in criticisms of it, some young men of color and women now seek to disassociate themselves from it, oblivious to its role in creating the life choices they assume as unremarkable givens in planning their lives.

Perhaps the right's leaders would not have achieved the success they did if the history of these struggles for fair treatment were more widely known; their project gained immensely from widespread collective amnesia. Jobs activists were too busy keeping their fingers in the dikes through the 1980s and 1990s to write down their stories. And since the 1970s, most scholars of people of color and women of all groups moved in different directions, leading to neglect of this history. For varied reasons, beyond the ranks of labor historians, most progressive scholars lost whatever interest they once had in issues involving work and the labor movement. Those who studied social movements tended to focus on the young activists of the Student Nonviolent Coordinating Committee (SNCC), Students for a Democratic Society (SDS), and women's liberation groups and largely wrote off the older members and staff of organizations such as the NAACP, the Urban League, NOW, and the GI Forum, let alone unions, on the assumption that young people were more interesting and the source of all the real innovation.

As a result, there are now literally dozens of books on SNCC, SDS, and women's liberation, yet no published histories of the NAACP and NOW, the largest membership-based organizations of their respective movements. Nearly all American social studies and history students today learn of the student-led lunch counter sit-ins, yet few know anything of the quest for good jobs that was such an important part of the black freedom movement. In part, we have the almost work-free popular narratives of the civil rights movement we do because historians have taken their cues from journalists, who were mesmerized by the dramatic confrontations that make news. As Charles Payne puts it in a pathbreaking counternarrative of the black freedom movement that focuses on ordinary people, although the journalists were sympathetic, in "rushing to tell the story, they missed much of its substance." Above all, they missed the day-to-day, face-to-face organizing that sustained the movement and made substantive change possible.[20] That pattern was then repeated with coverage of feminism: flashy youthful protests such as the 1969 Atlantic City demonstration against the Miss America pageant overshadowed the patient organizing by older women that yielded many of the movement's most noteworthy innovations in culture and achievements in policy. All told, the prevailing scholarly focus on youth and on headline-winning drama has contributed to memories of the civil rights movement in particular that leave out what the NAACP's chief lobbyist called "the chance to earn a living on an equal basis with other people."[21]

This slighting of the workplace and the drive for economic security has made the right's creation myth appear plausible. In an irony of unintended consequences, radical historians have assisted conservative proponents of that myth by writing off older activists as liberal elites interested only in formal equality and unconcerned with the needs of working-class people, a depiction that is grossly misleading. Being not students but adults responsible for their own and others' support, people like Bert Corona, Herbert Hill, and Eleanor Holmes Norton realized the need for economic security for personal, familial, and communal well-being—much more so than the young people who have attracted the lion's share of attention from historians.

The lack of interest in the quiet heroism of such adult working people compounds the tragic tendency in our market-driven culture to worship the new and toss out the old, in this case to value youth for its own sake and so lose the wisdom that elders glean from long experience and observation. Shocking as it may seem, we owe many of the most lasting and popular innovations of the era to them. In the jobs struggles of the past half century, older activists raised questions—some never asked before—about how we make goods, assess skill, run offices, transport people and products, decide our life plans, design and erect buildings, evaluate and disseminate knowledge, identify and broadcast news, choose leaders, conceive and administer justice, organize families, raise children, treat co-workers, imagine community, and more. They spearheaded critical and creative thinking about virtually every activity of our common life. Of all the movements of those years, they may have done the most to transform everyday experience. Their achievements should remind us that credit for the transformations of "the sixties" belongs to middle-aged working people as well as to middle-class student activists.

What probably contributed more to the widespread forgetting, though, was the hyperspecialization of the knowledge industry, such that it became hard to put the whole puzzle together. Political historians derived conclusions about the origins of policy without consulting the records of social movement organizations, while social historians stopped following reform struggles once they achieved policy victories. Scholars of blacks, Latinos, feminists, Jews, and unions operated in parallel universes that rarely met. However sensible as a mental survival strategy in the information age, compartmentalizing knowledge in this way limits understanding of the logic, even the magic, of how significant social change happens. Because although most published accounts follow only a single group, many groups fought both for and against inclusion, and their interactions shaped the process in ways that remain invisible when we look at only one.

Just as significant, few social movement scholars have welcomed the prospect of spending years in the virtual company of corporate leaders, let alone conservatives, so the enormous role of these groups in this history remains largely unexamined. Those interested in the obstacles that activists for equality faced have been far more likely to focus on white workers, trade unions, and government. Combating the romanticism that once induced progressives to believe that the New Deal ushered in equity for American working people and that labor struggle would inevitably dissolve any remaining racism and sexism, two generations of scholarship have documented the many ways in which white workers and the public policies their union and political activism helped win reinforced racial and gender inequality. Historians have shown how, for example, union contracts codified job segregation and how homeowners' loan policies impoverished black communities as they helped whites accumulate and pass on wealth.[22] As vital and important as this corrective was, it yields only a very partial picture. What is necessary now is to bring employers and activists on the right back into the picture, not only for an accurate understanding but also so that they, too, face accountability for their long-standing hostility to inclusion.

Yet in a world in constant motion, the ground shifts under all parties, making all victories ephemeral, not just those of one side. What is clear from the conservatives' appropriation of the language of civil rights is that now the genie will never go back into the bottle. Regardless of which administration is in power or how the courts rule, the pressures for inclusion are now too strong, and come from too many quarters, to go away.[23] Evidence of the dissemination of the value of inclusion abounds, even where it was once most resisted. In 1991 an amusing clash occurred at Yale University, a school built with proceeds from the slave trade and closed to women until the 1970s. When its prestigious Skull and Bones Society—whose alumni included then-president George H. W. Bush—prepared to admit six women, some alumni went to court to prevent this violation of 150 years of tradition. Among them was William F. Buckley, Jr., the founder of modern American conservatism. His arguments failed against the pragmatic reasoning of a current member. "We're not getting good people because they don't want to be part of an organization that would discriminate against women," the young man said. "You never know when you will have to explain it away."[24] As influential as Buckley was in shaping the contours of today's America, his enthusiasm for old ways had become an embarrassment to would-be elites being groomed for power. None was willing to be seen as someone who practiced exclusion.

By the turn of the century, even those who fought the policy of affirmative action felt a need to perform a commitment to inclusion. Bill Clinton promised a cabinet that "looks like America," but it was the Texas-based conservative Republican George W. Bush who appointed a black woman to the key strategic position of national security adviser. Fighting a war against an enemy that veiled and secluded women, Condoleezza Rice advised the president on strategy while female journalists covered a war front where female military personnel took and gave orders in defiance of ally Saudi Arabia and some American conservatives.[25] It was a world markedly altered from the 1950s, and not just superficially. As one affirmative action activist put it, "we'll lose bits here and there and sometimes they'll be important bits . . . but you can't turn this thing around."[26]

The value of inclusion had seeped deep into the culture. Even where affirmative action was outlawed, as it was on California campuses by popular referendum in Proposition 209, in the end, few were comfortable with the results, so support quickly built for alternative ways of ensuring diversity.[27] So much did so many Americans want diversity— even as they had been taught to disdain the main policy that achieved it—that they redefined terms in an Alice-in-Wonderland way. A 1996 survey of almost four thousand freshmen at over six hundred colleges and universities thus found that "more than two-thirds of the freshmen support using race as a criterion in college admissions, but 50 percent agree 'affirmative action in college admissions should be abolished.'" This is true not just of colleges but of corporate life as well, notes one observer of Wall Street: "Whether or not diversity pays in and of itself, it clearly pays to avoid the public perception that you lack it." As political campaigns against affirmative action grew more shrill at the opening of the new century, even some once vocal conservative critics recanted their earlier opposition, most prominently Nathan Glazer and Glenn Loury. "The most striking feature of the debate" in the 1990s, noted a writer in the *New York Times*, observing the changes at *Commentary*, which had led the fight against affirmative action in the early 1970s, "is that the impulse toward diversity—and, by extension, toward affirmative action—is a mainstream impulse, endorsed by varying degrees even by [some] conservatives who once saw it as the embodiment of evil."[28]

Such changes mean that not only is reversion to the old order almost unimaginable, but also even today's seeming stasis is unstable. As Americans of all groups interact regularly on the job as never before (as they do nowhere else), they find themselves stimulated to think and question as never before. It is not always comfortable, but it is a catalyst for deep, ongoing social and cultural change. As one observer quips, all the ominous warnings of balkanization notwithstanding, "we are having these cultural brawls not because we fragmented, but because we integrated." As he points out, "the life paths of women and men, and, to a lesser extent, of black and white Americans are more likely to be congruent than at any [other] time in history. Friction is not, after all, the consequence of separation."[29] James Baldwin would have appreciated the irony. Seeing how the subordination of blacks had undergirded the American social order since the founding of the Jamestown colony in 1619, he knew that when they fight free of their assigned place at the bottom, "everything is changed," such that the "white man . . . has to find out what *he* is." In the years since the 1950s, African Americans' challenge to their place unsettled every other location in the social hierarchy, creating new possibilities for white women, Mexican Americans, Jewish Americans, and even the conservatives who so resisted change.

Cumulatively, the resulting movements did their work so well that they altered the everyday life of millions and changed the culture. Recasting political identities and re-mapping historic allegiances, they also began to change the public face of power. From assembly lines and union halls to college lecture podiums and corporate boardrooms, African Americans and white women especially, and Latinos, Asian Americans, and lesbians and gays to a lesser degree, now have a presence and a voice as never before. If women of all groups and men of color are still far from having what activists would call a fair share, theirs is now a significant enough share to shame those in power who would exclude, and so make it unlikely that these institutions will ever go back to working the way they did before. Now that the genie is out of the bottle, not only are the nation's workplaces and alliances altered; so, too, are its dreams.

For now, those who would block further inclusion and avoid rec-ognizing the truth that freedom is not enough have considerable strength. But just as a movement that seemed vanquished by the mid-1950s defied doomsayers, so another one may manage a similar feat in the fullness of time. That it is incubating seems likely, for what was true fifty years ago is even truer now: the promise of full citizenship exists in constant tension with a labor market that delivers vastly uneven re-wards, when it delivers them at all.[30] Conservatives' very success in finally achieving the dismantling of the safety net guarantee of welfare and making employment the sole route to the entitlements of citi-zenship has drawn new attention to the millions of Americans who work full-time yet live in poverty, thus spurring campaigns to "make work pay."

Those growing up in a world that at last acknowledges the justice of equal opportunity for all yet does so amidst spiraling inequality of re-wards may sooner or later, as their forebears did, put to use the promise of the Declaration of Independence. Like those who came before them in the 1950s, that new wave of activists will likely find creative ways to navigate daunting new conditions. Whether they will enjoy anything like the same success is impossible to guess in advance, not least be-cause so much depends on how much help they attract and how tal-ented are the organizers they develop. Both will be needed in abun-dance to undo the damage of the exclusionists' successes, let alone realize the ambitious goals the earlier activists fought for but lacked enough power to achieve. It will not be easy. As one black worker who spent his life fighting for justice predicted with deep sadness, "There's going to be a lot more suffering here, because you have white folks who still believe they can make it without us."[31] Yet in the protected interior spaces where truth takes shelter in cynical times, millions of Ameri-cans—white along with black and brown, men along with women—know that freedom is indivisible, and that freedom is not enough.

Abbreviations in Notes

Abzug Papers	Bella Abzug Papers, 1970–1976, Rare Book and Manuscript Library, Columbia University, New York
ACLU Papers	American Civil Liberties Union Records, Seeley G. Mudd Manuscript Library, Princeton University, Princeton, New Jersey
AFSCME-PDD	American Federation of State, County, and Municipal Employees, Program Development Department Records, 1964–1977, Walter P. Reuther Library, Archives of Labor and Urban Affairs, Wayne State University, Detroit
AFT-OP	American Federation of Teachers, Office of the President Collection, 1960–1974, Walter P. Reuther Library, Wayne State University, Detroit
AHR	*American Historical Review*
AJCA	American Jewish Committee Archives, Jacob and Hilda Blaustein Human Relations Research Library, New York
AJC-OH	American Jewish Committee Oral History Collection, Dorot Jewish Division, New York Public Library
AJCongressR	American Jewish Congress Records, American Jewish Historical Society, Center for Jewish History, New York
AJS	*American Journal of Sociology*
Andow Papers	Paul Andow, National President Office Files, 1963–64, LULAC Collection, Nettie Lee Benson Latin American Collection, University of Texas at Austin
Aragon Papers	Joseph Aragon Papers, Staff Office Files, Jimmy Carter Presidential Library, Atlanta
Armstrong Papers	Anne L. Armstrong Papers, Staff Member Office Files, White House Special Files, Richard M. Nixon Presidential Materials, National Archives, College Park, Maryland

Barr Files   William L. Barr Files, 1982–83, Ronald Reagan
                             Presidential Library, Simi Valley, California
Benites Files   Joseph Benites National President Office Files, 1973–74,
                             LULAC Collection, Nettie Lee Benson Latin American
                             Collection, University of Texas at Austin
Boyte Papers   Boyte Family Papers, 1941–1981, Southern Historical
                             Collection, Wilson Library, University of North
                             Carolina–Chapel Hill
Browne Papers   Robert S. Browne Papers, 1960–1984, Manuscripts,
                             Archives, and Rare Books Division, Schomburg Center for
                             Research in Black Culture, New York Public Library
CASA Records   Centro de Acción Social Autónomo—Hermandad General
                             de Trabajadores Records, 1963–1979, Special Collections,
                             Stanford University, Stanford, California
CCR   U.S. Chamber of Commerce Records, 1912–1975, Hagley
                             Museum and Library, Wilmington, Delaware
Clark Papers   Ramsey Clark Personal Papers, Lyndon Baines Johnson
                             Presidential Library, Austin, Texas
CLUW Records   Coalition of Labor Union Women Records, 1972–1980,
                             Walter P. Reuther Library, Archives of Labor and Urban
                             Affairs, Wayne State University, Detroit
CNPR   Center for National Policy Review Papers, 1971–1986,
                             Manuscript Division, Library of Congress, Washington,
                             D.C.
Cooke Papers   Robert Bruce Cooke Papers, Southern Historical
                             Collection, Wilson Library, University of North
                             Carolina–Chapel Hill
CORE   Congress of Racial Equality (CORE), Southern Regional
                             Office Papers, 1954–1966, State Historical Society of
                             Wisconsin, Archives Division, Madison
Costanza Papers   Margaret Costanza Papers, Office of Public Liaison,
                             Jimmy Carter Presidential Library, Atlanta
CQ   *Congressional Quarterly*
Cribb Files   T. Kenneth Cribb, Jr., Files, 1981–1989, Ronald Reagan
                             Presidential Library, Simi Valley, California
DCRR   Department of Civil Rights Records, AFL-CIO, George
                             Meany Memorial Archives, Silver Spring, Maryland
Dole Papers   Elizabeth H. Dole Files, 1981–1983, Office of Public
                             Liaison, Ronald Reagan Presidential Library, Simi Valley,
                             California
Draper Papers   Anne Draper Papers, 1963–1994, George Meany
                             Memorial Archives, Silver Spring, Maryland
East Papers   Catherine East Papers, Schlesinger Library, Radcliffe
                             Institute for Advanced Study, Harvard University,
                             Cambridge, Massachusetts
Eastwood Papers   Mary O. Eastwood Papers, Schlesinger Library, Radcliffe
                             Institute for Advanced Study, Harvard University,
                             Cambridge, Massachusetts

Erlichman Files	John D. Erlichman Files, Staff Member Office Files, White House Special Files, Richard M. Nixon Presidential Materials, National Archives, College Park, Maryland
Ervin Records	Samuel James Ervin, Jr., Senate Records, Southern Historical Collection, Wilson Library, University of North Carolina–Chapel Hill
Finch Papers	Robert H. Finch Papers, Staff Member Office Files, White House Special Files, Richard M. Nixon Presidential Materials, National Archives, College Park, Maryland
Friedan Papers	Betty (Goldstein) Friedan Papers, 1933–1980, Schlesinger Library, Radcliffe Institute for Advanced Study, Harvard University, Cambridge, Massachusetts
Gaither Files	James Gaither Office Files, 1964–1969, Lyndon Baines Johnson Presidential Library, Austin, Texas
Galarza Papers	Ernesto Galarza Papers, 1936–1984, Special Collections, Stanford University, Stanford, California
García Papers	Dr. Hector P. García Papers, Special Collections and Archives, Bell Library, Texas A&M University–Corpus Christi
Garment Papers	Leonard Garment Papers, Staff Member Office Files, White House Special Files, Richard M. Nixon Presidential Materials, National Archives, College Park, Maryland
GRFL	Gerald R. Ford Presidential Library, Ann Arbor, Michigan
Gutierrez Papers	Annie Gutierrez, Domestic Policy Staff, Civil Rights & Justice Cluster, Jimmy Carter Presidential Library, Atlanta
Harding Papers	Bertrand M. Harding Personal Papers, 1958–1969, Office of Economic Opportunity, Lyndon Baines Johnson Presidential Library, Austin, Texas
Haughton Papers	James Haughton Papers, 1929–1984, Manuscripts, Archives, and Rare Books Division, Schomberg Center for Research in Black Culture, New York Public Library
Heide Papers	Wilma Scott Heide Papers, 1968–1974, Schlesinger Library, Radcliffe Institute for Advanced Study, Harvard University, Cambridge, Massachusetts
Holcomb Papers	Luther Holcomb Personal Papers, Lyndon Baines Johnson Presidential Library, Austin, Texas
ILWCH	*International Labor and Working Class History*
JAH	*Journal of American History*
JCPL	Jimmy Carter Presidential Library, Atlanta
JJKP	James J. Kilpatrick Papers, 1908, 1963–1997, University of Virginia, Special Collections, Charlottesville
JLC	Jewish Labor Committee Records, 1947–1973, Michigan Region Collection, Walter P. Reuther Library, Archives of Labor and Urban Affairs, Wayne State University, Detroit
JNH	*Journal of Negro History*
Jordan Papers	Hamilton Jordan Papers, Office of the Chief of Staff Files, 1977–1980, Jimmy Carter Presidential Library, Atlanta
JSH	*Journal of Southern History*

JWH	*Journal of Women's History*
Kaplan Collection	Kivie Kaplan Collection, 1948–1975, Manuscript Division, Amistad Research Center, New Orleans
Kruger Files	Robert M. Kruger Files, 1986–1988, Counsel to the President, Ronald Reagan Presidential Library, Simi Valley, California
LAT	*Los Angeles Times*
Layzer Papers	Judith Layzer Papers, 1969–1986, Robert F. Wagner Labor Archives and Tamiment Archives, New York University
LBJL	Lyndon Baines Johnson Presidential Library, Austin, Texas
LCCR	Leadership Conference on Civil Rights Papers, 1952–1990, Manuscript Division, Library of Congress, Washington, D.C.
MALDEF	Mexican American Legal Defense and Education Fund Records, 1967–1984, Stanford University, Special Collections, Palo Alto, California
Malson Papers	Robert Malson Papers, 1977–1981, Domestic Policy Staff Files, Jimmy Carter Presidential Library, Atlanta
Martin Papers	Louis Martin Papers, Special Assistant to the President, 1978–1981, Jimmy Carter Presidential Library, Atlanta
McPherson Files	Harry McPherson Office Files, Lyndon Baines Johnson Presidential Library, Austin, Texas
Meese Files	Edwin Meese III Files, Counselor to the President, 1981–1985, Ronald Reagan Presidential Library, Simi Valley, California
Miller Interviews	White Burkett Miller Center Jimmy Carter Project, University of Virginia, 1980–1989, Jimmy Carter Presidential Library, Atlanta
Mitchell Files	Martha (Bunny) Mitchell Files, Office of the Special Assistant, 1977–1981, Jimmy Carter Presidential Library, Atlanta
Morga Collection	Edward Morga Collection, 1971–1986, LULAC Archives, Nettie Lee Benson Latin American Collection, University of Texas at Austin
Murray Papers	Pauli Murray Papers, 1927–1985, Schlesinger Library, Radcliffe Institute for Advanced Study, Harvard University, Cambridge, Massachusetts
NAACP	National Association for the Advancement of Colored People Papers, 1909–1982, Manuscript Division, Library of Congress, Washington, D.C.
NABF Papers	National Alliance of Black Feminists Records, 1972–1986, National Archives for Black Women's History, Mary McLeod Bethune Council House, Washington, D.C.
NAM	National Association of Manufacturers Archives (U.S.), Hagley Museum and Library, Wilmington, Delaware

NAM-IRD   National Association of Manufacturers, Industrial
Relations Department Records, 1895–1975, Hagley
Museum and Library, Wilmington, Delaware

NCAC   U.S. Commission on Civil Rights, North Carolina
Advisory Committee Papers, Special Collections Library,
Duke University, Durham

NCCIJ   National Catholic Conference for Interracial Justice
Records, 1956–present, Special Collections and Archives,
Marquette University, Milwaukee

NCJW   National Council of Jewish Women, National Office
Papers, Manuscript Division, Library of Congress,
Washington, D.C.

NCNW   National Council of Negro Women Records, 1935–1980,
National Archives for Black Women's History, Mary
McLeod Bethune Council House, Washington, D.C.

Nicolau Papers   Siobhan Nicolau Papers, 1967–1994, Mexican American
Collection, Special Collections and University Archives,
Stanford University, Stanford, California

NOW NYC   National Organization for Women, New York City
Chapter Records, 1966–1984, Robert F. Wagner Labor
Archives and Tamiment Archives, New York University

NOW Papers   National Organization for Women Records, 1966–1992,
Schlesinger Library, Radcliffe Institute for Advanced
Study, Harvard University, Cambridge, Massachusetts

NPMP   Richard M. Nixon Presidential Materials Project, National
Archives, College Park, Maryland

NR   *National Review*

NUL   National Urban League Records, 1909–1985, Manuscript
Division, Department of Research, Library of Congress,
Washington, D.C.

NYT   *New York Times*

NYTWC Papers   New York Times Women's Caucus Papers, 1969–1980,
Schlesinger Library, Radcliffe Institute for Advanced
Study, Harvard University, Cambridge, Massachusetts

Parrish Papers   Richard Parrish Papers, 1950–1975, Schomberg Center
for Research in Black Culture, New York Public Library

Patterson Papers   Bradley H. Patterson, Jr., Staff Member Office Files,
White House Special Files, Richard M. Nixon Presidential
Materials, National Archives, College Park, Maryland

PRLDEF   Puerto Rican Legal Defense and Education Fund Papers,
Centro de Estudios Puertorriqueños, Hunter College,
City University of New York

Randolph Papers   A. Philip Randolph Papers, 1937–1968, Brotherhood of
Sleeping Car Porters Records, Manuscript Division,
Library of Congress, Washington, D.C.

Rauh Papers   Joseph Rauh Papers, 1913–1994, Manuscript Division,
Library of Congress, Washington, D.C.

RBCCOF	Ruben Bonilla, Corpus Christi Council Office Files, 1957–1979, LULAC Archives, Nettie Lee Benson Latin American Collection, University of Texas at Austin
RBDSDF	Ruben Bonilla, Ruben Bonilla Office Files, Deputy State Director, 1976–77, LULAC Archives, Nettie Lee Benson Latin American Collection, University of Texas at Austin
RB-GC	Ruben Bonilla Office Files, 1957–1979, LULAC Archives, Nettie Lee Benson Latin American Collection, University of Texas at Austin
Reedy Papers	George Reedy Office Files, Special Assistant, 1954–1964, Lyndon Baines Johnson Presidential Library, Austin, Texas
Rockefeller Records	Rockefeller Brothers Fund Records, Rockefeller Archive Center, North Tarrytown, New York
RRPL	Ronald Reagan Presidential Library, Simi Valley, California
Sánchez Papers	George I. Sánchez Papers, 1892–1972, Nettie Lee Benson Latin American Collection, University of Texas at Austin
SAV File	Social Action Vertical File, Archives Division, State Historical Society of Wisconsin, Madison
SCLC	Southern Christian Leadership Conference Records, 1954–1970, Microfilm Edition, Bethesda, Maryland
SHC	Southern Historical Collection, Wilson Library, University of North Carolina–Chapel Hill
Shiskin Papers	Boris Shiskin Papers, 1918, 1927–1971, Research Department, AFL-CIO, George Meany Memorial Archives, Silver Spring, Maryland
SIRW	Southwest Institute for Research on Women, Southern Historical Collection, Wilson Library, University of North Carolina–Chapel Hill
SOHP	Southern Oral History Program Collection, Southern Historical Collection, Manuscripts Department, Wilson Library, University of North Carolina–Chapel Hill
SRC	Southern Regional Council Papers, 1944–1968, Microfilm edition, Ann Arbor. [Originals held by Special Collections and Archives Division, Robert W. Woodruff Library, Atlanta University Center.]
SWEC	Southeast Women's Employment Coalition Records, 1968–1991, Special Collections Library, Duke University, Durham, North Carolina
TCTUW	Twentieth-Century Trade Union Women Oral History Project, Bentley Historical Library, University of Michigan, Ann Arbor
Torres Papers	Esteban Edward Torres Papers, Office of Hispanic Affairs, Jimmy Carter Presidential Library, Atlanta
TWUA	Textile Workers Union of America Papers, Archives Division, State Historical Society of Wisconsin, Madison

UT Papers	United Tradeswomen Records, 1979–1984, Robert F. Wagner Labor Archives and Tamiment Archives, New York University
VCHR	Virginia Council on Human Relations, Charlottesville-Albemarle Chapter Papers, 1956–1970, University of Virginia Library, Charlottesville
VPP-LBJL	Lyndon Baines Johnson, Vice Presidential Papers, Lyndon Baines Johnson Presidential Library, Austin, Texas
WEAL	Women's Equity Action League Records, 1966–1990, Schlesinger Library, Radcliffe Institute for Advanced Study, Harvard University, Cambridge, Massachusetts
Weatherford Papers	Willis Duke Weatherford Papers, Southern Historical Collection, Wilson Library, University of North Carolina–Chapel Hill
White Files	Lee White Office Files, Special Counsel, 1962–1966, Lyndon Baines Johnson Presidential Library, Austin, Texas
WFBP	William F. Buckley, Jr., Papers, 1951–2002, Manuscripts and Archives, Yale University, New Haven, Connecticut
WHCF	White House Central Files
White Files	Franklin E. White Files, Civil Rights and Justice Cluster, Domestic Policy Staff, Jimmy Carter Presidential Library, Atlanta
WHORM	White House Office of Records Management, Ronald Reagan Presidential Library, Simi Valley, California
WHSF	White House Special Files, Richard M. Nixon Presidential Materials, National Archives, College Park, Maryland
Wilkins Papers	Roy Wilkins Papers, 1901–1980, Manuscript Division, Library of Congress, Washington, D.C.
WOW Papers	Wider Opportunities for Women Records, 1965–1987, Schlesinger Library, Radcliffe Institute for Advanced Study, Harvard University, Cambridge, Massachusetts
WP	*Washington Post*
Wright Papers	Marion C. Wright Papers, Southern Historical Collection, Wilson Library, University of North Carolina–Chapel Hill
WSJ	*Wall Street Journal*
Young Papers	Whitney M. Young, Jr., Papers, 1960–1977, Rare Book and Manuscript Library, Columbia University, New York

Notes

Prologue

1. "Mississippi: 'Act of Savagery,'" *Time*, March 10, 1967, 25; Frank L. Dwyer to Roy Wilkins, March 14, 1967, box A36, group 4, NAACP; Stephanie Saul, "Her Quest for Truth," *Newsday*, Dec. 14, 1998, A6, A27; Jerry Mitchell, "Klan Fear Hampered Justice in Slayings," *Natchez Clarion-Ledger*, Feb. 13, 2000, 1. Jackson quoted in Southern Poverty Law Center, *Free at Last: A History of the Civil Rights Movement and Those Who Died in the Struggle* (Montgomery, Ala., 1989), 90.

2. See sources in note 1 and John Dittmer, *Local People: The Struggle for Civil Rights in Mississippi* (Urbana, Ill., 1995), 353–362; Jack E. Davis, *Race against Time: Culture and Separation in Natchez since 1930* (Baton Rouge, La., 2001).

3. See, for example, William Julius Wilson, *When Work Disappears: The World of the New Urban Poor* (New York, 1996); Robert H. Frank and Philip J. Cook, *The Winner-Take-All Society: Why the Few at the Top Get So Much More Than the Rest of Us* (New York, 1995); Eileen Appelbaum, Annette Bernhardt, and Richard J. Murnane, eds., *Low-Wage America: How Employers Are Reshaping Opportunity in the Workplace* (New York, 2003).

4. On traditions of exclusion, see Rogers M. Smith, *Civic Ideals: Conflicting Visions of Citizenship in U.S. History* (New Haven, 1997); and Evelyn Nakano Glenn, *Unequal Freedom: How Race and Gender Shaped American Citizenship and Labor* (Cambridge, Mass., 2002). For today's "multicultural military" as a global U.S. public relations tool, see Melani McAlister, *Epic Encounters: Culture, Media, and U.S. Interests in the Middle East, 1945–2000* (Berkeley, 2001).

5. The struggle to open good jobs to all has been overlooked by scholars of the modern black freedom movement, with the important exception of labor historians, whose pioneering scholarship includes Robin D. G. Kelley, *Race Rebels: Culture, Politics, and the Black Working Class* (New York, 1996); Roger Horowitz, "*Negro*

and White, Unite and Fight": A Social History of Industrial Unionism in Meatpacking, 1930–90 (Urbana, Ill., 1997); Timothy J. Minchin, *Hiring the Black Worker: The Racial Integration of the Southern Textile Industry, 1960–1980* (Chapel Hill, N.C., 1999), and *The Color of Work: The Struggle for Civil Rights in the Southern Paper Industry, 1945–1980* (Chapel Hill, N.C., 2001); Venus Green, *Race on the Line: Gender, Labor, and Technology in the Bell System, 1880–1980* (Durham, N.C., 2001); Bruce Nelson, *Divided We Stand: American Workers and the Struggle for Black Equality* (Princeton, 2001); Eric Arnesen, *Brotherhoods of Color: Black Railroad Workers and the Struggle for Equality* (Cambridge, Mass., 2002); Michael Keith Honey, *Black Workers Remember: An Oral History of Segregation, Unionism, and the Freedom Struggle* (Berkeley, 2002); and Ruth Needleman, *Black Freedom Fighters in Steel: The Struggle for Democratic Unionism* (Ithaca, N.Y., 2003).

6. For blacks as an island of social-democratic values in U.S. public opinion, see Michael C. Dawson, *Black Visions: The Roots of Contemporary African-American Political Ideologies* (Chicago, 2001), esp. 59, 83; Dona Cooper Hamilton and Charles V. Hamilton, *The Dual Agenda: The African-American Struggle for Civil and Economy Equality* (New York, 1997); Seymour Martin Lipset, *American Exceptionalism: A Double-Edged Sword* (New York, 1996), 113–150.

7. "Remarks of the President at Howard University, Washington, D.C.: To Fulfill These Rights," June 4, 1965, box 172, EX SP-93, WHCF, LBJL.

8. Quoted in Victoria Byerly, *Hard Times Cotton Mill Girls: Personal Stories of Womanhood and Poverty in the South* (Ithaca, N.Y., 1986), 160.

9. For classic treatments, see Richard Weiss, *The American Myth of Success: From Horatio Alger to Norman Vincent Peale* (Urbana, Ill., 1969); and Daniel T. Rodgers, *The Work Ethic in Industrial America, 1850–1920* (Chicago, 1974).

10. Judith Shklar, *American Citizenship: The Quest for Inclusion* (Cambridge, Mass., 1991), 100.

11. For the findings of a major multidisciplinary government study in the midst of these events, see *Work in America: Report of a Special Task Force to the Secretary of Health, Education, and Welfare* (Cambridge, Mass., [1973]), 4, xv, 17, also 51–58; for Western thought about work, see Sean Sayers, "The Need to Work: A Perspective from Philosophy," in *On Work: Historical, Comparative, and Theoretical Approaches*, ed. R. E. Pahl (London, 1988), 722–741; and Keith Thomas, ed., *The Oxford Book of Work* (New York, 1999).

12. Charlottesville NAACP, "The 1963 Revolution Comes to Charlottesville: A Statement of Grievances and Recommendations," Sept. 11, 1963, box 2, VCHR.

13. Susan Eisenberg, *Pioneering: Poems from the Construction Site* (Ithaca, N.Y., 1998), xii.

14. Barbara R. Bergmann, *The Economic Emergence of Women* (New York, 1986), esp. 8; Stephen Steinberg, *Turning Back: The Retreat from Racial Justice in American Thought and Policy* (Boston, 1995), 179–185. On work as a culture-shaping enterprise that helps define gender, see Ava Baron, "Gender and Labor History: Learning from the Past, Looking to the Future," in *Work Engendered: Toward a New History of American Labor*, ed. Ava Baron (Ithaca, N.Y., 1991), 1–46; for "race making," see Thomas Holt, "Marking: Race, Race-making, and the Writing of History," *AHR* 100 (Feb. 1995): 1–20.

15. Testimony by Martin Luther King, Jr., Eighty-ninth Congress, 2nd sess.,

The Federal Role in Urban Affairs: Hearings before the Subcommittee on Executive Reorganization of the Committee on Government Operations, pt. 14, Dec. 14–15, 1966 (Washington, D.C., 1967), 2991, 2981.

16. For overviews, see Jill Quadagno, *The Color of Welfare: How Racism Undermined the War on Poverty* (New York, 1996); Alice Kessler-Harris, *In Pursuit of Equity: Women, Men, and the Quest for Economic Citizenship in Twentieth-Century America* (New York, 1996); and Mae M. Ngai, *Impossible Subjects: Illegal Aliens and the Making of Modern America* (Princeton, 2003).

17. El Comite, "An Open Letter to Mexican American Employees of [the Freeport, Texas,] Dow Chemical Company," May 31, 1974, box 92, García Papers.

18. Edward T. Chase, "Preferential Hiring for Negroes: A Debate" (special issue), *American Child* 45 (Nov. 1963): 13.

19. Charles Whalen and Barbara Whalen, *The Longest Debate: A Legislative History of the 1964 Civil Rights Act* (Washington, D.C., 1985), 200–201.

20. *Conversations with James Baldwin,* ed. Fred L. Standley and Louis H. Pratt (Jackson, Miss., 1989), 73.

1. The Rightness of Whiteness

1. Quoted in Timothy J. Minchin, *The Color of Work: The Struggle for Civil Rights in the Southern Paper Industry, 1945–1980* (Chapel Hill, N.C., 2001), 1.

2. For surveys of the literature, see Nancy MacLean, "Postwar Women's History: The 'Second Wave' or the End of the Family Wage?" in *A Companion to Post-1945 America,* ed. Roy Rosenzweig and Jean-Christophe Agnew (London, 2002), 235–259; MacLean, "From the Benighted South to the Sunbelt: The South in the Twentieth Century," in *Perspectives on Modern America: Making Sense of the Twentieth Century* (New York, 2001), 202–226; Mae M. Ngai, *Impossible Subjects: Illegal Aliens and the Making of Modern America* (Princeton, 2004), 67–92.

3. Rogers M. Smith, *Civic Ideals: Conflicting Visions of Citizenship in U.S. History* (New Haven, 1997), 2–3, 7, 29; Ian F. Haney Lopez, *White by Law: The Legal Construction of Race* (New York, 1996), 1. Asian Americans organized for jobs later and to a lesser degree than Mexican Americans; see Chapter 7.

4. Elaine Tyler May, *Homeward Bound: American Families in the Cold War Period* (New York, 1988), 16–18.

5. See, for example, Nina C. Leibman, *Living Room Lectures: The Fifties Family in Film and Television* (Austin, Tex., 1995); on Cole, see Julie Salamon, "An Evolving Vision in Black and White," *NYT,* Feb. 2, 2002, B1; Nat "King" Cole, "Why I Quit My TV Show," *Ebony* (Feb. 1958): 29–34.

6. Walter Christmas, "Negroes in the Ads," *Negro Digest* (Dec. 1949): 70–73; for film quote, see *Current Biography* (New York, 1970), s.v. Herbert Hill, 183.

7. Martha May, "The Historical Problem of the Family Wage: The Ford Motor Company and the Five Dollar Day," *Feminist Studies* 8 (Summer 1982): 399–424; Linda Gordon, *Pitied but Not Entitled: Single Mothers and the History of Welfare* (New York, 1994); Linda K. Kerber, *No Constitutional Right to Be Ladies: Women and the Obligations of Citizenship* (New York, 1999).

8. Linda Gordon, *Women, the State, and Welfare* (Madison, Wisc., 1990); Alice Kessler-Harris, *In Pursuit of Equity: Women, Men, and the Quest for Economic Citizenship in Twentieth-Century America* (New York, 2001).

9. "The National Association for the Advancement of Colored People Appraises the First Year of the President's Committee on Equal Employment Opportunity," April 6, 1962, box 1, Reedy Papers; Jill Quadagno, *The Color of Welfare: How Racism Undermined the War on Poverty* (New York, 1994).

10. George Lipsitz, *The Possessive Investment in Whiteness: How White People Profit from Identity Politics* (Philadelphia, 1998).

11. Howard Kester, *Revolt among the Sharecroppers* (1936; reprint, Knoxville, Tenn., 1990), 17; Vivian W. Henderson, *The Economic Status of Negroes: In the Nation and in the South* (Atlanta, 1963), 17; Ray Marshall, "Black Employment in the South," in *Minorities, Women, and Employment Discrimination*, ed. Phyllis Wallace and Annette LaMond (Lexington, KY., 1977), 71; Jacqueline Jones, *Labor of Love, Labor of Sorrow: Black Women, Work, and the Family from Slavery to the Present* (New York, 1985), 260; Gavin Wright, *Old South, New South: Revolutions in the Southern Economy* (New York, 1986).

12. Southern Christian Leadership Conference, "Negro Ministers Launch Big Push in Employment, [1962], series 4, reel 23:0715, SCLC.

13. National Planning Association, Committee of the South, *Selected Studies of Negro Employment in the South*, Report no. 6 (Washington, D.C., 1955), 1:3.

14. Donald Dewey, "Four Studies of Negro Employment in the Upper South," ibid., 158–161, 209; National Planning Association, *Selected Studies*, 3:266; Leon Litwack, *Trouble in Mind: Black Southerners in the Age of Jim Crow* (New York, 1998), 142, 151–161, 159, 162.

15. Atlanta SCLC to John Feild, Nov. 1, 1962, series 4, reel 23: 0600, SCLC; Michael Honey, *Southern Labor and Black Civil Rights: Organizing Memphis Workers* (Urbana, Ill., 1993); "The Time Is Now: A Statement of the National Urban League" to John F. Kennedy, President-Elect, Dec. 29, 1960, box 85, VPP-LBJL; Kelly M. Alexander to North Carolina Advisory Committee of the U.S. Civil Rights Commission, [n.d., ca. 1960], NCAC.

16. Mrs. Helen Clinton to Dr. Rankin, Feb. 2, 1961, box 7, NCAC.

17. Herbert Hill to Roy Wilkins et al., April 1, 1957, box A309, group 3, NAACP; Martha Biondi, *To Stand and Fight: The Civil Rights Movement in Postwar New York City* (Cambridge, Mass., 2003), 19–25.

18. William H. Johnson to James P. Mitchell, Aug. 17, 1955, box 1, DCRR.

19. National Research Council, *A Common Destiny: Blacks and American Society*, ed. Gerald David Jaynes and Robin M. Williams, Jr. (Washington, D.C., 1989), 273; Darlene Clark Hine, "Black Professionals and Race Consciousness: Origins of the Civil Rights Movement, 1890–1950," *JAH* (March 2003): 1279–94; Robert E. Weems, Jr., *Black Business in the Black Metropolis: The Chicago Metropolitan Assurance Company, 1925–1985* (Bloomington, Ind., 1996).

20. Southern Regional Council, *The Negro and Employment Opportunities in the South: Houston* (Atlanta, 1961), 6; Wright, *Old South, New South*, 80, 177.

21. Marshall, "Black Employment," 71–72; National Research Council, *Common Destiny*, 334–335.

22. See, for example, J. H. Wheeler to McNeill Smith, July 6, 1961, box 7, NCAC; also Southern Regional Council [SRC], *The Negro and Employment Opportunities in the South: Chattanooga* (Atlanta, Feb. 1962), 5; SRC, *Negro and Employment Opportunities*, 16.

23. Douglas S. Massey and Nancy A. Denton, *American Apartheid: Segregation and the Making of the Underclass* (Cambridge, Mass., 1993).

24. Quoted in Abraham F. Citron, *The "Rightness of Whiteness": The World of the White Child in a Segregated Society* (Detroit, 1969), 3, 4.

25. Ngai, *Impossible Subjects;* David Montejano, *Anglos and Mexicans in the Making of Texas, 1836–1986* (Austin, Tex., 1987); see also Chapter 5.

26. See Jones, *Labor of Love,* 257–269; Vicki L. Ruiz, *From Out of the Shadows: Mexican Women in Twentieth-Century America* (New York, 1998); Alice Kessler-Harris, *Out to Work: A History of Wage-Earning Women in the United States* (New York, 1982); Lois Scharf, *To Work and to Wed: Female Employment, Feminism, and the Great Depression* (Westport, Conn., 1980).

27. Brett Harvey, *The Fifties: A Women's Oral History* (New York, 1993), 48–49; John H. Fleming and Charles A. Shanor, "Veterans' Preferences in Public Employment: Unconstitutional Gender Discrimination?" *Emory Law Journal* 26 (1997): 13–64.

28. Mary Bosworth to W. J. Schieffelin, Feb. 27, 1947, box 24, Wilkins Papers; J. S. McColl to W. J. Schieffelin, Feb. 20, 1947, ibid.; Mrs. William A. Murray to W. J. Schieffelin, March 5, 1947, ibid.; "Civil Rights Bill Opposition" [Minnesota], petition from Scott D. Drum et al., April 28, 1964, box 1, Civil Rights Public Opinion Mail, WHCF, LBJL.

29. Quoted in Vincent Harding et al., "We Changed the World, 1945–1970," in *To Make Our World Anew: A History of African Americans,* ed. Robin D. G. Kelley and Earl Lewis (New York, 2000), 445.

30. Harvard Sitkoff, *A New Deal for Blacks: The Emergence of Civil Rights as a National Issue* (New York, 1978), 315; William H. Harris, *The Harder We Run: Black Workers since the Civil War* (New York, 1982), 115–121; Jervis Anderson, *A. Philip Randolph: A Biographical Portrait* (New York, 1973), 248–261, quote on 248–249; Joe Trotter, "From a Raw Deal to a New Deal?" in Kelley and Lewis, *To Make Our World Anew,* quote on 444; Merl E. Reed, *Seedtime for the Modern Civil Rights Movement: The President's Committee on Fair Employment Practice, 1941–1946* (Baton Rouge, La., 1991).

31. Gary Gerstle, "The Working Class Goes to War," in *The War in American Culture: Society and Consciousness during World War II,* ed. Lewis A. Erenberg and Susan E. Hirsch (Chicago, 1996), 113; Sitkoff, *New Deal,* 324; Patricia Sullivan, *Days of Hope: Race and Democracy in the New Deal Era* (Chapel Hill, N.C., 1996), 103.

32. Lizabeth Cohen, *A Consumers' Republic: The Politics of Mass Consumption in Postwar America* (New York, 2003), 167, 180.

33. Eric Arnesen, *Waterfront Workers of New Orleans: Race, Class, and Politics, 1863–1923* (New York, 1991); Alex Lichtenstein, *Twice the Work of Free Labor: The Political Economy of Convict Labor in the New South* (New York, 1996); Tera W. Hunter, *To 'Joy My Freedom: Southern Black Women's Lives and Labors after the Civil War* (Cambridge, Mass., 1997); Daniel Letwin, *The Challenge of Interracial Unionism: Alabama Coal Miners, 1878–1921* (Chapel Hill, N.C., 1998); Steven Reich, "The Making of a Southern Sawmill World: Race, Class, and Rural Transformation in the Piney Woods of East Texas" (Ph.D. diss., Northwestern University, 1999). For how female workplace activists accepted the gender division of labor at mid-century, see Dorothy Cobble, *The Other Women's Movement: Workplace Justice and Social Rights in Modern America* (Princeton, 2003). Mexican Americans in these years organized mainly in farm work, taking the division of labor for granted while trying to improve conditions.

34. T. H. Marshall and Tom Bottomore, *Citizenship and Social Class* (London, 1992), 3–49; Wright, *Old South, New South;* Sitkoff, *New Deal,* esp. 76; Trotter, "From a Raw Deal."

35. Nelson Lichtenstein, *Labor's War at Home: The CIO in World War II* (New York, 1982), 233; Eric Arnesen, *Brotherhoods of Color: Black Railroad Workers and the Struggle for Equality* (Cambridge, Mass., 2001), 86, 226; Mason quoted in Honey, *Southern Labor,* 117.

36. Trotter, "From a Raw Deal," 429; Dona Cooper Hamilton and Charles V. Hamilton, *The Dual Agenda: The African-American Struggle for Civil and Economic Equality* (New York, 1997), 9; Beth Tompkins Bates, "A New Crowd Challenges the Agenda of the Old Guard in the NAACP, 1933–1941," *AHR* 102 (April 1997): 340–377; Erik Gellman, "Civil Rights in Hard Times: The National Negro Congress and Its Legacy, 1936–1948" (Ph.D. diss., Northwestern University, 2006).

37. August Meier and Elliott Rudwick, *CORE: A Study in the Civil Rights Movement* (Urbana, Ill., 1975), esp. 6; *American Social Leaders,* ed. William McGuire and Leslie Wheeler (Santa Barbara, Calif., 1993), s.v. Farmer, James Leonard, 164; Houston quote from Sitkoff, *New Deal,* 242.

38. Arnesen, *Brotherhoods,* quote from 2; Anderson, *A. Philip Randolph;* William H. Harris, *Keeping the Faith: A. Philip Randolph, Milton P. Webster, and the Brotherhood of Sleeping Car Porters, 1925–37* (Urbana, Ill., 1977).

39. Stephen Steinberg, *Turning Back: The Retreat from Racial Justice in American Thought and Policy* (Boston, 1995), 26–29; August Meier and John H. Bracey, Jr., "The NAACP as a Reform Movement, 1909–1965: 'To Reach the Conscience of America,'" *JSH* 59 (Feb. 1993): 15–19.

40. Winston McDowell, "Race and Ethnicity during the Harlem Jobs Campaign, 1932–1935," *Journal of Negro History* 69 (Summer–Autumn 1984): 134–146; Darlene Clark Hine, "The Housewives' League of Detroit: Black Women and Economic Nationalism," in *Hine Sight: Black Women and the Re-Construction of American History* (Bloomington, Ind., 1994), 129–145; Andor Skotnes, "'Buy Where You Can Work': Boycotting for Jobs in African-American Baltimore, 1933–34," *Journal of Social History* 27 (Summer 1994): 735–762.

41. Sitkoff, *New Deal,* 192, 199.

42. Trotter, "From a Raw Deal," 423–424.

43. National Research Council, *Common Destiny,* 273; Harris, *The Harder We Run,* 126–127, 130; Nicholas Lemann, *The Promised Land* (New York, 1991), 6.

44. National Research Council, *Common Destiny,* 233, 339; Meier and Bracey, "NAACP," 22, 27; Aldon D. Morris, *The Origins of the Civil Rights Movement: Black Communities Organizing for Change* (New York, 1984); Doug McAdam, *Political Process and the Development of Black Insurgency, 1930–1970* (Chicago, 1982), 65–116.

45. Biondi, *To Stand and Fight,* 1–2, 16; Penny M. Von Eschen, *Race against Empire: Black Americans and Anticolonialism, 1937–1957* (New York, 1997).

46. Robert Korstad and Nelson Lichtenstein, "Opportunities Found and Lost: Labor, Radicals, and the Early Civil Rights Movement," *JAH* 75 (1988): 786–811; Honey, *Southern Labor;* Robert Rodgers Korstad, *Civil Rights Unionism: Tobacco Workers and the Struggle for Democracy in the Mid-Twentieth-Century South* (Chapel Hill, N.C., 2003); Robert O. Self, *American Babylon: Race and the Struggle for Postwar Oakland* (Princeton, 2003); Josh Sides, *L.A. City Limits: African American Los Angeles from the Great Depression to the Present* (Berkeley, 2004); Stuart Svonkin, *Jews against Prejudice* (New York, 1997).

47. Sullivan, *Days of Hope*, 270; Jack M. Bloom, *Class, Race, and the Civil Rights Movement* (Bloomington, Ind., 1987), 74–76; Sitkoff, *New Deal*, 138.

48. Honey, *Southern Labor*, 244, 275; David Montgomery, *Workers' Control in America* (New York, 1979), 149–150; Thomas J. Sugrue, *Origins of the Urban Crisis: Race and Inequality in Postwar Detroit* (Princeton, 1996), 104; Korstad, *Civil Rights Unionism*.

49. Harris, *The Harder We Run*, 124, 137–139, 140–141; Robert H. Zieger, *The CIO, 1935–1955* (Chapel Hill, N.C., 1995), 108–111, 254, 372–377; Meier and Bracey, "NAACP," 24.

50. Westbrook Pegler, "As Pegler Sees It," *New York Journal American*, Feb. 27, 1945; Ellen Schrecker, *Many Are the Crimes: McCarthyism in America* (Boston, 1998), 282; Biondi, *To Stand and Fight*, 266; Jeff Woods, *Black Struggle, Red Scare: Segregation and Anti-Communism in the South, 1948–1968* (Baton Rouge, La., 2004).

51. Schrecker, *Many Are the Crimes*, 393, 390, 391; Biondi, *To Stand and Fight*, quote on 137; Sullivan, *Days of Hope*; Barbara Ransby, *Ella Baker and the Black Freedom Movement: A Radical Democratic Vision* (Chapel Hill, N.C., 2003).

52. Elizabeth A. Fones-Wolf, *Selling Free Enterprise: The Business Assault on Labor and Liberalism, 1945–1960* (Urbana, Ill., 1994); Kim McQuaid, *Uneasy Partners: Big Business in American Politics, 1945–1990* (Baltimore, 1994), 103–104; Risa Lauren Goluboff, "The Work of Civil Rights in the 1940s: The Department of Justice, the NAACP, and African American Agricultural Labor" (Ph.D., Princeton University, 2003), esp. 361–366, 381; Jennifer Klein, *For All These Rights: Business, Labor, and the Shaping of America's Public-Private Welfare State* (Princeton, 2003).

53. P. H. Moehrle, "Some Questions in Connection with Expansion of NAM Program re: Discrimination," box 13, NAM-IRD; NAM, "Some Reasons against Anti-Discrimination Laws," April 9, 1945, ibid.; Fones-Wolf, *Selling Free Enterprise*, 55.

54. Sara M. Evans, *Born for Liberty: A History of Women in America* (New York, 1989), 245; Betty Friedan, *The Feminine Mystique* (New York, 1963); May, *Homeward Bound*, 13; for the limits of containment, see Joanne Meyerowitz, ed., *Not June Cleaver: Women and Gender in Postwar America, 1945–1960* (Philadelphia, 1994).

55. Robert Booth Fowler, *Believing Skeptics: American Political Intellectuals, 1945–1964* (Westport, Conn., 1978), quote on 50; Rowan quoted in Walter A. Jackson, *Gunnar Myrdal and America's Conscience: Social Engineering and Racial Liberalism, 1938–1987* (Chapel Hill, N.C., 1990); James B. McKee, *Sociology and the Race Problem: The Failure of a Perspective* (Urbana, Ill., 1993), 2.

56. Arthur Miller, *Death of a Salesman; Certain Private Conversations in Two Acts and a Requiem* (New York, 1949); Paul Goodman, *Growing Up Absurd: Problems of Youth in the Organized Society* (New York, 1960), 17, xii, xv, 52; Herbert Marcuse, *One-Dimensional Man: Studies in the Ideology of Advanced Industrial Society* (Boston, 1964); C. Wright Mills, *White Collar: The American Middle Classes* (New York, 1951); Mills, *The Power Elite* (New York, 1956); see also Barbara Ehrenreich, *The Hearts of Men: American Dreams and the Flight from Commitment* (New York, 1983).

57. Sullivan, *Days of Hope*, 275.

58. Sitkoff, *New Deal*, 217; Arnesen, *Brotherhoods*, 207; Morton J. Horowitz, *The Warren Court and the Pursuit of Justice* (New York, 1998).

59. Michael S. Sherry, *In the Shadow of War: The United States since the 1930s*

(New Haven, 1995), 146; Mary L. Dudziak, *Cold War Civil Rights: Race and the Image of American Democracy* (Princeton, 2000), 79; Carol Polsgrove, *Divided Minds: Intellectuals and the Civil Rights Movement* (New York, 2001), xvi.

2. The Fight Begins

1. Harvard Sitkoff, *The Struggle for Black Equality, 1954–1980* (New York, 1981), quotes on 49, 53, 55–56; Robin D. G. Kelley and Earl Lewis, *To Make Our World Anew: A History of African Americans* (New York, 2000), quote on 464; Adam Fairclough, *To Redeem the Soul of America: The Southern Christian Leadership Conference and Martin Luther King, Jr.* (Athens, Ga., 1987), esp. 13–18, 33; Young quoted in Deborah Gray White, *Too Heavy a Load: Black Women in Defense of Themselves, 1894–1994* (New York, 1999), 233; Aldon D. Morris, *The Origins of the Civil Rights Movement: Black Communities Organizing for Change* (New York, 1984), 40–63.

2. Robert S. Graetz, *A White Preacher's Memoir: The Montgomery Bus Boycott* (Montgomery, Ala., 1998), 124; *The Montgomery Bus Boycott and the Women Who Started It: The Memoir of Jo Ann Gibson Robinson*, ed. David Garrow (Knoxville, Tenn., 1987), 80.

3. Gunnar Myrdal, *An American Dilemma* (New York, 1944), 61; Hugh Davis Graham, *The Civil Rights Era: Origins and Development of National Policy* (New York, 1990), 15; Josh Sides, *L.A. City Limits: African American Los Angeles from the Great Depression to the Present* (Berkeley, 2003), 148–151; Robert O. Self, *American Babylon: Race and the Struggle for Postwar Oakland* (Princeton, 2003), esp. 11–13, 182, 187.

4. John D'Emilio, *Lost Prophet: The Life and Time of Bayard Rustin* (New York, 2003), 239; Opinion Research Corporation, *The Controversy over Equal Rights for Negroes: A Report of the Public Opinion Index for Industry* (Princeton, Sept. 1956), 1–8, 19–20, NAM.

5. Bethune quoted in Dona Hamilton and Charles V. Hamilton, *The Dual Agenda: The African-American Struggle for Civil and Economic Equality* (New York, 1997), 57; "Statement of Mrs. Mary McLeod Bethune before the Committee on Education and Labor of the House of Representatives, May 20, 1949," in series 5, NCNW. On adaptation to the cold war, see Fairclough, *To Redeem the Soul of America*, 5, 29–31, 41.

6. Hamilton and Hamilton, *Dual Agenda*, 90; Alan Brinkley, *The End of Reform: New Deal Liberalism in Recession and War* (New York, 1995), 225, 268; *A Testament of Hope: The Essential Writings of Martin Luther King, Jr.*, ed. James Melvin Washington (New York, 1986), 107–108; Merl E. Reed, *Seedtime for the Modern Civil Rights Movement: The President's Committee on Fair Employment Practice, 1941–1946* (Baton Rouge, La., 1991), 339.

7. On LCCR, see Graham, *Civil Rights Era*, 15; on moderate coalitions, see Shana Bernstein, "Building Bridges at Home in a Time of Global Conflict: Interracial Cooperation and the Fight for Civil Rights in Los Angeles, 1933–1954" (Ph.D. diss., Stanford University, 2003).

8. Quoted in Roger Horowitz, *"Negro and White, Unite and Fight": A Social History of Industrial Unionism in Meatpacking, 1930–1990* (Urbana, Ill., 1997), 206, who documents the best case of civil rights unionism, esp. 220–227; Robert Clifton Weaver, *Negro Labor: A National Problem* (New York, [1946]), 249–265, 316.

9. "Statement by the AFL-CIO Executive Council on Civil Rights," Feb. 28, 1961, with Lyndon B. Johnson to George Meany, March 11, 1961, box 86, VPP-LBJL; James F. Findlay, "Religion and Politics in the Sixties: The Church and the Civil Rights Act of 1964," *JAH* (June 1990): 89; Opinion Research, "Controversy," 25.

10. Jack W. Gager to George Meany, Feb. 17, 1956, box 4, DCRR; Emory F. Via, "Race Relations in Georgia Unions," [1956], DCRR; Alan Draper, *Conflict of Interests: Organized Labor and the Civil Rights Movement in the South, 1954–1968* (Ithaca, N.Y., 1994); Nelson Lichtenstein, *State of the Union: A Century of American Unionism* (Princeton, 2002), 98–140.

11. Robert D. Reynolds, "A Career at Labor Headquarters: The Papers of Boris Shiskin," *Labor's Heritage* 1 (Oct. 1959): 69–70; Boris Shiskin to Walter Davis, Sept. 6, 1962, box 6, DCRR.

12. Philip S. Foner, *Organized Labor and the Black Worker, 1619–1981*, 2nd ed. (New York, 1982), quote on 334; A. Philip Randolph, "Memorandum on Civil Rights in the AFL-CIO" (June 1961), 5, box A180, group 3, NAACP; "Report to the Executive Council of the AFL-CIO by Its Subcommittee to Review the Memorandum on Civil Rights in the AFL-CIO Submitted by Vice President Randolph," June 1961, esp. 17, 25–30, box 24, Randolph Papers; George Meany to Roy Wilkins, Nov. 20, 1962, box A180, group 3, NAACP; Martin Luther King, Jr., "If the Negro Wins, Labor Wins," in *A Testament of Hope*, 204, 207.

13. Roy Wilkins to Emanuel Muravchik, Oct. 31, 1962, box 23, Randolph Papers; Roy Wilkins to George Meany, Dec. 7, 1962, box A180, group 3, NAACP.

14. For an overview, see August Meier, "Civil Rights Strategies for Negro Advancement," in Arthur Max Ross and Herbert Hill, eds., *Employment, Race, and Poverty* (New York, 1967), 175–204.

15. See, for example, Herbert Hill to Roy Wilkins, Feb. 27, 1957, box A309, group 3, NAACP; Herbert Hill, *NAACP Labor Manual: A Guide to Action* (New York, [1956?]); reports from the New York Labor and Industry Committee and the Negro American Labor Council (NALC), box 2, Haughton Papers. For rally, see Brotherhood of Sleeping Car Porters, "Mass Job Rights Rally Planned," Aug. 30, 1961, box 2, Haughton Papers.

16. Scores of examples can be found in CORE Papers and August Meier and Elliot Rudwick, *CORE: A Study in the Civil Rights Movement, 1942–1968* (Urbana, Ill., 1975), esp. 3–39, 183.

17. Nancy J. Weiss, *Whitney M. Young, Jr., and the Struggle for Civil Rights* (Princeton, 1989), 87–124; John G. Feild to Hobart Taylor, Jr., Nov. 14, 1962, box 139, VPP-LBJL; George R. Reedy to LBJ, June 15, 1963, box 9, VPP-LBJL; Robert J. Norrell, "Caste in Steel: Jim Crow Careers in Birmingham, Alabama," *JAH* 73 (Dec. 1986): 689–690; Colin J. Davis, "'Shape or Fight?': New York's Black Longshoremen, 1945–1961," *ILWCH* 62 (Fall 2002): 143–63; Foner, *Organized Labor and the Black Worker*.

18. "OIC: The OIC Story," in series 4, reel 23, frames 650–664, SCLC.

19. NAM-IRD, "States Barring Discrimination in Employment," July 20, 1964, box 8, NAM-IRD; see also Graham, *Civil Rights Era*, 149; Thomas J. Sugrue, "The Tangled Roots of Affirmative Action," *American Behavioral Scientist*, 41 (April 1998): 886–897.

20. Martha Biondi, *To Stand and Fight: The Civil Rights Movement in Postwar New York City* (Cambridge, Mass., 2003), 270; Graham, *Civil Rights Era*, 149.

21. Dr. Bruce H. Green to the President, Aug. 6, 1965, box 47, HU 2–1/ST, WHCF, LBJL.

22. Herbert Hill to [Glouster] Current, Jan. 13, 1958, box A309, group 3, NAACP; "Summary of Report on Negro Employment in Private Firms with Federal Government Contracts in North Carolina, 1961" (draft), Sept. 21, 1961, box 7, NCAC.

23. Herbert Hill to Arthur J. Chapital, Sr., Oct. 14, 1966, box A38, group 4, NAACP; Hill also quoted in "Plans for Progress: Atlanta Survey," Jan. 1963, series 4, reel 139: 1387, SRC; "The Time Is Now: A Statement of the National Urban League," to John F. Kennedy, President-Elect, Dec. 29, 1960, box 85, VPP-LBJL, 10; Graham, *Civil Rights Era*, 51–59.

24. Donald M. Kennedy, "Industry—The Responsible Citizen," Keynote Address to the Fifth Annual Conference of Plans for Progress, Jan. 23, 1967, box 150, Young Papers; Charles A. Kothe to Bennett E. Kline and Sam Berry, Jan. 20, 1964, box 13, NAM-IRD.

25. Herbert Hill, "Black Workers, Organized Labor, and Title VII of the 1964 Civil Rights Act: Legislative History and Litigation Record," in *Race in America: The Struggle for Equality*, ed. Herbert Hill and James E. Jones, Jr. (Madison, Wisc., 1993), 263.

26. Frank S. Meyer, "The Court Challenges the Congress," in *The Conservative Mainstream* (New Rochelle, N.Y., 1969), 163. The agreement stands out all the more because conservatives did seek to distinguish themselves from "kooks" such as members of the John Birch Society and ideological anti-Semites. See William F. Buckley, Jr., to Rev. C. N. Dombalis, Nov. 30, 1964, box 1, acc. 6626-e, JJKP. The lone challenger to the consensus was Garry Wills, who in time became a pariah among his former allies for his dissident views on race and the war in Vietnam. To take one example, he urged support for "the policy of *preferential* hiring of the Negro" as "an eminently moral one." It was an extraordinary yet logical position for a conservative, so well reasoned that it led Buckley to a short-lived flirtation with compensatory measures. Garry Wills, "Who Will Overcome?" *NR*, Sept. 22, 1964, 819; also Garry Wills to Buckley, March 9, 1963, box 28, WFBP; Patrick Allitt, *Catholic Intellectuals and Conservative Politics in America, 1950–1985* (Ithaca, N.Y., 1993), 261–66.

27. Frank S. Meyer, "Richard M. Weaver: An Appreciation," *Modern Age* 14 (Summer 1970): 243; Willmoore Kendall, *The Conservative Affirmation* (Chicago, 1963), 9–10; Felix Morley, *Freedom and Federalism* (Chicago, 1959), 171.

28. "The contribution of Southerners to modern conservatism is immense," writes one chronicler within the fold. Gregory Wolfe, *Right Minds: A Sourcebook of American Conservative Thought* (Chicago, 1987), 153. Among the few scholars of the national right to recognize how important race was even in the early years are Godfrey Hodgson, *The World Turned Right Side Up: A History of the Conservative Ascendancy in America* (Boston, 1996), and Patrick Allitt, *Catholic Intellectuals*.

29. W. J. Simmons to S. E. Brookings, May 21, 1956, box 8, acc. 6626-b, JJKP; James J. Kilpatrick to Harry F. Byrd, Dec. 28, 1955, box 7, acc. 6626-B, JJKP. For Kilpatrick's role, see Joseph J. Thorndike, "'The Sometimes Sordid Level of Race and Segregation': James J. Kilpatrick and the Virginia Campaign against *Brown*," in *The Moderates' Dilemma: Massive Resistance to School Desegregation in Virginia*, ed. Matthew D. Lassiter and Andrew B. Lewis (Charlottesville, Va., 1998), esp. 56, 61, and 62.

30. *Current Biography* (1980), s.v. Kilpatrick, James J(ackson), 184; John Hope Franklin, *The Militant South, 1800–1861* (Cambridge, Mass., 1956). For sample correspondence, see Kilpatrick to William F. Buckley, Jr., June 7, 1956; Buckley to Kilpatrick, Sept. 21, 1956; Kilpatrick to Buckley, Sept. 19, 1956; and Maureen L. Buckley to Kilpatrick, Sept. 30, 1957, all in box 8, acc. 6626-b, JJKP; Buckley to Kilpatrick, June 3, 1959, box 26, JJKP.

31. Buckley to W. J. Simmons, Sept. 10, 1958, box 6, WFBP; Simmons to J. P. McFadden, Sept. 5, 1958, WFBP. See also Kilpatrick to Buckley, July 10, 1958, box 22, acc. 6626-b, JJKP; Kilpatrick to William J. Simmons, with att., Oct. 10, 1963, box 6, acc. 6626-c, JJKP.

32. Robert Nisbet, "The Conservative Movement in Perspective," *Public Interest*, 81 (1985): 129; Frank S. Meyer, introduction to *What Is Conservatism?* ed. Frank S. Meyer (New York, 1964), 3; Russell Kirk, "Prescription, Authority, and Ordered Freedom," in Meyer, *What Is Conservatism?* 32–34, quote on 35; Frank S. Meyer, "Conservatism," in *Left, Right, and Center: Essays on Liberalism and Conservatism in the United States*, ed. Robert A. Goldwin (Chicago, 1966), 3, also 1; Richard M. Weaver, *Ideas Have Consequences* (Chicago, 1948), 35–51.

33. William F. Buckley, Jr., "Notes Towards an Empirical Definition of Conservatism," in Meyer, *What Is Conservatism?* 225; also Allitt, *Catholic Intellectuals*, esp. 82, 101.

34. John Court, "Integration in Historical Perspective," *Modern Age* 2 (Fall 1958): 365; Edward Stone, "A Backward and Forward Look at Integration," ibid., 372; Meyer, "Conservatism," 7; M. Stanton Evans, "A Conservative Case for Freedom," in Meyer, *What Is Conservatism?* 67.

35. William F. Buckley, Jr., "Birmingham and After," *NR*, May 21, 1963, 397; Donald Davidson, *Still Rebels, Still Yankees and Other Essays* (Baton Rouge, La.; reprint, 1972), 206, 264; Robert Y. Drake, "What It Means to Be a Southerner," *Modern Age* 2 (Fall 1958): 346.

36. William F. Buckley, Jr., "Why the South Must Prevail," *NR*, Aug. 24, 1957, 149; Kendall, *Conservative Affirmation*, 16–17; James Burnham, *Suicide of the West: An Essay on the Meaning and Destiny of Liberalism* (New York, 1964), 86.

37. Morley, *Freedom*, x.

38. William F. Buckley, Jr., "A Clarification," *NR*, Sept. 7, 1957, 199.

39. Kendall, *The Conservative Affirmation*, 8.

40. Richard M. Weaver, "The Regime of the South," *NR*, March 14, 1959, 587–589; Anthony Harrigan, "The South *Is* Different," *NR*, March 8, 1958, 225–227; Editor [Russell Kirk], "Norms, Conventions, and the South," *Modern Age* 2 (Fall 1958): 338–345.

41. Russell Kirk, *The Conservative Mind, from Burke to Santayana* (Chicago, 1953), 133; William F. Buckley, Jr., "A Counterrevolt?" *NR*, May 5, 1964, 348; Donald Davidson, "The New South," *NR*, Sept. 10, 1960, 145; Davidson, *Still Rebels*, 209.

42. Christine Benagh, "American Dream: A Southern Nightmare?" *Modern Age* 2 (Fall 1958): 377, 379, 282.

43. Frank W. Mann to the President, June 11, 1965, box 172, GEN SP3–93, WHCF, LBJL; William F. Buckley, Jr., "The Negro and the American Dream," *NR*, April 6, 1965, 273; Richard M. Weaver, *The Southern Tradition at Bay: A History of Postbellum Thought* (New Rochelle, N.Y., 1968), 167–168; Buckley, "Why the South Must Prevail," *NR*, Aug. 24, 1957, 149–150.

44. Henry Hazlitt, "Market Is Color-Blind," *Newsweek*, Nov. 23, 1964, 94; James T. Patterson, *Congressional Conservatism and the New Deal: The Growth of the Conservative Coalition in Congress, 1933–1939* (Lexington, Ky., 1967).

45. Jeff Woods, *Black Struggle, Red Scare: Segregation and Anti-Communism in the South, 1948–1968* (Baton Rouge, La., 2004).

46. John B. Judis, *William F. Buckley, Jr.: Patron Saint of the Conservatives* (New York, 1988), 140; Irving Kristol, "American Conservatism, 1945–1995," *Public Interest* (Fall 1995): 83.

47. Martin Luther King, Jr., *Why We Can't Wait* (New York, 1963), 54. On Birmingham, see Morris, *Origins*, 250–274; Sitkoff, *Struggle for Black Equality*, 127–156 (who notes the demand for jobs on 130, 140).

48. King, *Why We Can't Wait*, 84; Mary L. Dudziak, *Cold War Civil Rights: Race and the Image of American Democracy* (Princeton, 2000), 178; Charles Whalen and Barbara Whalen, *The Longest Debate: A Legislative History of the 1964 Civil Rights Act* (Washington, D.C., 1985), 233.

49. Sitkoff, *Struggle for Black Equality*, quotes on 141; Fairclough, *To Redeem the Soul of America*, 133–135; Robin D. G. Kelley, *Race Rebels: Culture, Politics, and the Black Working Class* (New York, 1994), 87–88.

50. King, *Why We Can't Wait*, 81, 135, 102–103; Martin Luther King, Jr., and Ralph D. Abernathy to Friend of Freedom, Oct. 25, 1962, reel 1, frame 207, SCLC.

51. New York NAACP, Labor and Industry Committee Report, Sept. 4, 1963, box 4, Haughton Papers. On Birmingham's impact, see Sitkoff, *Struggle*, 144–152.

52. Jack Greenberg, "An N.A.A.C.P. Lawyer Answers Some Questions," *NYT Magazine*, Aug. 18, 1963, 85.

53. Sitkoff, *Struggle*, 144; Meier and Rudwick, *CORE*, 232; Jack M. Bloom, *Class, Race, and the Civil Rights Movement* (Bloomington, Ind., 1987), 177.

54. Quoted in Timothy J. Minchin, *The Color of Work: The Struggle for Civil Rights in the Southern Paper Industry, 1945–1980* (Chapel Hill, N.C., 2001), 11.

55. Charles E. Silberman, "The Businessman and the Negro," *Fortune* (Sept. 1963): 3, 4; "The Negro Drive for Jobs," *Business Week*, Aug. 17, 1963, 52; John Perry, "Business: Next Target for Integration?" *Harvard Business Review* 41 (March 1963): 104–115.

56. See Biondi, *To Stand and Fight*.

57. John G. Feild, "A New Look at Employment," *North Carolina Law Review* 42 (1963): 160; Ray Marshall and Virgil L. Christian, Jr., eds., *Employment of Blacks in the South: A Perspective on the 1960s* (Austin, Tex., 1978), 227; for illustration, see Thomas J. Sugrue, *The Origins of the Urban Crisis: Race and Inequality In Postwar Detroit* (Princeton, 1996), 91–123.

58. Poll on "Racial Equality," July 21, 1963, in *The Gallup Poll: Public Opinion, 1935–1971*, vol. 3, 1959–1971 (New York, 1972), 1829; Opinion Research, *Controversy*, 3, 6, 7, 17.

59. SRC, "Plans for Progress: Atlanta Survey," Jan. 1963, series 4, reel 139: 1384–99; SRC, "Agency Investigations of Plans for Progress Companies' Atlanta Facilities," April 20, 1963, box 8, Reedy Papers, 8; also Charles C. Bolt and David M. Routh, "The Charlottesville Employer: His Attitudes and Policies Relevant to the Employment of Negroes in This City," 1961, box 1, VCHR.

60. Hon. Francis E. Rivers, "Confidential: Preferential Hiring," [Nov. 1963],

sent with Robert W. Sweet to Murray A. Gordon et al., Nov. 12, 1963, box A180, group 3, NAACP.

61. King, *Why We Can't Wait*, 134; also his statements in "Eggs Are Thrown at Dr. King Here," *NYT*, July 1, 1963, 1.

62. A. Philip Randolph, "The Civil Rights Revolution and Poverty," 8, June 13, 1964, box 3, Haughton Papers.

63. City Commission on Human Rights of New York, "Policy Statement on the State of the Negro Today," Oct. 23, 1963, box 4, Haughton Papers; "Draft: The Question of Morality," reel 24, CORE.

64. Risa Lauren Goluboff, "The Work of Civil Rights in the 1940s" (Ph.D. diss., Princeton University, 2003), esp. 306, 314.

65. William H. Harris, *The Harder We Run: Black Workers since the Civil War* (New York, 1982), 125–133; Vivian W. Henderson, *The Economic Status of Negroes: In the Nation and in the South* (Atlanta, 1963), 8, 15–16; Chicago Urban League, "Notes on Problems of Negro Employment," Aug. 20, 1964, series 4, reel 10, frames 169–176, SCLC.

66. Negro Ministers of Atlanta, press release, [1962], reel 3, frame 203, series 3, SCLC; Feild, "A New Look," 161.

67. Sugrue, *Origins of the Urban Crisis*, esp. 125–164.

68. Brotherhood of Sleeping Car Porters, press release, "Mass Job Rights Rally Planned," Aug. 30, 1961, box 2, Haughton Papers; Emergency Committee for Unity on Social and Economic Problems, "Economic and Social Demands," Aug. 29, 1961, ibid.; New York Branch NAACP, Program, "An Action Workshop . . . [on] Whither the Civil Rights Movement and the Trade Unions in the Developing Automation Revolution?" June 13, 1964, box 5, ibid.

69. Hill quoted in "The Negro's Search for a Better Job," *Newsweek*, June 8, 1964, 79; Whitney Young, *To Be Equal* (New York, 1964), 98.

70. For cumulative effects, see Dalton Conley, *Being Black, Living in the Red: Race, Wealth, and Social Policy in America* (Berkeley, 1999).

71. Hamilton and Hamilton, *Dual Agenda*, 123–128; Randolph, "Civil Rights Revolution," 7; Robert Theobald, "Cybernation, Human Rights, and the New Society," for release June 13, 1964, box 5, Haughton Papers.

72. "The Time Is Now: A Statement of the National Urban League," Dec. 29, 1960, box 85, VPP-LBJL; National Urban League, "A Statement. . . . Urging a Crash Program of Special Effort to Close the Gap between the Conditions of Negro and White Citizens," series 3, box 56, NUL; Young, *To Be Equal*, esp. 28–33; telegram from Whitney Young, Jr., to President Johnson, Jan. 4, 1964, box 36, Names File, WHCF, LBJL; Weiss, *Whitney M. Young*, quotes on 152.

73. Young, *To Be Equal*, 32, 33.

74. King, *Why We Can't Wait*, 94; Charlottesville NAACP, "The 1963 Revolution Comes to Charlottesville: A Statement of Grievances and Recommendations," Sept. 11, 1963, 4, box 2, VCHR.

75. Lizabeth Cohen, *A Consumer's Republic: The Politics of Mass Consumption in Postwar America* (New York, 2003).

76. Henderson, *Economic Status of Negroes*, 21; OIC, "The OIC Story"; Whitney M. Young, Jr., "Preferential Hiring for Negroes: A Debate," in *American Child*, 6.

77. Roy Wilkins to Herbert Hill, Jan. 22, 1962, box A309, group 3, NAACP;

Charles E. Silberman, *Crisis in Black and White* (New York, 1964), 118, 235; Marisa Chappell, "From Welfare Rights to Welfare Reform: The Politics of AFDC, 1964–1984" (Ph.D. diss., Northwestern University, 2002); Kim M. Blankenship, "Bringing Gender and Race In: Employment Discrimination Policy," *Gender & Society* 7 (June 1993): 206, 219.

78. Deborah Gray White, *Too Heavy a Load: Black Women in Defense of Themselves* (New York, 1999), 174, 178–181, 197.

79. On film, see Thomas Cripps, *Making Movies Black: The Hollywood Message Movie from World War II to the Civil Rights Era* (New York, 1993).

80. By 1994 that proportion dropped to fewer than one in five; Gallup poll cited in Carter, *Politics of Rage*, 466. For the public optimism, see James T. Patterson, *Grand Expectations: The United States, 1945–1974* (New York, 1996).

81. Murray Rothbard, "The Negro Revolution," *New Individualist Review* 3 (Summer 1963): 32–33; Robert Bork, "Civil Rights—A Challenge," *New Republic*, Aug. 31, 1963, 23.

82. Frank S. Meyer, "The Negro Revolution," *NR*, June 18, 1963, reprinted in Meyer, *Conservative Mainstream*, 204–206; Meyer to William F. Buckley, Jr., June 28, 1963, box 40, WFBP.

83. Buckley, "Birmingham and After," 397; Buckley quoted in Judis, *William F. Buckley, Jr.*, 269.

84. WFR [initials only in original] to Buckley, June 21, 1963, box 40, WFBP.

85. Robert J. Dwyer, "I *Know* About the Negroes and the Poor," *NR*, Dec. 17, 1963, 517; Weaver, *Southern Tradition*, 168; Meyer, *What Is Conservatism?*, dedication page, 32.

86. Kendall, *Conservative Affirmation*, 216, also 215; Clyde Wilson, review, *Modern Age* 16 (Winter 1972): 106; Burnham, *Suicide*, 278, 297–303.

87. James Jackson Kilpatrick, "The Hell He Is Equal," 7, 10, 11, 14, manuscript and correspondence in Thomas B. Congdon, Jr., to James J. Kilpatrick, Sept. 16, 1963, box 6, 6626-c, JJKP. (The piece was commissioned by the *Saturday Evening Post*, whose editors held it back after the Birmingham bombing as "in bad taste.")

88. James Jackson Kilpatrick, "View from a Southern Exposure," in *One Hundred Years of Emancipation*, ed. Robert A. Goldwin (Chicago, 1963), 103–128; *Current Biography* (1980), s.v. Kilpatrick, James J(ackson), 184–187.

89. "FYI" from Frank Meyer, "New Study Urged in Race Heredity," *NYT*, Oct. 18, 1966, box 40, WFBP; Ernest Van den Haag, "Intelligence or Prejudice?," *NR*, Dec. 1, 1964, 1059–63, esp. 1061, 1063; *Current Biography* (1983), s.v. Van den Haag, Ernest, 420–423; Van den Haag, "The Tortured Search for the Cause of Inequality," *NR*, Feb. 16, 1973, 200 n., 203.

90. On Buckley's lack of interest in genetic discussion yet his insistence on the need for "a racial vocabulary" in analysis, see Judis, *William F. Buckley, Jr.*, 192, 244.

91. Catherine B. Willis to the Editor, *NR*, Sept. 7, 1957, 310; Frank C. Naldrop to Editor, *NR*, Feb. 9, 1965, 101; Mary Lou Tyler to Editor, *NR*, Feb. 9, 1965, 101; Robert J. Alexander to Editor, *NR*, 101–102.

92. Lester Tompkins to Buckley, July 10, 1964, box 32, WFBP; Irving Kristol to Buckley, Nov. 23, 1964, box 31, WFBP.

93. DGMC to Buckley, Oct. 13, 1962, box 20, WFBP.

94. Graham, *Civil Rights Era*, 75–82.

95. Ibid., 19, 82–99, 139, quote on 83; Kevin Boyle, *The UAW and the Heyday of American Liberalism, 1945–1968* (Ithaca, N.Y., 1995), 171; on the broader "anti-poverty coalition," see Chappell, "Welfare Rights," 30–84.

96. Biondi, *To Stand and Fight*, esp. 15–16, 18; also August Meier and John H. Bracey, Jr., "The NAACP as a Reform Movement, 1909–1965: 'To reach the conscience of America,'" *JSH* 59 (Feb. 1993): 23–24.

97. Findlay, "Religion and Politics"; Whalen and Whalen, *The Longest Debate*, 233.

98. Joseph Cardinal Ritter to Dear Sister, May 6, 1965, series 13, box 11, NCCIJ; "National Catholic Conference on Interracial Justice," Agenda and Docket, RBF Semiannual Meeting, Nov. 17, 1966, series 4, box 66, Rockefeller Records; also National Catholic Council for Interracial Justice, *Project Equality: Affirmative Action for Equal Employment Opportunity through Churches, Synagogues, and Related Institutions*, Rockefeller Records.

99. Silberman, *Crisis*, 237, 241; Kim McQuaid, *Uneasy Partners: Big Business in American Politics, 1945–1990* (Baltimore, 1994), 102–131; Eli Ginzberg, ed., *The Negro Challenge to the Business Community* (New York, 1964), 81–103.

100. Southern Regional Council, *Negro and Employment Opportunities*, 6. The report concerned Chattanooga, but the pattern was common.

101. Walter F. Carey, "Moderates on the March," [published 1964 speech], box 22, CCR; Law Department, "Memorandum Regarding Civil Rights Bill," n.d., box 108, series 4, NAM; Coordinating Committee for Fundamental American Freedoms, press release no. 29 [n.d.], in file "CR—Industry Comments," NAM; Law Department, "Summary Analysis of Equal Employment Provisions (Title VII) of the Civil Rights Bill," [March 1964], box 101, NAM.

102. NAM, "Minority Program," box 13, NAM-IRD; Terry Smith, "Plight of Negroes Their Own Fault, A Negro Business Man Tells NAM," *New York Herald*, Dec. 7, 1963, ibid.; Charles A. Kothe to S. B. Fuller, Dec. 18, 1963, ibid.

103. Patrick M. Boarman, *Facts and Fancies about Automation*, NAM Industrial Relations Sourcebook Series (New York, 1965), 16, box 15, NAM-IRD; editorial, "Where Civil Rights Law Is Going Wrong," *Nation's Business* (Nov. 1965): 73; John T. Tabor to Hon. Stuart Symington, March 26, 1964, series 4, box 108, NAM.

104. Frank E. Young to the President, with attachment, March 12, 1964, box 46, HU 2–1, WHCF, LBJL.

105. Marianne Keyes to Charles A. Kothe, Sept. 19, 1963, box 13, NAM-IRD; National Planning Association Committee of the South, *Selected Studies of Negro Employment in the South*, vol. 3 (Washington, D.C., 1955), 318; "Forced Hiring of Negroes—How It Would Work," *U.S. News and World Report*, July 29, 1963, 83.

106. James Jackson Kilpatrick, "Civil Rights and Legal Wrongs," *NR*, Sept. 24, 1963, 231, 234; Virginia Commission on Constitutional Government, "Civil Rights and Legal Wrongs" (Richmond, 1963).

107. James J. Kilpatrick, remarks in debate with Roy Wilkins, University of Minnesota, 1964, box 3, acc. 6626-c, JJKP; Kilpatrick, "The Case for Conservatism," remarks before the St. Johns Dinner Club, Jacksonville, Fla., April 22, 1964, box 4, JJKP.

108. Bork, "Civil Rights," 22–24.

109. Quoted in Whalen and Whalen, *Longest Debate*, 142.

110. Bruce J. Schulman, *Lyndon B. Johnson and American Liberalism* (New York,

1995), 57–74, quotes on 64, 67, 73, 81; Whalen and Whalen, *Longest Debate*, 78–79, 121, 232–233, 241; Graham, *Civil Rights Era*, 133–140.

111. Whalen and Whalen, *Longest Debate*, 115–118, 116, 225, 122, 238. For the feminist effort to keep "sex" in the amendment, see the discussion in Chapter 4.

112. Graham, *Civil Rights Era*, 106–109, 139–151; Schulman, *Lyndon B. Johnson*, 74; Whalen and Whalen, *Longest Debate*, 149–193. For how these restrictions produced the need for the kinds of affirmative action policies about which the conservatives later complained, see Anthony S. Chen, "From Fair Employment to Equal Opportunity and Beyond: Affirmative Action and the Politics of Civil Rights in the New Deal Order, 1941–1972" (Ph.D. diss., University of California, Berkeley, 2002).

113. Whalen and Whalen, *Longest Debate*, Wilkins quoted on 238.

114. Sitkoff, *Struggle*, 152; Paul Burstein, *Discrimination, Jobs, and Politics: The Struggle for Equal Employment Opportunity in the United States since the New Deal* (Chicago, 1985), 55.

115. See, for example, Alfred W. Blumrosen, "Strangers in Paradise: *Griggs v. Duke Power Co.* and the Concept of Employment Discrimination," *Michigan Law Review* 71 (Nov. 1972): 67–71, 101n.

116. Adolph Reed, "Review: Race and the Disruption of the New Deal Coalition," *Urban Affairs Quarterly* 27 (Dec. 1991): 330–331; Sugrue, *Origins;* Kenneth D. Durr, *Behind the Backlash: White Working-Class Politics in Baltimore, 1940–1980* (Chapel Hill, N.C., 2003).

117. See also David Alan Horowitz, "White Southerners' Alienation and Civil Rights: The Response to Corporate Liberalism, 1956–1965," *JSH* 54 (1988): 186, 194.

118. Lisa McGirr, *Suburban Warriors: The Origins of the New American Right* (Princeton, 2001); also Hodgson, *World Turned.*

119. King, *Testament of Hope*, 373.

120. "Text of Goldwater Explanation of Vote against Civil Rights Bill," *Congressional Quarterly Weekly Report* 26 (June 26, 1964): 1297; Arthur Frommer, ed., *Goldwater from A to Z: A Critical Handbook* (New York, 1964), 73, also 35; Patterson, *Grand Expectations*, 544.

121. McGirr, *Suburban Warriors*, 142.

122. Henry Bockelman to William F. Buckley, Jr., July 4, 1964, box 32, WFBP; spelling errors in original.

123. William F. Buckley, Jr., "Black Madness," *NR*, April 7, 1964, 263; LBJ quoted in Schulman, *Lyndon B. Johnson*, 76, also 79; Lott quoted in Hodgson, *World Turned*, 108; Paul Gottfried and Thomas Fleming, *The Conservative Movement* (Boston, 1988), 32.

124. "Remarks of the President at Howard University, Washington, D.C.: To Fulfill These Rights," June 4, 1965, box 172, EX SP-93, WHCF, LBJL. The ensuing White House conference, "To Fulfill These Rights," stimulated cutting-edge thinking about what would become known as affirmative action, as documented in its voluminous records at LBJL.

125. On the assumptions of African American unworthiness that drive the opposition to affirmative action, see John David Skrentny, *The Ironies of Affirmative Action: Politics, Culture, and Justice in America* (Chicago, 1996), 63, 238. Long the very essence of public policy, targeted measures benefiting other groups include

crop payments to farmers, aid to victims of disasters, protective laws for women, employment preference for American Indians, textile import quotas, the GI Bill, and the Veterans' Preference Act.

126. Coordinating Committee for Fundamental American Freedoms, *Unmasking the Civil Rights Bill* (Washington, D.C., 1964), 56.

3. Civil Rights at Work

1. Herbert Hill to Branch Presidents, July 27, 1965, box A180, group 3, NAACP.

2. Richard B. Freeman, "Black Economic Progress after 1964: Who Has Gained and Why?" in *Studies in Labor Markets*, ed. Sherwin Rosen (Chicago, 1981), 269.

3. Equal Employment Opportunity Commission, *Making a Right a Reality: An Oral History of the Early Years of the EEOC, 1965–1972: In Celebration of the Twenty-fifth Anniversary, July 2, 1990* (Washington, D.C., 1990), 14; Alfred W. Blumrosen, *Black Employment and the Law* (New Brunswick, N.J., 1971), esp. 51–101; Jerold S. Auerbach, *Unequal Justice: Lawyers and Social Change in America* (New York, 1976), 263–308.

4. NAACP press release, Sept. 17, 1965, box A180, group 3, NAACP; Equal Employment Opportunity Commission, "Administrative History" (typescript), 139, LBJL; EEOC, *Making a Right*, 15; *Textile News*, Jan. 16, 1967, 1; Alice Kidder et al., "Changes in Minority Participation in the Textile Industry of North and South Carolina, 1966–1969," report submitted in compliance with EEOC Contract no. 70–18 (Greensboro, N.C., 1972), 140–141.

5. Jacquelyn Dowd Hall et al., *Like a Family: The Making of a Southern Cotton Mill World* (Chapel Hill, N.C., 1987), 66; Timothy J. Minchin, *Hiring the Black Worker: The Racial Integration of the Southern Textile Industry, 1960–1980* (Chapel Hill, N.C., 1999), 7, also 18; North Carolina Advisory Committee to U.S. Civil Rights Committee, typescript report, "North Carolina: Segregation-Desegregation: Current," 19, folder 619, Wright Papers.

6. F. Ray Marshall, *The Negro and Organized Labor* (New York, 1965), 190–191, 203; Allen Tullos, *Habits of Industry: White Culture and the Transformation of the Carolina Piedmont* (Chapel Hill, N.C., 1989), xiv, 13; Tera W. Hunter, *To 'Joy My Freedom: Southern Black Women's Lives and Labors after the Civil War* (Cambridge, Mass., 1997), 114–120; Bryant Simon, *A Fabric of Defeat: The Politics of South Carolina Millhands, 1910–1948* (Chapel Hill, N.C., 1998), esp. 220–239.

7. Aubrey Clyde Robinson to Charles S. Johnson and Howard W. Odum, "Remarks on Textile Policies Affecting Negro Employment at Points in Alabama," April 13, 1945, reel 67: 0327–0339, SRC; "Conferences on the Textile Labor Situation," ibid.; Winnie Mae Winfield interview, tape only, side A, SOHP.

8. Leonard R. Mitchell to Randolph T. Blackwell and Harry G. Boyte, Feb. 1, 1966, series 4, reel 23: 0550, SCLC; Victoria Byerly, *Hard Times Cotton Mill Girls: Personal Histories of Womanhood and Poverty in the South* (Ithaca, N.Y., 1986), 94; press release, "Atlanta SCLC to Launch 'Operation Bread Basket,'" Oct. 23, 1962, reel 23: 0713, SCLC.

9. Hugh Davis Graham, *The Civil Rights Era* (New York, 1990); 27–28; Kidder et al., "Changes," 87; also the "Scope" file of the President's Committee on

Equal Employment Opportunity, box 86, VPP-LBJL; North Carolina Advisory Committee, Draft Employment Report, Sept. 21, 1961, box 7, NCAC.

10. Harry Boyte, Sr., notes on conversation with Sarah Herbin, April 23, 1963, box 28, Boyte Papers; Byerly, *Hard Times*, 134, 150, 153; also Carl R. Harris to Colonel Virlyn Y. Jones, July 24, 1963, folder 11, Cooke Papers; Donnell K. Wolverton to Carl R. Harris, Aug. 23, 1962, folder 11, Cooke Papers; and the heavily annotated copy of the text of Executive Order 10925, folder 11, Cooke Papers.

11. Minchin, *Hiring*, 9; James J. Heckman and Brook S. Payner, "Determining the Impact of Federal Antidiscrimination Policy on the Economic Status of Blacks: A Study of South Carolina," *American Economic Review* 79 (March 1989): 138–176; Alice Kidder, "Federal Compliance Efforts in the Carolina Textile Industry: A Summary Report," in *Proceedings of the 25th Annual Meeting of the Industrial Relations Research Association* (Madison, Wisc., 1972), 353–361.

12. Byerly, *Hard Times*, 150, 138, 195.

13. Minchin, *Hiring*, 180, 219–220, 231; Kelly M. Alexander to North Carolina Advisory Committee, [1960], box 6, NCAC; Ada Ford Singleton interview, transcript, 2, SOHP; Lewis M. Durham interview, transcript, 42, SOHP; Daisy Bates interview, transcript, 59, SOHP; Sarah Herbin to Marion Wright, Aug. 4, 1961, folder 622, Wright Papers; Herbin to Smith, April 5, 1960, box 6, NCAC; American Friends Service Committee, "Employment Survey in Greensboro, North Carolina: Report to Employers," Sept. 1958, box 8, NCAC.

14. Minchin, *Hiring*, 169; *Sallie Pearl Lewis et al. v. J. P. Stevens & Co., Inc.*, no. 72–341, U.S. District Court, District of South Carolina, Greenwood Division (1981); *Lewis et al. v. Bloomsburg Mills, Inc.*, no. 73–324, U.S. District Court, District of South Carolina, Greenwood Division (1982).

15. *Textile News*, Jan. 16, 1967, 1; Kidder et al., "Changes," 140–141; Walter N. Rozelle, "The Mill and the Negro: Let's Tell It Like It Is," *Textile Industries* 132, no. 11 (Nov. 1968): 67.

16. EEOC, *Textiles Are Getting a New Look* (Washington, D.C., 1967); Minchin, *Hiring*, 31; William Henry Chafe, *Civilities and Civil Rights: Greensboro, North Carolina, and the Black Struggle for Freedom* (New York, 1980).

17. Reese Cleghorne, "The Mill: A Giant Step Forward for the Southern Negro," *NYT Magazine*, Nov. 9, 1969, 34–35; *NYT*, May 19, 1969, 147; also Rozelle, "Mill," 70–71.

18. Richard L. Rowan, *The Negro in the Textile Industry: The Racial Policies of American Industry*, Report no. 20 (Philadelphia, [1970]), 19; Kidder et al., "Changes," 78; *Daily News Record*, April 6, 1961, box 316, mss. 396, TWUA; box 417, Henderson Papers; boxes 49, 61, 71, Ervin Records.

19. Minchin, *Hiring*, 56.

20. Ethel Bowman Shockley interview, transcript, 25, SOHP; Mildred Shoemaker Edmonds interview, transcript, 33, SOHP.

21. Mildred Shoemaker Edmonds interview, transcript, 33–34; Nell Putnam Sigmon interview, 38–39, SOHP; Cleghorn, "Giant Step," 42.

22. Alan Draper, *Conflict of Interests: Organized Labor and the Civil Rights Movement in the South, 1954–1968* (Ithaca, N.Y., 1994), 27, but also 37, 46, 77; Minchin, *Hiring*, 106–107. The union's fitful conversion to equity is well captured in the TWUA Papers.

23. Quoted in *NYT*, May 19, 1969, 1; Minchin, *Hiring*, 67–97, 182–183, 265–266, quotes on 90–91.

24. TEAM, "Equal Employment Opportunity in the Textile Industry of South Carolina: Workbook for Community Leaders," box 28, Boyte Papers; also Southern Regional Council, *Annual Report* (1968), 26, folder 3668, Weatherford Papers; Mordecai Johnson to Jean Fairfax, "A brief history of the Textile Industry Project," Aug. 7, 1967, reel 163: 0313–0331, SRC.

25. Minchin, *Hiring*, 70, 111–112, also 161–162, 166.

26. Quoted in Minchin, *Hiring*, 105, 154, 133; 1962 complaint of Moses Mangum against Erwin Mills, folder 11, Cooke Papers; Mimi Conway, *Rise, Gonna Rise: A Portrait of Southern Textile Workers* (Garden City, N.Y., 1979), 109; Byerly, *Hard Times*, 138–139.

27. Whitney M. Young, Jr., speech on "Community Communications" to the National Industrial Conference Board, Jan. 10, 1968, box 165, Young Papers.

28. Quoted in Minchin, *Hiring*, 57 (emphasis added), 58, 64; Jack Greenberg, *Crusaders in the Courts: How a Dedicated Band of Lawyers Fought for the Civil Rights Revolution* (New York, 1994), 412; "Tactics Planned in Job Bias Fight," *NYT*, July 20, 1968, 17.

29. Greenberg, *Crusaders*, 304–305, 412–429 (quote on 414); Herbert Hill, "The Equal Employment Opportunity Commission: Twenty Years Later," *Journal of Intergroup Relations* 11 (Winter 1983): esp. 45–46. Other cases were brought by the NAACP, the Lawyers' Committee for Civil Rights under Law, and the National Employment Law Project. See also Paul Burstein, "Legal Mobilization as a Social Movement Tactic: The Struggle for Equal Employment Opportunity," *AJS* 96 (March 1991): 1201–25.

30. Barbara Carlisle Bigelow, ed., *Contemporary Black Biography*, vol. 3 (Detroit, 1993), s.v. Chambers, Julius"; Minchin, *Hiring*, 219–221, 39–40; Greenberg, *Crusaders*, 40, 375–376.

31. Quote from interview by Timothy Minchin of Corine Lyttle Cannon, March 11, 1996, Kannapolis, N.C. (in Minchin's possession); Minchin, *Hiring*, 4, 36, 219–221, 39–40, 135; Greenberg, *Crusaders*, 40. For a glimpse of the legal labor, see *Sledge v. Stevens*, U.S. District Court for the Eastern District of North Carolina, Wilson Division (1984), opinion of Judge Morgan.

32. Minchin, *Hiring*, 188, 204, 183, 185; Byerly, *Hard Times*, 99.

33. Conway, *Rise*, 127; Byerly, *Hard Times*, 138, see also 105, 155, 160; Mary Robinson interview, 32, SIRW; Cannon in Byerly, *Hard Times*, 160, 156.

34. Kidder et al., "Changes," vii, 19–20; Rowan, *Negro in the Textile Industry*, 1, 136; Mary Frederickson, "Four Decades of Change: Black Workers in Southern Textiles, 1941–1981," in *Workers' Struggles, Past and Present*, ed. James Green (Philadelphia, 1983), 62–82.

35. Minchin, *Hiring*, 32–33, 186; Heckman and Payner, "Determining," 138–175.

36. Summary of Southern TWUA Staff Survey, Dec. 1966, box 315, TWUA; Solomon Barkin to John Chupka, May 12, 1961, box 316, TWUA; Thomas McNamara to William Pollock, May 21, 1964, box 614, TWUA; Scott Hoyman to William Pollock, 15 May 1961, box 638, TWUA; Minchin, *Hiring*, 254, 233–263; Michelle Brattain, *The Politics of Whiteness: Race, Workers, and Culture in the Modern South* (Princeton, 2001), 232.

37. Rozelle, "Mill," 66; Carolyn Ashbaugh and Dan McCurry, "On the Line at Oneita," in *Working Lives: The Southern Exposure History of Labor in the South*, ed. Marc S. Miller (New York, 1980), 210, 212; Frederickson, "Four Decades," 69–70, 76; Cleghorn, "Giant Step," 142; Chip Hughes, "New Twist for Textiles," *Southern Exposure* 3 (1976): 76; Michael D. Schulman, Rhonda Zingraff, and Linda Reif, "Race, Gender, Class Consciousness, and Union Support: An Analysis of Southern Textile Workers," *Sociological Quarterly* 26 (1985): 187–204.

38. Byerly, *Hard Times*, 156; Minchin, *Hiring*, 55, 181; Margaret Holmes Turner interview, SOHP; interviews with Mary Robinson, Marva Watkins, and Mildred McEwen, SIRW; Cannon in Byerly, *Hard Times*, 156.

39. Bayard Rustin, "The Foundation: A Black Working Class," *Ebony* (Aug. 1975): 90–94; James J. Heckman, "The Central Role of the South in Accounting for the Economic Progress of Black Americans," *American Economic Review* 80 (May 1990): 242–246.

40. Herbert Hammerman, *A Decade of New Opportunity: Affirmative Action in the 1970s* (Washington, D.C., 1984), 5; Freeman, "Black Economic Progress"; also Jonathan S. Leonard, "The Impact of Affirmative Action and Equal Employment Law on Black Employment," *Journal of Economic Perspectives* 44 (1990): 47–63.

41. Vincent Whylie to President Nixon, Sept. 22, 1970, GEN HU 2–2, box 18, WHCF, NPMP; Jack Star, "A National Disgrace: What Unions Do to Blacks," *Look*, Nov. 12, 1968, reprint in box 82, Wilkins Papers; on lawsuit, see William B. Gould, *Black Workers in White Unions: Job Discrimination in the United States* (Ithaca, N.Y., 1977), 323–328.

42. Quoted in Whitney M. Young, Jr., *To Be Equal* (New York, [1964]), 71.

43. Leonard H. Carter to Samuel C. Jackson, Feb. 2, 1967, box A37, group 4, NAACP.

44. Statement of Herbert Hill, National Labor Director, NAACP, to the Subcommittee on Separation of Powers of the Senate Committee of the Judiciary, Oct. 28, 1969, box 24, Wilkins Papers (quote on 5); Elliot Leibow, *Tally's Corner: A Study of Negro Streetcorner Men* (Boston, 1967), esp. 11, 50, 71, 214. For the thinking of some in government who backed such efforts, see Lee Rainwater and William L. Yancey, *The Moynihan Report and the Politics of Controversy* (Cambridge, Mass., 1967).

45. Articles are too numerous for individual citation. See the annual volumes of the *NYT Index* for a sense of how many places saw such protests. For examples from Ohio, see William E. Pollard to Don Slaiman, May 11, 1967, box 6, DCRR; Robert M. McGlotten to Don Slaiman, June 14, 1967, DCRR; for Pittsburgh, see Irwin Dubinsky, *Reform in Trade Union Discrimination in the Construction Industry* (New York, 1973).

46. Boris Shiskin, "Civil Rights Developments Involving Building and Construction Trades Unions," July 1963, box 13, Shiskin Papers.

47. Clarence Taylor, *The Black Churches of Brooklyn* (New York, 1994), 139–163.

48. Robert J. Moore, Jr., "Showdown under the Arch: The Construction Trades and the First 'Pattern or Practice' Equal Employment Opportunity Suit," *Gateway Heritage* (Winter 1994–95): 30–43; Herbert Callender to Chapter Chairmen et al., March 22, 1966, reel 16: 1015, CORE.

49. Quote (describing firefighting, but applicable here) from Roxanne Brown,

"Black Women Firefighters," *Ebony* (March 1988), box 57, SWEC. On the trades, see Joshua B. Freeman, "Hardhats: Construction Workers, Manliness, and the 1970 Pro-War Demonstrations," *Journal of Social History* (Summer 1993): 725–745; Herbert A. Applebaum, *Royal Blue: The Culture of Construction Workers* (New York, 1981); Jeffrey W. Riemer, *Hard Hats: The Work World of Construction Workers* (Beverly Hills, Calif., 1979).

50. Freeman, "Hardhats," 725–745; Applebaum, *Royal Blue*, 77; Riemer, *Hard Hats*.

51. Hill, Statement to Subcommittee on Separation of Powers, 15; *Local 53, International Association of Heat and Frost Insulators and Asbestos Workers, Appellant v. Paul Vogler, Jr. et al., Appellees*, U.S. 5th Circuit Court of Appeals (1969), 1.

52. Staff to Edwin Berry, Sept. 15, 1969, box 56, Garment Papers; for quotes, see Edmund Newton, "Minorities and the Building Trades," *New York Post*, clipping [n.d.], 1, box 8, Haughton Papers; also E. E. LeMasters, *Blue-Collar Aristocrats: Life-Styles at a Working-Class Tavern* (Madison, Wisc., 1975), esp. 187–189, also 193.

53. Stephen Gayle, "Well-Schooled," *New York Post*, Dec. 7, 1976, series 25, box 5, NCNW Papers; Maurice R. Berube, *Breaking the Barrier in the Building Trades Unions: A Special Report on the WDL Apprenticeship Training Program* (n.p., n.d.), reel 2: 0010–0013, SCLC Papers; for limitations, see Napoleon Johnson to Adolph Holmes, Nov. 6, 1970, series 3, box 137, NUL; "Statement of the NAACP on 'The New York Plan' for Employment of Minorities in the Building Trades, 1 April 1970," box 27, Wilkins Papers.

54. See debate between Herbert Hill of the NAACP and Don Slaiman, "The Negro and the Labor Movement," *Congressional Record* 117 (July 12–16, 1971), 25496–25506; "pockets" in William E. Pollard to Don Slaiman, May 11, 1967, box 6, DCRR; Scott Green in Berube, *Breaking*. For comprehensive treatment, see Gould, *Black Workers in White Unions*; Blumrosen, *Black Employment*, esp. 304–327.

55. Graham, *Civil Rights Era*, 278–296, 322–326, 334–335; James E. Jones, Jr., "The Origins of Affirmative Action," *University of California–Davis Law Review* 21 (1988): 383–419.

56. Richard Blumenthal to Daniel P. Moynihan, Oct. 2, 1969, EX HU 2–2, box 17, WHCF, NPMP; *Asbestos Workers v. Vogler*, U.S. Court of Appeals for the 5th District (1969), 4–5; NAACP, press release, Aug. 7, 1969, box 27, Wilkins Papers; Whitney M. Young, Jr., to Daniel Patrick Moynihan, Dec. 24, 1969, EX HU 2–2, box 17, WHCF, NPMP; Charles Wright to Daniel P. Moynihan, Jan. 13, 1970, GEN HU 2–2, box 18, WHCF, NPMP; John R. Price to the President, Jan. 9, 1970, EX HU 2–2, box 17, WHCF, NPMP; John L. Wilks to the President, March 10, 1970, EX HU 2, box 2, WHCF, NPMP; Bruce Rabb to Leonard Garment, box 143, Garment Papers; Graham, *Civil Rights Era*, 327, 336–337; James E. Jones, Jr., "The Bugaboo of Employment Quotas," *Wisconsin Law Review* 1970 (1970): 341–403.

57. *Current Biography* (New York, 1971), s.v. Fletcher, Arthur A(llen), 133–136; address by Arthur A. Fletcher before the Pennsylvania League of Cities, Aug. 11, 1969, box 88, Garment Papers.

58. "Opening Statement of Senator Sam J. Ervin, Jr., Chairman, Subcommittee on Separation of Powers of the Committee of the Judiciary, Hearings on Administrative Agencies: The Department of Labor's 'Philadelphia Plan,'" Oct. 27,

1969, series 4, box 127, NAM; Lambert H. Miller to Sam J. Ervin, Oct. 24, 1969, series 4, box 98, NAM; on goals versus quotas, see John Evans to Ken Cole, Oct. 24, 1972, EX HU 2–2, box 17, NPMP; Graham, *Civil Rights Era*, 337.

59. Tom Wicker, "In the Nation: Quotas, Goals and Tricks," *NYT*, Dec. 23, 1969, C30.

60. Robert R. Semple, Jr., "Philadelphia Plan: How White House Engineered Major Victory," *NYT*, Dec. 26, 1969, A20; Graham, *Civil Rights Era*, 340.

61. Joe Califano to the President, March 5 and Nov. 30, 1966, EX LA 2, box 7, WHCF, LBJL; Thomas O'Hanlon, "The Unchecked Power of the Building Trades," *Fortune* (Dec. 1968): esp. 101, 214; NAM, Study Group on Labor Problems in the Construction Industry, Industrial Relations Committee, *Chaos in the Construction Industry: Analysis and Recommendations* (New York, 1969); meeting summary, Task Force on Construction Industry Problems, Sept. 17, 1969, box 8, NAM-IRD.

62. S. D. Bechtel, Jr., "Remarks to Business Council Re: Construction Industry Problems; Off the Record: Not for Publication," Oct. 16, 1970, EX BE 4, box 31, WHCF, NPMP; Business Roundtable Report, *Coming to Grips with Some Major Problems in the Construction Industry* (New York, 1974), esp. 54–57.

63. Daniel P. Moynihan to George P. Shultz, March 3, 1969, BE 4, box 31, WHCF, NPMP; Arthur F. Burns to the Staff Secretary, July 22, 1969, ibid.; Staff Secretary to Secretary Shultz et al., July 18, 1969, EX LA 8, box 23, ibid.

64. John R. Brown III to Alex Butterfield, Dec. 31, 1969, EX HU 2–2, box 17, WHCF, NPMP; John R. Price to John D. Ehrlichman, Dec. 22 [1969], box 143, Garment Papers; unsigned, "For Background on the Philadelphia Plan vote," [1969], box 143, Garment Papers; also John D. Ehrlichman, *Witness to Power: The Nixon Years* (New York, 1982), 228–229; J. Larry Hood, "The Nixon Administration and the Revised Philadelphia Plan for Affirmative Action: A Study in Expanding Presidential Power and Divided Government," *Presidential Studies Quarterly* 23 (Winter 1993): 145–167.

65. Herrick S. Roth and A. Toffoli to the President, Dec. 23, 1969, GEN HU 2–2, box 18, WHCF, NPMP.

66. George Meany to John N. Mitchell, March 19, 1971, series 4, box 27, DCRR; see scathing discussion of enforcement in R. Waldmann to Leonard Garment, Jan. 17, 1973, box 25, Patterson Papers. For an insider's bitter critique, see Leon E. Panetta and Peter Gall, *Bring Us Together: The Nixon Team and the Civil Rights Retreat* (Philadelphia, n.d.), esp. ix–x, 368–70; and the cynical Ehrlichman, *Witness to Power*, 220–240.

67. Marion K. Sanders, "James Haughton Wants 500,000 More Jobs," *NYT Magazine*, Sept. 14, 1969, 8; and plans in Arthur F. Burns to the Staff Secretary, July 22, 1969, BE 4, box 31, WHCF, NPMP.

68. Quoted in John R. Brown III to John Ehrlichman and Len Garment, Jan. 14, 1970, box 142, Garment Papers.

69. Daniel P. Moynihan to the President, Jan. 16, 1970, Presidential Handwriting File, box 5, WHSF, NPMP.

70. John D. Ehrlichman to the President, March 23, 1970, EX BE 4, box 31, WHSF, NPMP; Ehrlichman to the President, Oct. 21, 1970, John D. Ehrlichman, Staff Member and Office Files, WHSF, NPMP.

71. *NYT*, May 9, 1970, 1; *Nation*, June 15, 1970; Peter N. Carroll, *It Seemed Like Nothing Happened: The Tragedy and Promise of America in the 1970s* (New York,

1982), 57–58; Freeman, "Hardhats," 737; for rally call, see "Official Building Trades Rally," May 20, 1970, box 8, Haughton Papers. For evidence that such events were orchestrated by union leaders working with contractors and Nixon operatives, see Brian Kelly, "Workers for the War? Labor, the Antiwar Movement, and the New York Hardhat Riots of 1970" (unpublished paper in author's possession).

72. H. R. Haldeman to Charles Colson, Sept. 8 and 14, 1970, Confidential File, box 38, WHSF, NPMP; Colson to Haldeman, Sept. 14, 1970, ibid.; William Gould, "Moving the Hard-Hats In," *Nation*, Jan. 8, 1973, 41–43.

73. "Briefing Session for National Urban League Regional Directors and Labor Affairs Representatives to Explore Current Problems in the Construction Industry," Aug. 12, 1970, series 3, box 194, NUL; Gould, "Hard-Hats," 42; B. J. Widick, "Nixon's Hard Hat Strategy," *Nation*, Dec. 18, 1972, 614; for calculations, see Charles Colson to Ed Harper, May 17, 1971, EX HU 2-2, box 17, WHCF; Pat Buchanan to John Ehrlichman et al., Jan. 31, 1972, WHCF.

74. Fight Back efforts documented in detail in Haughton Papers; Joseph S. Harris to the President, Jan. 25, 1971, GEN FG 22, box 6, WHCF, NPMP; for LEAP, see, for example, Cecil I. Smith to Janiece Wright, Nov. 22, 1972, series 3, box 138, NUL Papers, and the many boxes on LEAP in the 1999 addition to the collection.

75. Paul Good, "The Brick and Mortar of Racism," *NYT Magazine*, May 21, 1972, 25, 57; data from the Bureau of Labor Statistics, which reports that categories have changed so as to make the data not fully comparable over time, reported in Askin, "Blood, Sweat and Steel," 40.

76. For a detailed listing, see the finding aid to series 1, Case Files, DCRR. For varied examples of the NAACP's aid, see, from Tennessee, Herbert Hill to Henry Moon, June 3, 1965, box A309, group 3, NAACP; from East St. Louis, David Owens to Herbert Hill, July 29, 1967, box A37, group 4, NAACP; and from Mississippi, Glouster Current to Herbert Hill, Feb. 10, 1965, box A309, group 3, NAACP.

77. On Natchez, see Akinyele Umoja, "'If a White Man Shoot a Black Man in Mississippi, We Will Shoot Back': The Natchez Model and Para-military Organization in the Mississippi Freedom Movement" (unpublished paper in author's possession); on Clarksdale, Mississippi, see the 1966–1969 branch records, box 17, group 4, NAACP; on Beaufort, see clippings, reel 5, frame 0977, SCLC Papers.

78. See "Playboy Interview: Jesse Jackson," *Playboy* (Nov. 1969), reprint in Andy Simons Collection, Amistad Research Center, New Orleans; for Operation Breadbasket's work, see SCLC Papers; for PUSH, see "Docket Memorandum," Oct. 25, 1976, box 213, Rockefeller Records.

79. *Morristown (Tennessee) Citizen Tribune*, May 15, 1970, box G2, group 6, NAACP; Grover Smith, Jr., to Herbert Hill, Report of Activities, April 1–30, 1970, ibid.

80. Bayard Rustin to Dear Friend [mass mailing], Nov. 1, 1966, box 33, Names File, WHCF, LBJL; for fullest statement, see A. Philip Randolph Institute, *A "Freedom Budget" for All Americans: Budgeting Our Resources, 1966–1975, to Achieve "Freedom from Want"* (New York, 1966); also Dona Cooper Hamilton and Charles V. Hamilton, *The Dual Agenda: The African-American Struggle for Civil and Economic Equality* (New York, 1997), 146–153.

81. Martin Luther King, Jr., *Why We Can't Wait* (New York, 1963), 137–138;

also *A Testament of Hope: The Essential Writings of Martin Luther King, Jr.*, ed. James Melvin Washington (New York, 1986), 366–368. See interview with Martin Luther King by Alex Haley, *Playboy* (Jan. 1965): 74–76; Jesse L. Jackson, "Three Challenges to Organized Labor," *Freedomways* (4th quarter 1972): 310.

82. A. Philip Randolph Institute, *A "Freedom Budget" for All Americans: A Summary* (New York, 1967), introduction.

83. Department of Justice, "Computer List of Riots and Civil Disorders for 1968," box 66, Clark Papers; the Field Community Tension Factors Reports in box 64 and 65 demonstrate this clearly.

84. A. Philip Randolph to President, July 18, 1967, box 33, Names File, WHCF, LBJL; Martin Luther King, Jr., to the President, July 25, 1967, box 8, EX LA 2, ibid.; Kerner Commission, *Report of the National Advisory Commission on Civil Disorders* (Washington, D.C., 1968); Harry C. McPherson, Jr., to the President, March 26, 1968, box 7, McPherson Files.

85. Whitney M. Young, Jr., speech to NAM, Dec. 6, 1967, box 149, Young Papers.

86. Harry C. McPherson, Jr., to the President, March 26, 1968, box 7, McPherson Files.

87. For a painstaking demonstration of how employer-backed and conservative-led resistance to enforcing fair employment produced the need for affirmative action goals and timetables, see Anthony S. Chen, "From Fair Employment to Equal Employment Opportunity and Beyond: Affirmative Action and the Politics of Civil Rights in the New Deal Order" (Ph.D. diss., University of California, Berkeley, 2002).

88. L. V. Bodine for NAM, "Brief Outline of Some Considerations Concerning Federal Government Handling of Equal Employment Opportunity," Feb. 28, 1969, series 4, box 101, NAM; Richard D. Godown to David G. Hemminger, Oct. 14, 1968, box 98, NAM; "Proposed Policy Recommendation," NAM Industrial Relations Committee Meeting," April 22, 1971, series 1, box 103, NAM; "Equal Employment Opportunity Reform: A NAM Analysis and Proposal, n.d. [1971], box 26, series 4, NAM; James W. Hunt, "Statement on S. 1308 . . . for the Chamber of Commerce of the United States," 9, May 5, 1967, box 10, CCR.

89. Graham, *Civil Rights Era*, 239; "Statement of Mr. Leonard H. Carter, NAACP West Coast Regional Director, to the 14th Biennial Personnel Management Conference," San Francisco, Nov. 13, 1967, box A37, group 4, NAACP; for the personal toll taken by the process, see Mrs. Leona Knox to Herbert Hill, July 27, 1966, box A38, group 4, NAACP; for critique of the individual complaints approach, see David Copus, "Long-Term Problems in Title VII Enforcement," [1977], box 57, CNPR.

90. *Report of the White House Conference on Equal Employment Opportunity*, Panel 7: "Affirmative Action," Aug. 19–20, 1965, box 46, HU2–1, WHCF, LBJL; for earlier efforts that anticipated these, see Martha Biondi, "Grassroots Affirmative Action: Black Workers and Organized Labor in Postwar New York City," *New Labor Forum* 2 (Spring 1998): 61–66.

91. Marshall C. Brown to Herbert Hill, Nov. 17, 1965, box A38, group 4, NAACP; EEOC, *News* (Press Release 69–51), "Chairman Brown Calls for New Business-Government Partnership" [Nov. 1969], box 86, Garment Papers; [Department of Defense], "Affirmative Action Recommendations," [n.d.], box 22, JLC.

92. Stokely Carmichael and Charles V. Hamilton, *Black Power: The Politics of Liberation in America* (New York, [1967]), 3–5, 31–32, 53–54, 167; Louis L. Knowles and Kenneth Prewitt, eds., *Institutional Racism in America* (Englewood Cliffs, N.J., 1969), esp. 126.

93. "What OFCC Expects," *NAM Reports in Depth*, June 17, 1968, series 4, box 98, NAM; PRLDEF, *Annual Report* (1972–73), 8, and (1973–74), 11.

94. Quotes from *Griggs et al. v. Duke Power Co.*, U.S. Supreme Court (1971), 430, 432; Alfred W. Blumrosen, "Strangers in Paradise: *Griggs v. Duke Power Co.* and the Concept of Employment Discrimination," *Michigan Law Review* 71 (Nov. 1972): 59–110; EEOC, *The First Decade: Equal Employment Opportunity Commission* [Washington, D.C., 1975], 18, in FG 109, box 152, WHCF, GRFL; Greenberg, *Crusaders*, 418–20.

95. Alfred W. Blumrosen, "Quotas, Common Sense, and Laws in Labor Relations: Three Dimensions of Equal Opportunity," *Rutgers Law Review* 27 (Spring 1971): 676, 688, and 692; U.S. Commission on Civil Rights, "Statement on Affirmative Action," 18–19, Nov. 17, 1972, box 17, EX HU 2–2, WHCF, NPMP; Jones, "Origins of Affirmative Action," 401–402.

96. Clarence Mitchell, "An Advocate's View of the 1972 Amendments to Title VII," *Columbia Human Rights Law Review* 5 (1973): 311–333; Graham, *Civil Rights Era*, 444.

97. Greenberg, *Crusaders*, 423; Mary Bralove, "Running Scared: Costly Lawsuits Spur Companies to Step Up Efforts to End Bias," *WSJ*, Aug. 2, 1974, 7, 21.

98. Freeman, "Black Economic Progress"; Jonathan S. Leonard, "The Impact of Affirmative Action Regulation and Equal Employment Law on Black Employment," *Journal of Economic Perspectives* 44 (1990): 47–63.

99. Frank Dobbin et al., "Equal Opportunity Law and the Construction of Internal Labor Markets," *AJS* 99 (Sept. 1993): 421, 422.

100. Richard P. Nathan, *Jobs and Civil Rights: The Role of the Federal Government in Promoting Equal Opportunities in Employment and Training* (Washington, D.C., 1969), quote on 14, also 3, 11–28, 57–67, 230.

101. Herbert Hill to Clifford L. Alexander, Jr., Sept. 19, 1967, box A30, group 4, NAACP; Joe Califano to the President, Dec. 19, 1968; Harry C. McPherson, Jr., to George Christian, June 28, 1968; Jim Jones to the President, June 25, 1968; and Roy Wilkins to Hon. John Rooney, March 3, 1966, all FG 655, box 381, WHCF, LBJL; Stephen N. Shulman to the President, Dec. 30, 1966, box 122, WHCF-Confidential File, LBJL; United States Commission on Civil Rights, "Statement on Affirmative Action," 2, Nov. 17, 1972, box 17, EX HU 2–2, WHCF, NPMP.

102. "Interagency 1968 Task Force on Civil Rights" (Ramsey Clark, Chair), 7, 2, box 26, Task Force Reports, WHCF, LBJL.

103. A. Philip Randolph Institute, *The Reluctant Guardians: A Survey of the Enforcement of Federal Civil Rights Laws*, Prepared for the Office of Economic Opportunity, typescript, Dec. 1969, quotes on 2, 35; William H. Brown III to Robert J. Browne, Nov. 23, 1970, box 84, Garment Papers; also Ray Waldman, "Preliminary Results of the Domestic Council Study of Federal Efforts to Reduce Employment Discrimination" (1972), box 25, Patterson Papers.

104. For political power as a factor, see Peter K. Eisinger, "Black Employment in Municipal Jobs: The Impact of Black Political Power," *American Political Science Review* 76 (June 1982): 380–392.

105. For a fascinating account of the full employment effort, see Marisa Chap-

pell, *From Welfare Rights to Welfare Reform: The Politics of AFDC, 1964–1984* (Philadelphia, forthcoming 2007).

4. Women Challenge "Jane Crow"

1. Nancy F. Cott, *The Grounding of Modern Feminism* (New Haven, 1987), esp. 117–142; Leila J. Rupp and Verta Taylor, *Survival in the Doldrums: The American Women's Rights Movement, 1945 to the 1960s* (New York, 1987), esp. 135–165; Dorothy Sue Cobble, *The Other Women's Movement: Workplace Justice and Social Rights in Modern America* (Princeton, 2004).

2. Cobble, *Other Women's Movement*, 65, also 175; Carl M. Brauer, "Women Activists, Southern Conservatives, and the Prohibition of Sex Discrimination in Title VII of the Civil Rights Act," *JSH* 49 (Feb. 1983): 43; Cynthia Harrison, *On Account of Sex: The Politics of Women's Issues, 1945–1968* (Berkeley, 1998), 20; for a historical overview, see Paula Giddings, *When and Where I Enter: The Impact of Black Women on Race and Sex in America* (New York, 1984).

3. On the exclusivity of women's liberation and greater diversity of so-called liberal feminism, see Sara Evans, *Tidal Wave: How Women Changed America at Century's End* (New York, 2003), 32, 54, 116.

4. Linda Gordon, "Black and White Visions of Welfare: Women's Welfare Activism, 1890–1945," *JAH* 78 (Sept. 1991): 559–590.

5. Quoted in Marilyn Bender, "Black Woman in Civil Rights: Is She a Second-Class Citizen?" *NYT*, Sept. 2, 1969, 42; Cobble, *Other Women's Movement*, 91, 127.

6. Pauli Murray, *Pauli Murray: The Autobiography of a Black Activist, Feminist, Lawyer, and Poet* (Knoxville, Tenn., 1989), 232. My interpretation builds on the path-breaking scholarship of Alice Kessler-Harris, *In Pursuit of Equity: Women, Men, and the Quest for Economic Citizenship in Twentieth-Century America* (New York, 2001), esp. 239–296, and other women's labor historians cited later in this chapter; Jacqueline Jones, *Labor of Love, Labor of Sorrow: Black Women, Work, and the Family from Slavery to the Present* (New York, 1985); Susan Hartmann, *The Other Feminists: Activists in the Liberal Establishment* (New Haven, 1998); Susan Lynn, *Progressive Women in Conservative Times: Racial Justice, Peace, and Feminism, 1945 to the 1960s* (New Brunswick, N.J., 1992); Joanne Meyerowitz, ed., *Not June Cleaver: Women and Gender in Postwar America, 1945–1960* (Philadelphia, 1994); Gerda Lerner, "Midwestern Leaders of the Modern Women's Movement: An Oral History Project," *Wisconsin Academy Review* 41 (Winter 1994–95): 11–15; Joyce Follet, *Step by Step: Building a Feminist Movement, 1941–1977* (Women Make Movies, 1998); Evans, *Tidal Wave*; Cobble, *Other Women's Movement*.

7. Murray, *Pauli Murray*, 360; Pauli Murray, *Dark Testament and Other Poems* (Norwalk, Conn., 1970), 70; Pauli Murray, "Why Negro Girls Stay Single," *Negro Digest* 5 (July 1947): 4, 5; Uche Egemonye, "Pauli Murray (1910–1985)," in *Significant Contemporary American Feminists: A Biographical Sourcebook*, ed. Jennifer Scanlon (Westport, Conn., 1999), 216. For growing recognition of Murray as pivotal, see the symposium "Dialogue: Pauli Murray's Notable Connections," *JWH* 14 (Summer 2002): 54–87.

8. Pauli Murray and Mary Eastwood, "Jane Crow and the Law: Sex Discrimination and Title VII," *George Washington Law Review* 34 (Dec. 1965): 232–256;

Harrison, *On Account of Sex*, 89–105; Brauer, "Women Activists," quotes on 48, 49; Kessler-Harris, *In Pursuit*, 239–241.

9. Murray, typescript, "Arguments Made in Behalf of Including 'Sex' in the Employment Section of the Civil Rights Bill," folder 7, Eastwood Papers; Pauli Murray to Marguerite Rawalt, April 14, 1964, ibid.; Cynthia Ellen Harrison, *On Account of Sex: The Politics of Women's Issues, 1945–1968* (Berkeley, 1988); also Pauli Murray to Richard Graham, March 28, 1966, box 1145, ACLU Papers; Murray, *Pauli Murray*, 356–360, 347; Susan M. Hartmann, "Pauli Murray and the 'Juncture of Women's Liberation and Black Liberation,'" *JWH 14* (Summer 2002): esp. 74, 77; on Murray's evolution, see Linda K. Kerber, *No Constitutional Right to Be Ladies: Women and Obligations of Citizenship* (New York, 1998), 185–193. For how government policy divided "blacks" and "women" and left black women out, see Eileen Boris and Michael Honey, "Gender, Race, and the Policies of the Labor Department," *Monthly Labor Review* (Feb. 1988): 26.

10. Ann Petry, "What's Wrong with Negro Men," *Negro Digest* 5 (March 1947): 4–6; Murray, "Why Negro Girls Stay Single," 5–6, 8; Gwendolyn Brooks, "Why Negro Women Leave Home," *Negro Digest* 9 (March 1951): 27–28; also Lorraine Hansberry, *A Raisin in the Sun: A Drama in Three Acts* (New York, 1959); Bart Landry, *Black Working Wives: Pioneers of the American Family Revolution* (Berkeley, 2000).

11. Quoted in Bender, "Black Women in Civil Rights," 42; Vicki L. Crawford, Jacqueline Anne Rouse, and Barbara Woods, eds., *Women in the Civil Rights Movement* (Bloomington, Ind., 1993); Deborah Gray White, *Too Heavy a Load: Black Women in Defense of Themselves, 1894–1994* (New York, 1999); Barbara Ransby, *Ella Baker and the Black Freedom Movement: A Radical Democratic Vision* (Chapel Hill, N.C., 2003); Giddings, *When and Where I Enter*, 311–324.

12. Bruce Fehn, *Striking Women: Gender, Race, and Class in the United Packinghouse Workers of America* (Iowa City, 2003).

13. Pauli Murray, "The Negro Woman in the Quest for Equality," in *Black Women in White America: A Documentary History*, ed. Gerda Lerner (New York, 1972), 599.

14. On "the radical consequences of incremental change," see Alice Kessler-Harris, *Out to Work: A History of Wage-Earning Women in the United States* (New York, 1982), 315.

15. *Mrs. Lorena W. Weeks v. Southern Bell Telephone & Telegraph Company*, U.S. District Court for the Southern District of Georgia, Swainsboro Division (1971) and U.S. Court of Appeals for the 5th Circuit (1969). On complaints, see EEOC, *First Annual Report* (Washington, D.C., 1966), 6, 62; Dennis A. Deslippe, *"Rights, Not Roses": Unions and the Rise of Working-Class Feminism* (Urbana, Ill., 2000).

16. Cobble, *Other Women's Movement*, 88; also Kessler-Harris, *In Pursuit of Equity*, 203.

17. Barbara Reskin, "Sex Segregation in the Workplace," *Annual Review of Sociology* 19 (1993): 241–71; Mary Eastwood to Dr. Elizabeth Drews, Oct. 6, 1967, box 5, Eastwood Papers.

18. Donald Allen Robinson, "Two Movements in Pursuit of Equal Employment Opportunity," *Signs* 4 (1979): 423.

19. Lee C. White to James F. Horst, Nov. 22, 1965, GEN HU 2–1, box 45, WHCF, LBJL; James F. Horst to Lee C. White, Nov. 3, 1965, ibid.; dissenting

opinion of Commissioner Luther Holcomb, Dec. 20, 1966,1–9, box 10, Holcomb Papers; Elizabeth Boyer, "Help-Wanted Advertising—Everywoman's Barrier," *Hastings Law Journal* 23 (Nov. 1971): 221–231.

20. Editorial, "Where Civil Rights Law Is Going Wrong," *Nation's Business* (Nov. 1965): 66; Charles B. Pekor to W. W. Keeler, June 17, 1970, box 101, series 4, NAM; Lambert H. Miller to Arthur A. Fletcher, Aug. 4, 1969, box 26, series 4, NAM.

21. Ernest Van den Haag, "Women: How Equal?" *NR*, Sept. 8, 1970, 945, 963; Russell Kirk, "From the Academy," ibid., Oct. 24, 1975, 1177; D. Keith Mano, "The Liberated Man," ibid., May 19, 1975, 513; Ernest Van den Haag, "Negroes and Whites: Claims, Rights, and Prospects," *Modern Age* 9 (Fall 1965): 354–362.

22. Press Release, text of address by Dr. Luther Holcomb, Nov. 16, 1968, box 8, Holcomb Papers; Boyer, "Help-Wanted," 221–222; also Barbara R. Bergmann, *The Economic Emergence of Women* (New York, 1986), esp. 117–118, 136–140; Reskin, "Sex Segregation."

23. Ava Baron, "Gender and Labor History: Learning from the Past, Looking to the Future," in *Work Engendered: Toward a New History of American Labor,* ed. Ava Baron (Ithaca, N.Y., 1991), 39; Judith Butler, *Gender Trouble: Feminism and the Subversion of Identity* (New York, 1990), esp. 140, 25, 136; on television news, see Jennifer Coburn, *The History of San Diego County National Organization for Women: Twenty-five Years of Feminism, 1970–1995* (San Diego, 1995), 5; also Vernon A. Stone, "Attitudes toward Television Newswomen," *Journal of Broadcasting* 18 (Winter 1973–74): 56.

24. Pauli Murray, "The Liberation of Black Women," reprinted in *Words of Fire: An Anthology of African-American Feminist Thought,* ed. Beverly Guy-Sheftall (New York, 1995), 190.

25. Sonia Pressman Fuentes interviewed by Sylvia Danovitch, Dec. 27, 1990, http://www.utoronto.ca/wjudaism/contemporary/articles/history_eeoc.htm, 2–10; Fuentes, "Representing Women," *Frontiers* 18 (1997): 94; also Aileen Hernandez, "E.E.O.C and the Women's Movement, 1965–1975," typescript paper for symposium on the tenth anniversary of the EEOC (1975), esp. 6.

26. Pauli Murray to Marguerite Rawalt, April 14, 1964, folder 7, Eastwood Papers; Eastwood to Lucy Komisar, Dec. 8, 1970, folder 57, ibid.; Betty Friedan, *It Changed My Life* (New York, 1976), 75–86, esp. 77, 80, 81; Maren Lockwood Carden, *The New Feminist Movement* (New York, 1974), 103–105; Myra Marx Ferree and Beth B. Hess, *Controversy and Coalition: The New Feminist Movement across Three Decades of Change* (Boston, 1985), 53–54; Harrison, *On Account of Sex,* 191–209.

27. Edith Evans Asbury, "Protest Proposed on Women's Jobs," *NYT,* Oct. 13, 1965, 32; Murray, *Pauli Murray,* 365–366; Friedan, *It Changed,* 75–86.

28. Kathryn Clarenbach and Betty Friedan to the President, March 14, 1969, box 30, Finch Papers; also *NYT,* Nov. 22, 1966, 1.

29. Fuentes interview, 11; Fuentes, "Representing Women," 101–103; Harry McPherson to Marvin Watson, Sept. 25, 1967, HU 3, box 58, WHCF, LBJL.

30. "Where Civil Rights Law Is Going Wrong," 64; National Association of Manufacturers, press release, Jan. 7 [1965], box 13, NAM-IRD; Will Lissner, "Help Wanted: Female, But Men May Apply," *NYT,* Sept. 13, 1964, clipping in box 13, NAM-IRD; Arelo Sederburg, "Real Rights Fight—Women; Sex Bigger Worry

Than Race, NAM Tells Firms," *Charlotte Observer,* Oct. 15, 1964, box 13, NAM-IRD.

31. NOW press release, [Oct. 1966], HU 3, box 58, WHCF, LBJL; NOW press release, Feb. 24, 1967, box 44, Friedan Papers; Betty Friedan to Dr. Elizabeth Drews, Sept. 13, 1967, box 44, Friedan Papers; Dorothy Haener, Chair, Report on Task Force on Equal Opportunity in Employment [ca. 1967], box 44, Friedan Papers.

32. Carden, *New Feminist,* 134; Cobble, *Other Women's Movement,* 28; Stewardesses for Women's Rights Papers, Robert F. Wagner Labor Archives, New York University.

33. For examples, see NOW NYC, box 1; Judith Adler Hennessee and Joan Nicholson, "NOW Says: TV Commercials Insult Women," *NYT Magazine,* May 28, 1972, 12–13, 48–51.

34. Robles in EEOC, *Making a Right a Reality: An Oral History of the Early Years of the EEOC, 1965–1972* (Washington, D.C., 1990), 16; Edelsberg quoted in Fuentes, "Representing Women," 98; Fuentes interview, 8; David A. Copus to Lynne Darcy, Sept. 19, 1973, box 19, NOW Papers.

35. Lois Kathryn Herr, *Women, Power, and AT&T: Winning Rights in the Workplace* (Boston, 2003), xix.

36. Alice Peurala, interview by Elizabeth Balanoff, Sept. 30, 1977, TCTUW, esp. 16, 28–33, 36–43; more generally, Kate Weigand, *Red Feminism: American Communism and the Making of Women's Liberation* (Baltimore, 2001); Daniel Horowitz, *Betty Friedan and the Making of Feminine Mystique: The American Left, the Cold War, and Modern Feminism* (Amherst, Mass., 1998).

37. Bonnie Halascsak interview, in *Nobody Speaks for Me: Self-Portraits of American Working-Class Women,* ed. Nancy Seifer (New York, 1976), 277–293; NOW, *Do It NOW* (Feb. 1974): 5, and (May 1974): 1; Elaine F. Solez, press release, April 11, 1974, box 13, NOW Papers; S. Stocking, "Steel Industry Action," Nov. 20, 1973, box 31, NOW Papers; Kay Deaux and Joseph C. Ullman, *Women of Steel: Female Blue-Collar Workers in the Basic Steel Industry* (New York, 1983), esp. 51; Mary Margaret Funow, *Union Women: Forging Feminism in the United Steelworkers of America* (Minneapolis, 2003).

38. Mary Kathleen Benét, *The Secretarial Ghetto* (New York, 1972), 1; David Copus, "Long-Term Problems in Title VII Enforcement" [1977], box 57, CNPR; NOW, "Affirmative Action: The Key to Ending Job Discrimination," April 28, 1971, box 44, NOW Papers.

39. Julianne Malveaux, "Tilting against the Wind: Reflections on the Life and Work of Phyllis Ann Wallace," *American Economic Review* 84 (May 1994): 93–97; Robin Armstrong, "Phyllis A. Wallace," in *Contemporary Black Biography,* vol. 9 (Detroit, 1995), 249–251; Herr, *Women,* 5.

40. EEOC, *"A Unique Competence": A Study of Equal Employment Opportunity in the Bell System* (Washington, D.C., 1972), 173; *The First Decade: Equal Employment Opportunity Commission* [1975], 28, FG 109, box 152, WHCF, GRFL; Herr, *Women,* esp. 62–67. See also Phyllis A. Wallace, ed., *Equal Employment Opportunity and the AT&T Case* (Cambridge, Mass., 1976); on limited results owing to automation, see Venus Green, *Race on the Line: Gender, Labor, and Technology in the Bell System, 1880–1980* (Durham, N.C., 2001), 195–263.

41. Hartmann, *Other Feminists,* 53–56, 78–86, 183; Murray, *Autobiography,*

386

Notes to Pages 134–139

363–364; Joan Steinau Lester, *Eleanor Holmes Norton: Fire in My Soul* (New York, 2003), 106.

42. Gwenn Brown Nealis, "Ruth Bader Ginsburg," in Scanlon, *Significant Feminists*, 119–120; Diana Klebanow and Franklin L. Jonas, eds., *People's Lawyers: Crusaders for Justice in American History* (Armonk, N.Y., 2003), 360; *Current Biography* (1994), s.v. Ginsburg, Ruth Bader; on "outsiders within," see Patricia Hill Collins, *Black Feminist Thought: Knowledge, Consciousness, and the Politics of Empowerment* (New York, 1991), 11.

43. Klebanow and Jonas, *People's Lawyers*, 361, 364–366, 368–371; Amy Leigh Campbell, "Raising the Bar: Ruth Bader Ginsburg and the ACLU Women's Rights Project," *Texas Journal of Women and the Law* 157 (Dec. 2002): 163–243.

44. Fuentes interview, 8; *Current Biography*, s.v. Ginsburg, 214.

45. Gretchen L. Kemp to Anne L. Armstrong, Nov. 5, 1973, EX HU 2–2, box 17, WHCF, NPMP.

46. Sederberg, "Real Rights Fight"; Neil Thomas, "NAM Members Air Views on Civil Rights," *Lynn (Mass.) Daily Evening Item*, Sept. 24, 1964, ibid.; John P. Carberg, "NAM Seminar Sets Record Straight on Civil Rights Law," *Boston Herald*, Sept. 24, 1964, ibid.

47. Haener, Report on Task Force; Trudy Hayden, *Punishing Pregnancy: Discrimination in Education, Employment, and Credit: Women's Rights Project* (New York, 1973), 1–76; for unionists' path breaking, see Nancy F. Gabin, *Feminism in the Labor Movement: Women and the United Auto Workers, 1935–1975* (Ithaca, N.Y., 1990), 21, 80, 225; Hartmann, *Other Feminists*, 15, 37, 43–46; Cobble, *Other Women's Movement*, 217.

48. Gordon, "Black and White Visions," 584; White House Conference, "To Fulfill These Rights," Council's Report and Recommendations to the Conference (Washington, D.C., 1966), 26, 27; Cobble, *The Other Women's Movement*, 131–139.

49. NOW, "Proclamation," Aug. 25, 1972, box 64, Armstrong Papers; NOW, "Bill of Rights," in *Sisterhood Is Powerful*, ed. Robin Morgan (New York, 1970), 576; Hartmann, *Other Feminists*, 39.

50. Mary Frances Berry, *The Politics of Parenthood: Child Care, Women's Rights, and the Myth of the Good Mother* (New York, 1993), quote on 137–139, more generally 123–146; Cobble, *Other Women's Movement*, 197, 219.

51. Mildred Jeffrey, interview by Ruth Meyerowitz, Aug. 13, 1976, TCTUW, transcript, 128; Gabin, *Feminism*, 188; Florence Peterson, interview by Ruth Meyerowitz, July 26, 1978, TCTUW, transcript, 46.

52. Hartmann, *Other Feminists*, esp. 20–21, 25, 14–52; Deslippe, *Rights, Not Roses*, 98–99.

53. Hartmann, *Other Feminists*, 34–39, 41, 43, 52; Deslippe, *Rights, Not Roses*, 166–190, quotes on 169, 189; Winn Newman and Carole W. Wilson, "The Union Role in Affirmative Action," *Labor Law Journal* 32 (June 1981): 323–342.

54. Ann Scott, "Feminism vs. the Feds," *Issues in Industrial Society* 2 (1971): 34; Lynne Darcy, "Questionnaire for Task Force Coordinators" (1975), box 32, NOW Papers.

55. Patricia Somers to Lynne Darcy, April 8, 1974, box 18, NOW Papers; Herr, *Women*, 98; Lynne Darcy, "Compliance Task Force Questionnaire Evaluation," [n.d.], box 18, NOW Papers; Lynne Darcy for the Task Force, *Job Equality*

NOW Kit (New York, 1975); NOW, Task Force on Compliance and Enforcement, "History and Statement of Policy," [ca. 1972], NOW Papers; Ann Scott and Lucy Komisar, . . . *And Justice for All: The Federal Equal Opportunity Effort against Sex Discrimination* (Chicago, 1971), 23–34.

56. See esp. "Sears Action Bulletin" (Oct. 1974), 4, box 9, NOW Papers; Mary Jean Collins-Robson and Ann Ladky to NOW Chapter Presidents et al., Nov. 9, 1974, ibid.; and Nancy MacLean, "The Hidden History of Affirmative Action: Working Women's Struggles in the 1970s and the Gender of Class," *Feminist Studies* 25 (Spring 1999): 55–58.

57. Herr, *Women*, 6, 8, 10, 50; for other reader response, see *Chicago Tribune*, June 28, 1972, box 51, Armstrong Papers.

58. Susan Davis, "Organizing from Within," *Ms.* (Aug. 1972): 92, 96. For other efforts, see Jewell George [for NBC's women's committee] to Jill Ruckelshaus, Nov. 7, 1973; *Media Report to Women*, Dec. 1, 1974; "Sexism Scorecard," *MORE* (Oct. 1977); and Women's Committee, press release, "Network Women Meet," Dec. 18, 1972, all box 18, GEN HU 2–2, WHCF, NPMP.

59. Discussion based on documents in the NYTWC Papers, in particular the opinion of Judge Werker in *Elizabeth Boylan et al., Plaintiffs, v. The New York Times, Defendant*, U.S. District Court, Southern District of New York (1977), and the expert witness depositions in box 1; "Betsy Wade, A Fondness for Facts," clipping of advertisement, ca. 1962, box 2; Wade to Grace Glueck and Joan Cook, Aug. 19, [1974], box 1; Wade to Yetta Riesel, May 30, 1974; Members of the Negotiating Committee to All Women at The New York Times, Dec. 1974; and typescript history, "Times Caucus," n.d. [1975], all NYTWC; *NYT*, Nov. 21, 1978, B7; *Nation*, Dec. 9, 1978, 635–637; Lindsay Van Gelder, "Women vs. The New York Times," *Ms.* (Sept. 1978): 66–68.

60. Aileen C. Hernandez to NOW Chapters, May 10, 1971, box 8, acc. 72, NOW Papers.

61. American Civil Liberties Union, in re: petition filed by NOW, before the Federal Communications Commission, Jan. 7, 1971, box 196, ACLU Papers; also Jan Goodman to Dora Freeman, Jan. 3, 1973, box 151, Abzug Papers.

62. Susan R. Brown to Mrs. Max Berg et al., Jan. 14, 1971, box 54, series 2, NCJW Papers.

63. The LDEF ads can be found in box 15, NOW NYC.

64. Davis, "Organizing from Within," 92, 93.

65. Mr. Paris's 9th Grade Science Class to the President, [Sept. 1969], GEN HU 2–5, box 22, WHCF, NPMP; Lucia Alongi and Diane Shuran to the President, Feb. 18, 1974, box 23, ibid.; Vicki Schultz, "Telling Stories about Women and Work: Judicial Interpretations of Sex Segregation in the Workplace in Title VII Cases Raising the Lack of Interest Argument," in *Feminist Legal Theory*, ed. Katherine T. Bartlett and Rosanne Kennedy (Boulder, Colo., 1991), 134; for education organizing, see Coburn, *Herstory of San Diego*, 18.

66. Patricia M. Vasquez to Eva Freund, Sept. 22, 1975, RG V, box 38, MALDEF; Vasquez to Joan Suarez, Oct. 9, 1975, ibid.; Vasquez to Vilma Martinez, Oct. 21, 1975, ibid.; Chicana Rights Project, *CETA: An Economic Tool for Women* (San Antonio, [1975?]); Field Community Tension Factors Report, New Orleans, Sept. 4, 1967, and St. Louis, Aug. 30, 1967, box 65, Clark Papers; Jill Quadagno and Catherine Forbes, "The Welfare State and the Cultural Reproduc-

tion of Gender: Making Good Girls and Boys in the Job Corps," *Social Problems* 42 (May 1995): 171–190.

67. Mary Bralove, "Running Scared: Costly Lawsuits Spur Companies to Step Up Efforts to End Bias," *WSJ*, Aug. 2, 1974, 7, 26.

68. NOW, "Sears Action Bulletin" (Nov. 1974), 5, box 9, NOW Papers.

69. Susan C. Els to Lynne Darcy, Sept. 20, 1974, box 18, NOW Papers; Susan Els, "How Polaroid Gave Women the Kind of Affirmative Action Program They Wanted," *Management Review* 62 (Dec. 1973): 11–15.

70. Aileen C. Hernandez to Karen DeCrow et al., Oct. 24, 1974, box 9, NOW Papers; Sonia Pressman Fuentes, *Eat First—You Don't Know What They'll Give You: The Adventures of an Immigrant Family and Their Feminist Daughter* (n.p., 1999), 142–150; Herr, *Women*, 53, 70–73, 88–89, 159.

71. Herr, *Women*, 163; Mary Roebling, "Women and Title VII," *Industrial Management* 8 (July 1966): 9–12; M. Barbara Boyle, "Equal Opportunity for Women Is Smart Business," *Harvard Business Review* 51 (May–June 1973): 85–95; Erin Kelly and Frank Dobbin, "How Affirmative Action Became Diversity Management," *American Behavioral Scientist* 41 (April 1998): 960–984.

72. Eleanor Holmes Norton, "Women's Rights: The Power of the Majority," text of address to EEOC, June 17, 1970, box 51, Armstrong Papers; Lillian Serece Williams, "Eleanor Holmes Norton," in *Leaders from the 1960s: A Biographical Sourcebook of American Activism*, ed. David DeLeon (Westport, Conn., 1994), esp. 275, 277; Lester, *Eleanor Holmes Norton*, 149, 177–178.

73. Eleanor Holmes Norton, "For Sadie and Maude," typescript mimeo, box 3, series 24, NCNW; *Current Biography* (1976), s.v. Norton, Eleanor Holmes, 297. African Americans also led in the innovative Mississippi prototype for Head Start. See Charles M. Payne, *I've Got the Light of Freedom: The Organizing Tradition and the Mississippi Freedom Struggle* (Berkeley, 1995), 233, 328–330.

74. Lester, *Eleanor Holmes Norton*, 207–208; Carrie N. Baker, "Sex, Power, and Politics: The Origins of Sexual Harassment Policy in the United States" (Ph.D. diss., Emory University, 2001), esp. 7, 19–20, 43, 51, 65, 487–505; Catharine MacKinnon, *Sexual Harassment of Working Women: A Case of Sex Discrimination* (New Haven, 1979); Kimberlé Crenshaw, "Race, Gender, and Sexual Harassment," *Southern California Law Review* 65 (1992). See also Deborah Gray White, *Ar'n't I a Woman? Female Slaves in the Plantation South* (New York, 1985), 27–46, and her *Too Heavy a Load*; also Darlene Clark Hine, "Rape and the Inner Lives of Black Women: Preliminary Thoughts on the Culture of Dissemblance," *Signs* 14 (Summer 1989): 912–920. One conservative California official commented to a complainant "that he didn't blame the man for propositioning her, that she was so good-looking that he . . . would proposition her, too!" Reported in Carol Benson to Lynne Darcy, Sept. 28, 1974, box 18, NOW Papers; similarly, see editorial, "Sex and Judicial Progress," *NR*, March 3, 1978, 299–300.

75. See, for example, Clara Bingham and Laura Leedy Gansler, *Class Action: The Story of Lois Jenson and the Landmark Case That Changed Sexual Harassment Law* (New York, 2002).

76. Lester, *Eleanor Holmes Norton*, 207–208; guidelines in *Sexual Harassment: Issues and Answers*, ed. Linda LeMoncheck and James P. Sterba (New York, 2001), 135, 351–361.

77. For her record in New York, see Ninety-fifth Congress, Hearing before

the Committee on Human Resources, U.S. Senate, May 24, 1977 (Washington, D.C., 1977), 1–53; on the EEOC years, see Lester, *Eleanor Holmes Norton*, 172–217 (174 on gay rights, 201 on backlog); also varied testimonials to her success in the EEOC records in WHCF, JCPL.

78. Halascsak interview, Seifer, *Nobody Speaks*, 290.

79. *NOW New York Chapter News* (July 1971): 1–2, box 64, Armstrong Papers; Dee Estelle Alpert to Miriam Kelber, Aug. 9, 1971, box 151, Abzug Papers; *Stewardesses for Women's Rights* (Feb. 15, 1973), SAV File.

80. Jeffrey interview, 128–33; Peurala interview, 36; Peterson interview, 45, also 69–70; Haener interview, 63; Susan Jacoby, "What Do I Do for the Next Twenty Years?" in *America's Working Women: A Documentary History*, ed. Rosalyn Baxandall et al. (New York, 1976), 384–389.

81. Peterson interview, 70; Herr, *Women*, 105; Lillian Roberts, interview by Susan Reverby, May 1978, transcript, 57, 101, TCTUW; Klebanow and Jonas, *People's Lawyers*, 355, 357–358.

82. Chicago NOW, *A Decade of Feminism: Chicago N.O.W. Highlights the 1970s* (Chicago, [1979]); Sherry Lurth to Lynne Darcy, Aug. 19, 1975, box 18, NOW Papers; Wendy Winkler to Mary Lynn Myers, Nov. 20, 1975, box 15, NOW Papers.

83. Kathryn F. Clarenbach et al. to the President, Oct. 27, 1967, HU 3, box 58, WHCF, LBJL.

84. Kathryn F. Clarenbach and Betty Friedan to W. Willard Wirtz, April 9, 1967, folder 15, Eastwood Papers; Scott, "Feminism vs. the Feds," 2 [copy]; Scott and Komisar, . . . *And Justice for All*; Catherine East, "Chronology of Inclusion of Sex in Executive Order 11246," box 627, Abzug Papers.

85. Kerber, *No Constitutional Right*, esp. 11, 304–310, also 203, 213–219; Virginia Sapiro, "The Gender Basis of American Social Policy," in *Women, the State, and Welfare*, ed. Linda Gordon (Madison, Wisc., 1991), 42; Ruth Lister, "Women, Economic Dependency, and Citizenship," *Journal of Social Policy* 19 (1990): 445–467.

86. NOW, press release [Oct. 1966], and "Statement of Purpose," Oct. 29, 1966, HU 3, box 58, WHCF, LBJL.

87. William E. Pollard, "Discussion Outline" for EEOC Conference, Sept. 21, 1974, box 32, DCRR; Cynthia Deitch, "Gender, Race, and Class Politics and the Inclusion of Women in Title VII of the 1964 Civil Rights Act," *Gender and Society* 7 (June 1993): 199; Ruth Milkman, "Union Responses to Workforce Feminization in the United States," in *The Challenge of Restructuring: North American Labor Movements Respond*, ed. Jane Jenson and Rianne Mahon (Philadelphia, 1993), 227; David Roediger, "What If Labor Were Not White and Male? Recentering Working Class History and Reconstructing Debates on Race and the Unions," *ILWCH* 51 (Spring 1997): 72–95.

88. Evans, *Tidal Wave*, 75; Giddings, *When and Where I Enter*, 307–309, 299–311. On divisions over sexual orientation, which played less of a role in the jobs struggle, see Alice Echols, *Daring to Be Bad: Radical Feminism in America, 1967–1975* (Minneapolis, 1990), 203–241.

89. Barbara Smith quoted in Guy-Sheftall, *Words of Fire*, 229.

90. Pauli Murray to Kathryn F. Clarenbach, Nov. 21, 1967, box 51, Murray Papers; Dorothy Haener to Betty Friedan, Dec. 26, 1967, box A46, group 4, NAACP.

91. Cobble, *Other Women's Movement*, 178, 190–195.

92. Diane K. Lewis, "A Response to Inequality: Black Women, Racism, and Sexism," *Signs* 3 (1977): 339–361; Evans, *Tidal Wave*, 33.

93. Guy-Sheftall, *Words of Fire*, 261.

94. Ibid., 285.

95. Joan Hull, coordinator, "Business and Industry Workshop," Feb. 17, 1973, box 18, NOW.

96. NUL, press release, "Jordan Charges Quota Issue Designed to Split Labor–Civil Rights Alliance," Sept. 19, 1972, box 1, series E, LCCR; also Thomas Johnson, "A Debate over Affirmative Action: Will Blacks Lose to Other Groups?" *NYT*, Aug. 12, 1980, B1, B6.

97. Juan José Nuñez Martínez to Sarah Weddington, March 6, 1979, box 17, GEN HU 1–6, WHCF, JCPL; Velma Brown and Karen Sinnreich to Al Blumrosen, Dec. 3, 1975, box 18, NOW Papers; *SHER (Self Help for Equal Rights—NIHOW)*, Sept.–Oct. 1973, folder 10, Eastwood Papers; petition from Los Angeles EEOC office to Frank A. Quinn, Oct. 31, 1974, box 27, series 4, DCRR; Giddings, *When and Where I Enter*, 317.

98. Bender, "Black Woman in Civil Rights," 42; Murray, "Liberation of Black Women," in the superb collection edited by Beverly Guy-Sheftall, *Words of Fire*, 197. Particularly helpful are Barbara Smith, "Some Home Truths on the Contemporary Black Feminist Movement" (254–269), and Deborah K. King, "Multiple Jeopardy, Multiple Consciousness: The Context of Black Feminist Ideology" (294–318), from the same collection.

99. Aileen C. Hernandez and Eleanor Spikes, "Report of the Task Force on Minority Women and Women's Rights," National Board Meeting, July 13–15, 1973, box 9, NOW Papers; WOW, minutes, Sept. 9, 1974, through the fall, box 9, WOW Papers; Joanne Omang, "YWCA Expands Its Arena of Activism," *WP*, June 5, 1973, box 9, Draper Papers.

100. NABF Papers; Giddings, *When and Where I Enter*, 344–345; White, *Too Heavy a Load*, 242–253; Alma M. Garcia, ed., *Chicana Feminist Thought: The Basic Historical Writings* (New York, 1997); Asian Women United of California, ed., *Making Waves: An Anthology of Writings by and about Asian American Women* (Boston, 1989).

101. Leaflet, "'Southern Bell' Is a Male Chauvinist," box 17, NOW Papers; Judith G. Stowers to Muriel Fox et al., Jan. 24, 1973, box 18, ibid.; G. Stocking, "Steel Industry Action—Preliminary Memo," box 31, ibid.; NOW, "The General Mills Story," box 15, ibid.; NOW and the National Urban League, "General Mills, Inc. . . . discriminates against ALL Women and Minority Men," box 18, ibid.

102. Ann Scott for Aileen Hernandez to Dean Burch, Oct. 6, 1970, box 17, NOW Papers.

103. Ann Scott and Lucy Komisar, . . . *And Justice for All: Federal Equal Employment Opportunity Effort against Sex Discrimination* (Chicago, 1971), 29; Responsible Corporate Action, "Corporate Apartheid—California, U.S.A. Style," Feb. 4, 1971, box 55, Galarza Papers; NOW, *Job Equality Kit*, 6, 15–16.

104. Kessler-Harris, *In Pursuit of Equity*, 267–275, Marisa Chappell, "Rethinking Women's Politics in the 1970s: The League of Women Voters and the National Organization for Women Confront Poverty," *JWH* 13 (Winter 2002): 155–179.

105. Barbara F. Reskind and Patricia A. Roos, eds., *Job Queues, Gender Queues: Explaining Women's Inroads into Male Occupations* (Philadelphia, 1990), 16, 56, 303, 317–319.

5. Are Mexican Americans "Whites" or "People of Color"?

1. Mario T. García, *Memories of Chicano History: The Life and Narrative of Bert Corona* (Berkeley, 1994), 200; see also minutes, California MAPA State Board of Directors, Aug. 24, 1963, box 14, Galarza Papers.

2. Alfredo Cuéllar, "Perspective on Politics: Part I," in *La Causa Política: A Chicano Politics Reader*, ed. F. Chris Garcia (South Bend, Ind., 1974), 44–46; "Campaign '72: The Rising Voice of Ethnic Voters," *Congressional Quarterly*, March 11, 1972, 534.

3. EEOC, *First Annual Report* (Washington, D.C., 1967), 58. In my research, I sought information about the involvement of these other groups, along with Native Americans and Asian Americans, but found little evidence of it, for reasons discussed later.

4. David Montejano, *Anglos and Mexicans in the Making of Texas, 1836–1986* (Austin, Tex., 1987), 4, 7.

5. For incisive accounts of how the law constructed race among Mexican Americans, see George A. Martínez, "Mexican Americans and Whiteness," in *The Latino/a Condition: A Critical Reader*, ed. Richard Delgado and Jean Stefanic (New York, 1998), 175–179; George A. Martínez, "The Mexican-American Litigation Experience," ibid., 355–358; Ian F. Haney López, "Race and Erasure: The Salience of Race to Latino/as," ibid., 180–195. On the role of the state in race-making, see Michael Omi and Howard Winant, *Racial Formation in the United States* (New York, 1994). For the white violence influencing LULAC's assimilationism, see Benjamin Heber Johnson, *Revolution in Texas: How a Forgotten Rebellion and Its Bloody Suppression Turned Mexicans into Americans* (New Haven, 2003).

6. For an example, see Marianne Keyes to Charles A. Kothe, Sept. 19, 1963, box 13, NAM-IRD. For contrasting ways of understanding such liminality, see David R. Roediger and James Barrett, "Inbetween Peoples: Race, Nationality, and the 'New Immigrant' Working Class," *Journal of American Ethnic History* 16 (Spring 1997): 3–44; Eric Arnesen, "Whiteness and the Historians' Imagination," *ILWCH* 60 (Fall 2001): 3–32. My research concentrated on Texas, where the national organizations in the jobs struggle were based. For California, where inter-group coalitions arose earlier, see Shana Bernstein, "Building Bridges at Home in a Time of Global Conflict: Interracial Cooperation and the Fight for Civil Rights in Los Angeles, 1933–1954" (Ph.D. diss., Stanford University, 2003); and Charlotte Brooks, "Ascending California's Racial Hierarchy: Asian Americans, Housing and Government, 1920–1955" (Ph.D. diss., Northwestern University, 2002), who finds more competition than cooperation.

7. Telegram from Texas Congressman Joe Eagle in *Testimonio: A Documentary History of the Mexican American Struggle for Civil Rights*, ed. F. Arturo Rosales (Houston, 2000), 172, also 173–175.

8. Daniel C. Roper to Richard M. Kleberg, Oct. 29, 1946, box 113, García Papers; Hector García to Ed Idar, June 29, 1953, box 141, and Dec. 23, 1953, box 142, ibid.; García to Morris Schwartz, Oct. 14, 1969, box 129, ibid. For earlier his-

tory, see Vicki L. Ruíz, *From Out of the Shadows: Mexican Women in Twentieth-Century America* (New York, 1998), 90; F. Arturo Rosales, *Chicano! A History of the Mexican American Civil Rights Movement*, 2nd rev. ed. (Houston, 1997), 95–96; Neil Foley, *White Scourge: Mexicans, Blacks, and Poor Whites in Texas Cotton Culture* (Berkeley, 1999), 209–211; Ignacio M. García, *Hector P. García: In Relentless Pursuit of Justice* (Houston, 2002), 96–97.

9. This is not to suggest that Title VII alone explains the change, but simply to foreground its neglected importance. For the drawbacks of claiming classification as white in education and jury selection, see Vernon M. Briggs et al., *The Chicano Worker* (Austin, Tex., 1977), 95; and the discussion of the 1954 Supreme Court case *Hernández v. Texas*, in Rosales, *Testimonio*, 207–210.

10. Joseph A. Califano, Jr., to W. Willard Wirtz, with enclosure, June 7, 1967, box 381, EX FG 655, WHCF, LBJL; Juan Gómez-Quiñones, *Mexican American Labor, 1790–1990* (Albuquerque, N.M., 1994), 39; Manuel G. Gonzales, *Mexicanos: A History of Mexicans in the United States* (Bloomington, Ind., 1999), 113, 137, quote on 225; Rosales, *Chicano*, 74.

11. Paul Bullock, "Employment Problems of the Mexican-American," in *Mexican-Americans in the United States: A Reader*, ed. John H. Burma (New York, 1970), 158; Mae M. Ngai, "The Architecture of Race in American Immigration Law: A Reexamination of the Immigration Act of 1924," *JAH* 86 (June 1999): 89–91.

12. Foley, *White Scourge*, 8; Linda Gordon, *The Great Arizona Orphan Abduction* (Cambridge, Mass., 1999), 102; Rosales, *Chicano!* 125; Montejano, *Anglos and Mexicans*, 181, 196.

13. Gómez-Quiñones, *Mexican American Labor*, esp. 65, 157, 161, 174, 204, 208; George T. Sánchez, *Becoming Mexican American: Ethnicity and Identity in Chicano Los Angeles* (New York: 1993), 12; Gonzales, *Mexicanos*, 148; also Henry A. J. Ramos, *The American GI Forum: In Pursuit of the Dream, 1948–1983* (Houston, 1998), 68–72; Gonzales, *Mexicanos*, 170–78; Foley, *White Scourge*, 207.

14. Montejano, *Anglos and Mexicans*, 193; "The Caste System of Employment: Report of the Equal Employment Opportunity Commission," in *Aztlan: An Anthology of Mexican American Literature*, ed. Luis Valdez and Stan Steiner (New York, 1972), 186–187; also Maclovio R. Barraza, "Mañana Is Too Late—Labor Standards," ibid., 189; Albert Armendariz, "Discrimination against Mexican Americans in Private Employment," testimony at Cabinet Committee Hearings on Mexican American Affairs, El Paso, Texas, box 72, García Papers; Alfred J. Hernandez, "Civil Service and the Mexican American," box 72, García Papers; Dr. J. A. García to Hobart Taylor, Aug. 18, 1965, box 112, García Papers.

15. Bullock, "Employment Problems," 151–152, 154; Gómez-Quiñones, *Mexican American Labor*, 164; Briggs, *Chicano Worker*, 63, 101; Louis G. Mayorga, complaint to Inspector General, May 7, 1962, box 60, García Papers.

16. Ngai, "Architecture"; Montejano, *Anglos and Mexicans*; esp. 159–160, 219, 262; Foley, *White Scourge*, xiv, 19, 39, 63; David G. Gutiérrez, *Walls and Mirrors: Mexican Americans, Mexican Immigrants, and the Politics of Ethnicity* (Berkeley, 1995), esp. 211; Rosales, *Chicano!* 174; Dennis Nodín Valdés, *Al Norte: Agricultural Workers in the Great Lakes Region, 1917–1970* (Austin, Tex., 1991); Zaragosa Vargas, *Proletarians of the North: A History of Mexican Industrial Workers in Detroit and the Midwest, 1917–1933* (Berkeley, 1993).

17. For Texas's political economy, see Montejano, *Anglos and Mexicans*.

18. Foley, *White Scourge*, xiii, 59–61, 208; Montejano, *Anglos and Mexicans*, 234, 315; Gutiérrez, *Walls and Mirrors*; Gordon, *Arizona Orphan Abduction*, 53–54, 98, 105, 148; and Michael McCoyer, "*Mestizaje* Meets the Color Line: Mexicans and Racial Formation in the Chicago-Calumet Region, 1917–1960" (Ph.D. diss., Northwestern University, 2006).

19. Julie Leininger Pycior, *LBJ and Mexican Americans* (Austin, Tex., 1997), 202; García, *Hector P. García*, xxi, xxiii; see Chapter 2 on blacks, and on churches, Aldon D. Morris, *The Origins of the Civil Rights Movement: Black Communities Organizing for Change* (New York, 1994).

20. Lewis W. Gillenson, "Texas' Forgotten People," *Look*, March 27, 1951; Helen Rowan, "A Minority Nobody Knows," *Atlantic Monthly* (June 1967): 41–45, reprints in box 87, García Papers (Rowan took due note of exceptions such as Carey McWilliams and Fred W. Ross); U.S. Commission on Civil Rights, "Justice in the Southwest," in Valdez and Steiner, *Aztlan*, 177.

21. Ernesto Galarza, "A Brief History of the Chicano Movement," box 55, Galarza Papers; Ramos, *American GI Forum*, 71; Project Equality, *Bulletin* (Aug.–Sept. 1965), box 11, series 13, NCCIJ; also Roger Mahony to Thomas H. Gibbons, Jr., April 28, 1969, box 4, series 13, NCCIJ; for critique of the Catholic Church, see Rosales, *Testimonio*, 370–371.

22. Rosales, *Chicano!* 74, 85–86; Gonzales, *Mexicanos*, 186–187, 223.

23. Cuéllar, "Perspective on Politics," 43–44; Ramos, *American GI Forum*, 20–21, 63; García, *Hector P. García*, xxii; Juan Gómez-Quiñones, *Chicano Politics: Reality and Promise, 1940–1990* (Albuquerque, N.M., 1990), 31–99; Gonzales, *Mexicanos*, 160–195.

24. Rosales, *Chicano!* 90; Clete Daniel, *Chicano Workers and the Politics of Fairness: The FEPC in the Southwest, 1941–1945* (Austin, Tex., 1991).

25. Sánchez, *Becoming Mexican American*, 229–252; Gutiérrez, *Walls and Mirrors*, 105–114, quote on 113; Gómez-Quiñones, *Chicano Politics*, 50–51; Gómez-Quiñones, *Mexican American Labor*, 183–186.

26. Ruíz, *From Out of the Shadows*, 72–98, quote on 101.

27. One contributing factor to black women's public leadership was that they were far more likely to hold jobs than Chicanas. Gómez-Quiñones, *Mexican American Labor*, 172. An exception that proves the rule is the CSO, influenced by the northern, CIO-linked Saul Alinsky. See Maria Linda Apodaca, "They Kept the Home Fires Burning: Mexican American Women and Social Change" (Ph.D. diss., University of California, Irvine, 1994).

28. Sánchez, *Becoming Mexican American*, 251; Gómez-Quiñones, *Chicano Politics*, 50–51.

29. Ed Idar, Jr., to Nicholas Ninnemacher, Oct. 16, 1952, box 141, García Papers. Yet for new, moderate inter-group alliances in Los Angeles as an answer to cold war conditions, see Bernstein, "Building Bridges."

30. Patrick J. Carroll, *Felix Longoria's Wake: Bereavement, Racism, and the Rise of Mexican American Activism* (Austin, Tex., 2003), 6; García, *Hector P. García*, xxxvi, 1–75, 101.

31. Cris Aldrete, "History of the American GI Forum" (1966), box 55, Harding Papers; Ernesto Galarza, "A Brief History of the Chicano Movement," box 55, Galarza Papers; Ramos, *American GI Forum*, esp. viii, 5–17, 21, 71.

32. Aldrete, "History of the American GI Forum"; Hector P. García to the

President, Feb. 1, 1966, box 43, HU 2–1, WHCF, LBJL; García, *Hector P. García*, 275–276; Galarza, "Brief History"; Ramos, *American GI Forum*, esp. viii, 5–17, 21, 71; Carl Allsup, *The American G.I. Forum: Origins and Evolution* (Austin, Tex., [1982]), 138, 152.

33. Carroll, *Felix Longoria's Wake*, 110; García, *Hector P. García*, 313.

34. "Racial Discrimination Exists in Local Postal System No Matter How Bigwigs Want to Cover It," unidentified clipping, June 21, 1961, box 113, García Papers; Manuel A. Valasco to Arthur J. Goldberg, Aug. 26, 1961, box 117, ibid.; García, *Memories*, 205.

35. Manuel H. Guerra to Julius F. Castelan, Feb. 21, 1963, box 14, Galarza Papers; Guerra to Glenn S. Dumke, June 14, 1963, ibid.; Rudolfo Loa Ramos to Lyndon Johnson et al., [1963], ibid.

36. LULAC, convention minutes, July 4–7, 1963, box 1, Andow Papers; minutes of National Council Meeting, Nov. 30, 1963, ibid.; Paul Andow, "Civil Rights 'Quid Pro Quo,'" ibid.; García, *Hector P. García*, 261.

37. Robert A. Goldberg, "Racial Change on the Southern Periphery: The Case of San Antonio, Texas, 1960–1965," *JSH* 49 (Aug. 1983): 362; Rosales, *Chicano!* 107; García, *Hector P. García*, xxvii, 259–260, 309.

38. Address of Bertrand Harding to Texas GI Forum Convention, July 5, 1968, box 55, Harding Papers; Bullock, "Employment Problems," 147–148; Gómez-Quiñones, *Mexican American Labor*, 170–171.

39. Nicholas C. Chriss, "Hopes for Latins Rise in Rights Panel Study," *LAT*, Dec. 16, 1968, sec. 1, 14; Bullock, "Employment Problems," 150.

40. Generalization based on minutes of 1963 meetings, box 1, Andow Papers; Rudolfo Loa Ramos, "Private Corporations Having Equal Employment Opportunities Agreements with the Federal Government," [1963 memo], box 13, Galarza Papers; Ramos to José Alvarado, May 17, 1963, box 13, Galarza Papers; Rudolfo Loa Ramos to Vice President Johnson et al., [1963], box 13, Galarza Papers.

41. Lloyd Larabee, "Peña Seeks Positive Anti-bias Action," *San Antonio Express*, Aug. 1965, 1.

42. Elias R. Luevano to MAPA California, March 30, 1966, box 14, Galarza Papers; "Albuquerque Declaration" to Lyndon B. Johnson, ibid.; Joseph M. Montoya to the President, April 1, 1966, HU2–1, box 45, WHCF, LBJL, and attachment, Rowland Evans and Robert Novak, "Inside Report . . . The Mexican Revolt," *WP*, March 31, 1966; "Walkout in Albuquerque: The Chicano Movement Becomes Nationwide," in Valdez and Steiner, *Aztlan*, 211–214.

43. Gonzales, *Mexicanos*, 186, 233; Rosales, *Chicano!* 223; Gutiérrez, *Walls and Mirrors*, 204.

44. Corona, *Memories*, 224; George I. Sánchez to "the Participants who 'walked out' of the Equal Employment Opportunity Commission conference at Albuquerque on March 28, 1966," box 108, García Papers.

45. Montejano, *Anglos and Mexicans*, 265; Gómez-Quiñones, *Chicano Politics*, 187.

46. Rudy L. Ramos to U.S. Civil Service Commission, April 22, 1966, box 59, García Papers; Pycior, *LBJ*, 167.

47. Bert Corona, "Press Release," March 8, 1967, box 11, McPherson Files; also Robert E. Gonzales to the President, March 13, 1967, box 45, HU 2–1, WHCF, LBJL; Aldrete, "History of the American GI Forum," 2; Hector P. García

to Hobart Taylor, June 28, 1965, box 112, García Papers; copies of charges filed with EEOC, boxes 62 and 64, García Papers.

48. Joseph A. Califano, Jr., to W. Willard Wirtz, with enclosure, June 7, 1967, box 381, EX FG 655, WHCF, LBJL; "Viva Ximenes," *WP*, May 10, 1971, box 28, DCRR; Vicente Ximenes to the President, Sept. 7, 1967, EX LA 2, box 8, WHCF, LBJL; press release, "Statement of the President," Feb. 23, 1968, EX PU 1/FG 687, box 21, WHCF, LBJL; video documentary of the El Paso Cabinet Committee hearings graciously provided to me by Dr. Vicente Ximenes. He ranked affirmative action for Mexican Americans as their most important achievement in the 1960s. E-mail communication, Aug. 18, 2004.

49. Ramos, *American GI Forum*, 111–119; SER/Jobs for Progress, "Changing the Faces of Progress" (brochure, ca. 1970), box 98, García Papers; U.S. Dept. of Labor, *Spanish-Speaking Americans: Their Manpower Problems and Opportunities* (Washington, D.C., 1973).

50. Mrs. Gertrude Grijalva to the President, April 21, 1967, box 46, EX HU 2–1/ST 5, WHCF, LBJL; video documentary of the El Paso Cabinet Committee hearings.

51. Marvin Rogoff to Gordon Chase, May 27, 1968, box 28, DCRR.

52. Field Community Tension Factors Report, San Antonio, Oct. 6, 1967, box 65, Clark Papers.

53. W. Willard Wirtz to George Thomas, April 11, 1967, with enclosure, GEN HU 2–1/ST 43, box 47, WHCF, LBJL.

54. Albert Pinon, press release, Feb. 12, 1967, box 11, McPherson Files; Rudolfo "Corky" Gonzales, "We Demand: Statement of the Chicanos of the Southwest in the Poor People's Campaign," in Valdez and Steiner, *Aztlan*, 220; Robert E. Gonzales to United Press International, July 27, 1970, box 18, GEN HU 2–2, WHCF, NPMP.

55. Sidney Kossen, "'Brown Power' Conferees Deplore Absence of White House Aids," *WP*, March 20, 1967, box 11, McPherson Files; U.S. Commission on Civil Rights, *Puerto Ricans in the Continental United States: An Uncertain Future* (Washington, D.C., 1976), 63–64, also 79. For a fascinating interpretation of the shift to brownness that complements the account here but explains less at the national level, see Ian Haney-López, *White by Law: The Legal Construction of Race* (New York, 1996).

56. Sherwin [Markman] to the President, June 22, 1968, box 386, FG 686, WHCF, LBJL; "Campaign '72," 534; Field Community Tension Factors Report, San Antonio, Jan. 6, 1968, box 65, Clark Papers; Alfredo Cuéllar, "Perspective on Politics, 46–51; Gómez-Quiñones, *Chicano Politics*, 104, 102–153; Gonzales, *Mexicanos*, 204–222; Rosales, *Chicano!* 176; Carlos Muñoz, Jr., *Youth, Identity, Power: The Chicano Movement* (New York, 1989), esp. 63.

57. Ruíz, *From Out of the Shadows*, 103; Rosales, *Chicano!* 221.

58. Ruíz, *From Out of the Shadows*, 115; Gonzales, *Mexicanos*, 211–213, 219; Allsup, *American G.I. Forum*, 161; García, *Hector P. García*, 286, 305; Edward J. Escobar, "The Dialectics of Repression: The Los Angeles Police Department and the Chicano Movement, 1968–1971," *JAH* 79 (March 1993): 1483–1514.

59. García, *Memories*, 257–258; Martin Sánchez Jankowski, "Where Have All the Nationalists Gone? Change and Persistence in Radical Political Attitudes among Chicanos, 1976–1986," in *Chicano Politics and Society in the Late Twentieth*

Century, ed. David Montejano (Austin, Tex., 1990), 201–233; Gonzales, *Mexicanos*, 220–221.

60. Ruíz, *From Out of the Shadows*, 119; Rosales, *Chicano!* 139, 151; Corona, *Memories*, 248.

61. Haney-López, *Racism on Trial*, 224–225; see also Ramón A. Gutiérrez, "Community, Patriarchy, and Individualism: The Politics of Chicano History and the Dream of Equality," *American Quarterly* 45 (March 1993): 44–72; Alma M. García, ed., *Chicana Feminist Thought: The Basic Historical Writings* (New York, 1997).

62. Field Community Tension Factors Report, San Antonio, Nov. 24, 1967, box 65, Clark Papers; Dec. 22, 1967, ibid.; Jan. 6, 1968, ibid.; Jorge Lara-Braud to George B. McCulloch, Feb. 4, 1968, box 114, García Papers.

63. "Attack Frito Bandito," *Hutchinson News*, Feb. 14, 1971, box 81, García Papers; Ramos, *American GI Forum*, 111; Ivan Vasquez, "Historical Synopsis of the American G.I. Forum Affirmative Action Team," Nov. 13, 1976, mimeograph, 15, box 140, García Papers.

64. EEOC, *First Annual Report*, 58.

65. Gilbert Pompa, San Antonio Field Community Tension Report, Nov. 24 and Oct. 20, 1967, box 65, Clark Papers; United Naval Air Station Employees to Paul Wright, Feb. 3, 1964, box 64, García Papers; M. H. Ferdin to Robert Watson, July 8, 1974, box 85, García Papers; Hector P. García to James J. Symbol, Sept. 15, 1976, box 125, García Papers.

66. Rowan, "Minority Nobody Knows," 299; García, *Memories*, 219–220.

67. James DeAnda to Hector P. García, Sept. 16, 1971, box 138, García Papers; Editors' News Service, Press Release, Jan. 26, 1966, box 94, ibid.; also Jesus Perez to Harvey R. Wehman, May 30, 1972, box 85, ibid.

68. Paul Morin to Dr. Hector García, Sept. 26, 1966, box 51, ibid.; "Black-Brown Friction Growing," *Los Angeles Times*, Oct. 26, 1969, box 87, ibid.; "Rights Unit Denounced by Mexican-Americans," *WP*, May 3, 1967, box 92, ibid.; also Allsup, *American G.I. Forum*, 136–137.

69. Rudy Ramos, Mexican-American Ad Hoc Committee on Equal Employment Opportunity, April 22, 1966 Report, box 59, García Papers.

70. Studs Terkel, *Race: How Blacks and Whites Think and Feel about the American Obsession* (New York, 1992), 91.

71. Ramos, *American GI Forum*, 111–116; Vasquez, "Historical Synopsis"; "Why Boycott Coors?" mimeograph leaflet, box 76, García Papers; Grace Lichtenstein, "Rocky Mountain High," *NYT Magazine*, Dec. 28, 1975, 14–18.

72. "Why Boycott Coors?"; Vasquez, "Historical Synopsis," box 140, García Papers; Dr. Hector P. García, "Coors Boycott in Texas," Nov. 11, 1975, box 76, García Papers; "The Coors Family Heritage," editorial, *Hays County Citizen*, Sept. 4, 1975, García Papers; Ramos, *American GI Forum*, 111–116; Molly Ivins, "Union's Survival Is at Stake in 14-Month Strike at Coors Brewery," *NYT*, June 12, 1978, A16.

73. Vasquez, "Historical Synopsis," 2–3; "Why Boycott Coors?"; *EEOC v. The Adolph Coors Company et al.*, U.S. District Court for District of Colorado (1975), copy of filing in box 2, RBCCOF; Ramos, *American GI Forum*, 111–116.

74. *Forumeer* editorial reprinted in Vasquez, "Historical Synopsis," 16–18;

correspondence in Vasquez, "Historical Synopsis," appendices; "Boycott Coors!" leaflet, March 1975, box 76, García Papers.

75. Vasquez, "Historical Synopsis," appendix, 3–4; Adolph Coors Company, press release, Feb. 9, 1976, box 76, García Papers; "Coors to Expand Hispano Role," *Denver Post*, Feb. 8, 1976, García Papers; Ernest C. Ayala to Antonio G. Morales, Feb. 3, 1977; Ezequiel Duran to Manuel D. Fierro, n.d. [1976], García Papers; Bert Lujan to Eduardo Morga, box 1, Morga Collection; Adolph Coors Foundation, "Grantee Agreement," Jan. 18, 1977, box 3, RBDSDF.

76. Benjamin Márquez, *LULAC: The Evolution of a Mexican American Political Organization* (Austin, Tex., 1993), esp. 86 and 110.

77. James C. Falcon to Jake Jacobsen, Dec. 2, 1966, box 43, HU 2–1, WHCF, LBJL; Barry Goldwater to Bryce Harlow, Jan. 6, 1969, box 1, EX HU 2, WHSF, NPMP; see also George Bush to Hector P. García, Aug. 6, 1970, box 119, García Papers.

78. Robert E. Gonzales to the President, March 13, 1967, box 45, HU 2–1, WHCF, LBJL.

79. Tony Castro, "Republican 'Chicano Strategy' Eyes Mexican-American Vote," *WP*, undated clipping, box 21, Finch Papers; Castro, *Chicano Power*, 185–214; H. R. Haldeman to Harry Dent, Oct. 31, 1969, box 2, EX HU 2, WHCF, NPMP; Gómez-Quiñones, *Chicano Politics*, 160–161, 181.

80. George Grassmuck to Clark MacGregor and George Schultz, May 10, 1971, box 15, Finch Papers; U.S. Civil Service Commission, Bulletin no. 713–16, Feb. 12, 1971, box 17, ibid.

81. Bill Marumoto to Dave Parker, Aug. 9, 1972, EX HU 2–2, box 17, WHCF, NPMP; Gómez-Quiñones, *Chicano Politics*, 160; Alex Armendariz to Henry Ramirez, "Spanish Speaking Study" for the Committee for the Re-Election of the President, June 19, 1972, box 72, García Papers.

82. Vicente T. Ximenes to Marvin Watson, Feb. 5, 1968, box 386, EX FG 686, WHCF, LBJL.

83. Ramos, *American GI Forum*, 124–139; García, *Hector P. García*, 212, 298; "Founder's Message to the American G.I. Forum of the U.S. on our 26th Anniversary," June 10, 1974, box 68, García Papers.

84. For Republican fear of labor movement influence on and assistance in "the previously disorganized Chicano movement," see Alex Armendaris to Anne Armstrong and George Bush, Dec. 4, 1973, EX HU 2, box 5, WHCF, NPMP. On GOP headway, see Pycior, *LBJ*, 241. For Reagan White House "Hispanic strategy," see Elizabeth H. Dole to Edwin Messe III et al., May 17, 1982, OA: 9454, Meese Files; Elizabeth Dole to the Vice President, July 15, 1981, OA: 5455, Dole Files.

85. Alex M. Saragoza et al., "Who Counts? Title VII and the Hispanic Classification," in Delgado and Stefanic, *The Latino/a Condition*, 47.

86. Louis Winnick to Franklin A. Thomas, "Program Review: Civil Rights," 6, box 1, Nicolau Papers; Desi Arnaz to Richard Nixon, Dec. 19, 1968, box 1, EX HU 2, WHCF, NPMP; Manuel Lujan, Jr., to Fernando DeBaca, Oct. 30, 1974, HU 2–2, box 7, WHCF, GRFL.

87. Field Community Tension Factors Report, Hartford, Conn., July 17 and June 26, 1967, box 64, Clark Papers; Puerto Rican Legal Defense and Education

Fund, *Annual Report*, 1972–73, box 6, Series: Annual Reports, PRLDEF; U.S. Commission on Civil Rights, *Puerto Ricans in the Continental United States: An Uncertain Future* (Washington, D.C., 1976), 44, 64; Clara E. Rodriguez, "Puerto Rican Studies," *American Quarterly* 42 (Sept. 1990): 441; Hector I. Vazquez, "Puerto Rican Americans," *Journal of Negro Education* 38 (Summer 1990): 248.

88. Carmen Teresa Whalen, *From Puerto Rico to Philadelphia: Puerto Rican Workers and Postwar Economics* (Philadelphia, 2001).

89. David S. North to Joseph Califano, Dec. 23, 1966, box 11, McPherson Files; Galarza, "A Brief History of the Chicano Movement," box 55, Galarza Papers; Vicente T. Ximenes to Alberto Pinon, n.d. [June 1967], box 686, EX FG 686, WHCF, LBJL.

6. Jewish Americans Divide over Justice

1. "Remarks of the President at Howard University, Washington, D.C.: To Fulfill These Rights," June 4, 1965, box 172, EX SP-93, WHCF, LBJL.

2. See report on conference with college presidents in American Jewish Congress [hereafter AJCongress], minutes of Executive Committee meeting, Jan. 8, 1973, box 6, AJCongressR; and "Over 40, White and Male," *NYT*, Aug. 26, 1973, box 186, Bertram H. Gold Papers, AJCA [hereafter Gold Papers].

3. Robert Weil, "Introductory Remarks," session on "Affirmative Action, Preferential Treatment, and Quotas," National Jewish Community Relations Advisory Council, June 28–July 2, 1972, Los Angeles, copy in box 35, JLC; Alexander F. Miller, "Some Reflections on Black-Jewish Relations," June 1972, box E1, LCCR; see also Jonathan Kaufman, *Broken Alliance: The Turbulent Times between Blacks and Jews in America* (New York, 1988), 209.

4. Speech notes attached to John Slawson to Morris Abram, Jan. 24, 1973, box 43, Gold Papers.

5. "Introduction to Discussion on Quotas" and "A Chronology of AJC Activities," with Natalie Flatow to Bert Gold, Sept. 26, 1972, box 186, Gold Papers, AJCA.

6. Hyman Bookbinder to Len Garment, Aug. 7, 1972, with attachment, box 118, Garment Papers; Rabbi Morris Sherer et al. to Samuel H. Solomon, March 8, 1973, box 42, Patterson Papers.

7. "Colleges' White Men Assail 'Preference' for Minorities," *Chronicle of Higher Education*, Feb. 5, 1973, box 186, Gold Papers, AJCA.

8. Bernice Sandler, *A Little Help from Our Government: WEAL and Contract Compliance* (Davis, Calif., 1974), 439; Martha P. Rogers, "The Role of the Equal Employment Opportunity Commission," in *Women in Higher Education*, ed. W. Todd Furniss and Patricia Albjerg Graham (Washington, D.C., 1974), 219.

9. Walter Goodman, "The Return of the Quota System," *NYT Magazine*, Sept. 10, 1972, 29–118; John P. Mackenzie, "Quotas and Politics," *WP*, Sept. 24, 1972, B3; Peter E. Holmes to Leonard Garment, April 18, 1974, box 38, Patterson Papers.

10. Anthony S. Chen, "From Fair Employment to Equal Employment Opportunity and Beyond: Affirmative Action and the Politics of Civil Rights in the New Deal Order, 1941–1972" (Ph.D. diss., University of California, Berkeley, 2002),

esp. 289; Martha Biondi, *"To Stand and Fight": The Civil Rights Movement in Postwar New York City* (Cambridge, Mass., 2003).

11. Aryeh Neier, 1974 interview, transcript, 35–36, AJC-OH; Patricia Roberts Harris interview, 15, ibid.

12. Bernice Sandler to Ann Wolfe, Aug. 24, 1973, box 212, Gold Papers, AJCA.

13. *A Testament of Hope: The Essential Writings of Martin Luther King, Jr.*, ed. James Melvin Washington (New York, 1986), 370.

14. Charles Silberman, *Crisis in Black and White* (New York, 1964), 237, 241.

15. See, for example, Murray Friedman to Samuel Rabinove, June 8, 1973, box 9, Intergroup Relations, AJCA; Jonathan Kaufman, "Inside Outsiders: As Blacks Rise High in the Executive Suite, CEO Is Often Jewish," *WSJ*, April 22, 1998, A1, 12; Milton Himmelfarb quip quoted in Marc Dollinger, *Quest for Inclusion: Jews and Liberalism in Modern America* (Princeton, 2000), 3.

16. Bernice Sandler to Eric F. Goldman, Feb. 25, 1976, box 1, WEAL; Bernice Resnick Sandler, *Sex Discrimination at the University of Maryland—Report Prepared for Women's Equity Action League* (n.p., fall 1969), 1025.

17. Blanche Linden-Ward and Carol Hurd Green, *American Women in the 1960s: Changing the Future* (Boston, 1993), 68, 69, 76, 82–83; Daniel P. Moynihan to the President, Aug. 20, 1969, EX HU 2–5, box 21, WHCF, NPMP; Diana Klebanow and Franklin L. Jonas, eds., *People's Lawyers: Crusaders for Justice in American History* (Armonk, N.Y., 2003), 364.

18. Helen S. Astin and Alan E. Bayer, "Sex Discrimination in Academe," *Educational Record* (Spring 1972): 115–116; Linden-Ward and Green, *American Women*, 88, 121; Alan Pifer, "Women in Higher Education," Speech before the Southern Association of Colleges and Schools, Miami, Nov. 29, 1971, 5; Ezorsky, "Hiring Women Faculty," 91; "Affirmative Action Program Submitted to Health, Education, and Welfare by the Ad Hoc Committee to End Sex Discrimination at Yale," [1971], box 1, WEAL.

19. Sandler to Goldman, Feb. 25, 1976; Sandler, "A Little Help from Our Government," 440–441; Catherine Stimpson, ed., *Discrimination against Women: Congressional Hearings on Equal Rights in Education and Employment* (New York, 1973); Joyce Antler, "Pauli Murray: The Brandeis Years," *JWH* 14 (Summer 2002): 80; Ann Scott, "Feminism vs. the Feds," *Issues in Industrial Society* 2 (1971): 32–46; "Academic Antidiscrimination Kit," box 12, NOW Papers.

20. Sandler to Goldman, Feb. 25, 1976; Bernice Sandler to Barbara Franklin, June 27, 1971, box 67, Armstrong Papers.

21. Walter J. Leonard to Arthur Hertzberg, December 28, 1972, box 144, Garment Papers; F. K. Barasch, "HEW, the University, and Women," in *Reverse Discrimination*, ed. Barry Gross (Buffalo, N.Y., 1977), 60, 63; Peter E. Holmes, in *Federal Higher Education Programs Institutional Eligibility*, Hearings of the Special Subcommittee on Education or the Committee on Education and Labor, House of Representatives, 93rd Cong., 2nd sess., pt. 2A, Civil Rights Obligations (Washington, D.C., 1974), 73–89.

22. Barasch, "HEW, the University, and Women," 61; Jo Freeman to Mary Eastwood, Sept. 17, 1969, box 5, Eastwood Papers; Myra Lockwood Carden, *The New Feminist Movement* (New York, 1974), 160.

23. Lillian Alexander et al. to Bertram Gold, April 14, 1972, box 9, Intergroup relations, AJCA.

24. Harriet Alpern to Philip Hoffman, n.d. [fall 1972], box 186, Gold Papers, AJCA.

25. Lillian Alexander et al. to Bertram Gold, April 14, 1972, box 9, Intergroup relations, AJCA.

26. Judith Herman to Seymour Samet, Nov. 10, 1972, box 9, Intergroup Relations, AJCA; see also, for AJCongress agreement, minutes, Executive Committee Meeting, Jan. 8, 1973, box 6, AJCongressR.

27. Sandler, "A Little Help."

28. Justine Wise Polier to Dr. Joachim Prinz, Feb. 27, 1960, box 45, AJCongressR; Will Maslow to Files, March 15, 1960, ibid.; Nathan L. Edelstein for the National Community Relations Advisory Council, "Jewish Relationship with the Emerging Negro Community in the North," June 23, 1960, ibid.

29. Oscar Handlin and Mary Handlin, "The Acquisition of Political and Social Rights by the Jews in the United States," in *The Characteristics of American Jews*, ed. Nathan Glazer et al. (New York, 1965), 267; Leonard Dinnerstein, *Uneasy at Home: Anti-Semitism and the American Jewish Experience* (New York, 1987), 50; Harold S. Wechsler, "The Rationale for Restriction: Ethnicity and College Admission in America, 1910–1980," *American Quarterly* 36 (Winter 1984): esp. 663; Marcia Graham Synnott, "Anti-Semitism and American Universities: Did Quotas Follow the Jews?" in *Anti-Semitism in American History*, ed. David A. Gerber (Urbana, Ill., 1986), 233–271; Biondi, *"To Stand and Fight,"* 16.

30. Lucy S. Dawidowicz, *On Equal Terms: Jews in America, 1881–1981* (New York, 1982), 131–132; Dinnerstein, *Uneasy at Home*, 49, 178–194; Handlin and Handlin, "Acquisition," 281, 282; Arthur Hertzberg, *The Jews in America: Four Centuries of an Uneasy Encounter* (New York, 1989), 321.

31. Dawidowicz, *On Equal Terms*, 125.

32. Report of the Executive Director to the Biennial National Convention of the American Jewish Congress, May 1968 and May 1970, box 12, AJCongressR; Nathan Glazer, "The Role of the Intellectuals," *Commentary* 51 (Feb. 1971): 55–61.

33. Stuart Svonkin, *Jews against Prejudice* (New York, 1997), 180; Waldo E. Martin, Jr., "'Nation Time!': Black Nationalism, The Third World, and Jews," in *Struggles in the Promised Land: Toward a History of Black-Jewish Relations in the United States*, ed. Jack Salzman and Cornel West (New York, 1997), 341–355.

34. Nathan Glazer, "Negroes and Jews: The New Challenge to Pluralism," *Commentary*, Dec. 1964, 30; Albert J. Weiss, testimony of ADL before the EEOC, Nov. 15, 1971, box D 64, LCCR.

35. Press release, Lee Stokes to Committee Members," box 19, Young Papers; minutes of meeting of the Temporary Committee on Black-Jewish Relations, May 7, 1969, ibid.; Alexander F. Miller (ADL), "Some Reflections on Black-Jewish Relations," June 1972, 1–7, series E, box 1, LCCR; Jerald E. Podair, *The Strike That Changed New York: Blacks, Whites, and the Ocean Hill–Brownsville Crisis* (New Haven, 2002).

36. Kaufman, *Broken Alliance*, 259; Michael E. Staub, *Torn at the Roots: The Crisis of Jewish Liberalism in Postwar America* (New York, 2002), esp. 66; Alan M. Wald, *The New York Intellectuals: The Rise and Decline of the Anti-Stalinist Left from the 1930s to the 1980s* (Chapel Hill, N.C., 1987), esp. 350, 352; on Boys Club, see John

B. Judis, *William F. Buckley, Jr.: Patron Saint of the Conservatives* (New York, 1988), 326; Norman Podhoretz, *Breaking Ranks: A Political Memoir* (New York, 1979), 302–305; Godfrey Hodgson, *The World Turned Right Side Up: A History of the Conservative Ascendancy in America* (Boston, 1996), 129, 137. For an effort to show that the historic alliance failed to benefit Jews, see Seth Forman, *Blacks in the Jewish Mind: A Crisis of Liberalism* (New York, 1998).

37. Glazer, "Role of the Intellectuals," 55–61. On how foreign policy beliefs led neoconservatives to the GOP, see John Ehrman, *The Rise of Neoconservatism: Intellectuals and Foreign Affairs* (New Haven, 1995).

38. Daniel Bell, ed., *The Radical Right* (Garden City, N.Y., 1963); William F. Buckley, Jr., *God and Man at Yale: The Superstitions of Academic Freedom* (Chicago, 1951); William F. Buckley, Jr., and L. Brent Bozell, *McCarthy and His Enemies: The Record and Its Meaning* (Chicago, 1954); Svonkin, *Jews against Prejudice*, 144. On the interwar right and its interpreters, see Leo P. Ribuffo, *The Old Christian Right: The Protestant Far Right from the Great Depression to the Cold War* (Philadelphia, 1983).

39. On Kilpatrick and Weaver, see Chapter 2; on the others, see Paul V. Murphy, *The Rebuke of History: The Southern Agrarians and American Conservative Thought* (Chapel Hill, N.C., 2001), 131, 133, 151–178, 174.

40. Quoted in Gillian Peele, *Revival and Reaction: The Right in Contemporary America* (London, 1984), 49.

41. "Liberalism and the Negro: A Round-Table Discussion," *Commentary* (March 1964): 25–42.

42. Glazer, "Negroes and Jews," 29–34; Milton Himmelfarb, "Is American Jewry in Crisis?" *Commentary* (March 1969): 33–42; Daniel J. Walkowitz, *Working with Class: Social Workers and the Politics of Middle-Class Identity* (Chapel Hill, N.C., 1999), 254–258, 286–287; Herbert Hill, "The ILGWU Today: The Decay of a Labor Union," in *Autocracy and Insurgency in Organized Labor,* ed. Burton H. Hall (New Brunswick, N.J., 1972).

43. Quoted in clipping included with appeal for "a firm stand against this latest evidence of discrimination against the Jewish people," Miriam H. Le Roy to Sirs, Sept. 12, 1972, box 186, Gold Papers, AJCA.

44. Norman Podhoretz, "A Certain Anxiety," *Commentary* 52 (Aug. 1971): 10.

45. Norman Podhoretz, "Is It Good for the Jews?" *Commentary* (Feb. 1972): 7–12.

46. "A Chronology: AJC Activities and Statements Regarding Quotas and Preferential Treatment," Sept. 16, 1972, box 186, Gold Papers, AJCA. *Commentary* issued a press release on Seabury's critique of HEW that proclaimed it was "fostering new forms of discrimination" and deplored the lack of resistance from the universities. Press release, Jan. 30, 1972, box 188, ibid.

47. Albert J. Weiss, testimony of ADL before the EEOC, Nov. 15, 1971, box D-64, LCCR; Stephen Steinberg, *The Academic Melting Pot: Catholics and Jews in American Higher Education* (New York, 1974), 102, 122–123; Dinnerstein, *Uneasy at Home*, 51.

48. Minutes of the Executive Committee, May 12, 1969, box 6, AJCongressR. For the implication that opposition to hard affirmative action in student admissions began among Jewish Americans and only later, by mid-decade, became "a non-Jewish concern," see Hyman Bookbinder to Naomi Levine, Sept. 2, 1975, box 187, Gold Papers, AJCA.

49. Podhoretz, *Breaking Ranks*, 334; for an example of continuing but flagging resistance in AJC discussions driven by neoconservatives who accused the recalcitrant of being "indifferent to Jewish interests," see Hyman Bookbinder to Seymour Samet, Jan. 24, 1972, box 186, Gold Papers, AJCA.

50. For student struggles, see Wayne Glasker, *Black Students in the Ivory Tower: African American Student Activism at the University of Pennsylvania, 1965–1978* (Amherst, Mass., 2002); Joy Ann Williamson, *Black Power on Campus: The University of Illinois, 1965–1975* (Urbana, Ill., 2003).

51. Naomi Levine and Martin Hochbaum, "Draft: Quotas and Preferential Admissions to Medical and Law Schools," Jan. 1972, 1, box 34, AJCongressR; Simon Podair to Bertram Gold, July 31, 1972, box 186, Gold Papers, AJCA; Arthur N. Horwich to Bertram H. Gold, May 15, 1972, box 186, Gold Papers, AJCA.

52. "Summary of [Convention] Workshops on Quotas and Preferential Treatment," May 6, 1972, box 186, Gold Papers, AJCA.

53. National Jewish Community Relations Advisory Council, "Jews in the Inner City," [Fall 1971], box 9, Intergroup Relations, AJCA; Israel Laster to Seymour Samet, Aug. 10, 1973, box 186, Gold Papers, AJCA; Max Fiks to Gentlemen, Sept. 3, 1972, box 186, Gold Papers, AJCA.

54. "Debate on Preferential Treatment in the Selection Process Excerpted from Minutes of the American Jewish Congress Executive Committee Meeting of March 16, 1972," box 6, AJCongressR.

55. Clipping from *American Examiner–Jewish Week* attached to Hyman Bookbinder to Leonard Garment, Dec. 11, 1972, box 144, Garment Papers; also David I. Caplan to Leonard Garment, Nov. 30, 1972, box 30, ibid.

56. Bernard Fryshman, "Affirmative Action: W(h)ither the Jewish Community?" A Report to the Association of Orthodox Jewish University Faculty, 1–10, with Fryshman to Bella Abzug, Sept. 24, 1973, box 407, Abzug Papers; Emanuel Rackman to President Nixon, June 28, 1972, GEN HU 2–2, box 18, WHCF, NPMP; Jack Fischel and Sanford Pinsker, eds., *Jewish-American History and Culture: An Encyclopedia* (New York, 1992), 524, s.v. Rackman, Emanuel.

57. Benjamin Epstein, 1974 interview, 28–30, transcript, AJC-OH.

58. Peter Novick, *The Holocaust in American Life* (Boston, 1990), 103–203, quote on 159; Dawidowicz, *On Equal Terms*, 145–146.

59. "Excerpted Summary of AJC Annual Meeting Discussions on Affirmative Action," May 31, 1972, box 9, Intergroup Relations, AJCA.

60. JDL ad, "Is This Any Way for Nice Jewish Boys to Behave?" *NYT*, June 24, 1969, 31; Staub, *Torn at the Roots*, 227; Rabbi Meir Kahane, *The Story of the Jewish Defense League* (Radnor, Pa., 1975). For concerns, see Gerald Baumgarten and Jerome Bakst, "ADL Press Survey: The Jewish Defense League," Feb. 1971, attachment to David A. Brody to Leonard Garment, Feb. 22, 1971, box 117, Garment Papers.

61. Sidney Hook, "Discrimination, Color Blindness, and the Quota System," in Gross, *Reverse Discrimination;* Eleanor P. Wolf to Preliminary Meeting, Jewish Community Council, Nov. 6, 1972, box 35, JLC; for origins in the early sixties, see Staub, *Torn at the Roots*, 77, 130.

62. "A Chronology: AJC Activities and Statements Regarding Quotas and Preferential Treatment," Sept. 16, 1972, box 186, Gold Papers, AJCA; Hyman Bookbinder, 1974 interview, 5, 13, AJC-OH; Richard Cohen, interview, 43, AJC-OH.

63. Hyman Bookbinder to Dear Friend, Sept. 1, 1972, box 188, Gold Papers, AJCA.

64. Hyman Bookbinder to Bert Gold, Sept. 14, 1972, box 186, ibid.

65. Seymour Samet to IRSA staff, Aug. 24, 1972, box 188, ibid.

66. Natalie Flatow to Bert Gold, Sept. 26, 1972, ibid.

67. Eugene Du Bow to Yehudah Rosenman, Sept. 8, 1972, box 186, ibid.; minutes, Consultation Meeting on AJC Approach to Jewish Academicians, Oct. 25, 1972, ibid.

68. Podhoretz, *Breaking Ranks*, 305, 334. Some neoconservatives similarly sought to deny that "social justice" was a defining element of Judaism, as was widely believed at the time. See Glazer, "Role of the Intellectuals," 60; Staub, *Torn at the Roots*.

69. For the positioning, see the panel discussion "Liberalism and the Negro." For empirical refutation of the notion of radical rupture, see Chapter 2 and also Chen, "From Fair Employment to Equal Employment Opportunity and Beyond," esp. 275–300; Thomas Sugrue, "The Tangled Roots of Affirmative Action," *American Behavioral Scientist* 41 (April 1998): 886–897.

70. Daniel Bell, "On Meritocracy and Equality," *Public Interest* (Fall 1972): 48, 63, 65, 31, 40; Robert F. Sasseen, "Affirmative Action and the Principle of Equality," in *New Egalitarianism: Questions and Challenges* (Port Washington, N.Y., 1979), 180, 186, 188; and see the acute discussion in Peter Steinfels, *The Neoconservatives: The Men Who are Changing America's Politics* (New York, 1979), 214–247.

71. Milton Metzger to William Van Alstyne, Jan. 10, 1973, box 184, ACLU Papers.

72. Paul Seabury, "HEW and the Universities," *Commentary* (Feb. 1972): 97–112; also Irving Kristol, "How Hiring Quotas Came to the Campuses," *Fortune*, (Sept. 1974): 203, 207; Miro M. Todorovich, exchange of letters with Howard Glickstein, reprinted in *Reverse Discrimination*, ed. Barry R. Gross (New York, 1977), 18, 32; Steinfels, *The Neoconservatives*, 228.

73. Philip Perlmutter to Seymour Samet, April 6, 1973, box 186, Gold Papers, AJCA.

74. Nathan Glazer, "Jews and Blacks: What Happened to the Grand Alliance?" in *Jews in Black Perspectives: A Dialogue*, ed. Joseph R. Washington (Teaneck, N.J., 1984), 108. Jews in the South differed, as noted by Forman, *Blacks in the Jewish Mind*, 47. For later fusion, see Seymour Martin Lipset, "A Unique People in an Exceptional Country," in *American Exceptionalism: A Double-Edged Sword* (New York, 1996), 151–175, who also calls blacks "the great exception to the American Creed" (113).

75. Equality Committee to Board of Directors, Nov. 29, 1972, 4, box 184, ACLU Papers; Samuel Walker, *In Defense of American Liberties: A History of the ACLU* (New York, 1990), 305–306.

76. Svonkin, *Jews against Prejudice*, 114, 132, 192, 149, 150.

77. Stephen Steinberg, *The Ethnic Myth: Race, Ethnicity, and Class in America* (Boston, 1981).

78. Charles V. Hamilton, "On Affirmative Action as Public Policy," in *Bakke, Weber. and Affirmative Action: A Rockefeller Foundation Conference* (New York, 1979), 183–187; Biondi, *"To Stand and Fight,"* 99. Biondi's work refutes the notion that the early black movement sought only color-blindness. As the discussion in this chapter illustrates, that idea has spread owing to a kind of ventriloquism in which white

observers have retrospectively defined its agenda. For the damage done in the name of color-blindness after emancipation, see John H. Cox and LaWanda Cox, "Andrew Johnson and His Ghost Writers: An Analysis of the Freedman's Bureau and Civil Rights Veto Messages," *Mississippi Valley Historical Review* 48 (Dec. 1961): esp. 469, 475; U.S. Supreme Court, *The Civil Rights Cases* (1983), esp. 24–25, 60.

79. See Chapter 2; also, on "the long civil rights era," Nikhil Pal Singh, *Black Is a Country: Race and the Unfinished Struggle for Democracy* (Cambridge, Mass., 2004); Adam Green and Charles M. Payne, introduction to Green and Payne, *Time Longer Than Rope: A Century of African American Activism* (New York, 2003), 1–9; Jacquelyn Dowd Hall, "The Long Civil Rights Movement and the Political Uses of the Past," *JAH* 91 (March 2005): 1233–63.

80. Mark Elliott, "Race, Color Blindness, and the Democratic Public: Albion W. Tourgée's Radical Principles in *Plessy v. Ferguson*," *JSH* 67 (May 2001): 299.

81. Roger Meltzer to Solomon Fisher, June 12, 1974, box 25, Intergroup Relations, AJCA; Murray Friedman to Solomon Fisher and Richard Fox, April 22, 1974, ibid.; Murray Friedman to Seymour Samet, Sept. 10, 1974, ibid.

82. Walter T. Hubbard, Sr., to Philip Hoffman, Sept. 20, 1972, box 188, Gold Papers, AJCA.

83. Benjamin Epstein, 1974 interview, transcript, 29, AJC-OH.

84. Paul Seabury, "The Idea of Merit," *Commentary* (Dec. 1972): 41.

85. Loretta Bass to Gentlemen, March 27, 1973, box 186, Gold Papers, AJCA.

86. Evelyn M. Avery to Norman Podhoretz, April 29, 1973, box 25, Intergroup Relations, AJCA.

87. For empirical data, see Richard B. Freeman, *Black Elite: The New Market for Highly Educated Black Americans* (New York, 1976), 195–213.

88. Hyman Bookbinder to Harry Fleischman, Sept. 25, 1972, box 186, Gold Papers, AJCA; Hyman Bookbinder to Bert Gold, April 1, 1976, box 187, ibid.

89. Gold quoted in National Jewish Community Relations Advisory Council, Executive Committee Minutes, Oct. 15, 1972, box 9, Intergroup Relations, AJCA; AJCongress, "A Program to Implement the 1972 Convention Resolution on Affirmative Action, Quotas and Goals in Employment and Education," Sept. 11, 1972, box 6, AJCongressR.

90. "Excerpted Summary of AJC Annual Meeting Discussions on Affirmative Action," May 31, 1972, box 9, Intergroup Relations, AJCA.

91. Minutes, Staff Coordinating Committee Meeting, Aug. 29, 1972, box 186, Gold Papers, AJCR; similarly, Podhoretz, "A Certain Anxiety," 10.

92. Margaret L. Rumbarger, "The Great Quota Debate and Other Issues in Affirmative Action," in Furniss and Graham, *Women in Higher Education*, 209–210, 214; J. Stanley Pottinger, "The Drive toward Equality," *Change: The Magazine of Higher Learning* 4 (Oct. 1972): 24–29.

93. Rogers, "Role of the EEOC," 221; Pifer, "Women in Higher Education," 10; Bernice Sandler, "Affirmative Action on Campus," 324–326.

94. Emanuel Rackman to Roland L. Elliot, attachments, Aug. 15, 1972, GEN HU 2–2, WHCF, box 18, NPMP; Committee on Academic Nondiscrimination and Integrity to "Dear Professor," with attachments, [n.d], box 151, Abzug Papers; Eleanor P. Wolf to Preliminary Meeting, Jewish Community Council, Nov. 6,

1972, 5, box 35, JLC; Benjamin Epstein to Leonard Garment, attachment, April 14, 1972, box 118, Garment Papers; Naomi Levine to Leonard Garment, April 2, 1973, box 42, Patterson Papers.

95. "Preferential Treatment and Other Improper Procedures in Admissions and Employment at Colleges and Universities: Illustrative Instances," Aug. 8, 1972, box 9, Intergroup Relations, AJCA; Seymour Samet to Bert Gold, May 22, 1972, box 188, Gold Papers, AJCA.

96. Quoted in "Colleges' White Men Assail 'Preference' for Minorities"; Kristol, "How Hiring," 203.

97. Sandler, "Affirmative Action on Campus," 325.

98. Pottinger, "Drive toward Equality," 29; Todorovich, exchange of letters with Glickstein, 36; Pifer, "Women in Higher Education," 8, 10.

99. Murray Friedman to Morris Fine, Nov. 14, 1972, box 186, Gold Papers, AJCA.

100. "Debate on Preferential Treatment in the Selection Process," 11; Esther G. Stone to Gentlemen, Dec. 26, 1972, box 186, Gold Papers, AJCA.

101. Hyman Bookbinder to Bert Gold, Sept. 14, 1972, box 186, Gold Papers, AJCA.

102. Seymour Samet to Bertram H. Gold, Oct. 23, 1972, with attached Sept. 26, 1972 news clipping, box 9, Intergroup Relations, AJCA.

103. Judith Herman to Seymour Samet, Nov. 10, 1972, ibid.

104. Speech by Congresswoman Bella Abzug on quotas at the Democratic Women's Club, Washington, D.C., March 13, 1973, box 151, Abzug Papers; Joyce Antler, *The Journey Home: Jewish Women and the American Century* (New York, 1997), 267–279; Hasia Diner and Beryl Lieff Benderly, *Her Works, Praise Her: A History of Jewish Women in America from Colonial Times to the Present* (New York, 2002), 394–396. The best examination of the neoconservatives' gambit is Staub, *Torn at the Roots.*

105. Quoted in NOW, *Compliance Newsletter,* no. 10 (Sept. 1973): 10; also Julia Graham Lear, March 30, 1973, box 17, NOW Papers; minutes of the meeting of the Coalition for Affirmative Action," April 5, 1973, box 17, NOW Papers.

106. Hyman Bookbinder to Seymour Samet, March 5, 1973, with attachments, box 186, Gold Papers, AJCA; also Bernice Sandler, "Is 'Affirmative Action' Penalizing Males?" *Chronicle of Higher Education,* May 14, 1973, ibid. For the pressure for an ombudsman, see Haskell Lazare to Seymour Samet, July 18, 1972, ibid.

107. John A. Morsell to Harry Fleischman, Sept. 29, 1972, with attached letter, box 188, ibid. The exception was Bayard Rustin, who by then depended on the AFL-CIO for his livelihood and echoed its top officials in treating "full employment" as a panacea for racial inequality, which even an AJC staff member criticized as insufficient. Harry Fleischman to Bayard Rustin, June 14, 1974, box 187, ibid. See also Jesse L. Jackson, "Three Challenges to Organized Labor," *Freedomways* (4th quarter 1972): 311–312; Eleanor Holmes Norton to Philip E. Hoffman, Nov. 3, 1972, "More on 'Quotas," Vertical File, s.v. Preferential Treatment, AJCA.

108. Natalie Flatow to Bert Gold, Sept. 26, 1972, box 188, Gold Papers, AJCA.

109. Ibid.

110. Payne's commentaries reproduced with an AJC complaint to the president of CBS, Richard S. Salent to Bertram H. Gold, Sept. 6, 1972, box 188, ibid.

111. William Raspberry, "Another View of Quotas," *WP,* Oct. 4, 1972, A23;

Marc Dollinger, *Quest for Inclusion: Jews and Liberalism in Modern America* (Princeton, 2000), 212.

112. Theodore M. Shaw, "Affirmative Action: African American and Jewish Perspectives," in Salzman and West, *Struggles in the Promised Land*, 326; Nathaniel S. Colley, "Affirmative Action or Quotas? It Depends upon Whose Bull Is Gored," 8, address delivered to the Professional Men's Club, Los Angeles, Nov. 15, 1972, box 22, Rauh Papers.

113. Vernon E. Jordan, Jr., to Patricia Roberts Harris, Jan. 19, 1973, and attachment, Harris to Hyman Bookbinder, Jan. 3, 1973, box 167, series 3, NUL; Patricia Roberts Harris to Samuel Rabinove, Dec. 18, 1972, box 188, Gold Papers, AJCA; Jon Katz, "Hobson Assails Opposition to Racial Job Quotas," *WP*, undated 1972 clipping, box 144, Garment Papers; Colley, "Affirmative Action or Quotas?" For AJC awareness of the critical timing, see Hyman Bookbinder to Neil Sandberg, Sept. 15, 1972, box 186, Gold Papers, AJCA.

114. Vernon E. Jordan, Jr., "Blacks and Jews: United and Unafraid," *Congress Bi-Weekly*, June 21, 1974, 5–6; *Contemporary Black Biography*, vol. 3 (Detroit, 1998), 116–117.

115. Rev. Emmett C. Burns to Philip E. Hoffman, Sept. 12, 1972, box 188, Gold Papers, AJCA.

116. Walter T. Hubbard, Sr., to Philip Hoffman, Sept. 20, 1972, box 188, Gold Papers, AJCA; Vernon Jordan, 1974 interview,, transcript, 6–7, AJC-OH; Patricia Roberts Harris, 1974 interview, transcript, AJC-OH.

117. Harris interview, 1974, 6, 11, 13, 16, 18, 19, 22, 29–30, AJC-OH.

118. Clipping with John M. Lavine to Bertram H. Gold, Oct. 29, 1973, box 186, AJCA.

119. Seymour Samet to Milton Himmelfarb, Nov. 16, 1972, ibid.

120. "Remarks of Joseph L. Rauh, Jr., before the Milwaukee Jewish Council Dinner," June 26, 1973, box 22, Rauh Papers; Hyman Bookbinder to Joseph Rauh, July 5, 1973, with attachment, ibid.

121. Quoted in Hyman Bookbinder to Bert Gold, Sept. 14, 1972, box 188, Gold Papers, AJCA; also Alexander J. Allen to Bayard Rustin, May 10, 1973, box 187, ibid.

122. William J. Greene to Bert Gold, Nov. 16, 1972, box 188, ibid.

123. Kenneth B. Clark in The Conference Board, *Equal Employment: Opportunity or Quotas?* transcript of a conference at the Waldorf Astoria, New York, June 6, 1973, 6 vols., Hagley Museum and Library, Wilmington, Del.; also Richard H. Mapp to Charles Sharpe, "Forum by the Capital Press Club on 'Quotas vs. Goals,'" Oct. 19, 1972, box 167, series 3, NUL; Alexander J. Allen to Adolph Holmes and Ronald H. Brown, Nov. 9, 1972, box 167, series 3, NUL (that meetings could deepen hostilities was clear from the handwritten notes: "Jewish leadership—if they don't accept our superior guidance, let them stew!").

124. Jewel Prestage, "Quelling the Mythical Revolution in Higher Education: Retreat from the Affirmative Action Concept," *Journal of Politics* 41 (1979): 765–766; Richard Chait and Cathy Tower, "Professors at the Color Line," *NYT*, Sept. 11, 2001, A27.

125. Leigh Beinen, Alicia Ostriker, and J. P. Ostriker, "Sex Discrimination in the Universities: Faculty Problems and No Solution," *Women's Rights Law Reporter* 2 (1975): 3; statement of Norma Raffel, WEAL, in *Federal Higher Education Programs* Hearings, 335.

126. Winifred D. Wandersee, *On the Move: American Women in the 1970s* (Boston, 1988), 115.

127. See, for example, Albert D. Chernin in National Jewish Community Relations Advisory Council, "Affirmative Action, Preferential Treatment, and Quotas," papers from the Plenary Session, June 28–July 2, 1972, Los Angeles, 26; also Nathan Glazer, "On Jewish Forebodings," *Commentary* (Aug. 1985): 34; Kaufman, *Broken Alliance*, 212.

128. Sam Rabinove to Bertram H. Gold, June 14, 1976, box 187, Gold Papers, AJCA.

129. Hyman Bookbinder interview, AJC-OH, 20; Hyman Bookbinder to Naomi Levine, Sept. 2, 1975, box 187, Gold Papers, AJCA.

130. Hyman Bookbinder to Robert Hampton, Aug. 28, 1972, box 1, series E, LCCR Papers; William H. Brown III to Leonard Garment, Nov. 13, 1972, box 144, Garment Papers; *Newsweek* quoted in briefing memorandum, "Philadelphia Plan vs. Quotas," by John Evans for Ken Cole, Oct. 24, 1972, EX HU 2–2, box 17, WHCF, NPMP.

131. Jack Greenberg, *Crusaders in the Courts: How a Dedicated Band of Lawyers Fought for the Civil Rights Revolution* (New York, 1994), 463; Marc Dollinger, *Quest for Inclusion: Jews and Liberalism in Modern America* (Princeton, 2000), 209; James J. Kilpatrick, "The DeFunis Syndrome," *Nation's Business* (June 1974): 13–14; Benjamin Epstein and Arnold Forster, *Preferential Treatment and Quotas* (New York, 1974), 31.

132. Peter Schnurman to Al Franco, Feb. 25, 1974, with attachment, box 26, Intergroup Relations, AJCA.

133. Samuel Rabinove to Gentlemen, March 28, 1974, ibid.

134. Greenberg, *Crusaders*, 463; Dollinger, *Quest*, 209–210.

135. Saul Goldstein to President, NCJW, May 1, 1974, box 16, group 2, NCJW; Laura Greenberg to Eleanor Marvin, March 6, 1974, ibid.; Eli Fox to Eleanor Martin, March 8, 1974, ibid.

136. AFT Resolution, "The Bakke Decision and Racial Quotas," [n.d.], box 8, AFT-OP; Peter Laarman to State and National Field Staff, Sept. 30, 1977, box 9, ibid.; Epstein and Forster, *Preferential Treatment*, 13; Glazer, "Jews and Blacks," 110; Jerome A. Chanes, "Affirmative Action: Jewish Ideals, Jewish Interests," in Salzman and West, *Struggles in the Promised Land*, 303.

137. Albert Vorspan to Social Action Chairmen [of UAHC] et al., March 19, 1974, box 2, Kaplan Collection.

138. Six agency leaders to Peter E. Holmes, May 20, 1974, box 25, Intergroup Relations, AJCA; Samuel Rabinove to Bertram H. Gold, Oct. 16, 1972, box 188, Gold Papers, AJCA; Levine and Hochbaum, "Draft: Quotas and Preferential Admissions," 11; Resolution on Inquiries and Surveys about Race, Religion, Ethnic Origin, and Sex, Feb. 12, 1973, box 6, AJCongressR; Morris U. Schappes to *Amsterdam News*, Aug. 3, 1974, box 26, Intergroup Relations, AJCA (also source of "means test").

139. Hyman Bookbinder to Seymour Samet, April 30, 1973, box 186, Gold Papers, AJCA.

140. Opinion of Justice Powell, *Regents of the University of California v. Bakke*, U.S. Supreme Court (1977), 267, 305, 307, 311–313, 317.

141. Hyman Bookbinder to Bert Gold, Sept. 14, 1972, box 186, Gold Papers, AJCA.

142. Joan Steinau Lester, *Eleanor Holmes Norton: Fire in My Soul* (New York, 2003), 151.

143. Naomi Levine and Martin Hochbaum, "Draft: Quotas and Preferential Admissions," 29.

7. *Conservatives Shift from "Massive Resistance" to "Color-Blindness"*

1. Richard L. Borden to James J. Kilpatrick, Dec. 27, 1971, and attached article by Kilpatrick, "An Appraisal of American Conservatism," 29–33, box 23, acc. 6626-g, JJKP; Buckley diary entry quoted in George H. Nash, *The Conservative Intellectual Movement in America since 1945* (New York, 1976), 325, who notes how the right seized on the conflicts in higher education (279–328); Donald Atwell Zoll, "The Future of American Conservatism: A New Revival?" *Modern Age* 18 (Winter 1974): 4. For poll data showing "a remarkable 'liberal leap' between 1970 and 1972 followed by steady positive change between 1972 and 1976," see Gerald D. Jaynes and Robin M. Williams, eds., for the National Research Council, *A Common Destiny: Blacks and American Society* (Washington, D.C., 1989), 120; also Barbara Ehrenreich, *Fear of Falling: The Inner Life of the Middle Class* (New York, 1990), 114; Thomas Ferguson and Joel Rogers, *Right Turn: The Decline of the Democrats and the Future of American Politics* (New York: 1986), 11–28.

2. On Buckley's urging Reagan to run for president from 1973 on, see John B. Judis, *William F. Buckley, Jr.: Patron Saint of the Conservatives* (New York, 1988), 382; on the rise of conservatism, see, among others works cited, Allen J. Matusow, *The Unraveling of America: A History of Liberalism in the 1960s* (New York, 1984); Thomas Byrne Edsall and Mary Edsall, *Chain Reaction: The Impact of Race, Rights, and Taxes on American Politics* (New York, 1991); Michael Kazin, *The Populist Persuasion: An American History* (New York, 1995); and Godfrey Hodgson, *The World Turned Right Side Up: A History of the Conservative Ascendancy in America* (Boston, 1996).

3. For two conservatives who note how anomalous the sudden turn to egalitarianism was, see Paul Gottfried and Thomas Fleming, *The Conservative Movement* (Boston, 1988), 41.

4. Clyde Wilson, book reviews, *Modern Age* (Winter 1972): 106, and (Spring 1975): 221–223; M. E. Bradford, "Faulkner's Last Words and 'The American Dilemma,'" ibid. (Winter 1972): 77, and "A Fire Bell in the Night: The Southern Conservative View" (Winter 1973): 9, 10.

5. R. J. Herrnstein, "On Challenging an Orthodoxy," *Commentary* 55 (April 1973): 52–54, 61–62; Ernest Van den Haag, "The Tortured Search for the Cause of Inequality," *NR*, Feb. 16, 1973, 200; James J. Kilpatrick, "A Conservative View of the Urban Crisis," notes for a talk at Auburn University, April 1, 1969, box 12, acc. 6626-e, JJKP. For defenses, see Gottfried and Fleming, *Conservative Movement*, 45; Norman Podhoretz, "The New Inquisitors," *Commentary* 55 (April 1973): 7–8; Charles Frankel, "The New Egalitarianism and the Old," *Commentary* 56 (Sept. 1973): 54–55; Daniel Bell, "On Meritocracy and Equality," *The Public Interest* (Feb. 1972): 32–33.

6. James Burnham, "Are American Blacks Natives?" *NR*, Feb. 9, 1971, 133; Burnham, "The Black Nation," *NR*, Oct. 20, 1970, 1102.

7. Michelle Brattain, *The Politics of Whiteness: Race, Workers, and Culture in the Modern South* (Princeton, 2001), 271; Hodgson, *World Turned Right*, 140–142; Jef-

ferson Cowie, "Nixon's Class Struggle: Romancing the New Right Worker, 1969–1973," *Labor History* 43 (2002): 257–283; Dan T. Carter, *The Politics of Rage: George Wallace, the Origins of the New Conservatism, and the Transformation of American Politics* (New York, 1995).

8. Kevin P. Phillips, *The Emerging Republican Majority* (New Rochelle, N.Y., 1969), 38, 472, 25, 31, 37, 39, 468; William F. Buckley, Jr., *Inveighing We Will Go* (New York, n.d.), 38; William A. Rusher, *The Making of the New Majority Party* (New York, 1975), 26–27, 31, 171. For Phillips's book as "the blueprint which was successfully followed in 1980," see Robert W. Whitaker, ed. *The New Right Papers* (New York, 1982), 2, xv.

9. *Current Biography* (1983), s.v. Richard A[rt] Viguerie, 427–430; Richard Viguerie, *The New Right: We're Ready to Lead*, rev. ed. (Falls Church, Va., 1981), esp. 219, 241–242.

10. Both quoted in Judis, *William F. Buckley*, 377–379.

11. Ibid., 38, 213, 436–437, 283, 285.

12. Jerome Himmelstein, *To the Right: The Transformation of American Conservatism* (Berkeley, 1990), 78; Mark J. Green and Andrew Buchsbaum, *The Corporate Lobbies: Political Profiles of the Business Roundtable and the Chamber of Commerce* (n.p., 1980), 8, 68; Ferguson and Rogers, *Right Turn*, 51–58, 76, 111–113; Thomas Byrne Edsall, *The New Politics of Inequality* (New York, 1984), 121; Kim McQuaid, *Uneasy Partners: Big Business in American Politics, 1945–1990* (Baltimore, 1994), 149, 128–131.

13. Kirkpatrick Sale, *Power Shift: The Rise of the Southern Rim and Its Challenge to the Eastern Establishment* (New York, 1975); Michael Goldfield, *The Decline of Organized Labor in the United States* (Chicago, 1987); Edsall, *New Politics*, 141–178, 23–106; Lisa McGirr, *Suburban Warriors: The Origins of the New American Right* (Princeton, 2001).

14. Matthew Lassiter, *The Silent Majority: Suburban Politics in the Sunbelt South* (Princeton, 2005).

15. William F. Buckley, Jr., "The New Conservatism," in Buckley, *The Governor Listeth* (New York, [1970]), 137–138; Irving Kristol, *Two Cheers for Capitalism* (New York, 1978), 136–139; James J. Kilpatrick to F. Evans Farwell, Feb. 20, 1974, box 4, acc. 6626-F, JJKP.

16. See the hostile exchanges between Buckley and the ADL's director, culminating with William F. Buckley, Jr., to Herman Edelsberg, June 27, 1960, box 10, WFBP; the clippings "ADL Tactics Cause Ill Will" and "The ADL's Own Extremism," box 18, WFBP; also Stuart Svonkin, *Jews against Prejudice* (New York, 1997), 181–183.

17. William F. Buckley, Jr., to Sidney Hook, Oct. 2, 1970, box 159, WFBP; Buckley, "Come On In, the Water's Fine," *NR*, March 9, 1971, 249. Hooks had written a few pieces for conservatives on higher education: Sidney Hook, "Politicized Universities Are Betraying Their Mission," *Human Events* 30 (1970): 12. For how Buckley spurned anti-Semitism from early on, see Judis, *William F. Buckley*, 59.

18. William F. Buckley, Jr., to Irving Kristol, July 8, 1970, box 180, WFBP; Kristol to Buckley, June 29, 1970, ibid.; William F. Buckley, Jr., to Norman Podhoretz, March 28, 1972, box 224, WFBP; Judis, *William F. Buckley*, 326, 327; Jacob Neusner to Buckley, June 11, 1970, box 212, WFBP.

19. Philip Gleason, "Minorities (Almost) All: The Minority Concept in Amer-

ican Social Thought," *American Quarterly* 43 (Sept. 1991): 408; *NYT,* Aug. 7, 1972, A20.

20. Frank Meyer to William F. Buckley, Jr., et al., Jan. 17, 1962, box 20, WFBP.

21. Paul Burstein, *Discrimination, Jobs, and Politics: The Struggle for Equal Employment Opportunity in the United States since the New Deal* (Chicago, 1985), 162; Alfred W. Blumrosen, "How the Courts Are Handling Reverse Discrimination Claims," *Daily Labor Report* (Bureau of National Affairs), no. 56 (March 23, 1995), E-1.

22. Charles C. Moscos and John Sibley Butler, *All That We Can Be: Black Leadership and Racial Integration the Army Way* (New York, 1996), 2. The Chamber of Commerce, for its part, was far more concerned about crime than about affirmative action, to judge from its files.

23. The work that affirmative action did for the right shows how "race consciousness is central . . . to whites' acceptance of the legitimacy of hierarchy and to their identity with elite interest." Kimberlé Williams Crenshaw, "Race, Reform, and Retrenchment: Transformation and Legitimation in Antidiscrimination Law," *Harvard Law Review* 101 (1988): 1369.

24. Bradford, "Faulkner's Last Words," 77; M. E. Bradford, "A Fire Bell in the Night: The Southern Conservative View," ibid. (Winter 1973): 11; Orrin Hatch, "Loading the Economy" [Heritage Foundation] *Policy Review* 12 (Spring 1980): 36; Mrs. M. C. Wilson to President Nixon, Aug. 23, 1972, GEN HU 2–2, box 18, WHCF, NPMP; Kilpatrick to James R. DeLay, May 27, 1974, with attachment, box 8, acc. 6626-F, JJKP.

25. Allan C. Ornstein, "Comment: Quality vs. Quotas," *Society* (Jan.–Feb. 1976): 16–17; Paul Seabury, "The Idea of Merit," *Commentary* 54 (Dec. 1972): 45.

26. Ernest Van den Haag, "Reverse Discrimination: A Brief against It," *NR,* April 29, 1977, 492–495; Jesse Helms, *When Free Men Shall Stand* (Grand Rapids, Mich., 1976), 11; on the rhetorical power of white "innocence," see Thomas Ross, *Just Stories: How the Law Embodies Racism and Bias* (Boston, 1996), xvi, 9, 21–25, 45–46.

27. Benjamin R. Epstein, presentation at the National Jewish Community Relations Advisory Council, "Affirmative Action, Preferential Treatment, and Quotas," Papers from the Plenary Session at Los Angeles (June 1972), 6, 11, box 35, JLC.

28. Van den Haag, "Reverse Discrimination," 493.

29. J. J. Kilpatrick, "Notes for Informal Talk to Association of Senate Press Secretaries," Jan. 30, 1969, box 12, acc. 6626-e, JJKP; Frank S. Meyer, "Equality Ad Absurdum," *NR,* Nov. 15, 1966, 1168; Felix Morley, "Equality Theory Insults the Common Man," *Nation's Business* (April 1964): 27–28.

30. Robert A. Nisbet, "The New Despotism," *Commentary* 59 (June 1975): 31–43, esp. 32.

31. Patrick J. Buchanan, *Conservative Votes, Liberal Victories: Why the Right Has Failed* (New York, 1975), 52, 69, 172, 71; James J. Kilpatrick to Harry F. Byrd, Dec. 28, 1955, box 7, acc. 6626-B, JJKP.

32. James J. Kilpatrick to Mr. Mason, April 27, 1983, box 30, acc. 6626-j-k-m, JJKP; Randall Kennedy to Kilpatrick, July 9, 1986, box 11, acc. 6626-N, JJKP; Kilpatrick to Kennedy, July 14, 1986, JJKP; Kilpatrick to Wubnig, July 10, 1985, box

11, acc. 6626-N, JJKP. Critics pushed him, in vain, to acknowledge the right's responsibility. See, for example, Ray Fleming to Kilpatrick, Jan. 1, 1989, acc. 6626-N, box 11, JJKP; David A. Leas to Kilpatrick, Nov. 22, 1974, acc. 6626-N, box 8, JJKP.

33. Irving Kristol, "Of Populism and Taxes," in *The New Egalitarianism: Questions and Challenges*, ed. David Lewis Schaefer (Port Washington, N.Y., 1979), 86–87; Richard A. Viguerie, *The Establishment vs. The People: Is a New Populist Revolt on the Way?* (Chicago, 1983); and, for analysis, see Peter Steinfels, *The Neo-Conservatives, The Men Who Are Changing America's Politics* (New York, 1979), 248–272.

34. James J. Kilpatrick to Mr. May, July 21, 1978, box 29, acc. j-k-m, JJKP; Kilpatrick to Ann S. Frentz, Dec. 1, 1974, box 8, acc. 6626-F, JJKP; Kilpatrick to Marie B. Cooper, Aug. 17, 1977, box 12, acc. 6626-H, JJKP; Kilpatrick to Brent Hall, March 19, 1979, box 30, acc. j-k-m, JJKP.

35. "Statement of Hon. James Buckley, a Senator from the State of New York," in *Federal Higher Education Programs Institutional Eligibility*, Hearings before the Special Subcommittee on Education or the Committee on Education, pt. 2A, Civil Rights Obligations and Labor, House of Representatives, 93rd Cong., 2nd sess. (Washington, D.C., 1974), p. 236; Van den Haag, "Reverse Discrimination," 495; also Robert F. Sasseen, "Affirmative Action and the Principle of Equality," in *The New Egalitarianism*, ed. David Lewis Schaefer (Port Washington, N.Y., 1979), 175–176; Nisbet, "The New Despotism," 40. See also Allan C. Ornstein, "Are Quotas Here to Stay?" *NR*, April 26, 1974, 480–481, 495.

36. Earlier, Kristol had tried to market *Public Interest* to precisely this "new class, a policy-making intellectual class." Irving Kristol, "About Equality," *Commentary* 54 (Nov. 1972): 42–43; also *Current Biography* (1974), s.v. Irving (William) Kristol, 224. See also Bell, "On Meritocracy and Equality," 64.

37. For the archaic, see Jarret B. Wollstein, "Civil Rights and Civil Riots," *New Guard* (April 1968): 10–13; Robert H. Bork, "The Supreme Court Needs a New Philosophy," *Fortune* (Dec. 1968): esp. 170.

38. Steinfels, *The Neo-Conservatives*, 10.

39. Ferguson and Rogers, *Right Turn*, 77, 89–92; also Thomas J. McCormick, *America's Half-Century: United States Foreign Policy in the Cold War* (Baltimore, 1989), 161–165.

40. McQuaid, *Uneasy Partners*, 149; Sidney Blumenthal, *The Rise of the Counter-Establishment: From Conservative Ideology to Political Power* (New York, 1986), esp. xiii; Ferguson and Rogers, *Right Turn*, 78–113; Edsall, *New Politics*, 107–140; Himmelstein, *To the Right*.

41. McQuaid, *Uneasy Partners*, 135; Ferguson and Rogers, *Right Turn*, 70–73, 86; "Egalitarianism: Threat to a Free Market," *Business Week*, Dec. 1, 1975, 62–65; David Vogel, *Lobbying the Corporation: Citizen Challenges to Business Authority* (New York, 1978).

42. Jean Stefanic and Richard Delgado, *No Mercy: How Conservative Think Tanks and Foundations Changed America's Social Agenda* (Philadelphia, 1996), quote on 137; Edsall, *New Politics*, 113; Mark J. Green and Andrew Buchsbaum, *The Corporate Lobbies: Political Profiles of the Business Roundtable and the Chamber of Commerce* (n.p., 1980), 14–15.

43. Robert Kuttner, quoted in Ferguson and Rogers, *Right Turn*, 102.

44. Joseph Coors to "Dear Fellow Americans" n.d., box 44, García Papers;

Grace Lichtenstein, "Rocky Mountain High," *NYT Magazine*, Dec. 28, 1975, 18; James Traub, "Potent Brew," *NYT Magazine*, Dec. 28, 2003, 37.

45. Stefanic and Delgado, *No Mercy*, 53–72; Ferguson and Rogers, *Right Turn*, *86–88;* Edsall, *New Politics*, 117–120.

46. BYN to WMD and Rockefeller Brothers Fund Files, "American Enterprise Institute," Dec. 5, 1979, box 72, series 4, Rockefeller Records; Blumenthal, *Rise of the Counter-Establishment*, 42–44; Steinfels, *The Neo-Conservatives*, 11, 261. Van den Haag became an Olin Professor and Distinguished Scholar at the Heritage Foundation and Hook a senior research fellow at the Hoover Institution. *Current Biography* (1983), s.v. Van den Haag, Ernest, 420–421; *American National Biography*, vol. 11 (New York, 1999), s.v. Hook, Sidney, 127.

47. Edsall, *New Politics*, 117; Eric Alterman, "The 'Right' Books and Big Ideas," *Nation*, Nov. 22, 1999, 16–21.

48. Letter reproduced in "Statement of George C. Roche III, President, Hillsdale College, Michigan," in *Federal Higher Education Programs*, 102–103; *Current Biography* (1981), s.v. Sowell, Thomas, 390–393; Thomas Sowell, "Affirmative Action Reconsidered: Was It Necessary in Academia?" *American Enterprise Institute Evaluative Studies* 27 (Dec. 1975): 1–45. For the larger pattern, see Angela D. Dillard, *Guess Who's Coming to Dinner Now? Multicultural Conservatism in America* (New York, 2001).

49. *Current Biography* (1992), s.v. Thomas, Clarence, 567–573; Linda Chavez, *An Unlikely Conservative: The Transformation of an Ex-Liberal (Or, How I Became the Most Hated Hispanic in America)* (New York, 2002); Blumenthal, *Rise of the Counter-Establishment*, 288.

50. Kevin Boyle, *The UAW and the Heyday of American Liberalism, 1945–1968* (Ithaca, N.Y., 1995), 180; John A. Ford to L. William Seidman, Feb. 26, 1975, HU 2–2, box 7, WHCF, GRFL.

51. Martin Luther King, Jr., *Why We Can't Wait* (New York, 1963), 134, 137, 138, 142. For the class grievances and cultural commitments that fed the backlash, see Kenneth D. Durr, *Behind the Backlash: White Working-Class Politics in Baltimore, 1940–1980* (Chapel Hill, N.C., 2003), esp. 190–191; and Thomas Frank, *What's the Matter with Kansas? How Conservatives Won the Heart of America* (New York, 2004).

52. See Chapter 2; also Dona Cooper Hamilton and Charles V. Hamilton, *The Dual Agenda: Race and Social Welfare Policies of Civil Rights Organizations* (New York, 1997).

53. James Baldwin, "Liberalism and the Negro," *Commentary* 37 (March 1964): 35–36.

54. On Reagan-era redistribution to the wealthy, see Edsall, *New Politics*.

55. Michael E. Staub, *Torn at the Roots: The Crisis of Jewish Liberalism in Postwar America* (New York, 2002), 96; Samuel Rabinov to Seymour Samet, Dec. 20, 1973, box 26, Intergroup Relations, AJCA; Irving Kristol, "American Conservatism, 1945–1995," *Public Interest* (Fall 1995): 80–91.

56. Paul M. Deac to Lee White, Aug. 16, 1965, box 4, White Files; Micaela di Leonardo, "White Ethnicities, Identity Politics, and Baby Bear's Chair," *Social Text* 41 (Winter 1994): 175. For white ethnics as initially more liberal than WASPS, see Richard J. Krickus, "The White Ethnics: Who Are They and Where Are They Going?" *City* (May–June 1971): esp. 29.

57. Jack Valenti to the President, July 13, 1965, EX HU 2–1, box 43, WHCF,

LBJL; Peter Flanigan to the President, Sept. 27, 1969, EX HU 2–2, box 17, WHCF, NPMP; Peter M. Flanigan to Harry Fleming, Jan. 27, 1970, EX HU 2–2, box 17, WHCF, NPMP; A. F. Kristovich to Robert Finch, Aug. 15, 1970, GEN HU 2–2, box 18, WHCF, NPMP.

58. Paul M. Deac to Lee C. White, March 19, 1964, box 4, White Files; Pat Buchanan to the President, May 26, 1969, box 2, President's Office File, White House Special Files, NPMP.

59. Richard K. Cacioppo for the National Italian-American Bar Association to Ronald Reagan, June 8, 1985, Alphabetical File, s.v. Scalia, WHORM, RRPL; also Frank D. Stella for the National Italian American Foundation to Red Cavney, March 19, 1981, ibid. I take the filing of Scalia's résumé by these organizations as evidence of his consent.

60. Russell Barta, "Are the Rules Changing?" *America*, Oct. 30, 1971, 341–345; George Lipsitz, *The Possessive Investment in Whiteness: How White People Profit from Identity Politics* (Philadelphia, 1998).

61. "CQ Political Report: Campaign '72: The Rising Voice of Ethnic Voters," *Congressional Quarterly* (March 11, 1972): 531–534; Pete Hamill, "The Revolt of the Lower Middle Class," *New York*, April 14, 1969, 26. Hamill's article was circulated in the Nixon White House for internal discussion; see Harry Dent to Bill Gavin, June 25, 1970, EX PU 2–3, box 17, WHCF, NPMP; also Cowie, "Nixon's Class Struggle."

62. Patrick J. Buchanan, *Conservative Votes, Liberal Victories: Why the Right Has Failed* (New York, 1975), 68, 52, 69, 172, 71; Antonin Scalia, "The Disease as Cure: 'In Order to Get beyond Racism, We Must First Take Account of Race,'" *Washington University Law Quarterly* 147 (1979): 152, 153.

63. Dierdre English, "The Fear That Feminism Will Free Men First," in *Powers of Desire: The Politics of Sexuality*, ed. Ann Snitow et al. (New York, 1983); on related concerns in anti-abortion circles, see Rosalind Pollack Petchesky, *Abortion and Women's Choice: The State, Sexuality, and Reproductive Freedom* (Boston, 1984), 241.

64. Quoted in Barbara Ehrenreich, *The Hearts of Men: American Dreams and the Flight from Commitment* (New York, 1983), 145; Jane J. Manbridge, *Why We Lost the ERA* (Chicago, 1986), esp. 92–93; Donald T. Critchlow, "Conservatism Reconsidered: Phyllis Schlafly and Grassroots Conservatism," in *The Conservative Sixties*, ed. David Farber and Jeffe Roche (New York, 2003).

65. Phyllis Schlafly, "What's Wrong with 'Equal Rights' for Women?" *Phyllis Schlafly Report* 5 (Feb. 1972): 3, 4; also Schlafly, "Unemployment—Causes and Solutions," ibid., 9 (Nov. 1975): 1–2; William F. Buckley, Jr., "Women's Lib," in *Inveighing*, 288; George Gilder, *Sexual Suicide* (New York, 1973), v, 92, 95, 98–99, 103, 100–101, 246–247; Steven Goldberg, *The Inevitability of Patriarchy* (New York, 1973), 226–229, 233–234.

66. Staub, *Torn at the Roots*, 271; also Joyce Antler, *The Journey Home: Jewish Women and the American Century* (New York, 1997), 267; Svonkin, *Jews against Prejudice*, 133.

67. Kristol, "About Equality," 47.

68. Himmelfarb quoted in Staub, *Torn at the Roots*, 261–262, also 70–72, 250–251; Decter in Alan M. Wald, *The New York Intellectuals: The Rise and Fall of the Anti-Stalinist Left from the 1930s to the 1980s* (Chapel Hill, 1987), 357; Kristol in

Nina Roth, "The Neoconservative Backlash against Feminism in the 1970s and 1980s: The Case of *Commentary*," in *Consumption and American Culture*, ed. David E. Nye and Carl Pederson (Amsterdam, 1991), 85, 88.

69. James Davison Hunter, *Culture Wars: The Struggle to Define America* (New York, 1991), 39–47; Christel J. Manning, *God Gave Us the Right: Conservative Catholic, Evangelical Protestant, and Orthodox Jewish Women Grapple with Feminism* (New Brunswick, N.J., 1999).

70. *Encyclopedia of Associations*, 16th ed. (Detroit, 1982), 358; Stefanic and Delgado, *No Mercy*, 47–52; Clint Bolick, *Unfinished Business: A Civil Rights Strategy for America's Third Century* (San Francisco, 1991), 141.

71. Lyle Denniston, "EEOC Offers 'Reverse Discrimination, Guidelines," *Washington Star*, Dec. 21, 1977, box 5, Malson Papers; Carl Cohen, "Why Racial Preference Is Illegal and Immoral," *Commentary* 67 (June 1979): 40.

72. *United Steelworkers v. Weber*, U.S. Supreme Court (1979), 193, 198–199; American Federation of State, County, and Municipal Employees et al., Brief *Amici Curiae*, 5, box 24, CLUW Records. On the long struggle of black steelworkers, see Bruce Nelson, *Divided We Stand: American Workers and the Struggle for Black Equality* (Princeton, 2001); Ruth Needleman, *Black Freedom Fighters in Steel: The Struggle for Democratic Unionism* (Ithaca, N.Y., 2003).

73. Steven V. Roberts, "The *Bakke* Case Moves to the Factory," *NYT Magazine*, Feb. 25, 1979, 100; *Brian F. Weber et al. v. Kaiser Aluminum et al.*, no. 76–3266, U.S. Court of Appeals, 5th Circuit (1977); Affirmative Action Coordinating Committee leaflet, "Affirmative Action: Some Facts about *Weber v. Kaiser Aluminum and United Steelworkers Union*" (New York, 1977), box 75, CLUW Records.

74. Howell Raines, "Evidence Questioned in White Factory Worker's Job Discrimination Suit," *NYT*, Dec. 18, 1978; Alan Citron, "Weber: Blue Collar Bakke Wants Rights for All," *New Orleans Times-Picayune*, Dec. 21, 1978, sec. 1, 14; *United Steelworkers v. Weber*, 193–197, 201.

75. Editorial, "Rethinking *Weber:* The Business Response to Affirmative Action," *Harvard Law Review* 102 (1989): 658–671.

76. Quoted in Charles V. Hamilton, "On Affirmative Action as Public Policy," in *Bakke, Weber, and Affirmative Action: A Rockefeller Foundation Conference* (New York, 1979), 194.

77. *United Steelworkers v. Weber*, 207.

78. Eleanor Holmes Norton, speech on "The *Bakke* Decision and Affirmative Action," July 5, 1978, box 36, Martin Papers; Cohen, "Why Racial Preference," 41.

79. Notes on memo from Griffin Bell to the President, n.d., [ca. Sept. 9, 1977], Handwriting File, Office of the Staff Secretary, box 48, JCPL; Sharon Stockard Martin, "Interview: Rashaad Ali," *Equal Opportunity Forum* (April 1979): 7.

80. *United Steelworkers v. Weber*, 194.

81. Miro M. Todorovich to Jules Kolodny, Feb. 12, 1979, box 9, AFT-OP; Cohen, "Why Racial Preference," 42–43; Terry Eastland and William J. Bennett, *Counting by Race: Equality from the Founding Fathers to Bakke and Weber* (New York, 1979), 198; Hatch, "Loading the Economy," 26–27. For discrimination, see Andy Rose, *The Weber Case: New Threat to Affirmative Action* (New York, 1979), 6–12. For a labor historian who echoes the conservatives' arguments, see Judith Stein, *Running Steel, Running America: Race, Economic Policy, and the Decline of Liberalism* (Chapel Hill, N.C., 1998), 186–192.

82. *United Steelworkers v. Weber,* 211–213; AFSCME et al., *Amici,* 5, 15; Abner W. Sibal et al., Petition for Certiorari, *United States of America and Equal Employment Opportunity Commission v. Brian F. Weber et al.* (1978), 6, 12–13; Raines, "Evidence Questioned," A14; Sharon Stockard Martin, "Interview: Rashaad Ali," *Equal Opportunity Forum* (April 1979): 7.

83. Martin, "Interview," 6; Cohen, "Why Racial Preference," 40, 51–52; Carl Cohen, "Justice Debased: The *Weber* Decision," *Commentary* 68 (Sept. 1979): 43.

84. Roberts, "*Bakke* Case Moves to the Factory," 37–38, 84–85, 100.

85. Miro M. Todorovich to various correspondents, Feb. 13, 1979, box 9, AFT-OP; Orrin Hatch, "Labor: Promoting Freedom in the Workplace," in *A Changing America: Conservatives View the '80s from the United States Senate* (South Bend, Ind., 1980), 61; *Current Biography* (1982), s.v. Hatch, Orrin G(rant), 145–146; Hatch, "Loading the Economy," 23, 36.

86. William F. Buckley, Jr., "*Bakke* in a Blue Collar," *NR,* Jan. 5, 1979, 16; James J. Kilpatrick, "The Color of One's Skin Now the Only Measure of Merit," text of Dec. 1977 column, box 29, acc. 6626 j-k-m, JJKP; Scalia, "Disease as Cure," 150; Cohen, "Why Racial Preference," 47; Committee on Academic Nondiscrimination and Integrity, brief of *amicus curiae* for *Weber* case, 22, copy in box 9, AFT-OP; Hatch, "Loading," 31.

87. *United Steelworkers v. Weber,* 194–195, 202–208 (quote on 204), 234; William F. Buckley, Jr., "Double Thought," *NR,* Aug. 3, 1979, 990.

88. Buckley, "*Bakke,*" 17. For how white expectations of entitlement shaped the affirmative action debate, see Cheryl Harris, "Whiteness as Property," *Harvard Law Review* 106 (June 1993): esp. 1714–15.

89. Hamilton Jordan et al. to the President, Jan. 13, 1979, Confidential File, EX JL-2, box JL-3, WHCF, JCPL; Scalia, "Disease as Cure," 151.

90. Citron, "Weber: Blue Collar Bakke,"14; James Burnham, "Black, White, Grey," *NR,* March 31, 1978, 393; Laurence Salomon, "South Africa in Our Future," *NR,* Oct. 15, 1976, 111–114.

91. William M. Horner to James J. Kilpatrick, July 4, 1975, box 9, acc. 6626-G, JJKP.

92. James J. Kilpatrick to Reginald D. Jones, Oct. 18, 1977, with attachment, box 12, acc. 6626-H, JJKP.

93. Carla Hall, "Bradford's Boosters," *WP,* Oct. 20, 1981, box 2, Dole Papers; Barbara Honegger to Elizabeth Dole, Oct. 23, 1981, ibid.; quotes from Bradford, "Fire Bell" and "The Lincoln Legacy: The Long View," reprinted in his *Remembering Who We Are: Reflections of a Southern Conservative* (Athens, Ga., 1985), 143–156. Bradford had founded Scholars for Reagan and served on Reagan's transition team for the National Endowment for the Humanities. Lott quotes from "A Partisan Conversation with Trent Lott" [interview], *Southern Partisan* 4 (Fall 1984): 44–48; Jon Kifner, "Lott and the Shadow of a Pro-White Group," *NYT,* Jan. 14, 1999, A9. For Buckley's exposure of anti-Semitism among paleo-conservatives, including Buchanan, brought on by critiques from Podhoretz, Kristol, and others, see his *In Search of Anti-Semitism* (New York, 1992).

94. Ryoji Mihara to J. J. Kilpatrick, Oct. 25, 1974, box 8, acc. 6626-F, JJKP.

95. Mike Masaoka and David E. Ushio to Richard M. Nixon, Nov. 16, 1971, with attachment, box 58, Garment Papers. Similarly, see Paul M. Li to Friends, Oct. 4, 1977, box 3, Gutierrez Papers; Harold T. Yee, "The General Level of Well-

Being among Asian Americans," Oct. 6, 1977, box 3, Gutierrez Papers; Asian and Pacific Federal Employee Council, "Fact Sheet: The *Bakke* Case and Asian/Pacific Americans," [Sept. 1977], box 3, Gutierrez Papers. On the history of state-sponsored discrimination against persons of Asian descent, see Kim Hyung-chan, *A Legal History of Asian Americans, 1790–1990* (Westport, Conn., 1974).

96. Quoted in Gary Y. Okihiro, *Margins and Mainstreams: Asians in American History and Culture* (Seattle, 1994), 140, also 32–33, 62; Helen Zia, *Asian American Dreams: The Emergence of an American People* (New York, 2000), 46–47, 117–118. So distorting was the model minority stereotype that it moved some Asian Americans to activism. See notes on meeting with Wayne Horiuchi et al., March 1, 1977, box 60, Costanza Papers; Mary Ann Yoden to Doug Huron, Oct. 6, 1977, box 60, Costanza Papers; Paul M. Li to Friends, Oct. 4, 1977, box 3, Gutierrez Papers. For how the vulnerability of Asian American citizenship affected organizing, see Charlotte Brooks, "Ascending California's Racial Hierarchy: Asian Americans, Housing, and Government, 1920–1955" (Ph.D. diss., Northwestern University, 2002).

97. Dana Y. Takagi, *The Retreat from Race: Asian-American Admissions and Racial Politics* (New Brunswick, N.J., 1992), 138–139; Frank H. Wu, "Neither Black nor White: Asian Americans and Affirmative Action," *Third World Law Journal* 225 (1995): 226, 272. For examples of the conservative argument, see Nathan Glazer, "Why *Bakke* Won't End Reverse Discrimination," *Commentary* 66 (Sept. 1978): 41; Elizabeth H. Dole to Michael K. Deaver et al., Dec. 2, 1982, box 6388, Dole Papers; John H. Bunzel, "Diversity or Discrimination? Asian Americans in College," *Public Interest* 87 (Spring 1987).

98. Lucy S. Dawidowicz, *On Equal Terms: Jews in America, 1881–1981* (New York, 1982), 158.

99. William A. Gamson and Andre Modigliani, "The Changing Culture of Affirmative Action," *Research in Political Sociology* 3 (1987): 137, 158. On the impact of color-blindness, see Michael K. Brown et al., *Whitewashing Race: The Myth of a Color-Blind Society* (Berkeley, 2003).

100. Edsall, *New Politics*, 107–108; McQuaid, *Uneasy Partners*, 150.

8. The Lonesomeness of Pioneering

1. Melinda Hernandez quoted in Susan Eisenberg, *We'll Call You If We Need You: Experiences of Women Working in Construction* (Ithaca, N.Y., 1998), 26–28. The title of this chapter comes from the poem "Pioneering (for the Tradeswomen of '78)" by Susan Eisenberg, in *Pioneering: Poems from the Construction Site* (Ithaca, N.Y., 1998), 4–5.

2. *Rocky Mountain News*, March 28, 1982, box 33, CNPR; Eisenberg, *We'll Call You*, 3.

3. M. D. Taracido, "The Puerto Rican Woman," May 29, 1980, 1–6, box 8, Series: Reports and Conferences, PRLDEF; Lynn Angel Morgan, "Access to Training Programs: Barriers Encountered by Hispanic Female Heads-of-Household in New York City" (New York, 1981), preface, 1–3, 21–22, ibid.; Eisenberg, *We'll Call You*, 95–96.

4. Wider Opportunities for Women, "A Proposal for WOW-CNPR Women in Construction Compliance Monitoring Project" (Jan. 1980), box 30, CNPR; Aileen Hernandez, "Small Change for Black Women," *Ms.* 3 (Aug. 1974): 16–18; All-Craft Center, "Evaluation of Training and Job Placement Program for Eco-

nomically Disadvantaged Women in Non-Traditional (Skilled Trades) Work," [n.d.], esp. 3, box 1, UT Papers; Committee for Women in Nontraditional Jobs, "An Interview and Dialogue with Judith Layzer and Miriam Ourin," Aug. 17, 1981, 13–14, box 1, Layzer Papers; Philip S. Foner, *Women and the American Labor Movement: From World War I to the Present* (New York, 1980), 538–540; Ronnie Steinberg, "The Unsubtle Revolution: Women, the State, and Equal Employment," in *Comparable Worth*, ed. Ronnie Steinberg (Philadelphia, 1989), 193–197.

5. Susan Eisenberg, "Tradeswomen: An Endangered Species?" in *Frontline Feminism, 1975–1995: Essays from Sojourner's First Twenty Years*, ed. Karen Hahn (San Francisco, 1995).

6. Dorothy Haener, "Task Force on Equal Opportunity in Employment," [ca. 1967], box 44, Friedan Papers; Judy Heffner, "A Conversation with Barbara Bergmann," *Women's Work* (March–April 1977): 12; Brenda Eichelberger, "Feminists Argue for Job Parity," *Chicago Defender*, May 8, 1978, box, NABF Papers.

7. *Advocates for Women Newsletter* 1, no. 1 (Dec. 1972); Rebecca A. Mills to Anne L. Armstrong, July 11, 1973, box 58, Armstrong Papers; Dorothea Hernandez to Joe O'Connell, June 25, 1974, box 19, Armstrong Papers; Advocates for Women, *The California Study on Women in Nontraditional Employment* (San Francisco, 1977).

8. Wider Opportunities for Women, introductory letter, Oct. 1966, box 6, WOW Papers; WOW, "Preliminary Proposal: Jobs 70," Aug. 15, 1972, box 3, ibid.; see also Wider Opportunities for Women, *Women Offenders in Non-Traditional Work: A Report* (Washington, D.C., 1978).

9. Testimony of Jane P. Fleming, House Committee on Education and Labor, Subcommittee on Employment Opportunities, Sept. 24, 1981, box 16, WOW Papers (the lawsuit later became *Advocates for Women v. Marshall*); Advocates for Women, *California Study*, 196; Eisenberg, *We'll Call You*, 19–20, also 25. "Nontraditional" designated jobs less than 25 percent female. On Revised Order no. 4, see Department of Labor, press release, Dec. 2, 1971, box 86, Garment Papers.

10. For Labor Department funding, see All-Craft Center, "Evaluation of Training and Job Placement Program"; "Conference Agenda," *Women's Work Force Report* (1979), 4–5, box 2, WOW Papers.

11. The Committee for Women in Nontraditional Jobs, "An Interview and Dialogue with Judith Layzer and Miriam Ourin," Aug. 1, 1981, 4, box 1, Judith M. Layzer Papers, Wagner Library, New York University; Wider Opportunities for Women, "A Proposal," 7; in the South, see Louisiana Bureau for Women, *Forty-six Pioneers: Louisiana Women in Non-Traditional Jobs* (Baton Rouge, La., 1977), 1; Chris Weiss, "Appalachian Women Fight Back: Organizational Approaches to Nontraditional Jobs Advocacy," in *Fighting Back in Appalachia: Traditions of Resistance and Change*, ed. Stephen L. Fisher (Philadelphia, 1993), 152–157.

12. "Conference Agenda," *Women's Work Force Report* (1979), 4, box 2, WOW Papers.

13. Wider Opportunities for Women, *National Directory of Women's Employment Programs: Who They Are, What They Do* (Washington, D.C., 1979); Betsy Cooley et al. to Weldon J. Rougeau, Nov. 16, 1979, box 1, WOW Papers; also Women's Work Force, "New Connections," Network Conference Report (Washington, D.C., May 21–23, 1979), box 2, WOW Papers; Maureen Thornton to Betsy Cooley, Nov. 1, 1979, box 18, WOW Papers.

14. Eisenberg, *We'll Call You*, 7 (more generally, 7–36); Jean Keith Schroedel,

Alone in a Crowd: Women in the Trades Tell Their Stories (Philadelphia, 1985), 8, 10, 206; Eisenberg, *We'll Call You*, 10, 3, 13; Mark Erlich, *With Our Hands: The Story of Carpenters in Massachusetts* (Philadelphia, 1986), 217; Women Working in Construction, *Blue-Collar Trades for Women* (Washington, D.C., 1977).

15. Wider Opportunities for Women, *Working for You: A Guide to Employing Women in Non-Traditional Jobs* (Washington, D.C., 1979), 1, box 6, WOW Papers; Sylvia A. Law, "'Girls Can't Be Plumbers'—Affirmative Action for Women in Construction: Beyond Goals and Quotas," *Harvard Civil Rights–Civil Liberties Law Review* 24 (1989): 54, n. 33; Eisenberg, *We'll Call You*, 17; also Schroedel, *Alone*, 9–10; Reyes quoted in Walter Ruby, "Contractors Make It Tough for Women," *In These Times*, Sept. 9–15, 1981, box 1, UT Papers; also Paulette Jourdan and Gay Wilkinson quoted in Eisenberg, *We'll Call You*, 7, 17.

16. Kathryn B. Stechert, "The Best Jobs for Women in the '80s," *Woman's Day*, Jan. 15, 1980, box 1, UT Papers.

17. Schroedel, *Alone*, 34–35, 152, 13; Center for Women's Services, *Hard Hats, Boots, and Goggles: Jobs that Pay; A Look at Nontraditional Jobs for Women* (Kalamazoo, Mich., 1985), 11; Angelika M. Sims, "Breaking the Sex Barrier: Women in Non-Traditional Jobs," *Ebony* (Dec. 1987): 98.

18. Eisenberg, *We'll Call You*, 11, 91.

19. Laura Berman, "The Struggles of Tradeswomen," *Detroit Free Press*, Aug. 26, 1979, box 9, CLUW Records.

20. Chicago Women in Trades, *Tools for Success: A Manual for Tradeswomen* (Chicago, 1994), 19; Apprenticeship and Nontraditional Employment for Women, *Renovations: Changing Your Shape for New Forms of Work* (Renton, Wash., 1982); Atlanta YWCA, *YWCA Women in Construction News* 1 [1987]: 2, box 52, SWEC; Eisenberg, *We'll Call You*, 23, also 129–139; Martin, *Hard-Hatted Women*, 53, 102, 107, 145; Carly Lund, "Women Build Careers in Construction," in Hahn, *Frontline Feminism*, 91; Schroedel, *Alone*, 63, 152; United Tradewomen, "News Brief," n.d. [early 1982], box 1, UT Papers.

21. Andra Medea and Kathleen Thompson, *Against Rape* (New York, 1974); Pauline M. Short, *Fight Back! A Self-Defense Training Program for Women* (Portland, Ore., 1974); *Nobody's Victim* (Studio City, Calif., 1972); Py Bateman, *Fear into Anger: A Manual of Self-Defense for Women* (Chicago, 1978); *Continental Directory of Martial Arts and Self-Defense Schools and Classes for Women*, compiled by *Black Belt Women*, the magazine of women in the martial arts and self defense (Medford, Mass., 1976).

22. U.S. Department of Education, *Title IX: Twenty-five Years of Progress* (Washington, D.C., 1997).

23. Joshua B. Freeman, "Hardhats: Construction Workers, Manliness, and the 1970 Prowar Demonstrations," *Journal of Social History* 26 (Summer 1993): 725–744; Martin, *Hard-Hatted Women*, 217; Center for Women's Services, *Hard Hats*, 1; Eisenberg, *We'll Call You*, 92–93.

24. Advocates for Women, *California Study*, 192; United Tradeswomen, "News Brief," n.d., [early 1982], box 1, UT Papers; leaflet, "Construction Boom: A Bust for N.Y.C. Women," [n.d.], box 1, UT Papers; Berenice Fisher, "United Tradeswomen Going Beyond Affirmative Action," *Womanews* (March 1982), box 1, UT Papers; Atlanta YWCA, *Women in Construction News* 1 [1987]: 1, box 52, SWEC Papers.

25. Ann Ramsbotham and Pam Farmer, "Women Working: The Building Trades Begin to Open Up," *Southern Exposure* 8 (Spring 1980): 36–37; Eisenberg, *We'll Call You*, 22; Kevin Bellows and Beryl Lieff Benderly, "WOW Spells Work (Not Whistles) for Women," brochure, box 6, WOW Papers.

26. Women's Work Force, *Connections* 4 (July 1983): 2, 14, box 6, WOW Papers; Martin, *Hard-Hatted Women*, 202–211, 143–149, 63–70; Miriam Frank, "Hard Hats & Homophobia: Lesbians in the Building Trades," *New Labor Forum* 8 (Spring–Summer 2001): 25–36.

27. Martha Tabor and Nancy Murray to William Sidell et al., March 5, 1979, box 1, UT Papers.

28. Erlich, *With Our Hands*, 209–10; Martin, *Hard-Hatted Women*, 171; Eisenberg, *We'll Call You*, 26.

29. On building trades, see Chapter 3; on the 1970s, Women Working in Construction, *Blue-Collar Trades*; Erlich, *With Our Hands*, 209.

30. Center for Women's Services, *Hard Hats*, 13; Eisenberg, *We'll Call You*, 129, 39–40.

31. Jennifer Coburn, *The Herstory of San Diego County National Organization for Women: Twenty-five Years of Feminism, 1970–1995* (San Diego, Calif., 1995), 18; Eisenberg, *We'll Call You*, 66, 78, 8, 51, 137, 44, 61–62; "Trip Report," Bennington Corp., Louisville, Ky., Oct. 13, 1987, box 57, SWEC; Center for Women's Services, *Hard Hats*, 13.

32. Schroedel, *Alone in a Crowd*, 79; Chicago Women in Trades, *Breaking New Ground: Worksite 2000* (Chicago, 1992), 13, 19; Eisenberg, *We'll Call You*, 16, also 45, 63.

33. Schroedel, *Alone*, 39, also 84–85; Bellows and Benderly, "WOW Spells Work"; Eisenberg, *We'll Call You*, 21, 33, 71–73, 82–84; Erlich, *With Our Hands*, 217; Chicago Women in Trades, *Breaking New Ground*, 14.

34. Eisenberg, *We'll Call You*, 37, 79; Schroedel, *Alone*, 78, 145–146. For a tragic example, see the poem "Tell Me," in Eisenberg, *Pioneering*, 32–33.

35. Eisenberg, *We'll Call You*, 85, 47–48; Martin, *Hard-Hatted Women*, 146; Eisenberg, "Limits," in *Pioneering*, 57; Brigid O'Farrell and Sharon L. Harlan, "Craftworkers and Clerks: The Effect of Male Co-Worker Hostility on Women's Satisfaction with Non-Traditional Jobs," *Social Problems* 29 (Feb. 1982): 259; Chicago Women in Trades, *Breaking New Ground*, 16.

36. United Tradeswomen, newsletter, Feb. 1983, 1–2, box 1, UT Papers; also Martin, *Hard-Hatted Women*, 13; Eisenberg, *We'll Call You*, 142–149; Schroedel, *Alone*, 134–135, 194.

37. Schroedel, *Alone*, 109, 138–139; Eisenberg, *We'll Call You*, 58–59.

38. For early writings, see Linda Gordon, "The Politics of Sexual Harassment," *Radical America* 15 (July–Aug. 1981): 7–16; Alliance against Sexual Coercion, "Organizing against Sexual Harassment," ibid., 17–36.

39. Eisenberg, *We'll Call You*, 54, 72, 74–75, 81–82.

40. Ibid., 76, 69; Schroedel, *Alone*, 60–61.

41. Chicago Women in Trades, *Breaking New Ground*, 12; U.S. Merit Systems Protection Board, *Sexual Harassment in the Federal Workplace: Is It a Problem?* (Washington, D.C., 1981); Eisenberg, *We'll Call You*, 32, 44–45, 75; Martin, *Hard-Hatted Women*, 14. For early organizing, see United Tradeswomen, "Workshop on [Sexual] Harassment of Blue Collar Women," Nov. 22, 1981, box 1, UT Papers.

42. Schroedel, *Alone*, 20–21; Ramsbotham and Farmer, "Women Working," 36; O'Farrell and Harlan, "Craftworkers," 254, 258, 262; Brigid O'Farrell and Suzanne Moore, "Unions, Hard Hats, and Women Workers," in *Women and Unions: Forging a Partnership*, ed. Dorothy Sue Cobble (Ithaca, N.Y., 1993), 78–83; Marian Swerdlow, "Men's Accommodations to Women Entering a Nontraditional Occupation: A Case of Rapid Transit Operatives," *Gender and Society* 3 (1989): esp. 384–386; Eisenberg, *We'll Call You*, 12, 70–71, 34–35; Louisiana Bureau for Women, *Forty-six Pioneers*, 21–22.

43. Eisenberg, *We'll Call You*, 28; Schroedel, *Alone*, 117, 191, 207.

44. Eisenberg, *Pioneering*, xi.

45. Eisenberg, *We'll Call You*, 62 ; Chicago Women in Trades, *Tools*, 15–18.

46. Eisenberg, *We'll Call You*, 88; Martin, *Hard-Hatted Women*, 11; Center for Women's Services, *Hard Hats*, 13.

47. Eisenberg, *We'll Call You*, 65, 97, also 83–84; Schroedel, *Alone*, 57–58; Martin, *Hard-Hatted Women*, 222–223.

48. Schroedel, *Alone*, 39, 214; Eisenberg, *We'll Call You*, 49, 68; Martin, *Hard-Hatted Women*, 107.

49. Schroedel, *Alone*, 59, also 63, 122, 197. On how the identification could be racially exclusive, see Eisenberg, *We'll Call You*, 76.

50. Eisenberg, *We'll Call You*, 99, 53, 105, more generally, 97–107.

51. Susan Eisenberg, "Assembling a Labor Chorus," in *Pioneering*, 34; Nancy Mason and Susan Eisenberg, "Lighting Up the Trades: A Seattle Local Brings Women into the Building Trades," *Dollars & Sense*, no. 184 (March 1993): 12–15; Eisenberg, *We'll Call You*, 6, 179.

52. Eisenberg, *We'll Call You*, 96, 113, 119; United Tradeswomen, "News Brief," [1982], 1, box 1, UT Papers; Martin, *Hard-Hatted Women*, 216.

53. Schroedel, *Alone*, 40; Martin, *Hard-Hatted Women*, 153; Ann Withorn, "Helping Ourselves: The Limits and Potential of Self-Help," *Radical America* 14 (May–June 1980): 25–39.

54. Based in San Francisco, *Tradeswomen Magazine* appeared quarterly from 1981 to 1999 and served as a national forum for women in the trades. See also Martin, *Hard-Hatted Women*, 254–262; newsletters in box 1, UT Papers.

55. Eisenberg, *We'll Call You*, 1.

56. S. D. Bechtel, Jr., "Remarks to Business Council Re: Construction Industry Problems" (1970), EX BE 4, box 31, WHCF, NPMP; Business Roundtable, *Coming to Grips with Some Major Problems in the Construction Industry* (New York, 1974), 54–57.

57. Testimony of Jane Fleming, 9; Schroedel, *Alone*, 11; Cynthia Marano to "Dear Friends," Aug. 7, 1980, box 1, WOW Papers.

58. Wider Opportunities for Women, *Working for You*; Chicago Women in Trades, *Breaking New Ground*, 24; for contrast, see testimony on New York's Shiavone Construction accompanying Jane P. Fleming to William Taylor, Jan. 29, 1980, box 30, CNPR.

59. For example, WOW, *Working for You*.

60. WOW, "Background Statement for Board Use in Approach to Corporations," n.d., box 13, WOW Papers; Wider Opportunities for Women, *WOW's Nontraditional Work Programs: A Guide* (Washington, D.C., 1980), 1–2; Chicago Women in Trades, *Breaking New Ground*, 24.

61. Quoted in testimony of Jane Fleming, 9. The crucial role of federal backing recurs throughout sources of every variety.

62. See Chapters 3 and 7; WOW, "Will CETA Support Affirmative Action Programs for Women? A Background Summary," Jan. 1979, box 9, WOW Papers.

63. Barbara Ehrenreich, *The Hearts of Men: American Dreams and the Flight from Commitment* (Garden City, N.Y., 1983), 145, 159; Jane J. Mansbridge, *Why We Lost the ERA* (Chicago, 1986), 92–93.

64. Eisenberg, *We'll Call You*, 62.

65. Ibid., 3, 20, 121; Chicago Women in Trades, *Building Equal Opportunity*, 5. See also Chicago Women in Trades, *Building Equal Opportunity*, 18, 27–29; and the exhaustive report by Dennis DeLeon, *Building Barriers: A Report on Discrimination against Women and People of Color in New York City's Construction Trades* (New York, 1993).

66. See Robert H. Zieger, *American Workers, American Unions, 1920–1985* (Baltimore, 1986), 163–164, 169; Deslippe, *"Rights, Not Roses": Unions and the Rise of Working-Class Feminism* (Urbana, Ill., 2000), 8, 166–191; Foner, *Women*, 438–477; Leon Fink and Brian Greenberg, *Upheaval in the Quiet Zone: A History of Hospital Workers' Union, Local 1199* (Urbana, Ill., 1989); Paul Johnston, *Success while Others Fail: Social Movement Unionism and the Public Workplace* (Ithaca, N.Y., 1994); James O'Connor, *The Fiscal Crisis of the State* (New York, 1973); Michael Goldfield, *The Decline of Organized Labor in the United States* (Chicago, 1987).

67. Statement of the National Organization for Women on the Balanced Growth and Full Employment Act of 1976, Submitted to the House Education and Labor Committee, Subcommittee on Manpower, Compensation and Health and Safety, April 26, 1976, box 2, NOW Papers; for debate in the labor movement, see Foner, *Women*, 525–527; Peggy Combs to Nancy Perlman, May 1, 1975, box 1, AFSCME-PDD.

68. Charles V. and Dona C. Hamilton, "Social Policies, Civil Rights, and Poverty," in *Fighting Poverty: What Works and What Doesn't*, ed. Sheldon H. Danziger and Daniel H. Weinberg (Cambridge, Mass., 1986); Margaret Weir, *Politics and Jobs: The Boundaries of Employment Policy in the United States* (Princeton, 1992), xiii, 4–5, 62–98, 168, 178.

69. Kim Moody, *An Injury to All: The Decline of American Unionism* (New York, 1988), 205; Thomas Byrne Edsall, *The New Politics of Inequality* (New York, 1984), 172; Robert H. Zieger, *American Workers*, 170–192.

70. Transcript of interview with Ray Marshall, May 4, 1988, 42, Miller Center Interviews, JCPL; also Edsall, *New Politics of Inequality*, 176; Peter N. Carroll, *It Seemed Like Nothing Happened: The Tragedy and Promise of America in the 1970s* (New York, 1982), 207–232. For full employment campaign, see Marisa Chappell, "From Welfare Rights to Welfare Reform: The Politics of AFDC, 1964–1984" (Ph.D. diss., Northwestern University, 2002); Gary Mucciaroni, *The Political Failure of Full Employment Policy, 1945–1982* (Pittsburgh, 1992); and Weir, *Politics and Jobs*, 99–162. On Carter's failure to pursue an industrial policy, see Judith Stein, *Running Steel, Running America: Race, Economic Policy, and the Decline of Liberalism* (Chapel Hill, N.C., 1998).

71. *National Urban League News*, Jan. 17, 1978, box 323, White Files; also Benjamin L. Hooks to Martha Mitchell, Feb. 3, 1978, box 16, Mitchell Files.

72. Stuart Eizenstadt to Jimmy Carter, June 29, 1977, box 35, Jordan Papers;

Hamilton Jordan to Jimmy Carter, June 29, 1977, ibid.; also Thomas Ferguson and Joel Rogers, *Right Turn: The Decline of the Democrats and the Future of American Politics* (New York, 1986), 85.

73. Deslippe, *"Rights, Not Roses,"* 195; David Harvey, *The Condition of Postmodernity* (Cambridge, Mass., 1990), 173; Thomas A. Kochan et al., *The Transformation of American Industrial Relations* (New York, 1986).

74. Austin Scott, "NAACP Building Ties with Business," *LAT,* July 11, 1978, box 16, Mitchell Files; Robert Putnam, *Bowling Alone: The Collapse and Revival of American Community* (New York, 2000), 15, 55. For Mexican American parallel, see Ignacio M. García, *Hector P. García: In Relentless Pursuit of Justice* (Houston, 2002), 294–295.

75. *Annual Report* (1980), box 6, Series: Annual Reports, PRLDEF. For their felt need to turn to corporate funding for survival, see Jack John Olivero to Thomas Wahman, Jan. 13, 1975, box 213, Rockefeller Records; Siobhan Oppenheimer-Nicolau to Lou Winnick, Sept. 2, 1981, box 9, Nicolau Papers.

76. I regret the need for such harsh characterization, but the record makes it inescapable. See, for example, Tony Bonilla to Santana Gonzalez, July 12, 1982, box 8, RB-GC; Tony Bonilla to Jesse Aquirre, Dec. 14, 1981, ibid.; on Jackson and PUSH, see Tony Bonilla to Ruben Bonilla, Jr., Aug. 2, 1983, with attachment, box 14, ibid.; Bob Walsdorf to Luke Meatte, Aug. 31, 1982, with attachment, ibid.

77. Putnam, *Bowling Alone,* 63, 158.

78. Putnam, *Bowling Alone,* 27.

79. Theda Skocpol, "Associations without Members," *American Prospect* (July–Aug. 1999): 66, 68–69; Skocpol, *Diminished Democracy: From Memberships to Management in American Civic Life* (Norman, Okla., 2003); John D. McCarthy and Mayer Zald, *The Trend of Social Movements in America: Professionalization and Resource Mobilization* (Morristown, N.J., 1973); Benjamin Márquez, *LULAC: The Evolution of a Mexican American Political Organization* (Austin, 1993), esp. 72, 109; Juan Gómez-Quiñones, *Chicano Politics: Reality and Promise, 1940–1990* (Albuquerque, 1990), 181; Judith Sealander and Dorothy Smith, "The Rise and Fall of Feminist Organizations in the 1970s: Dayton as a Case Study," in *Women, Class, and the Feminist Imagination,* ed. Karen V. Hansen and Ilene J. Philipson (Philadelphia, 1990), 249.

80. Debra C. Minkoff, *Organizing for Equality: The Evolution of Women's and Racial-Ethnic Organizations in America, 1955–1985* (New Brunswick, N.J., 1995).

81. Roberta Spalter-Roth and Ronnee Schreiber, "Outsider Issues and Insider Tactics: Strategic Tensions in the Women's Policy Network during the 1980s," in *Feminist Organizations: Harvest of the New Women's Movement,* ed. Myra Marx Ferree and Patricia Yancey Martin (Philadelphia, 1995), 106. The approach that posits cooptation, note Janet Gornick and David Meyer, "neglects both the real achievements that such bargains can entail, and the actual difficulties of mobilizing in the wake of success." Janet C. Gornick and David S. Meyer, "Changing Political Opportunity: The Anti-rape Movement and Public Policy," *Journal of Policy History* 10 (1998): 373, 393; also Putnam, *Bowling Alone,* 159–160.

82. Mitchell Sviridoff to Franklin A. Thomas, Oct. 24, 1980, 8, box 8, Nicolau Papers; Siobhan Oppenheimer-Nicolau to Lou Winnick, Sept. 2, 1981, box 9, ibid.; Siobhan Oppenheimer-Nicolau to Frank Thomas, Oct. 10, 1980, 17, box 1, ibid.; Louis Winnick to Franklin A. Thomas, "Program Review: Civil Rights," Dec. 29,

1980, 13, ibid. See also Gornick and Meyer, "Changing Political Opportunity," 386–390; Alice O'Connor, *Poverty Knowledge: Social Science, Social Policy, and the Poor in Twentieth-Century U.S. History* (Princeton, 2001).

83. See, for example, Spalter-Roth and Schreiber, "Outsider Issues," 117; Erlich, *With Our Hands*, 211; Thomas W. Wahman to RBF Files, Jan. 24, 1975, with attachment, box 213, Rockefeller Records; Sealander and Smith, "Rise and Fall," 249–250; Christine Marie Sierra, "The Political Transformation of a Minority Organization: The Council of La Raza, 1965–1980" (Ph.D. diss., Stanford University, 1983). For essential reading on the impact of government contracting, see Steven Rathgeb Smith and Michael Lipsky, *Nonprofits for Hire: The Welfare State in the Age of Contracting* (Cambridge, Mass., 1993), esp. 206–232. For later use of contracts to discipline dissent, see Elizabeth Dole to the Vice President, July 15, 1981; Henry Zuniga to Dole, Nov. 4, 1981; and Dole to Edwin Meese III, July 29, 1981, all box 5455, Dole Papers.

84. Dewey quoted in Putnam, *Bowling Alone*, 116; Board of Directors, minutes, Dec. 1, 1983, box 3, Series: Minutes, PRLDEF; *Nuestro* 8 (March 1984): 19–21, box 3, PRLDEF.

85. All-Craft Center, "Evaluation of Training and Job Placement Program for Economically Disadvantaged Women in Non-Traditional (Skilled Trades) Work," [n.d.], box 1, UT Papers; Law, "'Girls Can't Be Plumbers,'" 45, 53; "Trip Report," Louisville, Oct. 13, 1987, box 57, SWEC.

86. Wider Opportunities for Women, "Meeting [of seven women's groups] with Secretary of Labor Raymond J. Donovan," Aug. 26, 1981, box 16, WOW Papers. See also "WOW Leads Women from Welfare to Wages," *Capital Spotlight*, April 23, 1987, 9, box 25, ibid.

87. Wider Opportunities for Women, *Women Offenders*; Wider Opportunities for Women, *WOW's Nontraditional Work Programs*, epilogue; Eisenberg, *We'll Call You*, 5, 205.

88. Alice Echols, *Daring to Be Bad: Radical Feminism in America, 1967–1975* (Minneapolis, 1989), 203; Joreen [Jo Freeman], "Trashing: The Dark Side of Sisterhood," *Ms.* (April 1976): 49–51, 92–98, and ensuing letters; Barbara Epstein, "'Political Correctness' and Collective Powerlessness," in *Cultural Politics and Social Movements*, ed. Marcy Darnovksy, Barbara Epstein, and Richard Flacks (Philadelphia, 1995), 3–19. On factional fighting that paralyzed NOW for three years in the mid-1970s, see Winifred D. Wandersee, *On the Move: American Women in the 1970s* (Boston, 1988), 49–54.

89. Women's Work Force, *Connections* 4 (July 1983): 2, 14, box 6, WOW Papers; Gale Feinstein, "What about Whites? A Worksheet on Racism," *United Tradeswomen Newsletter* (Feb. 1983): 5–8, 9; United Tradewomen, "News Brief," n.d. [1982]; Eisenberg, *We'll Call You*, 116.

90. Wendy, for the Homophobia Workshop Coordinating Committee, to Staff and Steering Committee, Aug. 15, 1986, box 36, SWEC; Leslie Lilly, "On Being Who I Wish to Become," n.d., box 39, ibid.; "Flip Charts from Marydale, Oct. 14–18, 1986, Steering Committee Meeting," box 4, ibid.; [Mary Reynolds Babcock], "Staff Workplan on '85 Program Goals," May 30, 1985, box 39, ibid.; Weiss, "Appalachian Women," 160.

91. Tim Kraft to Phil Wise, July 7, 1978, with attachment, Confidential File,

box TR-19, WHCF, JCPL; Sheila Rowbotham, *The Past Is before Us: Feminism in Action since the 1960s* (Boston, 1989), 169–177; Edsall, *New Politics of Inequality*, 163, also 142; Zieger, *American Workers*, 182; Putnam, *Bowling Alone*, 80–92, 358–60. For how labor's default made the movements "more conservative, less oriented toward the welfare of average workers, and much more vulnerable to business/foundation decisions on what, where, and how much to fund," see Ferguson and Rogers, *Right Turn*, 64.

92. For a start on the vast literature regarding the rightward shift of the courts and the challenges it poses for progressives, see Lani Guinier and Gerald Torres, *The Miner's Canary: Enlisting Race, Resisting Power, Transforming Democracy* (Cambridge, Mass., 2002).

93. Martin, *Hard-Hatted Women*, 223; Eisenberg, "Pioneering (for the tradeswomen of '78)," in *Pioneering*, 4–5. As notable as their abandonment by others is the endurance of many tradeswomen and some allies. See NOW Legal Defense and Education Fund and Association for Union Democracy, Women's Project, *Manual for Survival for Women in Nontraditional Employment* (New York, 1993), and *http://www.tradeswomennow.org/*.

94. Spalter-Roth and Schreiber, "Outsider Issues," 126.

9. The Struggle for Inclusion since the Reagan Era

1. Speech to Conservative Political Action Dinner, March 20, 1981, box 1, Presidential Handwriting File, RRPL; on attendance, see *NYT*, March 21, 1981, A9; James L. Buckley to Ronald W. Reagan, Nov. 6, 1980, Alphabetical File, s.v. Buckley, RRPL. On Reagan's wing of the GOP, see William A. Rusher, *The Rise of the Right* (New York, 1984). It bears noting that myriad pertinent documents in the Reagan Library have been closed to researchers. What appears here is the tip of an iceberg that may someday come to light if court challenges succeed in contesting the peculiar and unprecedented secrecy of recent GOP administrations.

2. Robert Pear, "Goals for Hiring Split Reagan Aides," *NYT*, Oct. 23, 1985, A1, B5; "Administration Ignites New Conflict over Affirmative Action Enforcement," *CQ*, Oct. 19, 1985, OA: 18389, Kruger Files.

3. Robert Pear, "Rights Groups Assail Hiring Change Drafted by Reagan Aides," *NYT*, Aug. 16, 1985, B4; "Administration Ignites New Conflict on Affirmative Action Enforcement," *CQ*, Oct. 19, 1985, OA: 18389, Kruger Files; Howard Kurtz, "Minority Hiring Battle Illustrates Policy Stalemate," *WP*, Jan. 11, 1986, OA: 18389, Kruger Files; for 1985 poll data, see Ralph G. Neas to Members of the Press, Jan. 15, 1986, HU-010: 399315, WHORM; Paul M. Sniderman and Thomas Piazza, *The Scar of Race* (Cambridge, Mass., 1993).

4. Linda Chavez to Donald Regan and Patrick Buchanan, Aug. 14, 1985, HU-010: 579086, WHORM; Steven A. Shull, *A Kinder, Gentler Racism? The Reagan-Bush Civil Rights Legacy* (London, 1993), 40.

5. Kurtz, "Minority Hiring Battle."

6. Shull, *Kinder, Gentler Racism?* 4; for Republican gloating, see William French Smith, *Law and Justice in the Reagan Administration: The Memoirs of an Attorney General* (Stanford, 1991), esp. 89–90.

7. Barbara R. Bergmann, *The Economic Emergence of Women* (New York, 1986), 302, also 8. "Voluntary goals" became an explicit compromise strategy when

Reagan advisers "sharply divided" over whether to terminate Executive Order 11246. Gerald M. Boyd, "Accord in Cabinet Reported on Plan on Minority Jobs," *NYT*, Jan. 11, 1986, clipping in PQ: 382608, WHORM.

8. John B. Rhinelander to Caspar W. Weinberger, Nov. 26, 1980, s.v. Reynolds, William B., Alphabetical File, RRPL; résumé of William Bradford Reynolds, ibid.; John B. Rhinelander to James H. Cavanaugh, Jan. 13, 1981, ibid.; *Current Biography* (1988), s.v. Reynolds, William Bradford, 476–479; Drew S. Days III, "Turning Back the Clock: The Reagan Administration and Civil Rights," *Harvard Civil Rights—Civil Liberties Law Review* 19 (1984): 313, 318.

9. "Battle Heats Up over Sex, Race Bias in Jobs," *U.S. News & World Report*, May 27, 1985, 49; George Gilder, "The Myths of Racial and Sexual Discrimination," *NR*, Nov. 14, 1980, 1381, 1385. Gilder insisted that biological "differences between the sexes fully explain all gaps in earnings" (1389). Quotes also from his "Battling the Racial Spoils System," *Newsweek*, June 10, 1985, 96; see also Gilder, *Wealth and Poverty* (New York, 1981), 128–139. For Reagan's enthusiasm, see *Current Biography* (1981), s.v. Gilder, George, 166, 169. The idea that discrimination against blacks no longer exists and that whites are today's victims pervades conservative writing. For other examples, see Harvey Mansfield, "The Underhandedness of Affirmative Action," *NR*, May 4, 1984, 26–32, 61; Jim Buchanan, *Reverse Discrimination: A Resource Guide* (Monticello, Ill., 1985), esp. 1–3.

10. William Bradford Reynolds, *Toward Freedom and Dignity: Understanding the Misunderstandings about Affirmative Action* (Washington, D.C., 1989), 11, 6; also Reynolds, "The Justice Department's Enforcement of Title VII," *Labor Law Journal* 34 (May 1983): 259–265.

11. Washington Council of Lawyers, "Reagan Civil Rights: The First Twenty Months,"108 ["embargoed," Sept. 15, 1982], HU-010: 077500 CA, WHORM; Quentin Crommelin, Jr., to Vilma Martinez, June 16, 1981, 12, 25 of attached transcript, box 348, series 9, MALDEF; *Current Biography* (1982), s.v. Hatch, Orrin G., 144–148; Orrin G. Hatch to Ronald Reagan [hereafter RR], July 22, 1981, HU-012: 034758, WHORM; Hatch to RR, March 29, 1982, HU-012: 068820, WHORM.

12. Chester E. Finn, Jr., "'Affirmative Action' under Reagan," *Commentary* (April 1982): 17–28, which Reynolds praised as "'must' reading" and "absolutely correct" to Elizabeth Dole, April 26, 1982, box 1, Dole Files; Washington Council of Lawyers, "Reagan Civil Rights," esp. 106–107; Days, "Turning Back the Clock," 309, 347, 343.

13. Pear, "Rights Groups Assail," B4; Nathan Perlmutter to RR, Oct. 23, 1985, PQ: 339364, WHORM; Thomas C. Dawson to Al Kingon, Nov. 5, 1985, with attachment, HU-012: 381898, WHORM. More than a third of the eighteen groups in the coalition were construction contractors. Richard L. Lesher to Alfred H. Kingon, Nov. 25, 1985, PQ: 339394, WHORM.

14. Pat Buchanan to Miro Todorovich, Feb. 15, 1986, with attachment, PQ: 382608, WHORM; Howard L. Hurwitz, Professors for Academic Order, to RR, Sept. 8, 1986, OA: 18389, Kruger Files; John Pecoraro to Pat Buchanan, Aug. 18, 1985, PQ: 357071, WHORM. See also the editorials "Reynolds's Inquisition," *NR*, July 12, 1985, 18, and "A-K-A Quotas," *NR*, Dec. 13, 1985, 14.

15. Hubert Beatty to Linda Chavez, Aug. 26, 1985, HU-012: 343298, WHORM. For a sample of other letters, see Perry L. Nations to RR, Aug. 16,

1985, PQ: 327849; Charles E. Stevens, Jr., to RR, Dec. 5, 1985, PQ: 354499; and William J. Keogh to RR, Aug. 26, 1985, PQ: 328196, all WHORM.

16. James M. Rowell to Edwin Meese, Jan. 18, 1983, HU-010: 121772, WHORM; Nick Durastanti, Jr., to Patrick Buchanan, Feb. 11, 1986, HU-010: 397444, WHORM; Harris Saunders, Jr., to RR, Nov. 1, 1985, PQ: 350942, WHORM.

17. "Blacks Urge Reagan to Save Affirmative Action," *Jet*, Sept. 9, 1985, 4; "Battle Heats Up," 49; Franklin E. Breckenridge to RR, Aug. 23, 1985, HU-012: 328084, WHORM; Herbert J. Henderson to RR, Dec. 6, 1985, PQ: 354575, WHORM; John E. Jacob to RR, Nov. 27, 1985, PQ: 354055, WHORM; Julian Dixon et al. to RR, Aug. 21, 1985, HU-012: 327997, WHORM; Ralph G. Neas to Alfred H. Kingon, Feb. 12, 1986, PQ: 339421, WHORM.

18. Walter E. Fauntroy to RR, Aug. 20, 1985, HU-010: 328061, WHORM; John Conyers to Donald T. Regan, Oct. 23, 1985, PQ: 358668, WHORM; Frederick J. Ryan, Jr., to Clarence M. Mitchell, Oct. 2, 1985, HU-010: 328446, WHORM; Norman Hill to RR, Sept. 21, 1985, HU-012: 342317, WHORM; Pear, "Rights Groups Assail," B4.

19. Oscar Moran to RR, Oct. 23, 1985, PQ: 350359, WHORM; Esteban E. Torres et al. to RR, Nov. 20, 1985, PQ: 369076, WHORM; also Reinaldo A. Cardona to RR, Aug. 26, 1985, HU-010: 328481, WHORM.

20. Pear, "Rights Groups Assail," B4; Women's Action Alliance, "U.S. National Women's Agenda—1975," in *The Female Experience: An American Documentary*, ed. Gerda Lerner (Indianapolis, 1977), 458–462. For a White House insider's description of "a broad coalition of public interest groups, led by women's organizations, [who] are unalterably opposed to the changes," see Mel Bradley to Ed Harper, July 22, 1983, HU-010: 172991PD, WHORM.

21. Dorothy S. Ridings to Donald T. Regan, Sept. 27, 1985, PQ: 359198, WHORM; Sandra Porter to RR, Sept. 30, 1985, PQ: 340689, WHORM; Anne Steinbeck and Irma Finn Brosseau to RR, Aug. 29, 1985, HU-010: 328444, WHORM.

22. Lenard M. Black to Melvin Bradley, Oct. 30, 1985, FE-003: 369203, WHORM; Milton Bins to RR, Feb. 11, 1986, PQ: 375914, WHORM; also *Jet*, Nov. 11, 1985, 4.

23. Alan J. Dixon et al. to RR, Nov. 25, 1985, HU-012: 352920, WHORM; for listing of congressional opponents, see Ralph G. Neas to Members of the Press, Jan. 15, 1986, HU-010: 399315, WHORM; Augustus F. Hawkins and James M. Jeffords et al. to RR, Sept. 17, 1985, PQ: 346140, WHORM; Robert Stafford et al. to RR, Nov. 25, 1985, HU-012: 352920, WHORM; John C. Danforth to RR, Oct. 21, 1985, HU-012: 357542, WHORM; Pear, "Goals for Hiring," A1, B5.

24. Linda Chavez to Donald Regan and Patrick Buchanan, Aug. 14, 1985, HU-010: 579086, WHORM; Mary Fainsod Katzenstein, *Faithful and Fearless: Moving Feminist Protest inside the Church and Military* (Princeton, 1998); Bernice Resnick Sandler, interview, Nov. 18, 1985, 11–12, 47, AJC-OH; Bert Gold to Elmer Winter, June 10, 1974, Bertram H. Gold Papers [hereafter Gold Papers], box 212, AJCA. (Box 212 contains many examples of the feminist challenge.)

25. Sam Rabinove to Bertram H. Gold, June 14, 1976, box 187, Gold Papers, AJCA; Harry Fleischman to Members of the Affirmative Action Committee, July 19, 1979, s.v. "Preferential Treatment," Vertical File, AJCA; Jonathan S. Woocher,

"American Jewish Political Activism in the 1980s: Five Dilemmas," *Jerusalem Letter*, no. 30 (July 1, 1980), included with Stuart E. Eizenstat to Philip Klutznick, Nov. 2, 1980, Confidential File, box HU-1, WHCF, JCPL; Marc D. Stern, "Affirmative Action, the Law and the Jews," in *Survey of Jewish Affairs*, ed. William Frankel (London, 1990), 143, also 148, 157.

26. Howard I. Friedman to RR, Aug. 15, 1985, PQ: 328243, WHORM; Theodore R. Mann to RR, Aug. 26, 1985, PQ: 340786, WHORM; Hyman Bookbinder to Ralph Neas, Oct. 31, 1985, box 21, series 2, LCCR.

27. Maurice E. Culver and Dr. Yvonne Delk to RR, Aug. 16, 1985, PQ: 328017, WHORM.

28. Robert H. Atwell to RR, Sept. 18, 1985, HU-012: 340261, WHORM; Paul H. L. Walter to RR, Aug. 29, 1985, HU-010: 328526, WHORM; Sarah Harder to RR, Aug. 21, 1985, PQ: 328076, WHORM; Frank H. T. Hodes to RR, Dec. 2, 1985, PQ: 354331, WHORM; John E. Worthen to RR, HU-012: 340347, WHORM.

29. William Lucy and Gerald W. McEntee to RR, Oct. 4, 1985, PQ: 340736, WHORM; Charles A. Perlik, Jr., to RR, Dec. 3, 1985, PQ: 354287, WHORM; William H. Bywater to RR, Aug. 23, 1985, PQ: 328140, WHORM; Anna Padia in "Roundtable on Pay Equity and Affirmative Action," in *Women and Unions: Forging a Partnership*, ed. Dorothy Sue Cobble (Ithaca, N.Y., 1993), 63–66; Joyce D. Miller to RR, Sept. 4, 1985, PQ: 338213, WHORM; Pear, "Rights Groups Assail," B4; Fred Wertheimer to RR, Feb. 5, 1986, PQ: 374933, WHORM; also Sharon Simon, "The Survival of Affirmative Action in the 1980s," *Labor Studies Journal* 10 (Winter 1986): 277.

30. Patrick J. Campbell to RR, Sept. 17, 1985, PQ: 340181, WHORM; also, from the California State Council of Carpenters, Anthony L. Ramos to RR, April 14, 1986, PG: 389912, WHORM. For courtship of blue-collar voters, see Jack Burgess to Elizabeth H. Dole, April 6, 1982, box 6388, Dole Papers; Ronald Reagan, speech to Building and Construction Trades Department of AFL-CIO, March 30, 1981, box 1, series 2, Presidential Handwriting File, RRPL.

31. Linda Chavez to Donald Regan and Patrick Buchanan, Aug. 14, 1985, HU-010: 579086, WHORM.

32. James E. Burke to Donald T. Regan, Nov. 19, 1985, PQ: 369741, WHORM; Alexander B. Trowbridge to RR, Nov. 27, 1985, PQ: 354230, WHORM; "Administration Ignites," 4; "The New Rights War," *Newsweek*, Dec. 30, 1985, 86; Anne B. Fisher, "Businessmen Like to Hire by the Numbers," *Fortune*, Sept. 16, 1985, 26.

33. Gary L. Lubben et al., "Performance Appraisal: The Legal Implications of Title VII," *Personnel* 57 (May–June 1980): 20; Alan Farnham, "Holding Firm on Affirmative Action," *Fortune* 13 (March 1989): 87–88; on lawsuits, see Jonathon S. Leonard, "The Impact of Affirmative Action Regulation and Equal Employment Law on Black Employment," *Journal of Economic Perspectives* 44 (1990): 60.

34. Simon, "Survival," 262. For the refusal of administration officials to believe evidence from studies they had funded, see Edwin L. Harper to Edwin Meese III, July 27, 1983, HU-010: 153548, WHORM. For the "unanimous" internal view that the administration "should move away" from any empirical gauge of "doing a good job" in this area to protect the president, see Michael M. Uhlmann to Edwin L Harper, Jan. 5, 1983, HU-010: 102897, WHORM.

35. *BusinessWeek*, Sept. 2, 1985, 41; Pear, "Rights Groups Assail," B4.

36. Jeremiah O'Leary, "Regan May Referee Quota Fight," *Washington Times* [March 1986], PQ: 500980, WHORM; Pear, "Goals for Hiring"; Ralph G. Neas to Members of the Press, Jan. 15, 1986, HU-010: 399315, WHORM; "The New Rights War," *Newsweek*, Dec. 30, 1985, 66.

37. Kurtz, "Minority Hiring Battle"; address to Conservative Political Action Conference, Jan. 30, 1986, 4, box 22, series 2, Presidential Handwriting File, RRPL.

38. *Current Biography Yearbook*, s.v. Pendleton, Clarence M(cLane), Jr. (1984), 316–320; Michael Fumento, "Clarence Pendleton, RIP," *NR*, July 8, 1988, 18; Nathan Glazer et al., "Clarence's Critics," *New Republic*, 194 (June 9, 1986): 6; and, more generally, Angela D. Dillard, *Guess Who's Coming to Dinner Now? Multicultural Conservatism in America* (New York, 2001).

39. "Reagan Contradicted on Civil Rights Enforcement," *WP*, Sept. 28, 1982, HU-010: 097774, WHORM; Clarence Thomas, "Current Litigation Trends and Goals at the EEOC," *Labor Law Journal* 34 (April 1983): 208–215, esp. 212; Clarence Thomas, "Affirmative Action Goals and Timetables: Too Tough? Not Tough Enough!" reprinted in *Debating Affirmative Action*, ed. Nicholaus Mills (New York, 1994), 93–94, 97.

40. Clarence Thomas, "Why Black Americans Should Look to Conservative Policies," in *The Heritage Lectures* (Washington, D.C., 1987), 5.

41. M. V. Lee Badgett and Heidi L. Hartmann, "Effectiveness of Equal Employment Opportunity Policies," in *Economic Perspectives on Affirmative Action*, ed. Margaret C. Simms (Washington, D.C., 1995), 63; see also Institute for Women's Policy Research, "Affirmative Action in Employment: An Overview," briefing paper (Washington, D.C., [1995]).

42. Milton Coleman, "Administration Asks Blacks to Fend for Themselves," *WP* (undated clipping), box 69, CNPR; Days, "Turning Back the Clock," 309, 318, 347, 343 n. 168; Simon, "Survival," esp. 269–275. For a case study documenting Reagan administration fallacies, see Gary Orfield and Carole Ashkinaze, *The Closing Door: Conservative Policy and Economic Opportunity* (Chicago, 1991).

43. Leonard, "Impact," 58; Jonathon S. Leonard, "The Impact of Affirmative Action on Employment," *Journal of Labor Economics* 2 (1984), 460; Leonard, "Employment and Occupational Advance under Affirmative Action," *Review of Economics and Statistics* 66 (1984): 377–388; Leonard, "What Promises Are Worth: The Impact of Affirmative Action Goals," *Journal of Human Resources* 20 (1985), 3–20; Herbert Hammerman, *A Decade of New Opportunity: Affirmative Action in the 1970s* (Washington, D.C., 1984); Richard B. Freeman, "Black Economic Progress after 1964: Who Has Gained and Why?" in *Studies in Labor Markets*, ed. Sherwin Rosen (Chicago, 1981), esp. 281–283; John Bound and Richard B. Freeman, "What Went Wrong? The Erosion of Relative Earnings and Employment among Young Black Men in the 1980s," Working Paper no. 3778 (Cambridge, Mass., 1991).

44. Simon, "Survival," 261; Heidi Hartmann in "Roundtable on Pay Equity and Affirmative Action," 44–45; Francine D. Blau and Andrea H. Beller, "Trends in Earnings Differentials by Gender, 1971–1981," *Industrial and Labor Relations Review* 41 (July 1988): 513–529.

45. See *Alternative Press Index*, which recorded at least twenty to thirty articles a year on the subject through most of the 1980s.

46. Opinion of Justice Powell, *Regents of the University of California v. Bakke*,

U.S. Supreme Court (1977), 265, 305, 307, 311–313 (emphasis added), 317. On the consequences of Powell's ruling, see also Avery Gordon, "The Work of Corporate Culture: Diversity Management," *Social Text* 44 (Fall–Winter 1995): 24–25 n. 12; Nicholas Lemann, "The Empathy Defense," *New Yorker,* Dec. 18, 2000, esp. 50.

47. Hugh Davis Graham, *Collision Course: The Strange Convergence of Affirmative Action and Immigration Policy in America* (New York, 2002), 192.

48. R. Roosevelt Thomas, Jr., "From Affirmative Action to Affirming Diversity," *Harvard Business Review* (March–April 1990): 107–117; also Erin Kelly and Frank Dobbin, "How Affirmative Action Became Diversity Management: Employer Response to Antidiscrimination Law, 1961–1996," *American Behavioral Scientist* 41 (April 1998): 973, 977, 979.

49. William B. Johnston and Arnold E. Packer, *Workforce 2000: Work and Workers for the Twenty-first Century* (Indianapolis, 1987); The Conference Board, *In Diversity Is Strength: Capitalizing on the New Work Force* (New York, 1992); Mary J. Winterle, *Work Force Diversity: Corporate Challenges, Corporate Responses* (New York, 1992), 9; Michael L. Wheeler, *Diversity Training* (New York, 1994), 7; listing of "diversity leaders" at *www.fortune.com;* "Merrill Lynch Offers Portfolio Based on Diversity," Jan. 15, 1998, *www.mbnglobal.com/merrill_lynch.htm.//enottxt.*

50. Lawrence Perlman, "Turning Diversity into Opportunity," in Conference Board, *In Diversity,* 15–16; Kelly and Dobbin, "How Affirmative Action," 960–984.

51. Wheeler, *Diversity Training,* 7; Richard D. McCormick, "Making Sure Diversity Works at US West," in Conference Board, *In Diversity Is Strength,* 13–15.

52. Alfred W. Blumrosen, "How the Courts are Handling Reverse Discrimination Claims," in Bureau of National Affairs, *Daily Labor Report* 56 (March 23, 1995), 1; William L. Taylor, *"Brown,* Equal Protection, and the Isolation of the Poor," *Yale Law Journal* 95 (1986): 1704–5, 1707; Thomas F. Pettigrew, "Race and Class in the 1980s: An Interactive View," *Daedalus* 110 (1981): esp. 240, also 238–239, 244–245; Pettigrew, "New Patterns of Racism: The Different Worlds of 1964 and 1984," *Rutgers Law Review* 37 (1985): 677; Richard B. Freeman, *Black Elite: the New Market for Highly Educated Black Americans: A Report Prepared for the Carnegie Commission on Higher Education* (New York, 1976), 2, also xix–xx; personal narratives in Henry Louis Gates, Jr., *America behind the Color Line: Dialogues with African Americans* (New York, 2004).

53. Jonathan D. Glater, "Women Are Close to Being Majority of Law Students," *NYT,* March 26, 2001, A1, 16; Institute for Women's Policy Research, *Restructuring Work: How Have Women and Minority Managers Fared?* (Washington, D.C., 1995); Tamar Lewin, "Study Says More Women Earn Half Their Household Income," *NYT,* May 11, 1995, A13; Francine D. Blau, "Trends in the Well-Being of American Women, 1970–1995," *Journal of Economic Literature* 36 (March 1998): esp. 160–161.

54. Gordon, "Work of Corporate Culture," 16, 21; Wayne E. Hedien, "Managing Diversity: A Full-Time, Top-Down Commitment," in Conference Board, *In Diversity,* 11; Perlman, "Turning Diversity into Opportunity," 15.

55. See, for example, Exhibit 1 in Winterle, *Work Force Diversity,* 34; also Lauren B. Edelman, Sally Riggs Fuller, and Iona Mara-Drita, "Diversity Rhetoric and the Marginalization of Law," *AJS* 106 (May 2001): 1589–1641.

56. Wheeler, *Diversity Training,* 8; Jim Braham, "No, You *Don't* Manage Everyone the Same," *Industry Week* 238 (Feb. 6, 1989): quote on 28.

57. William Kristol quoted in Eric Foner, "Hiring Quotas for White Males

Only," *Nation*, June 26, 1995, 924; Bob Herbert, "Workaday Racism," *NYT*, Nov. 11, 1996, A11; Kurt Eichenwald, "The Two Faces of Texaco," *NYT*, Nov. 11, 1996, sec. 3, 1, 10–11; Howard Kohn, "Service with a Sneer," *NYT Magazine*, Nov. 6, 1994, 43–81; Steve Watkins, *The Black O: Racism and Redemption in an American Corporate Empire* (Athens, Ga., 1999); Steven Greenhouse, "Abercrombie & Fitch Bias Case Is Settled," *NYT*, Nov. 17, 2004, A12.

58. "The Not-Quite-Melted Pot," *NYT*, July 28, 1996, section 5, 5; Tom Squitieri, "Affirmative Action Still Divides Races," *USA Today*, Sept. 22, 1989, 2A; Howard Fineman, "Race and Rage," *Newsweek*, April 3, 1995, 25, 34.

59. Marjorie Austin Turner et al., *Opportunities Denied, Opportunities Diminished: Racial Discrimination in Hiring*, Urban Institute Report 91–99 (Washington, D.C., 1991), 61; Walter Goodman, "In St. Louis, the Camera Looks Racism in the Eye," *NYT*, Sept. 26, 1991, B5.

60. Joleen Kirschenman and Kathryn M. Neckerman, "'We'd Love to Hire Them, But . . .': The Meaning of Race for Employers," in *The Urban Underclass*, ed. Christopher Jencks and Paul E. Peterson (Washington, D.C., 1991), 204, 207; Devah Pager, "The Mark of a Criminal Record," *AJS* 108 (2003): 937–975; also William Julius Wilson, *When Work Disappears: The World of the New Urban Poor* (New York, 1996), 111–146.

61. Glater, "Women Are Close," A1, 16; Helen Rheem, "Equal Opportunity for Women: The Verdict Is (Still) Mixed," *Harvard Business Review* 74 (July–Aug. 1996): 12–13; Anne E. Preston, "Why Have All the Women Gone? A Study of Exit of Women from the Science and Engineering Professions," *American Economic Review* 84 (Dec. 1994): 1446–62; Patrick McGeehan, "Wall Street Highflier to Outcast: A Woman's Story," *NYT*, Feb. 10, 2002, C1.

62. Rebecca M. Blank, *It Takes a Nation: A New Agenda for Fighting Poverty* (New York, 1997), esp. 69–70; also Leslie McCall, "Gender and the New Inequality: Explaining the College/Non-College Wage Gap," *American Sociological Review* 65 (April 2000): 234–255.

63. Women Employed, *Two Sides of the Coin: A Study of the Wage Gap between Men and Women in the Chicago Metropolitan Area* (Chicago, 1994), 14; Francine D. Blau, "Gender and Economic Outcomes: The Role of Wage Structure," *Labour* (1993): 73–92, quote on 85; Margaret Hallock, "Unions and the Gender Wage Gap," in Cobble, *Women and Unions*, esp. 28–32.

64. Francine D. Blau and Lawrence M. Kahn, "Understanding International Differences in the Gender Pay Gap," National Bureau of Economic Research Working Paper no. W8200 (April 2001), quote on 4, also 7, 34–36; Lewin, "Study Says More Women," A13. On union contracts as responsible for "most of the progress toward pay equity," see Jean Ross in "Roundtable on Pay Equity and Affirmative Action," 50.

65. Speech by Vilma Martinez, "The Impact of Reaganomics on the Vitality of EEO/AAP," Aerospace Industry Equal Opportunity Committee, Feb. 16, 1982, 10, box 37, RG 2, MALDEF.

66. Joan Steinau Lester, *Eleanor Holmes Norton: Fire in My Soul* (New York, 2003), 231; Jerome M. Culp, "A New Employment Policy for the 1980s: Learning from the Victories and Defeats of Twenty Years of Title VII," *Rutgers Law Review* 37 (Summer 1985): 894. On how conservative foundations funded ideas to reshape debate while liberal ones funded social services or scholarship with no action agenda, see Jean Stefancic and Richard Delgado, *No Mercy: How Conservative Think*

Tanks and Foundations Changed America's Social Agenda (Philadelphia, 1996), esp. 140–157.

67. Wilson, *When Work Disappears*, xiii; on job losses, see Arthur A. Fletcher, "When Industry Goes South," *Ebony* (Aug. 1971): 168–172, esp. 169; Thomas J. Sugrue, *The Origins of the Urban Crisis: Race and Inequality in Postwar Detroit* (Princeton, 1996); Eric Arnesen, *Brotherhoods of Color: Black Railroad Workers in the Struggle for Equality* (Cambridge, Mass., 2001), esp. 232, 238, 249–250; Ruth Milkman, *Farewell to the Factory: Auto Workers in the Late Twentieth Century* (Berkeley, 1997); Roger Horowitz, *"Negro and White, Unite and Fight!" A Social History of Industrial Unionism in Meatpacking, 1930–90* (Urbana, Ill., 1997), esp. 245–279; Timothy J. Minchin, *The Color of Work: The Struggle for Civil Rights in the Southern Paper Industry, 1945–1980* (Chapel Hill, N.C., 2001), esp. 214; Mary Margaret Fonow, *Union Women: Forging Feminism in the United Steelworkers of America* (Minneapolis, 2003), esp. 7. For how blacks get locked out of jobs even when they are available, see Roger Waldinger, *Still the Promised City? African-Americans and New Immigrants in Postindustrial New York* (Cambridge, Mass., 1996).

68. William Julius Wilson in "Who Will Help the Black Man? A Symposium Moderated by Bob Herbert," *NYT Magazine*, Dec. 6, 1994, 74.

69. David Remnick, "Dr. Wilson's Neighborhood," *New Yorker*, April 29–May 6, 1996, 98; Freeman, *Black Elite*, 151–174.

70. Of the vast literature, see, for example, William H. Chafe, "The End of One Struggle, The Beginning of Another," in *The Civil Rights Movement in America*, ed. Charles W. Eagles (Jackson, Miss., 1986), 127–71; Freeman, "Black Economic Progress after 1964," 247–294; also Freeman, *Black Elite*, esp. 88; Bart Landry, *The New Black Middle Class* (Berkeley, 1987); Bound and Freeman, "What Went Wrong?"; Michael B. Katz, ed., *The "Underclass" Debate: Views from History* (Princeton, 1993), esp. 442–447; Taylor, *"Brown,"* esp. 1725–35; William Julius Wilson, *The Truly Disadvantaged: The Inner City, the Underclass, and Public Policy* (Chicago, 1987), esp. 46–62, 137; Pettigrew, "Race and Class," 248–249; Wilson, *When Work Disappears*. On the benefits of a tight labor market, see Sylvia Nasar with Kirsten B. Mitchell, "Booming Job Market Draws Young Black Men into Fold," *NYT*, May 23, 1999, A1, 21.

71. Donald Tomaskovic-Dewey, *Gender and Racial Inequality at Work: Sources and Consequences of Job Segregation* (Ithaca, N.Y., 1993), 147, 169.

72. William Julius Wilson, *The Declining Significance of Race: Blacks and Changing American Institutions* (Chicago, 1978), quotes on ix, 19, also 100, 165; Wilson, *The Truly Disadvantaged*, 118, 138–164. In the latter work, Wilson wrote more disparagingly of "the affirmative action agenda of the black middle class" (15, also 110). For earlier versions of this argument, see Bayard Rustin, "From Protest to Politics: The Future of the Civil Rights Movement," *Commentary* (Feb. 1964): 25–31; Tom Kahn, "Problems of the Negro Movement," *Dissent* (Winter 1964): 108–138. In more recent years, Wilson has argued for "comprehensive social reform that includes race-based *and* race-neutral programs." See Wilson, *When Work Disappears*, esp. 197–199, and *The Bridge over the Racial Divide: Rising Inequality and Coalition Politics* (Berkeley, 1999).

73. For an amusing example, see Remnick, "Dr. Wilson's Neighborhood," 100. One wonders how the debates might have differed if Wilson had titled his works, for example, *The Growing Significance of Class* and *The Most Disadvantaged*.

74. For a sampling, see Alexander Cockburn, "How Many Cheers for Affirma-

tive Action?" *Nation,* Aug. 14–21, 1995, 156–157; Troy Duster, "Individual Fairness, Group Preferences, and the California Strategy," *Representations* 55 (Summer 1996): esp. 41; Joanne Barkan in the debate "Affirmative Action under Fire: A Symposium," *Dissent* (Fall 1995): 461–475.

75. Stokely Carmichael, "What We Want," in *The New Student Left: An Anthology,* ed. Mitchell Cohen and Dennis Hale (Boston, 1967), 115; Adolph Reed, Jr., "Review: Race and the Disruption of the New Deal Coalition," *Urban Affairs Quarterly* 27 (Dec. 1991): 326, 332–333; and see the cogent discussion in Robin D. G. Kelley, "Identity Politics and Class Struggle," *New Politics* (Winter 1997): 84–96. For how earlier black struggles sought universal policies, see Dona Cooper Hamilton and Charles V. Hamilton, *The Dual Agenda: The African-American Struggle for Civil and Economic Equality* (New York, 1997).

76. Kenneth S. Tollett, "Racism and Race-Conscious Remedies," *American Prospect* 5 (Spring 1981): 91. As a civil rights attorney and activist puts it, "the limitations of race conscious civil rights remedies standing alone as a means of advancement for low-income black people are as apparent as the positive results such remedies have achieved." Taylor, *"Brown,"* 1725.

77. Coretta Scott King, "Man of His Word," *NYT,* Nov. 3, 1996, section 4, 15; for a sampling of the radical left's spirited defense, consult the *Alternative Press Index;* on the challenge, see Pettigrew, "Race and Class," esp. 238–239, 244–245; Pettigrew, "New Patterns of Racism," 673–706.

78. Manning Marable, "An Idea Whose Time Has Come," *Newsweek,* Aug. 27, 2001, 22; Robert Westley, "Many Billions Gone: Is It Time to Reconsider the Case for Black Reparations?" *Boston College Law Review* 40 (1998): 43. For an overview, see Martha Biondi, "The Rise of Reparations Movements," *Radical History Review* 87 (Fall 2003): 5–18; and, more generally, Roy L. Brooks, ed., *When Sorry Isn't Enough: The Controversy over Apologies and Reparations for Human Injustice* (New York, 1999).

79. See Kate Zernike, "Slavers in Yale's Past Are Focus of Reparations Debate," *NYT,* Aug. 13, 2001, A18, and ensuing letters; Randall Robinson, *The Debt: What America Owes to Blacks* (New York, 2000).

80. Westley, "Many Billions Gone," 429, 432; also Biondi, "Rise of Reparations." For reckonings, see George Lipsitz, *The Possessive Investment in Whiteness: How White People Profit from Identity Politics* (Philadelphia, 1998); Melvin L. Oliver and Thomas M. Shapiro, *Black Wealth/White Wealth: A New Perspective on Racial Inequality* (New York, 1995).

81. Biondi, "Rise of Reparations"; Westley, "Many Billions Gone," 436, 473–474.

82. Alan Freeman, "Legitimizing Racial Discrimination through Antidiscrimination Law," *Minnesota Law Review* 62 (1978): 1050.

83. "The minute any of you start to think of gov[ernmen]t as we, instead of as they," President Reagan told his own appointees, "we will have begun to lose the fight . . . [to] drain [the] swamp." Ronald Reagan, remarks to reception for women appointees, Feb. 10, 1982, box 1, series 2, Presidential Handwriting File, RRPL.

84. See Philip A. Klinker with Rogers M. Smith, *The Unsteady March: The Rise and Decline of Racial Equality in America* (Chicago, 1999).

85. Salim Muwakkil, "Affirmative Action, R.I.P.," *In These Times,* March 20, 1995, 19.

86. Quotes from Barbara Smith, "Some Home Truths on the Contemporary Black Feminist Movement," and Audre Lorde, "Age, Race, Class, and Sex: Women Redefining Difference," both in *Words of Fire: An Anthology of African-American Feminist Thought*, ed. Beverly Guy-Sheftall (New York, 1995), 256, 260, 261, 290, which offers an excellent sampling of the large literature. For policy implications, see Kimberlé Crenshaw, "Demarginalizing the Intersection of Race and Sex: A Black Feminist Critique of Antidiscrimination Doctrine, Feminist Theory, and Antiracist Politics," in *Feminist Legal Theory*, ed. Katherine T. Bartlett and Rosanne Kennedy (Boulder, Colo., 1991), 57–80; for the premier historical model of organizing in this tradition, see Barbara Ransby, *Ella Baker and the Black Freedom Movement: A Radical Democratic Vision* (Chapel Hill, N.C., 2003); for examples of successful recent activism animated by such thinking, see Kelley, "Identity Politics and Class," 84–96.

87. John Baker, *Arguing for Equality* (New York, 1987), quote on 46; David Cay Johnston, "Gap between Rich and Poor Found Substantially Wider," *NYT*, Sept. 5, 1999, A16.

Epilogue

1. Albert Camus, *The Myth of Sisyphus and Other Essays* (1955; reprint, New York, 1955), 89.

2. Sumner M. Rosen to Editor, *NYT*, July 13, 1999, A16; David Remnick, "Dr. Wilson's Neighborhood," *New Yorker*, April 29–May 6, 1996, 98. On the decline of real income for most Americans from 1973 to 2000, see Paul Krugman, "The Death of Horatio Alger," *Nation*, Jan. 5, 2004, 16; on blacks in particular, see Dedrick Muhammad et al., *The State of the Dream, 2004: Enduring Disparities in Black and White* (Boston, 2004); for less recent data but excellent analysis, see National Research Council, *A Common Destiny: Blacks and American Society*, ed. Gerald David Jaynes and Robin M. Williams, Jr. (Washington, D.C., 1989), 269–328.

3. On individualism and community, see Robert N. Bellah et al., *Habits of the Heart: Individualism and Commitment in American Life* (New York, 1985).

4. See Robin D. G. Kelley, "Identity Politics and Class Struggle," *New Politics* 22 (Winter 1997): 84–96; Ruth Milkman, "Union Responses to Workforce Feminization in the United States," in *The Challenge of Restructuring: North American Labor Movements Respond*, ed. Jane Jenson and Rianne Mahon (Philadelphia, 1993), 226–250; David Roediger, "What If Labor Were Not White and Male? Recentering Working-Class History and Reconstructing Debate on the Unions and Race," *ILWCH* 51 (Spring 1997): 72–95; Gregory Mantsios, ed., *A New Labor Movement for the New Century* (New York, 1998), esp. 147–215; and the pathbreaking study by Dorian T. Warren, "A New Labor Movement for a New Century? The Incorporation and Representation of Marginalized Workers In U.S. Unions" (Ph.D. diss., Yale University, 2004).

5. Richard Scotch, *From Good Will to Civil Rights: Transforming Federal Disability Policy*, 2nd ed. (Philadelphia, 2001); on the Pride at Work initiative in the AFL-CIO, see *http://www.prideatwork.org/story.html//enottxt*.

6. Lauren Edelman, "Legal Environments and Organizational Governance: The Expansion of Due Process in the American Workplace," *AJS* 95 (May 1990): 1435–36.

7. Erin Kelly and Frank Dobbin, "Civil Rights Law at Work: Sex Discrimination and the Rise of Maternity Leave Policies," *AJS* 105 (Sept. 1999): 487–488.

8. Chicago Urban League, "Notes on Problems of Negro Employment," Aug. 20, 1964, series 4, reel 10, frames 169–176, SCLC.

9. For job losses in industries where workers achieved headway with Title VII, see Chapter 9.

10. On the resistance from other quarters to movement-backed calls for full employment, see Margaret Weir, *Politics and Jobs: The Boundaries of Employment Policy in the United States* (Princeton, 1992); Dona Cooper Hamilton and Charles V. Hamilton, *The Dual Agenda: The African American Struggle for Civil and Economic Equality* (New York, 1997), esp. 262, 265–266.

11. For a cogent summary of how government policy since the 1970s has exacerbated racial economic inequality, see Martin Carnoy, *Faded Dreams: The Politics and Economics of Race in America* (New York, 1994).

12. Michael Lewis, "Rainbow, Inc.," *NYT Magazine*, Dec. 8, 1996, 54, 56.

13. For a representative iteration of this thesis by a prominent scholar, see Seymour Martin Lipset, *American Exceptionalism: A Double-Edged Sword* (New York, 1996), 119. Otherwise valuable works by more sympathetic scholars who use only inside-the-Beltway sources and so perpetuate the creation myth include Hugh Davis Graham, *The Civil Rights Era: Origins and Development of National Policy, 1960–1972* (New York, 1990); John David Skrentny, *The Ironies of Affirmative Action: Politics, Culture, and Justice in America* (Chicago, 1996), and his broader work *The Minority Rights Revolution* (Cambridge, Mass., 2002). These works also overlook the business and conservative opposition to equal employment that made tougher affirmative action policies necessary.

14. Whitney M. Young, Jr., "The Negro Revolt," special issue *American Child* 45 (Nov. 1963): 8. For the right's messages about race and poverty, see Thomas Byrne Edsall with Mary D. Edsall, *Chain Reaction: The Impact of Races, Rights, and Taxes on American Politics* (New York, 1992); Michael B. Katz, *The Undeserving Poor: From the War on Poverty to the War on Welfare* (New York, 1990).

15. Quoted in Jack M. Bloom, *Class, Race, and the Civil Rights Movement* (Bloomington, Ind., 1987), 212.

16. See, for example, the video by Citizens United for the Preservation of Civil Rights, *Gay Rights, Special Rights: Inside the Homosexual Agenda* (Nashville, Tenn., 1993).

17. James R. Kluegel, "If There Isn't a Problem, You Don't Need a Solution," *American Behavioral Scientist* 28 (July–Aug. 1985): 761–784. For a paradigm-altering discussion of how analogous collective forgetting affected the postwar labor movement and sixties left, see Jack Metzgar, *Striking Steel: Solidarity Remembered* (Philadelphia, 2000), 202–229.

18. Sidney Hook, "Discrimination, Color Blindness, and the Quota System," in *Reverse Discrimination*, ed. Barry R. Gross (New York, 1977), 86.

19. David W. Blight, "'For Something beyond the Battlefield: Frederick Douglass and the Struggle for Memory of the Civil War," *JAH* 75 (1989): 1171.

20. Charles M. Payne, *I've Got the Light of Freedom: The Organizing Tradition and the Mississippi Freedom Struggle* (Berkeley, 1995), 392.

21. Clarence Mitchell quoted in Charles Culhane, "Labor Report: Battle

over Enforcement Powers for EEOC Pits Business against Labor, Civil Rights Groups," *National Journal*, Nov. 13, 1971, 2249.

22. See, for example, Alexander Saxton, *The Indispensable Enemy: Labor and the Anti-Chinese Movement in California* (Berkeley, 1971); Robert L. Allen with Pamela P. Allen, *Reluctant Reformers: The Impact of Racism on American Social Reform Movements* (Washington, D.C., 1974); Herbert Hill, "Race, Ethnicity, and Organized Labor: The Opposition to Affirmative Action," *New Politics*, n.s., 1 (Winter 1987): 31–82; David R. Roediger, *The Wages of Whiteness: Race and the Making of the American Working Class* (New York, 1991); George Lipsitz, *The Possessive Investment in Whiteness: How White People Profit from Identity Politics* (Philadelphia, 1998). For how attention to employers can change understanding, see Brian Kelly, *Race, Class and Power in the Alabama Coalfields, 1908–21* (Urbana, Ill., 2002).

23. "Given the entrenched political and economic opposition movements are likely to encounter," notes one scholar of social movements, "it is often true that their biggest impact is more cultural than narrowly political and economic." Doug McAdam, "Culture and Social Movements," in *New Social Movements: From Ideology to Identity*, ed. Enrique Larana et al. (Philadelphia, 1994), 49.

24. Phyllis Theroux, "Man and Animal at Yale," *NYT*, Sept. 25, 1991, op ed page; "Yale Club Admits Women; Irate Alumni Bar the Door," *NYT*, April 15, 1991, A10.

25. Alessandra Stanley, "Walking a Fine Line in Showcasing Women and Dealing with Muslim Allies," *NYT*, Oct. 27, 2001, B9.

26. Bernice Resnick Sandler, interview, Nov. 18, 1985, transcript, 79, AJC-OH. Indeed, the movements for equality have gone global, as beautifully captured in Estelle Freedman, *No Turning Back: The History of Feminism and the Future of Women* (New York, 2002).

27. James Traub, "The Class of Prop. 209," *NYT Magazine*, May 2, 1999, 44–79. See also Lauren B. Edelman, "Legal Ambiguity and Symbolic Structures: Organizational Mediation of Civil Rights Law," *AJS* 97 (May 1992): 1531–76, esp. 1568.

28. Deb Riechmann, "College Survey Shows Shifting Social Views," *Chicago Sun-Times*, Jan. 8, 1996, 5; Michael Lewis, "Rainbow, Inc.," *NYT Magazine*, Dec. 8, 1996, 54, 56; Steven A. Holmes, "Re-thinking Affirmative Action," *NYT*, April 5, 1998, section 4, 5; Brent Staples, "The Quota Bashers Come in from the Cold," *NYT*, April 12, 1998, section 4, 12; Adam Shatz, "About Face," *NYT Magazine*, Jan. 20, 2002, 18–23; Gerald R. Ford, "Inclusive America, Under Attack," *NYT Magazine*, Aug. 8, 1999, section 4, 15.

29. Louis Menand, "Mixed Paint," *Mother Jones* (March–April 1995): 31, 33.

30. T. H. Marshall, *Citizenship and Social Class* (1950; reprint, London, 1992), esp. 40, 45.

31. Clarence Coe, quoted in Michael Keith Honey, *Black Workers Remember: An Oral History of Segregation, Unionism, and the Freedom Struggle* (Berkeley, 1999), 362.

Acknowledgments

In his "Letter from a Birmingham Jail," Martin Luther King, Jr., observed that whether we see it or not, "we are caught in an inescapable network of mutuality." Most often, Americans live the truth of these inevitable connections in reaping the costs of our failure to recognize that our fates are connected. Yet at some magical times, such as in social movements like those written about here, some get to experience the power of mutuality to clear away obstacles and achieve what had seemed impossible. I felt the power of community so many times over the ten years of researching and writing this book that it is a supreme pleasure now to thank collectively the many people and institutions that have contributed to it.

For encouragement early on, I am profoundly grateful to Mari Jo Buhle, Gerda Lerner, and Linda Gordon for launching me on a career as a historian, and to Mike Gordon, Linda Kerber, David Roediger, and Michael Sherry, whose support for this project enabled me to secure fellowships with which to carry out the research. For giving me the time away from teaching duties to travel to archives, research, and write, I thank the American Council of Learned Societies, the Hagley Museum and Library, the Lyndon B. Johnson Foundation, the Institute for Policy Research at Northwestern University, the Alice Berline Kaplan Humanities Center at Northwestern, and above all the Russell Sage Foundation for a vital writing year in the company of stimulating colleagues and staff spent in an idyllic environment for producing scholarship. I also thank my editor at Harvard University Press, Joyce Seltzer, whose probing questions and wise counsel helped shape this book, and whose rigorous reading of the manuscript immeasurably improved the final product. I thank Amanda Heller for her careful work, high standards, and commitment to the endangered art of copyediting.

Over the past fifteen years, Northwestern University has nurtured me as a scholar, and for this I acknowledge the many smart and challenging colleagues in the History Department from whom I have learned a great deal. For going out of their way to enable completion of this book, I am especially grateful to department chairs Jock McLane, Ed Muir, and Sarah Maza, and also deans Eric Sundquist and Dan Linzer.

The best part about teaching is learning from students. I thank the outstanding graduate students in U.S. history at Northwestern for educating me about new areas and deepening my understanding of topics covered in this book, especially Michael Allen on the political impact of historical memory; Wallace Best on how faith communities adapt to social change; Charlotte Brooks on Asian American history and comparative racial politics; James Burkee on the right-left struggle in mainline churches; Marisa Chappell on how the family wage norm shaped public policy and organizing from the 1960s to the 1980s; Marcus Cox on the military as a vehicle of mobility for African Americans; Leslie Dunlap on gender and social movement mobilization; Brett Gadsden on the complexities and ironies of desegregation; Erik Gellman on black-Jewish relations and grassroots black activism in the interwar years; Deborah Holland on the failures of federal civil rights policy before passage of the Civil Rights Act; Seth Jacobs on how faith and race shaped postwar American political culture; David Johnson on sexuality in cold war politics; Karen Leroux on the influence of employment on women's citizenship; Anastasia Mann on how veterans' politics shaped the American welfare state; Christopher Manning on African Americans and Democratic Party politics; Michele Mitchell on gender and black nationalism; Steven Reich on race and class formation in the South; Christopher Tassava on government-industry collaboration in economic development; and James Wolfinger on the ways Republicans exploited the racial fault lines of the Roosevelt coalition beginning in the 1940s.

Lyndon Johnson and Sargent Shriver understood that working to end poverty would help all Americans; one example of the wider benefits of their War on Poverty is the Federal Work-Study Program that helps so many undergraduate students learn as they earn, while also aiding their lucky employers. I am grateful to this visionary initiative for the stream of bright and talented research assistants whose conscientiousness contributed so much to this project, especially Wendy Torigoe, Alana McDonough, Dan Corstange, Tim Gaylord, and in the last key stages, with additional summer support from Northwestern's Institute of Policy Research, Katherine Turk and Martin Zacharia, whose initiative and resourcefulness particularly impressed me. Special thanks to Martin for his assistance with the photographs and other last-minute matters, and to Erik Gellman for careful checking of quotations.

Polls find that pharmacists are the most trusted professionals; they would have tougher competition if more Americans had the pleasure of working with the archivists who tend the raw materials of our history. In the course of this project, I have worked in repositories large and small in all parts of the country, and have never left without being struck by the vast knowledge, commitment, professionalism, and hospitality of the staff members who process these precious records and guide researchers to finding the riches their files contain. Grateful thanks to all those who assisted me at the American Jewish Historical Society; Amistad Research Center; Archives Division, State Historical Society of Wisconsin; Bentley Historical Library; Centro de Estudios Puertorriqueños; Dorot Jewish Division, New York Public Library; George Meany Memorial Archives; Gerald R. Ford Presidential Library; Hagley Museum and Library; Jacob and Hilda Blaustein Human Relations Research Library; Jimmy Carter Presidential Library; Lyndon Baines Johnson Presidential Library; Manuscript Division, Library of Congress; Manuscripts, Archives, and Rare Books Division, Schomburg Center for Research in Black Culture; Manuscripts and Archives, Yale University Library; National Archives for Black Women's History, Mary McLeod Bethune Council House; Nettie Lee Benson Latin American Collection, University of Texas at Austin; Rare Book and Manuscript Library, Columbia University; Richard M. Nixon Presidential Materials, National Archives; Rockefeller Archive Center; Robert F. Wagner Labor Archives and Tamiment Archives,

New York University; Ronald Reagan Presidential Library; Schlesinger Library, Radcliffe Institute for Advanced Study; Seeley G. Mudd Manuscript Library, Princeton University; Southern Historical Collection, Wilson Library, University of North Carolina–Chapel Hill; Special Collections, Stanford University Library; Special Collections and Archives, Bell Library, Texas A&M University–Corpus Christi; Special Collections and Archives, Marquette University; Special Collections Library, Duke University; University of Virginia, Special Collections; and the Walter P. Reuther Library, Archives of Labor and Urban Affairs, Wayne State University.

By far the hardest thing about doing history is the actual writing, and what makes it worthwhile is the invigorating engagement of wise critics. My deepest debt and most abiding gratitude goes out to those who generously agreed to review drafts of this work. My first and best reader, as always, was Bruce Orenstein, whose close attention to drafts beyond number convinced me I could do this book and helped me through many discussions to see how. For reading the first, unconscionably long full draft of the book and offering sage advice, I am eternally grateful to my peerless colleagues Laura Hein and Mike Sherry. For incisive and extremely helpful guidance about how to improve the next draft, I offer heartfelt thanks to Eric Arnesen, Martha Biondi, Leon Fink, Joyce Follet, Wally Hettle, Brian Kelly, Laura McEnaney, Jack Metzgar, Leslie Reagan, Leo Ribuffo, and the anonymous readers for Harvard University Press. For giving me the benefit of their varied expertise on particular chapters, I am grateful to Shana Bernstein, Charlotte Brooks, Michelle Couturier, Maureen Fitzgerald, Erik Gellman, Rick Halpern, Steven Hahn, Jane Latour, Raymond McAlonan, Stephanie McCurry, Regina McGraw, Leisa Meier, Aldon Morris, Michelle Nickerson, Marc Rodriguez, Jennifer Salazar-Biddle, and students in my "State and Society in Modern America" and "Affirmative Action at Work" seminars.

For help with research queries and for alerting me to sources, I thank Martha Biondi, Charlotte Brooks, Bobby Buchanan, Paul Kenneth Longmore, Dwight McBride, and Marc Rodriguez. Penny Weaver of the Southern Poverty Law Center helped me find additional information on the murder of Wharlest Jackson, and Denise Ford generously provided me with a photo of her father. Former EEOC commissioner Vicente Ximenes volunteered to send me visual resources as he filled in the story of the Mexican American struggle. Tim Minchin graciously shared transcripts of his oral histories of textile workers. William F. Buckley, Jr., granted me permission to quote from his papers. My thanks to all of them.

For the opportunity to present work in progress and receive helpful feedback, I thank the American Historical Association, Auburn University, the Cambridge University American History Seminar, the Carter G. Woodson Regional Library in Chicago, the College of William and Mary, Duke University, the Institute for Policy Research at Northwestern University, the Newberry Library, the North American Labor History Conference, the Organization of American Historians, the Oxford University American History Research Seminar, the Social Science History Association, the Southern Historical Association, Tulane University, the University of Pennsylvania, the University of Michigan, the University of Mississippi, the University of New Hampshire, the University of Notre Dame, the University of Toronto, and Women's and Gender Historians of the Midwest.

As my editor will attest, about one third of the original draft consisted of documentation, a suicidal ratio in today's publishing business. In order to make the book inviting to general readers and manageable for classroom use, I had to cut back radically on references to the vast number of articles and books on which it builds and from whose authors I learned so much. In the final draft the principle of acknowledgment had to be Spartan: only sources directly quoted or providing specific information used in the text could be cited. All the "see also" chains of elaboration so painstakingly compiled in earlier drafts had to go. I ask forbearance from those who have written important work in these areas yet do not see it cited here. Please know that you are in excellent company. I am aware of my debts and deeply sorry that I could not use the notes to guide readers through the rich scholarship that made this book possible.

It is customary that the dearest come last, perhaps because words are so inadequate to honor their contributions. I feel infinitely grateful to my father, Jack MacLean, who died in 2000. His loyalty, love, and playful spirit carried us through, and his principled conservatism challenged and stretched me. It was my father who first taught me fairness and who showed me the power of meaningful work, so his example guided this book as it has my life. For matchless friendship for as long as I can remember, I am indebted to my beloved sister and stalwart champion, Mary Anne McAlonan. I learned solidarity from her. No one else did more to help me with this book than Bruce Orenstein, and I thank him for endless patience and astute advice on every aspect of the project. But most of all I thank him for being the best person I know and the finest partner in life I could imagine. His wit makes this strange era bearable, and the good he does in the world inspires me to try harder. This book is for him, with deepest love and appreciation.

Index